This book is based on the premise that the foreign policy of any country is heavily influenced by a society's evolving notions of itself. Applying his analysis to Russia, Poland, and Ukraine, the author argues that national identity is an ever-changing concept, influenced by internal and external events, and by the manipulation of a polity's collective memory. The interaction of the narrative of a society and its foreign policy is therefore paramount. This is especially the case in East-Central Europe, where political institutions are weak, and social coherence remains subject to the vagaries of the concept of nationhood. Ilya Prizel's study will be of interest to students of nationalism, as well as foreign policy and politics in East-Central Europe.

# NATIONAL IDENTITY AND FOREIGN POLICY

## Cambridge Russian, Soviet and Post-Soviet Studies

*Series list continues after index*

# NATIONAL IDENTITY AND FOREIGN POLICY

## Nationalism and leadership in Poland, Russia and Ukraine

ILYA PRIZEL

CAMBRIDGE
UNIVERSITY PRESS

PUBLISHED BY THE PRESS SYNDICATE OF THE UNIVERSITY OF CAMBRIDGE
The Pitt Building, Trumpington Street, Cambridge CB2 1RP, United Kingdom

CAMBRIDGE UNIVERSITY PRESS
The Edinburgh Building, Cambridge, CB2 2RU, United Kingdom
http://www.cup.cam.ac.uk
40 West 20th Street, New York, NY 10011-4211, USA    http://www.cup.org
10 Stamford Road, Oakleigh, Melbourne 3166, Australia

First published 1998

Printed in the United Kingdom at the University Press, Cambridge

Typeset in Palatino 10/12.5pt [CE]

ISBN 0 521 57157 X hardback
ISBN 0 521 57697 0 paperback

Dedicated to my parents, Zoya and Chaim Prizel,
who encouraged me to love books
at an early age

# Contents

# Preface

This book was originally conceived as an attempt to bridge the gap in the political science literature, which tends to deal with nationalism and foreign policy as separate phenomena. My endeavor to address such an enigmatic theme would not have been possible without the support of friends and colleagues who graciously read parts or all of this manuscript.

I would like to express my profound gratitude to my colleagues, Professors Karen Dawisha, Nikolai Rudenksy, Bruce Parrott, Orest Subtelny, Vladimir Tismaneanu, Arthur Rachwald, Mark Katz, Daniel Chirot, Andrew Michta, Zoya Vatnikova-Prizel, Maya Latynski, and Taddeus Zachurski, and others who have chosen to remain anonymous. While the responsibility for all errors and omissions are mine alone, I am certain that their kind advice and counsel has helped me to avoid many pitfalls and mistakes. I would like to thank Florence Rotz and Paula Smith, who patiently devoted long hours to helping me to revise the various versions of this book.

In addition, I would like to thank my research assistants who diligently performed what at times must have been long and tedious tasks. I would like to acknowledge the contributions of: Marek Michalewski, Alexandra Doroshenko, Helen Fessenden, Steven Guenther, Ray Branden and Alexis Martin-Ruehle.

This project would have been far more difficult to accomplish without the support of my home institution, The Paul H. Nitze School of Advanced International Studies of The Johns Hopkins University. My colleagues have generously allowed me a year's leave to concentrate on this effort. I would also like to thank the Woodrow Wilson Center for International Scholars at the Smithsonian Institution for providing a research award which enabled me to successfully complete it. Special thanks go to Michael Holdsworth and John Haslam of Cambridge University Press, who were enthusiastic about the undertaking and graciously accepted what must have often seemed interminable delays.

Finally, I would like to thank my wife, Kate Rothko, and my children, Peter, Natalie, and Lauren, who had to endure my prolonged absences, and did so with understanding and aplomb.

# Introduction: statement of arguments

In analyzing the development of the foreign policy of a given polity, the political science community has tended to view the process as rational and pragmatic. The theory is that these policies reflect geopolitical realities and stem from clearly defined national interests.

While it is certainly true that all states pursue what they perceive as a rational foreign policy, the parameter of what constitutes rational choice is a flexible and elusive concept. In addition to such objective factors as geostrategic position, geography, economic factor endowments, which indeed do impact on the formation of foreign policy, there are broad subjective criteria which guide the political choices made by states. Even within the framework of Western civilization, a civilization ostensibly based on eighteenth-century rationality, arbitrary factors such as moral and cultural values and national identity underlie many aspects of foreign policy. It is my contention that in order to understand the dynamics of foreign policy formation, it is vital to assess how the identity of a polity has evolved, and what new intellectual parameters the polity has internalized.

Given the prevalence of the "rational" model of policy formation, the most irrational concept of nationalism and national identity as a vital element of foreign policy formation is generally shunned by modern scholars. On the rare occasions that nationalism, let alone national identity, has been incorporated into the analysis of a specific foreign policy, it has been viewed as an outburst of irrationality that passed once rationality returned. Such an explanation has been given for the behavior of Germany in the two world wars and for the jingoistic yellow journalism in the United States on the eve of the Spanish-American War.

At the end of the twentieth century, "nationalism" has become a loaded term, generally associated with xenophobic ethnonationalism smacking of fascism. For this reason, there is a tendency to avoid

1

discussing nationalism, national identity, and the power of ethnicity in shaping politics. However, as I argue, the interaction between national identity and foreign policy is a key element in both established and nascent polities, but this interaction is particularly important in newly emerging or re-emerging states since nationalism and national identity are often the main, if not the sole force binding these societies together.

Some scholars, such as John Breuilly, who tackle the issue of nationalism as a living force, argue that it is primarily a form of politics.[1] While this is clearly true, two essential points need elaboration. First, a polity cannot exist in a state of prolonged anomie; it needs an identity to provide a psychological frame of reference in which to function. Therefore all polities, whether or not they are aware of it, have an identity that helps define their values and serves as the basis for ranking their priorities. These values and priorities, along with a host of objective factors, shape foreign as well as domestic policy. Second, despite the popular notion that national identities are either fixed or evolve very slowly, national identities, like those of individuals, are as stable as the environment around them. Polities experience "teachable moments" when confronted with crisis, either internal or external. Thus, sometimes within as little as a generation, a polity's identity may be redefined, leading to a new self-vision and a new set of priorities. These two key observations form the basis for the thesis of this book – that in Poland, Ukraine, and Russia rapid changes in the internal and external environments spawned the development of new definitions of self and the reordering of priorities, which in turn led to core changes in foreign policy.

Poland, Ukraine, and Russia, despite their common Slavic roots and extensive cultural cross-pollination, are markedly different polities. Over the centuries Poland has developed a strong concept of national identity, but its attempts at statehood have been weak and fugitive. Conversely, Russia's history has been marked by a powerful and overbearing state but a weak, and even uncertain, national identity. Ukraine has not developed strength in either arena – its national identity has not been well defined, and it has enjoyed only short periods of quasi-statehood.

What these three countries have in common is a lack of abiding institutions on which to anchor their political personas, making them

---

[1] John Breuilly, *Nationalism and the State* (Chicago: University of Chicago Press, 1994).

heavily reliant on their collective memories as the bases for their national identities. The absence of independent statehood or freedom has meant that collective memories, as well as notions of identity, have had to be articulated through historiography and literature. Historians and authors served as curators of the collective memory, and authors often played an active role in the development of political consensus within a polity, setting its current parameters, as well as prophesying the future. Both Russia and Poland became multinational entities (or empires) before they developed their own ethnic identities. As a result, both the Polish Commonwealth and the Russian empire, despite their very different political structures, developed an elite whose identity was linked to an extra-national entity, an attachment that was generally not shared on the popular level even by the core ethnic group, creating a permanent schism between the identity of the elites and that of the masses. Given the very different concepts of identity of Poland's multinational *szlachta* or Russia's (either tsarist or Soviet) imperial elite and their respective broad nativist and parochial masses, it is not surprising that the foreign policy agendas of the elite and the masses became increasingly contradictory as the political consciousness of the general populace awakened. In addition, the collapse of Poland and Russia as multinational entities led to a prolonged disorientation of the elite and a search for a workable paradigm.

It is my contention that nationalism and national identity are the glue that gives coherence to these, and indeed all polities. A flux in national identity is caused by a shift in the collective memory, which often reflects a transfer of a polity's collective consciousness from one group or level of a polity to another. The political and intellectual democratization that occurred during this century caused a gradual shift in the custodianship of national identity, and with it a shift in the foreign policy orientation of these states.

## The concept of national identity in contemporary politics

Since World War II, a curious consensus has evolved among liberal and Marxist historians. The defeat of the Axis and the emergence of a bipolar world order convinced historians on both sides of the Iron Curtain that nationalism had ceased to be a potent political force in shaping the course of human events. Followers of Karl Marx considered nationalism a product of bourgeois capitalism, a part of modernity that would wither away along with the state once society reached the post-capitalist phase of history and embraced class consciousness, not nationality, as the prime source of identity.[2] Soviet historians and ideologists continually spoke about the emergence of a supranational "Soviet people,"[3] while Western scholars, Marxists and non-Marxists alike, believed that growing global economic interdependence was diluting nationalism as a decisive political force. Writers such as Raymond Vernon in *Sovereignty at Bay: The Multinational Spread of US Enterprises*, contended that multinational organizations and multinational corporations were undermining the appeal of both the nation-state and nationalism.[4] E. J. Hobsbawm argued that "[history] will see nation states and nations or ethnic/linguistic groups primarily as retreating before, resisting and adapting to, being absorbed or dislocated by, the new supranational restructuring of the globe."[5] Francis Fukuyama, in his controversial article "The End of History," described the twentieth century as a relentless struggle between Marxism and Western liberalism that was finally resolved only by the collapse of communism and the embrace of liberal capitalism as the new universal ideology.[6]

Despite the prevalent view that nationalism has become an anachronistic force, a dissenting school has emerged that holds that nationalism will remain a potent force in shaping events. This strain of thought traces its roots to prescient thinkers such as Arnold Toynbee, who observed:

> [The] factor that played the greatest part in defeating communist hopes and expectations – and this both in the Soviet Union and everywhere else – has been the triumph of nationalism. Communism has been worsted by nationalism as decisively as liberal democracy has been.[7]

Lenin, in his analysis of the Soviet defeat in the Soviet–Polish War

[2] See Walker Connor, *The National Question in Marxist-Leninist Theory and Strategy* (Princeton: Princeton University Press, 1984), especially chs. 1 and 2.
[3] See Gerhard Simon, *Nationalism and Policy Toward the Nationalities in the Soviet Union: From Totalitarian Dictatorship to Post-Stalinist Society* (Boulder, CO: Westview Press, 1991), ch. 9.
[4] David Held, "Farewell Nation State," *Marxism Today* (December 1988); Raymond Vernon, *Sovereignty at Bay: The Multinational Spread of US Enterprises* (New York: Basic Books, 1971).
[5] E. J. Hobsbawm, *Nations and Nationalism since 1780: Programme, Myth, Reality* (Cambridge: Cambridge University Press, 1992), 182.
[6] Francis Fukuyama, "The End of History," *National Interest*, no. 16 (Summer 1989), 3–18.
[7] Quoted by Hugh Seton-Waton in *The Influence of Bolshevism on the World Outside Russia* (London: Oxford University Press, 1967), 177.

(1920), was startled that the Poles "acted not in a social, revolutionary way, but as nationalists and imperialists."[8] John Lukacs argued that Marxism and the entire notion of universal workers' solidarity died in August 1914, when, despite the slogan "The worker has no country," Europe's, and later America's workers joined the bourgeoisie and took up arms without hesitation against fellow workers in the name of the fatherland.[9]

Indeed, history will remember the twentieth century as the century of nationalism. Not only did the century witness two world wars that originated with the nationalist ambitions of newly ascending powers and the declining powers' unwillingness to accommodate them,[10] but it also saw the collapse of an ideology – communism – that stemmed from a-nationalist forces. This collapse does not represent so much the victory of liberal democracy over communism but rather the implosion of a "universalist" polity when confronted with the nationalist idea. Even among polities that share the mythology of a common ethos, such as the Arab world, the past thirty years have seen a constant drift away from the universalist pan-Arab ideologies of Ba'athism and Nasserism toward regional nationalism. Iran's Islamic revolution, despite its claims to a universalist ideology, owed much of its success to its ability to graft pan-Islamic ideology onto Persian nationalism.[11] Similarly, the ideology of Algeria's Islamic Salvation Front is primarily a nativist reaction to the Western universalist pseudo-socialist ideology of the Front Liberacion Nacional that has governed the country since the defeat of France in 1962.[12] In India, as the binding collective memory of British colonial rule fades, supporters of parochial nationalism are asserting themselves from Kashmir to Karela, tearing at the fabric of what was hitherto a relatively stable polity.

The clash between universalism and nationalism is not confined to the postcommunist societies of Central and Eastern Europe or the developing world. It also lies at the source of the conflict between

---

[8] Quoted in Richard Pipes, *Russia Under the Bolshevik Regime* (New York: Alfred A. Knopf, 1993), 192.

[9] John Lukacs, *The End of the Twentieth Century and the End of the Modern Age* (New York: Ticknor & Fields, 1993), 5.

[10] See Paul Kennedy, *The Rise of Anglo-German Antagonism, 1860–1914* (London and Boston: Allen & Unwin, 1980).

[11] See H. E. Chehabi, *Iran's Politics and Religious Modernization: The Liberalization Movement of Iran under the Shah and Khomeini* (Ithaca: Cornell University Press, 1990).

[12] Mark Jurgen Meyer, *The New Cold War? Religious Nationalism Confronts the Secular State* (Los Angeles, Berkeley, London: University of California Press, 1994), ch. 1.

Great Britain, in its desire to widen and thereby dilute the meaning of
European Union membership, and France and Germany, in their drive
to deepen the integration of the European Union. Despite powerful
economic and political arguments for full integration with its European partners, Great Britain's island-based national identity, forged
over a millennium of quasi-detachment from the continent, has
greatly hindered the pursuit of a seemingly pragmatic foreign policy
and still requires considerable psychological adjustments on the part
of the British public.[13]

Few historians would argue that the Bolshevik system legitimized
itself on ideological merits anywhere, either in the Soviet Union or in
its satellite states. During the seventy-four years of the Soviet experiment, the regime managed to survive through a mix of coercion,
material co-optation, and carefully tailored appeals to national sentiments. The breakup of the Soviet Union, Yugoslavia, and Czechoslovakia occurred not along ideological lines but along ethnic ones. In his
book, *Reinventing Politics: Eastern Europe from Stalin to Havel*, Vladimir
Tismaneanu argues that if the original challenge to Soviet-style
Marxism did indeed come from intellectuals eager to re-create a
liberal civil society,[14] nationalists soon came to dominate the process
of transition and turned nationalism into the "political coin of the
realm" in postcommunist Europe. With the notable exception of
Václav Havel, who can rely on his dissident credentials as a source of
legitimacy (and even in Havel's case this legitimacy did not extend
beyond the Czech lands), most of the leaders who emerged from the
wreckage of communism have turned to nationalism in varying
degrees as their source of political legitimacy. Even Lech Wałęsa,
perhaps the most authentic opponent of communism in Eastern
Europe, felt compelled to rely on nationalism, rather than liberalism,
to build a political base. Thus, the collapse of communism generally
resulted not in the immediate triumph of tolerant, liberal democracy,
but in a clear victory for nationalism over universalist ideology.

This transformation of revolutions from broad liberal endeavors to
nationalist expressions is not limited to recent events in Eastern
Europe but has international precedents. The great revolutionary
upheavals of the late nineteenth century in Italy and Ireland also
started as broad liberal movements opposed to foreign rule, only to be

[13] Sir Nicholas Henderson, "Mad John Bull Disease," *The Economist*, 23 November 1996.
[14] See Vladimir Tismaneanu, *Reinventing Politics: Eastern Europe from Stalin to Havel*
(New York: Free Press, 1992).

overwhelmed by exclusionary nationalist politicians.[15] Even further
back, the battle cry of the French Revolution – "Liberté, Egalité,
Fraternité" – originally conceived as a cosmopolitan-universalist
appeal, quickly became an ethnocentric and nationalist slogan.[16]
Although a case can be made that French nationalism retained a large
dose of civic rather than ethnic nationalism, it is noteworthy that it
was in France that "scientific" anti-Semitism and racism made their
first appearance, started by Joseph-Arthur de Gobineau and perpetuated by Jean-Marie Le Pen to this day.

Current examples of the strain on states because of ethnic conflicts
can be found in Mexico, the United Kingdom, Sri Lanka, Canada,
Nigeria, the successor states to the Soviet Union, and Angola. These
countries testify to the vitality of nationalism. The disintegration of
multiethnic states started with the end of World War I and the collapse
of the multinational Habsburg, Romanov, and Ottoman empires and
gathered momentum after World War II as nationalist forces in Asia
and Africa triumphed over the European colonial empires. Now the
century is ending with the dissolution of the USSR, the last multinational empire in Europe. Despite its remarkable ability to assimilate
disparate groups of people, the Russian state that began its imperial
career with the conquest of Kazan in 1552 ultimately succumbed to
the forces of nationalism and – almost without bloodshed – disintegrated overnight.

Nationalism will likely remain the world's most potent political
force for the foreseeable future. Although there is a rich and diverse
body of work on the concept of nationalism, literature on the role of
national identity in the formation of foreign policy remains in an
embryonic state. The main obstacle in linking nationalism or national
identity to foreign policy is that sociologists and political scientists
who study nationalism rarely venture into foreign affairs as a major
issue. Historians, while often paying attention to outbursts of nationalism, rarely follow the evolutionary process of nationalism over a
long period.

Admittedly, the study of nationalism and its impact on foreign
policy presents serious difficulties, since there is no single universal
source of national identification or, for that matter, any uniformity in

[15] For a case study illustrating the tendency of the chauvinist right to usurp the power
of nationalism, see Yael Tamar, *Liberal Nationalism* (Princeton: Princeton University
Press, 1993).
[16] Joseph Rothschild, *Ethnopolitics: A Conceptual Framework* (New York: Columbia
University Press, 1981), 12.

its effect on foreign policy. Furthermore, nationalism and national identity, like all living intellectual trends, are subject to constant redefinition. While the redefinition of national identities is generally a gradual process, under situations of persistent stress even well-established identities can change at a remarkable rate, and a people's collective memory can be "rearranged" quite quickly. The ability of the Zionist movement to redefine millennia-old notions of Jewish identity is an extreme, yet by no means the only, example of rapid national redefinition.[17] Because the sources of national identity are unique for each nation, and indeed are subject to constant re-creation, each study of nationalism and its impact on a given nation's foreign policy must be treated separately. Few generalizations are applicable to the international system as a whole.

It is clear, however, that national identity, by definition, reflects a nation's relationship to "the other,"[18] that national identity is an outgrowth of contact between at least two distinct groups. The sense of the other generally intensifies as linguistic, cultural, and racial differences increase. For example, Herodotus, in his *History*, describes the Persians as follows:

> They honor most of all those who dwell nearest to them, next those who are furthest removed, and so going ever onwards they assign honor by this rule; those who dwell the furthest off they hold least honorable of all; they deem themselves in all regards by far the best of all men, the rest have a proportionate claim to merit, till those who dwell furthest away have least merit of all.[19]

Hence, the conduct of foreign policy – namely, the relations a state has with foreign states – has a strong dialectical relationship with national identity, the cornerstone of nationalism. This book will examine the interaction between national identity and foreign policy in three major states in Eastern and Central Europe: Poland, Russia, and Ukraine. Each will serve as a test case for this phenomenon as each lies at a historic juncture in redefining its national identity and national interests. Poland, for the first time in centuries, returns to the international system as both a democratic and a national state. Ukraine has only recently embarked on the slow process of nation building, attempting

---

[17] See Yael Zerubavel, *Recovered Roots: Collective Memory and the Making of Israeli National Tradition* (Chicago and London: University of Chicago Press, 1994); also David N. Myers, *Re-Inventing The Jewish Past* (New York: Oxford University Press, 1995).

[18] See Iver Neumann, "Russia as Central Europe's Constituting Other," *East European Politics and Society* 7: 2 (1993) 349–69.

[19] Quoted by Tzvetan Todorov, *On Human Diversity: Nationalism, Racism, and Exoticism in French Thought* (Cambridge and London: Harvard University Press, 1993), 173.

to create cohesion out of an atomized and disoriented population. Russia, for the first time in history, is having to define what Russia is and what its interests are.

Though among the oldest states in Europe, Poland is today, in many ways, a new nation. First and foremost, Poland has very little of what Tony Judt calls a "usable past" that can be called upon in its quest for a new international role and identity.[20] Historically, it has served as a bastion of Roman Catholicism, isolated from the rest of the Catholic world by Lutheran Germany and bogged down in a bitter and draining "civilizing mission" to its east. Today, however, for the first time since the Counter-Reformation, Poland is no longer isolated from Europe. Internal divisions along ethnic and class lines have finally come to an end. Hitler's savage racial policies and Stalin's barbarous population shifts allowed Poland to re-emerge in the 1990s as a relatively homogeneous state, free of its enervating struggle to subdue the peoples east of the Bug River.[21] The demise of the Russian and Soviet empires and the emergence of the new states of Ukraine, Belarus, and Lithuania have given Poland the opportunity to establish "normal" relations within its traditional sphere of political and cultural influence for the first time in 600 years. Poland's international behavior will depend both on its new self-perception and on external conditions largely beyond its control. None of Poland's present-day neighbors existed six years ago: Germany united; Czechoslovakia dissolved; and four new states emerged to Poland's east.

A far more elusive situation confronts Ukraine. Stepping out onto the world stage for the first time, it is a nation beset with a weak national identity further weakened by profound regional divisions and a low international profile. Far more than Russia or Poland, it will have to rely on foreign policy as a means of establishing its presence within the international system. Simultaneously, Ukraine must determine its national interests for the first time in its history after centuries of foreign domination, first by Lithuania and Poland and later by Russia and Austria. Given the varying experiences of the people of Ukraine, different segments of the population have different notions of what constitutes Ukraine's "other," making it hard to forge a national identity that will prevent it from becoming a junior partner to

---

[20] Tony Judt, "The Unmastered Future: What Prospects for Eastern Europe," *Tikkun* (May 1990).

[21] One could argue that the European Community, founded on the basis of the Christian Democratic ideas of DeGasperi, Monet, and Adenauer, would fit very well with Poland's own political psychology.

either of its better-established neighbors, Poland and Russia.[22] Ukraine's dilemma of national identity is further complicated by its overwhelming economic dependence on Russia. Unlike Poland, Ukraine has to wrestle with external tensions as well as far more profound internal divisions. Given its political, security, and economic realities, a prolonged period of tension with its neighbors seems almost a necessity as Ukraine shapes its identity and determines corresponding national interests. A potentially rich and powerful country, it will have to choose whether to resume an intimate relationship with Russia – albeit on different terms – or to attempt a "return to Europe." Such questions will not be resolved until a single, predominant national identity emerges from several competing identities.[23]

The situation in Russia, a land where imperial consciousness preceded national consciousness and where the entire national ethos centered around the denial of distinct national identities to Russian and non-Russian peoples within the empire, is no less complex. (Poles and Finns provided the notable exceptions to Russia's elite a-national ideologies; even hard-line Slavophiles conceded that these two peoples could not be assimilated.) In the years to come, the process of shaping a national identity in Russia is bound to be tortuously slow. The disintegration of the Russian empire has left Russians facing a profound identity crisis, with virtually no extra-imperial identity, no defined borders, and a large and increasingly vocal diaspora of 25 million. Under these circumstances, Russia will be indefinitely preoccupied by its search for a new identity, with the only certainty being that its national self-definition will depend on its interaction with "the other."

The collapse of the Russian empire gave birth to several competing analyses of Russia's situation. Some feel that Russia will not be able to retain its truncated integrity without at least a partial resurrection of the empire, while others believe that the demise of the empire has had a liberating effect on Russia that will allow it to become a normal nation pursuing its own national interest rather than imperial demands. Proponents of this school of thought see the present as an opportunity for Russia's return to the international system. Another group, whose views are often articulated by the writer and essayist

---

[22] Ilya Prizel, "Ethnicity and Foreign Relations: The Case of Ukraine," in *The International Politics of Eurasia: National Identity and Ethnicity in Russia and the New States of Eurasia*, ed. Roman Szporluk (Armonk, NY: M. E. Sharpe, 1994).

[23] Andrew Wilson, *Ukrainian Nationalism in the 1990s: A Minority Faith* (Cambridge: Cambridge University Press, 1997).

Tatiana Tolstaya, argues that there are actually several distinct Russian identities and that the historical imperative for Russia is to devolve even further. Each new Russia would then formulate its own foreign policy, reflecting its own distinct needs and identity. Finally, a fourth school views the demise of the empire as an opportunity to return to Russia's nativist roots and to withdraw from the international system altogether. The common strand connecting these groups is that they attempt to use foreign policy as a tool to advance their vision of Russia's national identity. This dialectical process between national identity and foreign policy will ultimately shape Russia's world outlook.

In these three old yet new countries, the debate over national identity and the concomitant definition of "the other," and the emergence of a intellectual center of gravity which will claim the custodianship of the national identity will determine their relations with one another, their foreign policies, and ultimately, their profile within the European order and in the world. In all three, a strong dialectical relationship exists between the definition of national identity and the formulation of foreign policy. All three states have to cope with new, often unexpected, realities and have precious little "usable past" to serve as a guide.

Fouad Ajami has observed that in the Arab world, "None of the talk about authenticity or ancestors has given the Arab world the self-confidence to sort out its relationship to the West or to choose among the ideas, technologies and development models tantalizingly held before it and come up with a viable mix."[24] A similar dilemma haunts Russia, Ukraine, and – to a much lesser extent – Poland, creating the potential for internal instability and external strife.

While I base much of my argument on the current intellectual debates in these countries, I do not intend to provide a survey of contemporary intellectual history in Eastern and Central Europe. Rather my purpose is to delineate the ongoing transformations and debates in each country, and the emerging perceptions of each country's place within the international system.

---

[24] Fouad Ajami, *The Arab Predicament: Arab Political Thought and Practice since 1967* (Cambridge: Cambridge University Press, 1981), 195.

# 1 National identity and foreign policy: a dialectical relationship

> Science and reason have, from the beginning of time, played a secondary and subordinate part in the life of nations; so it will be to the end of time. Nations are built up and moved by another force which sways and dominates them, the origin of which is inexplicable.
>
> Fyodor Dostoyevsky, *The Possessed*

> A portion of mankind may be said to constitute a Nationality, if they are united among themselves by common sympathies which do not exist between them and others – which make them cooperate with each other more willingly than with other people, desire to be under the same government, and desire that they should be governed either by themselves or a portion of themselves exclusively . . . the strongest of all identity is that of political antecedents . . .
>
> John Stuart Mill[1]

The language of political science contains few concepts more fugitive than that of nation. For every definition proposed, a host of examples appear to qualify or reject it. Ernest Renan defined a nation as

> a grand solidarity constituted by the sentiment of sacrifices which have been made in the past and those that one is disposed to make again. It supposes a past, renews itself especially in the present by a tangible deed, the approval, the desire, clearly expressed, to continue the communal life. The existence of a nation (pardon the expression) is an everyday plebiscite.[2]

Walker Connor, in a simple, elegant way, defined a nation as a group of people "who believe that they are related by ancestry. It is the

---

[1] John Stuart Mill, "Considerations on Representative Government," in *The Nationalism Reader*, ed. Omar Dahbour and Micheline R. Ishay (New Jersey: Humanities Press, 1995), 98.

[2] Ernest Renan, "Que'est-ce qu'une nation?" reproduced in *The Dynamics of Nationalism: Readings in its Meanings and Developments*, ed. Louis L. Snyder (Princeton: D. Van Norstand, 1964), 9–10.

largest group that shares that belief."[3] In darker tones, the Yugoslav novelist Danilo Kis described nationalism as first and foremost paranoia. Collective and individual paranoia. As collective paranoia it results from envy and fear and most of all from the loss of individual consciousness; this collective paranoia is therefore simply an accumulation of individual paranoias at the pitch of paroxysm.[4]

The simplest, and thus broadest, definition of national identity is offered by Barrington Moore, Jr., as "membership in a group that can save an individual from the anxieties of carving out his own meaningful place in the world, especially when the realistic chances of doing so are tiny."[5]

Just as elusive as the definitions of nation and nationalism is the origin of either concept. There exists little consensus over when and where nationalism and national identity became a political force. While many scholars link the birth of nationalism to the French Revolution and the subsequent transfer of loyalty from the institution of the monarchy to the institution of the state, this definition is by no means universally accepted. Hans Kohn, for example, dates the rise of modern political nationalism to the English Revolution in the seventeenth century;[6] Benedict Anderson to the American Revolution and the Creole republics of the New World;[7] and Lord Acton to the Polish partition.[8]

Similarly, scholars do not agree on which social forces propelled the national ideal into the force that it became. Kohn sees nationalism as a substitute for the decline of religion and the rejection of "Cold Etatism" after the Peace of Westphalia.[9] Ernest Gellner, on the other hand, considers cultural bonds and linguistic links in a highly literate, modern society as the key to national assertiveness,[10] while Anthony D. Smith argues that the driving force of nationalism is industrialization's dislocation of the intelligentsia and subsequent creation of

---

[3] Walker Connor, "From Tribe to Nation," *History of European Ideas* 13:. 1/2 (1991), 6

[4] Danilo Kis, "On Nationalism," in *A Paper House: The Ending of Yugoslavia*, ed. Mark Thompson (New York: Pantheon Books, 1992), 337.

[5] Barrington Moore, Jr., *Injustice: The Social Bases of Obedience and Revolt* (New York: M. E. Sharpe, 1978), 488.

[6] See Hans Kohn, "The Origins of English Nationalism," *Journal of the History of Ideas* 1 (1940), 69–94.

[7] See Benedict Anderson, *Imagined Communities* (London and New York: Verso Press, 1993), ch. 4.

[8] See John Acton, *Essays on Freedom and Power* (London: Thames & Hudson, 1956).

[9] See Hans Kohn, *The Idea of Nationalism: A Study in Its Origins and Background* (New York: Macmillan, 1945), 188–89.

[10] See Ernest Gellner, *Nations and Nationalism* (Ithaca and London: Cornell University Press, 1983).

ethnocentric nationalism as a means of reinstatement.[11] Miroslav Hroch, analyzing the dynamics of the birth of national identity, sees a three-stage process, occurring primarily in "non-historic" nations (i.e. nations who either lack an indigenous elite, or whose elites were assimilated into an imperial culture).[12] The first stage occurs when the local intelligentsia develops an interest in artifacts of a distant past and peasant traditions to validate a sense of national separateness; the second witnesses the spread of the idea of cultural separateness from a narrow circle of intellectuals to the masses, usually peasants; and the third takes place when overtly political organizations result, fusing the intellectuals and the masses and creating a broad-based national movement, following the path common throughout the nineteenth century.[13]

Despite the elusiveness of the subject, however, a general consensus has evolved concerning the existence of a powerful link between romanticism and nationalism. In the words of Mostafa Rejai, "Romanticism rejects the idea of the self-sufficiency of the individual and emphasizes the identification with the external whole, with something outside oneself. . . Nationalism is the political expression of Romanticism."[14] This chapter contends that this emotional, albeit irrational, sense of nation and national identity plays a vital role in forming a society's perception of its environment and is an extremely important, if not driving, force behind the formation of its foreign policy because national identity helps to define the parameters of what a polity considers its national interests at home and abroad.

A polity's national identity is very much a result of how it interprets its history – beliefs and perceptions that accumulate over time and constitute a society's "collective memory." Since the memories of societies, much like those of individuals, are inconsistent and selective, the national identity is subject to what layer of a polity has the custodianship of the collective memory. As will be shown later, a transfer of the custodianship of a polity's collective memory will often lead to a fundamental redefinition of the "national idea" and, with it, the parameters of a polity's national interest.

The prevailing theory of what motivates nations to adopt a specific

[11] See Anthony D. Smith, *Theories of Nationalism* (New York: Holms & Meier, 1983).
[12] For example, the Czech elite were Germanized, the Slovak elite were Magyarized, and the Ukrainian elite were either Polonized or Russified.
[13] Miroslav Hroch, *Social Preconditions of a National Revival in Europe* (Cambridge: Cambridge University Press, 1985).
[14] Mostafa Rejai, *Political Ideologies: A Comparative Approach* (New York: M. E. Sharpe, 1991), 29.

course of action in international conduct is that of the Realist school. While scholars stress different specific factors, mainstream scholarly analysis of the forces shaping international behavior generally agrees that the state is a rational actor. Hans Morgenthau, the father of modern political Realism, asserted that man's political behavior is motivated by two primeval instincts: selfishness and lust for power.[15] Henry Kissinger, along with many others, emphasizes the balance of power among states as the prime determinant of states' behavior.[16] Marxist political scientists tend to see foreign policy as an external reflection of the power-based "correlation of forces" between classes within a society.

Given the dominance that Realist thought enjoys in academic circles, scholars often overlook the psychological aspects of foreign policy. Furthermore, although every member of the international system may strive to enhance its wealth and power, there exists no objective definition of "national interest." As Max Weber observed, some polities seem to be willing to sacrifice a great deal of wealth for an undertaking that may not enhance the state's security or economy but will satisfy "irrational" psychological needs. Expanding his examination of links between ideas and policy, Weber noted:

> Not ideas, but material and ideal interests directly govern men's conduct. Yet very frequently the world images that have been created by ideas have, like switchmen, determined the tracks along which action has been pushed by the dynamic of interests.[17]

The study of international relations often neglects what William Bloom refers to as "identification theory," a psychological bond that motivates an entire population to support certain external policies even if they cause a great deal of social pain and bring few visible rewards.[18] Harold Isaacs, in *Idols of the Tribe: Group Identity and Political Change*, cites Erik Erikson:

> [Erikson] says Freud is speaking of identity in a most central ethnic sense suggesting a deep commonality known only to those who share in it, and only expressible in words more mystical than conceptual. Identity, he says here, is a process "located" *in the core of*

---

[15] See Michael J. Smith, *Realist Thought from Weber to Kissinger* (Baton Rouge: University of Louisiana Press, 1986), ch. 6.

[16] Henry Kissinger, *Diplomacy* (New York: Simon and Schuster, 1994).

[17] Quoted in Judith Goldstein and Robert O. Keohane, eds., *Ideas and Foreign Policy: Beliefs, Institutions and Political Change* (Ithaca and London: Cornell University Press, 1993), 11.

[18] William Bloom, *Personal Identity, National Identity and International Relations* (New York: Cambridge University Press, 1990).

*the individual and yet also in the core of his communal culture*, a process which establishes, in fact, the identity of these two identities.[19]

Although all nations possess, to some degree, a national identity, these identities vary greatly in their intensity and origin. Nations may derive their sense of identity from common language, religion, geographic location, collective memory, cultural practices, or a myth of common ancestry. Indeed, one can hardly imagine the emergence of an Italian national identity without Dante's *Divine Comedy*, the emergence of a German national identity without Luther's translation of the Bible into the vernacular, or the emergence of a Ukrainian national identity without Taras Shevchenko's *Kobzar*. Nevertheless, while a polity must meet a set of preconditions to form a nation, it is interaction with the outside world, namely the acceptance or rejection of "the other," that allows polities to develop a sense of national uniqueness.

Hans Kohn, in his classic study of nationalism, notes that the distinctive monotheism of the Jews and the ancient Greeks' sense of cultural superiority gave the former the concept of *Amamamim* (non-monotheism) and the latter the concept of *te ethnie* (heathens).[20] This sense of superiority, or at least fundamental difference from other peoples, gave these two groups, along with many others, an identity that transcended clan or tribal identities.[21] Nations such as Great Britain, the Netherlands, the United States, and France (according to Hugh Seton-Watson, "continuous nations," whose identity formation was greatly facilitated by institutions that predated their nationalism) can trace the induction of an identity to prolonged contact with the "other"; an identity that shaped their outlook on the world and formed their policies *vis-à-vis* their neighbors. As William Bloom illustrates, England and France initially forged their national identity as a result of the Hundred Years War, which fostered in England the notion of the "Island of Virtue" and in France the national symbol of the "Maiden of Orleans."[22] Over 100 years later, the prolonged conflict with Spain proved a key factor in the early emergence of the Dutch national identity. The Poles date the birth of their national identity from their conversion to Christianity in 966, reinforced by the battle of

---

[19] Quoted in Daniel Patrick Moynihan, *Pandemonium: Ethnicity in International Politics* (New York: Oxford University Press, 1994), 64 (emphasis in the original).
[20] See Kohn, *The Idea of Nationalism*, ch. 2.
[21] In an interesting departure, Zia Sardar, Ashis Nandy, and Merryl Davies, in their pamphlet *Barbaric Others* (Boulder, CO: Westview Press, 1993), claim that this notion of "the other" is strictly a Western one.
[22] Bloom, *Personal Identity*, 65.

Grunwald in 1410; the Magyars date theirs from the Battle of Mohács in 1526; the Serbs from their defeat at Gray Falcon Fields in Kosovo in 1389; the Australians from the battle of Gallipoli in 1917; Brazil from the War of the Triple Alliance of 1865–67; and the United States from the "era of good feelings" following the War of 1812 (although most scholars, including Kohn and Liah Greenfeld, argue that the process of identity formation in the United States did not end until the Civil War).[23]

It should be noted, however, that while all nationalist births require a contact with an "other," the contact does not necessarily have to be a short and cataclysmic event as in the above-mentioned cases. National identity may emerge slowly, after incubating for centuries, as in the case of Ireland. There, in addition to a clash of cultures between native Gaelic Catholicism and British Protestantism, the emergence of national identity had other causes. D. George Boyce described these forces, saying, "[A] large culturally, politically and economically advanced country existed side by side with a small culturally, politically and economically retarded (or, to use a less pejorative phrase, less developed) country."[24] In other words, it was the clash with the "economic other" that sharpened the concept of national identity in Ireland. In short, while most nationalisms emphasize a common cultural or historical denominator to a certain degree, most date back to a conflict with an outside power. However, while war may be the fastest and most effective method of engendering a national identity, it is the prolonged contact with other cultures, not war itself, that stirs an awareness of "the other" hitherto dormant. Another important component of the concept of the "other" is that, often, the recognition of the contact's impact is used by nationalist historians to rebuild the concept retrospectively; for example, the revival of the myth of Bar-Kochba and Massada by the Zionists or the revival of Africanism in Brazil.

Using Nietzsche's concept of *ressentiment*, Greenfeld notes that, in many cases, national identity emerges after the introduction (or importation) of one culture into another. Ultimately, the indigenous culture reacts to, and partially rejects, the alien culture.[25] It is generally

[23] Liah Greenfeld, *Nationalism: Five Roads to Modernity* (Cambridge, MA: Harvard University Press, 1992); Hans Kohn, *The Idea of Nationalism* (New York: Macmillan, 1945).

[24] D. George Boyce, *Nationalism in Ireland* (London and New York: Routledge Press, 1995), 383.

[25] Liah Greenfeld, *Nationalism: Five Roads to Modernity* (Cambridge, MA: Harvard University Press, 1992).

assumed that economic modernization produces cultural homogeni-
zation on a universal Western model. In fact, modernization may
produce precisely the antithetical effect, in essence re-enforcing
Samuel Huntington's argument that, "Modernization and economic
development neither require nor produce cultural Westernization. On
the contrary they promote a resurgence of a renewed commitment to
the indigenous culture."[26]

This dynamic and its subsequent impact on foreign policy can be
seen throughout modern history. In Russia, for example, both Peter I
and Catherine II imposed foreign culture on Russia, but this imposition actually helped to crystallize a sense of Russian identity among
the Russian elite. Although the regimes had hoped to use the new
elite as harbingers of Westernization, it instead inculcated on *the*
Russian rural masses their own identity, and, for them, the Westernized elite became the "other." In Japan, after centuries of isolation
and cultural insularity, the people were confronted with the nation's
rapid economic and cultural integration into the world community.
This gave rise to a sense of national identity based on Japanese
national characteristics (*minzokuteki tokushitsu*), stressing the uniqueness of the Japanese while underplaying the characteristics of the
outside world.[27]

Although the common perception is that *ressentiment* results from
Western cultural imperialism, this phenomenon has occurred in
Western Europe as well. As the German historian Karl Bracher argues,
the imposition of the French political and cultural model on the
traditional German polities in the eighteenth and early nineteenth
century led to the birth of a collective German nostalgia that, in turn,
culminated in the German romantic movement and with it a rejection
of French rationalism, a process that profoundly affected German
domestic and foreign policies.[28] As the German case illustrates,
*ressentiment* of the "other" is a constantly evolving concept. Using
Hroch's model, one can see that when the German national identity
stemmed primarily from a rejection of French cultural hegemony and
rationalism (driven primarily by Herter and his fellow intellectuals),
the "other" was France. By the mid nineteenth century however,
when custodianship of the German national idea was appropriated by

[26] Samuel F. Huntington, "The West and the World," *Foreign Affairs* 75: 6 (November/
December 1997), 37.
[27] Kosaku Yoshino, *Cultural Nationalism in Contemporary Japan: A Sociological Inquiry*
(London and New York: Routledge Press, 1995).
[28] See Karl Dietrich Bracher, *The German Dilemma* (New York: Praeger, 1975).

the political and commercial classes of Germandom, the national interest acquired a far more utilitarian goal, emphasizing the creation of an autarkic economy. The "other" then shifted from the French to the free-trading British. Friedrich List attacked Adam Smith's views of economics, and by inference Britain, because of its "boundless cosmopolitanism, dead materialism, and a disorganizing particularism . . . *A nation must be cemented by a national economy.*"[29]

A spectacular example of how a foreign presence can spawn a new national identity is India. The national identity of the diverse peoples of the Indian subcontinent resulted directly from a reaction to the British Raj, giving these peoples a collective experience, as well as inducing the *ressentiment* process among India's British educated elite. The Nehru family's decision to burn their British manufactured clothing in favor of native dress, while at the same time remaining champions of Westminster democracy, illustrates the process of nation building. Similarly, the birth of an Algerian identity among Arabs and Berbers, traditional rivals, grew out of resistance to French colonial rule.

In short, national identity serves not only as the primary link between the individual and society, but between a society and the world. Foreign policy, with its role as either the protector or the anchor of national identity, provides the political elite with a ready tool for mass mobilization and political cohesion. This cohesion is essential for all societies to function. There are those who have argued that the routine use of foreign policy to secure legitimacy is unique to countries where the political elite feels particularly vulnerable and national identity is rooted not in institutions, but in a romantic national movement. This notion, however, is misplaced. All countries frequently use national identity to articulate their foreign policies and in turn, rely on foreign policy as a foundation of their legitimacy.

William Pfaff, in *The Wrath of Nations*, perceptively notes that the United States, founded on an ideological basis with a constitution and a commitment to universal values, has always used a distinctly American moralism in its foreign policy as a source of national identity.[30] Its hostility to the Bolshevik regime in the 1920s was based not only on a perceived threat to the country's security but also on the

---

[29] Louis L. Snyder, *Roots of German Nationalism: The Sources of Political and Cultural Activity* (New York: Barnes & Nobel Books, 1996), 15 (emphasis added).

[30] William Pfaff, *The Wrath of Nations: Civilization and the Furies of Nationalism* (New York: Simon & Schuster, 1993), 163.

potential communist assault on the American mythos of universal mission. As Gordon S. Wood wrote, The Bolsheviks "threatened nothing less than displacement of the United States from the vanguard of history. The Russians, not the Americans, now claimed to be pointing the way toward the future."[31]

Similarly, Margaret Thatcher's efforts to block deeper European integration were an attempt to preserve British integrity; in her eyes, any transfer of powers to Brussels would undermine Britain's courts and parliament, both vital components of Britain's institution-based national identity. France's spirited objections to subjecting its entertainment industry to the competitive regulations of the General Agreement on Tariffs and Trade were presented not as a defense of an economic asset, but as a policy dictated by the need to preserve France's culture. Generations of French citizens have considered their culture part of France's universal profile and a cornerstone of its national identity.

Most modern polities rely on a legitimizing mythology. The conduct of foreign policy, by extension, is one means of affirming that mythology and thereby legitimizing a governing elite. This relationship is, however, more central in countries in which legal institutions play a relatively marginal role in the process of nation building. In countries where romantic nationalism is prevalent, foreign policy assumes disproportionate importance; by enhancing national prestige, the political elite can appropriate national symbols and retain control over the dynamics of national identity. Since the symbols of national identity hold great political power, the political elite jealously guards them from usurpation by non-governmental actors.

Once mobilized, though, such symbols can trigger great pressures and may force decisions the elite would rather not make. One example is Egypt's President Nasser's decision to harness pan-Arab nationalism in May of 1967 to buttress the sagging popularity of his regime. A case can be made that this tactic created a momentum in the country toward a confrontation with Israel, for which Egypt was not militarily prepared and which resulted in a humiliating defeat. Following this debacle, the Egyptians, who until 1967 had based their identity on their leadership of the Pan-Arab movement, were forced to redefine themselves *vis-à-vis* the other Arab states, and indeed, the rest of the world, focusing on their Egyptian rather than their Arab identity.

[31] Ibid., 185.

## Typologies of nationalism

Although nationalism has no specific ideology and no two cases of national identity are the same, one can discern five separate categories of relationships between national identity and the conduct of foreign policy. The first group consists of national identities based on political institutions rather than mythologies of common blood ancestors, religion, and language. These are English-speaking countries such as the United States and Great Britain, whose political institutions were built on the foundations of eighteenth-century rationalism, which remains the underpinning source of legitimacy. Because of their Enlightenment origins, these polities assume that their political systems are rational and their political values universal. As a result, the foreign policies of these countries tend to be simultaneously legalistic and endowed with a sense of mission.

Grounded in these core beliefs, early American policy soon gave rise to Manifest Destiny and, 100 years later, Wilsonian idealism – the former committing the United States to export its values throughout its hemisphere in the nineteenth century[32] and the latter extending the commitment to a universal scale in the twentieth century. As Robert Osgood wrote, "With a mixture of self-righteous and genuine fervor [Americans] interpreted their own history as a prime example of this truth [of American moral superiority] and based their assertion of the American mission upon faith that their lofty example would shed enlightenment abroad."[33] Despite the oft-stated observation that, under the façade of moralism, Washington pursued a Machiavellian foreign policy, Tony Smith, in his book *America's Mission*, argues convincingly that the United States is unique in its consistent association of universal democracy with its own national well-being.[34]

Although Britain's foreign policy has rarely reached the rhetorical level of America's, it nonetheless has also sought to spread the universal values of rationalism. This British attitude was perhaps best articulated by Daniel O'Connell on the floor of the House of Commons. Commenting on the merits of the 1832 Reform Bill, O'Connell said,

---

[32] Albert Katz Weinberg, *Manifest Destiny: A Study of Nationalist Expansionism in American History* (Gloucester, MA: Peter Smith, 1958).

[33] Robert E. Osgood, *Idealism and Self Interest in America's Foreign Relations* (Chicago and London: University of Chicago Press, 1953), 17–18.

[34] Tony Smith, *America's Mission: The United States and the Worldwide Democracy in the Twentieth Century* (Princeton: Princeton University Press, 1994).

The effect of the Reform Bill would be to give the democratic principle in this country an impulse it had not yet received, and that spirit, urged on by the sympathy the people had for liberty, would press upon the government of this country – would press too, upon the stock-jobbing government of France – and would compel the unpopular monarch there to sympathize with the feelings of the people of France, and encourage the people of Germany . . . to range themselves with every rational government and insist upon justice being done to Poland.[35]

Thus, British pronouncements ranging from "white man's burden" within the colonial empire to upholding "the rule of law" and defending "little Belgium" (which led to Britain's entry into World War I) were framed in the language of universal values.

The Anglo-American world's faith in its institutional superiority reached a level of triumphalism in the late nineteenth and early twentieth centuries, as Anglo-Saxon politicians continually evoked divine providence as the source of authorization for specific foreign policy decisions. Justifying Britain's international role, William Gladstone (who belonged to the anti-imperialist camp) declared, "It is in the nature of things – it is in the design of Providence, that besides the concerns of the vast empire over which this little island rules, we should be meddling in the business of almost every portion of the Globe."[36] In a similar vein, US Senator Albert J. Beveridge described America's global mission in the following manner: "We will not renounce our part in our mission of our race, trustee, under God, of the civilization of the world."[37] In even more extreme fashion, President William McKinley claimed that an angel called on the White House and urged the United States to take up arms against Spain, thus precipitating the Spanish–American War in 1898.

Although the Anglo-Saxon democracies often combine moralism with Machiavellian skills in their conduct of foreign policy (and both Great Britain and the United States have provided numerous examples of cynicism, hypocrisy, and perfidious manipulation of national values), the universal application of their values has played a role in the formation of policy in these countries. A rhetorical bias in favor of democracy, human rights, and international law, however selectively applied, remains a vital element in foreign policy formation and

---

[35] Quoted in A. J. P. Taylor, *The Trouble Makers: Dissent over Foreign Policy 1792–1939* (Bloomington: University of Indiana Press, 1958), 43.

[36] Ibid., 85.

[37] Louis Leo Snyder, *The Dynamics of Nationalism: Readings in its Meaning and Development* (Princeton: Van Norstrand, 1964), 278.

legitimization. The rhetorical use of these values to rationalize the Gulf War is a recent example of the Anglo-Saxon tendency to use morality as a justification for policy choices.

Consistent with their belief in the Anglo-Saxon universal mission, the United States and Britain, during their expansionary phases, were not so much interested in exporting their language or culture as they were in advancing their brand of parliamentarism, political account-ability, and impartial justice. This had a profound impact on the British empire and on the early development of the United States. For example, although Thomas Jefferson showed enormous interest in expansion across North America, the crucial issue for him was not the creation of a single state, but rather that the new states shared similar institutions. In fact, young Jefferson expected that several institution-ally similar republics would emerge across the continent, rather than a single continent-wide state.[38]

For the British, as well, the advancement of their institutions took precedence over the maintenance of their empire. In his defense of American independence, Edmund Burke argued that a common notion of liberty and constitution was what bound the people of Britain and America: "Deny [the Americans] this participation of freedom, and you break the sole bond which originally made, and must still preserve, the unity of the empire."[39] Emphasizing the centrality of institutions, Richard Cobden, a founder of the Manche-ster School, argued that the purpose of British imperialism was not to create a vast, single entity governed from London, but rather entities that shared the same enlightened institutions and values and a commitment to free trade with Britain. For both Britain and the United States, free trade and democratic institutions, as opposed to possession of territory, are the primary guarantors of peace and prosperity.[40]

A second category of national identity is found in polities emerging from imperial or colonial domination. Not surprisingly, such nations express a strong sense of cultural and political *ressentiment* directed at the intruding entity and are generally found in Central and Eastern Europe, Mexico, and parts of Central and South America. In these

---

[38] See Merrill D. Peterson, *Thomas Jefferson and the New Nation: a Biography* (New York: Oxford University Press, 1970).

[39] Quoted in Richard Hofstadter, *Great Issues in American History: A Documentary Record* (New York: Vintage Books, 1958), 43 (emphasis added).

[40] See Richard Cobden, *England, Ireland and America* (Philadelphia: Institute for the Study of Human Issues, 1980).

cases, *ressentiment* has produced an intense feeling of political and social injustice inflicted on the indigenous peoples, profound cultural defensiveness, and a fascination with the past. The East Europeans tend to stress their eighteenth century roots; Mexicans and Peruvians, their pre-Columbian past; and Brazilians, their African heritage. Both Latin America and Eastern Europe keenly resent their treatment as peripheral European civilizations and their marginalization within the international system.[41] Nationalism in Eastern and Central Europe, where the issue of national identity only appeared following the revolutions of 1848 and has not yet fully crystallized, tends to take a profound cultural form stemming from mythologies of common ancestry, kinship of blood, shared language, and linkage to native soil. The "father" of cultural romantic nationalism, Johann Gottfried von Herder, firmly believed that ethnonationalism brings out the genius in every people, as long as the people remain in their natural habitat, retaining the mythical link between blood and soil. Thus, according to Herder, biblical Israelites possessed a "genius" that eighteenth-century East European Jews did not.[42]

Herder's fascination with the drive for cultural authenticity stretching to the "dawn of history" drew a far less sanguine response from more contemporary East European thinkers. To the Romanian historian of religion Mircea Eliade, this drive for "roots and authenticity" led to the cultural degeneration of Central and Eastern Europe:

> At the dawn of the modern World the "origin" enjoyed an almost magical prestige. To have a well established "origin" meant, when all is said and done, to have an advantage of a noble origin. "We find our origin in Rome!" the Romanian intellectuals of the eighteenth and nineteenth centuries proudly repeat. In their case consciousness of Latin descent was accompanied by a kind of mythical participation in the greatness of Rome. Similarly, the Hungarian intelligentsia found a justification for the antiquity, nobility and historical mission of the Magyars in the origins of Hunor and Magor and the heroic saga of Arpad . . . This anxiety [to be ancient and ergo noble] is perceptible in all national historians of Central and Eastern Europe.

[41] Andre Gunder Frank's dependence theory is but one manifestation of the frustration felt by the continent as a result of marginalization within the international community. See Andre Gunder Frank, *On Capitalist Underdevelopment* (Bombay: Oxford University Press, 1975). Similar resentment toward the West can be observed in the essay by the Hungarian novelist Gyorgy Konrad, "Den westlichen Höhlenforschern zür Aufmerksamkeit empfehlen," in *Mittleuropa: Traum ober Trauma*, ed. H. P. Burmeister, F. Boldt, and G. Meszaros (Bremen, 1989).

[42] See Daniel Chirot, "Herder's Multicultural Theory of Nationalism and Its Consequences," *East European Politics and Society* 10: 1 (Winter 1996).

> Then too, it was transformed into an instrument of propaganda and
> political warfare . . . with a few exceptions all respective historians
> confined themselves to national history and finally wound up in
> *cultural provincialism.*

The passion for "noble origins" also explains the racist myth of
"Aryanism" which periodically gained currency in the West, especially in Germany. The "Aryan" model was the exemplary model that
must be imitated in order to recover racial "purity," physical strength,
nobility, and heroic "ethics" of the glorious and creative "begin-
nings."[43] While this notion of defending national identity against an
inferior "other" may not be unique to Eastern Europe or Latin
America, it does play a special role in these regions.[44] Herder, in his
defense of the German culture against the French, urged Germans to
"[S]peak German! Spew out the Seine's ugly slime."[45] Citing Poland,
Rudolf Jaworsky notes that its traumatic history and lack of a strong
civil society has given rise to "a tradition of [external] enemies" that
serves as the key element of Poland's national identity.[46]

By extension, the historical development of East and Central
European national identities has had a unique impact on the development and exercise of foreign policy in the region. As Hans Kohn noted
in his classic *The Idea of Nationalism,* nationalism in Eastern Europe
was first and foremost a cultural process, often a protest against
external political and cultural domination.[47] Thus, while West European nationalism remained a political development that took on a
rationalist, cosmopolitan, modernist, and even positivist character
after World War II, East European nationalists adopted the notion of
an idealized society that had tragically succumbed to pressure from
the outside. Central European nationalism rejected political pragma-
tism and embraced historical, romantic sentiments. Describing the
unique characteristics of East European nationalism, the Hungarian
philosopher G. M. Tamas observed:

> [E]thnocultural nationalism, particularly in the extreme shape, has
> taken hold in Eastern Europe, and cannot and does not answer

[43] Mircea Eliade, *Myth and Reality* (New York: Harper Torchbooks, 1975), 182–83
(emphasis added).
[44] For historical reasons the notion of defending the nation differs between Eastern
Europe and Latin America. While the East Europeans fear physical annihilation by
Russia or Germany, Latin Americans tend to fear economic aggression.
[45] Quoted by Daniel Chirot, "Herder's Multicultural Theory," 12.
[46] Rudolf Jaworsky, "History and Tradition in Contemporary Poland," *East European
Quarterly* 19: 3 (September 1985), 351.
[47] Kohn, *The Idea of Nationalism.*

political questions. It is mostly a reaffirmation of identity. Nineteenth century nationalism strengthened the state; twentieth century ethno-cultural nationalism is contemptuous of institutions; it is anarchic, that is, it is anarchic in regard of state institutions and especially in regard of supreme state authority.[48]

With the exception of Poland – and to some degree Hungary, whose elites generally perceived themselves as part of the West[49] – East and Central European nationalists historically rejected, in varying degrees, the Western legalistic-national model in favor of nativism or Slavo-philia. This trend has found expression in musical and cultural populism, ranging from the efforts of the Russian "Mighty Five" to create a distinctly Russian classical music, to Dvořák and Smetana in the Czech lands, to Liszt and Bartók in Hungary, to Enescu in Romania. But far beyond music, East and Central European nation-alism bears heavy burdens of cultural and political *ressentiment* toward external pressures. Granted, no generalization about the emergence of East European national identities is precise, given the different histories and experiences of East Europeans. Poland and Hungary experienced an early emergence of national identity, while in Russia imperial identity preceded national identity. For the Czechs, national identity reawakened in the mid nineteenth century; in contrast, fragmented collective memory and the absence of sustained statehood delayed the emergence of national identity for Ukrainians and Belarussians until the early twentieth century. Nevertheless, the *ressentiment* model of external domination and romantic nationalism has proven consistent in the development of all East European national identities.

In stark contrast to English and American identification with political legalism (which is self-contained and does not rely on the concept of an "other"), East and Central Europeans identify with ideals almost universally determined by rejection of the "other." Unlike the West European, "horizontal" form of nationalism, which developed over time through bureaucratic incorporation by an aristo-cratic elite, Eastern Europe's nationalism evolved on a "vertical-vernacular" plane that cut across class lines.[50] Given the multiethnic

---

[48] Gaspar M. Tamas, "Old Enemies and New: A Philosophic Postscript to Nationalism," *Studies in East European Thought* (1993).

[49] Poland's case may be unique: unlike the rest of the region, where *ressentiment* was directed at Western cultural domination, Poland, dominated by Russia and Prussia, directed its national *ressentiment* toward the East and became very pro-Western.

[50] See Anthony D. Smith, *National Identity* (Reno, Las Vegas, and London: University of Nevada Press, 1991), 55–61.

nature of Eastern Europe, the definition of "other" can be both internal and external, and defined culturally, racially, politically, or economically. Furthermore, a polity may develop a hierarchy of "others" ranging from the external, such as the dominating empire, to the internal, for example, an ethnic minority.

These primordial nationalisms have often been manipulated by the elite to either seize new political and economic privileges (as in Poland, the Czech Republic, and Slovakia) or to preserve traditional ones (Hungary and Russia).[51] Poland has identified itself as the "Christ-nation" (bastion of Catholicism in a sea of heresy, with a civilizing mission thrown in for good measure); Russia as the "Third (and last) Rome"; Romania as "heir to the Roman civilization engulfed by the sea of Slavic and Magyar adversity"; Hungary as "an island of true civilization in a sea of Slavs"; Ukraine as a "bulwark against Muscovite Tartar despotism."

Given this blend of culture and politics in Eastern Europe, the nearly perpetual state of cultural mobilization, and the resentment of real and perceived pressures from the outside, the foreign policies of these countries have continually reflected goals beyond the commonly defined national interests, such as self-preservation and enhancement of economic prosperity. For the foreign policy of almost every East European country to remain credible at home, a government must also zealously defend the nation's identity. Due to weak political institutions and, therefore, a perennially precarious basis for the political legitimacy of the state, the ruling elites repeatedly have had to "reaffirm [the national] identity" through a distinctly nationalist foreign policy. Issues that would go unnoticed in the West become litmus tests of a government's commitment to the nation.[52] Does the Cathedral of St. Theresa in Przemyśl in eastern Poland belong to the Latin Catholic or Greek Catholic Church? Will Slovakia allow Hungarian language street signs in southern Slovakia? Will the statue of Magyar King Matyas remain in the center of the Romanian city of Cluj? Will Poland tolerate German language church services in Silesia?

Another central factor in the development of national identity, noted by Gale Stokes, is the role of a "zero hour" from which a nation can create a modern identity. In the case of Eastern Europe, the

---

[51] Robin Okey, *Eastern Europe 1740–1985: Feudalism to Communism* (Minneapolis: Minnesota University Press, 1986).

[52] For background, see Janusz Bugajski, *Nations in Turmoil: Conflict and Cooperation in Eastern Europe* (Boulder, CO: Westview Press, 1993).

imposition of Stalinist uniformity in 1948 deprived the entire region of a liberating *stunde null* that would have enabled it to forge new relations and identities, as did Western Europe following the catharsis of World War II.[53] Instead, the centrality of nationalism and national identity in Eastern and Central Europe gained prominence during the nearly forty years of Soviet domination to become the key weapons in the fight against Soviet hegemony. A disparate group of actors – from Poland's Cardinal Stefan Wyszyński to Romania's neo-Stalinist Nicolae Ceauşescu – used nationalism to defy the Kremlin and thus ensured that nationalism would continue to be a vital force in the politics of Eastern Europe.

Maria Todorova, in her essay "Ethnicity, Nationalism and the Communist Legacy in Eastern Europe," argues convincingly that the main cause of growing tension among the ethnic groups of Eastern Europe stems from Soviet domination. As long as the USSR existed, it provided Eastern Europe with a collective "other" against which all East Europeans developed an inverted nationalism; namely, the idea that "a more backward metropolis served as a catharsis from inferiority complex for a while."[54] Todorova posits that twentieth-century East European nationalism went through three distinct phases: (1) before World War II, a deep sense of inferiority to the West; (2) after World War II, a sense of superiority over the USSR and, by extension, over Russia; and (3) the post-Cold War era, a return to a sense of inferiority to the West. The collapse of the communist monolith not only made the need for redefining national identity inevitable, it also demanded the creation of a new "other" that would become the focus of growing nationalist pressures in Eastern and Central Europe. This new hostility toward the "other" has turned westward, spurred by feelings of rejection, resentment over the region's marginalization, and anger over the West's "betrayal" of Eastern Europe at Yalta, and the perceived failure of the West to appreciate its sacrifices for the cause of freedom. Furthermore, as Owen Harries points out, the West itself has ceased to exist as a cohesive political entity since the disintegration of the Soviet bloc.[55] This has deprived the Eastern European countries of a fixed reference point from which to redefine

[53] Gale Stokes, "Lessons of East European Revolutions of 1989," *Problems of Communism*, no. 40 (September 1991), 19.
[54] Maria Todorova, "Ethnicity, Nationalism and the Communist Legacy in Eastern Europe," *East European Politics and Societies* 7: 1 (Winter 1993), 153.
[55] Owen Harries, "The Collapse of the West," *Foreign Affairs* (September–October 1993).

their national identities and has instead further complicated relations between Eastern Europe and the West.

In many ways Eastern Europe finds its position in the international system analogous to the 1920s Harding–Coolidge era of "normalcy." Interest in Eastern Europe peaked between 1917 and 1919, when leaders such as Ignacy Jan Paderewski, Tomas Masaryk, and Alexander Kerensky captured the imagination of the West. Between 1989 and 1991, Wałęsa, Havel, and Gorbachev contributed to a similar burst of interest in Eastern Europe. This interest has now waned. Europe, to which the East European liberal leaders had hoped to return, has fragmented both politically and economically. East European leaders perceive the West European inability to respond credibly to the Balkan crisis or to speed the process of opening the European Union to Central European democracies as signs of continuing indifference. After a half century of exhausting international activism, the United States has withdrawn into a period of introspection, searching for answers to internal economic difficulties and redefining its own global role.

US policy in Europe also mirrors that of the 1920s, when the United States, the patron saint and role model to East Europeans, concentrated on the integration of Weimar Germany into the international system and ignored the new states of Eastern Europe. In the early 1990s, America's efforts seem to be heavily focused on "Weimar Russia," once again trying to integrate a former enemy into the international system, to prevent its reversion to an anti-status-quo power, while neglecting the smaller states of Eastern Europe. As a result of this perceived neglect and the absence of a larger framework in which to develop a new identity, the East European polities have drawn on the predominant image in their "usable past" – that of the victim. This preoccupation with their historical sense of "damaged self" has led to self-absorption in their unique experience of victimization and has fueled resentment toward Western indifference, cynicism, and betrayal. Even the possibility of NATO's expansion eastward is viewed by many East Europeans as part of a "deal" with Russia. All of these factors are bound to shape their emotion-laden foreign policies for a long time to come.

A third form of national identity can be found in modern France. On the one hand, France is an ancient state, with a venerable political tradition providing a stable reference point for its national identity. On the other hand, the country's tumultuous history has left it with few of the continuous political institutions of the Anglo-Saxon countries. Therefore, if the Anglo-Saxon countries require acceptance of the legal system of the host country as the price of being "admitted" to host society, and if the ethnic nation-states in Eastern and Central Europe claim that a genetic commonality forms the basis of the nation, the French marker of its national identity is its universal culture. The centrality of culture as a marker of "authentic Frenchness" is a constant refrain in France's definition of itself. Even during the collaborationist fascist regime of Vichy, its leaders claimed that "Frenchness" was a cultural construct. The Vichy constitution overtly stated that, "The French community requires from its members an absolute allegiance. It does not accept into its breast as a constitutive element a race that conducts itself as a distinct community that resists assimilation."[56]

During the late nineteenth century, France experienced a precipitous decline as Europe's premier power. After World War II, the loss of its colonies (in the view of the French, a consequence of their decline in Europe) and the shift of Western culture to the Anglophone world dealt a severe blow to the French historic sense of universalism. Today, French national identity lies at a crossroads. The French Revolution may have bequeathed to France a universal sense of mission, but France's relative decline in power has increasingly put this pursuit out of reach. Summing up the French dilemma, Henry Kissinger noted: "Since the end of Napoleon III's reign, France has lacked the power to impose the universal aspirations it inherited from the French Revolution, or the arena to find an outlet for its missionary zeal."[57] While to the outsider, France's preoccupation with its cultural uniqueness and seeming obsession with *grandeur* often appears incomprehensible or even comical, it is an important feature of the French national identity that is often misunderstood. Because France is a nation created out of diverse and multiethnic peoples, molded by an overbearing central state, it relies on its belief in the superiority of its culture and on the *grandeur* portrayed by its leaders as pillars of its national legitimacy.[58]

The shift from a universal mission to a posture *of raison d'état* engendered in French national identity a defensiveness of cultural heritage combined with a determination to pursue a foreign policy

---

[56] Richard Weisberg, "Leon Blum in Vichy France," *Partisan Review*, no. 3 (1996), 553–70.

[57] Henry Kissinger, *Diplomacy* (New York: Simon & Schuster, 1994), 120.

[58] Robert Gilda, *The Past in French History* (New Haven and London: Yale University Press, 1994), ch. 3.

affirming France's status as a unique culture and a great power. In their search for legitimacy, successive French governments have called for policies that have provided France with few tangible benefits and thus could be deemed irrational.[59] Nevertheless, these policies enjoyed the broad support of the French public because they responded to a psychological need for a sense of universal mission. France's insistence on maintaining the franc zone and a direct military presence in Africa, costly overseas departments, and a military doctrine alleging full French independence are all burdens on France's economy. Even when France, chastened by the unimpressive performance of its forces in the Gulf War and the European-led debacle in Bosnia, felt compelled to return to the integrated structure of NATO, it did so under the guise of an ill-defined promise to enhance the "European persona" of NATO. While to the outsider these policies may appear irrational, they have enabled the French to overcome a legacy of decline and defeat and have restored its national cohesion and sense of purpose.[60] Attempts to reconcile the needs of France's national identity with the country's limited resources have resulted in a paradoxical foreign policy, parochial in content but universal in its trappings.

A fourth and newer form of national identity emerged in the twentieth century among the former European colonies in Africa and Asia. The genesis of this nationalism is unique. Owing to the manner of colonial partitioning and subsequent multiethnic development, these new countries generally cannot use the East European romantic nationalist model, which implies a certain level of ethnic homogeneity, as a basis of political mobilization. These polities also lack traditional institutions that could serve as reference points for a national identity. Rather, national identities have resulted from rebellion against the colonial power by an intermediary group on behalf of the native population. Generally indigenous themselves, the intermediary group is detached from the rest of the population by virtue of their education or experience abroad. One example can be found in the Arab nationalism of the early twentieth century, which was led disproportionally by Greek Orthodox Christian Arabs who historically mediated between the colonial powers and the Arab masses.[61]

---

[59] France's expenditure of $7 billion in transfers to Francophone Africa is a case in point.

[60] Stanley Hoffmann, *Decline or Renewal? France since the 1930s* (New York: Viking Press, 1974); Philip H. Gordon, *A Certain Idea of France: French Security Policy and the Gaullist Legacy* (Princeton: Princeton University Press, 1993).

[61] George Antonius, *The Arab Awakening* (London, 1938)

India, however, provides the most vivid example of a "denatura-lized" elite taking the lead in creating a national identity. Given the enormous size of India, Britain's only hope of administering the vast subcontinent was through the creation of what Thomas Macaulay described in 1835 as "a class of persons, Indian in blood and color, but English in taste, in opinions, in morals, and intellect."[62] The creation of this intermediary group, as illustrated in E. M. Forster's novel, *A Passage to India*, ultimately led to the emergence of a new, educated elite, imbued with the European concept of nationalism and resenting its subordinate position to colonial overlords. By the 1920s, India's viceroy Lord Lytton was lamenting that the Anglicized elite in India had not only failed to shore up the British empire, but had actually turned against it. Lytton described the Anglicized Indians as "Babus, whom we have educated to write semi-seditious articles in the native press."[63] Nehru himself admitted that India's national identity was an "anti-feeling" fueled by the colonial experience rather than an identity built around a common ethnicity or national political institutions.[64]

In general, these kinds of nations create unique models of foreign policy. Once they attain independence, their leaders splinter under the pressure of divergent agendas. This process of disintegration has proven the most severe in post-colonial countries, since they often lack either institutional supports or ethnic homogeneity. As a result of these weaknesses, their traditional relationship – often tension-ridden – with the former colonial power continues to serve as the only unifying element, with notable examples such as Zimbabwe, India, Indonesia, Guinea, and Guyana. In each of these cases, the ruling elite desperately clings to its tenuous identity by repeatedly exploiting the legacy of colonialism's abuses, the inherent injustices within the international system, and general issues of economic and cultural imperialism. Another aspect of post-colonial countries' foreign poli-cies is their attempt to find a broader context for national existence along a regional basis. Thus, membership in such institutions as the Arab League, the Organization of African Unity, and the Non-aligned Movement not only provides post-colonial states with a greater presence within the international system, but also legitimizes and reinforces their "anti-feeling" sense of national identity.

A fifth form of nationalism is theocratic nationalism, which gener-ally emerges in countries whose religion falls outside the mainstream

---

[62] Quoted in Nigel Harris, *National Liberation* (Reno, Las Vegas, and London: University of Nevada Press, 1993), 168.
[63] Ibid., 168.     [64] Rejai, *Political Ideologies*, 7.

of a world religion; namely, tsarist Russia and contemporary Iran. Russia, the only major Orthodox country, used its religious uniqueness to define the rest of Christendom as the "other." By virtue of being the only "true" Christian country, it claimed the right to project its influence beyond its frontiers. Similarly, contemporary Iran, the sole major Shiite Muslim country, grafted national identity onto its unique form of religion while simultaneously claiming the role of "defender of the faith" for the entire Islamic world. Being religious splinters within a larger context, both Russia and Iran used their minority status as a means to acquire legitimacy by asserting themselves as the last bastion against the "degeneration" that allegedly afflicted Sunni Islam or Western Christianity. This reliance on religion as a source of cohesion is particularly intriguing in the case of Iran and the Russian empire, since in both cases the dominant ethnic groups, the Persians and the Russians, were declining pluralities within a multinational state. In short, although both Russia and Iran claimed universal messianic roles based on their theocratic ideologies, both used their state religions to shore up a distinct national identity and the legitimacy of their regimes.

These five categories of national identity are by no means exhaustive. Some national identities do not fall into any of the above categories or they contain only some elements of them. Nevertheless, a remarkable degree of consistency remains between Weber's "governing ideas," despite their malleability, and the formation of foreign policy. Nigel Harris argues that "National claims summarize complex economic and social interests and classes, a coalition that is rarely the same in different times and places; so nationalism does not in and of itself indicate any self-evident aims."[65]

In sum, national identity is neither constant nor immutable, but rather constantly redefined, in part by foreign policy. The relationship between national identity and foreign policy experiences is highly dialectic. Several factors can contribute to these dialectical changes in national identity. Perhaps the most common element altering the national identity of a polity is the metamorphosis or the total disappearance of "the other." The collapse of the Habsburg empire, the disintegration of the USSR, and the withdrawal of European powers from their overseas possessions sharply redefined the "other" for scores of polities. For example, between 1848 and 1948, Czech intellectuals resented the Germans' political and cultural domination and

[65] Harris, *National Liberation*, 22.

tended to stress their Slavic roots and their solidarity with fellow Slavs. After World War II, the definitive "other" of the Czechs shifted from their German-speaking neighbors to the hegemonic, Russian-dominated Soviet Union. In this case, the change in the "other" fundamentally altered the Czechs' national identity. Recent tension between the Czech Republic and Germany over the question of the expulsion of the Sudeten Germans, has reawakened again the notion of the Germans as the "other." In the late twentieth century, following four decades of Soviet domination, the Czechs stress their Central European identity. A parallel mutation of a national identity can be observed in the case of the Palestinians who historically viewed themselves as a part of Muslim–Ottoman civilization, however the clash with Jewish Zionists following World War I, and the introduction of a specific "other" led to the substitution of the former identity with an Arab–Palestinian identity.[66] Similarly, late-nineteenth-century Russia saw the German-speaking world as its defining "other," furnishing for the Russians a standard by which they judged their identity. After the defeat of Germany in World War II and four decades of the Cold War, Germany receded in Russia's national consciousness, and the United States became "the other" by which Russians defined their success and failure.

The pursuit of a specific foreign policy may also over time induce a change in the national identity of a polity. When Austria came into being in 1918, most Austrians did not identify with the new state. In fact, Austria's declaration of statehood explicitly stated that Austria's goal was to merge into Germany, ironically making the declaration both a birth certificate and an obituary. However, Austria's successful maintenance of neutrality since 1955 has led most Austrians to internalize the notion of neutrality to such a degree that many objected to membership in the European Union on the grounds that it might compromise the country's neutrality and weaken its identity.

As previously noted, national identities can undergo rapid transformation as a result of military defeat. France's shift from a national identity based on the concept of a civilizing empire to one of a component of a larger European entity can be directly traced to its defeats in Indochina (1954) and Algeria (1962). Polities, though, may respond differently to the same stimulus. The 1956 Suez fiasco taught Great Britain that it was no longer a major power. Hence, it willingly

---

[66] See Rashid Khalidi, *Palestinian Identity: the Construction of a Modern National Consciousness* (New York: Columbia University Press, 1997), *passim*, esp. ch. 7.

assumed the role of a junior partner to the United States under the guise of a "special relationship." France, whose national identity has suffered far more during this century, responded to the Suez debacle by denying its decline within the international system and pursuing a policy of global assertiveness, even if its impact proved more symbolic than real. Finally, there are times when mere disappointment in a foreign policy can radically alter a polity's perception of its role within the international system. The profound disappointment of the United States in the Treaty of Versailles and the collapse of Wilsonian diplomacy led to a fundamental change in self-perception as it ceased to believe in a universal mission and withdrew into isolationism and unilateralism.

Generational changes can also alter the identity of a polity. The independence of India in 1947, the creation of ANZUS (Australia, New Zealand, United States – but not Britain) in 1948, and the 1956 Suez crisis clearly demonstrated that the British empire was no longer tenable. British politicians of Churchill's generation, whose formative experience was the Boer War, could not imagine Great Britain as a mere component of a larger European entity, shorn of its global mission and forced to subordinate its venerable institutions to the dicta of Brussels. Britain's difficulty in recasting its national identity led former US Secretary of State Dean Acheson to note in 1962 that "Britain [has] lost an empire, and has not found a destiny." It was far easier for prime ministers Harold Wilson and Edward Heath, whose formative political experiences occurred during the Marshall Plan and European reconstruction, to initiate the move from a global to a regional orientation. Even so, nearly a generation after Britain's entry into the European Union, recasting Britain's national identity remains a slow and fitful process.

The concept of national identity is a derivative of a real or imagined collective memory of a polity. Since memory is highly selective, it is vital to consider who has the custodianship of that memory. When the custodian of a national identity changes, so do perceptions of the past and, consequently, the parameters of the national interest. Iran under the Shah utilized the collective memory of Persian empire, Emperor Darius and his universalist, enlightened policies to justify the modernization of Iran and its cultural integration into the "World civilization" under the Palahvi dynasty. The Shah's use of the nation's memory of Darius justified Iran's role as a supporter of the existing world order. After the fall of the Shah, the custodianship of Iran's national identity shifted to the Shiite clerics, who found in their collective memory an image of Iran as the universal protector of Islam, endowed with a messianic mission to fight against the betrayal of the true Islamic dogma by the infidels, the Sunni Muslims. For the Shah, Iran's "other" was the "backward" Third World from which Iran was trying to break away. For the clerics, the "other" is the godless West, locked in a struggle with "true Iranian" values.

The democratization of Brazil and the decline in the monopoly on power and education of the criollo elite resulted in a shift in that country's identity. While it had viewed itself as a part of the 'enlightened' West ( a myth which was bolstered by Brazil's token participation in World War II), it shifted to a greater identification with Africa, Latin America, and the Portuguese-speaking world. Not only does Brazilian culture no longer seek to mimic European patterns, but the country's foreign policy orientation is far different than it was but a generation ago. The demise of Nasserism following the 1967 Arab–Israeli war and the re-emergence of the Egyptian bourgeoisie as the dominant political class led to a shift in the custodianship and hence the definition of Egypt's identity. Nasser had stressed Egypt's Arab heritage and Third World position, charging Egypt with a pan-Arab mission and leadership of the Non-Aligned Movement. Nasser's death in 1970 led to a rediscovery of a distinct Egyptian identity stretching back to Pharoanic times, seeing Egypt as superior to the "young" Arab states and setting much more narrow parameters around Egypt's national interests.

France may well serve as an example of a consistent custodianship of a national identity and therefore, a remarkably consistent set of psychological parameters have set the country's foreign policy. Despite a stormy history of revolutions, defeat, and political turmoil, France's highly centralized state, dirigist economy, and ubiquitous political-bureaucratic elite produced by the Ecole Nationale d'Administration (ENA) and similar institutions dominating the civil service, industry, and financial institutions have resulted in a relatively consistent (however distorted) "collective memory." While France has adapted to the changing realities of the world, the parameters and rhetoric of French policy have remained consistent, though leading to policies which may strike outside observers as pretentious or even quixotic. Robert Osgood once observed:

> Great changes in the way a nation thinks of itself, and acts, come like a tide. They come gradually, almost imperceptibly, in a series of surges and recessions, unevenly, like the waves on the shore. But they come steadily and surely, so that if one fixes one's attention on a

landmark upon the shoreline one can measure the advance in the course of time . . . .[67]

Although the collapse of the Soviet bloc and the Soviet Union occurred with dazzling speed, the emergence of a sovereign Poland, an independent Ukraine, and a post-imperial Russia was the result of a slow, almost imperceptible evolution much like Osgood's metaphoric tide. The subsequent chapters explore the evolution of national identity in Poland, Ukraine, and Russia and trace how the evolution of their identities is reflected in these countries' foreign policies.

[67] Osgood, *Idealism and Self Interest*, 429.

# 2 Polish identity 1795–1944: from romanticism to positivism to ethnonationalism

> All men, as beings of one and the same nature, have equal rights and equal obligations; all are brethren, all are children of the one father – God; all are members of one family – Mankind . . . The reborn independent Poland will be democratic. All, irrespective of faith and origin, will receive mental, political, and cultural emancipation . . .
>
> Manifesto of a Democratic Society, 1836[1]

> Sooner or later [the Jews] will be fused with us in a uniform society.
>
> Bolesław Prus, 1886[2]

> Even if Jews were moral angels, mentally geniuses, even if they were people of a higher kind than we are, the very fact of their existence among us and their close participation in our life is for our society lethal (*zabójczy*) and they have to be got rid of (*Trzeba się ich pozbyć*).
>
> Roman Dmowski, 1934[3]

Poland is a "historic" nation with an indigenous national elite and a powerful sense of distinctiveness and identity. However, until World War II, its national identity to a large degree remained in the repository of a small social and political elite that perpetuated a peculiar collective memory of the idea of Poland – a Poland that was rooted in a commonwealth with Lithuania, that covered vast areas of contemporary Ukraine and Belarus and perceived itself as a great military power, armed with the messianic notion of having been endowed with a civilizing mission and a racially superior ruling class. It was the collective memory and the state of mind of this elite that

---

[1] See Krystyna M. Olszer, ed., *For Your Freedom and Ours: Polish Progressive Spirit from the 14th Century to the Present* (New York: Frederick Ungar Publishing Co., 1981), 65.

[2] Bolesław Prus, "The Jewish Little Question," in Olszer, *For Your Freedom and Ours*, 108.

[3] Quoted in Alexander J. Groth, "Dmowski, Piłsudski and Ethnic Conflict in Pre-1939 Poland," *Canadian Slavic Studies* 3: 1 (Spring 1969), 76.

gave content to the domestic and foreign policies of the Polish Second Republic (1919–39). It was not until the twentieth century that the Polish national idea filtered into the popular consciousness, and it was not implemented until the re-emergence of an independent Poland in 1989. Thus, the story of the evolution of the Polish national identity is also the story of the transfer of that identity from the elite to the popular level and the emergence of a different collective memory, different priorities, and, ultimately, a different foreign policy. This chapter will review the evolution of the Polish national identity from universalism to ethnonationalism and the impact of this mutation on both the internal relations in Poland and its external relations. As noted in chapter 1, many ingredients – including language, religion, geography, and institutions – help forge a national identity by serving as cardinal points of convergence among an otherwise diverse people. Most important, however, is the national "collective memory" that defines the essence of the nation's experience, especially in countries lacking strong political and legal institutions. But collective memory is a highly subjective matter. National memories, like those of an individual, can prove extremely selective and arbitrary. Edward Said, in his book *Orientalism*,[4] observed that the ability to manipulate the narrative of collective memory gives politics moral as well as political power. Accordingly, since various elements within a polity remember different events at different times and in differing ways, the concept of national identity is inherently unstable.

Few polities are more sensitive to the vagaries of collective memory than Poland, a country where, as Andrzej Walicki observed, "Everything has a historic dimension."[5] Walicki argued that a Polish national identity is particularly problematic because of centuries of alienation from Europe and domination by foreign rulers. As a result, Polish loyalties have tended to remain localized and provincial or to embrace an abstract vision of "the nation" without the distracting impact of other intermediate institutions. Thus, the issue of national identity has had far greater emotional impact in Poland than in many Western countries with more developed civil societies.[6]

The definition of Poland's national identity is complicated by its

[4] Edward Said, *Orientalism* (New York: Vintage Books, 1979).
[5] Andrzej Walicki, "The Three Traditions of Polish Patriotism," in *Polish Paradoxes*, ed. Stanisław Gomułka and Antony Polonsky (London and New York: Routledge Press, 1990).
[6] Ibid.

history and geography. Located at the crossroads of three main branches of Christianity (Catholicism, Orthodoxy, and Lutheranism), for centuries home as well to more than half the world's Jewry, and periodically engaged in battles against the encroachment of Islam from the east and south, Poland has one of Europe's most turbulent and tortured histories. Poland's enormous economic and ethnic diversity, combined with the divergent experiences of Poles under the Russian, Austrian, and Prussian regimes during the nineteenth century, further deepened the cleavages in Polish society. Although it was one of the first European states to introduce an "aristocratic democracy" (which enfranchised a surprising 8 percent of the population) and to promote a significant degree of religious tolerance, and in fact to become one of the largest states in Europe, it disappeared from the map altogether at the end of the eighteenth century.

Over the past two centuries, Polish identity has been splintered by two interrelated developments – the 1795 partition by Russia, Austria, and Prussia and the growth of national consciousness among social groups traditionally excluded from the magnates and enfranchised gentry (*szlachta*) classes. Only two institutions consistently preserved national identity throughout Poland's tortured history of partition – the Roman Catholic Church and the Polish elite, with its distinctive collective memory of the past. Divided on so many levels, Poles found it increasingly difficult to agree on the crucial issues of how to proceed in regaining their statehood and even on what constitutes a Pole. Consequently, they were also sharply divided over which Poland to revive.

Poland's travails from its 1795 partition to its rebirth in the aftermath of World War I resulted in a fundamental redefinition of the notion of "Polishness." Originally this notion was neither exclusively ethnic nor exclusively religious and was grounded in the traditions and the collective memory of the Commonwealth. The failure of the 1863 Uprising to unite the Commonwealth and the subsequent displacement of romanticism by positivism resulted in a new concept of Polishness based on a "civilizational" notion that envisioned the ultimate convergence of peoples living across the partitioned lands. They would be united, not by class, but by the superiority of Polish culture and would be defined by Polish language and customs. By the late nineteenth century, when it became clear that the hopes of the positivists would not be realized, the concept of Polishness became even narrower, based on ethnicity and the myth of Polish genetic commonality.

## Polish romanticism and its notion of Polish nationalism

Well before the partitions, the privileged *szlachta* had developed the romantic vision of the Aristocratic Commonwealth (*Rzecz-pospolita Szlachecka*)[7] that became the matrix of a national ideal. Central to this vision was the belief that Roman Catholic Poland was destined to battle the Tartars, Turks, and Russians, acting as the Christian rampart (*antemurale christianitatis*) of Western civilization. In keeping with these beliefs, the elite accepted the defeats and partitions of Poland in the late eighteenth century as a sacrifice for a transcendent goal – security for the civilized West as a whole. Because the Polish elite tirelessly clung to the belief that Poland's cause was the cause of the entire civilized world, they concluded that a "rescue" by the civilized world was Poland's right. A unique feature of Polish romanticism was the fact that, unlike most of its counterparts in Central and Eastern Europe, it was devoid of ethnonationalism. Andrzej Walicki, in describing the *Weltanschauung* of Polish romantics, wryly noted,

> Polish thinkers of the "romantic epoch" were convinced that Poland *had* to *prove* that her restoration was necessary for mankind. The existence of a nation, they thought, is not of value as such; on the contrary, only such nations have an indisputable right to existence which can claim to represent universal value. . .[8]

This "internationalist" element of the Polish romantic national ideal manifested itself in a variety of ways. Poles were perhaps the most enthusiastic supporters of the universal cause of freedom, not only in the American Revolution, but also in the Napoleonic campaigns. They enlisted in droves in Napoleon's armies and died by the thousands for his causes in areas as disparate as Haiti, Italy, and Russia; and Poland may be the only country whose national anthem still lauds Napoleon. Perhaps nothing symbolized the internationalist element of the Polish romantic tradition more than this challenge to the West – *Za wolność waszą i naszą* (For Your Freedom and Ours) – which became the battle cry of the romantics throughout the nineteenth century.

[7] The Commonwealth (or technically the Commonwealth of Both Nations) was created as a result of the Union of Lublin (1569) which united the crown lands of Poland and the Grand Duchy of Lithuania, covering vast areas of contemporary Poland, Lithuania, Ukraine, and Byelorussia. The Commonwealth was governed by a multi-ethnic yet Polonized gentry. It was dismembered by the Third Partition in 1795.

[8] Andrzej Walicki, "Adam Gurowski: Polish Nationalism, Russian Pan-Slavism and American Manifest Destiny," *Russian Review* 38: 1 (1979), 1 (emphasis in the original).

Despite Poland's role as "defender of the faith" and its ardent participation in liberation movements in North America and Western Europe, its commitment to the West remained unreciprocated. When the Poles rose up against Russian rule in 1830, they discovered that the West was virtually indifferent to their fate. This disappointment led to a new twist in the Polish romantic perception of Poland's national identity. If the Polish–Lithuanian Commonwealth had, indeed, been the *antemurale christianitatis*, then the partitioned, betrayed, suffering Poland was the "Christ of Nations," atoning for the sins of Europe. Poland's romantic nationalist poet Adam Mickiewicz described his country's predicament thus: "Verily I say unto you, it is not for you to learn civilization from foreigners, but it is you who are to teach them civilization . . . You are among the foreigners like the Apostles among the idolaters."[9]

To the *szlachta*, therefore, the only path to redemption lay in the restoration of the Polish Commonwealth as both a moral and a political imperative. The fact that Polish nationalism derived almost exclusively from the *szlachta* and its Commonwealth ideals profoundly affected the nature of Polish national identity. Since the *szlachta* represented approximately 8 percent of the population and traditionally expanded to the east, the local elite, whether Lithuanian, Belarussian, or Ukrainian, invariably became Polonized. As a result, the national identity of the Polish elite was based on class and geography, rather than ethnicity. In the eighteenth century, the *szlachta* even perceived itself as being from a different genetic stock than the peasantry. Members of the *szlachta* claimed to be the offspring of Noah's son Japhet and believed that the peasants were the offspring of Ham. Accordingly, the elite had little interest in ethnographic Poland, namely Prussian Poland, which had never belonged to the Commonwealth. At the same time, they could not envision a Polish rebirth without the reacquisition of the eastern borderlands (*kresy*), despite the fact that the *kresy*'s peasantry was neither Catholic nor Polish-speaking.

The unique economic realities of the *kresy* further distorted Poland's national identity. In ethnic Poland, roughly the territory between the Oder and Bug rivers, the continual scarcity of land meant that the economic position of the *szlachta* remained only marginally better than that of some of the wealthier peasants. In the *kresy*, however, the

[9] Adam Mickiewicz, *Księgi narodu i pielgrzymstwa polskiego* [The Books of the Polish National Pilgrimage], vol. II (Warsaw: PWN, 1950), 26–46.

abundance of land and peasants to work it led to the creation of a *latifundia* economy, in which the Polish (or Polonized) elite held vast tracks of land cultivated by numerous peasant sharecroppers. In the east, the aristocracy's economic and political strength enabled it to co-opt the identity of the Commonwealth and forge its agenda. As Janusz Tazbir has argued, the Union of Lublin (1569) and the subsequent expansion into the *kresy* reinforced the *szlachta's* national and class consensus in its eastern power base and also shaped the tradition of Samartism.[10] In the realm of foreign policy, the romantic paradigm argued that the challenge in the east was not a clash with the indigenous peoples of the borderlands, who ostensibly shared the Polish romantics' nostalgia for the Commonwealth, but rather a clash between Russian autocracy and Polish freedom.

Although only a minority of ethnic Poles ever resided in the borderlands east of the Bug River, this relatively small but highly influential group was pre-eminent in molding Poland's national identity and shaping its politics until 1945. The significance of the *kresy* and the dominance of the *Szlachta Kresowa* was so strong that in 1815, despite offers of relatively generous freedoms and broad autonomy, the Polish elite rejected the Congress of Vienna's Polish Kingdom (*Kongresówka*) as a fraud because it excluded the stolen lands (*ziemie zabrane*) in the east. This affront spurred the Poles to rise up against the Russian crown in 1830. Since Russia, Prussia, and Austria were the pro-status-quo, partitioning powers, and since Britain all but withdrew from European affairs, France, Europe's premier anti-status-quo power, soon became the model for Poland, while conservative, autocratic Russia was cast as the quintessential foe. Consequently, during much of the nineteenth century, Paris served as a magnet for exiled Polish nationalists, inspiring the Polish elite to imitate French customs.

The Western orientation of the Poles in the mid nineteenth century made them an anomaly among Slavs. While Slavophilism spread west to engulf Czech and Balkan nationalists, the Poles remained ambivalent. Although some Polish thinkers did envision a pan-Slavic entity with Russia becoming a constitutional monarchy and serving as the core of a Slavic commonwealth, others, such as Bronisław Trentowski,

---

[10] A pseudo-historic concept claiming the Polish nobility are the descendants of an Iranian–Samartian people who colonized the Vistula and the Dnieper valleys and turned the native Slavs into slaves. According to this thesis, the nobility had a hereditary right to rule over the lower castes and retain their special freedoms. This concept is generally associated with xenophobia, self-adulation, national megalomania, and a belief in Poland's special mission. See George J. Lerski, *Historic Dictionary of Poland* (Westport, CT and London, Greenwood Press, 1996) 524.

attempted to counter the Russian version of pan-Slavism by calling for a confederation of Slavic republics. Most of the Polish elite rejected pan-Slavic doctrine as a Russian scheme to divert "small Slavic rivers and streams into the great Russian ocean."[11] Because of its overwhelming presence, Russia remained anathema even to those Poles professing pan-Slavic feelings. Franciszek Duchiński, a Ukrainophile Pole who did embrace the notion of Slavic brotherhood, went to great lengths to prove that the Russians were not a Slavic people, but rather an Ugro–Finnish people who had adopted the Orthodox faith and with it some Slavic customs.

Throughout the first half of the nineteenth century, the romantic school of Polish nationalism continued to dominate, embracing an inclusive, non-ethnic vision of the Polish national ideal and advocating a return to the Commonwealth that included historically Polish territory in Belarussia, Lithuania, and Ukraine. The collective memory of those who formed the Polish romantic school dictated the resurrection of the Polish–Lithuanian Commonwealth, not just the establishment of a state based on the Polish ethnographic area (*Piast* Poland). As Wiktor Weintraub observed:

> Polish national consciousness in the Romantic era differed from contemporary national consciousness in one important aspect. Usually the basic element of national consciousness is the language shared by compatriots. In Poland, during the first half of the nineteenth century, this was not so. To be a Polish patriot then did of course mean to be attached to the Polish language as well as its literature and folklorist tradition, but *above all it meant to believe in the revival of the old Polish Commonwealth in its pre-partition frontiers – that is, the Commonwealth as a multinational state encompassing large territories belonging to contemporary Ukraine, Belarussia, and Lithuania.*[12]

In short, although the romantics clearly cherished the distinct Polish cultural heritage, remaining devoutly (if unconventionally) faithful to the Roman Catholic Church, their concept of the Commonwealth's bond was not based on an ethnolinguistic identity but on notions of political freedom and tolerance.

This romantic notion of Poland as a "mosaic of peoples" also surfaced in the literature of the period. The Ruthenian Stanisław Orzechówski exemplified this belief with his reference to *"gente*

---

[11] Wacław Lednicki, "Poland and the Slavophile Idea," *Slavonic and East European Review*, 7 (1928), 120–40.

[12] Wiktor Weintraub, "National Consciousness in Polish Romantic Literature," *Cross Currents* 6 (1987), 53 (emphasis added).

*Ruthenus, natione Polonus"* (ethnicity Ruthenian, nationality Polish). Despite the clear dominance of the Polish language within the romantic literature, ethnically Polish poets and prose writers – including Antoni Malczewski, Seweryn Goszczyński, Michał Grabowski, Michał Czajkowski, and Juliusz Słowacki – formed the so-called Ukrainian School of Polish literature that often sided with the Ukrainians in their grievances against the Poles.[13] This school not only reaffirmed the multinational consciousness of the Polish romantics but inspired Ukrainian romantic poetry and ultimately aided in the rise of a distinct Ukrainian nationalism.[14] Some Polish poets took an overtly Semitophilic view. In his drama *The Ancestors*, Adam Mickiewicz described the future savior of Poland with reference to King David (forty-four are King David's initials in Hebrew numerology) and his "foreign" mother was his *Moabite* grandmother Ruth:

> Born of a foreign mother, and his blood
> Derived from godlike heroes of the past
> and his name shall be FORTY AND FOUR.[15]

The poet Juliusz Słowacki, in his work *Ksiądz Marek* (Father Marek), depicted the Jewess Judyta as a symbol of integrity and Polish patriotism.[16] Works lauding the legacy of Jewish Colonel Berek Joselewicz, who led Jews into combat against tsarist troops in the 1794 Uprising, also remained ingrained in the romantic consciousness of Poland.

The romantic emphasis on a multiethnic Poland did not, however, address several issues that were to become problematic for Polish nationalists. First, to its great detriment, Polish nationalism remained class bound. While it glorified the "pure" peasantry (*Lud*), the *Weltanschauung* of both Mickiewicz and Słowacki remained deeply ingrained in the *szlachta* world[17] that ignored both the ethnic Polish peasants and the slowly growing urban population that had little or no attachment to the Commonwealth. Furthermore, the romantics ignored nascent Lithuanian and Ukrainian nationalism, confusing the

---

[13] See Józef Łobodowski, "A Polish View of Polish–Ukrainian Influences" in *Poland and Ukraine: Past and Present*, ed. Peter J. Potichnyj (Edmonton and Toronto: Canadian Institute of Ukrainian Studies, 1980), 106.

[14] Piotr S. Wandycz, *The Lands of Partitioned Poland: 1795–1918* (Seattle and London: University of Washington Press, 1984), 101.

[15] See Frank H. Forty, *Gems of Polish Poetry* (Warsaw, 1923), 94–99.

[16] See Joanna Rostropowicz Clark, "Judyta and Other Israelite Spirits in the Poetry of Juliusz Słowacki," *The Polish Review* 39: 2 (1994).

[17] Piotr S. Wandycz, *The Lands of Partitioned Poland: 1795–1918* (Seattle and London: University of Washington Press, 1984), 183.

anti-tsarist sentiments of the Lithuanians and Ukrainians with nostalgia for the Commonwealth.[18]

The painfully slow emergence of a coherent national identity was not limited to Poland. As Walker Connor noted, "The delay – in some cases stretching into centuries between the appearance of national consciousness among sectors of the elite and the masses – reminds us of the obvious but all too often ignored fact that nation formation is a process, not an occurrence or event."[19] Even in France, Europe's oldest nation-state, the process of national consolidation was not complete until the end of the nineteenth century.[20] Within rural areas of Poland, this delay meant that until the late nineteenth century, the term *pole* meant *gentry*.[21] In short, although the national values of the *szlachta* did eventually seep into peasant consciousness,[22] the elite's isolation, both physical and psychological, from the *Lud* resulted in the development of a serious rift between the two classes. Exacerbated by mutual misunderstanding, this rift had tragic results.

The uprisings of 1830, 1846–48, and 1863 demonstrated two irreversible realities. A fundamental weakness of romantic Polish nationalism was its perpetually optimistic anticipation of Western support against Russia. The nineteenth-century uprisings against Russia proved that the West had neither the capacity nor the will to shore up Polish aspirations. They also demonstrated that the Polish peasant remained indifferent to an identity that was based on a collective memory of the Commonwealth and gentry democracy. As a Polish peasant leader observed during the 1830 Uprising, "The Polish nationality is excluded today from the rank of nations, but the Polish peasant lost nothing by this."[23] As a result of the failure to enlist Western support in shaking off Russian domination and the failure to build a more economically inclusive vision of the Polish national idea, national identity among Polish peasants did not emerge in Prussian

[18] For example, see the exchange between the Pole Bolesław Limanowski and the Ukrainian Mykola Drahamov, in Kazimiera Janina Cottam, *Bolesław Limanowski (1835–1935): A Study in Socialism and Nationalism* (New York: Columbia University Press, 1978), 75–77.

[19] Walker Connor, "When Is a Nation?" *Ethnic and Racial Studies* 13: 1 (1990), 99.

[20] See Eugene Weber, *Peasants into Frenchmen: The Modernization of Rural France, 1870–1914* (Stanford: Stanford University Press, 1976).

[21] Janusz Tazbir, "Polish National Consciousness in the 16th–18th Centuries," *Acta Poloniae Historica, no. 46* (1982), 63.

[22] See Janusz Tazbir, *Kultura szlachecka w Polsce. Rozkwit-Upadek-Relikty* [Culture of the Szlachta in Poland – Rise, Fall and Traces] (Warsaw, 1976).

[23] Quoted by Peter Brock, "Polish Nationalism," in *Nationalism in Eastern Europe*, ed. Peter F. Sugar and Ivo Lederer (Seattle and London: University of Washington Press, 1969), 318.

Poland until the late nineteenth century. In Russian and Austrian Poland, this process was delayed until 1905–14.[24] Repeated Polish uprisings failed to shake the indifference of the peasantry toward the partitioning powers. In 1846–48, the Polish peasants in Galicia supported the Habsburg empire and defended the emperor against the rebellious "Poles" – whom they considered the gentry – and in 1863, Polish peasants refused to resist agrarian reform in Russian Poland.

The uprising of 1863 may have been the last gasp of the romantic notion of a multinational Poland. The manifesto of the 1863 Uprising specifically appealed to "brother Ruthenians and Lithuanians."[25] Because of its anti-Russian character, the uprising was widely supported by Poland's urban Jews and revived the Semitophilic orientation reminiscent of the romantic era. The image, popularized by Michał Landy's literary work *Żyd który zginął z krzyżem w ręku* (The Jew Who Died with a Cross in his Hands), resonated strongly among many Polish intellectuals. The insurrection's government even appealed to the Jews as *Braci Polaków wyznania mojżeszowego* (Brothers of the Poles of the Mosaic Persuasion).[26] Immediately after the uprising, Polish literature lionized the brotherhood of the "two Israels," the old ( Jews) and the new (Poles). Jews were depicted as heroic partisans, a part of the Polish nation selflessly sacrificing their lives for the cause of Polish independence.[27]

The failure of the 1863 Uprising and the demise of the landed *szlachta* as the country's dominant political and economic class led to a reappraisal of Poland's predicament and a redefinition of Polish identity. This new concept of Polishness had far-reaching consequences for the non-ethnic Poles who constituted a majority within the historic boundaries of the Commonwealth and recast ethnic relations within it. The defeat of 1863 also signaled the end of the notion of a triune Poland built on an equal partnership of Lithuanians, Poles, and Ukrainians. This re-partition along ethnic lines implied an inevitable auto-partition of the nationalities and with it, a reduction in Polish presence in the east.[28]

[24] Jan Molenda, "The Formation of National Consciousness of the Polish Peasants and the Part They Played in Regaining the Independence of Poland," *Acta Poloniae Historica*, no. 64 (1991), 125.

[25] Olszer, *For Your Freedom and Ours*, 73.

[26] Ibid., 52.    [27] Ibid., ch. 2.

[28] Roman Szporluk, "Polish–Ukrainian Relations in 1918: Notes for Discussion," in *The Reconstruction of Poland 1914–1923*, ed. Paul Latawski (New York: St. Martin's Press, 1992), 42–43.

### The rise of positivism: an identity redefined

The philosophic underpinnings of Polish positivism were in many ways no different from those of positivist schools across Europe. Believing that progress is synonymous with improvement, European positivists embraced Auguste Comte's assertion that all societies pass through three stages of development – the theological, the metaphysical, and the positive – before reaching a stage of "objective" knowledge based on the physical, "positive" sciences. Comte described this final stage as one where societies cease to be composed of autonomous, unique individuals and instead become ordered organisms governed by necessary laws. All positivist philosophies were heavily conditioned by the imprint of the scientific inquiry on social thought, particularly Herbert Spencer's application of Charles Darwin's theory of perpetual competition among the species and the survival of the fittest among them.[29] For the Polish intelligentsia, this meant abandoning the traditional theological-metaphysical outlook on the world, which had bestowed upon the Polish people a "chosen mission," in favor of "scientific laws" for a new "organic society." In practical terms, this meant avoiding confrontation with the partitioning powers and focusing instead on addressing internal, "objective" problems through industrialization and application of the scientific method.

Polish positivism was also strongly influenced by the conservative historians of the Kraków historical school. Partisans of the Kraków school opposed the traditional romantic notion that blamed Poland's travails on its unfortunate geographic location or the messianic mission bestowed on its people. Instead, they believed that Poland would regain a normal existence only when it objectively faced its internal shortcomings and ceased spinning myths about itself and its foes. Rather than indulging in nostalgia for a long-defunct Commonwealth, Poles should concentrate on "organic work" and devote their energies to improving their educational and economic infrastructure as a means of preserving Polish identity. Instead of indulging in repeated uprisings, the partisans of "organic work" argued that Poles ought to take advantage of the structures of the respective empires to advance their own political and economic interests.

Although the Polish positivists believed that social improvement

---

[29] For an excellent study of the political and intellectual climate of the time, see Carlton J. H. Hayes, *A Generation of Materialism 1871–1900* (New York: Harper's Torch), 1963.

meant the uplifting of society across class and ethnic chasms, they failed to create bonds with either the peasantry or the minorities and over time drifted toward authoritarianism and ethnonationalism. Their detachment from the masses resulted in a continued division between the elite and the *Lud*, even though much of the positivist intelligentsia consisted either of impoverished gentry forced from their estates by the tsars after the 1863 Uprising or members of the educated middle class who had acquired the cultural attributes of the *szlachta*. The exclusion of the Polish peasantry meant that the vast majority of the population remained outside the political process and intellectual debates.

Addressing the issue of class, historian Stefan Kieniewicz noted, "We must not remain blind to scores of pieces of evidence provided by peasants from various regions and sectors of partitioned Poland which are unanimous in indicating that in the early twentieth century a Polish peasant-patriot was an exception rather than something typical."[30] Indeed, in the 1870s, according to one careful estimate, no more than 30 percent of the Polish-speaking Catholic population had a sense of national identity.[31] Most peasants tried to avoid friction with the Prussian and Russian authorities and shied away from overt displays of religious and national sentiment. Although a national revival among peasants did begin at the turn of the century, its expression was limited to those who went abroad as seasonal workers and immigrants.[32]

In short, the gap between the intelligentsia and the peasantry remained as wide as the historic gap between the *szlachta* and the *lud*, despite the dramatic shift in nationalist intellectual discourse. Writing in 1886, the positivist novelist Bolesław Prus lamented:

> It is an undeniable fact, pitiable beyond expression, that the intelligentsia has no common unity with the peasant; it knows him not; does not understand him; does not see and does not influence him. The Jewish innkeeper, the loan-shark, the clandestine advisor, even the thief . . . possess greater trust and confidence among the peasantry than does the intelligentsia which styles itself as the leader of society.[33]

As Prus concluded, the entire notion of a distinct Polish national identity remained the concern of a relatively small elite. While the

---

[30] Stefan Kieniewicz, *Historyk a świadomość narodów* [Historian and National Identity] (Warsaw, 1982), 248.

[31] Tazbir, *Kultura szlachecka*, 70.

[32] Benjamin P. Murdzek, *Emigration in Polish Social Political Thought, 1870–1914* East European Quarterly Monographs (New York): Columbia University Press, 1977), 169.

[33] Ibid., 167.

*szlachta's* romantics dreamed of Commonwealth and the Jagiellonian tradition and the middle-class positivists called for a "modern-national state," the Polish peasantry, burdened by a social structure that it perceived as exploitative and brutal, remained outside the political arena.

The positivists were no more successful in addressing the minority issue. Their approach to the multinational character of Poland was to assume that in an era of education, science, and technology, ethno-national and religious differences would "wither away" and super-stition and traditionalism would retreat. Thus, early positivists assumed that modernity would inevitably lead to the assimilation of minorities. The Ukrainian and Belarussian "tribes" would assimilate rapidly upon contact with Polish culture, and Jews, although more resistant to enlightenment, would ultimately also join the mainstream of Polish society. According to prominent positivist authors such as Eliza Orzeszkowa and Bolesław Prus, the "Jewish Question" would resolve itself. They believed that if the Jews were allowed to partici-pate in the "organic society," exposure to "scientific laws" would lead them to abandon their metaphysical attachment to a mystical religion and assimilate into Polish society.[34] Most positivists welcomed the emancipation of the Jews in the 1860s as a step toward the dissolution of Jewish identity and assimilation into mainstream Polish society. But this sentiment was not universally shared. During the 1850s, when capitalism was beginning to develop, some early positivists consid-ered it their role to use the economic revival to free Poland, not only from the hegemony of the partitioning empires, but also from what the poet Korzeniowski in 1857 called the *niewola Żydowska* (Jewish captivity).[35] As the nineteenth century progressed, the positivists, who had initially advocated the assimilation of minorities into a Polish ethnos, increasingly turned to narrow, defensive nationalism.

## The fall of positivism and the rise of ethnonationalism

By the 1880s, the forces of ethnonationalism were displacing positivism, and the "organic society" was acquiring an increasingly

---

[34] Bolesław Prus's essay, "The Little Jewish Question," and Eliza Orzeszkowa's pamphlet, "The Jews and the Jewish Question," are both reproduced in *For Your Freedom and Ours: Polish Progressive Spirit through the Centuries*, ed. Manfred Kridl, Władysław Malinowski, and Józef Wittlin (New York: Frederick Ungar, 1943), 123–26.

[35] Magdalena Opalski and Israel Bartal, *Poles and Jews, A Failed Brotherhood* (Hanover and London: Brandeis University Press, 1992), 16.

narrow ethnic definition throughout Europe. A major contributing factor was the introduction of social and "objective scientific" criteria based on the social theories of Charles Darwin, the genetic experiments of Gregor Mendel, and the microbiological discoveries of Louis Pasteur. Charles Darwin's twin theories of evolution and survival of the fittest and Louis Pasteur's breakthroughs in bacteriology, which demonstrated how invisible organisms can invade and ultimately destroy a healthy organism, accelerated the mutation of positivism throughout Europe.

The intellectual hegemony of positivism in Poland lasted no more than a generation and by the 1890s had fallen into a steep and irreversible decline brought about by both internal and external forces. Internally, the assimilationist paradigm had lost its appeal by the late 1800s. The popularity of the notion of an interspecies struggle for survival grew throughout Europe as a result of the depression of 1873 and continued until the end of the nineteenth century. Although the difficulties that many positivist intellectuals experienced in finding an economic niche in the emerging capitalist world also contributed to their rejection of assimilation, even before the depression of 1873, thousands of young Poles, often from impoverished aristocratic families, expressed reservations about the Western orientation of positivism. Andrzej Walicki noted:

> Economically, however, it [positivism] was a Westernism with qualifications. Its Positive heroes were the intelligentsia rather than "captains of the industry" and its image of "organic work" was modeled on disinterested public service, rather than the liberal conception of furthering worthy private interests in a spontaneously regulated civil society. Hence they took from Spencer, their favorite thinker, the ideas of organicism and evolutionism, but rejected his unbending "laissez faire" position; they listened rather to J. S. Mill's arguments against unrestricted competition, and were ready to learn even from the socialists. Characteristically, their attitude toward capitalists and the bourgeoisie as a whole was rather suspicious. Apart from general distrust, there were local reasons for such an attitude: the bourgeoisie of [the] Congress Kingdom was composed of Germans and unassimilated Jews, whose loyalty to Poland was often suspect.[36]

The positivist notion that progress leads to improvement proved bitterly disappointing. Although Poland did industrialize rapidly in

---

[36] Andrzej Walicki, *Poland Between East and West: The Controversies of Self-Definition and Modernization in Partitioned Poland* (Cambridge, MA: Ukrainian Research Institute, Harvard University, 1994), 21.

the last decade of the nineteenth century, the status of the ethnic Poles remained unchanged. In both industrial and commercial activities, they remained on the lowest rung compared with either Jews or Germans. The failure of modernization to address the needs of ethnic Poles was captured by Bolesław Prus in his 1886 novel *Placówka* (The Outpost), in which the protagonist, a poor Polish peasant, resists the intrusion of a railroad and German settlers and refuses to sell his land despite advantageous terms.

The bankruptcies resulting from the Great Depression of 1873 led many positivists to consider themselves victims of unscrupulous Jewish competition at home or financial manipulation abroad. This belief was reinforced by the very visible Jewish presence in textiles, food processing, and other industries.[37] Many of the new urban Poles were uprooted *szlachta* (*wysadzeni z siodła*) who resented the need to compete with the successful Jewish bourgeoisie. The growing clout of the urban Jewish elite created the perception that the Jews had benefited the most from the post-1863 order in Poland. The patrician novelist Józef Ignacy Kraszewski lamented, "The insurrection fell in a pool of blood and the Jews, guided by the experience of millennium, arose over our corpse."[38] Positivists such as Prus, Orzeszkowa, and Aleksander Świętochowski, who initially supported Jewish assimilation, all retreated from Semitophilism.[39] Nobel prize-winning author Władysław Reymont, who depicted Jews as *krajowy cudzoziemiec* (domestic foreigners), was but the most prominent representative of an increasing trend in Polish literature. This change in attitude toward the Jews was graphically captured by a character in Prus's 1890 novel *Lalka* (The Doll):

> In general, I have noticed over the last year or two that dislike of Hebrews is increasing; even people who a few years ago called them Poles of Mosaic Persuasion now call them Jews. And those who recently admired their hard work, their persistence, their talents, today only see their exploiting and deceit.[40]

For many Polish positivists, the lesson of the depression of 1873 was that although capitalist development might be essential to the modernization of Polish society, this modernization would be unattainable as long as Jews and Germans retained hegemony in economic life, acting like two "foreign bodies" infiltrating the "organic" Polish society.

---

[37] Wandycz, *The Lands of Partitioned Poland*, 281.
[38] Opalski and Bartal, *Poles and Jews*, 100.
[39] Ibid., 102.     [40] Ibid., 132.

Reflecting the Social Darwinist views of the late nineteenth century, Roman Dmowski, the father of Polish right-wing nationalism, stated:

> The surface of the globe is not a museum to preserve ethnographic displays in order, utility, each in its place. Humanity is moving forward swiftly, and in the contest of nations . . . the greatest factor in progress is competition and the need to improve continually the weapons which enable one to defend one's own existence.[41]

Analogous to Pasteur's observation that an organism can be infiltrated by aliens and annihilated, Dmowski objected to the assimilation of the Jews, fearing that:

> [The] character of this race which has never lived the life of societies of our type [with] so many distinctive characteristics [that] have been accumulated and established themselves which are alien to our moral code and are in fact harmful to our life that pouring in of the bulk of this element would destroy us.[42]

This "zoological" nationalism was echoed in Poland's positivist literature, which developed a strong "naturalist streak" often associated with the French novelist Émile Zola. The concept that human groups are perennially locked in a struggle for survival was a constant feature of the naturalist literary school. Adolf Dygasiński, in his 1883 story "Wolves, Dogs, and Humans" (*Wilki, psy, i ludzie*), tells how dogs attack a young domesticated wolf that the human wants to protect. The human is restrained, however, by the recognition that the aggression of the hounds is "natural." Using this allegory of Polish attitudes toward the Jews, the human observes:

> Although anti-Semitism did not exist at the time when I raised Butt [the wolf], even then Christians held Jews in contempt. Such and similar reflections cooled my anger at the hound. How can you expect animals to achieve equality, I thought, if humans seem unable to achieve it? Let my wolf experience the bitterness of civilized life in his youth; let him have some tragic memories![43]

External events also drove Polish nationalism toward a defensive, narrow definition of Polishness. Germany's inability to modernize its social structure, the government's increasing reliance on German *volkish* nationalism for legitimacy, and a growing sense of impending struggle between the "Slavic and Teuton races" made Polish–German

---

[41] Antony Polonsky, "Roman Dmowski and Italian Fascism," in *Ideas Into Politics: Aspects of European History, 1880–1950*, ed. R. J. Bullen, H. Pogge von Strandmann, and Antony Polonsky (London and Sydney: Croom Helm, 1984), 131.
[42] Ibid., 133–34.    [43] Ibid., 110.

relations even more tense and acrimonious. In Prussian Poland, efforts to Germanize the educational system resulted in a massive backlash. The resulting enhancement of Polish national solidarity not only led to a significant re-Polonization of many Germanized Poles, but also solidified the alliance between the Polish national movement and the Roman Catholic Church. This resistance to Germanization was immortalized in Maria Konopnicka's poem *Rota* (The Oath), in which she states, "We shall not allow the Germans to spit in our face, nor Germanize our children."[44]

In Russia, Alexander II's Polish policy, which was bent on eradicating Polish identity altogether, was followed by Alexander III's policy of state patriotism (*gosudarstvenyi patriotism*). This policy increased the Romanovs' reliance on Russian nationalism as a source of legitimacy, leading to ever-stronger Russification and thus the further alienation of non-Russians within the Russian empire, particularly those residing along the western fringe of the empire in Finland, the Baltic states, and the Vistula Land (*Previslianskii Krai*) – Poland.

The 1867 *Ausgleich* (equalization) in Austria which was meant to address the grievances of the Magyars, led instead to a cascade of nationalist demands across the Habsburg empire. In the Austrian province of Galicia, this meant a growing Ukrainian challenge to the Habsburg-sanctioned Polish hegemony there.

This rise of nationalism across Europe, especially the partitioning of empires, rendered the early positivist notion of "triple loyalty" untenable and humiliating to many educated Poles. It soon became clear that the only way for Poles to meet the challenges to their society was to seize the instruments of power within the state and use them to redress what they perceived as the increasingly unfavorable circumstances of the Polish nation. The popularity of "narrow nationalism" in Poland accelerated with the growing urbanization of the country in the late nineteenth century and the rise of mass politics. Urbanization and industrialization, combined with growing literacy in the countryside, created an interest in politics among the masses (*lud*) for the first time. As in other European countries, the changing demographics and the legacy of positivism as a scientific social doctrine laid the foundation for the rise of socialism.[45] Given the failure of positivism and its mutation into socialism or Marxism, which alienated much of the

[44] See Maria Konopnicka, *Poezje* (Warsaw: Czytelnik, 1974).
[45] Norman M. Naimark, *The History of the "Proletariat": The Emergence of Marxism in the Kingdom of Poland, 1870–1887* (New York: East European Quarterly Monographs, Columbia University Press, 1979), ch. 3.

Polish intelligentsia, "narrow nationalism" began to work as a bridge between the intelligentsia and the masses. Even for ethnic Poles such as Józef Piłsudski who joined the socialists at the turn of the century, the attraction of socialism was not its "universalism" but its implacable hostility to tsarism. The shift of national elites from universalist, leftist positions to narrow, nationalist, rightist positions was a Europewide phenomenon and served as an important means for them to retain control over the emerging mass politics.[46]

As with most late-nineteenth-century nationalisms, the key ingredients in the formation of Polish nationalism were the creation of a national myth and a sense of grievance against the "other." The national myth that emerged was the desire to reconstitute an independent Polish state within the boundaries of the old Commonwealth. Unlike the Commonwealth, a reconstituted Poland would be based on the Poles as an ethnic group rather than on a common ruling class and shared institutions. Instead of seeing Poland as a multinational entity based on the notion of one people, one faith (*jeden naród, jedna wiara*), the newly emerging Polish national identity reflected the belief of many post-positivists that only a clear, ethnonational self-definition would give the Poles sufficient cohesion to face the pressures of the partitioning empires. It is important to note that the definition of a nation advocated by Poland's conservative nationalist elite envisioned a theistic entity resulting from the "supreme will ruling the world, and its purpose is metaphysical." They believed that political societies do not rest on a social contract but rather exist by divine will and thus should rest on the foundation of religious ethics.[47]

This shift away from the "cosmopolitan" national identity envisioned by the Polish romantics and some positivists was soon reflected in the arts. The programmatic statement of the *Towarzystwo Ludoznawcze* (Polish Folklore Society) published in 1895 stated:

> History teaches us that the nation will not die as long as its people live, this people which is able to revive the withered limbs of national life and instill a new life into the works of its intellectual toil; when cosmopolitan truths clash with this fortress of nationality, may it be a holy endeavor of each to watch over this fortress and strengthen it.[48]

[46] Brian A. Jenkins and Spyros A. Sofos, eds., *Nation and Identity in Contemporary Europe* (London & New York: Routledge Press, 1996), 21.
[47] Szymon Rudnicki, "The Polish Conservative Idea after 1918," *Acta Poloniae Historica*, no. 40 (1979), 136.
[48] Jerzy Jedlicki, "Polish Concept of National Culture," in *National Character and National Ideology in Interwar Eastern Europe*, ed. Ivo Banac and Katherine Verdery (New Haven: Yale Center for International and Area Studies, 1995), 13.

The increasingly nationalist demands on the artist in late-nineteenth-century Poland caused the critic Ludwik Szczepański to complain that "imagination and individuality at once elicit accusations of unnationality."[49]

## The search for a foreign policy paradigm on the eve of independence

Historians generally view the 1863 Uprising as the historic watershed marking the decline of the romantic school and the rise of positivism.[50] Although it is clear that events in Poland and the emergence of politically and ethnically conscious classes certainly affected the relative strength of the two competing paradigms, the controversy between the romantics and the positivists (between a multiethnic commonwealth and a monoethnic state) continued to haunt Poland's sense of nationhood and foreign policy throughout the interwar period and did not end until after World War II.

The collapse of positivism and the concomitant realization that the only way to ensure Poland's national survival was to regain political independence led to a serious debate over the Polish role within the international system. The consensus among those claiming to be heirs of the positivists was that the primary external threat to Poland was Germany, which, with its efficient colonization policy and enormous powers, could assimilate segments of the Polish population. They assumed that Poland could guarantee its survival primarily through internal institution building and the development of links with other Slavs. Their leader, Roman Dmowski, maintained that the only way Poland could recover and retain its independence was through an alliance with Russia. To Dmowski and his followers, the only means by which Poland could hope to attain Western support for its sovereignty lay in its ability, along with that of Russia, to contain an ever-restless and aggressive Germany. As far as the fate of the peoples of the eastern borderlands was concerned, the post-positivists continued to believe that Poland must not be bound by an ethnographic border to the east, insisting that the "weak" indigenous cultures could be Polonized.

By contrast, Józef Piłsudski, the founding father of modern Poland, continued to subscribe to the romantic tradition, viewing the Jagiello-

---

[49] Ibid., 3.
[50] See Adam Bromke, *Poland's Politics: Idealism vs. Realism* (Cambridge, MA: Harvard University Press, 1967).

nian period as the national ideal to be replicated. In Piłsudski's view, Poland could not be whole until it recreated a commonwealth or a confederate structure with Ukraine, Lithuania, and Belarussia.[51] Believing that Poland was locked in a perennial battle with Russia, Piłsudski continued to trust in Poland's Promethean "civilizing mission" in the East, which required a powerful Poland and deserved Western support for a latter-day *antemurale christianitatis* against Soviet Bolshevism.[52] Poland's romantic self-definition was further complicated by a deep-seated ambivalence toward both its Western and Slavic links. On the one hand, Polish romantics endorsed the cult of nativism and remained suspicious of Western-originated ideas. On the other, they rejected Russian-style Slavophilia as an Asian aberration. As a result, because Poles were both Roman Catholic and Slavic, the romantics believed that they were the "chosen people" destined to civilize the Slavs and save the world.[53] It was because of the depth of this conviction that Piłsudski launched his disastrous war against the Bolshevik state in 1920, a move that nearly resulted in Poland's occupation by Soviet troops.[54]

Although Polish romantics such as Piłsudski were far more Poland-centered than their eighteenth-century predecessors, the multinational Jagiellonian notion remained deeply rooted. Proszyński, in describing his childhood in interwar Poland, encapsulated the mental state of the Polish polity:

> We grew up with the conviction that we were heirs to a great motherland . . . which although defeated stretched from sea to sea . . . Were we told that Gdańsk is not Polish, we would have been terribly surprised. Were we told that Kiev is not Polish, our surprise would have been greater. But had we been told that our motherland is nationally uniform – that it covers the area around the Vistula from

---

[51] For Piłsudski's views of federalism, see Piotr S. Wandycz, "Polish Federalism 1919–1920 and its Historic Antecedents," *East European Quarterly*, no. 4 (1970), 25–39; see also Marian Kamil Dziewanowski, *Joseph Piłsudski: A European Federalist, 1918–1922* (Stanford: Hoover Institution Press, 1969).

[52] Some Polish politicians, such as Jan Paderewski, were clearly committed to the notion of commonwealth. There is a body of evidence, however, supporting the claim that Piłsudski viewed the notion of commonwealth as merely an "American palaver." See Piotr Wandycz, "Poland's Place in Europe in the Concepts of Piłsudski and Dmowski," *East European Politics and Society* 4: 3 (1990).

[53] Jerzy Jedlicki, "Native Culture and Western Civilization: Essay from the History of Polish Thought of the Years 1764–1863," *Acta Poloniae Historica*, no. 28 (1973).

[54] See Dziewanowski, *Józef Piłsudski*; Piotr Wandycz, *Soviet–Polish Relations, 1917–1921* (Cambridge, MA: Harvard University Press, 1969); Norman Davies, *White Eagle, Red Star: The Polish–Soviet War, 1919–1920* (New York: St. Martins, 1972); also Richard Pipes, *Russia Under the Bolshevik Regime* (New York: Alfred Knopf, 1993), 177–83.

the Carpathians to the sea, but that there is room in it neither for Ruthenian peasants nor for Russian Orthodox churches, nor even for old Mrs. Szomstein – we would certainly have been most surprised of all. Our generation is probably the last to have grown up with the ideals of the 1863 insurrection, of Poland-Lithuania-Ruthenia.[55]

By the beginning of this century there was consensus among the elite that Poland must strive for independence, but the peasantry remained inert and apathetic. As late as 1914, the partitioning empires managed to draft almost 600,000 Poles into their armies, while Piłsudski's 1914 attempt to trigger an uprising in Russian Poland by marching from Kraków to Kielce evoked little response from the population.[56] In fact, the rebirth of Poland in 1918 was greeted by many Polish peasants with apprehension and outright fear. Aleksander Hertz noted that the population of Poland was so bewildered by the sudden re-emergence of a Polish state, that all ethnic groups (including ethnic Poles) experienced the sensation of being "native strangers."[57]

Wincenty Witos, the leader of the Polish peasants and a prime minister during the interwar period, cautioned, "Poland fell as a state of nobility . . . and rises as a peasant state, as such it can and must survive."[58] Witos' reminiscences of the reaction of the Polish peasantry to the rebirth of the Polish state are illustrative of the differing collective memories of the peasants of pre-partition Poland. He recalls that "the majority of peasants were very concerned, fearing once the Polish state was restored, back would come serfdom and total enslavement to the nobles."[59] Clearly, the gap between the elites and the rural masses remained as wide as ever.

### National identity of independent Poland

The Poland that emerged from the ruins of World War I was an extraordinarily heterogeneous society, divided across ethnic, class, and urban versus rural lines, and burdened by the legacies of the

---

[55] Quoted by Adam Michnik, "Shadows of Forgotten Ancestors," in *Letters from Prison and Other Essays*, trans. by Maya Latynski (Berkeley and Los Angeles: University of California Press, 1987), 216.

[56] Richard M. Watt, *Bitter Glory: Poland and Its Fate, 1918 to 1939* (New York: Simon and Schuster, 1979), 45.

[57] Aleksander Hertz, *The Jews in Polish Culture* (Evanston, IL: Northwestern University Press, 1988).

[58] Ibid., 147.

[59] Wincenty Witos, *Moje wspomnienia* [My Reminiscences], vol. I (Paris, 1964), 132.

partitioning powers. Like any complex society, Poland spawned numerous ideologies, concepts of statehood, and national paradigms. Yet the Polish state that emerged in 1918 remained both psychologically and politically dominated by the mind-set of a rather narrow sliver of the society. Writing on the personality patterns in interwar Poland, the sociologist Aleksandra Jansina-Kania noted that during the 1920s and 1930s:

> The land-owning class remained at the top of the social hierarchy of the Second Republic. Made up of old aristocratic and gentry families, this class maintained its image as the leading class of the nation, although the political elite was composed from individuals of differentiated social background.[60]

Describing the mind-set of the political elite that came to dominate Poland during most of the interwar decades, Joseph Rothschild wrote:

> The inner core of Piłsudski's entourage, like the Marshal himself, originated from *szlachta*-become-intelligentsia families from the eastern *kresy* borderlands, where memories [remained] of the old Commonwealth and its traditions of aristocratic stewardship of power over "immature" and ethnic elements.[61]

As Rothschild observed, this caused "a rift between the Piłsudskist 'state-bearing elite' and the rest of society."[62] Poland's elite was far more interested in "state building" than in building a society and had no strategy for building a broad-based political model. In a manner reminiscent of Kuomintang founder Sun Yat-sen, who opted for what he called "political tutelage" to a technocratic elite driven by nationalism,[63] Poland's political elite preferred technocrats to politicians, abhorred political parties, and considered the democratic process a nuisance. Piłsudski, himself, unlike most authoritarian rulers, abhorred mass politics. Two examples of this aversion were his efforts to create the "non-party" bloc BBWR (*Bezpartyjny Blok Współpracy z Rządem*) and his successors' attempt to establish the Camp of National Unity OZN (*Obóz Zjednoczenia Narodowego*), composed of "outstanding people of the Polish Nation." The Polish military-backed regime scrupulously avoided the ritualistic mass mobilizations char-

[60] Aleksandra Jansina-Kania, "National Identity and Personality Patterns in Poland Between the Wars," in *Poland Between the Wars: 1918–1939*, ed. Timothy Wiles (Bloomington: University of Indiana Polish Studies Center, 1989), 118.
[61] Joseph Rothschild, "Marshal Piłsudski on State/Society Dialectics in Restored Interwar Poland," in Wiles, *Poland Between the Wars: 1918–1939*, ed. Wiles, 30.
[62] Ibid., 35.
[63] John Breuilly, *Nationalism and the State* (Chicago: University of Chicago Press, 1993), 236.

acteristic of the totalitarian regimes of Germany and the Soviet Union. Even when compared with the mild authoritarian regimes of Latin America – such as Getulio Vragas's *Estado Novo* in Brazil or the Mexican Institutional Revolutionary Party – the Piłsudski government was remarkable for its lack of effort in generating even a limited degree of controlled mass mobilization. This absence of a uniform ideology or structure caused Italy's ambassador to Warsaw to dismiss Piłsudski's potential as a fascist, referring to him as "a liberal democrat in the clothes of an old-world knight."[64] As a result, the majority of Poland's population – its peasants, its socialists, and its numerous minorities – was excluded from discussions of the Polish national identity during the interwar period. In the absence of a national grassroots organization or a political ideology, the debate between Piłsudski and Dmowski described previously was, in fact, little more than a discussion between two elites over how to reconcile their specific paradigms with the reality of the Second Republic.

Despite their differences, the Piłsudski and Dmowski camps were able to reach a broad consensus on the structure of the new Polish state. First of all, both sides agreed that the Polish Commonwealth had ceased to exist primarily because it lost its coherence as a result of internal divisions and corrosive multinationalism. Thus, although there was some disagreement over how to achieve the goal, both sides recognized that the new Poland had to be based on the principle of the nation-state, and both exhibited a fascination with authoritarianism. Both also rejected the notion of limiting the new state's borders to those of ethnographic Poland. Beyond this point of agreement, however, there were sharp differences. Piłsudski claimed the Commonwealth borders on historic grounds, a position that was strongly opposed by the right-wing National Democratic Party (*Endecja*), led by Dmowski. Members of the *Endecja* considered themselves heirs to the positivist-realist tradition. Their critique of the romantic vision argued that the Commonwealth was a class-based entity that had diluted the Polish character of the state and had sapped its vitality by neglecting ethnic Poland's historic core. As a result, Poland had suffered a massive German infiltration. In their view, Russia might be the enemy of the Polish gentry, but Germany was the real threat to the Polish nation.

However, as far as attitudes toward the eastern territories were

---

[64] Antony Polonsky, "Roman Dmowski and Italian Fascism," in *Ideas Into Politics: Aspects of European History, 1880–1950*, ed. R. J. Bullen, H. Pogge von Strandmann, and A. B. Polonsky (London and Sydney: Croom Helm, 1984), 137.

concerned, the differences between the Piłsudski and Dmowski camps were more apparent than real. Both leaders were contemptuous of Ukrainians and Belarussians, believing that their assimilation into the superior Polish culture was as desirable as it was inevitable. While Piłsudski argued for a federal structure with the non-Polish-populated *kresy*, Dmowski believed that Poland's frontiers should not be limited to the Polish ethnographic area since borders were nothing more than a reflection of a nation's power relative to its neighbors.[65] Whereas Piłsudski supported the idea of creating an independent, albeit subordinate, Ukrainian state, Dmowski thought the notion of a Ukrainian state was a fiction that could only serve the interests of Berlin.[66] It is noteworthy that although Piłsudski and Dmowski might have disagreed about the configuration that a reborn Poland should take, both men envisioned the *kresy* under Polish domination.[67]

Piłsudski never fully accepted his failure to resurrect the Commonwealth, and interwar Poland became a national entity existing within a multinational state characterized by increasingly antagonistic relations with its restless minorities. Piłsudski refrained from using anti-Semitism as a means of nation building, but Dmowski made vicious anti-Semitism part of his ideology. Both leaders, though, considered the 3.5 million Jews in Poland a foreign body whose presence would have to be substantially reduced. Communal rights for minorities, to which Poland had committed itself at Versailles, were never implemented.[68] As the Polish historian Andrzej Garlicki aptly noted, it is a historic irony that it was Piłsudski the federalist who implemented Dmowski's program of minority incorporation.[69] Despite his early associations with socialism, Piłsudski steadily drifted to the right during his years in power, abandoning his erstwhile liberal allies.[70] Norman Davies, in his profound and rather sympathetic *God's Play-*

---

[65] See Brian A. Porter, "Who Is a Pole and Where Is Poland? Territory and Nation in the Rhetoric of Polish National Democracy before 1905," *Slavic Review* 56: 4 (1992).

[66] See Wandycz, "Poland's Place"; also Konstantin Symmons-Symonolewicz, "Polish Political Thought and the Problem of Eastern Borderlands of Poland (1918–39)," *Polish Review* 4, no. 1, 65–81.

[67] For a history reflective of Poland's mind-set in the interwar period, see Stanisław Mickiewicz, *Historia Polski od 11 listopada 1918 r do 17 września 1939 r* [History of Poland from 11 November 1918 to 17 September 1939] (London: 1961).

[68] See Marian Marek Drozdowski, "The National Problem in Poland in 1918–1939," *Acta Poloniae Historica*, no. 22 (1970), 226–51. For a different perspective, see Stephen Horak, *Poland and Her National Minorities, 1919–39* (New York: Vantage Press, 1961).

[69] Andrzej Garlicki, "The Second Republic: Hopes and Their Fulfillment," in Wiles, *Poland Between the Wars: 1918–1939*, 20.

[70] See Alexander J. Gorth, "Polish Elections, 1918–1928," *Slavic Review* 34: 4 (December 1965), 653–65.

*ground: A History of Poland,* argues that although Piłsudski triumphed over Dmowski politically, Poland's inability to recreate the Common-wealth and to come to terms with its minorities eroded the credibility of Piłsudski's Jagiellonian ideal and accelerated the drift toward Dmowski's concept of Poland as an ethnonational state.[71] Com-menting on Dmowski at the time of his death in 1939, the prestigious conservative newspaper *Czas* wrote:

> His influence on public views, on the psychology of the nation is enormous. The ideals propagated by Dmowski are believed by a very substantial portion of the whole society, and particularly adhered to by the great majority of the youth . . . For all of us who belonged to the camp of Marshall Piłsudski the national ideology which Dmowski enunciated has exerted a great influence. [Dmow-ski's] heritage has become the *general treasury of the nation.*[72]

Poland's inability to come to terms with its minorities turned out to be the most destabilizing element in its internal politics. Article 109 of Poland's constitution assured every citizen "The right to preserve his nationality and cultivate his nationality and to cultivate his language and national characteristics by means of autonomous minority organi-zation of public legal status."[73] But the impact of this article was short-lived at best. In response to the startling election of Gabriel Narutowicz to the presidency on the strength of minority support in the *Sejm,* the Polish political elite passed the 1922 Lanckorona Pact, which ensured that Poland's minorities would be excluded from the corridors of power. Despite the fact that more than one-third of Poland's citizens were not ethnic Poles, of the 350 people to attain ministerial rank in the 31 coalition governments of interwar Poland, not a single one was drawn from the minority communities. Similar ethnic exclusivity prevailed among provincial officials of the *Woje-wodes* and *Starosts.*[74]

Even though it was not consistently implemented, the interwar policy of Poland's Second Republic remained bent on a self-contra-dictory goal – the creation of a "Polish" state within the territories of the Commonwealth. To attain that goal, successive Polish govern-ments, whether or not dominated by Piłsudski, maintained a consis-

---

[71] Norman Davies, *God's Playground: A History of Poland,* vol. II (New York: Columbia University Press, 1982), ch. 19.
[72] Alexander J. Gorth, "Dmowski, Piłsudski, and Ethnic Conflict in Pre-1939 Poland," *Canadian Slavic Studies* 3: 1 (1969), 78 (emphasis added).
[73] Quoted in Richard Blanke, *Orphans of Versailles: The Germans in Western Poland, 1918–1939* (Lexington: University of Kentucky Press, 1994), 58.
[74] Ibid., 62.

tent attitude on the nationality issue. Millions of Ukrainians and Belarussians were to be Polonized, while the number of Jews was to be reduced to a "tolerable" level. To that end, the Second Republic pursued a variety of policies. In order to reduce the number of Belarussians, the Polish authorities devised a distinction between Belarussians and locals (tutyśnie). To deal with the far more numerous Ukrainian population, they tried to accentuate the distinction among Ukrainians, Lemkos, and Ruthenians. In a ploy to reduce the number of minorities in Poland, the Polish government changed its census methodology. Whereas initially national identity was a matter of self-definition, in 1931, after more than a decade of widespread Polish language schooling, national designation became contingent on a person's native tongue (język ojczysty).[75]

Despite the profession of a multiethnic Jagiellonian principle, Poland failed to come to terms with any of its minorities. With the exception of Silesia, where some autonomy was granted as a result of the plebiscite, Poland's geographic minorities – Slavs in the east and Germans in the west – remained resistant to Polonization. In eastern Galicia and Wolynia, where Ukrainians were the majority, the entire interwar period was marked by an endless, low-grade struggle between Ukrainian nationalists and a "pacifying" Polish army. The weak and unassuming nationalism of the Belarussians was initially welcomed by the Polish state as a means of weakening Russian influence. In the early 1920s, 400 Belarussian schools were opened, but by 1928 the Belarussian National Association (Hramada) was closed, and by 1931 so was the Belarussian School Society.[76]

The Polish strategy for dealing with the Jewish population was to increase economic pressure while simultaneously attempting to find outlets for mass emigration. Prime Minister Count Aleksander Skrzyński, writing in 1926 to Zionist leader Nahum Skolov, noted, "The Polish government is following with interest the progress made by the Zionist organization in its effort to resurrect the national individuality and culture of the Jews in Palestine."[77] Following the growing Arab–Jewish strife in Palestine that led the British government to curtail Jewish access to Palestine, and after the failure of the

---

[75] Joseph Rothschild, East Central Europe Between the Two World Wars (Seattle, WA: University of Washington Press, 1992), 31.

[76] See Jan Zaprudnik, Belarus at the Cross Roads of History (Boulder, CO, San Francisco, Oxford: Westview Press, 1993).

[77] Harry Rabinowicz, The Legacy of Polish Jewry (New York and London: Thomas Yoseloff, 1965), 188.

Polish government's lobbying efforts to reverse the US quota system that limited East European immigration, hopes of solving the "Jewish problem" through conventional emigration faded. Therefore, in an effort to find a new outlet for its Jews, the Polish government pursued a scheme to support Jewish colonization of Madagascar.

Although interwar Poland was divided along a left–right axis, there was remarkable consensus between the two groups that the Jewish population must be reduced. The rightist newspaper *Gazeta Warszawska* declared, "If we want to be a great nation we must get rid of the Jews as the Spaniards did in the fifteenth century,"[78] and even the leaders of the Polish Socialist Party, which vocally protested the pogroms and anti-Jewish policies pursued by the regime, conceded that Poland could not be reconciled with 3.5 million Jews in its midst. In 1937, the socialist J. M. Borski stated, "Only those Jews who are thoroughly integrated into Polish culture and political life will be able to remain and live freely in Poland."[79] Although the socialists believed that assimilation was the solution to the Jewish minority issue, to the intellectual mainstream in interwar Poland assimilation had become synonymous with "alien infiltration," which endangered the Polish ethnos. Throughout the interwar period, the Roman Catholic Church and right-wing politicians remained at odds over how to resolve the vexing Jewish question. To the Church hierarchy, the gravest danger to "Christian Poland" was the cultural assimilation of the Jews, because it would invariably lead to the secularization of the society, the erosion of Catholic values, and the promotion of the Jewish–Bolshevik, anti-Christian conspiracy known as *Żydokomuna* (Judaic communist conspiracy). Therefore, the Church's strategy was to promote the conversion of Jews to Catholicism, while segregating those Jews who continued to cling to their "Talmudist" tradition or adopted socialist atheism.[80] The position of the Polish nationalist right was not without paradox. This was perhaps best exemplified by Zofia Kossak. Along with Władysław Bartoszewski and Henryk Wolińksi, Kossak organized a special underground unit called *Żegota*[81] devoted to the rescue of Jews during the Holocaust. But in 1936 she maintained that the Jewish question in Poland was a racial one, writing, "The Jews are so terribly foreign to us, foreign and unpleasant because they

---

[78] *Gazeta Warszawska*, 19 April 1935.
[79] Rabinowicz, *The Legacy of Polish Jewry*, 55.
[80] See Ronald Modras, *The Catholic Church and Antisemitism, Poland, 1933–1939* (Chur, Switzerland: Harwood Academic Press, 1994).
[81] Żegota is the code name for the Council for Aid to Jews (Rada Pomocy Żydom).

are of another race."[82] To Kossak and many right-wing nationalists the issue was not religious affiliation, but *Zażydzenie* (Judification) of the authentic Polish culture by an alien race. This racial rejection of the Jews within Polish society was perhaps best encapsulated in a letter from the liberal avant-garde artist Stanisław Witkiewicz to his son, who intended to marry a thoroughly Polonized Jewish woman: "Between you and her a gap will open immediately . . . because the feelings of racial superiority will erupt impulsively in you, and in her will erupt the feeling of contempt which Jews have for the rest of humanity. . . Think of it. What will you do when she bears you a half dozen little Jews, your children?"[83]

The rejection of Jews on both religious and racial grounds did, indeed, result in a reversal of assimilation in interwar Poland. In fact, while there was a significant increase in Jewish assimilation across Europe, with intermarriage reaching nearly 50 percent in Germany and one-third in Hungary, in interwar Poland there was actually a decline. According to the 1921 census, 74.2 percent of Poland's Jews declared their native language as either Yiddish or Hebrew (the rest presumably viewing Polish as their native tongue); by 1931 the number of Jews declaring Yiddish or Hebrew as their native language had risen to 87 percent.[84]

Ethnic Poles also had a difficult relationship with the German minority. Poland's post-World War I acquisition of former German territories resulted in the reversal of centuries of "dominant–subservient" relations between the Germans and the Poles. Although there is ample evidence that the Germans in western Poland never resigned themselves to their new status, the policies of successive Polish governments exacerbated the situation and made the treatment of Poland's Germans a *cause célèbre*, both in Germany and in the League of Nations. Successive Polish governments vacillated in their attitudes toward the German minority. On the one hand, Prime Minister Władysław Sikorski believed that "the great historic process which one calls the de-Germanization of the Western provinces [of Poland] must be completed in the shortest possible time and at the most rapid pace. . . It is always the case that the strong [*sic*] is right

---

[82] Ibid., 277.
[83] Quoted in Celia S. Heller, *On the Edge of Destruction: Jews of Poland Between the Two World Wars* (Detroit: Wayne State University Press, 1994), 61.
[84] Włodzimiez Rozenbaum, "The Status of the Jews in Poland Between the Wars, 1918–1939: An Overview," in Wiles, *Poland Between the Wars: 1918–1939*, 163.

and the vanquished must take a back seat."[85] On the other hand, Piłsudski opted for an assimilationist solution: "[The Germans] demonstrated in the course of their history an ease of assimilation and possess an innate streak of loyalty toward the state. The utilization of this minority for the state with the prospect of assimilation is possible and probable."[86]

Throughout the interwar period, Polish regimes not only failed to develop a strategy to accommodate the German community but also failed to distinguish between the "irreconcilable" Germans in the western provinces and the German communities in the eastern part of the country who had immigrated over centuries and had adjusted to their minority status. This undifferentiated approach to the German question resulted in an unprecedented coalescence of Polish–Germans that further delegitimized the Second Republic in the eyes of its minorities.

In a historic paradox, Poland, which had pioneered the notion of a multinational polity, adopted an ethnocentralizing (assimilationist) policy during the Second Republic that was reminiscent of that of Bourbon France. Successive Polish governments tried to create a single polity, oblivious of the fact that, unlike the prerevolutionary French, ethnic groups in the age of nationalism would not disappear to meet the agenda of the state. The prevailing view of the Polish political elite on options available to minorities was bluntly stated in *Nationality Issues (Sprawy Narodowościowe)*, published by the Institute for the Study of the Nationality Question (*Instytut Badań Spraw Narodowościowych*):

> The minorities must adjust to the needs of the state of which they are a part; they must renounce those aspirations which are particularistic from the state's point of view, in favor of the whole state. As the state draws them into the sphere of its leveling activities, it crushes one minority, bends another, and transforms them all, including the main nationality, according to its common and general needs.[87]

In the final analysis, neither Piłsudski's nor Dmowski's vision served the country well. To their dismay, Poland's elites discovered that the Lithuanians' collective memory of the Commonwealth differed sharply from their own, with the Lithuanians opting for outright independence. Similarly, the Ukrainians were neither the "ethnographic mass" that Dmowski envisioned as being easily assimilated nor, in the case of those outside Galicia, in the USSR, sufficiently

---

[85] Blanke, *Orphans of Versailles*, 64.      [86] Ibid., 91.      [87] Ibid., 92.

nationalist to join Piłsudski's campaign to resurrect a Ukrainian state within Poland's sphere of influence. Domination of Ukraine, either through assimilation or confederation, proved to be beyond Poland's grasp. Summing up the interwar Polish state of mind, Jerzy Tomaszewski observed, "Poles never understood or accepted the national aspiration of the peoples to the East, seeing always a foreign hand."[88]

This myopia on the part of the Polish political elite had catastrophic results, both domestically and internationally. Within Poland the attempt to create a national – or, more accurately, nationalist – state within a multinational polity resulted in the alienation of one-third of the population. Even before the outbreak of World War II, Poland was plagued by constant ethnic violence and was engaged in a prolonged "pacification" campaign in the eastern borderlands.[89] By the 1930s, all the minorities in Poland were seeking solutions outside the Polish state. Ukrainians wanted an independent Ukraine; Germans a return of German authority (by 1937, 80 percent of them supported Nazism);[90] Belarussians looked across the border to the Soviet Union; and Jews were polarized between Zionists seeking a national state in Palestine and Bundists and communists seeking to replace Poland with an ideological rather than a national state. Yet despite its numerous failures and shortcomings, the Polish Second Republic left one indisputable legacy as far as ethnic Poles were concerned. Whereas in 1919 the notion of a Polish state was the domain of a minority, twenty years of independence gave the Polish nation a new identity and new confidence. If, in 1919, most Poles were apathetic and even indifferent to Polish independence, by 1939 there was a deeply felt need across the Polish nation, even including its atomized peasantry, for an independent Polish state, making the revival of an independent Poland irreversable and shifting the custodianship of the national identity from a narrow elite to the broad masses.

World War II demolished the illusion that Poland's minorities could be either assimilated or forced to emigrate. Not only was Hitler's *Wehrmacht* welcomed by euphoric *Volksdeutsch* crowds under the banner *Deutsch Blüt in Danzig*, but in eastern Poland, as Jan T. Gross has pointed out, the native populations, whether pro-Soviet (as some

[88] Jerzy Tomaszewski, "The National Question in Poland in the 20th Century," in *The National Question in Europe in Historical Context*, ed. Mikulas Teich and Roy Porter (Cambridge: Cambridge University Press, 1993), 298.

[89] See Mikołaj Siwicki, *Dzieje Konfliktów Polsko-Ukraińskich* [History of Polish–Ukrainian Conflicts] (Warsaw: Tyras Press, 1992).

[90] Blanke, *Orphans of Versailles*, 163.

Jews were) or anti-Soviet (as many Ukrainians were) greeted the demise of the Polish state with relief, if not enthusiasm. Gross noted that "the last battles in the these [eastern] territories were fought [by the Polish army] against Ukrainians, Belarussians and Jews, and 'locals.' "[91]

The massive "ethnic cleansing" of Poles in Volhynia by the SB (*sluzhba bespeky*) security units of the Organization of Ukrainian Nationalists was the most visible symbol of the abandonment, if not outright betrayal, of the Polish state by its minorities.[92] Poland's bitter experience with its minority population during World War II finally convinced much of the Polish elite that in the age of mass politics and national self-determination, Poland could never maintain a presence in the *kresy*. Hence, it would once again be necessary to redefine the notions of Poland and Polishness. Although the Polish elite found it difficult to accept the calamity of 1939, in 1941 General Władysław Sikorski, then prime minister of the Polish government-in-exile in London, confessed to Stalin, "It is not the Ukrainians [in formerly eastern Poland] who matter to me, but the territory in which the Polish element is dominant."[93] This statement by Sikorski may well have been the first official recognition of Poland's desire to reorient itself into an ethnographic state.

### Interwar identity and foreign policy

The differing perceptions of Piłsudski and Dmowski concerning Russia and Germany are well documented. Briefly stated, Piłsudski saw Poland as a latter-day *antemurale christianitatis* in the crusade against Russian Bolshevism, while Dmowski viewed Poland as a partner of Russia in containing Germany. Nevertheless, both based their approach to foreign policy on two assumptions. First, they maintained that Poland was a great military power capable of affecting the balance of power in Europe and therefore a major actor in the international arena. Second, both believed that in order to retain its major-power status, the Polish state must not be territorially

---

[91] Jan T. Gross, *Revolution From Abroad: The Soviet Conquest of Poland's Western Ukraine and Western Belorussia* (Princeton: Princeton University Press, 1988), 19.

[92] See Ryszard Torzecki, *Polacy i Ukraińcy: Sprawa ukraińska w czasie II wojny swiatowej na terenie II Rzeczpospolitej* [Poles and Ukrainians: The Question of Ukrainians on the Territory of the Second Republic during World War II] (Warsaw: Wydawnictwo Naukowe PWN, 1993).

[93] Sarah Meiklejohn Terry, *Poland's Place in Europe: General Sikorski and the Origin of the Oder–Neisse Line, 1939–1943* (Princeton: Princeton University Press, 1983), 130.

confined to ethnographic Poland. As Dmowski declared, "To anyone who had even the slightest understanding of [the] political geography of Europe, it should have been clear that the region where Western Europe ends and the vast Plains of the East begin, in a region placed as of late between two great powers, Germany and Russia, there is no room for a *państewko* (small state)."[94] Piłsudski, in turn, asked sardonically "whether Poland was to be a state equal to the powers of the world, or a small power needing the protection of the mighty?"[95]

The emergence of Poland as Europe's fourth-largest state reinforced the notion that was accepted by nearly the entire interwar political and diplomatic elite – including such key foreign policy makers as Józef Lipski (ambassador to Berlin, 1932–39), Juliusz Łukasiewicz (ambassador to Moscow, 1934–36, and Paris 1936–39), and Józef Beck (foreign minister, 1932–39) – that Poland was once again destined to play the role of a great power (*mocarstwo*).[96] As Piłsudski noted in 1919, "[Poland] would be the greatest power not only militarily, but also culturally in the East."[97] In the 1920s, the French military attaché in Warsaw, General d'Arbnneau, observed that Poland's leaders "have imbibed the elixir of greatness."[98] This sense of *grandeur*, combined with the mind-set of the Polish elite described previously, contributed to the scrappy diplomacy that resulted in Poland's perpetually poor relations with all of its neighbors except Romania. The Polish elite's obsession with their country's great-power status was captured in Józef Beck's 1939 statement: "There is only one thing in the life of men, nations, and states which is without price, and this is honor."[99] Warsaw was averse to joining any sort of "collective security" arrangement, fearing that Poland's stature would be reduced because any such arrangement was bound to be dominated by the truly great powers.[100]

The prevailing belief among the political elite of the interwar period was that Poland derived its great-power status not only from its historic role as the rampart of Christianity defending Europe against the Bolshevik–Russian menace, but also from its new, Promethean role of liberating the little nations of the East from communist oppression. Based on the important international role that Poland

[94] Quoted by Piotr Wandycz, "Polish Foreign Policy: An Overview," in Wiles, *Poland Between the Wars: 1918–1939*, 65.
[95] Ibid.
[96] For an example of the view that Poland is a great power, see Juliusz Łukasiewicz, *Polska jest mocarstwem* [Poland is a Great Power] (Warsaw: Gebethner & Wolff, 1939).
[97] Piotr Wandycz, *Polish Diplomacy 1914–1945* (London: Orbis Books, 1988).
[98] Wandycz, "Poland's Place in Europe."
[99] Wandycz, "Polish Foreign Policy," 68.    [100] Ibid.

ascribed to itself, its leaders assumed that they were entitled to Western, and particularly French, support in their struggle against Soviet Bolshevism. Piłsudski's attitude toward Russia was reinforced by a belief that Russia's culture and social structure precluded the possibility of a democratic transformation. He was firmly convinced that even if Russia did miraculously achieve democracy, it would still be condemned to remain an imperial chauvinist power. However, Piłsudski, along with many other political actors of the time, assumed that Russia's ability to rise to the status of a truly great power would be stymied for an extended period of time. It should be noted that this contempt for Russia as a great power, was by no means unique to Poland. Even in Finland, a country that had not suffered the brutal Russian repression experienced by Poland, the interwar attitude toward Russia and its culture was described by Max Jakobson as "a time of Finnish McCarthyism."[101] Finnish and Polish interwar leaders suffered from a similar blind spot concerning the Soviet Union. As David Kirby noted in his study of Finnish foreign policy:

> The story of Finnish foreign policy between 1918 and the conclusion of the mutual assistance treaty with the Soviet Union thirty years later was one of tragic failure to appreciate the apprehensions and the desire for security of an isolated great power, and the inability to understand that in spite of its isolation, the Soviet Union was a *great power*.[102]

The Polish political elite had fewer doubts that Germany would regain its standing as great power, a process that would require a major readjustment of the European landscape that was potentially dangerous to Poland. During much of the interwar period, however, most of the Polish elite continued to believe that either Germany could be contained by a Polish-led coalition that would include the countries between the Black and Baltic seas, backed by the French-led *mini entente*, or that Germany's energies could be harnessed for an anti-Bolshevik crusade. In either scenario, Warsaw was sure to play a vital role in Western Europe's containment efforts.

Poland's perception of itself as a great power facing what Piłsudski described as the "twin enemies" – Russia and Germany – from whom it had to remain equidistant was confirmed by the Rapallo Agreement concluded by Germany and the Soviet Union in 1922. This agreement

---

[101] Max Jakobson, *Finnish Neutrality: A Study of Finnish Foreign Policy Since the Second World War* (London: Hugh Evelyn, 1968), 9.

[102] David G. Kirby, *Finland in the Twentieth Century* (Minneapolis: University of Minnesota Press, 1979), 107 (emphasis in the original).

aroused Western fears regarding the possibility of an anti-status-quo "coalition of pariahs" and revealed the shallowness of the Western commitment to Poland. During a visit to Warsaw soon after the conclusion of Rapallo, France's Marshal Foch suggested that Paris' military commitments to Poland should be modified in case of German aggression and should be inoperative regarding Russia.[103] The Locarno Agreement, negotiated in 1925 by Western powers reeling from the shock of Rapallo, provided for the reintegration of Germany into Europe as a great power without demanding a German commitment to its eastern frontiers. Piłsudski responded to this with the blunt statement that "Every good Pole spits with disgust at the name [Locarno]."[104] Poland's sense of having been abandoned by its Western allies was expressed by Jan Karski: "[France, Poland's historic ally] sought to preserve the status quo, trying to maintain the new détente as the most essential requirement for general peace and national security. Poland could not contribute to that détente; in fact the frequent Polish–German disputes and frictions in the League of Nations represented an annoying *dissonant*"[105] even if success in this struggle meant severely compromising the position of Poland within the international system.[106]

Although the interwar Polish leadership was disinclined to attach itself to either of its immediate neighbors, it did not entirely rule out the possibility of an alliance with Germany. This position was articulated by Piłsudski, who considered Russia a "cadaver," and by the influential historian Adolph Bocheński, who argued that Poland's sole hope of attaining stability and security lay in an alliance with Hitler's Germany.[107] The belief that Poland should form part of an anti-Bolshevik, right-wing coalition was echoed by the influential Kraków newspaper *Czas*. Conservative nationalist Polish publicist Władysław Studnicki, associated with the Wilno publication *Słowo*, advocated an alliance with Nazi Germany against the Soviet Union, prophetically

[103] Jan Karski, *The Great Powers and Poland: 1919–1945: From Versailles to Yalta* (Lanham, New York, London: University Press of America, 1985), 108.
[104] Quoted by Henry L. Roberts, "The Diplomacy of Colonel Beck," in *The Diplomats 1919–1939*, ed. Gordon A. Craig and Felix Gilbert (Princeton: Princeton University Press, 1994), 588.
[105] Karski, *The Great Powers and Poland*, 113.
[106] There is a wealth of literature on Poland's interwar diplomacy, including Stanisław T. Bębenek, *Myślenie o przeszłości* [Thoughts about the Past] (Warsaw, 1981); Josef Korbel, *Poland Between East and West: Soviet and German Diplomacy toward Poland, 1919–1923* (Princeton, Princeton University Press, 1963).
[107] Adolf Bocheński, *Między Niemcami a Rosją* [Between Germany and Russia] (Warsaw: Nałęcz, 1994).

noting that a war between Poland and Germany would lead to a Polish defeat and that "Russia alone will emerge as victor from a war of Central Europe against Eastern Europe."[108] The policies advocated by the right were adopted by Foreign Minister Józef Beck and resulted in the Polish–German Non-Aggression Pact of 1934, strenuous opposition to Soviet Foreign Minister Maxim Litvinov's efforts to contain Germany through a scheme of collective security, and the unfortunate Polish participation in the partition of Czechoslovakia. Historians such as A. J. P. Taylor believe that Poland's quest to be a great power led to its alliance with the ultimate anti-status-quo power – Hitler's Germany – and brought about the collapse of the European order and a fourth partition of the Polish state.[109] Yet, as Piotr Wandycz has pointed out, although it was not entirely clear that the Soviet Union would have offered Poland an option to escape an increasingly precarious position, such a possibility could not have been explored in light of the *Weltanschauung* of the Polish polity.[110] It is interesting to note, however, that apparently there was a major gap between the elite's enthusiasm for Nazi Germany and the views of the Polish public. In March 1936, Poland's deputy foreign minister, Jan Szembek, stated that "Polish opinion is thoroughly hostile to Germany and, in contrast, is favorable to France and even Sovietophile."[111] However, given the obsession of the Polish elite, and the non-democratic nature of the state, the popular repulsion toward the embrace of Nazi Germany had no impact on policy.

### The lessons of the failed 1944 uprising

Much as 1863 was a watershed year in Polish identity, a year in which many previously perceived truisms were swept aside, the calamity of World War II, and particularly the 1944 Warsaw Uprising, signaled the unsustainablity of several key assumptions that guided the Second Republic. The defeat of the 1863 Uprising led to a profound re-evaluation of the tenets of the romantic school and its implications for Poland's domestic politics and international relations. Similarly, the failure of the Polish uprising in 1944 dealt the final blow to both the internal and external paradigms that had guided Poland since its rebirth after World War I. The 1863 fiasco demonstrated both

---

[108] Blanke, *Orphans of Versailles*, 194.
[109] A. J. P. Taylor, *The Origins of the Second World War* (New York: Athenaeum, 1983).
[110] See Wandycz, *Dyplomacja Polska*.
[111] "The Diplomacy of Colonel Beck," in *The Diplomats, 1919–1939*, 606.

the peasants' indifference to the ideals of the Commonwealth and the inability of romantic notions about the wishes of the peoples of the *kresy* to support the re-creation of a Polish-led Commonwealth. The experiences of 1939–45 showed that Poland's attempts to force assimilation on the Ukrainians and the Belarussians merely fostered nationalism among them and ultimately resulted in their collaboration with both the Soviets and the Nazis and in the "ethnic cleansing" of the ethnically Polish population of the *kresy*. The failure of the 1863 Uprising and the Nazi occupation graphically demonstrated that in the age of popular nationalism, Poland lacked the means to either co-opt or permanently coerce the peoples of the *kresy*. The Poles were left with no alternative but to reverse nearly 500 years of national experience and abandon the lands and the concepts that had shaped the Polish identity since the Reformation. The experiences of World War II also forced a major reconsideration of Poland's perception of itself and its role within the international system. Although Poland's prime minister in exile, General Władysław Sikorski, did not embrace Dmowski's notion of realism, he did point the way to a new vision of its place in the international system. Sikorski advocated three basic shifts of orientation: elimination of the doctrine of "two enemies" through expansion to the West at the expense of Germany; reconciliation with Russia, even if that meant a departure from the Jagiellonian heritage and a substantial loss of the *kresy*; and the creation of a Central European federation or confederation.[112] Although the last may have seemed less dramatic than the other two, the notion of a federation with Czechoslovakia represented a significant departure for Poland, given the traditional Polish view that Czechoslovakia was an artificial, pro-Russian creation.

Most Poles found the reversal of the country's 500–year-old tradition difficult and painful to accept, particularly in light of Stalin's brutal behavior. Poland's World War II experience was one of trauma and betrayal. Defeat in 1939 by a combined Nazi–Soviet assault, cold indifference on the part of the Western allies to the 1944 Warsaw Uprising, and the relegation of issues concerning their future to a secondary status at the Teheran and Yalta conferences, left the Poles bitter and dejected. Although the Polish people made an honorable contribution to the Allied war effort, heroically fighting Nazi Germany from the streets of Warsaw to the Battle of Britain, from the

---

[112] See Terry, *Poland's Place in Europe*, also *Integracja Europy*, ed. Lech Zacher and Piotr Matusak (Warsaw: Fundacja Edukacyjna Transformacja, 1996), 2–11.

hills of Monte Casino to the beaches of Normandy, the West did not lobby to grant Poland the "victor power" status granted to France. The "gratitude" of the West to Poland expressed by President Franklin D. Roosevelt when he told Stalin at the Yalta Conference that "Poland . . . has been a source of trouble for over 500 years"[113] made it clear that the West did not consider Poland either a great military power or of central importance to the international system. The paradigm that dominated the political life of the Second Republic was annihilated along with the combatants of the Warsaw Uprising.

Following the experiences of 1939–45, the remnants of the Polish elite – democrats in exile, national communists in Poland, and the Roman Catholic Church – all recognized that Poland needed a conservative paradigm based on a "usable history" and a new definition of Polish statehood. The development of this new paradigm would be further complicated by the fact that the Poles would once again be forging their identity under foreign domination. Publicist Marcin Król acknowledged that the task would be inherently painful and difficult because "To be a conservative in a time of national slavery is *ipso facto* contradictory."[114] Nevertheless, as we shall see in chapter 3, Poland did finally manage to separate itself, both physically and psychologically, from the eastern borderlands and lay the foundation for a modern European nation-state.

[113] Piotr Wandycz, "Poland in World History: Inspiration or a Trouble Maker?" *Cross Current* 5 (1986), 195.

[114] Marcin Król, *Style politycznego myślenia: wokół 'Buntu młodych' i 'Polityki'* [Styles of Political Thought] (Paris: Libella, 1978), 30.

## 3 Poland after World War II: native conservatism and the return to Central Europe

> Poland has a thousand year history and no yesterday to which to refer.
>
> Juliusz Mieroszewski

### The aftermath of World War II

The suffering, destruction, and humiliation endured by the Polish people during World War II recast Poland. Geographically, it was moved west, and its population changed from one of the most heterogeneous to one of the most homogeneous in Europe. Much of the prewar political and cultural elite of the nation was annihilated by Stalin and Hitler, and its remnants were forced into long, involuntary exile. The Poland that emerged from the war was psychologically, sociologically, and economically different from the Second Republic. In psychological terms, World War II, unlike Piłsudski's struggle for independence, was a truly national war embracing every layer of Polish society and embodying a powerful collective experience on an unprecedented scale. Economically, the harnessing of Poland's economy to the Reich's war machine resulted in significant industrialization of the country (in the area between the Oder and Bug rivers, the number of industrial workers increased threefold during the war) as well as the establishment of economic etatism, which did not exist before the war.[1]

Sociologically, the Polish elite that emerged from the ruins of the war developed a very different sense of Poland's place within the international system, as well as a notion of Polishness that differed markedly from that of the interwar elite. Not only were the old Polish intelligentsia and elite annihilated or driven abroad, but also, as

---

[1] Jan T. Gross, "The Experience of War in East Central Europe: Social Disruption and Political Revolution," *East European Politics and Society* 3: 2 (1989).

Krystyna Kersten noted: "The middle class ceased to exist as a social stratum, as did the land owners, as a result of the land reform, more than 10,000 landowners were expropriated, 13,243 estates were either parceled out or placed under state control."[2] The remnants of the Home Army (Armia Krajowa) representing the last vestiges of the authority of the government-in-exile in London was reduced to a beleaguered force fighting for its physical survival, prompting the anti-communist, socialist leader Zygmunt Zaremba to lament that: "The moral border that then divided the soldiers from bandits began to blur more and more."[3] The moral authority of the Home Army, and with it, that of the Polish government-in-exile in London, was degraded and rapidly eliminated as a force in Polish politics. In an environment of crisis and confronted with the demise of their traditional leadership, the Polish people were being rapidly transformed.

Although communist-dominated Poland indeed resembled a "saddled cow" in its first two years, the communists managed to gain a degree of acceptance. The communist leadership had several advantages. Since the party leadership was initially dominated by "home communists" rather than by those who returned from exile in the USSR ("Mosovites"), they could claim a degree of authenticity. Bolesław Bierut was able to declare that: "[The Polish economic model] is not based on any foreign model or imitation, it is not the socialist model of the Soviet economy or the classical form of the great capitalist states . . ." Władysław Gomułka went even further, asserting that, "Our [Polish] democracy is also not similar to the Soviet democracy."[4]

The broad Polish *lud*, after years of suffering and travail, reluctantly accepted and indeed welcomed the new order in Poland. The rural population welcomed the accelerated redistribution of land brought about by the confiscation of large estates. Landless rural Poles were moved to the "regained" cities (formerly German), thereby accelerating Poland's urbanization and industrialization. Thousands of Poles benefited from the new job opportunities and the wider availability of education. One symptom of the change in the Polish mind-set was the wholesale abandonment of the Catholic Church, as the Kraków based church scholar Jan Jerschina observed:

[2] Krystyna Kersten, *The Establishment of Communist Rule in Poland 1943–1948* (Berkeley, Los Angles, Oxford: University of California Press, 1991), 166.
[3] Ibid., 223.     [4] Ibid., 176.

It is significant that that was the time, the only historical era since the Reformation, when there was a mass exodus of believers from the Church. In the 1940s and 1950s, the exodus took place even among those upwardly mobile young people from the villages (traditionally so religious) and from small towns, not to mention the new young intelligentsia.[5]

The position of the Church as a counterweight to communist usurpers was weakened by the stand of Pope Pius XII, whose formative career was shaped by serving first in Munich and later in Spain during the cvil war. Seeing communism as the ultimate evil, the pope appeared to be inclined to stress the needs of the Cold War over Poland's particular needs. The Vatican's refusal to transfer the parishes in the "new territories" to the Polish church gave the communists a pretext to annul the 1925 concordat in 1945. The pope's letter to German bishops in March of 1948, questioning the legitimacy of the Polish state as it emerged after World War II, asserted that 12 million "guiltless" Germans had been driven from their homes. Noting Germany's potential as a bloc against Bolshevism, the Pope stated: "Were the measures [the expulsion of the Germans] taken politically justified and economically defensible, considering the urgent needs of the German people and the safety of all of Europe? It is unrealistic to desire and hope that all concerned may come to a peaceful understanding and forget the past . . ."[6] The fact that the Vatican openly sided with the Germans in the territorial dispute with Poland enabled the home communists to question the patriotism of the church as a whole, forcing it to a defensive position.

The symbiosis between the new regime's policies and the feelings of the population may explain why, between 1945–47, Poland reconstructed itself faster than any other European state recovering from the war.[7] In 1947 incomes rose by 14 percent over the previous year, and in 1948 salaries grew an additional 40 percent.[8] Furthermore, aside from the narrow fringe of the intelligentsia that mourned the demise of multicultural Poland, most of the population did not regret

[5] Jan Jerschina, "The Catholic Church, the Communist State and the People," in *Polish Paradoxes*, ed. Stanisław Gomułka and Antony Polonsky (London and New York: Routledge, 1991), 84.

[6] Quoted in Hermann Schreiber, *Teuton and Slav: The Struggle for Central Europe* (New York: Alfred A. Knopf, 1963), 364.

[7] Wiktor Herer and Władyslaw Sadowski, "The Incompatibility of System and Culture," in *Polish Paradoxes*, ed. Stanisław Gomułka and Antony Polonsky (London: Routledge, 1990), 120.

[8] Kersten, *The Establishment of Communist Rule in Poland 1943–1948*, 421.

the disappearance of the Germans, Jews, and Ukrainians. The series of violent attacks against the Jews, culminating with the pogrom in Kielce (1946); the murder of hundreds, if not thousands, of Ukrainians during their eviction to the Soviet Union;[9] and the population's general support for Operation Vistula, which removed the Ukrainian minority from its historic homelands in the southeast and scattered it throughout Poland, are a reflection of the popular mind-set of the time. Nazi brutality against the Poles and the "ethnic cleansing" campaign by the Ukrainians in Vohlynia had aroused feelings of fear and malice toward these groups. The disproportionately high representation of Jews among the new communist leadership and in the regime's security apparatus gave new impetus to Poland's endemic anti-Semitism, causing a reflexive association between Jews and the Soviet-imposed regime.[10]

The government-in-exile in London, representing the enlightened and tolerant element of Poland's prewar intelligentsia, demonstrated how far it was out of touch with the existing Polish realities. In a declaration entitled "What Is the Polish Nation Fighting For?" (*O co walczy naród Polski?*), the government-in-exile offered a concept of a multinational Poland that promised:

> The Polish nation will fully take into consideration the interests of other nations living in the territory of the state. While demanding that they should be loyal and faithful to the Polish state and sympathetic to the rights and interests of the Polish nation, Poland will base its relations to these nationalities on the principle of equal political rights and will guarantee them conditions for full economic and cultural development within the framework of unity and common good of all citizens.[11]

The London government's blueprint for postwar Poland failed to consider the attitudes of both the Poles and Poland's prewar minorities. The Polish masses, themselves subject to some of the largest population transfers in modern history, adapted to Poland's new frontiers remarkably easily. Despite the Polish romantics' deep emotional attachment to the eastern borderlands and the obvious pain caused by the loss and de-Polonization of historically Polish cities such as Lwów (Lviv) and Wilno (Vilnius), most Poles accepted these

---

[9] Krystyna Kersten, "The Polish–Ukrainian Conflict Under Communist Rule," *Acta Polonicae Historica*, no. 73 (1996).

[10] Jaff Schatz, *The Generation: The Rise and Fall of Jewish Communists of Poland* (Berkeley: University of California Press, 1991).

[11] Kersten, "The Polish–Ukrainian Conflict," 126.

changes, and quickly forgot the German origins of the "recovered" territories.[12] Describing the Poles' attitude toward their country's postwar territorial configuration, Jan Jerschina writes:

> Poland within its new [post-World War II] boundaries was a terri-torial, economic, and social entity, whose integration and develop-ment could be achieved more rapidly and more completely than that of the territorial-social creation which was a result of the First World War. It is not surprising that in the consciousness of modern Poles, irrespective of their political sympathies, this new homeland is the most natural, proper nest, and they meet any doubt cast on this idea not only with hostility, but simply with astonishment.[13]

Despite the prevalent view of the communist regime as both alien and suspect, Adam Michnik asserted that the communists succeeded in imposing their system "because of its deadly mixture of terror and social promise."[14] During its first two years in power, the regime secured a grudging acquiescence from the Polish populace, and many of its policies provided the ruling elite with an important source of legitimacy.

The outlook of the Polish intelligentsia paralleled popular percep-tions in several important ways.[15] The romantic school, the embodi-ment of the Polish spirit that had played a key role in Polish thought since the partitions, had been annihilated in the forests of Katyń and in the rubble of the Warsaw Uprising. This tragic experience aside, the mere fact that Kraków survived the war unscathed meant that its tradition of conservative realism was better positioned to dominate the intellectual debate in postwar Poland.

The intelligentsia that emerged in postwar Poland consisted of two distinct strands: the traditionally conservative, Catholic "Kraków" intellectuals and the young, leftist intellectuals, often of proletarian or Jewish origin. Both could cite intellectual precedents that allowed them to come to terms with the territorial configuration of postwar Poland. For Catholic conservatives, the emergence of an ethnically and religiously homogeneous state that did not leave major Polish minorities outside Poland appeared to fulfill the ideal advocated by Roman Dmowski earlier in the century. For the leftist intelligentsia,

---

[12] See Rafal Bubiński, "Ziemia Nieznana Wrocław," *Rzeczpospolita*, no. 9, September 1995.

[13] Jerschina "The Catholic Church," 81.

[14] Adam Michnik, *Letters from Prison and Other Essays* (Berkeley, Los Angeles, and London: University of California Press, 1987), 44.

[15] See Maria Dąbrowska, *Dzienniki Powojenne 1945–65* (Warsaw: Czytelnik, 1996).

the arrangement seemed to fulfill a 1943 commitment to the right of self-determination for the people of the eastern borderlands.[16]

But the Catholic intellectuals could hardly approve of a regime that they perceived as a creature of "Byzantine Bolshevism." In 1945 the Polish primate, Cardinal Hlond, clashed with the communist authorities over his insistence on reading Pope Pius XII's letter criticizing the regime's decision to annul the 1925 Concordat between Poland and the Vatican. During the elections in the following year, the Church hierarchy obliquely supported the opposition led by Stanisław Mikołajczyk.[17] For the most part, however, the church hierarchy avoided direct confrontation with the regime, and lay Catholic intellectuals adopted a decisively neo-positivist outlook. Nevertheless, the Catholic intelligentsia, which had a right-wing orientation during the interwar years, split into two distinct groups, *Pax* and *Znak*.

*Pax* was led by Bolesław Piasecki, whose prewar followers (known as "progressivists") took strongly nationalist, anti-capitalist, anti-communist, and anti-Semitic positions. During the war, Piasecki and his followers fought against both the Germans and the Soviets. Piasecki was captured by the Soviets in 1944, but released the following year. During his imprisonment, he came to be perceived by the communists as a useful tool to co-opt Catholic support.[18] The ideology of *Pax* was based on the notion of "multiformity," which in essence argued that Marxism's socioeconomic program could be separated from the rest of its ideology; hence Catholics could cooperate with the communist regime. *Pax*, perhaps more than any political group in Poland except the communists themselves, rejected the romantic tradition's ideas regarding the Polish tragedy. Launching one of the first broadsides at the romantic school in his book, *The History of Foolishness in Poland*,[19] Alexander Bocheński claimed that Poland's string of tragedies stemmed from its delusions of *grandeur*, messianism, and overestimation of its importance within the international system. In his opinion, Poland's security lay in an alliance with one of its two powerful neighbors – Russia or Germany. Given the geopolitical conditions of 1947, it was clear that Bocheński was advocating an alliance with Russia. Bocheński's critique is not surprising given the desire of the

---

[16] Kersten, "The Polish–Ukrainian Conflict."

[17] Vincent C. Chrypiński, "The Catholic Church in Poland 1944–1989," in *Catholicism and Politics in Communist Societies*, ed. Pedro Ramet (Durham and London: Duke University Press, 1990), 122.

[18] Tadeusz N. Cieplak, ed., *Poland Since 1956: Readings and Essays on Polish Government and Politics* (New York: Twayne, 1972), 185.

[19] Alexander Bocheński, *Dzieje głupoty w Polsce: Pamflety dziejopisarskie* (Warsaw, 1947).

communist regime to discredit the prewar order and the author's association with the pro-government (yet Catholic) publication *Dziś i Jutro*.

A far more important segment of the Catholic intelligentsia clustered around the periodicals launched by Kraków Cardinal Sapieha – the *Tygodnik Powszechny*, *Znak*, and later, *Więź*. The group that published and read these publications developed the neo-positivist ideology typical of the Catholic leadership during much of the communist era. Under the intellectual leadership of Stefan Kisielewski, Stanisław Stomma, and Tadeusz Mazowiecki, the *Znak* group believed that although the romantics provided Poland with a unifying national mythology without which a nation cannot survive, the Polish people confronted a set of realities that made the continuation of that tradition inappropriate. Before World War II, both Kisielewski and Stomma had belonged to conservative groups that advocated reliance on the West and rejected an alliance with Russia, but their wartime experiences forced them to recast their view of Poland's place in Europe, if not its national identity. While insisting that Poland was part of the Western cultural mainstream, members of *Znak* felt that the Poles had been abandoned by the West. US support for West Germany's non-recognition of the Oder–Neisse line was a particularly sore point. Since the Anglo-Saxons had always supported the Curzon line (approximately the new Soviet–Polish border), only an alignment with the Soviet Union assured Poland that it would not be reduced to a rump state such as Congress Poland, similar to the one that emerged following the 1815 Congress of Vienna. According to *Znak* partisans, Colonel Józef Beck's notion of Poland as a "third force" between Russia and Germany was an impractical alternative, which had contributed to the 1939 tragedy. Although *Znak* advocated a Soviet alliance, it did so on the basis of geopolitical reality rather than out of any ideological conviction. Realizing that their ultimate goal of a truly independent Poland would have to await a realignment in the international system, these Polish Catholic intellectuals embraced the traditional positivist position that they could best serve their nation by investing their energies in Poland's economic and social improvement.[20] Stomma, the leader of the Catholic faction in the *Sejm*, observed that if it wanted to survive, Poland had no option other than to embrace realism. Any attempt to bring about change militarily

---

[20] For a discussion of *Znak*'s views, see Adam Bromke, *Poland's Politics: Idealism vs. Realism* (Cambridge, MA: Harvard University Press), ch. 12.

would result in another catastrophe. Carefully reminding his readers that he was neither a Marxist nor a socialist, Stomma observed:

> Undoubtedly, after a period of lesser or greater friction, we shall witness the establishment of new forms of even closer coordination between all Western states. Independently of this we know that they have joined in a political and military union: NATO.
>
> If such is the case in the West, it would be naive to think that the same tendency toward uniformity would not prevail in the Eastern socialist bloc, which, as all know, is a much more closely knit structure. It is therefore perfectly obvious to every sensible person that the logical and irrefutable consequence of Poland's belonging to the Eastern bloc must be the adaptation of the socialist system, *as a historical and political necessity*.[21]

In addition to *Pax* and *Znak*, a third political group emerged in postwar Poland – the leftist intellectuals. Only a small number of them were actual Marxist–Leninists, but the prevailing view among much of the leftist intellectual community in post-World War II Europe was that only socialism could have ameliorated the economic deprivations of the interwar period, which were seen as a key cause of World War II. Although they were aware that the Soviet Union deviated from socialist standards in many respects and were often appalled by the Stalinist practices prevalent in the USSR, the leftists tried to overlook these flaws. As a result, leftist intellectuals were torn between the socialist myths that they forced themselves to believe and the reality of communist authoritarianism, a predicament depicted in Czesław Miłosz's *The Captive Mind*.[22]

### The Stalinization of Poland: the end of symbiosis

The synergy between the state and society that emerged in postwar Poland did not last long. The outbreak of the Cold War and the declaration of the "two camps" doctrine[23] by Andrei Zhdanov, Stalin's chief ideologue, resulted in the imposition of direct Soviet-style conformity on all facets of life and caused a bitter reaction across the political spectrum in Poland. The imposition of Russian culture on the endemically Russophobic Poles completely offended national

---

[21] See Alexander Stomma, *Myśli o polityce i kulturze* (Crack: Znak, 1960) (emphasis added).

[22] Czesław Miłosz, *The Captive Mind* (New York: Vintage Books, 1990).

[23] Andrei Zhdanov, "The Two Camp Policy," (1947) in *From Stalinism to Pluralism: A Documentary History of Eastern Europe Since 1945*, ed. Gale Stokes (New York and Oxford: Oxford University Press, 1991), 38–42.

sensibilities. Most Poles had always considered Russia an inferior imitator of European civilization. Miłosz captured the attitude of Central Europeans (particularly Poles) toward Russia: "[The Poles] are more intelligent; most of their land is under cultivation; their system of communication and their industry are more highly developed. Measures based on absolute cruelty are unnecessary and even pointless."[24]

The Stalinization of Poland was comparatively free of the extreme brutality characteristic of the process in the Soviet Union and other Eastern bloc states, but the immediate post-World War II era was a dark period for the Polish polity. The Catholic Church and the intellectuals associated with it were among the first victims of the Cold War. In 1949, reacting primarily to events in Italy, the Vatican issued a papal bull forbidding all co-operation between Catholics and communists.[25] Although communism had always been anathema to the Church, in the immediate postwar years a certain degree of Church–communist cooperation had developed. But under the so-called Pacelli–Spellman alliance to combat world communism, the Vatican became a direct participant in the anti-communist struggle, condemning Cardinal Wyszyński's efforts to deal with the authorities[26] and making the neo-positivist position of Polish Catholic intellectuals untenable. The confrontation between the Stalinist authorities and the Church resulted in the suppression of Znak;[27] a Soviet-style show trial and conviction of Kielce's bishop, Czesław Kaczmarek; and the banishment of Cardinal Wyszyński to a monastery in southern Poland. With these measures, the Polish Communist Party laid the groundwork for an assault on the Church, the most authentic national institution in Poland.

The imposition of Stalinism on Poland also led to growing disillusionment among the working class, which had initially benefited from the communist transformation. The total subjugation of the Polish economy to the Soviet Union, increasing demands for more rapid industrialization, overt Soviet intrusion into Polish industrial enter-

---

[24] Miłosz, The Captive Mind, 62.
[25] Hansjakob Stehle, The Independent Satellite – Society and Politics in Poland Since 1945 (New York and London: Frederick A. Prager, 1965), 64.
[26] See George Weigel, The Final Revolution: The Resistance Church and the Collapse of Communism (Oxford: Oxford University Press, 1991), 66. Eugenio Pacelli is the original name of Pope Pius XII; Francis Cardinal Spellman was the Cardinal of New York and a strong advocate of anti-communist states during the Cold War.
[27] Adam Bromke, "The 'Znak' Group on Poland," in Poland Since 1956, ed. Tadeusz N. Cieplak (New York: Twayne, 1972), 81.

prises, and an economic slowdown led to ever greater tension and hostility among blue-collar workers. Polish wages, which rose steeply during the first three postwar years, collapsed after 1950, declining between 1950 and 1953 at 3.7 percent per annum.[28] The Kremlin's frequent calls for the collectivization of Polish agriculture fostered fear and disillusionment among the peasantry and resulted in lower rural investment and productivity and food shortages in the cities. Poland's rapid economic recovery of the years 1945–47 slowed, sharply curtailing the co-optive ability of the communist regime. Writing in 1947 on regime efforts to co-opt the working class, the Polish sociologist Józef Chałasiński noted that "the [regime's] efforts to produce a workers' and peasants' intelligentsia failed. The most important factor in this failure was the unattractive type of culture which one tried to use as the basis of this effort."[29] The working class, in whose name the communist authorities claimed the right to govern, felt increasingly alienated from the regime and soon came to view the *nomenklatura* as a new exploiting elite.

The heavy-handed Sovietization of Poland even offended the leftists, who were intellectually prepared to accept both scientific socialism and the practical necessity of an alliance with the Soviet Union. Many communists, including Władysław Gomułka, were charged with "nativism" and either purged or arrested. Leszek Kołakowski, a professor of Marxism at the University of Warsaw in 1947, complained:

> Soviet-type communism was so obviously incompatible with the Polish cultural legacy, and the Soviet version of Marxism so primitive and boorish, that apart from other reasons, it was simply impossible for intellectuals, bred in what essentially was West European civilization, to adopt it lock, stock, and barrel.[30]

The gap between the state and society deepened after Gomułka's purge and the replacement of the "native" communists with those who spent the war years in the USSR. Many of these new leaders were of Jewish origin, and far more identified with Stalinism than with Poland. Stalinist conformity, which demanded near worship of every-

---

[28] Michael Bernhard, *The Origins of Democratization in Poland* (New York: Columbia University Press, 1993), 35.

[29] Quoted by Aleksander Gela, "The Life and Death of the Old Polish Intelligentsia," *Slavic Review* 30 (1971), 3.

[30] Quoted by Anna R. Dadlez, *Political and Social Issues in Poland as Reflected in the Polish Novel 1946–1985* (New York: East European Monographs, distributed by Columbia University Press, 1989), 130.

believed that they could change the nature of the Polish state from above by engaging the state. The Catholics' neo-positivist strategy sought to extract concessions from the regime slowly and steadily, a process that would reinforce authentic Polish cultural and political traditions and ultimately lead to a transformation of the state. Leftist intellectuals adopted a "revisionist" strategy, believing that the thaw that followed Stalin's death and accelerated under Khrushchev would lead to the slow democratization of communism, ultimately producing what Czechoslovakia's Alexander Dubček would later call "communism with a human face."[32]

Although their philosophies differed, both the leftist intellectuals and the Catholics agreed that change would have to come from above as a result of the slow evolution of the regime and that it was necessary to avoid a recurrence of the notion of romantic martyrdom. The latter seemed likely because the postwar search for authentic Polish roots had combined with anti-Soviet sentiment to rekindle the Polish infatuation with certain aspects of romanticism, excluding a revival of the Jagiellonian tradition.

There was no return to romantic ideals when it came to foreign affairs. The collapse of the national paradigm based on the legacy of the Polish–Lithuanian Commonwealth and the bitter experience of abandonment by the West during World War II led to a reconsideration of Poland's international position. Ukrainian and Lithuanian hostility to the Poles during World War II had made it all too evident that Poland was not considered a "civilizing force" by its immediate neighbors to the east. The Polish pretension of being an *antemurale christianitatis* for the West, holding back the Russian and Ottoman empires, was also shattered. The Western powers had chosen the goodwill of Moscow over that of Warsaw, partitioning Europe in the aftermath of World War II and reinforcing a new consensus that the Polish question was actually a Central European question. As Maria Todorova noted, because the Soviet Union was a single, unified "other" confronting all of the countries of East-Central Europe, a distinct Central European identity began to emerge. As a result, it soon became clear that Poland's liberation could only be achieved as part of the liberation of the rest of East-Central Europe.[33] That, in turn,

<hr/>

[32] See Adam Michnik, "The New Evolutionism," *Survey* 22: 3/4 (Summer/Autumn 1976), 267–77; also Jan Bielasiak, *Poland Today: The State of the Republic* (Armonk, NY: M. E. Sharpe, 1981).
[33] See Marian S. Wolański, *Europa Środko-Wschodnia w myśli politycznej emigracji polskiej* (Wrocław: Wydawnictwo Unywersytetu Wrocławskiego, 1996).

hinged on the decline of bipolarity between the Soviet Union and the West. Recognizing that Poland's drive to democratization was contingent on a relaxation of tensions and democratization of the region, both the Catholic neo-positivists and the leftist revisionists attempted to develop policies that would reduce regional tensions and give the Poles freedom to maneuver. The first attempt to loosen the constraints imposed on Poland by its external environment was the so-called Rapacki Plan, a move initiated by the revisionist communists. Launched in 1957 by Poland's foreign minister, Adam Rapacki, the plan was to denuclearize Central Europe, a move that, if implemented, would have thawed the Cold War in the region and given Poland a modicum of diplomatic freedom. Although rejected, the Rapacki Plan was an important landmark in Polish diplomatic history. First of all, it was a genuine Polish proposal, not one in which Poland served as a "front" for the Kremlin, as was the case with the 1955 "Czech"–Egyptian arms deal. Second, the plan explicitly linked Poland's security and future to three other Central European states (the two Germanys and Czechoslovakia), rather than to either the West or the Soviet Union. Finally, the Rapacki Plan was based on a multilateral concept of collective security,[34] a major change from Poland's interwar diplomatic tradition of insisting on bilateralism. But the West rejected the plan, fearing that it was a ploy to detach West Germany from the North Atlantic Treaty Organization (NATO) and decouple the United States from Western Europe. Although the Soviet Union nominally supported Rapacki's initiative, the Western reaction encouraged Moscow to tighten its grip on Eastern Europe. If there was any lasting lesson to be learned from the saga of the Rapacki Plan, it was that Poland's sovereignty would remain hostage to the vagaries of the Cold War.

Like the revisionists, the Catholic Church recognized that as long as Poland remained trapped on the front line between two blocs in a bipolar world, it could never achieve full sovereignty and political liberalization. Church leaders recognized that only the normalization of Polish–German relations could erode bipolarity. With that in mind, during the 1966 celebration of the millennium of Christianity in Poland, the Polish bishops released a letter to their German counterparts declaring that Poland's Catholics "Forgive [the Germans], and

---

[34] See Piotr Wandycz, "Adam Rapacki and the Search for European Security," in *The Diplomats 1939–1979*, ed. Gordon A. Craig and Francis L. Loewenheim (Princeton: Princeton University Press, 1994), 289–318.

ask for forgiveness."[35] But that magnanimous gesture did little to thaw the international system in Central Europe. The Vatican, following its own Cold War policies, refused to recognize the Oder–Neisse line, thereby limiting the authority of the Polish Church in the "new territories" and enhancing the communists' argument articulated in the slogan *"Socjalizm Gwarancją Pokoju i Granic"* (Socialism, the guarantor of peace and borders).[36]

Despite the attempts of both Rapacki and the Polish bishops to ease tensions in Central Europe, Poland's diplomatic options remained limited. West Germany continued to insist on the restoration of Germany's 1937 frontiers and the enforcement of the Hallstein Doctrine, which denied recognition to any state that established diplomatic relations with East Germany. In order to ensure its territorial integrity, Poland had no option but to toe the Kremlin line in the international arena. Even the Vatican refused to come to terms with Poland until 1972, when the Polish government normalized relations with Germany.[37] Polish hopes that changes in the international climate would ease the burden of being a quasi-sovereign country trapped on the fault line between two blocs were crushed.

Internally, the hopes for democratization, be it from the revisionist or positivist perspective, were also dashed. The gains that had been achieved in October 1956 proved to be short-lived. In September 1957, the authorities closed down the iconoclastic *Po Prostu*, a weekly popular among the young intelligentsia. In November of the same year, delegates to the Conference of Communist Parties in Moscow agreed that the parties must close ranks against any challenges to such fundamental tenets of Marxism–Leninism as the dictatorship of the proletariat, the leading role of Marxist–Leninist parties, democratic centralism (Lenin's ban on factionalism), and fraternal aid among the communist parties.[38] China's aversion to revisionism, direct challenges to communist rule in Hungary and Poland, and Khrushchev's power struggles in Moscow combined to dash hopes for greater revisionism and put an end to the possibility of democra-

[35] Piotr Madajczyk, *Na drodze do pojednania: wokół orędzia biskupów polskich do biskupów niemieckich z 1965 roku* (Warsaw: Wydawnictwo Naukowe PWN, 1994).

[36] Weigel, *The Final Revolution*, 72.

[37] It is noteworthy that despite Poland's devout Catholicism, the Vatican's support for Polish aspirations was always an uneven affair. Regardless of the severe repression of the Polish Catholic Church following the uprising in 1863, in 1882 the Vatican established diplomatic relations with Russia, without even raising the issue of Polish Catholics.

[38] Adam Ciołkosz, "The Rise and Fall of 'Modern Revisionism' in Poland," *New Politics* 4: 1 (1965), 27.

tizing East-Central Europe in the near future. In October of 1957, Gomułka declared that revisionism posed a greater danger than communism and 200,000 "revisionist" party members were purged.[39]

Initially, the October 1956 compromise between the communist regime and the Catholic opposition had improved the position of the Catholic Church. Primate Wyszyński was released from banishment, and the Catholic group *Znak* was allowed to run for the *Sejm*, where it won nine seats. The weekly *Tygodnik Powszechny* was taken away from the state-sponsored *Pax* group and returned to its original owners. In 1957 Cardinal Wyszyński traveled to Rome and received limited authorization from Pope Pius XII to collaborate with the regime,[40] a gesture that led the government to sanction voluntary religious instruction in state schools in 1958.

But the rapprochement between the communist state and the Catholic Church did not last long. In 1961 the regime again conducted a series of assaults on the Church. Measures curtailing the availability of religious instruction ended in its elimination, thereby abrogating the 1956 agreements between Wyszyński and the state.[41] In the same year, circulation of *Tygodnik Powszechny* was curtailed, and the *Znak* faction lost four seats in the *Sejm*.

The Polish legislature, which had shown signs of becoming a genuine parliamentary institution between 1957 and 1961, underwent a rapid re-communization that rendered it largely irrelevant.[42] The authorities closed two popular literary journals – *Nowa Kultura* and *Przegląd Kulturalny* – and party leader Gomułka demanded that writers "build socialism." In 1966 there was a purge of the universities, and in March 1968 the "Anti-Zionist" campaign was launched. The latter soon widened into an assault on all intellectuals that led to the collapse of the revisionist paradigm. The crushing of the Prague Spring and the formulation of the Brezhnev Doctrine in 1968 destroyed the revisionist paradigm across most of the Soviet bloc, but by that time Poland's revisionist illusions had long faded.

Although some Catholic intellectuals continued to subscribe to neo-positivism, the regime's ideological offensive in the mid-1970s produced a revision of the constitution and re-emphasized the leading

---

[39] Bernhard, *The Origins of Democratization in Poland*, 38.
[40] Stehle, *The Independent Satellite*, 78.
[41] Jan Kubik, *The Power of Symbols Against the Symbols of Power: The Rise of Solidarity and the Fall of State Socialism in Poland* (University Park, PA: University of Pennsylvania Press, 1994), 108.
[42] Bromke, *Poland's Politic*, 167–8.

role of the communist party. This rededication to the ideological transformation of the nation made it clear that the neo-positivist paradigm had exhausted its usefulness. The Catholic Church retained its role as the repository of Poland's national identity during the entire communist period and, in the 1970s, regained its centrality in Poland's intellectual and moral life. At no time did the Church abandon its conservative, gradualist approach of presenting itself as a mediator between the state and society. Although very active in politics, the Polish Church, unlike its Latin American counterparts, did not embrace revolutionary ideologies. There was no Polish version of liberation theology.

In fact, as Norman Davies observed, *Tygodnik Powszechny* and *Znak* embodied Poland's adaptation to the new reality in many ways, making a careful distinction between the Polish state, with which they could cooperate, and communist ideology, with which they could not.[43] This position earned those publications scorn from both the extreme left and right, leading Kisielewski to complain: "The rationalist economic arguments of Lubieński, the rationalist historical arguments of Stomma, the rationalist 'ecumenical' arguments of Turowicz, and the rationalist social arguments of Mazowiecki fall upon deaf ears. It is time for Quixote to retire."[44]

But the position of these publications reflected the *modus vivendi* arrived at by Polish society under Soviet domination. Given Poland's status as a Soviet satellite, ecclesiastical debate often took Aesopian form, but it did sometimes spill into the open. One notable example was Dominik Morawski's attack on the *Znak* group and its leader Stanisław Stomma for their failure to articulate the needs of Polish Catholicism and for timidity in dealing with state authority, published in the Paris-based *Kultura*.[45] The challenge by *Kultura* drew a response from *Znak*'s leader, Andrzej Micewski, in *Tygodnik Powszechny*. Defending Stomma's neo-positivist attitude, he noted that "one has to stick to Polish political realities deriving from the international setup," and that in the past, Poland might well have been over-exposed to "heroic episodes."[46] Criticism of *Znak*'s neo-positivism was not limited to *émigré* intellectuals. Increasingly, Polish dissidents

[43] See Norman Davies, *God's Playground: A History of Poland*, vol. II (New York: Columbia University Press, 1982), 615.
[44] Bromke, *Poland's Politics*, 251.
[45] Dominik Morawski, "Powstanie, dekadencja i rozpad Znaku," *Kultura* (January–February 1977), 109–14.
[46] See Andrzej Micewski, "About True and False Maximalism," *Tygodnik Powszechny*, 29 May 1977.

at home found *Znak*'s position hard to sustain. Adam Michnik, writing in 1976, observed:

> A policy of conciliation makes sense only if both sides take it seriously. In relation to a Communist power, whose political vocabulary lacks the word *conciliation*, such a policy has meaning only if it is conducted from a position of strength. Otherwise, conciliation turns into capitulation . . . [*Znak*] deputies followed a path that proceeded from compromise to loss of credibility . . .[47]

Yet while Poland's formerly leftist, "revisionist" intellectuals lost all hope of reforming the regime by 1968, the Church remained true to its new positivist strategy until the early 1980s. In fact, when the Intellectuals' Committee to Defend Workers (KOR) was formed, the reaction of the Church was to accuse KOR and Solidarity of a Trotskyite infiltration, a statement laden with anti-Semitic overtones.[48]

### The rise of the unified opposition

As long as the bipolar system prevailed in Europe, the question of Poland's national identity and its role in the international system remained academic. In the early 1970s, however, the situation began to change. Willy Brandt launched his *Ostpolitik*, which was soon followed by détente between the superpowers. This gave Poland far more room to maneuver. But despite the new freedoms granted to the Poles by détente and *Ostpolitik*, the post-1969 changes failed to relieve tensions in Central Europe, and Poland continued to fear German revanchism. In the pre-détente days, the Poles could count on moral support from the West in their struggle against the communist regime, but after the onset of détente, massive Western loans helped to legitimate the regime. Although millions were moved by Brandt's gesture of falling to his knees at the monument to the Warsaw Ghetto, to many Central Europeans the changes that occurred in the 1970s seemed to represent a latter-day Congress of Vienna settlement, not real progress.[49] The Poles, along with the other Central Europeans, were offered "bipolarity with a human face."

By the late 1960s, the internal and external paradigms of both the

---

[47] Adam Michnik, "A New Evolutionism," in *Letters from Prison*, 141 (emphasis in the original).
[48] See Andrzej Korboński, "The Revival of the Political Right in Post Communist Poland," in *Democracy and Right-Wing Politics in Eastern Europe in the 1990s*, ed. Joseph Held (Boulder, CO: East European Monographs, 1993), 25.
[49] Wolfram Hendrier, *Germany, America, Europe: Forty Years of German Foreign Policy* (New Haven and London: Yale University Press, 1989), ch. 7.

revisionists and the positivists had run their courses. In domestic affairs, it was clear that the communist elite intended to maintain the totalitarian character of the regime. In foreign affairs, all attempts by Poles to reduce the tensions arising from bipolarity were either rejected or ignored. When an East–West rapprochement finally did occur, it was based on the premise that Europe would remain frozen in bipolarity. It was under these circumstances that the Polish opposition undertook a reassessment of its goals and tactics.

Early recognition that the concessions gained in October 1956 were a "false spring" had induced the Catholic Church to take steps that in the long run reshaped the outlook of Polish society. Beginning in 1957, when Poland's primate declared the *Great Novenna* in anticipation of the 1966 millennium, the Church organized a massive program of teaching campaigns, pilgrimages, so-called Christian weeks, and other events. By reviving Poland's Marian tradition, the Church sought to "re-Catholicize" the Polish populace.[50] The revival, which included relentless travel by Cardinal Wyszyński and a procession of the "Black Madonna" across Poland, had two interrelated consequences. It reversed the decline that the Polish Catholic Church had experienced in the 1940s and 1950s, transforming it from an insecure, defensive institution into the country's largest and most trusted political entity, one that no government dared ignore. This reinvigorated Church was then able to use its enhanced prestige, as well as its university, seminaries, and publishing houses, to help Poland regain its history and identity long before the collapse of communism.

The Church's involvement in the recovery of Polish national history also altered its relationship with the country's secular intelligentsia. The Church was traditionally viewed as a conservative institution, advocating "tri-loyalism" and supported by peasants or narrow-minded xenophobes. But by the 1970s, it had adopted the May Third[51] traditions of democracy and pluralism and was becoming a haven for many disenchanted leftists. In 1977, 54 percent of people with higher education described themselves as "believers"; by the mid-1980s the number had climbed to 87 percent.[52]

The neo-positivist tradition was thoroughly discredited, and the gap between the state and society was unbridgeable. Deteriorating economic conditions had played a key role in the final discrediting of the communist *nomenklatura*. Poland owed its relative economic

---

[50] Weigel, *The Final Revolution*, 115.
[51] Jan Kubik, *The Power of Symbols*, 122.
[52] Herer and Sadowski, "The Incompatibility of System and Culture," 147.

prosperity in the late 1950s and early 1960s to the extensive growth model, which required ever-increasing inputs to produce higher levels of output. By the late 1960s, when the stock of readily available inputs had been exhausted, the economy began to falter. Poland could not take advantage of the so-called third industrial revolution (in which economic growth is based on increases in productivity realized through advanced technology) because this model is largely incompatible with the structures of a command economy. Edward Gierek, the new first secretary of the Communist Party, sought to restore the regime's credibility with the working class through massive borrowing from the West designed to transform Poland into an export-promoting, capital-intensive economy. But this effort failed for two reasons. First, much of the borrowed capital was either stolen by the elite or used to support general consumption. Second, with the quadrupling of energy prices in 1974, the West slipped into its deepest recession since the 1930s, making it a poor market for the goods Poland produced with its borrowed capital. By the early 1970s the regime was dependent on coercion, threatening workers through direct intimidation or the specter of Soviet intervention.

The years between 1970 and 1990 were unique in Polish history. It was a time when the intelligentsia, the Church, and the working class shared a common vision and purpose, increasingly marginalizing the regime and forcing it on the defensive. During this period, romanticism regained its position as the cardinal referent of Polish society. But this new romanticism did not include quixotic notions regarding Poland's universal mission. Although Poles recognized that romanticism could not unilaterally alter the realities of the international system, dissidents such as Adam Michnik were unwilling to jettison the romantic tradition as an anachronism. In his treatise, *The Dispute over Organic Work*, Michnik concluded:

> Irredentism that was limited to planning for insurrections and that on principle rejected organic work was tantamount to adventurism. Irredentism that lacked a program of social change, a program for the education of peasant and the urban poor, had no chance of working for independence . . . But programs of organic work that abandoned the struggle for an independent Poland and for reform of social relations served as justification for passivity and conformism.[53]

The dispute between romantics and positivists would not end. Edmund Lewandowski, writing in the mid-1980s in a damning attack

---

[53] Michnik, "The Dispute over Organic Work," in *Letters from Prison*, 248.

on Polish romanticism, quoted the poet Cyprian Norwid in observing that Polish romanticism was a personality defect that causes "intelligence to be always surpassed by energy – that's why in each generation uprisings and slaughter are repeated. The Poles get drunk on 'unenlightened patriotism'; they know how to strike but not how to fight and this is why they win battles but lose wars . . ."[54] Attacking the traditional Polish elite for seeking a "life of gesture and fantasy, which leads to vanity along with bravery if there is an audience," Lewandowski concluded that only the Polish *kmiotek* (peasant) was responsible and industrious. But Andrzej Kijowski may have best articulated the intellectual consensus that emerged in post-World War II Poland when he wrote, " 'Realists' knew how to spare the country from tragedies; 'romanticists' saved it from extinction."[55]

Although the universalistic romantic tradition could not be revived, Polish intellectuals had been coming to terms with a new concept of Polishness and Poland's role within the international system since the mid-1960s. Rejecting the state of perpetual quasi-independence and totalitarianism of the "People's Republic" and unwilling to revive the tradition of romantic martyrdom built around a notion of universalist messianism, Poles were developing an East-Central European identity for the first time in centuries. They recognized that their freedom could come only with the democratization of their immediate neighbors.

But the debate on how to free East-Central Europe from totalitarianism could not take place in communist Poland. Therefore, the Paris-based *émigré* journal *Kultura* opened its pages to the question of how a free Poland could avoid the pitfalls and tragedies of interwar Poland. *Kultura* editor Jerzy Giedroyć and other authors articulated a new vision of Poland as a nation and of its place in a post-bipolar world. The traditional communist paradigm held that the only way to guarantee Polish security was through a firm alliance with the Soviet Union and continued joint US–Soviet pseudo-occupation of Germany.[56] *Kultura* viewed this arrangement as temporary and ultimately damaging to both Poland and Europe. Its authors maintained that Poland must come to terms with Russia, separate its identity from

---

[54] Edmund Lewandowski, "Polski Character Narodowy: Dusza Anielska i Czerep Rubaszny," *Polityka*, vol. 28, August 1984.

[55] Andrzej Kijowski, "On Fools and Non-Fools," *Tygodnik Powszechny*, 4 September 1977.

[56] For a sophisticated presentation of such an argument, see Michal Jaranowski, "Polska W Europie," *Polityka*, 21 March 1984, 14.

that of its immediate eastern neighbors, and abandon romantic visions of the West.

Writing in *Kultura* in 1967, Juliusz Mieroszewski made several iconoclastic observations that challenged many of the fundamental assumptions of Polish thought throughout much of the twentieth century.[57] Mieroszewski noted that the territorial changes imposed on Poland after World War II were not only irreversible, but, as Czesław Miłosz had stated, also dealt the final blow to the ideal of the Commonwealth. Furthermore, Mieroszewski conceded, "An independent Poland is necessary for [the Poles], but not for Europe." Therefore, if Poland were to regain its independence, it would have to restructure both its image of itself and its role within the international system completely. If it tried again to play the role of an *antemurale christianitatis*, defending Europe from Russia, Poland would never assume any importance in Europe. Russia was simply far more significant to the West than Poland could ever be. Poland's self-proclaimed role as a Western bastion accomplished little more than to feed Russia's imperialism. It could maintain an anti-Russian posture only if it were willing to recast itself as a multinational state, a proposition rejected by both the Poles and their immediate eastern neighbors. Instead, Poland should exploit its position as both a Roman Catholic and a Slavic state and serve as a bridge between Russia and the West. It should devote its energies to "Europeanizing" Russia, since only a process of Europeanization would enable Poland to escape its fate as a Russian satellite or keep it from becoming the object of Russo-German competition. "Poland must win a peace with Russia because it cannot win a war," Mieroszewski argued.[58]

Comparing Khrushchev to Metternich, a conservative leader "terrified by the spring of nations," Mieroszewski made the prophetic observation that no empire can resist the pressures of nationalism forever and that the Soviet empire would probably be no different from its predecessors and would ultimately break up: "Neither the Soviet Union nor the most liberal and enlightened colonial policy of the Western states will manage the nationality problem; they will not manage to persuade people on five continents that only certain nations have the right to independence . . ."[59] Although Mieroszewski remained skeptical about whether there could be a short-term reconci-

---

[57] For the English language version, see Juliusz Mieroszewski, "The Political Thoughts of Kultura," in *Kultura Essays*, ed. Leopold Tyrmand (New York: Free Press, 1970).

[58] Ibid., 320.    [59] Ibid., 321.

liation between Poland and Germany, he believed developments in Russia would ultimately shape the future of Poland and Europe:

> The liquidation of the "cold war" on our continent, including Russia in a broader European system, normalizing Polish–Russia relations – all of this depends on the decolonialization of the Soviet Union . . . Russia is in a significantly better position than France and England because she has greater possibilities for making partners out of her satellites. As a consequence, decolonialization would make Russia stronger, not weaker.[60]

Whether or not Russia succeeded in retaining its empire, it would most likely remain the most powerful state in Europe. In an interesting observation, Mieroszewski noted that even if the Cold War were to end and communism to collapse, Russia and Poland would retain a historic link as post-communist states trying to find a broader venue in the international arena. One of *Kultura's* principal contributors, Gustav Herling-Grudziński, noted that the "common suffering under communism of the Russians and Poles will also lead to the rise of common hope."[61]

The themes of Russo–Polish relations and the Jagiellonian tradition were addressed by Mieroszewski again in 1974, when he stressed that although Poland could become independent only if the Soviet empire broke up, Poland itself was not fully cured of an imperial complex in its attitude toward Ukraine, Belarussia, and Lithuania. Based on his view that Poland's security and freedom were ultimately tied to its ability to come to terms with its eastern neighbors, Mieroszewski was convinced that Poles would have to abandon the hate-cum-contempt attitude toward their eastern neighbors that had long been a part of their national ethos. Poland had to accept the loss of the *kresy* as the price to be paid for normal relations with Ukraine, Belarussia, and Lithuania. It could not insist on its pre-1939 frontiers in the east and the Oder–Neisse border in the west.

Poland's self-designation as a Western nation and its hero worship of the West, championed by generations of Polish romantics at home and in exile, were challenged in the pages of *Kultura* by novelist Witold Gombrowicz and Nobel poet laureate Czesław Miłosz. Gombrowicz noted that Western proclamations of the universality of art and culture were perfidious: "It is not art for art's sake, it is art for the West's sake."[62] Miłosz argued that there was such a thing as Central

---

[60] Ibid., 267.     [61] Ibid.
[62] Quoted in Robert Kostrzewa, ed., *Between East and West: Writings from Kultura* (New York: Hill & Wang, 1990), 18.

Europe, located between Germany and Russia, but that it was neither the *Mitteleuropa* advocated by Friedrich Naumann nor an anti-Russian bloc, but a cultural bloc and an antidote to the region's obsession with the West.[63] Mieroszewski felt that Poland's devotion to the West only begot tragedy and disappointment, stating, "We have been betrayed by our own history to which we had built altars in literature, in painting, in music."[64]

*Kultura*'s rejection of the West as the ideal for Poland even extended to economics. While remaining implacably opposed to communism, numerous *Kultura* authors continued to insist that pre-1939 Poland was far from being a paradise and that the return of unbridled capitalism would not advance Poland's national character and aspirations. They opted instead for a welfare state built around the concept of co-operatives and union co-management.[65] It is noteworthy that this aversion to a return of naked market capitalism was echoed by other opponents of the communist regime, ranging from Pope John Paul II to the founders of KOR, such as Jacek Kuroń and Adam Michnik.[66]

*Kultura* also introduced another important innovation to concepts of Poland's future. From its inception in 1947, *Kultura* argued against all irredentist claims to Lwów and Wilno, while adamantly defending the cultural rights of Poles in the east and acknowledging the cultural rights of minorities in Poland that, according to popular belief at that time, did not exist. Although *Kultura*'s authors accepted the loss of the eastern territories as an inevitable price of normalcy, not all were willing to give up the Jagiellonian tradition altogether. Innocenty Maria Bocheński, in an article titled "What Does It Mean To Be a Pole?"[67] noted that Poland should differentiate between abandoning irredentist claims and abandoning the multinational Jagiellonian tradition because an outright rejection of that tradition would reduce Poland to a uni-national, narrow-minded, undemocratic, anti-Semitic, and intolerant polity. Therefore, even though Poland must abandon its dreams of a resurrected Commonwealth, it had to return to the tradition of the broadest possible definition of Polishness if it wanted

[63] Czesław Milosz, "About Our Europe," *Kultura*, no. 4 (1986).
[64] Juliusz Mieroszewski, "Rosyjski 'Kompleks Polski' i Obszar ULB," *Kultura*, no. 9 (September 1974), 3–14. Appeared in its English version as "Imperialism: Theirs and Ours," in Kostrzewa, ed., *Between East and West*.
[65] Konstanty A. Jeleński, in Kostrzewa, *Between East and West*, 16.
[66] Bernhard, *The Origins of Democratization in Poland*, 88.
[67] Maria Bocheński, "Co to znaczy być Polakiem?" [What Does It Mean To Be a Pole?], *Kultura* (April 1993), 3–18.

to be a modern Western nation. This argument, that Poland must separate its cultural identity from the political identity of the Polish state and strive for the broadest possible Jagiellonian definition of Polishness, was echoed by Zdzisław Najder in *Tygodnik Powszechny*.[68]

The communists residing in Warsaw rejected *Kultura*'s contention that Poland continued to be a multinational state with minorities whose rights were abused. They also dismissed the notion that true Polish independence was tied to the break-up of the Soviet Union. Although *Kultura*'s visions were rejected by Poland's traditional left and right, they were warmly embraced by dissident movements both within and outside the Solidarity movement. By the late 1970s and early 1980s, many of the positions advocated by Jerzy Giedroyć's publication had been adopted by the intellectuals clustering around KOR and Solidarity.

The impact of Kultura was especially important with regard to the question of the *kresy*. Jan Józef Lipski, one of the founders of KOR and later a senator in post-communist Poland, expanded on the belief that Poland was an East-Central European state that must come to terms with its eastern neighbors and stressed that Poland would have to reorient its perception of the East fully. If it failed to do so, it could not become a normal, democratic nation. According to Lipski, one of the most damaging features of Poland's attitude toward the East was its unwarranted sense of cultural superiority to the Russians, engendered by the Polish romantic view of the Russian people as a quasi-European admixture with an ethos of subordination and collectivism. Lipski reminded his readers that it was Russia, not Poland, that coined the term *samizdat* and that without a democratic Russia there could be no democratic Europe. As far as the peoples of Lithuania, Belarussia, and Ukraine were concerned, Lipski believed that the Poles should drop their insistence on the Jagiellonian tradition and the notion of a "special role" for Poland among those peoples because that attitude served only to evoke a sense of being a historic people among them, thereby poisoning the relationship. Unlike Gombrowicz and Miłosz, Lipski, who accepted the notion that Poland was indeed a Western country and part of the West European spiritual community, believed that in order to return to Europe, the Poles would have to be reconciled with Germany and admit that the post-World War II settlement had also inflicted injustices on the Germans.[69]

[68] Zdzisław Najder, "Naród jako wartość," *Tygodnik Powszechny*, 12 March 1989.
[69] Jan Józef Lipski, "Dwie Ojczyzny - Dwa Patriotyzmy," *Kultura*, no. 10 (October 1981).

Poland's relations with its immediate eastern neighbors began to undergo a remarkable change in the 1970s. In the nineteenth century, the Poles had considered Ukrainians a Polish offshoot whose assimilation was regarded as an "indisputable, natural, generally understood fact."[70] Elements of the interwar intelligentsia asserted in *Słowo Polskie* that the entire notion of Ukrainian identity was fictitious: "the Ukrainian] has neither a sense of political individuality, which only centuries of political life can produce, nor clear awareness of his individual political needs . . . nor is he capable of imagining how a free Ukraine will look – in reality his ideal is mere cant, having no substance in life, which arose through imitation."[71] During the communist period, the Polish regime virtually denied the existence of a Ukrainian minority in Poland and kept its direct dealings with Ukraine to a minimum. Poland's emerging intellectual elite, however, not only embraced the notion of Ukrainian nationhood, but saw in it the seeds of a new historiography challenging the general Polish perceptions and attitudes toward Ukraine. Polish historians, including Teresa Chyńczewska-Hennel, produced a study arguing that a distinct sense of national identity had existed among the Ukrainian elite as early as the seventeenth century.[72] Equally important was Kazimierz Podlaski's book, *Białorusini, Litwini, Ukraińcy*, which called for a revision of the Poles' attitude toward their eastern neighbors and advocated reconciliation.[73] This change among Poland's intellectuals had been clearly detectable since the late 1960s, when the intelligentsia abandoned its traditional smugness toward Ukraine and its culture[74] and displayed fascination instead.[75] In the political sphere, Adam Michnik, at the time a Solidarity adviser and later the editor of *Gazeta Wyborcza*, stated:

> After many years of terror and subjugation, the Ukrainian nation is attempting to return to a free life. This great nation, a nation that is

[70] Janusz Radziejowski, "Ukrainians and Poles," *Acta Polonicae Historica*, no. 50 (1984), 117.

[71] Ibid., 128.

[72] See Teresa Chyńczewska-Hennel, *Świadomość narodowa szlachty ukraińskiej i kozaczyzny od schylku XVI do polowy XVII w.* (Warsaw: 1985).

[73] Kazimierz Podlaski (Bohdan Skaradziński), *Bialorusini, Litwini, Ukraińcy* (Białystok: Versus Press, 1990). (The work was initially published in 1983.)

[74] For a discussion of Polish historiography of Ukraine see Stephen Velychenko, *Shaping Identity in Eastern Europe and Russia: Soviet-Russian Accounts of Ukrainian History, 1914–1991* (New York: St. Martin's Press, 1993).

[75] For example, see Andrzej Sulima Kamiński, "W Kręgu Moralnej i Politycznej Ślepoty: Ukraina i Ukraińcy w Oczach Polaków," *Suchasnist'* (Polish edition), no. 12 (Summer 1985).

our neighbor, has now risen from its knees. By this very fact it produces a new situation that demands Polish–Ukrainian dialogue and the abandonment of constant repetitions of Brezhnev's formulas about "Ukrainian nationalism."[76]

The sympathy of Polish intellectuals for the plight of the Ukrainians was by no means limited to the predicament of the Ukrainians in the Soviet Union. The intellectuals maintained that Poland could not become a true democracy until it addressed the issue of its treatment of the Ukrainian minority within its borders. The historian and diplomat Maciej Kozłowski drew the attention of the Polish populace to the war of cultural annihilation waged by their state against the Ukrainian Lemko clan, whose language, religion, and institutions were all but destroyed.[77] In 1989, Zdzisław Najder, Lech Wałęsa's foreign policy advisor, urged the Poles to concentrate on cultural national bonds and eschew the notion of political nationalism, which is by definition hostile to neighbors and other ethnic groups.[78] Andrzej Wincenz went further, asserting that Poland was morally obliged to allow the return of Ukrainians displaced by World War II to their native lands even if such action challenged Poland's current mythology of the monoethnic state.[79]

The Polish Catholic Church, historically perceived by Poland's eastern neighbors as a tool of Polish hegemony, transformed itself under Pope John Paul II into a champion of the freedoms and national rights of Poland's neighbors. During his 1979 visit to Poland, the Pope himself set the tone of the Church's new activism among its neighbors. Addressing his remarks to the Ukrainians, Belarussians, and Russians, the Pope personified the new identity emerging in his native land:

> I hope, dear brothers, that you can hear us. I hope they can hear me, because I cannot imagine that any Polish or Slav ear in any part of the world would not be able to hear words spoken by a Polish Pope, *by a Slav!* I hope they can hear me because we live in an epoch where freedom to exchange information is so precisely defined, as is the exchange of cultural values.[80]

In Opole, in lower Silesia, the Pope spoke to a mainly German community about "the right to exist, the right to self-determination,

---

[76] *Gazeta Wyborcza*, 18 September 1989.
[77] Maciej Kozłowski, "Łemkowie," *Tygodnik Solidarność*, 14 September 1981.
[78] Najder, "Naród jako wartość."
[79] Andrzej Vincenz (interview), "Zrozumieć Ukraińców" [To Understand the Ukrainians], *Kultura* (June–July 1991), 139–55.
[80] Quoted in Weigel, *The Final Revolution*, 133 (emphasis added).

then the right to one's own culture."[81] Pope John Paul's political activities, together with his identification as a Slav, energized the Greek Catholic Churche in Ukraine and Belarussia, contributing yet another source of opposition to communism and weakening the established order in East-Central Europe. His activism similarly inspired the underground Catholic Church in Czechoslovakia and in Lithuania, further undermining the bipolar international system.

The actions of the Church in Central Europe were complemented by the activities of Polish dissidents who, like the Church, assumed that Polish freedom was inseparable from that of East-Central Europe. In July 1988, activists of Polish Solidarity met with their Czechoslovak counterparts in the mountains along the Polish–Czechoslovak border and committed themselves to dismantling the barriers between their countries, as well as between the two blocs.[82] These "mountain operations" significantly reinforced both the Catholic and secular components of the much smaller Czechoslovak dissident movement.[83] Another element of the Polish opposition – the Solidarity movement of blue-collar workers – made a deep impression on the working class throughout the communist bloc, but its effect was particularly felt in Ukraine and the coal-producing regions of Siberia.

In the Soviet Union, awareness of Solidarity among the blue-collar population was primarily confined to the western borderlands. But despite the difficulties in reaching Soviet workers elsewhere, Solidarity's defiance of communism greatly energized both secular and religious dissidents. Soviet *samizdat* systematically followed events in Poland, declaring support for Polish Solidarity. The Moscow-based Helsinki monitoring group released a statement signed by several key dissidents including Andrei Sakharov, addressed to "our Polish friends," that declared, "We are sympathetically following your brave struggle for civil and economic rights . . .Your struggle is restoring the honor of the working class and sets an example of unity between the workers and intellectuals."[84] Russia's embryonic independent labor union, the Council of Representatives of the Free Interprofessional Association of Workers, declared in a letter to a Russian *émigré* journal, "A free Russia is unimaginable without an independent

[81] Ibid.
[82] "Border Declaration (July 10, 1988) of members of Polish–Czechoslovak Solidarity and Representatives of Independent Circles," *East European Reporter* 3: 3 (1988), 61–2.
[83] Jan Kavan, "In Solidarity: Interview with Mirek Jasiński" *East European Reporter* 4: 1 (1989/90).
[84] Elizabeth Teague, *Solidarity and the Soviet Worker: The Impact of Polish Events of 1980 on Soviet Internal Politics* (London, New York, Sydney: Croom Helm, 1988), 161.

Poland."[85] On the first anniversary of Solidarity, thirty-five Lithuanian dissidents issued a statement greeting Lech Wałęsa, stating that "The heroic movement of Poland's working people is . . . significant for the Baltic nations as well."[86] In western Ukraine, Iosyp Terelya, writing to Wałęsa in the underground publication *Chronicles of the Catholic Church in Ukraine*, declared, "The steadfastness and courage of the leaders and workers' movement and of the Catholic Church in Poland give courage to us here, in Satan's very lair."[87] The ultimate collapse of communism may well have resulted from internal decay in the Soviet empire, the war in Afghanistan, and Mikhail Gorbachev's contradictory efforts to legitimate a quasi-totalitarian regime through democratic means, but it was Poland's unified opposition and its East-Central European orientation that not only consistently provided an example for others, but also served as a catalyst to undermine the legitimacy of Bolshevism, both in Eastern Europe and in the Soviet Union.

### Paradigms of a sovereign Poland

When Poland regained its full independence in 1989, the break with the exclusionary mind-set of interwar Poland seemed to be broad-based and fairly complete. Krzysztof Gawlikowski, writing in *Kultura*, reminded the Poles that the only way their country could become a modern state was to shed its notions of national exclusivity and accept the fact that it was but one part of a mighty European culture, which by definition must be tolerant and pluralistic. Gawlikowski stressed that Poland's traditional self-image as the frontier of European civilization offended the Russians, Bulgarians, and all its eastern neighbors and did not really correspond with the European ideal, which would remain unattainable if Europe were believed to "end on the Bug."[88] Roch Kowalski echoed the view that Poland could be of importance to the West only if it maintained close links with the East. Kowalski chided the Polish elite for assuming that "civilization is in the West, while the East is not interesting" and forgetting that Poland's ability to communicate with its powerful yet unstable neighbors to the east was vital if it wanted to become useful to Europe as a whole.[89] Marcin Król, a luminary of Polish intellectual

---

[85] Ibid.     [86] Ibid., 162.     [87] Ibid., 163.
[88] Krzysztof Gawlikowski, "Europejska wspólnota kulturowa a nacjonalizmy," *Kultura*, (April 1990); 1–13. The Bug, being Poland's eastern frontier, is perceived by some Poles as the cultural limit of European civilization.
[89] Roch Kowalski, "Kompleks Budrysa," *Kultura*, (July 1991).

circles, wrote in an important article entitled "Fatherland" that although nationalism might resurface in Poland, its polity had risen above its interwar levels when Poles were "drunk with independence." Król argued that for Poland to enter the post-modern world as a healthy state, Poles must develop a new sense of national awareness and a new collective memory. They should be proud of their cultural and historic achievements and stop oscillating between hubris and despair. Simultaneously, however, Poles must broaden their collective memory to include their history of anti-Semitism and the fact that the "recovered" territories had been inhabited by Germans for many centuries. Only by acknowledging its own past, Król argued, could Poland be transformed into a modern state while avoiding the pitfalls that bedeviled previous generations of Poles.[90]

But Poland's 1990 presidential election campaign was an indication that it was not fully cured of its prewar nationalism. President Lech Wałęsa resorted to anti-Semitic attacks on his opponent Tadeusz Mazowiecki. The third candidate, Stanisław Tymiński, made xenophobia a theme of his electoral campaign. Cardinal Glemp's homily at Jasna Góra monastery attacked "Polonophobia" and Jewish domination, an indication that psychological change within any polity is a slow and fitful process. Yet Poland appears to have made radical and complete changes in the definition of its international identity. By the early 1990s, a new Polish self-image seemed to have totally eclipsed the images common in Polish politics before World War II. Jerzy Giedroyć's three pillars of modern Polish orientation – support for an independent Ukraine, normalized relations with Germany, and the recognition of Poland's current frontiers – were thoroughly internalized by Poland's body politic, as was the dismissal of the notion that Poland is a great West European power. The overwhelming majority of Poles accepted Poland's permanent separation from the eastern borderlands. So did right-wing political leaders such as Senator Jan Zamoyski of the National Democratic Alliance, who stated that he was "personally enthusiastic about our eastern and western borders and see them as 100 percent solid. I miss Lwów. Yet these are sentimental views, not rational."[91]

A survey of the foreign policy positions of Poland's six largest political parties revealed that although these parties represent a broad spectrum of Polish political attitudes, there is fundamental agreement

[90] Marcin Król, "Ojczyzna," *Tygodnik Powszechny*, 9 February 1993, 1, 6.
[91] Marcin Masny, "Słuszny nacjonalizm," *Ład*, 13 December 1992.

on foreign policy, with the exception of the Confederation for an Independent Poland, which advocates the creation of a third force between Russia and Germany consisting of Poland, Ukraine, and other smaller states.[92] The parties agreed that Poland should accept its current frontiers and espouse good relations with all its neighbors; that it should maintain close relations with Russia, Ukraine, and its other eastern neighbors, while simultaneously striving to affiliate with the European Union, NATO, and other West European organizations; and that it must reach a final reconciliation with Germany. Only fringe groups such as Samo Obrona, Friends of Lwów, and other splinter groups objected to this vision of Poland within the international system. At the end of the twentieth century, the Polish political mainstream has finally broken with both Józef Piłsudski's Jagiellonian view of Poland as a great power and a multinational Commonwealth engaged in a struggle between Germany and Russia and Roman Dmowski's notion that the frontiers of Poland were a reflection of its military prowess. Poland has finally resigned itself to the status of a medium-sized country that wants to expand its ties to Western Europe for cultural and economic reasons while accepting the fact that these ties must be conditioned by Warsaw's relations with Moscow.

While the redefinition of Poland's national identity and its place in Europe was being conceived and articulated, first by émigré intellectuals and subsequently by non-communist intellectuals in Poland itself, a pattern reminiscent of the nineteenth century was being repeated. In the 1800s, the Polish bourgeoisie drew much of its nationalist ideology from the szlachta but modified it to reflect the needs and aspirations of collective memory. Similarly, in the late twentieth century, as Poles were beginning to accept the general notions of their country's new identity and international status, a difference between elite and popular attitudes became increasingly apparent. Today, Poland's intellectuals almost uniformly consider Poland's economic and cultural integration into Europe a key element of its new national identity. Yet a study carried out by the Center for Public Opinion Studies revealed that two-thirds of the Polish population objected to foreign ownership of property in Poland; one-third felt that Germany had too much influence in Polish affairs; and

---

[92] The parties questioned were the Democratic Union (UA), Alliance of the Democratic Left (SLD), Christian National Alliance (ZChN), Center Alliance (PC), and Confederation of Independent Poland (KPN). See "Our Questionnaire: Polish Political Parties on Foreign Policy," *Polish Western Affair* 1 (1992).

another third felt that US influence was excessive.[93] This difference in attitudes may well be a reflection of differing collective memories. Polish intellectuals tend to recall the seventeenth century, when Poland was a major figure in Europe's cultural and political life. The Polish masses, whose primary contact with the West in that period was as illegal migrant workers or peddlers, have been left with a residual sense of inferiority and impotence.

The shift in the Polish attitudes toward Western Europe was documented by Elżbieta Skotnicka-Iliasiewicz in her controversial book *Polish Complex*. According to Skotnicka-Iliasiewicz, Poles, particularly the young, continue to believe that their country will not catch up with Western Europe for a long time, but at the same time a profound "demythologizing of the West" has taken hold in the Polish psyche. The slogan "return to Europe" has been replaced by "adjustment to the European Union." The general population recognizes the economic advantages of affiliation with Western Europe but is far less culturally enthralled with the West than is the intellectual elite.[94]

There is a similar gap between elite and popular perceptions of Ukraine and Russia. Poland's intellectuals lionize Ukraine and its culture, seeing an independent Ukraine as a vital guarantor of Poland's own independence. But in their discussions of Polish–Ukrainian relations, they are fond of recalling the days of the Commonwealth, when a Ukrainian would identify himself as *"gente Ruthenus, natione Polonus"* (ethnicity Ruthenian, nationality Polish). They continue to believe that the collapse of the Treaty of Hadżiacz, which would have made Ukraine a Commonwealth member on an equal footing with Poland and Lithuania, was one of the great tragedies of Poland's history. By contrast, the Polish popular attitude toward Ukraine is based on the memory of Polish–Ukrainian violence during World War II and includes ambivalence and outright fear of an independent Ukraine. In two recent surveys, 38 percent of Poles said they feared Ukraine,[95] and 65 percent expressed antipathy toward Ukrainians.[96] Given this profound level of ambivalence among the Polish masses toward Ukraine, issues of symbolic importance, such as Church property and perceptions of irredentism or cultural slights, tend to aggravate Polish–Ukrainian animosities, particularly in the

---

[93] "Support for Integration with the EEC Dwindling," *Rzeczpospolita*, 16 September 1993, 5.
[94] Elżbieta Skotnicka-Iliasiewicz, "Polacy i Europejczycj," *Znak*, no. 461 (October 1993).
[95] Dominika Wielowiejska, "Who the Poles Fear," *Gazeta Wyborcza*, 14 February 1992.
[96] *PAP*, 8 September 1993.

thing Soviet or Russian, in the arts as well as daily life, was reflected in W. Hen's description of a Russian engineer in the novel *W dziwnym mieście*: "The Russian was a youngish man, tall, slim, with tawny complexion and dark eyes. . . . Owadko [a Pole] could not take his eyes off him. He was astonished by the Russian's refinement, his restrained manners, his pleasant . . . baritone."[31] After 1948, the Polish regime mandated this kind of sycophantic hero worship toward both Stalin and Russia and pressed writers to produce "social realist" art, reflecting the "unbreakable bond" of the Poles with the "fraternal Soviet people." The policy only served to discredit the communist regime in the eyes of the writers and the reading public. The defection of Czesław Miłosz in 1951 was a harbinger of the growing alienation of Polish intellectuals from the Stalinist state. By 1953, the conformist policies imposed on Poland had created a rapidly growing gap between the state and society, with the ruling class holding power almost solely on the basis of its ability to coerce and intimidate.

### A precarious equilibrium: 1956–1968

The death of Stalin in 1953 and Nikita Khrushchev's "Secret Speech" at the Twentieth Congress of the Communist Party of the Soviet Union in 1956, which denounced Stalin and Stalinism, had a profound impact on Poland. The Soviet regime had admitted that its ability to govern both its inner and outer empires would depend largely on the ability of Marxist–Leninist regimes to narrow the gap between the state and society. In the case of Poland, the post-Stalinist thaw had several implications. Following the turmoil in Poland in October of 1956, when what began as a labor strike threatened to spill over into an insurrection far more explosive than the Hungarian uprising, Moscow curtailed its cultural, political, and economic presence in Poland and grudgingly accepted Gomułka's return to power, the establishment of a *modus vivendi* with the Catholic Church, and greater freedom of expression. Although the Gomułka regime did manage to narrow the divide between the state and society, particularly during its first two years (1956–58), the gap remained. Polish intellectuals, both leftist and Catholic, remained determined to wear down the Stalinist legacy in Poland, albeit by different means.

Between 1956 and 1968, both Catholic and leftist intellectuals

---

[31] Ibid., 43.

border regions. This alarming gap between elitist and popular perceptions of Ukraine induced Jerzy Giedroyć and the Ukrainian intellectual Bohdan Osadchuk to publish in *Wysoki Zamek* (Castle on the Hill) a Polish–Ukrainian dialogue aimed at breaking the historic cycle of acrimony and stereotyping.

Poles are no less ambivalent about Russia. The collective memory of the Polish elite remains focused on the Russian imperial presence in Poland, which began in the eighteenth century. As a result, they are concerned about the possible rebirth of an imperial Russia. To the Polish masses, Russia is personified by the thousands of petty traders now flooding Polish cities.

The Poland of the late twentieth century may have fully abandoned historic notions regarding its identity and its place within the international system, but it now stands at a historic crossroads where it must choose between integration with the West and a return to narrow nationalism and particularism. Although it is difficult to imagine Poland reverting to the illusion of being a great power, disappointment with the progress of integration with the West or tension within the Commonwealth of Independent States could force the Polish populace to revert to defensive national egoism. Yet, despite disappointments in its dealings with the outside world and impatience with the pace of economic recovery, contemporary Poland is fundamentally different from its predecessors. Analyzing the new Poland, the influential journal *Polityka* observed:

> There is, however, a major difference between today's Poland and those of the interwar period or the Commonwealth of Two Nations. Both of the predecessors were endangered from the East and the West, while Poland at the same time was striving to be a regional superpower recognized by all parties. Wałęsa's Poland does not pretend to be a superpower, we do not long for a "from sea to sea" Poland, and we do not want to be anybody's policemen. Nor do we want to "save" anyone. The appreciation of our own predicament is far less pathetic than before 1939, and on this score we are far more "European" than ever before.[97]

But Poland has not fully joined the European mainstream. Although, unlike France, Germany, Hungary, Austria, and Italy, Poland does not have well-organized, extreme right-wing political groupings, resistance on some levels to a broadening of the Poles' horizons continues. The classic manifestation of frustration-aggression

---

[97] Adam Krzemiński and Wiesław Władyka, "Czym Polska Stoi?" [On What does Poland Stand?], *Polityka*, 1 August 1993, 16.

typical of societies haunted by a sense of uncertainty is still evident in Poland: 87 percent of the Poles feel wronged by the Germans, 71 percent by the Russians, 67 percent by the Ukrainians, and 20 percent by the Jews.[98] The prevailing feeling of victimization among many Poles makes it difficult to consolidate the emerging European national identities.

Nevertheless, despite setbacks such as outbreaks of violence between Poles and Ukrainians over the ownership of Church properties or occasional outbursts of anti-Semitism among some clerics and people in the entourage of former president Wałęsa, Poland's new Central European identity appears to have been internalized. Wałęsa's appeal to anti-Semitism and xenophobia backfired, contributing to his electoral defeat. In addition, although most Poles retain an emotional link to the Catholic Church, its attempts to institutionalize itself as a political actor were not well received and actually provoked a decline in its popularity. Finally, despite the region's bloody history, as many as 400,000 Ukrainians now reside in Poland as guest workers. There are also tens of thousands of Russian peddlers. The Polish response to the presence of the Ukrainians and Russians seems to be one of sympathy based on a remembrance of similar Polish experiences in the 1980s. Pope John Paul II's decisions to reverse the 1946 appointment of a Pole as head of the Eastern churches in Poland and to establish the Przemysł-Warsaw metropolis of the Ukrainian Greek Catholic Church[99] are highly significant for the future of Polish–Ukrainian relations. The establishment of a Ukrainian metropolis undercuts the post-World War II myth of Poland as a uni-national state and reinforces the independent status of Ukrainian culture.

Poland has not cured itself of anti-Semitism and indeed remains an anomalous case of "anti-Semitism without Jews," but this curse also seems to be waning, albeit fitfully. Since the late 1980s, reconciliation with the Jews has been one of Pope John Paul II's highest priorities, and he has increasingly adopted Adam Mickiewicz's romantic description of the Jew as "our older brother." In Kraków, festivals of Jewish Klezmer music have become regular events attended by thousands, and exhibits dealing with the vanished Jewish community draw large crowds of young, educated Poles.

Although anti-Semitism continues to exist, it is no longer considered to be in good taste or viewed as an act of patriotism. After

[98] Paweł Śpiewak, "Do Poles Dislike Jews?" *Sztandar*, no. 80, 23 April 1996.
[99] *Rzeczpospolita*, no. 127, 1–2 June 1996, 2.

decades of evasion, the Polish government has taken the first steps in coming to terms with the pogrom in Kielce and the history of Polish anti-Semitism in general. One of Poland's greatest directors, Andrzej Wajda, has produced a movie called *The Holy Week* that raises the issue of Polish indifference to, if not culpability in, the destruction of Jewish life in Poland. Finally, although Polish universities were hotbeds of anti-Semitism in the interwar years, contemporary universities have become the focus of interest in Poland's Jewish history. In a recent survey of Polish students, 59.7 percent willingly accepted the concept of a dual identity as Jew and Pole, and another 10.8 percent reluctantly accepted this identification as legitimate. For Ukrainians, the figures were 50 percent and 6 percent respectively; for Germans 45.9 percent and 35.8 percent (87.8 percent of the respondents believed that one can have a dual Polish and European identification).[100] These figures, which are comparable to those obtained in surveys conducted in Western Europe, are grounds for optimism, as are the results of the last presidential elections, in which former communist *apparatchik* Aleksander Kwaśniewski, running on a platform of competence, unseated the heroic persona Lech Wałęsa. Both are an indication that Poland is becoming a normal European state where history and collective memory are being replaced by realistic assessments of current realities and of the future.

Under different circumstances, Poland, the oldest state in East-Central Europe, had undergone a change akin to that of France, the oldest state in Western Europe. During the first two decades following World War II, both were forced to withdraw from their civilizational spheres while simultaneously coming to terms with the upstart powers. For France this meant dealing with Germany and the Anglo-Saxons; for Poland it meant dealing with Germany and the Eastern Slavs. Poland, like France, has had to re-invent itself. Although both have historically considered their polities as civilizations, both have had to adopt a much narrower definition of themselves as nations. Both states have found this kind of devolution both difficult and painful. In Poland, however, the tragedy of World War II has allowed for fewer illusions about the country's past and future and enabled Poland to develop a new, modern identity faster and more easily than France or most of the other countries that have historically viewed themselves in a universal-civilizational paradigm.

---

[100] Antonia Kłoslowska, *Kultury Narodowe u Korzeni* (Warsaw: Wydawnictwo Naukowe PWN, 1996), 360.

# 4    Polish foreign policy in perspective: a new encounter with positivism

> Before our very eyes Communism, the curse of the twentieth century, is dying, and with it the Soviet empire, the curse of my nation, but I cannot be happy. I am scared.                                    Adam Michnik[1]

The collapse of communism transformed Poland's neighbors beyond recognition and revolutionized Poland's geopolitical position. In October 1990, Germany reunited and undertook a massive reconstruction program of the eastern provinces. The Soviet Union suddenly ceased to exist in December 1991, creating four new countries on Poland's border. Poland and the international system found themselves facing the German economic powerhouse in the west and an unstable and insecure Russian state in the east, still imposing in size despite the loss of the constituent Soviet republics. In January 1993, Czechoslovakia's contentious experiment with a multinational state finally came to an end as the "velvet divorce" made two states out of one.

Despite the storm of change in Eastern and Central Europe and chronically weak governments in Poland, Polish foreign policy has remained remarkably consistent. Although Poles have yet to agree on central questions, such as how to create a market economy, the role foreign capital should play in the new economy, or the role of the Catholic Church in a democratic Poland, Poles of all political orientations have managed to reach a consensus on foreign policy. This consensus evolved over the years through the efforts of both leftist intellectuals and the Catholic Church and reflects Poland's acceptance of its identity as a mid-size European state, its renunciation of a mission beyond its frontiers, an understanding of the restrictions imposed by its geopolitical position between Germany and Russia,

---

[1] Adam Michnik, "Na skraju czarnej dziury" [On the Verge of a Black Hole], *Gazeta Wyborcza*, 23 December 1991.

and attempts to limit itself to those events which Warsaw can affect. Adhering to this new paradigm, Foreign Minister Krzysztof Skubiszewski and his successors have competently and consistently guided Poland's foreign policy through the first years of the postcommunist era.

At the very beginning of the postcommunist era, Polish policy makers set four goals for their country. The first was to guarantee Poland's long-term independence. Most Poles agreed that this would require, at the very least, the decentralization and democratization of the Soviet Union and that the best scenario for achieving this end would include its dissolution. Second, Polish policy makers understood that Poland could not completely free itself from Russian hegemony until it had settled its differences with Germany. This meant addressing the controversial issue of Poland's German minority. Third, in order to assure its long-term economic prosperity, policy makers realized that Poland would need to integrate itself into Western Europe. Fourth, in order to break out of its role as the perennial weak leg of the Berlin–Warsaw–Moscow triangle, policy makers in Warsaw aimed to join the North Atlantic Treaty Organization (NATO) at the earliest possible moment. Warsaw hoped to use the US presence in the alliance as leverage against Poland's most powerful neighbors.

It should be noted that Poland's desire to join NATO does not stem from a fear of a Russian invasion. Very few in Poland foresee a Russian attack. The Poles, however, perhaps more than any other European people, recognize the historic reality that the United States, despite its public affection toward Poland, will always consider Russia a potential partner in the global arena. This means that at some point the United States might pursue this partnership at the cost of Polish interests. In 1863 the United States was the only power to reject a diplomatic reprimand of St. Petersburg following its suppression of the Polish Uprising. Tsar Alexander II wrote President Abraham Lincoln that "[Russia] appreciates the firmness with which the government of the United States maintains the principle of non-intervention [sic]."[2] The post-World War II settlement was another indication that Polish interests could be sacrificed to US global interests. Polish political leaders see NATO membership as a means of ensuring that Poland's interests are not sacrificed to the interests of greater powers.

Concern that the United States will revert to isolationism is another

[2] Alexander Tarsaidze, *Czars and Presidents* (New York: McDowell, 1958), 192.

factor in Poland's enthusiasm for NATO expansion. A US withdrawal from Europe could create an insecure Germany that would seek rapprochement with Russia, thereby creating the possibility of a second Rapallo.[3] The fear of a Russo-German accord concluded without Polish participation is deeply ingrained among the elites and the general public.[4] Polish officials generally refuse to speculate on the possibility of US isolationism or a Russo-German rapprochement, but in an article authored by the men who shaped the first years of postcommunist Polish foreign policy, it was explicitly stated:

> It is of paramount importance that official US policy should accept and declare in public [its support] for full integration of Central European states with the Western system . . . While emphasizing and appreciating the momentous progress of Polish–German relations, we must not lose sight of the German elites' widely varied positions on the future of NATO and the foundations of the European security structures?[5]

Although the overall direction of Poland's foreign policy is toward a "return to Europe," successive Polish governments have been mindful that in the field of security, Poland, and indeed Europe, remains hostage to the tumult in Russia. This dilemma was succinctly articulated by one former foreign minister, Andrzej Olechowski, who observed, "We are looking for a formula capable of uniting Europe, without excluding the United States or isolating Russia."[6] This goal would be attainable only if Poland carried through economic reforms at home and maintained good relations with its neighbors. The latter was particularly important because the Poles recognized that they could not pursue this agenda unilaterally. To succeed, they would have to join their efforts with those of their immediate neighbors – the Czechs, the Slovaks, the Balts, the Hungarians, and, if possible, the Ukrainians and Belorussians. The Skubiszewski team realized that in order to achieve this type of cooperation, the Poles had to overcome their resentment of historical wrongs inflicted on them by their neighbors. Furthermore, despite Poland's prominence in the post-

---

[3] See Zbigniew Lentowicz, "What Defence Doctrine for Poland?" *Rzeczpospolita* (supplement), no. 170, 21 July 1992.

[4] See "State of the Nation Report – Presidential Chancellery," PAP News Wire, 9 November 1994.

[5] Andrzej Ananicz, Przemysław Grudziński, Andrzej Olechowski, Janusz Onyszkiewicz, Krzysztof Skubiszewski, and Henryk Szleifer, "Poland-NATO Report," *Rzeczpospolita*, no. 246, 23 October 1995, 7.

[6] Andrzej Olechowski, "Europe's Unification Challenge," *Polityka*, no. 50, 10 December 1994.

communist international system, they needed to remember that their country was a mid-sized European state with limited resources. Under no circumstances could Poland act beyond its real capabilities.[7] Among other things, this meant that it could not repeat its interwar mistake of offering itself as either a counterweight to Germany or a *cordon sanitaire* against Russia.

Throughout the Cold War, Polish intellectuals agreed that Poland would not be able to normalize its relationship with the West in general, and Germany in particular, until the situation in the East changed. Therefore, Polish intellectuals applauded and supported Mikhail Gorbachev's policies of *perestroika* and *glasnost*, seeing in them the first steps toward democracy in the Soviet Union, an essential prerequisite for its decentralization, if not outright break-up. Despite Polish sympathy for Russian liberals, as well as for nationalists in the Baltics, Ukraine, and Belarus, Poland's foreign policy in the East remained reactive. Surprisingly, it was in the West that independent Poland faced its first test in implementing the new paradigms that its intellectuals had been discussing for decades.

### Poland's German policy

Poland's long history of relations with Germany has made by far the largest contribution to Polish collective memory. Relations with Russia assumed significance only in the sixteenth century, but Polish–German relations go back 1,000 years and are fundamentally different from those with Russia. The latter relationship was marked by an underlying Russian belief that Poland was a wayward branch of the Slavic family. Even the Russian Decembrists, who supported the separation of Poland from the Russian empire, envisaged a Poland closely linked to Russia. But the official Russian attitude toward Poland was never based on a sense of racial superiority.[8]

By contrast, Polish–German relations have been colored by Polish perceptions of the Germans as an expansionist, ruthless horde, consumed by a *Kulturkampf* against the Poles. This attitude was ingrained in the Polish national consciousness long before Hitler's Polish campaign. For almost ten centuries, the Germans expanded

---

[7] Antoni A. Piotrowski, "Wokół Polityki Zagranicznej," *Polityka Polska*, March–April 1991.
[8] Since the late seventeenth century the second largest segment (24.3 percent) of recognized nobility *(Dvorianstvo)* was the Polish *szlachta*. See Richard Pipes, *Russia Under the Old Regime* (New York: Collier Books, 1974), 182.

into the east. Therefore, the Battle of Grunwald in 1410, where a combined Polish–Lithuanian force defeated the Teutonic Knights, is one of the key moments both in Polish history and in the formation of the Polish national identity. Polish–German relations have been further complicated by powerful linguistic, cultural, and religious differences. Perhaps nothing better expresses the Polish sense of insult and indignation toward the Germans than Maria Konopnicka's patriotic poem (often referred to as the country's unofficial anthem) *Rota* (1908): "We shall not let the Germans spit in our faces nor Germanize our children."

German attitudes toward the Poles were mixed. Intellectuals from Schiller to Engels admired Poland and saw the emergence of an independent Polish state as a means of separating Germany from autocratic Russia, thereby contributing to German democratization. But a far more typical reflection of German attitudes is found in the remarks of the German historian Ernst Moritz Arndt: "The Pole remains forever a big, wild boy." He went as far as to ask why God created "such people as the Irish and Poles who remain forever minors."[9]

The horrors of World War II left Poland with a chronic fear of a resurgent Germany. The murderous policies of the Third Reich lent credence to Bismarck's statement that the only solution to the Polish question was the extermination of the Poles.[10] As late as 1960, Poland's primate, Cardinal Wyszyński, referred to Chancellor Konrad Adenauer as "that man from the far west who will replicate the faith of the Teutonic Knights."[11]

This historical legacy combined with the constraints of the Cold War to make Polish–German rapprochement extraordinarily slow. Until the 1960s, domestic politics in both countries precluded any public dialogue between Bonn and Warsaw. The Polish communist government found tension with Germany politically useful because the perception of German hostility was its only source of legitimacy. Adenauer, beholden to the German expellees (*Vertriebene*) from territories east of the Oder–Neisse Line, claimed to be the sole spokesman for all Germans and rigidly enforced the Hallstein Doctrine which forbade relations with any government that recognized East

---

[9] Quoted in Harry Kenneth Rosenthal, *German and Pole: National Conflict and Modern Myth* (Gainesville: University of Florida Press, 1976), 20.

[10] Erik Eyck, *Bismarck and the German Empire* (New York: Norton and Co., 1968), 68.

[11] *Tygodnik Powszechny*, no. 39 (1960).

Germany.[12] Throughout the 1960s, Poland and West Germany crept toward rapprochement at a glacial pace. A West German trade bureau opened in Warsaw in 1963. Catholic bishops from both countries exchanged letters calling for reconciliation in 1965, an appeal that was reinforced in 1968 by the Bensberger Kries Memorandum in which German lay Catholics joined lay Protestants in urging the Bonn government to recognize the Oder–Neisse line.

The process of Polish–German reconciliation got under way in the early 1970s with Willy Brandt's *Ostpolitik*, but even this initiative was subject to domestic and foreign policy constraints. For West Germany, recognition of the status quo in Europe would mean abandoning the claims of the expellees. Furthermore, unilateral West German recognition of the Oder–Neisse line would be tantamount to acceptance of the legality of the division of Germany and the postwar order. For Poland, the situation was even more complex. Reconciliation with Germany would deprive the communist regime of its legitimacy. In addition, the Brandt government insisted on recognition of the minority rights of ethnic Germans resident in Poland. This posed a particularly vexing problem because admitting the existence of a German minority would destroy the postwar myth that all of the Germans had fled, making the People's Republic ethnically homogeneous. Poles feared that irredentist claims by Germany might follow. Despite these difficulties, a Polish–West German treaty was signed in December 1970. Although this treaty was a crucial step toward Polish–German reconciliation, it was not without shortcomings.

Germany did not relinquish claims to its 1937 frontiers, it merely acknowledged the Oder–Neisse line as the border between East Germany and Poland. Although Bonn renounced the use of force to alter that border, this decision left the permanent settlement of the border question unresolved until German unification. The West German position on this issue helped ease Poland's fears, but it clearly did not end the anxiety in Warsaw. For its part, the Polish government agreed to facilitate the emigration of ethnic Germans from Poland, but refused to address the concerns of Germans who remained. The agreement also made no reference to the injustices suffered by millions of Germans after World War II. Therefore, although Germany could finally drop the Hallstein Doctrine and establish diplomatic and economic ties with Warsaw, the Polish–West German Treaty post-

---

[12] The USSR, as one of the four victor powers, was exempted from the restrictions of the Hallstein Doctrine.

poned rather than resolved the key issues separating them.[13] Furthermore, Poles and Germans had very different interpretations of the treaty, which rekindled mutual suspicion and animosity.

The Americans and Russians had suspicions of a different kind. During the Cold War, both West Germany and Poland were the most important junior partners in their respective alliances, but they remained *de facto* semi-sovereign countries. US policy makers, such as former Secretary of State Dean Acheson and President Richard Nixon's National Security Adviser, Henry Kissinger, deeply distrusted *Ostpolitik* and exerted pressure on West Germany to limit its initiatives in the east, particularly as the fortunes of détente declined. Although the West German government was willing to defy the United States in order to maintain new contacts with East Germany, it had no desire to jeopardize US–German relations over Poland. On the Polish side, the collapse of Edward Gierek's economic policy, the deepening of economic relations with the Soviets and East Germans, and the souring of superpower relations led to a decline in interest in improving ties with Bonn. While the West considered *Ostpolitik* Germany's final break with its historical disposition toward its eastern neighbors, dissidents in East-Central Europe saw it as German affirmation of the Yalta settlement. As Timothy Garton Ash argued, the main purpose of West Germany's *Ostpolitik* was to normalize Bonn's relationship with Moscow and East Berlin; improving links with Poland was only a byproduct of that policy.[14] The aloofness of the Polish opposition toward West Germany during the 1980s stemmed not so much from historical *ressentiment* as from bitterness over Chancellor Helmut Schmidt's refusal to embrace US President Jimmy Carter's human rights policy in Eastern Europe and Schmidt's support for the Jaruzelski government's imposition of martial law.[15] Although Mikhail Gorbachev began improving Soviet–West German relations in 1987,[16] Polish–West German relations remained stagnant right up to the collapse of communism in Poland.

---

[13] See Louis L. Ortmayer, *Conflict, Compromise, and Conciliation: West German Polish Normalization 1966–1976*, University of Denver Monograph Series in World Affairs (Denver, CO: University of Denver, 1977).

[14] For an exhaustive study of *Ostpolitik* see Timothy Garton Ash, *In Europe's Name: Germany and the Divided Continent* (New York: Random House, 1993); also Wolfram Handrier, *Germany, America, Europe: Forty Years of German Foreign Policy* (New Haven and London: Yale University Press, 1989), ch. 7.

[15] Handrier, *Germany, America, Europe.*

[16] See Ilya Prizel, "Russia and Germany: The Case for a Special Relationship," in *Post Communist Europe: Crisis and Adjustment*, ed. Andrew Michta and Ilya Prizel (New York: St. Martin's Press, 1993).

As Soviet–German relations warmed, the specter of a reunited Germany along Poland's western border forced Poles to direct their attention to the German question. By 1989 they agreed that if Poland was to become a normal European country, it must reject its policy of confrontation and normalize relations with Germany.[17] Continued confrontation would leave Poland a semi-sovereign Soviet protectorate. Although both West Germany and Poland had abandoned key tenets of their historical national identities, reconciliation would prove difficult because it would challenge the foundations of their post-World War II self-images.

For Germany, the prospect of reunification not only implied an end to its status as a semi-sovereign nation, but also provided an opportunity to address the suffering inflicted on Germans at the end of World War II. As soon as the East German regime started to crumble, the West German government adopted an independent and assertive posture that took its neighbors and allies by surprise. The French were flustered when Chancellor Helmut Kohl proposed his ten-point plan for German unity without consulting the allies in advance. In the same statement, the chancellor alarmed the Poles by failing to mention the Oder–Neisse line and insisting that this question could be addressed only by a united Germany. Tension increased when Poland insisted that the four victorious powers could guarantee Germany's frontiers, implying that the Germans were less than fully sovereign, while the Germans treated Poland as a mere object of the emerging European order. Chancellor Kohl's decision to visit the Saint Annaberg shrine in Silesia during a state visit to Poland further disconcerted the Poles because it seemed to indicate a renewal of German irredentism. As Adam Krzemiński wryly observed: "Prospects of Polish–German relations now look just like the visit – neither continuous nor unambiguous. On the one hand, there is goodwill demonstrated by many people, on the other, the fact that others see no intrinsic value in relations with Poland."[18]

Kohl's refusal to agree *a priori* to Germany's post-World War II frontiers and his demands for a Polish apology to the German expellees and renunciation of all reparation claims for Polish citizens led the Polish foreign ministry to refrain from joining Prague and

---

[17] It is interesting to note that in a public opinion poll carried out by the newspaper *Rzeczpospolita* on 21 March 1990, 69 percent of those responding expressed fear of a united Germany, while at the same time 48 percent supported German reunification.

[18] Adam Krzemiński, "Dismantling the Walls: Chancellor Helmut Kohl's visit," *Polityka*, 18 November 1989, as reported in FBIS-EEU-89–225.

Budapest in asking the Soviet Union to withdraw its troops from East Germany. At one point, Foreign Minister Skubiszewski even suggested that Warsaw Pact troops should remain in the territory of the German Democratic Republic as a guarantee of Polish security.[19] Nevertheless, the Poles understood that the only way to guarantee normal relations with Germany was by supporting German integration into the West. This has remained a fundamental feature of postcommunist Polish foreign policy. In fact, Warsaw's reaction to German reunification was far more pragmatic than that of either France or Britain. Only Poland seemed to understand from the start that German reunification was unstoppable and that Warsaw's interests would be best served by accepting the inevitable and using the unification process to normalize Polish–German relations.

But the interwar notion that Poland could use its relations with France, Britain, or the United States to contain Germany did re-emerge. Solidarity's own weekly *Tygodnik Solidarność* had to remind readers that "Poland, if she wants to meet the challenge of crossing the threshold of civilization, which is possible only through integration with Western Europe, must open itself to wide cooperation and involvement with Germany."[20] Grzegorz Kostrzewa-Zorbas, the head of the Policy Planning Office in the Polish Ministry of Foreign Affairs, foresaw two possible scenarios for the evolution of Europe with a neutral Germany: either the European Community (EC) itself would become a tool of German domination, or it would disintegrate under German hegemony. Both options would lead to the expansion of Germany's role in Europe.[21] Kostrzewa-Zorbas saw membership in NATO, with its implicit US guarantee of security, as the ultimate solution to Poland's dilemma, noting that although the Anglo–Polish pact of 1939 did not prevent the outbreak of war, it did draw Britain, and ultimately the United States, into the conflict, thereby assuring Poland's ultimate liberation.

No longer willing to be used by others to contain Germany, Warsaw made several fundamental concessions to accommodate its western neighbor. Despite Poland's reliance on Soviet protection, Skubiszewski broke with Gorbachev, endorsing German membership in

---

[19] Nicholas Doughty, "Polish Minister Calls for New Warsaw Pact Units in East Germany," Reuters, 22 March 1990.

[20] Jan Rylukowski, "Między Niemcami a Rosją," *Tygodnik Solidarność*, 21 September 1990.

[21] Jeffrey Simon and Joshua Spero, "Executive Summary," Institute for National Strategic Studies, 28 January 1992.

NATO in order to prevent the creation of an "isolated giant."[22] Warsaw considered the Soviet position on German neutrality a sure way to return to Rapallo. Accommodation with Germany came mainly as a result of Poland's ability to adapt to international realities and to recognize its inability to affect events. Although the Polish government refused to apologize to the German expellees, the daily *Rzeczpospolita* on 9 October 1990 openly declared:

> The state (in 1945) confiscated property of people of German nationality, regardless of whether they regarded themselves as loyal Polish citizens, tied to Poland in various ways, whose attitudes during the war deserved great appreciation . . . Polish authorities, after examining claims in detail, are willing to make up for any losses.[23]

In November 1990, Poland and a united Germany finally signed a border treaty which committed each side to respect the other's "sovereignty and territorial integrity."[24] This was followed in June 1991 by a treaty of "friendship and cooperation." To the Poles, these treaties were bittersweet. The latter made no mention of reparations to the million-odd Poles who endured slavery in the Third Reich, but explicitly admitted, for the first time, the existence and rights of the hitherto "non-existent" German minority in Poland.[25] The notion of German minority rights remained particularly difficult for Poles to accept because ethnic homogeneity was a founding principle of the postwar Polish state. Since there was no precise way of determining the number of people who considered themselves to be German,[26] Warsaw feared that it might soon confront a large minority whose demands for cultural autonomy would be little more than a starting point for complete separation from Poland. There were rumors that significant numbers of Poles had obtained documentation certifying their German origins and were therefore entitled to benefits from the German welfare state.[27] As Timothy Garton Ash observed: "Germans in Poland multiplied like relics of the true cross."[28]

---

[22] See Paul Lewis, "Upheaval in the East: The Poles Favor One Germany in NATO," *New York Times*, 2 February 1990.

[23] Poland–Germany, "Broken Silence," *Rzeczpospolita*, 9 October 1990.

[24] See "Polska i RFN odpisały układ o potwierdzeniu istniejącej między nimi granicy," *Polska Zbrojna*, 15 November 1990.

[25] "'Experts' of German–Polish Treaty," *Die Welt*, 15 May 1991, as reported in FBIS WEU-91–099, 22 May 1991.

[26] The estimated number of ethnic Germans in Poland ranged from as few as 200,000 to over 1 million.

[27] "You Can Become German in Opole," *Sztandar Młodych*, 11 October 1990, 1. According to that publication, in 1990 alone, 30,000 Poles "mutated" into Germans.

[28] Ash, *In Europe's Name*.

Although the Poles have committed themselves to the protection of German communal rights, relations remain difficult.[29] Ethnic Germans in western Poland have been particularly assertive, erecting monuments to Germany's war dead. This action prompted a warning from then President Lech Wałęsa's spokesman, Andrzej Drzycimski:

> Actions that undermine the principles of coexistence in the state are manifestations of chauvinism, are in violation of Polish law, international agreements and standards, and do not promote the cause of building a European community . . . Poland, with Polish Silesia, wants to be in a Europe to which Germany already belongs. The borders, however, have been set forever. . .[30]

The local government responded to the challenge by outlawing the right-wing German group *Nationale Offensive* and banning the publication of the German-language *Schlesien Report*.[31] But the central government was willing to make some concessions to prevent German minority issues from becoming a source of confrontation between the two countries. For example, when Poland revamped its electoral law, it excluded the ethnic Germans from the requirement that a minority party receive a minimum of 5 percent of the vote in order to qualify for membership in the *Sejm*, thereby assuring German representation in the national legislature.

Despite the official reconciliation between Bonn and Warsaw on Silesia, Polish and German historians have continued to offer opposing interpretations of its history. Polish historians insist that Silesia was Polish for a millennium, while their German colleagues stress that for eight centuries Germans dominated the region, turning Silesia into one of the most industrial areas in Europe. As Johann Kroll, the leader of the region's German population, noted: "The question is, who is the visitor here and who is the host?"[32] In Germany, when President Herzog in a 1995 speech to expellees categorically stated that Germany's lost lands will not be regained, hecklers responded by calling him a "traitor."[33] In a similar vain, Henryk Kroll, the chairman of the Socio-Cultural Association of Germans in Opole (Poland), noted that no Polish–German reconciliation is complete as long as it "lacks a pillar named the expelled."[34] On the Polish side of the border, Poles

---

[29] For the text, see *ADN*, 17 June 1991.
[30] *Gazeta Wyborcza*, 8 December 1992, 2.     [31] PAP, 14 January 1993.
[32] Tyler Marshall, "German Poles Assert Their Restored Identities," *Los Angeles Times*, 30 December 1990.
[33] Hanna Suchocka quoted in Reuters Newswire, 8 September 1996.
[34] PAP Newswire, 17 June 1996.

living in former German lands fear that when the original leases for many buildings expire, their German former owners will seek to reclaim them using European Union (EU) laws which by then may well apply to Poland as well. This fear has resulted in the creation of lobbying groups on behalf of thousands of Polish families in these territories.[35]

The prevailing Polish view that it must bind itself to the West and Germany was elaborated by Foreign Minister Skubiszewski during a 1992 briefing for the *Sejm*. He noted that unless Warsaw cooperated with Bonn, German policy toward Eastern Europe and Russia would increasingly become a unilateral policy pursued "over our heads."[36] Some Polish nationalist groups, such as the Confederation for an Independent Poland (KPN) and the Christian-National Union (ZChN), objected to Skubiszewski's diplomacy. Their suspicions were heightened by Brandenburg Prime Minister Manfred Stolpe's proposal to create a regional bloc *(Oderraum)*. Many viewed this as the beginning of German domination, a fear fueled by Germany's relatively heavy investments in the former German territories. But the Polish leadership remains convinced that Poland will have to support continued German membership in NATO while simultaneously pressing for its own. Should Russia revert to imperial ambitions, particularly following an American withdrawal from Europe, Germany, as the most exposed European power, would attempt to deal with the situation either through confrontation with Russia or through a revival of their historic symbiosis in Central Europe. Polish fears of a Russo-German condominium in East-Central Europe were heightened when Germany attempted to dissuade the Central European states from forming the Višegrad group because it might offend Moscow. Warsaw had to turn to Washington before Bonn withdrew its objections.[37]

German policy, especially following Hans Dietrich Genscher's departure from the foreign ministry, has been to internationalize the crisis in the East by expansion of both the EU and NATO. Germany's defense minister Volker Rühe has become one of the most ardent advocates of early NATO expansion. This German commitment to push the problems of the former Soviet Union away from its frontiers

---

[35] *Gazeta Wyborcza*, no. 195, 24 August 1996, 1.
[36] *Życie Warszawy*, 18 March 1992.
[37] Grzegorz Kostrzewa-Zorbas, "The Russian Troop Withdrawal From Poland," in *The Diplomatic Record 1992–1993*, ed. Allen E. Goodman (Boulder, San Francisco, Oxford: Westview Press, 1994), 130.

was articulated by the chairman of the Bundestag's Foreign Affairs Committee, Hans Stercken, who confirmed that Germany's "image of the future is different from the image the Russians have. We will strive to provide the countries neighboring Russia with their due place [in Europe]."[38] Welcoming his Polish counterpart, Waldemar Pawlak, to Bonn, Chancellor Kohl went further, stating: "The Federal Republic is fighting for the Polish–German border, not the border of the European Union." Objecting to the inclusion of Poland among the states of Eastern Europe, Kohl added: "Kraków is the rock of Central Europe."[39]

Currently, Poland and Germany concur on the question of Polish membership in NATO. For the Poles, membership provides a link with the United States and an assurance that Germany will remain "bound." The Germans favor Polish membership as a means of ensuring that should chaos break out in Eastern Europe, it will not be treated as a singularly German problem. Therefore, they have supported the demands of successive Polish governments for NATO membership. Poland's current attitude toward Germany reflects not only changing perceptions among the Poles, but also an awareness of Poland's limited options. The creation of the Tashkent Pact, consisting of most of the members of the Commonwealth of Independent States, including hitherto neutral Belarus, further stimulated Poland's desire to join NATO at the earliest possible moment. As Arthur Rachwald has noted, Poland's failure to gain admission into NATO would ultimately result in "a strategic alliance between NATO and a re-centralized Commonwealth of Independent States (CIS), leaving Central Europe caught between two powerful supranational institutions, a twenty-first century version of the Holy Alliance."[40] Over 80 percent of the Polish population supports NATO membership, but it remains to be seen whether or not the US Congress will extend American security guarantees farther east or that NATO will risk offending Russia.

By 1993 German–Polish relations had entered a new phase, one increasingly free of the burdens of history and more responsive to new realities. On the Polish side, the initial infatuation with the West had faded. Warsaw was able to deal with the West without awe or fear. The universal expectation that a united Germany would turn into an economic juggernaut overnight failed to materialize. On the

---

[38] PAP, 28 March 1994.    [39] PAP, 14 April 1944.
[40] Arthur Rachwald, "Poland Looks West," in *Post-1989 Poland: Challenges of Independence,* ed. Andrew Michta and Ilya Prizel (New York: St. Martin's Press, 1995).

German side, the flood of asylum seekers, a recession in West Germany, and the free fall of the East German economy impressed upon Bonn the fact that it was not immune to events east of the Oder. The growing chaos in the new countries of the former Soviet Union and increasing Russian assertiveness have made Bonn and Warsaw more aware of their political and economic interdependence.

The new relationship with Germany has changed Poland's relations with France and the United States, both of which had been sources of inspiration. France, concerned that bringing the Central European states into the EU would tilt the balance in Brussels toward Germany and stir up the volatile French farmers, proved reluctant to extend EU membership to Poland. The United States, at least until late 1993, remained deeply committed to a Russia-first policy, making it clear that relations with Moscow would come before Central European interests.[41] On the political level, following the model of the Franco-German rapprochement, Poland and Germany, together with France, formed a new political bloc, known as the Weimar Triangle, charged with deepening Poland's relationship with both West European countries and developing a common security concept. When the United States tried to pressure Poland to sell tanks to Bosnia, Warsaw refused, siding with Paris and Bonn. Given their desire to find a safe harbor within the West European political, economic, and security system, the Poles will have to rely on Germany, "our liaison in contacts with EC and NATO."[42]

But the two countries cannot simply gloss over seven centuries of warfare in five years. When Edmund Stoiber, the prime minister of Bavaria, suggested that Germany should reassert its own national interest and halt the growth of "an overshadowing, undermining European federal state,"[43] many Poles panicked. Stoiber's statement raised fears that Genscher's maxim, "The more European our foreign policy is, the more national it is" might not survive in a united Germany. The fact that efforts to make Goerlitz and Zgorzelec on the Neisse River "sister cities" continue to be marred by misunderstandings and the burden of history has made these fears even more credible. [44]

[41] The Višegrad group was stunned when the United States forbade Belgium to sell Hungary surplus US-made F-16 aircraft, forcing Hungary to continue its reliance on Russia.
[42] Hanna Suchocka speech at the Catholic University of Lublin, 18 October 1992.
[43] Neal Ascherson, "Unity or Chaos – The Choice that Germany Must Make for Europe," *The Independent*, 14 November 1993.
[44] *Swiss Review of World Affairs*, 1 October 1996.

Despite the disappointments and difficulties that Poland has suffered in the early stages of its relationship with united Germany, successive Polish governments have maintained that the best hope of recasting Poland's identity and avoiding marginalization within Europe lies in continuously improving relations with Germany. In many ways, Polish policy resembles the road to reconciliation pioneered by French President Charles de Gaulle, who also used rapprochement with Germany to recast his country's national identity as a European power. Polish analysts continue to insist that only through continued integration into Western Europe will Poland avoid being drawn into the abyss of irredentist claims and ethnic conflict currently gripping the Balkans and some of Poland's eastern neighbors.[45] As Janusz Reiter noted, the only way Poland can contribute to the stability of the deteriorating East is if it is firmly embedded in the West.[46]

The Polish public's perceptions of Germany have improved tremendously. In early 1990, 67 percent of Poles felt that a united Germany presented a clear and present danger to Poland,[47] and in 1991, one in two Poles doubted the permanency of the Oder–Neisse border. Only 51 percent believed that Germany would remain democratic.[48] When questioned about the German minority, though, an overwhelming majority of Poles stated that Polish Germans ought to have full cultural and linguistic freedom, despite expectations of growing tension.[49] By mid-1992 there was a fundamental change in Polish perceptions of Germany. In a poll carried out by *Gazeta Wyborcza*, only 28 percent expressed fear of Germany.

The improvement of Polish–German relations may well be one of the greatest diplomatic achievements in post-World War II Europe. Anchored in their new European identities, the two have not only managed to overcome the legacy of their tortured past, but have also created a special relationship similar to that of France and Germany. The relationship between them appears to have become institutionalized. Joint training exercises between Polish and German troops have become commonplace. Germany has become Poland's largest trading partner, by far, and its third largest investor. In 1996, 77 percent of

---

[45] See Kazimierz Dziewanowski, "On Polish–German Relations," *Polish Review* 37: 4 (1992). At the time, Dziewanowski was Poland's Ambassador to the United States.
[46] Janusz Reiter, "This Was Europe: A Polish View," *Polish Review* 37: 4 (1992).
[47] Jan de Weydenthal, "The Polish German Reconciliation," *RFE/RL Research Reports*, 5 July 1991, 20.
[48] *Der Spiegel*, 2 September 1991, 48–57.
[49] See "Polacy o Niemcach," *Konfrontacje*, no. 5 (1991).

Polish respondents identified Germany as the most desirable economic partner; 67 percent as the best military partner.[50] Both Richard
von Weizaecker's last trip abroad as German president and his
successor's first official foreign visit were to Poland. Aleksander
Kwaśniewski's first foreign trip as the president of Poland was to
Germany. Poland's foreign minister Władysław Bartoszewski was
asked to address a joint session of the German parliament, a privilege
rarely granted to a foreigner. Bartoszewski recounted not only the
Nazi atrocities in Poland, but also the suffering inflicted on the
Germans at the end of the World War II. In so doing, he broke a fifty-
year-old taboo of Polish politics, saying, "I wish to state openly that
we are sorry for the individual fates and suffering of innocent German
casualties of the war *who lost their native lands*."[51] Bartoszewski, also a
survivor of Auschwitz, would later be quoted as saying: "[The]
change wrought in Polish–German relations is one of the most
positive transformations in European history."[52] Despite the occasional reappearance of suspicions and anxieties in both countries,
Bonn and Warsaw agree that to sustain their post-World War II
European identity, they must accept one another.

### Eastern policy revisited

Poland's relationship with Germany is qualitatively different
from its relationship with Russia. Despite German expansion to the
east and numerous wars, the Poles and the Germans have enjoyed
long periods of cooperation and peace. The Poles might have feared
the Germans, but they always felt that they shared a common
civilization with their western neighbor, and they never defined their
standing as a state in terms of their relationship with the Germans.
Accommodation with Germany could be reduced to the issues of
borders and security, but accommodation with Russia required abandoning key elements of Polish national identity and formulating a
new definition of Polish civilization. Although the physical wounds
inflicted upon the Poles by the Germans were deeper and far more
brutal than those inflicted by the Russian and Soviet empires, the
psychological wounds inflicted by Russia and the Soviet Union were
more deeply ingrained in the Polish national identity.

---

[50] PAP Newswire, 26 September 1996.    [51] Ibid.
[52] Anthony Baker, "Poland, Germany Draw Away from Bloodstained Past," *Reuters*, 4
July 1995.

Through its success in stemming the expansion of the Ottoman empire into Europe, Poland became the premier military power in Europe and acquired its identity as a defender of Christianity. In its own expansion into the East, Poland acquired an identity as a distinct civilization and a force of republicanism against Russian despotism.[53] As a result of this encounter with the East, Poland developed a profound attachment to these borderlands, where a large number of Poland's elite ultimately moved. This attachment to the eastern borderlands is not the only complicating factor in Poland's relationship with the East. Because of their contempt and sense of cultural superiority toward the Russians, the Poles found Russian rule considerably more humiliating than German domination. Describing the pervasiveness of this Polish attitude, Czesław Miłosz observed, "Russia is something *outside*, beyond the orbit of the civilized world. Consequently, [the Poles'] defeat at the hands of Russia shocked them . . ."[54] The bitter memory of Russian domination from 1793 to 1918 and from 1945 to 1989 still haunts the Polish national consciousness.[55]

As observed in chapter 3, Polish intellectuals, trying to devise a post-communist foreign policy for Poland, acknowledged that attitudes toward the East would have to undergo a fundamental revision. For Poland to become a truly normal and independent country, they recognized that it would first be necessary to abandon all claims to the *kresy* and accept the current eastern frontiers as permanent. Second, they maintained that Poland would have to abandon the notion that the Ukrainian and Belorussian peoples were merely an "ethnographic mass" devoid of authentic culture, recognize the national aspirations of the people of Lithuania, Belarus, and Ukraine, and support their aspirations for independence from both Moscow and Warsaw. Finally, they recognized that Poland would have to separate the Russian state from the Soviet Union and despite its loathing for communism and the "inferior" Russian culture, offer itself as a bridge and a catalyst for the "Europeanization" of Russia.

Although Poland's post-communist elite had internalized these precepts in theory, implementing the reorientation proved to be

---

[53] See Kaminski, *Republic vs. Autocracy* (Cambridge, MA: Harvard University Press).

[54] Czesław Miłosz, *Native Realm: A Search for Self-Definition* (Berkeley: University of California Press, 1981), 130 (emphasis in the original).

[55] Norman Davies even argues that, with the exception of the period between 1918 and 1939, Russia exercised either hegemony or direct rule over Poland from 1714, when Peter the Great put Augustus the Strong of Saxony back on the Polish throne, through the 1980s.

complex. First of all, this policy required a profound transformation of the Soviet Union, a process in which Poland could play only a marginal role at best. Second, because the question of the German frontier remained unsettled, Poland's postcommunist government felt that it still needed the Soviet military for its defense. This limited Poland's support of democratization within the Soviet Union and the development of relations with Ukraine, Belarus, and Lithuania. Third, despite the overwhelming support for reconciliation with Ukraine and Lithuania, parts of the Polish polity found it hard to resign themselves to the loss of Lwów and Wilno (Lviv and Vilnius). Memories of the ferocious and bloody fighting between the two peoples during World War II made it difficult for many Poles to free themselves from a latent fear of an independent Ukraine. The conflicting pressures exerted on Poland's postcommunist regime led to the adoption of a two-track policy. In the West, while striving for reconciliation with Germany, Warsaw simultaneously requested that Soviet troops remain on its soil. In the East, while making no secret of its sympathies for the aspirations of the Baltic peoples and the Ukrainians, Poland limited its support so as not to jeopardize its relationship with the Soviet government.

The extraordinarily rapid metamorphosis of Europe made it imperative that Poland develop a response to the changing situation in the East, yet few in Poland were prepared to do so. In 1990, in one of the first academic analyses of Poland's relationship with the East, Agnieszka Magdziak-Miszewska and Jerzy Marek Nowakowski, director of the Institute of Foreign Affairs attached to the Polish Senate, observed that although the break-up of the Soviet Union might well be under way, it would be a mistake for Poles to indulge in a senile policy (*zdziecinnienie starcze*) based on an interwar reality that had long ceased to exist. Poland must treat all Soviet citizens equally and avoid any appearance of paternalism. Because the new states emerging on Russia's fringe would most likely remain economically and militarily dependent on Moscow, the authors urged the Polish government to conduct a multidimensional foreign policy, reaching out to Gorbachev and Yeltsin, as well as to the leaders of the non-Russian republics. According to Magdziak-Miszewska and Nowakowski, Poland's road to normality and its acceptance by the West was contingent on good relations with Russia.[56]

---

[56] Agnieszka Magdziak-Miszewska and Jerzy Marek Nowakowski, "Droga do Rosji," *Polityka Polska* (November 1990), 10–17.

Therefore, with the prospect of a united Germany casting a shadow across Poland, Warsaw advocated the integration of the Soviet Union as a whole into Europe, stressing that the key to Poland's long-term security lay in the victory of the Westernizers in Russia. The aspirations of the peoples of the borderlands remained secondary.[57] At the same time, the Poles, nervous about German intentions, continued to advocate the maintenance of the Warsaw Pact, albeit in a new form. Only after the resolution of the German border issue in the autumn of 1990 did Poland reverse its position and advocate the dissolution of the alliance.[58] Thus the two-track policy, which was not intended to be a long-term approach, condemned Poland to passivity throughout much of 1990. The perceived need for the presence of Soviet troops in Poland disappeared after the German government accepted the Oder–Neisse line and signed a friendship treaty with Poland. As a result, within a short period of time the Poles came to view the continued Soviet military presence on Polish soil as anachronistic at best and humiliating at worst. In addition, after the Soviet crackdown on Lithuania in January 1991, Poland's measured policy toward its immediate eastern neighbors came under public criticism.

Yet the Polish population remained divided over the question of whether the demise of the Soviet Union would serve Poland's interests. Some groups saw an independent Ukraine as a guarantor of genuine Polish sovereignty, while others considered it a potential security threat.[59] In September 1990, during hearings on Poland's Eastern policy, the Polish Senate criticized the government's lack of contacts with the individual republics of the Soviet Union. The Sejm *refused*, however, to extend full support to the western Soviet republics' aspirations for independence and continued to hope that the Soviet Union would evolve as a "genuine confederacy."[60] Because of these constraints and ambiguities, the two-track policy did little to inspire Baltic and Ukrainian nationalists seeking independence or to please the Polish electorate.

By the time Lech Wałęsa declared his candidacy for president, challenging his hand-picked prime minister, Tadeusz Mazowiecki, the entire question of Poland's Eastern policy had become a hotly

---

[57] See Ronald Asmus and Thomas Szayna, *Polish National Security Thinking in a Changing Europe* (Santa Monica: Rand/UCLA Center for Soviet Studies, 1991), 22.
[58] Ibid.
[59] See Stephen R. Burant, "International Relations in a Regional Context: Poland and its Eastern Neighbors – Lithuania, Belarus, Ukraine," *Europe-Asia Studies* 45: 3, 395–418.
[60] PAP, 5 September 1990.

contested electoral issue. Once elected, President Wałęsa, on the advice of Zdzisław Najder,[61] an advocate of a far more activist approach to Poland's eastern rim, signaled a fundamental change of policy. At his inauguration, Wałęsa startled his audience by extending his greetings to Lithuania, Belorussia, and Ukraine, ignoring the Soviet Union altogether. Wałęsa's apparent challenge to the integrity of the Soviet Union drew an angry response from the Soviet media. Yet, despite Moscow's obvious displeasure, Poland's new government continued to pursue with enthusiasm the cause of Belorussian, Ukrainian, and Russian independence, as demonstrated by the dramatic increase in mutual exchanges and visits between the countries. Even before the collapse of the Soviet Union, the Polish government appropriated to itself the role of Europeanizing these emerging countries and bringing them into the West, seeing it as an opportunity to bolster Poland's international role. It should be noted that in Najder's view, by Europeanizing Ukraine, Poland would help to Europeanize itself and improve its position within the international system. This belief was reinforced by the nearly universal assumption that Ukraine, unlike Russia, would make the transformation to democracy and a market economy relatively quickly and painlessly, and that without Ukraine, Russia would cease to be a superpower.[62]

The difference between the Polish concept of nationhood in the 1980s and that of the interwar years should be noted. Whereas the latter sought legitimacy in reclaiming the Jagiellonian tradition, which demanded expansion to the east, postcommunist leaders sought legitimacy by turning Poland into a normal European state. The interwar leaders viewed Poland as a rampart against Russia, but the new Polish elite recognized that Poland's integration into the West was contingent on Russia's Europeanization and subsequent integration into Europe.

Yet despite Polish attempts to maintain cordial relations, the last year of the Soviet Union was marked by controversies between the two countries. On the symbolic level, the Poles were infuriated by the Kremlin's lack of forthrightness on the issue of the massacre of thousands of Polish officers in 1940 in Katyń and Mednoye forests. On a practical level, Warsaw refused to follow Romania's lead and commit itself to avoiding any alliance that Moscow perceived as anti-

---

[61] For Najder's views, see Zdzisław Najder "Spór o Polską Politykę Wschodnią," *Rzeczpospolita*, 1 November 1991.

[62] See Andrzej Romanowski, "Independence of the Ukraine," *Tygodnik Powszechny*, 15 December 1991.

Soviet – the so-called Kvitsinskii Doctrine – believing that this was an assault on Polish sovereignty and relegated Poland once again to the status of a "buffer state."[63] Moscow was in turn irked by what it perceived as Polish obstructionism regarding the movement of Soviet troops across Polish territory as they were leaving Germany. Poland's insistence on a rapid withdrawal of Soviet troops from its own soil further soured relations. Moscow perceived this as ungratefulness on the part of the Poles, while Warsaw considered Moscow's demands for compensation for alleged improvements left by the departing Soviet forces excessive and high-handed.

### Poland and Russia

The collapse of the Soviet Union in December 1991 provided Poland and its eastern neighbors with an opportunity for a final reconciliation. Poland was the first country outside of the Commonwealth of Independent States to recognize the independence of Ukraine, Belarus, and Russia. Based on the belief that there can be no stability in Eastern Europe without reconciliation with its eastern neighbors,[64] Poland signed friendship treaties with all of them, achieving stability along its frontiers for the first time in a millennium. The independence of the Baltics, Belarus, and Ukraine gave Poland the final assurance that it would not be doomed to being an immediate neighbor of an East ruled directly by Russia. Once Poland no longer bordered Russia, except for a short border in the Kaliningrad district, its prospects of joining NATO and the EU improved dramatically.

Yet despite the dramatic improvement in its geopolitical situation and its genuine desire to recreate a cultural and economic partnership with its new neighbors, Poland's Eastern policy was more a study in constraints than bold initiatives. Mirosław Głogowski, writing a few weeks after the disintegration of the Soviet Union, observed that in this new geopolitical environment Russia might well become Poland's partner in maintaining the status quo in Central Europe. Noting that Russia shared no border with Poland, with the exception of the Kaliningrad district, Głogowski believed that the probability of territorial tensions emerging between Poland and Germany, Ukraine, Belarus, or Lithuania was far greater than with Russia. Furthermore,

---

[63] See Adam Michnik, "What Next for Russia?" *Gazeta Wyborcza*, 20 February 1990, as reported in FBIS EEU-90–035, 21 February 1990.
[64] See *Gazeta Wyborcza*, 19 May 1992.

Głogowski stressed that when seeking strategic alliances, the newly independent states of the commonwealth would always view Poland as a "second-best alternative." The Baltic states would opt for Scandinavia, and Ukraine would always prefer Germany. Therefore, Poland should retain close links with Moscow in order to avoid isolation within the region.[65]

Post-communist Poland's Eastern policy reflected its new self-image as a mid-sized European state in search of anchorage within the West European context. Unlike Józef Piłsudski's interwar Poland, which considered the power of Soviet Russia equivalent to that of a "cadaver," postcommunist Poland firmly believed that Russia would remain a great power despite the collapse of the Soviet empire. While Piłsudski saw Poland as a European power that would supplant Russia in dominance of the region, President Wałęsa described contemporary Polish–Russian relations in the following manner: "Yeltsin and I are like drivers on a strange road at night, without road markings. The difference between us is that I am driving a baby Fiat and he a huge juggernaut."[66] This acceptance of the enduring power of Russia was the primary foreign policy postulate of all post-communist Polish governments.

The second assumption of the Polish foreign ministry was that the new states of Ukraine and Belarus would continue to be an area of strategic interest to Russia. Warsaw was anxious to bolster its relations with these states, but it was willing to do so only so long as this did not compromise relations with Moscow. Finally, although Poland's ultimate goal was membership in NATO and the EU, membership in the former could be achieved far more easily if it did not involve NATO in tensions between Poland and the western states of the former Soviet Union. This issue was particularly salient in light of the special attention given to Moscow by both Bonn and Washington.[67]

These were the conditions under which Poland's post-communist governments strove to normalize relations with Russia. Just a few months after the collapse of the Soviet Union, Poland and Russia negotiated the withdrawal of former Soviet troops from Polish soil. The terms of the agreement were controversial. Poland agreed to drop all financial claims resulting from the ecological damage inflicted on it

---

[65] Mirosław Głogowski, "Kłopot Na Wschodzie," *Prawo i Życie*, 7 September 1991.
[66] Nick Thorpe, "Why the Poles (and Others) Are Pulling for Yeltsin," *Gazette* (Montreal), 30 April 1993.
[67] See Skubiszewski's report to the *Sejm*'s Foreign Affairs Committee, PAP, 18 November 1992.

by Soviet troops and accepted that former Soviet bases should be turned into joint stock Polish–Russian companies. Many Poles considered the latter a vestige of Russian colonial presence, and, following direct intervention from Yeltsin, the notion of joint stock companies was dropped. Wide sectors of the Polish polity were also dismayed that the Polish–Russian Treaty of Friendship and Good Neighbor Cooperation made no mention of the murders at Katyń. President Wałęsa had to content himself with a joint declaration that both Poles and Russians were victims of Stalinism. Although Wałęsa, prior to his departure for Moscow, admitted that the treaty was "not future-oriented," he nevertheless supported the accord because he felt it was an essential step "to break with the past."[68] In reality, President Wałęsa's office remained far more skeptical about Russia's intentions and thus far more eager than the foreign ministry to embrace NATO or some other subregional organization that might enhance Poland's security. Wałęsa's national security adviser, Jerzy Milewski, noted that Poles "should not forget Russia . . . Whether we want it or not, Russia has not ceased to be a big power and is treated as one by the United States, Western Europe, the whole world."[69] Prime Minister Hanna Suchocka echoed this view, noting, "All long-term planning must, however, be based on the assumption that Russia, regardless of the scope of its current problems, will also in the future be a great country co-shaping [along with Germany] the situation in our region."[70]

Believing that Poland can integrate itself into Western Europe only if it becomes a catalyst for the Europeanization of Russia, Poland's political mainstream continues to support rapprochement with Moscow, making a conscious effort to avoid linking the current Russian government with Stalinist crimes. Similarly, although Poland has managed to reorient most of its trade to the West, Russia remains its principal source of oil and natural gas and a major importer of Polish textiles, coal, grain, and pharmaceuticals – sectors of the Polish economy that do not appear capable of competing in the West. The growing economic interdependence of Russia and Poland has revived in both a lobby of directors of state-owned enterprises pushing for deeper economic ties. In an analysis of Russo–Polish economic relations, Marek Henzler observed that even if Poland could free itself from its dependence on Russian oil and natural gas, it would never-

---

[68] PAP, 22 May 1992.
[69] *Gazeta Wyborcza*, 22 September 1992.
[70] Hanna Suchocka, "We Count on Understanding Not Only of Unity of Aims But Also of Unity of Interests," speech at Lublin Catholic University, 18 October 1992.

theless remain dependent on the Russian market for a long time to come.[71] In 1995 economic relations between Moscow and Warsaw improved dramatically. Poland and Russia signed the Yamal pipeline deal, an agreement that committed the two partners to build a pipe from the Yamal fields in northern Russia to Germany and specified that Poland would double its purchases of Russian natural gas over the next twenty-five years.[72] Simultaneously, small-scale traders in both countries resumed massive cross-border trade, making Russia Poland's third largest trading partner.[73] In fact, even as the Suchocka–Skubiszewski team worked toward a balanced relationship with both East and West, leftist members of the *Sejm* expressed concern that Poland's Western orientation ignored the fact that since the West's policy remained pro-Russian, Poland had to retain close ties with the East in order to avoid falling out of the loop.[74]

Despite the recognition that Poland must establish cordial relations with Russia, Warsaw remains concerned that the Russian democratic experiment might fail and that Russia might revert to its historical imperialism. Although some rightist groups, such as Leszek Moczulski's Confederation for an Independent Poland (KPN), believed that the only way for Poland to secure its integrity was to create a Polish-led bloc of states located between the Baltic and Black seas, the majority of Poles rejected this idea as a dangerous throwback to Poland's interwar doctrine. Consequently, successive Polish governments have sought to join NATO as soon as possible. Russian publication of a defense doctrine classifying Poland as a potential threat to its security and placing it within Russia's sphere of interest intensified that desire.[75] Sixty-one percent of Poles feel that Russia poses a long-term danger to their country,[76] while 80 percent remain convinced that despite the breakdown of the Soviet empire, Russia continues to influence Polish politics.[77]

When Boris Yeltsin, during an August 1993 trip to Poland, appeared to accept Polish membership in NATO, most Poles were elated, and

[71] Marek Henzler, "Na Czarną Godzinę" [For the Black Hour], *Polityka*, 16 October 1993.
[72] "Poland Signs Landmark Gas Deal with Russia's Gazprom," *New Europe*, 29 September–5 October 1996, 23.
[73] Paweł Tarnowski, "Who Wants Flourishing Polish–Russian Trade?" *Polityka*, no. 16, 20 April 1996.
[74] See interview with Józef Oleksy, *Przegląd Tygodniowy*, 7 February 1993.
[75] See Stephen Foye, "The Army Gets a Doctrine: Updating Russian Civil–Military Relations," *RFE/RL Reports*, 11 November 1993.
[76] *Życie Warszawy*, no. 56, 6 March 1996, p. 1.
[77] *Rzeczpospolita*, no. 65, 16–17 March 1996, p. 1.

Skubiszewski renewed Poland's demands that NATO admit Poland expeditiously. But this apparent concession triggered a barrage of criticism across the political spectrum in Russia,[78] forcing Yeltsin to reverse himself, thereby undermining his credibility and underscoring Russia's endemic instability. Yeltsin's violent confrontation with the Russian parliament convinced the Polish government that a Yeltsin beholden to the armed forces for his political survival was bound to pursue an increasingly imperialist foreign policy.

Paradoxically, Poland's foreign policy remained remarkably consistent despite the turbulence in Russia. Even as the rise of Russian nationalism increased the desire for admission into NATO, the new Polish government, dominated by former communists, continued to insist that building a more profound understanding with Russia remained a priority. Making his debut before the Foreign Affairs Committee of the *Sejm* in 1993, incoming Foreign Minister Andrzej Olechowski announced that he was committed to enshrining greater cordiality in Poland's relations with Moscow and warned that its relations with Russia and Germany should be *at least* as good as those between the countries themselves.[79] Olechowski went on to state that there could be no European security system without Russia. This view was reaffirmed by outgoing Foreign Minister Władysław Bartoszewski who stated that "Poland does not imagine a future security system without NATO agreements with Russia and the Ukraine."[80]

Moscow's ability to delay Polish membership in NATO provoked an indignant response throughout the country, with most politicians declaring that Poland would continue to lobby for membership in NATO regardless of Russia's objections. But Social Democratic leader Aleksander Kwaśniewski, whose Socjaldemokracja Rzeczpospolitej Polskiej (Social Democracy of the Republic of Poland – SDRP) is the senior partner in the ruling coalition, observed that although he found Yeltsin's position "incomprehensible," in order to guarantee its security, Poland would need "a clearly defined vision of cooperation with Russia, so as to rule out the threat that Russia might be our enemy."[81] The view that Russia was reverting to a more stridently nationalist mode was shared by some of Poland's best-known political

---

[78] It was not only General Pavel Grachev and the military who objected to the inclusion of Poland in NATO. For a liberal critique see Aleksei Pushkov, "Do Not Make an Enemy," *Moscow News*, 22 September 1993.

[79] *Rzeczpospolita*, no. 263, 10–11 November 1993, 2 (emphasis added).

[80] *Rzeczpospolita*, no. 266, 17 November 1995.

[81] Anna Wielopolska and Zbigniew Lentowicz, "Politicians of Yeltsin's Statement," *Rzeczpospolita*, no. 231, 2–3 October 1993.

analysts. Yadwiga Staniszkis observed that Russia's foreign policy would become more "collective," a situation in which Yeltsin's preferences would be of diminishing importance.[82] Jerzy Marek Nowakowski went further, asserting that, given Yeltsin's weak position, Poland would face a set of dynamics with "Europe connecting to Russia."[83] This weakness of Yeltsin's has already adversely affected Poland's position *vis-à-vis* the West:

> Regardless of whether Yeltsin is a "collective" leader or figurehead, the West will move to accommodate Yeltsin. The Germans already proved it to us when overnight they changed their position regarding Poland's membership in NATO. Russian reservations are for them the fundamental issue in the same way they are is for the Americans. In this situation cooperation with Poland will decrease in the eyes of the West. . .[84]

Inasmuch as Yeltsin was bound to practice what Vladimir Zubok called the "tyranny of the weak,"[85] blackmailing the West into supporting Russia by threatening anarchy, Poland's options were limited. Although the Poles should insist on a deepened partnership with the West, this can be attained only if Poland does not attempt to engage in building a *cordon sanitaire* around Russia. Karol Modzelewski of the Labor Union (UP) warned the Poles that "one should not tease the Russian national pride by getting engaged in their internal affairs. Anyway, the army will not forget the pleasure Poland got during the withdrawal of Soviet troops." Modżelewski reminded his countrymen that "Poland will have to live with the understanding that it is not a superpower. Poland will have to make efforts to maintain good relations with the East."[86]

The electoral results in Russia, in which nationalists and communists showed surprising strength, prompted Poland to dispatch Foreign Minister Andrzej Olechowski to the United States to intensify Poland's lobbying for NATO membership. Olechowski continued to stress that whereas Poland's ultimate security lay in NATO, ultimate world stability lay in the democratization of Russia. Speaking in Washington he observed: "Unless Russia is a democratic country with a market economy, no US strategic partnership with her will be truly

---

[82] Yadwiga Staniszkis, interview by author, Kazimiez, June 1993.
[83] Piotr Jędroszczyk interview in Jerzy Marek Nowakowski, "Przyłączenie Europy do Rosji," *Słowo Powszechne*, 12 October 1993.
[84] Ibid.
[85] Vladimir Zubok, "Tyranny of the Weak: Russia's New Foreign Policy," *World Policy Journal* 9: 2 (Spring 1992), 191–218.
[86] *Rzeczpospolita*, no. 233, 5 October 1993.

advantageous to the world's security." Olechowski then urged the United States to "lead the world in an effort to help Russia to build its democratic identity and presence in the world." To attain that goal he urged permanent membership for Russia in the Group of Seven, greater economic aid, and access to Western markets.[87] Olechowski concluded his remarks by noting that inasmuch as Poland was unconditionally tying its future to NATO, the Atlantic alliance would have to build a strategic relationship with Russia. Although the Poles were angered by NATO's decision not to admit the Višegrad group, their anger appeared to be primarily directed at the West rather than at Russia. This bitterness was pointedly reflected in Kazimierz Pytko's editorial in *Życie Warszawy* under the sardonic title "When Saxophone Players Rule."[88]

Russia's increasingly assertive foreign policy, particularly within the CIS, but also in the Balkans, the Middle East, and the Korean peninsula increased Warsaw's sense of anxiety. Relations between Poland and Russia reached their nadir during Foreign Minister Andrei Kozyrev's visit to Kraków in March 1994, when the two sides failed to come to any understanding. Russia continued to object to Polish membership in NATO, suggesting instead that the CIS and NATO should be co-guarantors of Polish security. Kozyrev's position prompted President Wałęsa's National Security Advisor, Jerzy Milewski, to complain that Russia "is returning to the imperialist policy once followed by the tsars and later by the Soviet Union."[89] Despite the unease over Russian diplomatic pressure, however, Poland refused to deviate from the position that its ultimate security lay in a good relationship with Russia. President Wałęsa's complaints that Russia's forces in the Kaliningrad District were unduly large and hence a threat to Polish security had no effect on Polish diplomacy. Within days of Kozyrev's visit to Kraków, the Polish government signaled that it had no intention of isolating Moscow by inviting Russia to join the Weimar Group, a consultative body of French, German, and Polish parliamentarians. President Wałęsa, in an oblique recognition of geopolitical reality, told Russian journalists that "neither Russia nor Poland can be transferred to America. We are destined to be together." He added: "[Poles] have learned from

---

[87] Andrzej Olechowski, "Seven Statements on Poland's Security," address at the Center for Strategic and International Studies, Washington, DC, 14 December 1993.
[88] *Życie Warszawy*, 28 October 1993.
[89] Juliusz Urbanowicz, "Kozyrev in Kraków: The Bridges Are Still Burning," *Warsaw Voice*, 6 March 1994.

history that it is wrong to pin serious hopes on the West."[90] The speaker of the *Sejm*, Józef Oleksy, supported Wałęsa's position and upon his return from Moscow declared that "there are no matters which could stand . . . in the way of Polish–Russian relations."[91]

The war in Bosnia is another factor influencing Warsaw's determination to sustain working relations with Russia. This war has affected Poles in two ways. First, they have witnessed the destruction of a European state while the West stood by, incapable of acting. Second, they have seen dexterous Russian policy makers defend their Serbian allies. The lesson drawn by the Polish elite is that a West that cannot muster the resolve to confront Serbia is unlikely to confront Russia. Therefore, good relations with Russia are imperative.[92]

The election of Aleksander Kwaśniewski to Poland's presidency did not alter its foreign policy agenda, although he did tone down some of the anti-Russian rhetoric used by Lech Wałęsa during the electoral campaign. Poland remained committed to gaining membership in NATO and the EU as soon as possible. Kwaśniewski demonstrated his intention to deepen the Weimar Triangle by traveling to Bonn and Paris. Both Poland and Russia made efforts to improve relations, but misunderstandings and recriminations continued. The offer by Polish Defense Minister Stanisław Dobrzański to form a joint Polish–Russian battalion triggered a political storm in Poland and led to acrimonious exchanges between Russia's Defense Minister Pavel Grachev and his Polish counterpart. Russia's proposal to build a link to Kaliningrad via Poland's so-called Suwałki Corridor evoked Polish memories of Nazi demands for an extra-territorial corridor to Danzig and led to a sharp, emotional reaction from Warsaw. Russia ultimately opted for an alternative link.[93]

The past continues to cast a shadow over Warsaw. Interaction between Moscow and Warsaw remains at a level that the Polish communist Witold Pawłowski described as a "neurotic dialogue" between a "rejected big brother" and a "scrappy newly independent state."[94] In this climate, gestures meant to lighten the burden of history are often misinterpreted. The Poles saw their invitation to Yeltsin to participate in the commemoration of the 1944 Warsaw

---

[90] ITAR-Tass, 31 March 1994.     [91] BBC World Service, 5 April 1994.

[92] Konstantyn Gebert of *Gazeta Wyborcza*, interview with the author, Washington, DC, 2 May 1994.

[93] *New Europe*, 29 September–5 October 1996, 14.

[94] Witold Pawłowski, "Neurotic Poland–Russia Dialogue," *Polityka*, no. 16, 20 April 1996.

Uprising as an opportunity to demonstrate Poland's new relationship with its neighbors. The Russians, however, considered the invitation of Yeltsin and Germany's President Roman Herzog an attempt to equate Russia and Germany as co-culprits in the tragedy. Russia continues to refuse to assume responsibility for the Katyń massacre, claiming that the Russians were also victims of Stalin. Demands by the Russian Military Archival Center that Poland apologize for the Polish–Bolshevik war of 1920[95] have reopened deep wounds, while attacks on Soviet war cemeteries in Poland and the removal of a monument to Marshal I. S. Koniev in Kraków triggered indignation in the Russian media.

Yet post-communist Poland has remained remarkably consistent in its approach to Russia. A report authored by the leading policy makers of the Wałęsa era stated: "The [present] conflict with Russia is far from being an incidental quarrel [and] reflects different visions of the European future. Reaching a compromise on this issue, although exceedingly difficult, is possible nevertheless . . . Poland's policy is not and must not be focused on 'rolling back' or 'containing' Russia."[96] Although Poland is anxious to join NATO, Poles do not want to see their country become a frontier state. Instead of attempting to gain international stature by acting as a rampart against Russia, modern Poland is determined to be a bridge to Russia, however difficult the task may be.

### Relations with Ukraine and Belarus

The final disintegration of the Soviet Union in December 1991 fulfilled a dream long cherished by much of Poland's elite. For the first time in four centuries, Poland no longer stood on the border of an overpowering neighbor to the east. The rebirth of independent states in Ukraine, Belarus, and Lithuania transformed Poland from an East European buffer state separating the Soviet Union from the heart of Europe into a Central European state in the orbit of Germany and Scandinavia. By accepting that it must not alter its post-1945 frontiers and recognizing that the peoples to the east were more than an

---

[95] PAP News Wire, 19 July 1996.
[96] Andrzej Ananicz, Przemysław Grudziński, Andrzej Olechowski, Janusz Onyszkiewicz, Krzysztof Skubiszewski, and Henryk Szleifer, "Against Military and Political Isolation: Poland–NATO Report," *Rzeczpospolita*, no. 246, 23 October 1995.

ethnographic mass or Russified Poles,[97] Poland was able to re-establish its historical and cultural links with the region. The emergence of these newly independent states afforded Poland greater political and military security. Yet, although Warsaw had long been a window to the West for millions of Ukrainians and Belarussians, Poland's relationship with the countries of the *kresy* could not fully transcend either the burden of history or the geopolitical realities of the post-Cold War world. On the one hand, significant numbers of these peoples, especially in Lithuania and western Ukraine, were haunted by the history of their relationships with the Poles. On the other, despite heartfelt support of the independence of all three of its new neighbors in the east, Polish policy continued to be constrained by Warsaw's far more important relationship with Moscow.

Nowhere were these contradictory pressures and constraints more visible than in the Polish–Ukrainian relationship. Ukraine's sheer size and its drive for separation from Russia put Poland's diplomacy to its hardest test. The collapse of the Polish communist regime inspired Ukrainian nationalists with great hopes that postcommunist Poland would champion Ukrainian independence.[98] Under the leadership of Tadeusz Mazowiecki, a longtime Catholic dissident supported by Lech Wałęsa, Poland's initial moves toward its eastern neighbors were encouraging. In 1989 the *Sejm* declared that Poland had no claims on the territory of any of its eastern neighbors, a move that helped to alleviate Ukraine's lingering suspicion of Poland. Pope John Paul II and Cardinal Glemp's energetic efforts to revive the Greek Catholic Church in Belarus and Ukraine impressed many in the East.

But the initial policy of Poland's first postcommunist government was bound to disappoint its eastern neighbors. Facing imminent German unification and Chancellor Helmut Kohl's resistance to recognition of the Oder–Neisse line as Germany's eastern border, the Mazowiecki government not only refused to join Hungary and Czechoslovakia in demanding the withdrawal of Soviet troops, but actually requested their continued presence on Polish soil. This greatly circumscribed Poland's ability to conduct a policy that might offend the Kremlin. It also indicated that Poland's eastern policy

---

[97] For an excellent discussion of the traditional Polish attitude toward Ukrainian statehood, see T. Mackiw, "Problem Ukraińskiej Państwowości w Publicystyce Polskiej" [The Problem of Ukrainian Statehood in Polish Journalism], *Kultura*, May 1987, 93–9.

[98] Iwan Drach, "Nasza droga wiedzie przez Polskę," *Tygodnik Powszechny*, 10 November 1991.

would remain subordinate to its relationship with Germany, the Soviet Union, and subsequently, Russia.

In order to reconcile Poland's precarious geopolitical position with strong public support for Ukrainian aspirations, Foreign Minister Skubiszewski launched his so-called two-track policy. While Poland would continue to maintain its links with the Soviet regime, it would also expand its ties to the peoples of the western Soviet territory.[99] Poland's reluctance to offend Moscow was accompanied by uncertainty over how deep the aspirations for full independence ran in either Belarus or Ukraine. The communist governments in those two republics continued to take evasive positions on this issue, and Ukrainians and Belarussians voted in favor of Gorbachev's March 1991 referendum on preserving a "reformed union" in convincing majorities – 70 percent in Ukraine. Poland's political elite was also split over whether the break-up of the Soviet Union would serve Polish interests. Some groups considered an independent Ukraine a guarantor of genuine Polish sovereignty, while others foresaw a potential threat to Poland's security.[100]

Nevertheless, Poland was the first country to recognize Kiev's independence. Polish analysts initially envisioned that their country would serve as a "bridge" between Ukraine and Europe, but many Ukrainian nationalists saw Poland as an escape hatch from Russian domination.[101] Because of these subtle but important differences, the relationship failed to develop beyond broad declarations of principle. Poland and Ukraine signed several economic protocols and an agreement on joint defense purchases. They also agreed to establish a "Euro-region" along their mutual frontier and a consultative body at the presidential level. But even after Ukrainian independence, geopolitical realities forced Warsaw to adhere to its two-track policy.

Russia was not the only influence on Polish–Ukrainian relations. Despite the lack of any major divisive issue and the existence of a strong symbiotic relationship between the two peoples, ethnonationalist history continued to influence Polish–Ukrainian relations. The re-emergence of the Ukrainian Greek Catholic Church (Uniate) produced several clashes with Poland's Roman Catholic Church over property. The confrontation was especially bitter in the dispute over

---

[99] See Anna Swidlicka, "Senate Calls for Changes in Eastern Policy," *RFE/RL Report on Eastern Europe*, no. 39, 28 September 1990.
[100] Burant, "International Relations," 395–418.
[101] See Wojciech Pieciak and Andrzej Romanowski interview with Rukh leader Ivan Drach, "Nasza droga wiedzie przez Polskę," *Tygodnik Powszechny*, 13 October 1993.

the Carmelite Cathedral of Saint Theresa in Przemyśl, a site that had originally belonged to the Greek Catholic Church. Some Polish nationalists found it offensive that the Ukrainian State Independence Organization, a self-proclaimed successor to the interwar, fascist-oriented Organization of Ukrainian Nationalists, would lay claim to territories currently part of Poland.[102]

Despite overwhelming support in Poland for the Polish–Ukrainian accord, which officially recognized the present Polish–Ukrainian border, some splinter irredentist groups continued to question the current arrangement, thereby keeping old fears and distrust alive. The Polish Society of Friends of Lwów challenged President Wałęsa's right to give up Poland's claim to Lwów (Lviv). In an open letter to President Wałęsa, the president of the society wrote: "You are the first politician in our thousand-year-old history who as head of state officially abandoned claims by the Polish nation to parts of the Father-land and to 'the most Faithful City' without consultation with the nation and against the *raison d'être*."[103] The speaker of the Ukrainian parliament further aggravated the situation when, during Prime Minister Suchocka's visit to Ukraine in January 1993, he insisted on additional information about Operation Wisła, yet refused to address "ethnic cleansing" by Ukrainian nationalists in Galicia and Volhynia during World War II.[104] Ukraine's position on this issue prompted Poland's Christian-National Union to demand that Poland freeze its relations with Ukraine until Kiev revealed all the data about the massacre of the Poles in Volhynia and formally apologized for the incident.[105]

Contemporary issues also hindered the development of Ukrainian–Polish relations. Ukraine's maintenance of a 400,000-man army and the ambiguity of its position on nuclear weapons further alarmed the Polish population. In a public opinion poll conducted in Poland in June 1992, 53 percent of respondents considered Ukraine the greatest threat to Poland.[106] It appears that Poland's relationship with Ukraine is affected to a large degree by the very different collective memories

---

[102] See Janusz Bugajski, *Nations in Turmoil: Conflict and Cooperation in Eastern Europe* (Boulder, CO: Westview Press, 1993), 43.
[103] J. Kresowiakow, "Nie można przemilczać zbroni nacjonalistów Ukraińskich," *Słowo Powszechny,* 17 December 1992.
[104] Radio Warsaw, 25 January 1993.
[105] *Gazeta Wyborcza*, 10 January 1994.
[106] PAP, 20 June 1992. A similar poll carried out by the US-based D-3 organization in June 1992 noted that 34 percent of Poles felt that Ukraine was most threatening, 13 percent Russia, and 11 percent Germany (Radio Warsaw, June 1992).

of Polish society. While the Polish elite sees the disintegration of the Soviet Union as an opportunity to re-establish a cultural Commonwealth and to replace Russia as the cultural center of the region, the general public sees only the region's bloody twentieth-century history. Despite two years of good neighborliness between Poland and Ukraine, in a poll conducted by the prestigious Center for Public Opinion Studies in September 1993, 65 percent of Poles responding expressed antipathy toward the Ukrainians.[107] Paradoxically, in Ukraine, Poland is one of the most admired countries.

But Ukrainians resent the activities of Polish right-wing organizations that have irredentist agendas in the East. Both the Kiev and Moscow patriarchates of Ukraine's Orthodox Church were angered by what they perceived as Polish Cardinal Glemp's missionary zeal in Byzantine lands. As a result, Moscow's Patriarch Aleksei II and Cardinal Glemp exchanged bitter words, and the papal nuncio to Ukraine, Archbishop Antonio Franco, was forced to issue an official renunciation of any ambition to convert Orthodox Christians to Roman Catholicism.[108] By the summer of 1992, the Orthodox Church and the Vatican were seeking improved relations, and Cardinal Glemp made a reconciliatory trip to Moscow. Nevertheless, both sides agreed that under the circumstances, it would be inappropriate for the Polish pope to visit the CIS.[109]

Relations between the Greek Catholic Church of Ukraine and the Vatican have also deteriorated as a result both of Vatican policies and those of the Polish Catholic Church. The 1991 decision of the council of the Ukrainian Greek Catholic Church to return to the ritualistic style of the 1720s (the high point of Latinization of that Church resulting from the synod of Zamość) was perceived by many Ukrainians as an effort by the Polish pope to Latinize and hence Polonize the Church. Tensions were further heightened by Pope John Paul II's instruction to Lviv's Metropolitan Sterniuk forbidding the ordination of married priests, even for service in his own archeparchy, an order that, if carried out, would lead to a sharp decline in the number of young Ukrainian priests, thereby forcing greater reliance on Polish Latin priests. In addition, some Ukrainian Greek Catholics, abiding by an understanding with the Russian Orthodox Church proscribing the expansion of the Greek Catholic Church outside of western Ukraine, responded with dismay to the Vatican's decision to create a Latin

[107] PAP, "Poles Do Not Like Their Neighbors," 8 September 1993.
[108] Interfax (Moscow), 1 November 1992.
[109] *La Stampa*, 4 March 1992.

Catholic bishopric in Kiev. All of these actions were perceived by Ukrainians as Polish cultural irredentism.

In fact, the question of Polish cultural presence in the *kresy* is far more contentious than generally assumed. Even publications such as *Kultura* and *Tygodnik Powszechny*, which have consistently called for a reconciliation with Ukraine on the basis of the current border between the two countries, have made this reconciliation conditional on guarantees of minority rights to ethnic Poles in the eastern border states and on strong cultural links with Poland. Both the Catholic Church and the Polonia Society have spent substantial resources to revive Poland's cultural presence east of its borders. Although the Ukrainian government has pursued an admirably enlightened policy toward its minorities, it has been unable to allay concerns in western Ukraine that Poland's cultural activism could lay the foundation for a political presence. Resentment and fear remained so strong that Prime Minster Suchocka was forced to cancel a planned meeting with representatives of the Polish community in Lviv.

Although Polish and Ukrainian intellectuals have developed a high level of mutual sympathy and admiration, these sentiments are not shared by the general populations of their countries. Opinion polls in Poland, and to a lesser degree in Ukraine, continue to reveal unease concerning the reconciliation, making it politically difficult to sustain good relations. Although more sympathetic than the general public, the Polish political elite is also ambivalent about the nature of relations with Ukraine. One segment of the elite, including former Defense Minister, Jan Parys; Leszek Moczulski, leader of the KNP;[110] and, to a lesser extent, former President Lech Wałęsa, believes that the only viable economic and security structure for the region is what Moczulski called *Międzymorze* (between the sea), a bloc of countries between the Baltic and Black seas,[111] combined with a Polish–Ukrainian alliance to "save European civilization from Russia. . ."[112] At the other extreme is the position articulated by Tomasz Gabis and Zdzisław Winnicki of the rightist Union of Polish Realpolitik (UPR)

---

[110] See Leszek Moczulski, *U progu niepodległości* [On the Threshold of Independence] (Lublin: EMBE Press, 1990).

[111] It should be stressed that the concepts of President Wałęsa and those of Moczulski are by no means identical. President Wałęsa sees a Central European alliance between the Visegrad group, or "NATO-bis," as a means to bring Poland into the West. Moczulski's KPN, with a strong similarity to the pre-World War II Endecja, is highly nationalistic and sees a Polish–Ukrainian bloc as an anti-Western as well as anti-Russian third force.

[112] PAP, 29 April 1992.

that Russia is Poland's natural ally and that the existence of an independent Ukraine only serves sinister German interests while compromising the interests of the Polish minority in the east.[113] The views of mainstream political elites tend to fall between these two positions.

Although the principal factor inhibiting Poland's commitment to Ukraine and, to a lesser extent, to Belarus is the unease generated by the history of its relations with these eastern neighbors, Polish policy toward them is also directly influenced by the impact it may have on relations with Russia and on Poland's desire to improve its relations with the West. The Poles do not want to be caught in the quarrel between Russia and Ukraine. Foreign Minister Krzysztof Skubiszewski, in an interview in *Polityka*, bluntly stated: "Russia has remained a major power, despite its current limitations and problems, and it is going to reinforce this position . . . Poland does not want to side with either party in the Russo-Ukrainian conflict."[114] During Leonid Kravchuk's presidency, Ukraine proclaimed itself Europe's bastion against "Asiatic" Russia, a position that conflicts with Poland's views on Russia's role in Europe. Many Poles fear that a complete Russian disengagement from Europe could lead to a German-centered configuration. Poland's adamant opposition to any change in the status of the Kaliningrad district is a measure of the level of their concern. Another factor inhibiting closer Polish–Ukrainian security ties is the anxiety voiced repeatedly by Polish officials and academics that a Polish–Ukrainian military alliance, based on a combined population of over 80 million and possibly including nuclear weapons, would be perceived by both Russia and Germany as a security threat. Such a threat could lead to a rebirth of the Russo-German axis – the ultimate nightmare of Polish policy makers. During an explanation of the guiding principles of Polish foreign policy in the *Sejm*, Skubiszewski asserted that Poland's first priority is to avoid a repetition of the Molotov–Ribbentrop pact.[115]

Poland's policy toward Ukraine and Belarus is also constrained by its declared policy of returning to the West. Although Polish officials continue to insist that their country has a historic right to be admitted into the EU and NATO, they realize that the ultimate criteria for admission will be the degree to which Poland reforms its economy and presents itself as a stable European state. Ukraine's faltering

[113] PAP, 14 September 1993.
[114] *Polityka*, 17 October 1993.        [115] PAP, 18 November 1992.

economic reforms, its contentious relations with Russia, and the international controversy surrounding its nuclear weapons have made Poland reluctant to seek closer ties. Although some Polish analysts initially believed that their country could help Europeanize its eastern neighbors, political developments in the former Soviet Union have shown that any involvement with the new border states could compromise Poland's fundamental interests.

Finally, there is a strong economic factor limiting Poland's level of engagement with the states on its eastern border. Despite chronic political instability, successive Polish governments have consistently sought to redirect Polish trade from East to West. By 1992 over 70 percent of Poland's trade was with the West, and many believed that trade with the East could only retard Polish modernization. In recent years, though, trade with Russia and Belarus has revived, with Russia supplying Poland with energy and minerals in exchange for food and consumer goods, thereby providing welcome relief for Poland's non-competitive industries and agriculture. Official Ukrainian trade with Poland has stagnated, but hundreds of thousands of Ukrainians are working in Poland and many more are involved in barter and "informal" trade. Thus the level of economic exchange between these countries is probably far greater than official figures indicate.

Poland must strike a balance between supporting the sovereignty and independence of Ukraine and Belarus and maintaining good relations with Russia and the West. But Ukraine and, to a lesser degree, Belarus consider Poland a vital partner in extricating themselves from Russian domination. For Ukraine, Poland is the natural gateway to integration into Europe and differentiation from Russia. Upon gaining independence in 1992, Ukraine immediately sought to establish a close relationship with Poland as a means of freeing itself from client status *vis-à-vis* Moscow and anchoring itself in the international system. While in Warsaw on one of his first trips outside the CIS, President Leonid Kravchuk declared: "The degree of cooperation with Poland will be higher than with any other country of the CIS, including Russia."[116]

But the Polish response was lukewarm. Poland, which was still negotiating the terms of Russian troop withdrawals while striving for integration into the West, showed little interest in moving Polish–Ukrainian relations beyond symbolic gestures. Two days after Kravchuk's departure, President Wałęsa traveled to Moscow, where he

---

[116] *Życie Warszawy*, 20 May 1992.

declared that he "would like Poland and Russia to be the pillars of Eastern Europe. Poland is ready for this and wants it, but it takes two to tango."[117] To the dismay of the Ukrainians, Wałęsa failed to include Ukraine in that configuration. Poland continued its policy of accommodating Moscow at the expense of Ukrainian interests by offering to build a natural gas pipeline from Russia to Germany across Belarus and Poland, bypassing the "capricious" states of Ukraine and Lithuania.[118] In response, Prime Minister Leonid Kuchma accused Poland of conducting an anti-Ukrainian policy,[119] reminding Ukrainians of the treaties of Andrusovo (1667) and Riga (1921), two occasions when Poland, confronted with Russian might, opted to accommodate Moscow at the expense of Kiev.

During the first year of Ukraine's independence, officials in the Polish foreign ministry did advocate that Poland remain aloof from Ukraine. They feared that an open alliance with the Ukrainians could jeopardize relations with Moscow, particularly the negotiations on the withdrawal of its troops from Poland. Polish politicians recognized that trade with Russia was far more important than trade with Ukraine, and they were also concerned that over-identification with Ukraine would compromise Poland's efforts to join the West.

As mentioned previously, former Defense Minister Jan Parys and KPN leader Leszek Moczulski advocated a regional economic and security arrangement based on what Moczulski has described as *Międzymorze* – a bloc of countries between the Baltic and Black seas. Ex-President Wałęsa supported this notion with some reservations. Whereas Moczulski saw an alignment of Poland, Ukraine, Belarus, the Baltic states, Hungary, the Czech Republic, and Slovakia as an effort to create a "third force" in Europe between Russia and NATO, Wałęsa saw this kind of alignment as a "halfway house" that would enhance these countries' prospects of entering NATO. This proposition received enthusiastic support from Ukrainian President Kravchuk and Deputy Foreign Minister Borys Tarasiuk and some qualified support from Prime Minister Jozsef Antall of Hungary.

Yet, despite the support of some political leaders in Poland, Ukraine, and Hungary, the idea of a regional defense alignment in Central Europe encountered fierce resistance. The United States, concerned that this kind of an alignment would be construed by

[117] PAP, 22 May 1992.
[118] See Jan de Weydenthal, "The Troubled Polish–Russian Economic Relationship," *RFE/RL Research Report*, 5 March 1993.
[119] See Rustam Narzikulov, "An Anti-Ukrainian Policy," *Segodnia*, 3 September 1993.

Moscow as an attempt to isolate Russia from the European main-stream, openly discouraged the idea.[120] The Polish foreign and defense ministries were also resistant to the notion of a Black Sea–Baltic alliance, fearing that it would not only ruin Polish prospects for NATO membership by alienating Russia, but actually condemn Poland to once again inhabiting a "gray zone" between Russia and the West. Former Polish Defense Minister Janusz Onyszkiewicz summed up the situation, observing: "A Poland at odds with Russia will not be an attractive partner for NATO."[121]

Although Warsaw is concerned that Ukraine may feel increasingly isolated and either turn inward or follow the Belarussian lead back to the Russian fold, it is willing to ease Ukrainian entry into the international mainstream only to the extent that this effort does not complicate its links with either Russia or the EU. The Russians, in turn, are increasingly taking advantage of this divergence between Polish and Ukrainian interests. Boris Yeltsin's August 1993 declaration that Russia would no longer stand in the way of NATO membership for Poland was an example of this type of manipulation. The state-ment produced a flurry of activity in Warsaw. Polish officials scurried to accelerate entry into NATO while simultaneously distancing them-selves even further from Ukraine.[122] There is also credible evidence that in exchange for Russia's decision to build a natural gas pipeline across Poland – the so-called deal of the century – Poland has agreed to lessen its support for Ukraine and Belarus. According to *Rossiiskaia Gazeta*, there was even talk of a Russian–Polish pact to contain Ukraine.[123] At a September summit meeting, Boris Yeltsin extracted a promise from President Kravchuk to "sell" Ukraine's share of the Black Sea Fleet and to turn all of its nuclear warheads over to Russia. Although most Ukrainian commentators would concede that Krav-chuk's negotiating position was severely weakened by his country's poor economic performance, the lack of diplomatic support from the outside, particularly from Poland, also contributed greatly to under-mining Ukraine's position *vis-à-vis* Russia.

Poland itself is coming to terms with the reality that despite its long-held belief that it has a right to be part of the West, one result of

---

[120] See *Gazeta Wyborcza*, 25 May 1993.
[121] *Życie Warszawy*, 25 May 1993.
[122] When Premier Suchocka stated that Ukraine was a priority of Poland during a lecture in Lublin (PAP, 18 August 1993), Foreign Minister Skubiszewski "corrected" the prime minister noting that one cannot address Ukraine without dealing with Russia's interests. *Gazeta Wyborcza*, 1 September 1993.
[123] *Gazeta Wyborcza*, "Poland–Russia–Ukraine," 3 March 1994.

the end of the Cold War has been the collapse of the West as a coherent entity.[124] As a result, Poland once again finds itself on the fault line of Europe. Its leaders acknowledge that Poland will not be able to become a normal country without a permanent reconciliation with Ukraine. They also recognize that an independent Ukraine would help to guarantee Polish sovereignty by inhibiting the reconstitution of a Russian-dominated empire.

Leonid Kuchma's election to the Ukrainian presidency eased the conditions for an improvement in Polish–Ukrainian relations, as did Kiev's decision to rid itself of its nuclear weapons and to introduce a modicum of economic reform. Although the relationship between Ukraine and Russia remained difficult, President Kuchma managed to lower the level of tension and acrimony that typified the Kravchuk era. The United States, which had all but ignored Ukraine, steadily improved its relations with Kiev, thereby changing Ukraine's status in the international system, particularly with respect to Poland. Whereas in the past the Polish drive toward NATO membership had all but ignored Ukraine's concerns, following the US–Ukrainian rapprochement, analysts in Warsaw recognized that Poland would have to secure some degree of Ukrainian support for NATO expansion.

Poland's need to secure Kiev's cooperation regarding the NATO issue resulted in an exchange of visits between Kwaśniewski and Kuchma, deepening military cooperation, and Poland's invitation to Ukraine to participate in both the Weimar Triangle deliberations and a summit of Central European leaders. But Polish Foreign Minister Dariusz Rosati's proposal to form an eastern "Brest Triangle" with Ukraine and Belarus met with fierce resistance from former Foreign Minister Skubiszewski and much of the Polish foreign policy establishment, who feared that excessive preoccupation with the East would distance Poland from the West, thereby hindering Warsaw's aspirations to join NATO and other Western institutions.[125]

Although the acceptance of a narrower definition of Polishness did end the historic feud between Poland and Ukraine, their relationship did not deepen and mature in a manner parallel to Poland's relationship with its Višegrad partners – Hungary, the Czech Republic, and Slovakia. In concert with the other members of the Višegrad group, Poland resisted the Kvitsinskii Doctrine, a strategy for resisting Soviet efforts to limit its sovereignty following the troop withdrawals. The

---

[124] See Owen Harries, "The Collapse of the West," *Foreign Affairs* (September/October 1993).
[125] Andrzej Romanowski, *Tygodnik Powszechny*, no. 36, 8 September 1996.

Poles subsequently received support from the countries of the former Czechoslovakia when a dispute arose between Warsaw and Moscow over transit rights for Soviet troops departing Germany. The four central European states have also maintained a modicum of coherence in their common approach to the EU and NATO.

By contrast, the relationship with Ukraine, although high on symbolic gestures and expressions of goodwill, has largely lacked substance. Describing Polish–Ukrainian relations in August 1996, former Solidarity KOR advisor to and parliamentarian Bronisław Geremek lamented:

> We [Poland] have not done enough, primarily because we failed to translate into practice the explicitly articulated objectives which spoke of "strategic" cooperation between Poland and Ukraine. There were gestures and there were meetings, but the concept of "strategic partnership" was never fulfilled with substance . . . Unfortunately, some political communities persist in cultivating fears that contacts with Ukraine might damage our standing with Russia.[126]

In a sense, Poland's Eastern policy has come full circle, from a limited two-track policy in the waning days of the Soviet Union, to a short-lived embrace of Ukraine as a possible ally in enhancing Polish integration into the West and lifting the shadow of the Russian giant, and finally to another circumscribed policy conditioned by Ukraine's faltering reforms and Russia's growing assertiveness.

### Relations with Lithuania

Although Lithuania does not cast as long a shadow on Poland as either Russia or Germany, relations with that small country have nevertheless had a profound impact on Poland's national consciousness and self-definition. The two countries were part of the same state for nearly 400 years, an experience which left very different imprints on the collective memories of Poles and Lithuanians. To the Poles, the "Commonwealth of Two Nations" is the high point of their history, a period when Poland was among the largest states in Europe, prosperous and setting standards for democracy and tolerance. Many of Poland's interwar political leaders, including Józef Piłsudski, came from Lithuania, and successive generations of Poland's leading men of letters have considered Lithuania an integral part of the Polish national heritage and a source of inspiration. In his epic *Pan Tadeusz*, Adam

---

[126] Interview with Bronisław Geremek, *Życie Warszawy*, no. 185, 8 August 1996, p. 1.

Mickiewicz, Poland's national poet, encapsulates the Poles' attachment to Lithuania with the words *Litwo! Ojczyzno moja* (Lithuania! My Fatherland). This nostalgia for Lithuania continued well into the twentieth century. In a fictionalized autobiography, Tadeusz Konwicki, who is Lithuanian-born and one of Poland's most influential contemporary authors, describes Lithuania as the cradle of what made Poland a reality.[127] Similarly, Czesław Miłosz, in his evocative *Search for a Fatherland*, sees Lithuania, with its mélange of peoples, languages, and cultures, as a magnificent monument to the Commonwealth.[128]

By contrast, the Lithuanian collective memory of the Polish–Lithuanian Commonwealth (*Rzeczpospolita Obojga Narodów*) focuses on the fact that it resulted in the Polonization of Lithuania's nobility and the cultural deprivation of the country. Whereas Poland, searching for a "usable past," sees the Commonwealth as a means of reasserting its role in European civilization, Lithuania, anxious to develop a distinct identity, is keen to obliterate all remnants of that relationship.[129] Thus, while Polish intellectuals stress the common history of the two nations, Lithuanian intellectuals continue to distance their country from Poland as a means of bolstering their national identity. Lithuania is also haunted by the memory of the forced annexation of Vilnius led by Poland's General Lucjan Żeligowski in 1920, as well as by the 1938 Polish ultimatum forcing Lithuania to recognize Polish sovereignty over its historic capital.

When Lithuania took its first bold steps toward independence, the Polish public reacted enthusiastically. The Polish government, anxious to avoid provoking the Kremlin, pursued a cautious policy, but Polish parliamentarians and other public figures did travel to Vilnius to offer moral support to the defiant Lithuanians. When Lithuania declared itself independent in March 1990, both chambers of the Polish parliament passed resolutions endorsing its right to self-determination.[130]

Despite the sincere Polish enthusiasm for Lithuania's independence struggle, the burden of their shared history has continued to frustrate efforts to establish normal relations between the two countries. The relationship between Warsaw and Vilnius has been inhibited by Poland's concern for the cultural rights of the approximately 250,000 Poles who live in Lithuania. This minority took a far dimmer view of

---

[127] Tadeusz Konwicki, *Bohin Manor* (London: Faber, 1992).
[128] Czesław Miłosz, *Szukanie ojczyzny* (Kraków: Znak, 1992).
[129] See Stephen R. Burant, "Polish–Lithuanian Relations: Past, Present and Future," *Problems of Communism* (May–June 1991).
[130] PAP, 22 March 1990.

the rise of Lithuanian nationalism than the Poles themselves. They responded by demanding autonomy within Lithuania, and some actually supported the attempted coup in Moscow in August 1991.[131] Poland's visionaries once assumed that if Poland abandoned all claims to the territory of its eastern neighbors, these states would tolerate and indeed encourage the cultural rights of their Polish minorities. However, activities that the Poles consider a normal exercise of cultural affinity toward people of the same ethnic stock across a political border were perceived by the Lithuanians as a harbinger of irredentist cultural expansion that could lead to territorial claims.

Initial attempts to improve relations between the two countries were derailed by historical legacies. Poland refused to make a public acknowledgment of its 1920 aggression and recognize the legal status of interwar Vilnius as a Lithuanian city. Lithuania resented the implication that Vilnius had become a Lithuanian city merely as a result of the odious Molotov–Ribbentrop Pact and the consequent "ethnic cleansing" by Hitler and Stalin. The burden of their difficult historic relationship was further manifested when the Lithuanian government refused to register the social club of the veterans of the Polish resistance to Nazi occupation, the "Home Army" (*Armja Krajowa*), alleging that the Polish partisans were an anti-state organization because they fought for Polish independence and thus opposed Lithuanian territorial integrity. Poland met this challenge by accusing the Lithuanians of collaborating with the Nazis during World War II.

In January 1992, the foreign ministers of the two countries, Krzysztof Skubiszewski and Algirdas Saudargas, issued a joint communiqué confirming a commitment to the existing borders between Poland and Lithuania and adherence to European standards of minority rights. But the issues dividing the two countries were far from resolved. Poland's demand for a Polish–language university in Lithuania provoked the chairman of the Lithuanian Supreme Council, Vytautas Landsbergis, to accuse the Poles of being "nationalist and expansionist."[132] Other Lithuanian officials claimed that there were no Poles in Lithuania, only Polonized Lithuanians. Warsaw's decision to redeploy some of its troops from western Poland to the east, and the statement by Polish ambassador Jan Widacki that "the Poles in Lithuania never left Poland, but rather Poland left this place,"

---

[131] Tim Snyder, "National Myth and International Relations: Poland and Lithuania," *East European Politics and Society* 9: 2 (Spring 1995), 317–43.
[132] TASS, 25 September 1991.

triggered indignant accusations in Vilnius that Poland was engaging in an irredentist campaign against Lithuania. The election of former communists in both Poland and Lithuania, together with a joint perception of a growing Russian threat, finally enabled both countries to sign a treaty of "good neighborliness" in April 1994. Although it took three long years for the two countries to overcome their historic legacies, Poland and Lithuania have evolved into partners providing mutual support in the face of Russian demands for passage rights to Kaliningrad, and Poland has started to advocate Lithuanian membership in NATO.

### Place and reorientation

Poland's self-redefinition, which was imposed partly by the post-World War II settlement and more substantially through a long and painful debate starting with the émigré publication *Kultura* and carried on in Poland itself in earnest beginning in the mid-1950s, resulted in a fundamental reorientation of its place in the world. The last vestiges of both an imperial mission in the east and a great power role within the European concert were permanently abandoned in favor of the concept of a mid-sized European state, which can only ensure its sovereignty and advance its interests through continuous accommodation with its immediate neighbors and concerted efforts to rejoin the European mainstream. Unlike their Romantic forebears who believed that Poland must enlighten Europe, today's Poles are eager students of Europe's mores and structures, seeking their identity in a commonality with Europe.

The emergence of a democratic "European Germany" on Poland's western rim and the demise of the Bolshevik empire to the east has granted Poland what is possibly its best geopolitical situation in centuries. Poland is no longer "the valley between the mountains," but increasingly part of a democratic continuum. When the Poles regained their autonomy after more than 100 years of partition and the Second Republic was formed, British Prime Minister David Lloyd-George observed that they were "drunk with the new wine of liberty."[133] By contrast, the Third Polish Republic, grounded in Poland's "Piast" legacy, is no longer eager to civilize the Ukrainians and Belorussians, no longer interested in foisting a Commonwealth on the Lithuanians, no longer perceiving itself as a rampart of "Western

---

[133] Jan Zaprudnik, *Belarus: At a Crossroads in History* (Boulder, CO: Westview, 1993), 82.

civilization" confronting Russia, and no longer viewing itself as an "apostle among the adulterers" in its dealings with Western Europe. The new Poland has finally managed to put to rest five centuries of Promethean delusion and to build a national polity with a sober diplomacy reflecting its new identity as a European nation-state.

# 5    Russia's national identity and the accursed question: a strong state and a weak society

The Russian people is not a people; it is a humanity.

Konstatin Aksakov

Before Peter the Great Russia was merely a people (*narod*); she became a nation (*natsiya*) thanks to the changes initiated by the reformer.

Visarion Belinskii

Our Fatherland is suffering, not from the incursion of a score of foreign tongues, but from our own acts, in that, in addition to the lawful administration, there has grown up a second administration possessed of infinitely greater powers than the system established by law.

Nikolai Gogol, *Dead Souls*

At first glance, the development of national identity in Russia and Poland appears to run along parallel lines. Both peoples converted to Christianity in the second half of the tenth century; the church helped to shape each country's national identity; for a long time both the Poles and the Russians saw themselves as bastions of Christendom, defending European civilization from Asiatic hoards; they have both felt at one time or another unappreciated by the West Europeans; and until recently the Poles and the Russians tended to characterize themselves as "civilizations" rather than narrow ethnic polities.

Despite these similarities, a tremendous gulf divides these two Slavic nations. For example, the founders of the Polish state embraced the Roman Catholicism of Western Europe, whereas the rulers of Kievan Rus adopted Orthodox Christianity from the Byzantine empire. The Asiatic hordes from which the Russians protected Europe were the Mongols, while the Asiatic hordes from which the Poles protected Europe were the Russians. More importantly, Poland's aristocratic democracy and civic institutions – supported by the *szlachta*, the politically relevant class – shaped the Polish tradition of a strong society and weak state. In Russia, on the other hand, the state

153

shaped the Russian autocracy from above and served as the midwife of all institutions, including serfdom.[1] Mikhail Pogodin (1800–73), a Slavophile and apologist for Russian autocracy, claimed that the state, not the people, would lead Russia to universal glory.[2] Although Poland and Russia both succumbed to the temptation of empire building, imperialism produced radically divergent results in each country. Poland's eastward expansion created a land-owning elite whose power grew at the expense of the central government in Warsaw. In Russia, an almost perpetual state of war from Ivan the Terrible to Nicholas II strengthened the autocratic center, leading the Russian historian Vasilii Kliuchevskii to lament that whereas the Russian state expanded, the Russian peoples shrank.

The notion of a Polish civilization transcending ethnic identity began to recede in the late nineteenth century. The dismemberment of the Polish Commonwealth at the end of the eighteenth century and the disastrous uprisings against the partitioning powers during the nineteenth century produced the positivist school of Polish thought and a reconsideration of empire. Despite the messianic tendencies in Polish intellectual history, Poles continued to view their country as a component of a larger entity, namely Roman Catholicism. Not until the 1960s, almost a century later than in Poland, did a similar process occur in Russia when Russian nativists and nationalists began to question the burdens of empire on Russia and attempted to devise a paradigm with Russia's distinct needs and interests as its center. Until then, Russian intellectuals, whether nationalist Slavophiles or liberal Westernizers, believed in the permanence of the imperial structure. The émigré historian George Fedotov, in one of the early critiques of the Russian imperialist mentality, lamented, "From the humanitarian and liberal point of view, the intellectuals condemned the Russian empire, as well as all other empires, as representing the subjugation of nations by force. The result of this subjugation was nevertheless accepted as unquestionable."[3] Russians viewed their civilization as distinct from and contrary to European culture.

One of the enduring paradoxes of the Russian historic experience is that while the Russian people have a strong belief in a Russian civilization and a clear association of the concept of that civilization with the concept of empire, when it comes to a distinct Russian

---

[1] See Boris N. Chicherin, *Oblastnye uchrezhdenii a v rossii XVIII veka* (Moscow, 1856).
[2] See Andrzej Walicki, *The Slavophile Controversy* (Oxford: Oxford University Press, 1975).
[3] George Fedotov, "The Fate of Empires," *Russian Review* 12: 2 (1953), 84.

national identity, the notion of "Russianness" becomes vague and uncertain. Although debates over Russia's national identity and interests have raged since the eighteenth century, the ideal of Russia as a superior civilization and a transcendent empire with a universal mission has remained. Indeed, a Russian national identity without this vision has yet to emerge. Were the Russians to establish such a concept of national identity, it would allow Russia to make peace with itself and the international system. Several factors have made Russia's search for a new national identity particularly problematic.

### The Russian Orthodox Church

The Russian Orthodox Church, much like the Polish Catholic Church, played a pivotal role in shaping the national identity of its people. Poland, however, by virtue of Roman Catholicism, perceived itself as a part of a broader civilization. Russian Orthodoxy, on the other hand, instilled a sense of otherness in the Russians *vis-à-vis* the rest of European civilization and created a dual sense of siege and universalism. The severing of the Russian Orthodox Church's ties with Western Christianity at the Council of Florence in 1439 and the theological innovation proclaiming Muscovy the *"Third Rome"* and last bastion of Christianity with a unique mission helped to sacrifice a distinct Russian national identity to a universalist mission cum imperialism. Although, as Edward Keenan pointed out, the doctrine of the Third Rome had little immediate impact on Russian political life, it was later utilized as justification for imperial expansion and exerted a profound influence on Russians.[4] Thus, the role of the Russian Orthodox Church within Russian society further complicated the emergence of Russia's national identity.

Although nominally a national church, the Russian Orthodox Church developed from a defensive, nativist institution to the ideological foundation of an imperial idea. In the mid seventeenth century, the priest Arsenius Sukhanov revived the ideology of the *Third Rome* following several visits to sister Byzantine churches. His motivation stemmed from the discovery of corrupting influences from Latinizing and Ottoman pressures.[5] With the expulsion of Polish rule from

---

[4] Edward L. Keenan, "On Certain Mythological Beliefs and Russian Behaviors," in *The Legacy of History in Russia and the New States of Eurasia*, ed. S. Frederick Starr (Armonk, NY: M. E. Sharpe, 1994), 19–40.

[5] James H. Billington, *The Icon and the Ax: An Interpretive History of Russian Culture* (New York: Vintage Books, 1970), 142–43.

modern Ukraine and Belarussia, the imperial vocation of the Russian Orthodox Church was further institutionalized by the import of clerics from these newly acquired territories. The arrival of these well-educated clerics in Muscovy could be justified only in an imperial and messianic context. The Belarussian priest, Simeon Polotsky, court preacher and tutor to the tsar's children, popularized the notion of Russia's imperial destiny, stressing the tsar's inevitable imperial future and destiny as victor "all over the world."[6] The Ukrainian cleric Archmandrite Gizel of the Caves Monastery in Kiev, in an officially commissioned history of Russia called *Synopsis*, overtly attributed the Russian victory over Poland to God's preference of autocracy to Poland's divided sovereignty, stating that, "'Hetmans' and 'senators' led Poland 'from tsardom to princedom, and from princedom to voevodism,' but the Tsar of Muscovy has now delivered 'the mother of Russian cities' from its bondage to Catholic Poland, and emerged as the 'strongest of monarchs.' The true Christian empire has thus returned to the East since the fall of Byzantium."[7] As James Billington observed, the graduates of the Kiev-Mohyla Academy in Kiev (Peter Mohyla himself being a Moldovan) energized the Muscovite church with a new anti-Catholic and anti-Lutheran zeal. These transplanted Ukrainian scholars introduced the entire genre of polemics into Russian writings. Among these Ukrainian clerics and courtiers were G. Skibinskii, Stepan Yavorskii, Dmitrii Tuptalo, and Theofan Prokopovich.[8] Prokopovich, both rector and alumnus of the Kiev-Mohyla Academy, had spent several years as a student of theology in Rome. In his capacity as the archbishop in the court of Peter I, Prokopovich upheld the notion of Russia's imperial and universalist vocation, even coining the term *Rossianin* (as opposed to *Russkii*) and thus creating a supranational imperial identity, as distinct from an ethnic identity.

Nikolai Berdaiev, in *The Russian Idea*, criticized this linking of the Church with imperialism, observing, "The whole idea of Moscow as the Third Rome contributed indeed to the power and the might of the Moscow State and to the autocracy of the Tsar, but not to the well-being of the Church and not to the growth of spiritual life. *The vocation of the Russian people was distorted and despoiled*."[9] By injecting into the Church a foreign cultural influence and reducing it to a supranational

---

[6] Ibid., 146.    [7] Ibid.

[8] See *Kratkaia literaturnaia entsiklopediia* (Moscow: Sovetskaia Entsiklopediia, 1972), 768.

[9] Nikolai Berdaiev, *The Russian Idea* (New York: Lindisfarne Press, 1992), 28 (emphasis added).

imperial institution, Tsars Aleksei and Peter created an enduring rift between the populace and the Church. This rift manifested itself in a variety of ways. Despite Mohyla's scorn for the traditional Russian superstition of indulgence toward the possessed "holy-simpleton," the tradition of admiration of the "*Urodivyii*" persisted. The Old Believers, that minority who despite terrible persecution resisted the Westernization of the Russian Church and remained true to the traditional Church, captured the Russia of later Russian authors and artists as an enduring symbol of righteousness and dignity. The image of the Old Believer as a symbol of integrity, dignity, and authenticity is immortalized in Dostoyevsky's novella *Notes from the House of the Dead*. In contrast, the official Church is often treated by Russian writers and painters with a derision reserved for state institutions. V. G. Perov's famous painting *Monastyrskaia Trapeza* (Monastery's Refectory), depicting Orthodox monks as obese drunkards oblivious to hunger and poverty, typified the prevailing perception among many Russian intellectuals of the Church. This disdain arose mainly as a consequence of the successful "recruitment" of the church by the state as an imperial institution, which denuded it of its national role.

### The annexation of Ukraine and the institutionalization of the empire

Russia became an empire in 1552–56, when Ivan IV ("the Terrible") captured the Tatar cities of Kazan and Astrakhan, incorporating for the first time large numbers of people who were neither Orthodox nor Russian-speaking. The early imperial expansion resulted in Russia acquiring an imperial identity before it developed a national individuality. However, it was the incorporation of Ukraine following the Pereiaslav Accords (1654) that fused Russia's national identity with an imperial identity, where the entire legitimization of the Russian state rested on the possession of the western borderlands.

The ongoing debate over the origins of the Russian state also contributes to Russia's difficulties in delineating a post-imperial national identity. Ukraine played but a minor role in Muscovy's consciousness and politics until the seventeenth century.[10] The great Russian historians, such as Nikolai Karamzin, Sergei Solovyev, Vasilii Kliuchevskii, and George Vernadsky,[11] have taken the position that

---

[10] Keenan, "On Certain Mythical Beliefs."
[11] See Vasilii O. Kluchevskii, *Kurs Russkoi Istorii*, vol. II (Moscow: Mysl', 1988); Sergei M.

Vladimir-Suzdal, and later Muscovy, were the true dynastic and cultural successors to Kievan Rus. Thus, possession of Ukraine, the heart of the lands of Rus, became a vital ingredient in legitimizing the Russian empire. To sustain this national myth, Russian historians have consistently denied the existence of a separate Ukrainian national identity, claiming instead that the inhabitants of what is present-day Ukraine were actually Russians. That Kiev, conquered first by the Mongols, then by the Lithuanians, and finally by the Poles, could not reassert itself provided Moscow with further justification for its claim as successor to Rus. As Charles Halperin concluded, "The city of Kiev that now existed in the fourteenth and fifteenth centuries had no claim upon the Kievan inheritance, which no longer resided in Kiev, but in Moscow."[12] The people of the western borderlands, the "Little Russians," had no distinct identity of their own, according to most Russian historians. To the Russian elite, Ukrainian culture was little more than a Polonized version of an original "Russian Culture," caused by centuries of Polish domination over the Russian borderlands.

Nineteenth-century Ukrainian historians, led by Mykhailo Hrushevskyi, claimed that the true successor to Kievan Rus was Galicia-Volhynia. In their view, Muscovy was a product of a different civilization altogether.[13] Extremist interpreters of Russian historiography, such as Pogodin, countered by arguing that modern Ukrainians had absolutely no relationship to the inhabitants of Kievan Rus, since the original inhabitants had ostensibly migrated to Russia after the fall of Kiev in 1240. Not to be outdone, some Ukrainians seized upon a theory put forth by the Polish ethnographer Franciszek Duchiński, who posited that the Russians were not a Slavic people at all, but rather a Finno-Ugric people whose sole relationship to Kievan Rus was limited to a family dynasty. Today, while few Russians go as far as Pogodin, many argue that Ukraine, Belarussia, and Russia are the same people with distinct linguistic characteristics, which developed as a result of the Mongol and Polish occupations, and therefore equal heirs to the Kievan legacy, but since Russia alone retained throughout

---

Solovyev, *Istoriia Rossii s drevneishikh vremen*, vol. VII (Moscow: Mysil, 1960); George Vernadsky, *A History of Russia* (New Haven: Yale University Press, 1961).

[12] Charles J. Halperin, "Kiev and Moscow: An Aspect of Early Muscovite Thought," *Russian History* 7 (1980), 312–20.

[13] See Mykhailo Hrushevskyi, "Traditional Scheme of 'Russian' History and the Problem of Rational Organization of History of Eastern Slavs," reproduced in *From Kievan Rus' to Modern Ukraine: Formation of the Ukrainian Nation*, Ukrainian Millennium Series, Ukrainian Studies Fund (Cambridge, MA: Harvard University, 1984).

the period its political independence, its claim to the legacy of Rus is more authentic.[14]

While some observers may find this debate an exercise in hair splitting, its impact on the formation of Russian national identity cannot be underestimated. The question also entails within it another question: whether Russia belongs to Europe or exists as a separate Eurasian civilization. The answer to this question hinges on the historical significance accorded Ukraine. Kliuchevskii described Russia's attitude toward the West prior to Peter I as "inveterate antipathy."[15] That changed, however, as large numbers of Westernized, yet fiercely anti-Roman Catholic, Ruthenians (Ukrainians) reached Moscow, creating a cultural bridge between the Russian hinterlands and the West. Ukrainians flowed into Moscow and assumed important offices in Russia's ecclesiastical and secular institutions. This influx of Ukrainians facilitated the Westernization of Russia during the reigns of both Tsar Aleksei Mikhailovich and Tsar Peter I. Liah Greenfeld, in her study of Russian nationalism, observed, "In Saint Petersburg and Moscow, literally in the front ranks of the nascent Russian intelligentsia, the humble youth from Little Russia forged the Great Russian national consciousness."[16] The cultural impact of the Ukrainian immigration on Russia continued unabated well into the twentieth century. Ukraine, along with Siberia and the Caucasus, remained a land of enchantment for many Russian artists, inspiring, for example, Aleksandr Pushkin and Peter I. Tchaikovsky. However, in art as in politics, Ukraine was generally treated as a variation of Russian culture in general, rather than a distinct entity. While there were some Russian thinkers who recognized that the acquisition of Ukraine was simultaneously leading to the denationalization of Russia and the strengthening of autocracy, the rejection of Ukraine as a separate entity within eastern Slavdom hindered not only the development of a distinct Ukrainian identity, but the development of Russia's own national identity as well. Nikolai Trubetskoi argued that the cultural union of Ukraine with Russia and the arrival of Ukrainian courtiers in Russia possibly deprived both Ukrainians and

---

[14] This position is held not only by Soviet historians but by dissident Russians as well. See Aleksandr I. Solzhenitsyn, *Kak Nam Obustroit Rossiiu?* (Moscow: Pravda Press, 1990).
[15] Quoted by Mark Bassin, "Russia Between Europe and Asia," *Slavic Review* 50: 1 (Spring 1991), 4.
[16] Liah Greenfeld, *Nationalism: Five Roads to Modernity* (Cambridge MA: Harvard University Press, 1992), 239.

Russians of their true cultural identity, creating instead a psychological gulf between the ruling class and the masses. As a result, nation building became far more difficult for both Russians and Ukrainians. Recognizing that a dominant institution can negate individual political traditions, Trubetskoi promoted Orthodox Christianity as a glue for the denationalized ruling class that Peter had arbitrarily created.[17] According to Trubetskoi's adherents, the Westernizing influence of Ukraine is alien to Russia rather than indigenous. Therefore, the combination of Byzantine Orthodoxy and Asian despotism provided Russia with more genuine political and cultural parameters and an entirely different international orientation than the Westernization induced by the influx of Ukrainians.[18] Adherents of this group deliberately downplayed Russia's Slavic roots and stressed instead the importance of Russia's Turanian heritage from the Ural-Altai region. Some of this school's more notable members, such as Trubetskoi and Vernadsky, even considered Russia the natural heir to the Mongol empire.[19] The recognition of the incompatibility of national development and the denial of distinct identities to the peoples of the borderlands, however, was recognized by very few.

### Westernizers and Slavophiles and the notion of empire

The possession of Ukraine was intellectually vital for both the Westernizers and the Slavophiles who dominated the Russian intellectual discourse throughout the nineteenth century. For the Westernizers, to separate Ukraine from Russia would destroy Russia's tie to Europe. To admit a separate Eurasian heritage would likewise marginalize Russia's place within the European mainstream. For the Slavophiles, the answer to the question of whether an indigenous or foreign people modernized Russia depended upon whether one considered Ukraine an integral or alien part of Russia, linking the question directly to the heart of the Slavophile ideology.

The Westernizers believed that Russia was an integral part of the Western cultural mainstream, which was merely separated from the West as a result of the Mongol yoke and hence must return to the

---

[17] See Nikolai Trubetskoi, "K Ukrainskoi probleme," *Evraaziatskii vremennik*, no. 5 (1927).
[18] For an analysis of the cultural impact and its historic implications, see David Saunders, *The Ukrainian Impact on Russian Culture, 1750–1850* (Edmonton: Canadian Institute of Ukrainian Studies, University of Alberta, 1985).
[19] Boris Ishboldin, "The Eurasian Movement," *Russian Review* 5:. 2 (1946), 69.

European orbit. The intellectual foundation of the Westernizers rested on two assumptions: first, that Russia was an integral part of the West and, second, that Russia's mission transcends its narrow ethnic parameters. Both arguments required the continued incorporation of the western borderlands. The Westernizers, therefore, had little interest in acknowledging a unique political and cultural heritage for either Ukraine or Russia. The Westernizers had to confront two problems in their argument for ownership of Ukraine. First, if one accepted the notion of a distinct identity for Ukraine, one would then have to agree that Peter's reforms were an alien imposition on Russia by a variety of unsavory influences ranging from Westernizing tsars, sophisticated, proselytizing Ukrainians, freemasons, Judaizers, Jesuits, and others. Therefore, only if one accepts that Ukraine is a Westernized part of Russia can Peter the Great's reforms be accepted as part of a natural process by which Russia, having shed the Mongol yoke, returned to its historical cultural orbit. By this interpretation, Peter's legacy may well serve as a useful guide for the future. Furthermore, the Russian intellectuals embraced the idea, favored by late-nineteenth-century Westernizers, of Russia's role as "universal-regenerative," saving Europe from merciless capitalism. Therefore the fragmentation of Russia from Ukraine would contradict their goals, that is, Russia itself had already been corrupted.

Vissarion Belinskii (1811–48), a major literary critic and Westernizer, dismissed the notion of a distinct Ukrainian identity by stating that "the history of Little Russia is no more than an episode from the reign of [Tsar] Aleksei Mikhailovich."[20] It should be noted however, that Belinskii's rejection of Ukrainian nationalism was based primarily on a nationality theory according to which nations exist in order to prepare people for participation in a higher modern cultural community of all humankind. Therefore, to indulge in a nationalism rooted in rural particularism was merely to retard an inevitable historic process.[21] Most Russian liberals agreed with this view well into the twentieth century. Petr Struve, despite his impeccable liberal credentials, continued to insist that Russia was a national state rather than a multinational entity and saw Ukrainian nationalism as a mortal threat to Russia. Reacting to the growing assertiveness of Ukrainian nationalists, Struve emphatically stated:

[20] Saunders, *The Ukrainian Impact on Russian Culture*, 238.
[21] See Andrea Rutherford, "Vissarion Belinskii and the Ukrainian Question," *The Russian Review*, 54 (1995), 500–15.

> Should the "Ukrainian idea" . . . strike the national soil and set it on
> fire . . . a gigantic unprecedented schism of the Russian nation,
> which, such is my deepest conviction, will result in veritable disaster
> for the state and the people. All our "borderland" problems will pale
> into mere bagatelles compared to the prospect of bifurcation and –
> should the "Belarussian" follow the "Ukrainians" – trifurcation of
> *Russian culture.*[22]

Not until 1905 did the Russian Academy of Sciences finally recognize Ukrainian as a language rather than a dialect of Russian. Ambiguity toward Ukraine's distinct national identity, however, remained a feature of the Russian national consciousness. George Fedotov observed, "The awakening of Ukraine, and especially its separatist character . . . astonished the Russian intelligentsia and to the end remained not comprehensible to it. Above all because we loved Ukraine, its land, its people, its songs, considering them our own."[23]

If the notion of a distinct identity for Ukraine did not suit the paradigm of the Westernizers, it was even less conceivable to the Slavophiles. The Slavophile idea, based on a reinforcing relationship between Orthodoxy, autocracy, and pan-Slavisim, would have been inconceivable without a Russo-Ukrainian union. If a Slavophile believed that the cardinal legitimizing pillar of the autocracy was not an integral part of Russia but only a religion imported from an alien Kievan Rus, he would have to deny the mutually re-enforcing relationship between Russian autocracy and Orthodoxy. Thus, he would reduce the Russian tsar to a mere head of state. This, in turn, would undermine the Slavophile school, which heavily relied on its view of Russia as a force of "liberation and renewal." Describing the essence of Russia, Laddis K. D. Kristof noted, "The orthodox idea, not the Russian tongue or civilization, was the *spiritus moves* of the Tsardom. Russia was first of all Holy Russia, not Russian."[24] Therefore, Kristof argued, "Russification was based on the state of ideology of orthodoxy, not Russianism." This helps to explain why the tsarist

---

[22] Quoted in Richard Pipes, *Struve: Liberal on the Right, 1905–1944* (Cambridge, MA: Harvard University Press, 1980), 211–12 (emphasis added).
[23] See George Fedotov, "The Fate of Empires," reprinted USIA Research memorandum, 11 June 1992, 5.
[24] Laddis K. D. Kristof, "The Russian Image of Russia: An Applied Study in Geopolitical Methodology," in *Essays in Political Geography*, ed. Charles Fisher (London: Methuen, 1968), 351. See also Nicholas Riasanvosky, *Nicholas I and Official Nationality in Russia 1825–1855* (Berkeley, Los Angeles, London: University of California Press, 1959)

regime eagerly translated Orthodox theological texts into the Tatar language.[25] The legitimacy of the Russian state, according to most Slavophiles, rested squarely on the tsar's claim to the patrimony of Kievan Rus; therefore, a notion of a distinct identity for either Russia or the Western borderlands amounted to heresy.

As a result of these legacies, there was almost an unspoken agreement between both Westernizers and Slavophiles to avoid issues of nationalism and national identity. It is a paradox that while in Poland and, indeed, across Central Europe, the growth of educated classes enhanced and broadened the concept of a "national idea," in Russia the educated classes, both left-wing and right-wing, continued to cling to denationalizing ideologies. Feodor M. Dostoyevsky in fact applauded the weak national identity of the Russians, as did many other Slavophiles, since the absence of a clear national identity left the Russian people without national egotism and thus made them particularly fit to carry out a universalist Christian mission.[26] Most Westernizers never went far enough in their liberalism to question the notion of empire, while Slavophiles continued to justify the notion of empire through Orthodoxy. As Hugh Seton-Watson observed, Russian nationalism did rear its head several times in the nineteenth century. Nicholas I's minister of education, Sergei Uvarov, advocated "Autocracy, Orthodoxy, and National Outlook (*narodnost'*)," while the Polish uprising of 1863 and German unification also stirred Russian national feelings among certain strata of society.[27] The house of Romanov did not come to promote Russian nationalism for its legitimization until the reigns of Alexander III (1881–94), when the crown introduced "state nationalism" [*kazennyi natsionalizm*],[28] and Nicholas II (1894–1917).[29] Even then contradictions abounded. As Sergei Maksudov and William Taubman noted, the embrace of nationalism during the twilight of both the tsarist and Soviet empires represented the last gasp of a decadent government. Failing to satisfy the national aspirations of either the Russians or the nationalities, it only further

[25] Ibid., 350. See also Wayne Dowler, "The Politics of Language in Non-Russian Elementary Schools in the Eastern Empire 1865–1914," *The Russian Review*, 54 (1995), 516–38.
[26] See D. V. Grishin, *Dostoyevsky–Chelovek Pisatel' i mify: Dostoyevsky i ego 'dnevnik pisatelia'* (Melbourne: University of Melbourne Press, 1971), 92.
[27] Dietrich Geyer, *Russian Imperialism: The Interaction of Domestic and Foreign Policy* (New Haven: Yale University Press, 1987), 53–54.
[28] Sergei G. Pushkarev, *Rossiia v XIX veke* (New York: Chekhov, 1956), 287.
[29] Hugh Seton-Watson, "Russian Nationalism in Historic Perspective," in *The Last Empire: Nationality and the Soviet Future*, ed. Robert Conquest (Stanford: Hoover Press, 1987), 20.

delegitimized the prevailing universal ideology.[30] The persecution of minorities prior to the reign of Alexander III, whether that of the Jews as a challenge to Christianity or the Ems Decree of 1876 banning Ukrainian language, can be interpreted as an effort to contain the perceived conspiracy of the Poles and the Austro-Hungarian monarchy, rather than an act of overt Russification.

The regime's preference for an imperial-religious identity, rather than a distinct national one, stems from two legacies: the traditional notion of divine rule, common to imperial European courts, and the non-Russian ethnicity of the Russian court and the Romanov family. Stressing ethnicity as a source of legitimacy would have merely undermined the *ancien régime* further.[31] Pospielovsky pointed out that the word "nationalism" did not appear in print in Russia until the early twentieth century. Moreover, prior to the reign of Alexander III:

> "Russian" tended to mean a subject of the Russian Emperor of whatever ethnic group, creed (except Judaic), language or race, with however a preference for Orthodoxy as a state religion. Adoption of the Russian language, and with it culture, became a necessary ingredient of the concept from the late nineteenth century.[32]

An illustrative example of the regime's ambiguity toward a distinct Russian identity was the traditional practice that all imperial institutions, from the emperor down, referred to themselves as *rossiskii* (of the lands of Rus,) rather than *russkii* (ethnic Russian). The equation of the term *narod* (the people) with *gosudarstvo* (the state) also reflects this ambiguity.[33] This frustrated some Russian liberals, such as Struve, who complained that the term *rossiiskii* enabled the Russian intelligentsia to "decolourize itself."[34] Nonetheless, the use of *rossiskii* persisted among the ruling classes until the very end of the Romanov dynasty. As late as 1910, Petr N. Durnovo, one of the luminaries of the Russian

---

[30] Sergei Maksudov and William Taubman, "Russian–Soviet Nationality Policy and Foreign Policy: A Historic Overview of Linkage Between Them," in *The Rise of Nations in the Soviet Union*, ed. Michael Mandelbaum (New York: Council on Foreign Affairs, 1991).

[31] Richard Pipes noted that in the seventeenth century only 4.6 percent of Moscow's *dvoriane* consisted of Great Russians. Given the great influx of foreigners during the Romanov dynasty, it stands to reason that the role of Great Russians did not change substantially. See Richard Pipes, *Russia Under the Old Regime* (New York: Collier, 1974), 182. As late as 1897, fewer than half of Russia's *dvoriane* were native speakers of Russian. See Richard Pipes, *The Russian Revolution* (New York: Knopf, 1990), 84.

[32] Dimitry Pospielovsky, "Ethnocentrism, Ethnic Tension, and Marxism–Leninism," in *Ethnic Russia in the USSR: The Dilemma of Dominance*, ed. Edward Allworth (New York: Pergamon Press, 1980), 125.

[33] Kristof, "The Russian Image," 350.

[34] See Jeffrey Brooks, "Vekhi and the Vekhi Dispute," *Survey* 86, no. 1 (Winter 1973), 33.

imperial court, stated: "If we want to preserve the unity of the Russian state, it would be madness to weaken the force that binds it together – that is, the Russian Orthodox Church . . . [The Church] teaches people not only Christ's truth, but also the need for obedience to the imperial power."[35] As Kliuchevskii observed, Russia's relentless expansion made colonization the prime force in Russian history, permanently blurring the distinction between Russia proper and its periphery.[36] Instead, from the start, nationalism in Russia was a manipulated state ideology. Russian nationalism failed to develop from below, that is, from the bourgeoisie, as in most other polities. The liberal historian Pavel Miliukov argued that even in the early twentieth century, Russian nationalism remained a product of a small alien minority, while the masses remained indifferent.[37] The rather diffuse state of Russian identity had several long-lasting effects on the formation of the Russian consciousness and its ability to create an identity separate from the empire. Regardless of their specific orientation, Russian thinkers across the spectrum – from Pavel Pestel, the liberal leader of the 1825 Decembrist uprising, to Konstatin Pobedonostsev, the arch-reactionary nineteenth-century procurator of the Holy Synod – remained attached to the belief that Russia is a civilization, rather than a nation, into which all peoples of the empire should be brought.

Between Westernizers and Slavophiles, differences in opinion over imperialist aims were limited to the question of Poland. Westernizers, such as Pestel and Alexander Herzen, conceded that Poland's separate identity was far too developed to be brought into an overarching Russian civilization and advocated limited independence for the Poles, under the guise of a confederacy.[38] The Slavophiles, though, urged Poland's complete separation from Russia, arguing that Polish Catholicism polluted Russian culture. Ivan Aksakov, a Slavophile, observed that "Russia swallowed Poland and became poisoned in the process."[39] Paradoxically, despite the well-documented Polonophobia among the Russian elite, during the 1863 Polish Uprising, Russians volunteered in larger numbers than any

---

[35] Quoted in Dominic Lieven, *Russia's Rulers Under the Old Regime* (New Haven: Yale University Press, 1990), 225–26.

[36] See Vasilii O. Kliuchevskii, *Kurs Russkoi Istorii*, vol. I (Moscow: Mysl', 1987), 49–62.

[37] See Pavel N. Miliukov, *Ocherki po Istorii Russkoi Kultury*, vol. II (St. Petersburg, 1909).

[38] While recognizing the fact that Poland is indeed a separate nation, the Decembrist envisioned an independent Poland allied to and sharing a political system with Russia.

[39] Nikolai A. Gerdeskul, *Rossiia i ee narody* (Petrograd, 1916), 29.

other nationality.[40] Toward other nationalities, Russian intellectuals remained uniformly imperialist in attitude. Thus, the banning of the Uniate Church in Belarussia (1839) and the notorious Ems Decree (1876), which outlawed the Ukrainian language, drew no protest from Russian intellectuals. In fact, since both the Belarussians and Ukrainians were perceived as West Russians whose culture had been contaminated by Polonisms, attacks on the "Polonizing" Uniate Church or on the Ukrainian "dialect" (*narechie*) were considered an act of redemption, rather than assimilation.

### The emergence of national identity in Russia

Although a Russian national identity started to emerge as early as the eighteenth century under Peter I and Catherine II, contemporary conditions hindered rather than promoted the development of a Russian national identity distinct from the Russian state. Exposure to the West in the eighteenth century did initially create in Russia an enthusiastic emulation of the West European model (mainly French), but, as Greenfeld has illustrated, by the end of the eighteenth century a process of *ressentiment* had set in. Russian thinkers, while no longer able to disengage from the West, recognized that Russia would not be able to implement the Western model in Russia. Vasilii Kliuchevskii, in his analysis of the Petrine reforms, wrote:

> [Peter I] hoped through the threat of his authority to evoke independence in an enslaved society and establish European science and public education in Russia via slave-owning nobility, conditions so essential to social independence; he wanted slaves to act consciously and freely while remaining slaves. The combined action of despotism and freedom, of enlightenment and slavery, is the political equivalent of squaring the circle, a riddle which historians have been attempting to solve for two centuries since the time of Peter but which still remains unsolved.[41]

Russia's ambiguity toward itself and the West was captured by the eighteenth-century Russian satirist Denis Fonvizin, who asked, "How can we remedy the two contradictory and most harmful prejudices; the first being that everything with us is awful, while in foreign lands everything is good; the second that in foreign lands everything is

---

[40] Piotr S. Wandycz, *The Price of Freedom: A History of Central Europe from the Middle Ages to the Present* (London and New York: Routledge, 1993), 164.
[41] Quoted in Evgenii V. Anisimov, "Petr I: Rozhdenie imperii," *Voprosy istorii*, no. 7 (1989), 3–20.

awful and with us everything is good?"[42] This lingering sense of inferiority *vis-à-vis* the West drove Russian intellectuals to seek solace in Russia's unique version of Christianity, as well as from the fact that Russia, however backward, remained a *Velikaiia Derzhava* (a Great Power), further linking the notion of Russianness with the imperial Russian state.

This profound pessimism about the ability to transplant a Western model to Russia resulted in a relatively brief flirtation with the West, with Russia's Westernizers gradually abandoning their infatuation and retreating back to a Slavophilic orientation. A succession of Westernizers from Karamzin (who reversed his positive attitude toward Peter's domestic policies) to Herzen (the doyen of Russian Westernizers) migrated from unabashed admiration of the West to enthusiasm for the purity of the Russian village and rejection of the decadent West.[43] The historian Timofei Granovskii (1813–55) may well have personified the ambivalence that many Russian *zapadniki* (Westernizers) felt toward reforming the Russian state. While accepting the West as a model and teacher of organization and science, Granovskii was reluctant to jettison Russia's political heritage and, despite bitter reservations about the autocratic rule of Nikolai I, continued to believe in the viability of the Russian political system and its ability to evolve along a unique Russian path.[44]

The slow pace of Russian urbanization and industrialization in Russia, unlike in Western Europe and parts of Central Europe, translated into a similarly slow growth of a nationalist bourgeois class, a modernizing force. Until the late nineteenth century, Russia's society consisted of two key classes: the service nobility, heavily dominated by Baltic Germans and dependent upon the a-national imperial regime, and the all but enslaved peasants, some 80 percent of Russia's population. Mikhail Speranksy went so far as to write to Tsar Alexander I that there were two classes in the Russian empire: the slaves of the sovereign and the slaves of the landowners.[45] The fact that the peasantry formed the bulk of Russia's conscript army hampered Russia's ability to project force. "The Russian peasant of 1900 owed loyalty to his village," Richard Pipes pointed out. "[At] most he

---

[42] Greenfeld, *Nationalism*, 223.
[43] Andrzej Walicki, *A History of Russian Thought: From the Enlightenment to Marxism* (Stanford: Stanford University Press, 1979), 162–83.
[44] See Nicholas Ratchets, "A Moderate Among Radicals: Timofei Nikolaevich Granovskii," *Studies in Soviet Thought* 24 (1982), 117–46.
[45] Hugh Seton-Watson, *The Russian Empire 1801–1917* (Oxford: Oxford University Press, 1990), 103.

was conscious of some vague allegiance to his province."[46] The Russian peasantry, with its communal structure, making many villages *de facto* extended families, tended to view all outsiders as aliens of a different *Rod* (caste) and the government (often Viking, Tatar, Baltic German, or Westernized Russians) as a manifestation of the anti-Christ, which allowed little possibility for the emergence of a national identity.

Despite the intense anti-German propaganda of World War I, "Russian peasant-soldiers failed to identify with national objectives, with the result that the Russian army found itself in a comparative disadvantage with armies that exhibited a greater degree of modern nationalism."[47]

The Russian intelligentsia that began to emerge in the 1830s exhibited a far greater interest in universal causes rather than in narrowly defined Russian issues, and thus failed to contribute to the development of a distinct Russian identity. Furthermore, the intelligentsia, despite its enduring commitment to social issues, remained fairly isolated from the Russian masses, insisting on its own utopian dreams regardless of their impact on the people. Nikolai Berdiaev noted that the Russian intelligentsia's attitude "remains one of a monastic order or sect with its own very intolerant ethics."[48]

Although no single event can explain the rise of a national identity, a distinct Russian identity started to emerge after the Napoleonic wars of 1812–15 and was clearly reinforced by the flowering of Russian music, painting, and, most notably, Russian literature in the nineteenth century. As Anatole Mazour noted, "[Russian nationalism] came as an answer to the fiasco of the cosmopolitan idea of the French Revolution and the failure of Napoleon to bring Europe to a federation of states and bend Russia to that scheme."[49] Mazour convincingly argued that the powerful Hegelian influence contributed to the assertive nature of Russian nationalism. Most early Russian nationalist intellectuals were educated in Germany and impressed by Hegel's *Lectures on the Philosophy of History*, in which Hegel divided history into three periods: the oriental, symbolized by despotism; the classical, symbolized by law and order; and the last phase, "man and

---

[46] Pipes, *Russia Under the Old Regime*, 91.
[47] Allan K. Wildman, *The End of the Russian Imperial Army: The Old Army and the Soldier's Revolt, March–April 1917* (Princeton: Princeton University Press, 1980), 93.
[48] Nikolai Berdiaev, *The Origins of Communism in Russia* (Ann Arbor: University of Michigan Press, 1972), 21.
[49] Anatole G. Mazour, *Russia Past and Present* (New York: D. Van Nostrand, 1955), 30.

freedom," dominated by Germans. Russian nationalists accepted the Hegelian division of history, but countered the notion of an approaching German hegemony with that of a Russian-centered Slavophilism.[50] Nikolai Danilevsky, a nationalist strongly influenced by Hegel and an adamant Slavophile, asserted that the third historic phase was bound to be dominated by the Orthodox Slavs (not Russians *per se*), since they were not as contaminated by Western ideas as the "Germano-Roman" world was.[51] Russia's cultural flowering, which was separate from both autocracy and Orthodoxy, contributed immensely to the creation of a Russian identity. This cultural flowering, however, became a tool of empire building. Russia's imperial expansion failed to produce a group analogous to Richard Cobden's "Little Englanders" or the Fabians, or a persona comparable to Charles William Eliot in the United States.

The combination of Napoleonic wars and the end of all reforms in Russia after 1830 led to an enduring controversy about the legacy of Peter I as well as the ultimate purpose of the Russian state. This debate over Russia's identity was illustrated by Nicholas V. Riasanovsky in his study of the image of Peter the Great in Russian history:

> A new situation emerged only in the 1830's. The Russian government had lost all its liberal promise, having consciously followed extremely conservative policies. . . . Inside Russia, too, the simple Enlightenment beliefs in education and progress appeared to bear little relationship to reality. Moreover, the ideology of the Age of Reason itself had been challenged, and in part, replaced by traditionalist doctrines and by German idealistic philosophy and Romanticism in general. In these circumstances, three basic images of Peter the Great arose in Russia. The Enlightenment image split into two. The government and its supporters retained faith in Peter the Great, the victorious creator of the Russian empire and its might, the sage organizer of the state, the lawgiver of modern Russia. But they rejected any further imitation of the West, dynamic development, progress. The Westernizers by contrast, hypostatized precisely the other part of the original Petrine image as the true aim and hope of their country and its people. In addition, a third Petrine image, the first full scale negative one to emerge among the educated Russian public, was postulated by the Slavophiles. They declared the entire Petrine reforms a perversion and a disaster and clamored to return to true Russian principles . . . The celebrated debate between the Westernizers and the Slavophiles was carried out not in the quasi-

---

[50] Ibid., 33.
[51] Nikolai Danilevsky, "The Nature of Russian Nationalism," in *The Dynamics of Nationalism*, ed. Louis L. Snyder (Princeton: D. Van Nostrand, 1964), 209.

empirical framework of the Age of Reason, but in a metaphysical one, that of German idealism.[52]

The schism in the image of Peter in Russian history reflected not so much a dispute about the emperor as a basic dispute about the essence of the Russian state and society.

The rise of the Russian arts and literature, particularly in the first half of the nineteenth century, coincided with the rise of German Romanticism and its "orientalism" and further legitimated the imperial vocation of the Russian state. Russian authors such as Radishchev, Lermontov, Griboiedov, and Gogol readily challenged the inequities and the absurdities of Russian society. However, rarely did the critique of Russian society expand to a critique of imperialism. When it came to commenting on Russia's state policy, Russian literature was consistently pro-imperial. Despite his contempt for Catherine II's personality, Pushkin lauded her imperial foreign policy as a great and eternal achievement: "Sweden humbled and Poland annihilated – these are Catherine's great claims to the Russian people's gratitude."[53] The poet and diplomat Fedr Tiutchev similarly lauded the Russian imperial idea. Exalting Russia's messianic role, he stated:

> What is the Eastern Empire? It is the legitimate and direct descendent of the authority of the Caesars . . . Ours is an Empire, which by design or chance, knows no historic equal; it represents two entities: The fate of an entire race, and the best and most sacred half of the Christian Church.[54]

In terms of foreign policy, the Slavophiles and Westernizers both were profoundly committed to an ever-expanding Russian empire. Even Aleksandr Herzen, who sympathized with the Poles' political aspirations, assigned to Russia the role of saving the decadent West. He went so far as to envision a Russian empire extending to the banks of the Rhine and the shores of the Bosporus.[55] The synergy between Russian literature and the notion of empire was further manifested during the long wars to "pacify the Caucasus." Despite some reserva-

---

[52] Nicholas V. Riasanovsky, *The Image of Peter the Great in Russian History and Thought* (New York and Oxford: Oxford University Press, 1985), 304.

[53] Marcus Wheeler, "Pushkin: Ideologist of Post-Petrine Russia or European Humanist," in *The Search for Self-Definition in Russian Literature,* ed. Ewa Thompson (Houston: Rice University Press, 1991), 151.

[54] Alexander Ospovat, "Tiutchev's Political Memorandum Rediscovered," *Elementa,* no. 1 (1993), 91–97.

[55] Aleksandr Herzen, "O razvitii revoliutzionnykh idei," in *Sobranie sochinenii* (Moscow: Mysl', 1957).

tions about the methods used by the tsars, Russia's romantic poets – Pushkin, Bestuzhev-Marlinski, Lermantov, and numerous others – endorsed Russia's quest to "civilize" the Caucasus.[56]

Dostoyevsky, despite his declared pacifism, exempted Russia's military expansion from charges of aggression. For him, wars were fought in the pursuit of a sacred idea [of Russia's universalist Christian mission] that would ultimately lead to perpetual peace.[57] Some giants of Russian literature disagreed. Tolstoy, in his novella *Haji Murat* sided with the Chechen rebels against Russia's might and in *Cossacks*, he depicted Russia's imperial adventure as cruel and shameful. The satirist Mikhail Slatykov-Shchedrin in his *Letters to the Peoples of Tashkent* ridiculed the notion of Russia's "civilizing mission." However, the authors who openly challenged the notion of empire were a minority. As the Anglo-American literary critic John Garrad noted: "It is hard to find a Russian writer bold enough to take exception to the comforting platitudes of national preeminence – Turgenev and later Chekhov are noteworthy exceptions."[58] Vladimir Zhabotinskii, who prior to his conversion to revisionist Zionism was a novelist and literary critic, complained that Russian culture and arts, despite their uncanny ability to reach into the human soul and describe human suffering, remained oblivious to the multinational character of the Russian empire and the diverse aspirations and interests of its peoples.[59]

Russian composers took a decisively pro-imperial view. Works such as those of the "Mighty Five" composers – Balakirev, Borodin, Cui, Mussorgsky, and Rimsky-Korsakov – and the *Marche Slav* by Tchaikovsky took on a nationalist, as well as imperialist, character. Russian operas – Glinka's *A Life for the Tsar*, Borodin's *Prince Igor*, or Mussorgsky's *Boris Godunov* and *Khovanshchina* – displayed an obsession with Russia's history and its relentless struggle against its various neighbors, similar to Wagner's work in Germany. One particular recurring theme in Russian opera, especially in Glinka and

---

[56] Susan Layton, *Russian Literature and Empire: Conquest of Caucasus from Pushkin to Tolstoy* (New York: Cambridge University Press, 1994).

[57] See Feodor M. Dostoyevsky, *The Diary of a Writer*, vol. II (New York: Charles Scribner, 1949).

[58] John G. Garrad, "A Conflict of Visions: Vasilii Grossman and the Russian Idea," in *The Search for Self-Definition in Russian Literature*, ed. Edward Thompson (Houston: Rice University Press, 1991), 58.

[59] Vladimir (Ze'ev) Zhabotinskii, "O iazykakh i prochem," in *Izbrannoe* (Jerusalem: Aliya Press, 1978), 136.

Mussorgsky, is a deep-seated *Polonophobia*.[60] Both Russia's instrumental music and its romantic poetry have shown a fascination with "orientalism."

Similarly, Russian painting during the nineteenth century includes a healthy dose of exhaltation of Russian military powers and military exploits, though there are noted exceptions where the futility and horror of war are stressed. On the whole, the flowering of the Russian arts not only reinforced the notion of empire in Russia's psyche, it actually provided additional justification for imperial expansion on the basis of *mission civilisatrice*, further linking the Russian identity and empire.

This frustration with the realities of Russia, together with the ambiguity concerning Russia's role in Europe, created in the Russian psyche a strong dependence on Russia's military powers in order to compensate for the sense of inferiority *vis-à-vis* the West. When Petr Chaadaev suggested that Russia's sole contribution to world civilization was its size and military might and that its cultural contribution amounted to nothing, he drew the wrath of Russian society. Russia's sense of inferiority cum superiority was brilliantly encapsulated by Nikolai Nekrasov in his description of Russia: "Thou art wretched. Thou art bountiful. Thou art mighty. Thou art impotent. Mother Russia."[61] Dostoyevsky observed that Russia must maintain a powerful Asian empire because "in Europe we are hangers-on and slaves."[62] The views of Sergei Witte, Russia's first prime minister, did not differ much from those of "the mad" Chaadaev. Writing in his memoirs, Witte declared, in the early twentieth century:

> In truth, what is it that has essentially upheld Russian statehood? Not only primarily but exclusively the army. Who has created the Russian Empire, transforming the semi-Asiatic, Muscovite Tsardom into the most influential, most dominant, grandest European power? Only the power of the army's bayonet. The world bowed not to our culture, not to our bureaucratized church, not to our wealth and prosperity. It bowed to our might.[63]

Struve, the leader of the Russian Cadet Party, and the philosopher Semen Frank, summarized Russian feelings toward the West in the following manner: "Before Western Europe, the Russian man feels himself in a position of a school boy and ignoramus; even when he

[60] See Solomon Volkov, *Saint Petersburg: A Cultural History* (New York: Free Press, 1995), 85.
[61] Nikolai Nekrasov, "Komu na Rusi Zhit' Khorosho," in *Isbrannye proizvedeniia* (Leningrad: Lenizdat, 1969).
[62] Dostoyevsky, *Diary of a Writer*, 1043.    [63] Pipes, *The Russian Revolution*, 80.

hates it as something foreign and antipathetic to him, he cannot avoid valuing it and feeling ashamed before it."[64] Karen Dawisha and Bruce Parrott observed that because the formation of the Russian nation:

> did not precede the process of Tsarist colonial expansion, but rather coincided with it, the simultaneity of the process blurred ethnic and cultural definition of Russian nationality, and made Russia's political identity dependent on the Tsarist state's imperial exploits. During most of the twentieth century Russian identity continued to hinge on the international power of the state.[65]

Perceptively, they noted that despite Dostoyevsky's statements that expansion into Asia was a means of escaping the role of "hanger-on" in Europe, most Russian nationalists viewed expansion as a way of affirming Russia's status as a great European power.[66] Kliuchevskii, who lamented the legacy of expansionism and colonialism, did not fully distinguish between Russia and the Russian empire. Kliuchevskii complained that Russia's restless expansion created a "bloated state with an emaciated people" and asserted that because of this tumultuous history, "Russia has yet to live a normal national life."[67] Yet as Robert Byrnes observed, Kliuchevskii remained virtually oblivious to the presence of non-Russians in the empire. To the extent that Kliuchevskii criticized the imperial expansion of Catherine II, he felt that instead of acquiring Catholic Poland, while ceding "Russian-populated" Galicia to the Austrians, Russia should have concentrated its efforts on building a universal Orthodox empire.[68]

In contrast to nineteenth-century Western and Central European nationalist historians, who increasingly asserted an integralist nationalism, emphasizing common primeval origins and a racist exclusivity, Russian historians continued to follow Karamzin's line praising Russia's ability to absorb and Russify other peoples. Nineteenth-century Russian historians praised the policy of cultural expansion along with extensive miscegenation as long as the "natives" were willing to become Orthodox Christians. As Nikolai Polevoi noted, "Henceforth a single will, a single faith, a single language were the

---

[64] Brooks, "Vekhi," 32.
[65] Karen Dawisha and Bruce Parrott, *Russia and the New States of Eurasia: The Politics of Upheaval* (New York: Cambridge University Press, 1994), 26.
[66] Ibid., 29.
[67] Vasilii O. Kliuchevskii, *Kurs Russkoi Istorii*, vol. I (Moscow, 1911), 338.
[68] Robert Byrnes, "Kliuchevskii and the Multi-national Russian State," *Russian History* 13: 4 (Winter 1986), 313–30.

insoluble bonds uniting Russian lands."[69] Russian thinkers firmly
believed that Russian civilization must permeate the empire, since, as
A. D. Gradovskii asserted, a multicultural state was "'artificial' and
cannot satisfy the most elementary needs of national development."[70]
Even among those Russians who insisted that Orthodox Christianity
and the Russian language could serve to hold the empire together, the
imperial Russian attitude resembled the Portuguese imperialism
based on massive intermarriage and cultural assimilation rather than
the West European imperialism based on racist exclusivity or the
physical annihilation of other ethnic groups. Even during the brutal
and nationalist reign of Alexander III, physical coercion played a
minor role in the policies of Russification.[71]

In contrast to West and Central European nationalists, who accepted
the notion of annihilation – which the German historian Heinrich von
Treitschke referred to as *Völkermord* – or Bismarck's call for the
"extermination" of the Poles,[72] Russian nationalists continued to
eschew an ethnic or racial definition of Russia. Russian historians
supported the suppression of the Uniate Church, which they viewed
as a renegade branch of Orthodoxy, and generally did not oppose the
persecution of the Jews, as heretics,[73] or the Poles, as traitors to
Slavdom and lackeys of the West. The tsarist regime, however,
avoided coerced Russification of peoples of the empire. As Marc Raeff
described:

> The goal of social, economic and political uniformity remained
> constant in the policy of the imperial government. At no point was it
> conscious or aware of the dynamic forces of nation and nationality.
> Yet, the Russian government did not aim at eradicating nations and
> nationalities. It simply felt that their way of life should change in a
> process of natural evolution which their membership in the empire
> could speed up.[74]

At the end of the nineteenth century, when nationalism became a

---

[69] Seymour Becker, "Contribution to a National Ideology: Histories of Russia in the First
Half of the 19th Century," *Russian History* 13: 4 (Winter 1986), 331–59.
[70] A. D. Gradovskii, *Natsional'nyi vopros v istorii literatury* (St. Petersburg, 1873), 28–29.
[71] See Tuomo Polvinen, *Imperial Borderland: Bobrikov and the Attempted Russification of
Finland, 1898–1904* (Durham: Duke University Press, 1995).
[72] Erich Eyck, *Bismark and the German Empire* (New York and London: W. W. Norton,
1968), 68.
[73] See Hans Rogger, *Jewish Policies and Right-Wing Politics in Imperial Russia* (Berkeley:
University of California Press, 1986), 1–24.
[74] Marc Raeff, "Patterns of Russian Imperial Policy Toward the Nationalities," in *Soviet
Nationality Problems*, ed. Edward Allworth (New York: Columbia University Press,
1971), 37.

potent global force shaking the foundations of all existing empires, the Russian people were ill-prepared to separate their own identity from that of the empire in general and its Slavic core in particular.

It is worth noting that until the reign of Alexander III (1881–94), the regime categorized the population of the empire into three broad categories: "Russians" (a category that, according to the regime, included Ukrainians and Belorussians), "Inorodsty" the non-Slavic people in the eastern and southern parts of the empire (whom the regime sought to convert to Orthodoxy, but not actually Russify) and peoples of the western borderlands, where German culture and Lutheranism were allowed to flourish unmolested. During his reign, however, a messianic urge to rescue the smaller peoples from the clutches of cultural Germanic and Ottoman hegemony came to dominate segments of Russian intellectual life. By the late nineteenth century, tsarist colonial policy consisted of systematic Russification of groups including the Baltic Germans, the Finns, and other western borderlands people, populations that had been spared previous policies of Russification. However, even these policies remained half-hearted and far less systematic than the efforts of the central French government to suppress regional languages or England's efforts to eradicate Gaelic languages and culture.

As the twentieth century began, Russian intellectuals split into two camps. The Slavophilistic right, increasingly relying on religion and xenophobia as a means of holding together the empire, stressed Slavicism and Orthodoxy as the empire's key sources of legitimacy. They continued to advocate an organic community, which included all Orthodox Slavs, Russians, Ukrainians, Belarussians, Bulgarians, Serbs, and, at times, Catholic Czechs.[75] The left, increasingly nihilist and, later, Marxist in its orientation, stressed Russia's destiny to save the decadent West. Whether traditional Westernizers or Marxists, they continued to assign to Russia a global mission and a universal ideology, paying little attention to a Russian identity. The link between Russian national identity and the empire remained the most constant feature of Russian national psychology. The preamble to the Basic Law of 1906, which was supported by politicians ranging from the

---

[75] It is important to note that there was a profound difference between Polish romantic messianism and Russian Slavophile messianism. Whereas the former was viewed as an admixture of state and religious conviction, the latter considered the political state as a mere reflection of human imperfection, placing its notion of messianism outside the context of history. See Andrzej Walicki, *Russia, Poland and Universal Regeneration* (Notre Dame: University of Notre Dame Press, 1991), 146–57.

conservative Stolypin, who insisted that "We need a Great Russia," to the liberal Struve, who insisted that Russia preserve its imperial shape and called for the preservation of a "one and indivisible Russia."

A conservative Slavophile attitude can be observed in *Vekhi*,[76] the famous collection of essays by Russian intellectuals written in reaction to the turbulent years of 1905–07. In this volume, one sees yet again the rejection of the Western democratic model in favor of a broader religious-civilizing polity. The attachment of Russia's liberal educated elite to the perpetuation of the Russian state in its current form must be understood in terms of the *Zeitgeist* of early twentieth-century Russia, where the events of 1905 were prophetically perceived by Russia's intellectual elite – including symbolist poets such as Andrei Belyi, Fedr Sologub, and others – as forces leading to the destruction of the existing order and ushering in an endless nightmare.

A minority school of Russian thinkers argued that the historic epoch of imperial and cultural expansion had exhausted itself and that the national minorities could not be Russified. Boris Chicherin, for example, stated, "To destroy the consciousness of an ethnic nation and force it to bend to another nation is a means to force it to deny itself, forget its own past, its collective memory, its greatness, its language, its interests . . . Such a task is beyond human strength."[77] Nikolai Gerdeskul, while rejecting the breakup of multiethnic empires as a turn toward greater intolerance, cautioned that the only way Russia could survive as a modern state was to become the fatherland (*otechestvo*) to all its ethnic groups. Gerdeskul warned that unless Russia replicated the model of the British commonwealth, it would exhaust itself and ultimately fail in its effort to "denationalize" its minorities.[78] These voices of moderation, however, remained a minority and had little impact on Russia's politics.

As a result, while nationalism spread and rapidly became a universal ideology for the minorities, Russia's own national identity remained opaque and unprepared to face the challenge. Hugh Seton-Watson correctly asserted that the 1905 rebellion represented "a revolution of non-Russians against Russification."[79] Yet the response

---

[76] For an English language translation of *Vekhi*, see Boris Shragin and Albert Todd, eds., *Landmarks: A Collection of Essays on the Russian Intelligentsia* (New York: Krazt Howard, 1977). It should be noted, however, that it would be simplistic to give a single characterization for the collection of essays. Bogdan Kistiakovskii's article "In the Defense of Law" can be viewed as a "Westernizing" call for a civil society.

[77] Boris N. Chicherin, *O narodnom predstavitel'stve* (Moscow, 1899), 227.

[78] Nikolai Gerdeskul, *Rossiia i ee narody* (Petrograd, 1916).

[79] Hugh Seton-Watson, *Nations and States* (Boulder, CO: Westview Press, 1977), 87.

of the Russian intellectual elite was not to formulate a distinct Russian identity but to retreat to a pre-national paradigm for Russia. Fedotov noted, "Perhaps, if a federal structure for Russia had been realized in 1905, through the triumph of a liberation movement, it might have prolonged the existence of the empire for several generations."[80] The inability of the tsarist regime to address either Russian or minority national aspirations left the Russian nation, despite the wealth of its language, arts, and history, the ethnic group least prepared to develop a post-imperial identity. Prime Minister Witte wearily observed: "[We] still have not realized that ever since the time of Peter the Great and Catherine the Great, there has not been such a thing as Russia, only a Russian empire."[81] Roman Szporluk correctly noted, "The Tsarist empire ultimately did not succeed in establishing a *modus vivendi* with the Russian nation."[82] The link between Russia's identity and the empire helped to trigger the Civil War of 1918–21. General Anton Denikin, the commander of the White armies, stated: "As far as I am concerned I will not fight for the form of government. I am leading a struggle for Russia only."[83] Echoing that sentiment, Struve in 1919, observed that a solid link between the Russian state and the Russian empire had to endure even if it meant forswearing acceptance by the democratic West.

> The long-standing hostility of Western democratic elements to "tsarism" very lightheartedly and swiftly was applied to Russia as a great state after the dissolution of the Russian state. These circles reasoned in the following manner: The fall of Russia is the fall of Tsarism, and [they] accepted this as a positive development. Many of us Russians, on the other hand, thought the exact opposite. Because for the Russians the fall of the monarchy meant the fall of Russia, many educated Russians, not being monarchists, became monarchists out of Russian patriotism.[84]

Given that Russia had become an empire before it was a state and given the relentless drive to acquire new peoples, the process of defining and building a Russian state was never completed. The notion of incompleteness, along with a powerful sense of what Alfred

---

[80] Fedotov, "The Fate of Empires," 6.
[81] Sergei Witte, *Vospominaniia*, vol. III (Moscow, 1960), 273.
[82] Roman Szporluk, "The Imperial Legacy and the Soviet Nationalities Problem," in *The Nationalities Factor in Soviet Politics and Society*, ed. Lubomyr Hajda and Mark Beissinger (Boulder, CO: Westview Press, 1990), 2.
[83] Anna Procyk, *Russian Nationalism and Ukraine: The Nationality Policy of the Volunteer Army During the Civil War* (Edmonton and Toronto: Canadian Institute of Ukrainian Studies Press, 1995), 59.
[84] Ibid., 172.

J. Rieber described as "cultural marginality," resulted from the physical and psychological location of the Byzantine, Muslim, and Western civilizations.[85] In Russia, this led to deep insecurity and, hence, to a need to cling to empire, not so much because of its alleged benefits, but because of a fear of the unknown. One of the paradoxes and tragedies of Russia's national development was that while the empire was unable to satisfy the growing needs of Russian nationalism, the Russian national consciousness remained fused to the empire. Since the eighteenth century, the educated class in Russia has pondered the meaning and purpose of the Russian state. Although the educated class in Russia rarely agreed on the essence of "Russianness" or the purpose of the Russian state, there was a nearly universal consensus that Russia must have a mission that transcends its confines, and that it must not be reduced to its ethnographic core.

For the great majority of Russian people, overwhelmingly peasants, the Russian empire was no more meaningful than the British empire was to the peasantry of western Ireland. Many, and perhaps most, Russians, much like the clerk Yevgenii in Pushkin's *The Bronze Horseman*, perceived the imperial Russian state as a chimera exacting a frightening toll for purposes unfathomable to the *temnyi narod* (dark masses). Because of the fact that, as late as 1897, only roughly 25 percent of the population was literate (compared to over 90 percent in the Baltics), the bulk of the Russian people had little notion of the world beyond their village and felt no commonality with the urban intellectual elites.[86]

Leo Tolstoy, in his essay "Christianity and Patriotism," described the atomized nature of society and the weak sense of nationhood among the Russian masses:

> Thus, for example, in Russia, where patriotism, in the form of love and loyalty for the faith, the Tsar, and the country, is inculcated in the masses with extraordinary tension and with the use of all the tools at the command of the governments, such as the church, the school, the press, and all kinds of solemnities, the Russian laboring classes – one hundred million of the Russian nation – in spite of Russia's unearned reputation as a nation that is particularly devoted to its faith, its Tsar, and its country, are most free from the deception of patriotism and from loyalty to its faith, the Tsar, and its country. The men of the

[85] Alfred J. Rieber, "Persistent Factors in Russian Foreign Policy," in *Imperial Russian Foreign Policy*, ed. Hugh Ragsdale (Cambridge: Cambridge University Press, 1993), 344.

[86] See Robert J. Kaiser, *The Geography of Nationalism in Russia and the USSR* (Princeton: Princeton University Press, 1994), 69.

masses for the most part do not know their Orthodox state faith, to which they are supposed to be so loyal, and when they come to know it, they immediately give it up and become rationalists, that is, a faith which is impossible to attack or defend; on their Tsar, in spite of the constant and persistent influences brought upon them, *they look as upon all powers of violence*, if not with condemnation, then with absolute indifference; but their country, if by that we do not mean their village or township, they do not know at all, or, if they do, they do not distinguish from any other countries.[87]

It is noteworthy that Tolstoy and Dostoevsky, despite their profoundly different convictions and outlooks, agreed on the fact that despite the vast empire created in the name of Russia, the national identity of its masses remained very weak.

On the eve of World War I, the Russian society remained divided into four distinct groups. The reactionary nationalists such as the Union of Russian Peoples clung to an ideology of theocratic absolutism in a society that had outgrown it. The liberal intelligentsia, traumatized by the events of 1905–06, fearing a peasant uprising,[88] and shaken by the nationalism awakening in minorities of the empire, were paralyzed by their apocalyptic vision and hence incapable of presenting a viable challenge to the autocracy. The nihilist revolutionaries lived for the day they would build a new utopia. And the great mass of apolitical rural Russians were oblivious to the storm about to engulf them.

Chekhov immortalized the sense of impending doom among Russia's non radical educated class and its pathological helplessness in his plays *The Three Sisters*, *The Cherry Orchard*, and *The Sea Gull*. In the tragic decade between 1914 and 1924, millions of young Russians would die for "Holy Russia," but few were able to define it. This task was left to future generations.

---

[87] Leo Tolstoy, "Christianity and Patriotism," *Collected Works* (New York: AMS Press, 1968), vol. XX, 421.

[88] See Shmuel Galai, "The Kadet Quest for the Masses," in *New Perspectives in Modern Russian History*, ed. Robert McKean (New York: St. Martin's Press, 1992), 80–99.

# 6    Russian identity and
the Soviet period

> Russian national consciousness has been suppressed and humiliated
> to an extraordinary degree.                     Alexander Solzhenitsyn

> The history of Russian culture is all made up of interruptions, of
> paroxysms, of denials or enthusiasms, of disappointments, betrayals,
> raptures.                                          Georgi Florovsky[1]

> Russia is a country without beliefs, without tradition, without the
> culture and skills to do a job.                        Andrei Amalrik

The seventy-four years of the Soviet experiment did not help the
Russians to resolve their "accursed question" (*proklyatyi vopros*). The
policies of the Bolshevik regime toward Russian nationalism in many
ways repeated those of its tsarist predecessors. Initially the regime
attempted to legitimize itself by relying on a universalist ideology;
under these circumstances a distinct Russian national identity was
perceived by the revolutionary regime as an impediment to its
ideological premise. Therefore, the Bolsheviks attempted at first to
repress the Russian identity in favor of an "internationalist" identity
incorporating the minority nations.

The communist regime "discovered" Russian identity and nationalism only when it perceived that the Marxist–Leninist ideology was
no longer a sufficient source of legitimacy. However, much as tsarist
regime before, the state-inspired Russian nationalism was tolerated
only so long as it could be grafted by the regime to the notion of
empire and an internationalist ideology, making the distinction
between Russia and the USSR fuzzy and often unrecognizable.

The Russian national identity that evolved during the Soviet period,
on the elite level, especially after World War II, was organically linked

---

[1] Quoted in Tim McDaniel, *The Agony of the Russian Idea* (Princeton: Princeton University Press, 1996), 21.

to the imperial Soviet identity. The wellspring of Russian popular nationalism, which was not articulated until the 1950s, was energized by a sense of resentment toward minority nationalisms, perceived by many Russians as the beneficiaries of the empire, and by a growing sense of alienation from the regime, which since Khrushchev's "secret speech" in 1956 was suffering from progressive delegitimization. Khrushchev's anti-religion campaign along with the doctrine of fusion into one "Soviet people" irritated many Russians on the popular level, who felt that all these policies were tantamount to their denationalization. Brezhnev, confronted with a deepening ideological atrophy, increasingly came to rely on Imperial Great Russian nationalism as a means to legitimize the regime, reverting to some of the verbiage of the period of high Stalinism.

The Soviet policy of shifting populations did result in mass migrations across ethnic lines, as Robert J. Kaiser aptly points out, but those migrations did not create a supranational Soviet people.[2] Instead, they actually heightened national awareness throughout the Soviet realm. The genesis of nationalisms proceeded far more rapidly among the minorities than among the Russians. However, despite the slower pace of the development of a Russian identity, Roman Szporluk perceptively observed that it was precisely the inability of the Russian-based empire, both under tsarism and communism, to resolve the "Russian question" that ultimately led to the demise of the Russo-centric empire.[3]

The swift collapse of the USSR did not permit the development of an extra-imperial Russian identity, let alone the internalization of a new post-imperial paradigm for Russia. Given the pace of the demise of the Soviet Union, Russia's people initially sought new paradigms among its intellectuals, its multilayered diaspora, and its own historic experience. Five years of independence and of limited democracy saw a progressive decline in the role of the intelligentsia and diaspora and the rise of a new political elite, less encumbered by either the Soviet past or burdened by association with the demise of the Soviet Union. A new "nativist" elite, especially on the local level, is emerging. The process of transformation, however, is far from complete. As with all

[2] See Robert J. Kaiser, *The Geography of Nationalism in Russia and the USSR* (Princeton: Princeton University Press, 1994).
[3] Roman Szporluk, "The Fall of the Tsarist Empire and the USSR: The Russian Question and Imperial Overextension," in *The End of Empire? The Transformation of the USSR in Comparative Perspective*, ed. Karen Dawisha and Bruce Parrott (Armonk, NY: M. E. Sharpe, 1997), 65.

other former empires, the process of devising a new post-imperial paradigm is slow and fitful. Russia's weak national identity compounded by its close association with an imperial identity makes the process of "nationalization" particularly protracted, and it will probably require a generational change within the Russian polity before it is fully complete.

This chapter will trace the evolution of Russian nationalism since the 1917 Revolution and the impact of these mutations of Russia's identity on its sense of self and its place in the international system.

## The October Revolution and Russia's national identity

The collapse of the Russian empire under the strain of World War I and the subsequent revolution did little to enhance the emergence of a distinctly Russian national identity from that of an historically imperial people.

One of the greatest paradoxes of modern time is the fact that despite Lenin's cynical manipulation of nationalism among Russia's minorities as a means of weakening the Romanov dynasty, ultimately the Bolsheviks owed the survival of their revolution to Russian nationalism. Despite rhetoric concerning the rights of self-determination and separation of minorities, and initial attacks on "Great Russian chauvinism," the Bolsheviks' long-term nationalities policy further blurred the Russian identity and bonded it to a "civilizing" role both universally and within the empire.

Before the 1917 revolution, Lenin, like most Russian Marxists, did not devote much attention to nationalism, seeing it as a mere by-product of capitalism that would wither away in due time. Unlike the Austrian socialists, who devoted a great deal of thought to the question of nationalities, Lenin initially had only a perfunctory interest in the nationality question. He rejected the federalist position of the Austrian socialist Karl Renner, who argued that "nations are indestructible and undeserving for destruction." Renner believed that nations would not disappear with the advent of socialism, and therefore a joint economic space would have to be created out of the empires in order to avert the slide toward national-based economies, which would thwart socialism. Otto Bauer, rejecting the notion that nationalism is a by-product of bourgeois capitalism, called for a community of cultures. Lenin, although contemptuous of nationalism, was keen to utilize the Russian minorities' disdain for the empire as a means of undermining the regime and opted to endorse the right of minorities to acquire self-determination, even including secession from Russia. In reality, Lenin, a firm believer in a materialist view of history, remained convinced that the powerful economic links binding the Russian empire, along with proletarian internationalism, would hold the empire together on a voluntary basis.[4] Lenin's hard-line attitude toward minorities' specific agendas was demonstrated in 1903 when he broke with the Mensheviks over the question of the separate status of the Jewish socialist Bund. The 1917 October Revolution therefore remained very much a Russian affair. The Communist Party of Russia was by far the most "Russian" in terms of membership and political base, and the revolutionaries in Saint Petersburg paid scant attention to potential fallout from their activities on the rest of the empire. Once Lenin realized that the collapse of the old regime was rapidly leading to the disintegration of the empire, he reversed himself, adopting federalism as "a compromise between doctrine and reality; an attempt to reconcile Bolshevik striving for absolute centralism of all power in the party hands with the recognition of the empirical fact that nationalism did survive the collapse of the old order."[5]

While the Bolsheviks avoided the slogan of the Whites calling for an indivisible Russia, it was the Bolsheviks' ability to exploit Russian national sentiments that enabled them to survive the civil war and emerge victorious. The withdrawal from World War I, a war perceived by many Russians as a foreign imposition that did not serve Russia's interests, evoked significant support among many nationally conscious Russians, as well as from the a-political peasantry exhausted by the travails of war. The Bolsheviks' ability to capitalize on foreign intervention during the civil war enabled the Red Army to portray itself as the defender of Russia from foreign invasion. Finally, the 1920 Polish war enabled the communists to enlist Russian nationalists in their cause. True believers in the Marxist process of history, the Bolshevik elite were not nationalists and, indeed, as Mikhail Agursky observed, although the Bolsheviks at times utilized Russian nationalism, they "treated the Russian people itself as a natural resource

---

[4] See Gerhard Simon, *Nationalism and Policy Toward Nationalities in the Soviet Union: From Dictatorship to Post Stalinist Society* (Boulder, CO: Westview Press, 1991), 21. See also Hans Kohn, "Soviet Communism and Nationalism: Three Steps of Development," in *Soviet Nationality Problems*, ed. Edward Allworth (New York: Columbia University Press, 1971).

[5] Richard Pipes, *The Formation of the Soviet Union: Communism and Nationalism 1917–1923* (Cambridge, MA: Harvard University Press, 1954), 296.

which could always be replenished by simple reproduction."[6] Nor did Lenin appear to be committed to the retention of Russia's status as a leading socialist power, believing that once the socialist revolution took hold in Germany, "Russia will cease to be a model country and will again become a backward country."[7]

The question of how to accommodate the inherently conflictual situation between Russian nationalism and that of the dozens of other minorities living in the territory of the Russian empire remained perhaps the most difficult and insoluble issue to bedevil the Soviet regime. Instead of eliminating nationalism as a political force, Russia's communists during their seventy-four years in power further blurred Russia's intra-imperial identity, yet at the same time constructed a system that turned out to be a parody of federalism. On the one hand, the Kremlin enhanced, and at times actually created, the national identity of many of its minority peoples; on the other hand, the notion of "democratic centralism" frustrated the growing national aspirations of these emerging nations. In essence, the structure of the USSR resulted in a double frustration. The Russians, their identity increasingly grafted to a supranational structure, viewed themselves as a mere "natural resource" exploited by that structure. At the same time, the other nationalities of the USSR, whose identities were bolstered by the existence of nominally sovereign union republics, felt that they were experiencing growing cultural denudation and ever greater subjugation to the Russian center. This frustration on the part of the minorities, occurring against a background of ever-growing national awareness and consciousness, increasingly convinced the non-Russian population that Soviet federalism was a hollow sham and a mere façade for Russian hegemony.

The Soviet nationalities policy underwent several distinct phases. Having discovered the potency of nationalism and the inherent threat that it posed to the integrity of the new Soviet state, Lenin moved to adopt a modified version of federalism as advocated by the Austrian socialists Karl Renner and Otto Bauer before World War I. Lenin accepted, albeit reluctantly, Renner's comments on the indestructibility of nations, even under socialism, as well as Bauer's position that cultural autonomy must be granted to avoid disintegration, and

---

[6] Mikhail Agursky, "Soviet Communism and Russian Nationalism: Amalgamation or Conflict?" in *The Soviet Union and the Challenge of the Future*, vol. III, ed. Alexander Shtromas and Morton Kaplan (New York: Paragon House, 1989), 153. See also Mikhail Agursky, *Ideologia natsional-bolshevism* (Paris: YMCA Press, 1980).

[7] Kohn, "Soviet Communism and Nationalism," 49.

showed remarkable flexibility on an issue that, before 1913, he had deemed utterly unimportant.

In the early 1920s, major national groups in the Soviet state were awarded a status equal with that of Russia. In order to broaden the regime's overwhelmingly Russian power base and expand it across the state, the role of Russians was de-emphasized while a deliberate policy of affirmative action to create native communist elites under the title of *Korenizatsiia* was vigorously pursued. This policy was officially affirmed at the Tenth Congress of the Communist Party of the Soviet Union (CPSU) in 1921, where it was explicitly stated: "The Congress calls to mind that without overcoming colonizing and [Russian] nationalist survivals in party ranks it is impossible to create in the borderlands a strong and truly communist organization."[8]

During the 1920s, the historiography of the Russian empire and its dealings with minorities was fundamentally rewritten. Whereas nineteenth-century Russian historians portrayed Russia's expansion against its neighbors as a civilizing mission which in the process often saved "smaller peoples" from more ruthless colonizers – be they the Poles, Swedes, Persians, or British – turning the history of a multinational empire into Russian history,[9] the new Marxist historiographers, led by Mikhail Pokrovsky, "developed an orthodox Marxist interpretation of Russian history, which serves today as the historic justification for the Soviet Union."[10] According to that interpretation, Russian nationalism was based on imperialism and chauvinism. As Pokrovsky himself stated, "The Russians had no cultural advantages to offer their new subjects – all the more reason why annexation to Russia for the non-Russians was an absolute evil."[11] On another occasion Pokrovsky asserted, "In the past we Russians – and I am a pure-blooded Great Russian – were the biggest robbers imaginable."[12] At the Twelfth Congress of the CPSU in 1923, it was declared that once Russian nationalism was defeated, all other nationalisms would lose their reason for being, a position reaffirmed by Stalin at the Sixteenth Congress of the CPSU in 1930.[13] To the extent that there was a role for the Russian nation within the USSR, it was declared at the

---

[8] Robert Conquest, ed., *Soviet Nationality Policy in Theory and Practice* (London: Bodley Head Press, 1967), 53.
[9] See Szporluk, "The Russian Question," 70.
[10] Kohn, "Soviet Communism and Nationalism," 56.
[11] Lowell Tillett, *The Great Friendship: Soviet Historians on the Non-Russian Nationalities* (Chapel Hill: University of North Carolina Press, 1969), 26.
[12] Kohn, "Soviet Communism and Nationalism," 56.
[13] Simon, *Nationalism and Policy,* 73.

Twelfth Congress that the "Russian proletariat has an obligation to help the less developed parts of the USSR."[14] While Georgian delegate Budu Mdivani demanded "reparation to the proletariat and working peoples whose nationalities were repressed," Nikolai Bukharin appealed to the Russians to "pretend" to be content with their inferior role.[15] Thus, during the 1920s, when most ethnic groups of Eastern and Central Europe were experiencing political and cultural revivals, Russian nationalism was subjected to a series of major blows, with attacks on Russian imperialism, the Russian Orthodox Church, and much of Russian cultural heritage profoundly disorienting and weakening a distinct Russian identity. The choice of German as the official language of the Comintern and the nihilist attempt to create a proletarian culture (*Proletkult*) not linked to pre-1917 further denuded Russia's uncertain identity.

Even the Russian peasantry, which during the nineteenth century was seen by Slavophiles as the unspoiled preserve of true Christianity and by some Western Marxists as a prototype of non-capitalist development, came under attack. Maksim Gorkyi, in many ways the spiritual godfather of the Bolshevik revolution, perceived the Russian people as possessing two souls: one Slavic, full of dynamism and creativity; the other Mongol, apathetic and destructive. According to Gorkyi, the peasant was the most Mongol of the Russian people and therefore dead weight, retarding Russia's mission of universalism; hence the only solution to the peasant problem was an "amputation" of this malignant element.[16] In a 1922 interview, Gorkyi blatantly stated, "The half-savage, stupid, difficult people of the Russian people will die out . . . and their place will be taken by a new tribe of the literate, the intelligent, the vigorous."[17] Given this state of mind within the Bolshevik regime, Russia's national identity was shorn of its most authentic institutions and increasingly redefined in terms of its relationship with the new universalist entity of the USSR.

It was this state of affairs of the Russian spiritual predicament that induced many Russian *émigrés* to join Petr Struve in the belief that the most urgent task facing the Russian diaspora was the preservation of Russian culture.[18] Despite the emigrants' deep commitment to preser-

---

[14] Ibid., 24.     [15] Ibid.
[16] Agursky, "Soviet Communism and Russian Nationalism," 152.
[17] Mikhail Heller and Aleksandr M. Nekrich, *Utopia in Power: The History of the Soviet Union from 1917 to the Present* (New York: Summit Books, 1982), 121.
[18] Richard Pipes, *Russia under the Bolshevik Regime* (New York: Alfred A. Knopf, 1993), 140.

ving Russian culture, much like the Polish immigration of the nineteenth century, the Russia diaspora embraced a messianic rather than national ethos for its homeland. Russian *émigré* intellectuals continued to advance the cause of an empire fortified by an "ideocracy" as a basis for the Russian state. The Eurasian school, which appeared in Sofia, Bulgaria, in the early 1920s, continued to argue that Russia was a civilization stretching from the Carpathian Mountains to the Great Wall of China, held together by the ideology of Orthodoxy, and these intellectuals rejected the notions of a state and society developed by the "German–Roman" civilization.[19]

Prince Nikolai Trubetskoi, a leading proponent of the Eurasian movement, argued that Russia's misfortunes lay in its attempts to take "leaps" in order to catch up with the West. Since these leaps exhausted Russia, they were invariably followed by prolonged periods of stagnation. Furthermore, these leaps not only served to humiliate Russia and destroy its self-esteem, they also fragmented Russian society between those who were more and less Westernized. He was convinced that before long the socialist idea would negate itself and the Orthodox idea would prevail.[20]

Although politically conservative and viewing Orthodox Christianity as the ideal philosophy for the state, the champions of the Eurasian school differed profoundly from the nineteenth-century Slavophiles. Whereas the Slavophiles dreamed of a pan-Slavic state, the Eurasians rejected pan-Slavism as being too European and too confining for Russia's young and vigorous culture, preferring instead the *assimiliatsionnyi kotel* (melting pot) of the Eurasian landmass, with its blend of Orthodox and Muslim culture, as the basis for a new and pure culture.[21] Nikolai Berdiaev went even further, linking Bolshevik-Marxism with the "Russian idea" and seeing it as a stem toward a "New Jerusalem."[22] Therefore the Russian diaspora, whether as partisans of the old Romanov empire or as advocates of the new Eurasian school, continued to stymie the appearance of a specific Russian identity separate from that of the empire. A small but intellectual group of émigrés, impressed by the ability of the Bolsheviks to preserve the Russian empire, embraced the ideology of

---

[19] Boris Ishboldin, "The Eurasian Movement," *Russian Review* 5 (1946), 64–73.
[20] See Jane Burbank, *Intelligentsia and Revolution: Russian Views of Bolshevism 1917–1922* (New York and Oxford: Oxford University Press, 1986), 212–16.
[21] Mark Bassin, "Russia between East and West," *Slavic Review* 50: 1 (Spring 1991), 15.
[22] Nikolai Poltoratzky, "The Russian Idea of Berdiaev," *Russian Review* 21 (1962), 121–36.

National Bolshevism (discussed below). Although they disagreed on many issues, most émigrés would have agreed with Trubetzkoi's statement that "Romano-German culture is our [Russia's] worst enemy."[23] Thus, the role of Russian émigrés was radically different from that of most other East and Central European émigrés; while the latter served as a catalyst to Westernize their homelands, the former continued to perpetuate the notion of Russia's unique cultural and historic mission.

The Bolsheviks' initial policies further obstructed the development of a Russian identity. The Soviet affirmative action policy for the minorities, *Korenizatsiia*, was intended to broaden the Bolshevik's power base and enhance the regime's appeal beyond ethnic Russia. Early Bolshevik leaders realized that, in order to maintain cohesiveness in the state, they needed to create native Soviet elites. *Korenizatsiia*, however, was doomed as a policy because it failed to provide the most important ingredient for a multiethnic polity, which in Ernest Gellner's words must consist of a "mobile, literate, culturally standardized, interchangeable population."[24] In fact, not only did *Korenizatsiia* fail to meet the above criterion, in reality it fueled the centrifugal forces of a multinational USSR.

The severe criticism of the Russian imperial past, along with a deliberate policy of stressing the national mythology of minority groups, soon deteriorated to the point where cultural separatism started to spill over into politics. The election of Mykhailo Hrushevsky to head the history department of the Ukrainian Academy of Science was a symptom of the centrifugal potential of this policy. Hrushevsky had pioneered the Ukrainian historiography school, which challenged the legitimacy of the unity of the Russian – and, by extension, the Soviet – state, and he had served briefly as president of an independent Ukraine. Among many of the ethnic groups living in the USSR, the depiction of Russia as a chauvinist and imperialist juggernaut increasingly posed the question, "What advantages are there in remaining tied to the empire?" Cultural nationalism among the minority peoples, as it is wont to do in all multiethnic empires, soon acquired political overtones, an occurrence that created foreboding in the Kremlin.

Bolshevik leaders worried that the issue of Russia's imperial past, whatever its merits, would degenerate into an anti-Russian campaign

---

[23] Burbank, *Intelligentsia and Revolution*, 216.
[24] Ernest Gellner, *Nations and Nationalism* (Ithaca: Cornell University Press, 1983), 46.

and eventually challenge the integrity of the centralized state. It was this fear that led Stalin to declare in 1934 that the issue of Russian nationalism belonged to the historians.[25] The implication was, of course, that the nationalities problem had been solved, a policy which required a retreat from *Korenizatsiia*. The end of *Korenizatsiia* had tragic consequences for the minorities, who were thereafter openly repressed. In the non-Russian lands many of the indigenous cultural and political elites (including Mikhailo Hrushevsky, Mykola Skrypnik and Mirza Sultan-Galiev) were politically and even physically purged. Although advocates of this policy, such as Porkrovsky, were attacked posthumously, the Soviet nationalities remained divided until World War II.

### The rehabilitation of the Russian imperial idea: the theory of a lesser evil

With Stalin's policy mutating from communism to Russian nationalism,[26] the historiography of Russia's relationship with its empire underwent a revision. Imperialism continued to be condemned, yet it was presented as a lesser evil when compared with the alternative imperialisms of Poland, Sweden, Persia, Britain, and others.[27] Although first articulated in 1937, even the modest rehabilitation of Russian nationalism, under the aegis of the theory of a lesser evil, did not receive official recognition until 1951.[28] As Russian nationalist émigré S. Dmitrievsky observed, after 1937 there was a return to patriotism, Soviet in theme, with a muted admission of the centrality of Russia to that patriotism. Before 1941 the regime stressed the imperial identity rather than a distinct Russian identity. Despite Bolshevik propaganda, which stressed Russia's altruistic role toward "less developed" people, instruction in the Russian language became compulsory across the USSR in 1938. However, until the outbreak of World War II, Russian nationalist sentiments were treated with suspicion. The practice of damning tsarist Russian imperialism, along with the perception of transfer of resources out of Russia to bolster the social and economic progress of the non-Russian periphery, laid the

---

[25] Conquest, *Soviet Nationality Policy*, 55.
[26] Heller and Nekrich, *Utopia in Power*, 248.
[27] See Tillett, *The Great Friendship*, ch. 3.
[28] Konstantin F. Sheppa, "The Lesser Evil Formula," in *Rewriting Russian History: Soviet Interpretation of Russia's Past*, ed. C. E. Black (New York: Praeger, 1956), 110.

foundation for the emergence of Russian feeling of victimization within the empire.

The Soviet regime resurrected Russian nationalism only when its ideological base had become bankrupt and incapable of meeting the demands imposed by World War II. It was during the war that Stalin fused the Russian idea with that of the USSR, depicting the war as a struggle for the preservation of the Russian culture against German hordes. Similarly, the war against Japan was portrayed as a war to avenge the defeat of Russia by Japan in 1904–05. During World War II the regime started to refer to Russians as the "older brother" and "first among equals," and to hail the unity of the peoples of the USSR with the "Great Russian people." It was during this period that Soviet historians "not only outdid the Slavophiles . . . but exceeded all bounds of probability, arguing the originality of the Russo-Slavic culture from its sources, and expanding to infinity the boundaries of this culture, both geographic and chronological."[29] This policy of glorifying Russia justifiably embittered many non-Russians. Yet for the Russians it was hardly a boon, since such a policy once again tied Russian identity to that of the empire and continued to demand from Russia significant sacrifices in the name of "friendship among peoples." In cultural terms, as Stalin increasingly equated Soviet culture with Russification, Russia was expected to lead in its own Sovietization, further stripping away any distinct Russian national identity. By 1950 Stalin openly demanded the imposition of the Russian language throughout the USSR, expressing the fear that otherwise the Soviet state would become like the empires of Cyrus and Alexander, Caesar and Charlemagne, "temporary and unstable military and administrative combinations, conglomerates of tribes and peoples, lacking economic unity and a language understood by all members of the empire."[30] While this integrative Stalinist policy aiming at the creation of a Soviet people led to violent attacks on the bourgeois nationalist non-Russians, it simultaneously tightened the link between "Russianness," empire, and xenophobia, as manifested in the anti-cosmopolitan campaign, and increased the pressure on Russia to Sovietize.

Despite the adulation of Russia during the last decade of Stalinism, Stalin remained aware that stoking Russian nationalism might well

[29] Konstantin F. Sheppa, *Russian Historians and the Soviet State* (New Haven: Yale University Press, 1962), 367.

[30] Quoted in Conquest, *Soviet Nationality Policy,* 61.

lead to the creation of a "sorcerer's apprentice" situation. As a result, unlike the rest of the republics of the USSR, Russia alone was denied its own trappings of a sovereign state, such as a nominally separate communist party, a ministry of foreign affairs, and a vote in the United Nations. Thus, although the immediate postwar period saw unprecedented glorification of Russianness, in reality this pro-Russian policy was a repeat of the state-directed nationalism *(kazennyi natsionalism)* of the early twentieth century and did little to help Russia separate its identity from that of the empire and the notion of a great power.

### Post-Stalinist USSR and the re-emergence of the two paradigms

The thaw that followed Stalin's death had a perverse impact on Russian nationalism and national identity. On the one hand, Nikita Khrushchev's "secret speech" during the Twentieth Congress of the CPSU debunked the notion of Marxist–Leninist infallibility and allowed Soviet intellectuals of all nationalities to take a fresh look at their histories. On the other hand, Khrushchev's intrinsic ideological optimism, bolstered by a period of relatively fast economic growth, along with several spectacular technological breakthroughs in space, allowed the regime to revert to greater reliance on ideology as a source of legitimacy while downplaying nationalism. Inasmuch as the doctrine of the "great friendship" between the Russians and the other peoples of the Soviet Union was not fully scrapped, the references to Russia as the older brother and the first among equals were not repeated after 1956. Convinced that nationalism was a product of capitalism that would wither away with the onset of communism, Khrushchev, in the 1961 Party Program, went so far as to declare that the USSR's nationality problem would be resolved through fusion *(sliianie)* of the nationalities: "Nations will draw together, until complete unity is achieved."[31]

It was during the Khrushchev period (1953–64) that the birth of a struggle between Russian nationalism and the "universalist" ideology of the governing elite was born. Simultaneously, the relatively tolerant atmosphere of Khrushchev's thaw saw the re-emergence of liberal intellectuals striving for greater decompression and openness in

---

[31] Walker Connor, *The National Question in Marxist-Leninist Theory and Strategy* (Princeton: Princeton University Press, 1984), 399.

Soviet society, with democracy rather than nationalism being their key concern. The new climate of relative political freedom, along with the shock administered by Khrushchev's "secret speech," for the first time in a generation encouraged groups to question openly the state of affairs in the Soviet Union. The most divisive question to arise out of Khrushchev's thaw was whether the tragedy that befell the USSR was the result of Stalin's perversion of Bolshevik principles, the nature of Bolshevism altogether, or an endemic feature of the Russian body politic.

This debate about the source of evil, although muted, was of enormous importance, since the entire question of appropriate "usable history" hinged on its outcome. Initially, however, partisans of all three views could find some comfort in the Khrushchev regime. The campaign of de-Stalinization appealed to those who believed that Stalin perverted a basically ideal social structure. Khrushchev's attempts to improve the living conditions of the peasants and to stop treating the countryside as an "internal colony" – including such measures as the abolition of the Machine Tractor Stations and the granting of internal passports to *kolkhozniks* – appealed to the Russian nationalists, whose greatest grievance against the regime was the destruction of the rural districts. Furthermore, the 1956 establishment of a distinct Russian bureau within the Communist Party of the Soviet Union (though a distinct Russian Communist Party was not to be allowed until 1990) and the founding of such Russian-specific publications as *Sovetskaia Rossiia* and *Literaturnaia Rossiia* were seen by Russian nationalists as a partial rectification of Russia's status within the USSR, since hitherto Russia had been deprived of institutions that all the other republics had. To those who viewed the West as a political model, the greater cultural freedoms, along with a growing openness to foreign cultural influence, as in events such as the World Youth Festival, foreign film festivals, and performances of foreign jazz bands, were perceived as nascent steps toward democratization.

The first group of dissidents to emerge consisted primarily of believers in Marxism–Leninism, who sought to ensure that the Soviet system would return to "Leninist norms" and avoid Stalinist aberrations. Thus, old Bolsheviks such as the novelist Yuri Kosterin took up the cause of the various deported ethnic groups, citing such deportations as violations of Leninist norms. General Petr Grigorenko, in his attacks on the re-emerging interest in the cult of personality, created a league whose aim was "to do away with all distortions of Lenin's doctrine, to restore Leninist norms in party life, and give real power back to the Soviets of toilers' deputies."[32] Even Andrei Sakharov, who never was a member of the Communist Party, initially spoke out for the convergence of the socialist and capitalist systems, to avoid the negative traits of both.[33] The belief that there could be a synthesis of socialism and capitalism was also shared by liberal dissidents such as Yuri Orlov.[34] It is noteworthy that among the dissidents engaged in the debate over the future of Russia, virtually all envisioned some form of a "mixed" economy rather than a return to Western capitalism.[35] Similarly, early underground publications of the *samizdat* were mainly works of old Bolsheviks who attempted to come to terms with the perversion of Leninism by Stalin. Yevgenia Ginzburg's *Journey into the Whirlwind*, Varlam Shalamov's *Kolima Tales*, and Roy Medvedev's "The October Revolution as Law-Governed Process," while all acknowledging the horrors of Stalinism, continued to affirm belief in Marxism–Leninism. The liberal aspirations of the generation of the 1960s probably peaked with the 1962 publication of Aleksandr Solzhenitsyn's anti-Stalinist novel *One Day in the Life of Ivan Denisovich*.

By the early 1960s, however, it was becoming quite clear that Khrushchev's thaw would turn out to be a false spring.[36] There were clear indications – such as the bloody suppression of the Hungarian uprising in 1956, the hounding of Boris Pasternak following his 1958 publication abroad of *Doctor Zhivago*, and the use of the army to crush a workers' strike in Novocherkassk in 1962 – that a return to "Leninist norms" would be tenuous and uneven. By 1963 there was a marked increase in repression of intellectuals, culminating in the 1966 show trials of the authors Yuli Daniel and Andrei Siniavsky, and the crushing of the "Prague Spring" in 1968. These events motivated many former Marxists toward embracing Western democracy and discarding communism altogether.

A second challenge to the regime came from disenchanted Russian nationalists. Khrushchev's vicious anti-religion campaign, which resulted in the closure and demolition of thousands of Orthodox

[32] Quoted in Heller and Nekrich, *Utopia in Power*, 583.
[33] Andrei Sakharov, *Progress, Coexistence and Intellectual Freedom*, ed. Harrison E. Salisbury (New York: Norton, 1968).
[34] See Pavel Litvinov, Mikhail Aksenov-Meerson, and Boris Shragin, *Samosoznanie: sbornik statei* (New York: Khronika Press, 1976).
[35] See Vladislav Krasnov, "Images of the Soviet Future: The Émigré and Samizdat Debate," in *The Soviet Union and the Challenge of the Future*, vol. I, ed. Alexander Shtromas and Morton A. Kaplan (New York: Paragon, 1988), 391.
[36] For an excellent evaluation of Khrushchev's ambiguous legacy, see Aleksei Kiva, "Epokha Khrushcheva: illiuzii i realii," *Rossiiskie vesti*, 21 April 1994.

churches and most seminaries, embittered Russian nationalists, who saw in the campaign an assault against the last vestiges of authentic Russian heritage and identity. Morever, Khrushchev's revival of the doctrine of ethnic fusion or *slianie* was perceived by Russian nationalists as an effort to dilute the Russian people ethnically and replace Russian culture with an ersatz Soviet culture. Even Khrushchev's seemingly benign policies, such as the opening up of the virgin lands of Kazakhstan, provoked among many Russians a sense of being once again called to serve other peoples' interests. A common refrain of the mid-1950s – *"Nikita, Nikita gde tvoi ochi? Russkie na tsylinie a zhidy v Sochi!"* – complained that while Russians were being sent to the virgin lands, Jews were being sent to the resort city of Sochi on the Black Sea. The Russian sense of slight was not directed at Jews alone, but was directed also at the fresh-fruit peddlers, mainly from Central Asia and the Caucasus, whose presence in Russian cities was perceived as exploitative. Similar resentment was directed at the small yet visible number of foreign students from the newly independent countries of Africa and Asia. This sense of victimization among the Russians was further heightened by Khrushchev's activist foreign policy in the Third World, which led to massive Soviet aid to China, Egypt, Syria, and India, among other nations. To many Russian nationalists, this transfer of resources indicated yet another example of support for a universalist alien ideology that further impoverished Russia's long-suffering people. It was during the Khrushchev era that the so-called Village Prose emerged as a force in Russian literature for the first time, raising the question of Russia's future, as opposed to that of an empire, or other universalist creation. The emergence of the literary Village Prose school was the first time in Russia's thousand year history that a totally nativist intellectual body, devoid of imperial or missionary zeal had emerged.

## Brezhnev: regime decay and co-optation of nationalism

The post-Khrushchevian USSR in many ways resembled twilight tsarist Russia. To the liberals, the aborted, self-limiting reforms of Khrushchev-era "thaw" signaled the limits of reform possible under the existing system, and they became further alienated from the political order in Russia. To the Russian nationalists, the growing psychological void visited upon the system during the Brezhnev years proved that the regime was too constrained by both external and internal pressures to allow a full-blooded revival of Russian nationalism; they also grew more and more alienated from the existing order in Moscow. As a result, the USSR of the 1980s in many ways resembled Russia exactly one hundred years earlier, far too unreformed to please the Westernizers and far too accommodating to foreign influences to please the increasingly frustrated Russian nationalists.

Marked by ideological ossification and inertia, as well as growing tension with an irreconcilably hostile China, the Brezhnev era elite gradually came, once again, to rely on Russian nationalism as a source of legitimacy. Russia's designation as the older brother was again reinstated, cultural and linguistic Russification was intensified, and the role of other languages was further curtailed. Leonid Brezhnev's increasing reliance on Russian nationalism as a source of legitimacy and greater repression of Western-oriented liberal dissidents, however, never approached either the intensity of state-directed Russian nationalism or the repression of the Stalinist era. This milder re-Russification of the Soviet political elite reflected several counter-forces constraining the regime's ability to accommodate Russian nationalism. First, the growing economic weakness of the USSR made détente essential and required greater patience with the aspirations of minorities, who could rely on the vocal diaspora in the West to defend their cultural autonomies. Second, Brezhnev, cautious by nature, was very much aware that an unrestrained adulation of Great Russian chauvinism would fuel increasingly assertive nationalism among other ethnic groups, who after two generations of nominal sovereignty were rapidly acquiring greater self-confidence. Thus, during the Brezhnev era, the regime tolerated and even tacitly supported mounting Russian nationalist, anti-Semitic, and xenophobic expressions in the media. Nevertheless, the regime remained aware that the utilization of Russian nationalism was a double-edged sword that if unchecked could undermine the entire structure of the Soviet Union.

An equally interesting parallel can be observed between Soviet liberals and nationalists and their tsarist predecessors in terms of their attitude toward the imperial structure of the country. Contemporary Soviet liberals, looking at the United States and the European Community as models, assumed that common human values were the wave of the future and that with the exception of the Baltic states all the other peoples of the USSR would want to remain within a democratic federal structure that would succeed the USSR. Conversely, Russian nationalists, firmly believing that Russia had indeed played the role of a selfless older brother through whose generous efforts the other peoples of the Soviet Union were uplifted in both economic and cultural terms, took it for granted that the "little peoples" of the USSR would happily continue to rely on their older brother. Much as with the nineteenth-century opposition to the regime, Russia's dissidents, whether liberal or nationalist, while cognizant and sympathetic to the travails of the peoples of the "outer empire," saw little linkage between the imperial configuration of the country and the nature of the regime.

## National identity and Russian dissent: the rebirth of dichotomy

One of the paradoxes of modern history is that despite the fact that the Bolshevik October Revolution of 1917 was a coup organized by a tiny minority – who upon seizing power proceeded to terrorize the country, causing millions of martyrs – by the early 1950s it had managed to attain a degree of legitimacy. The physical destruction or exile of the old intelligentsia, the advancement opportunities resulting from the purges, and rapid industrialization created a new elite, which owed much of its success to the regime. Soviet victory in World War II and the re-creation of the USSR as a great power further legitimized Bolshevik rule in the country. Finally, although the Soviet population was aware of the famine inflicted by collectivization and of the brutality of the "Great Terror," the Slavophiles' mythology of the good tsar versus the bad boyars continued to pervade the public view.

There was a persistent belief that the regime in general and Stalin in particular were benevolent, and all the misfortunes to befall the USSR were little more than a product of vicious bureaucrats. The belief in the good tsar struggling against wicked boyars, nourished by the Stalinist regime and depicted in Stalin's favorite movie, *Ivan the Terrible*, was by no means limited to the simple people, however. The notion of a benevolent Stalin thwarted by mean bureaucrats continued to be believed by many intellectuals in Russia as well as in the West. The grief manifested at Stalin's death was genuine and even included the foremost victims of the regime, the inmates of the gulag. Therefore, Khrushchev's "secret speech" at the Twentieth Congress of the CPSU not only shook the country and the party, but, more important, fundamentally delegitimized the regime. The dissident intellectual Yuri Glazov observed that Khrushchev's 1956 speech, along with the

1958 publication abroad of Boris Pasternak's novel *Doctor Zhivago*, rekindled the democratic movement in Russia.[37]

The delegitimization of Soviet ideology was facilitated by the suppression of the Prague Spring and the intellectual atrophy of the Brezhnev era (1964–82). During these years, the regime survived in power mainly through a careful titration of co-optation and coercion, with ideological legitimacy reduced to a mummified relic, and a substantial decline occurred in the number of those dissidents who still sought a return to "Leninist norms." Broadly speaking, competing liberal and nationalist paradigms for the future of Russia emerged.

The debate that surfaced in Brezhnev's Soviet Union in many ways resembled the nineteenth-century debate between the Westernizers and Slavophiles. Much like their nineteenth-century predecessors, both the liberals and the nationalists generally saw the Russian people as the *Staatsvolk* of the Soviet Union and gave little thought to the multinational character of the USSR. Beyond this attitude, however, there was a fundamental dividing line between these two groups. The nineteenth-century Westernizers and the twentieth-century liberals felt that Russia was a victim of a millennium-old autocracy, and that the root of Russia's tragedy lay in its failure to join the mainstream of Western civilization. Liberal intellectuals argued that the autocratic tradition not only stymied the political development of Russia, but also stymied the maturation of a sense of individualism, creating a propensity within the Russian populace to eagerly embrace ideologies as a means of evading responsibility.[38] Increasingly, the liberals argued, the October Revolution was but another form of traditional Russian authoritarianism.

Conversely, twentieth-century Russian nationalists, much like their Slavophile predecessors, argued that the source of Russia's misfortune was the repeated effort to foist upon Russia an alien ideology and culture. Thus, whereas nineteenth-century Slavophiles lamented the Westernization of Russia during the reigns of Peter I and Catherine II, contemporary Russian nationalists rued the 1917 October Revolution, when a tiny "non-Russian minority" forced an alien Western ideology on that country and turned Russia into a guineapig for theoretical writings of cosmopolitan abstract philosophy. As their philosophies would indicate, the agendas of the two were profoundly different.

[37] Yuri Glazov, "Chto takoe demokraticheskoe dvizhenie," *Novyi zhurnal*, no. 109 (1972), 216–39.
[38] See Margarita Riurikova, "Ishchushchemu opory v samom sebe," interview with Grigori Pomerants, *Novoe russkoe slovo*, 20 May 1994.

The liberals or Westernizers, who often consisted of former communist intellectuals, with a significant number of non-ethnic Russians
among their ranks, arose out of the dismay induced by Khrushchev's
exposure of the brutality of Stalinism. Following the events of
1966–68, when the regime ended all hopes for a continuing thaw of
"socialism with a human face," the alienated liberals increasingly saw
their mission as one of restoring human rights in the USSR, which
ultimately evolved into calls for a pluralist system, and the establishment of a society based on law. Speaking for thousands of disenchanted former Marxists, Vladimir Bukovsky lamented:

> After tanks with the red star, dream and pride of our childhood, had
> crushed our peers in the streets of Budapest, everything we saw was
> stained in blood. The entire world betrayed us, and we no longer
> believed anyone. Our parents turned out to be agents and informers,
> our military leaders were butchers and even the games and fantasies
> of our childhood seemed to be tainted with fraud.[39]

Marxism, once the prevalent dogma among wide circles of the
intelligentsia, had been largely delegitimized by the late 1960s.

Believing that Russia was a victim of centuries of autocracy, liberal
human rights activists felt that they were "inspired by such authors as
Nikolai Berdiaev, Sergei Bulgakov, Pavel Miliukov, and Petr Struve
. . . [continuing] the struggle for human rights in the USSR against the
arbitrariness of tsarism that had been going on since Radishchev
(1749–1802)."[40] Russian liberals believed that the only way Russia
could break its tragic cycle of oppression was to abandon all claims to
a special mission within the international system and join the family
of Western pluralist democracies. In their political program, the
liberals laid the source of Russia's trauma at the doorstep of the
Russian tradition of despotism. Examining the course of Russian
history, the framers of the liberal *Program of the Democratic Movement of
the Soviet Union* noted: "The USSR is an imperialist amalgamation
created around the nucleus of Great-Russian nationalism . . . the
hegemony of the Russian state over other nationalities and their lands
is a result of 500 years of expansion." Explaining the causes of Russia's
expansionism, the authors of the declaration stated: "Russia was
permanently haunted by internal failure, a weak economy compared
with European states. Culturally Russia was a stagnant backwater . . .

---

[39] Heller and Nekrich, *Utopia in Power*, 626.
[40] Krasnov, "Images of the Soviet Future," 369.

with semi-barbarous social relationships, and a political despotism assimilated from the oriental hordes."[41]

While strongly advocating the adoption of Western standards, most Westernizers relegated nationality issues, other than the rights of deported peoples and emigration issues, to a secondary concern. Much like Petr Chaadayev over a century before, Russian liberals increasingly came to believe that Russia had little in terms of usable history and that its sole hope of becoming a normal country lay in its ability to adopt the West's cultural and political mainstream. Andrei Stakhanov, in his rebuff to Solzhenitsyn's nationalist doctrines calling for an end to Russia's imperial role as well as avoidance of foreign models, noted "Only under democratic conditions is it possible [for the Russian people] to develop a national character capable of reasonable existence . . ."[42] As the years went on, they recognized that to accommodate the non-Russian peoples, the USSR would have to move toward a genuine federal system. This issue, however, they believed was manageable.

The shift away from the quest to create a socialist political system, adhering to Leninist norms and leaning toward the West became a recurring theme in the literary output of the generation of the 1960s. Vassily Aksyonov (Yevgenia Ginzburg's son), in his novel *The Burn*, explained the quest of his generation to return to the Western civilization orbit: "I was not alone and could feel behind me the presence of mother Europe. She did leave me, her flesh and blood; silent great nocturnal she was there. Where are you now?" The poet Yevgeni Yevtushenko expressed the liberals' quest to rejoin the Western world, complaining:

> Frontiers are in my way
> It's awkward
> Not to know Buenos Aires
> or New York.[43]

The view that Russia's tragedy was the result of its autocratic history rather than any specific event such as the October Revolution was

[41] *Programma Demokraticheskogo Dvizheniia Sovetskogo Soiuza* (Amsterdam: Herzen Foundation, 1970), 45.
[42] Frederick C. Barghoorn, *Détente and the Democratic Movement in the USSR* (New York: Free Press, 1976), 63.
[43] Both the Aksyonov and Yevtushenko quotes are from Nicholas Hayes, "A Crisis of Belief: Reflections in Soviet Youth Culture," in *The Soviet Union and the Challenge of the Future*, vol. II, ed. Alexander Shtromas and Morton A. Kaplan (New York: Paragon, 1989).

echoed by the poet/balladeer Bulat Okudzhava, who described the typical Muscovite as an "ant" whose oppression had not lifted for the past three hundred years, and even more poignantly by Vasili Grossman, who in his novel *Forever Flowing* linked the tragedy of Russia to a millennium-long chain of Russian servitude and authoritarianism.

This historic disassociation from Marxism among Russian liberal intellectuals led to the wholesale revision of their view of Russia's nineteenth-century intelligentsia. Dissident Soviet intellectuals broke not only with the Marxism fashionable among much of the late-nineteenth-century intelligentsia, but also with the populist notions common in the nineteenth century. Instead of worshiping the common people *(narod)* as the eternal source of goodness and values, Andrei Amalrik warned that the *narod* was spiritually devoid of the ability to build a democracy: "Whether because of its historic tradition or for some other reason, the idea of self-government or equality before the law and the personal freedom and responsibility that goes with it, are almost incomprehensible to the Russian people . . . In Russian history man has always been the means, not the end."[44] In a similar vein Nadezhda Mandelstam complained that "the intelligentsia had excessive belief in the ability of man to transform himself."[45]

By the early 1970s the transformation of the Russian liberal intelligentsia was profound. Sakharov, who as late as 1968 still believed that one could salvage parts of Marxism via fusion with capitalism, had by 1970 come to the conclusion that democracy and Marxism were incompatible, and Russia must join the international system. In 1970, shortly after joining with Valery Chalidze and Andrei Tverdokhlebov to form the Human Rights Committee, Sakharov observed, "The salvation for our country is interdependence with the rest of the world . . . [The USSR] must have democratic reforms affecting all aspects of life."[46] Similarly, the authors of the *Program of the Democratic Movement of the Soviet Union* called for "rapprochement and convergence with capitalist countries in order to attain the friendship and collaboration of the United States and Western Europe."[47]

By the 1970s the liberal opposition was in a situation somewhat

[44] Andrei Amalrik, *Will the Soviet Union Survive until 1984?* (New York: Harper and Row, 1976), 33–34.
[45] Jan Bergman, "Soviet Dissidents on Russian Intelligentsia, 1956–1985: The Search for a Usable Past," *Russian Review* 51: 1 (January 1992), 19.
[46] Andrei D. Sakharov, *My Country and the World* (New York: Alfred Knopf, 1976), 45.
[47] *Programma Demokraticheskogo Dvizheniia*, 63.

analogous to that of the pre-World War I intelligentsia, rejecting the old intelligentsia's enthusiasm for populism and violence, yet thoroughly alienated from the regime and skeptical about its ability to reform. The deepening repression of dissidents after 1973 increasingly forced the Russian liberal intelligentsia to turn abroad for support. Thus, Sakharov supported the Jackson–Vanik amendment tying improved relations with the USSR to the status of human rights in the Soviet Union.[48] The authors of the *Program of the Democratic Movement of the Soviet Union* insisted that an essential step toward bringing to an end centuries of suffering in Russia was the abolition of the monopolist role of the Communist Party and the introduction of a political system based on competitive politics.[49]

A consistent feature of the liberal-democratic opposition was the conviction that the West would be repeating a historic error if détente were to become another effort to co-opt the USSR, as was the case with the Yalta agreements. Andrei Amalrik warned, "Rapprochement between the United States and the Soviet Union would make sense only after serious steps toward democracy were taken in the USSR . . . Genuine rapprochement must be based on similarity of interests, culture, and traditions, and on mutual understanding."[50]

### The rise of nationalist opposition and its co-optation

Although also traceable to the post-Stalinist thaw, the genesis of the Russian nationalists as well as the impetus to this group's activity were fundamentally different from that of the liberals. The communist regime of the USSR did, especially in moments of weakness, turn to Russian nationalism as a source of legitimacy, but the relationship remained an uneasy one (as noted above). The manipulation of Russian nationalism by the communist regime had a perverse impact on Russian national identity. On the one hand, communist historiography reinforced the psychological link between the Russian identity and the empire, and the notion of Great Russia (*velikaia Rus'*) enshrined the endemic sense of messianism in the Russian national mythos. On the other hand, the constant stress of Russia's fraternal help to the rest of the Soviet Union increasingly irked Russian nationalists in light of Russia's growing impoverishment. The emerging Russian nationalists viewed Russia as a victim of the current

[48] Sakharov, *My Country*, 55.
[49] See *Programma Demokraticheskogo Dvizheniia*, 70–72.
[50] Amalrik, *Will the Soviet Union Survive?*, 55–58.

structure of the USSR, which reduced the republic to the role of a "wet nurse" *(Kormilitsa)* for the rest of the USSR. To the nationalists, Russia was the most denationalized republic in the Soviet Union. Whereas in all other republics there were national institutions (academics, parliaments, etc.) dominated by indigenous peoples, in Moscow these institutions were considered all-Union institutions where, as a result of affirmative action favoring minorities, the status of ethnic Russians never reflected their numbers or economic contribution. Scholars in the West, however, as well as minorities within the USSR, believed that all-Union institutions were tantamount to Russian institutions anyway.[51] The Russian nationalist increasingly found the blending of a Russian and an all-Union identity unacceptable.

This sense of anger and hostility on the part of Russian nationalists was vividly captured by Vasili Grossman in his novel *Life and Fate*, in which the character Dementi Getmanov complains:

> Quite frankly, all this makes me puke. In the name of friendship of peoples we keep sacrificing the Russians. A member of a national minority barely needs to know the alphabet to be appointed a people's commissar, while our Ivan, no matter if he is a genius, has to "yield to minorities." The Great Russian people is becoming a national minority itself. I'm all for the friendship of peoples, but not on these terms. I am sick of it.[52]

Although both liberals and nationalists collided with the regime, their goals remained quite different. The nationalists' key concern was far narrower, limited to the status of Russians within the Soviet Union. Unlike the liberals, they saw no utility in emulating Western models.

Another fundamental difference between liberals and nationalists was their assessment of the impact of Soviet rule on Russia. The liberal dissidents, when they denounced the horror that befell Russia during the reign of Stalin, concentrated almost exclusively on the so-called Great Terror of 1937. Russian nationalists perceived this obsession as perfidious and self-serving, arguing that the terror of 1937 was unique only in the sense that many of its victims were old Bolsheviks from whom many liberal dissidents stemmed. The liberals, they

---

[51] See articles by Oleh Fedyshyn, Seweryn Bialer, Michel Rywkin, and Vadim Medish in *Soviet Nationality Problems*, ed. Edward Allworth. All of these authors agree with the view that the Russians are comfortable with the notion of "Soviet people" in light of the Russians' dominating role.

[52] John G. Garrard, "A Conflict of Visions: Vasilii Grossman and the Russian Idea," in *The Search for Self-Definition in Russian Literature*, ed. Ewa Thompson (Austin: University of Texas Press, 1991), 61.

argued, ignore the fact that the Red Terror started as early as 1918 and that by 1929, as Solzhenitsyn asserted, the back of the Russian nation was broken by precisely the same people who would be consumed by the terror of 1937. Furthermore, whereas the liberals attributed the phenomenon of terror to Russia's autocratic tradition, nationalist thinkers stressed that Bolshevik terror was rooted in Western (Marxist) doctrine, which in its "scientific" self-righteousness had no compunction about the delivery of these brutal blows to Russia and its cultural heritage.[53] Aleksandr Tsipko, at that time the director of the prestigious Institute of Economics and the World Socialist System, asserted in his study of the sources of Stalinism that it was "bourgeois intellectuals" with their scientific schema who introduced mass terror to Russia and not Russia's autocratic tradition, as Aleksandr Yanov and others would argue.[54]

Given the different nature of the two groups' grievances toward the regime, that their visions of an ideal Russia should also be fundamentally different was only natural. Although rumblings of a Russian nationalist backlash could be sensed as early as the 1950s when some of the forerunners of the Village Prose started to lament the disaster that befell the Russian countryside,[55] the articulation of the nationalist dissent to a large degree was triggered by the position of the Westernizers and their critique of Russia's past. Nikolai Berdiaev's comment that in the "process of engendering [Russian] self-consciousness, next to them [the Slavophiles] is that of [westernizer] Chaadaev,"[56] proved to be equally true for the dissidents of the mid-twentieth century.

Unlike the liberals, whose initial rhetoric often had an apologetic, *mea culpa* tone, the nationalists originally coalesced around the issue of the destruction of historic buildings and the depopulation of the Russian countryside, and from the very beginning their attitude took on a strong nativist and anti-intellectual character. Reacting to statements such as Grossman's judgment that the "historic road of Russia is a road toward slavery" and Amalrik's assertion that "Russia is a

---

[53] See Vadim Kozhinov's review of Anatoli Rybakov's *Children of the Arbat* in *Nash sovremennik*, April 1988. For a broader analysis of the nationalist critique of liberals' historiography, see Vladislav Krasnov, *Russia Beyond Communism: A Chronicle of National Rebirth* (Boulder, CO: Westview Press, 1991).

[54] Aleksandr Tsipko, "Istoki stalinizma," *Nauka i zhizn'*, nos. 11, 12 (1988) and nos. 1, 2 (1989).

[55] For an excellent analysis of the role of Village Prose in the Russian cultural context, see Kathleen F. Parthe, *Russian Village Prose: The Radiant Past* (Princeton: Princeton University Press, 1992).

[56] Quoted in Dimitri Pospielovsky, "The Resurgence of Russian Nationalism in Samizdat'," *Survey* 86: 1 (1973), 57.

country without belief, without traditions, without the culture and the skills to do a job,"[57] Russian nationalists saw their first task as the defense of Russia's political heritage against the denationalized liberals. Like the liberals, the nationalists covered a broad spectrum of opinion, from moderate patriots such as Dmitrii Likhachev, who refused to equate patriotism with xenophobia, to nativists who sought an inward-looking Russia, to fascists and neo-Stalinists, who saw Russia's future tied to a powerful and assertive Russian state.

Several broad themes, however, were common to virtually all nationalists. Most believed that the tragedy of Russia lay in the fact that small minorities had repeatedly imposed an alien ideology on the country, reducing the Russian people to mere bystanders and victims of their own history. Unlike the liberals, who felt that Russia had no usable history, the nationalists firmly believed that Russia's history contained a glorious past that had been usurped by the imposition of foreign ideology, and therefore that this past should be a guide to the future. It is noteworthy that the precise point when that alien ideology was imposed on Russia remained controversial, even among the nationalists. While most nationalists agreed that the revolution of 1917 was a brazen and brutal imposition of an ideology alien to Russia's core beliefs, others viewed Peter I's reforms as the start of a series of foreign cultural encroachments on Russia, and still others reached as far back as the conversion of Kievan Rus to Christianity as the start of this pattern.[58]

A second belief common to many nationalists was the belief that if Russia was not to lose its national identity (*natsionl'nyi oblik*), Orthodox Christianity had to regain its central position within Russia's spiritual life. As the former dissident Michael Aksenov-Meerson explained, "No ethnocentric Russian movement can bypass Orthodoxy, for only there can it find historic roots."[59] It was partisans of the nationalists who pioneered the concept of *Russkost'*, defining a Russian as Orthodox, East Slav, and nativist.

A third common thread among Russian nationalists was the belief that Russia was the prime victim of the USSR. Although it was the Russians who came to dominate the rest of the USSR, politically and

[57] Ibid., 56.
[58] See Andrei Siniavsky, "Russian Nationalism," *Radio Free Europe/Research Library (RFE/RL) Reports*, 19 December 1988.
[59] Michael Aksenov-Meerson, "The Influence of the Russian Orthodox Church on Russian Ethnic Identity," in *Ethnic Russia in the USSR: The Dilemma of Dominance*, ed. Edward Allworth (New York: Pergamon Press, 1980), 111.

culturally, the price of this leadership was the denial of authentic cultural expression.[60] In fact, the self-image of most Russian nationalists remained "not the identity of a great people, responsible for their history, but rather a stymied identity of a subordinate ethnic group oppressed under the yoke of a conqueror and unable to liberate itself."[61]

A fourth common nationalist belief was that Russia was being forced to subsidize the ersatz cultures of Central Asia as well as the rest of the USSR, yet instead of earning gratitude it got abuse for its alleged imperialism. Similarly, the perceptions of Russian relations with the outside world were remarkably consistent across the nationalist spectrum. Unlike the liberals, who were eager to integrate Russia into the West, the nationalists believed that Russia's efforts to join the West were futile and bound to fail because successful integration would require an intolerable cultural mutation, and the West had no real intention of accommodating Russia anyway. In fact, throughout the nationalist camp there was a thread of bitterness toward the West, which had its source in the belief that Western prosperity was possibly the result of Russia's shielding of Europe from the Tatars, the Swedes, the Turks, Napoleon, Hitler, and Maoist China.

Instead of expressing its gratitude, however, the West remained haughty and arrogant in its dealings with Russia. This sense of bitterness toward the West, which was commonly articulated by nineteenth-century Slavophiles as well as by Eurasians and national Bolsheviks, was reaffirmed by the poet Aleksandr Blok, who in his powerful poem *The Scythians* (1922) stated that Russia, in return for shielding Europe, got little more than cold contempt.[62] The treatment of Russia by the Allies in the final days of World War I, as well as Western support for the Polish invasion of 1920, only confirmed the notion of the West's duplicitous attitude toward Russia. This theme of Western contempt and betrayal of Russia was revived by the poet G. Seribriakov more than fifty-five years later, as he berated the participation of Genoese soldiers in the Tatar–Mongol invasion as a Western conspiracy against Russia.[63]

Although this sense of slight was shared by virtually all Russian nationalists, the conclusion drawn from this conviction was far from

---

[60] See S. Enders Wimbush, "The Russian Nationalist Backlash," *Survey* 24: 3 (1979).
[61] Aksenov-Meerson, "The Influence of the Russian Orthodox Church," 112.
[62] See Babette Deutsch and Avrahm Yarmolinsky, *Russian Poetry* (New York: International, 1927).
[63] See G. Serbriakov, "Rubezhi pamiati," *Nash sovremennik*, no. 4 (1979), 44.

uniform, as noted above. There was, however, a fundamental consensus in the nationalist camp that Russia was not, nor should it seek to be, a part of the Western-dominated world order. In fact, Russian nationalists across the spectrum endorsed Yuri Bondarev's Spenglerian view that "European culture has probably reached its zenith and for the last twenty years has steadily been slipping into the darkening twilight."[64] On the issue of minorities in the USSR, the position of Russian nationalists, despite their consensus that the Russians were victims of the Soviet state, was sharply fragmented. At one end of the continuum were those who wanted to abolish the federal structure of the USSR and return to a unitary state, with the Russians becoming the *Herrenvolk* of that state; on the other hand were thinkers, foremost among them Solzhenitsyn, who favored decolonization of Central Asia and the Caucasus and reduction of the Soviet Union to its Slavic core.[65]

Although the Russian nationalist movement was a result of a reaction to perceived attacks on Russian identity by the Soviet regime, liberal intelligentsia, and increasingly restive nationalist-minded minorities in the USSR, the strength, diversity, and depth of the nationalist movement far exceeded that of either the liberals or the true Leninists. As Dina Rome Spechler observed, dissident Russian nationalism was qualitatively different from previous presentations of Russian nationalism. Unlike the bouts of Russian nationalism during the reign of Alexander III or the late Stalin years, which were initiated from above and thus perceived as state-guided nationalism, the latest wave of nationalism, even if initiated by literati of the village school or Orthodox intellectuals, soon spread among the population to become a genuine mass movement.[66] The 1960s may have been the first time that a broad Russian national consciousness emerged. Unlike the liberals, who sought, albeit non-violently, to recast the USSR as a Western state, nationalists concerned themselves with preventing Russia's cultural and religious heritage from being subsumed by the "new Soviet man" and perpetuating Russia's role as a great power.

[64] Mikhail Agursky, "Contemporary Russian Nationalism – History Revisited," Research Paper no. 45, Soviet and East European Research Centre, The Hebrew University of Jerusalem, 1982.

[65] Aleksandr I. Solzhenitsyn, *Kak nam obustroit' Rossiiu: poslednie soobrazheniia* (Paris: YMCA Press, 1990).

[66] Dina Rome Spechler, "Russian Nationalism and Soviet Politics," in *The Nationalities Factor in Soviet Politics and Society*, ed. Lubomyr Hajda and Mark Beissinger (Boulder, CO: Westview Press, 1990), 281–309.

With the agenda of the nationalists being far more modest, mainly aimed at changing the status of ethnic Russians in the Soviet Union rather than the structure of the Soviet regime, most nationalist dissident groups attempted to come to terms with the regime. Furthermore, since their agenda was often non-contradictory and actually supportive of the regime's own goals, some segments of the nationalist camp managed not only to arrive at a *modus vivendi* with the regime but actually to become part of the establishment.

In a sense, during their evolution liberal and nationalist dissidents crossed paths only to take up each other's positions. The liberals largely started as a loyal opposition, attempting to rectify Stalinist excesses before ultimately degenerating into outright opponents of the regime, the nationalists began as implacable opponents of the regime but by the mid-1970s, through compromise with the regime, had actually become pillars of Soviet power.

The first dissident nationalist groups to emerge in the USSR were bona fide opposition groups. Reacting to Khrushchev's anti-religion campaign and the prospect of ethnic fusion, *slianie*, the initial nationalist group clustering around the All-Russia Social Christian Union for the Liberation of the People (VSKhSOM) emerged in Leningrad in 1964. Its main aim was a coup against the Soviet regime and the creation of a theocratic system, with the Holy Synod playing a key role in the governance of Russia.[67] By the mid-1970s, after the VSKhSOM was suppressed by the regime, the Russian nationalist movement basically split into two camps. On one side were the protagonists of Village Prose and nativists *(pochviniki)*, whose agenda consisted of reasserting Russian cultural and ethnic traditions and demanding Russian withdrawal from the world arena, even at the cost of possible dissolution of the Soviet Union. On the other side, the national Bolsheviks embraced the theory of émigrés belonging to the Change of Signs *(Smenovekhovtsy)* group of the early 1920s, whose 1921 Prague program stated that despite the trappings of internationalism the Bolshevik revolution was a purely Russian national process leading toward the restoration of Russia as a great power with a universal mission. According to the *Smenovekhovtsy*, the "Russification of October" was an ongoing process that would ultimately lead to the re-creation of a "one and indivisible Russia" across the territory of the Soviet Union, without the internationalist verbiage brought in by

---

[67] See "Vserossiiskii Sotsial'no-Khristianskii soiuz osvobozhdeniia naroda" (Paris: YMCA Press, 1975).

cosmopolitan foreigners. Although nearly forgotten today, the impact of the *Smenovekhovtsy* on the Russian mindset must not be understated. Led by White émigrés in Sofia, Bulgaria, the group recognized early on, as Vasili Shulgin, the former publisher of the rabidly monarchist and anti-Semitic publication, *Kievlianin*, observed in 1920, that "under the shell of the Soviet state there is a process which has nothing to do with Bolshevism."[68] The *Smenovekhovsty* living in exile may well have been the first group to systematically fuse the Russian Idea with Bolshevism, recognizing the October Revolution as the "Great Russian Revolution."[69]

Even in the early years of the Bolshevik regime, when internationalism was at its apex, the *Smenovekhovtsy* had a profound impact on Soviet politics. The Soviet novelist Marietta Shaginian saw in the October Revolution a new synthesis of "Slavophile-Bolshevik consciousness."[70] The importance of the *Smenovekhovtsy* was not lost on parts of the early Soviet leadership, with Leon Trotsky declaring, "The Smenovekhovtsy from patriotic considerations came to the conclusion that the salvation of Russia lies in the Soviet state, and nobody can defend the Russian people . . . besides the Soviet state."[71] The flirtation by Lenin as well as Trotsky with Russian nationalists abroad drew bitter opposition to that policy from communists of minority background, such as Grigory Zinoviev, Joseph Stalin, and Mykola Skrypnik. Although the notion of the fusion of the Russian national idea with Bolshevism never became the official state ideology of the USSR, it remained a strong political undercurrent in the Soviet body politic. A vital residue of the *Smenovekhovtsy* in the thinking of many later Russian nationalists was their belief that following the destruction of the Russian Church and countryside, the Russian (Soviet) armed forces remained the repository and defender of enduring Russian values.[72] This belief helped cement the relationship between Russian nationalists and the Brezhnev regime, a relationship that Solzhenitsyn characterized as "attempts to salvage the disintegrating communism, fusing it with Russian nationalism . . . This current recognizes no blemishes in either the Russian communist or national past."[73]

---

[68] Mikhail Agursky, *The Third Rome: Bolshevism in the USSR* (Boulder, CO: Westview Press, 1987), 238.

[69] Hilde Hardman, *Coming to Terms with the Soviet Regime: The 'Changing Signposts' Movement among Russian Émigrés in the Early 1920s* (DeKalb: Northern Illinois University Press, 1994), 191.

[70] Agursky, *Third Rome*, 275.      [71] Ibid., 260.

[72] See Agursky, "Contemporary Russian Nationalism," 63.

[73] Pospielovsky, "Some Remarks," 74.

Explaining the ideological niche of contemporary Russian national Bolsheviks, Mikhail Agursky noted, "National Bolshevism is the Russian etatist ideology that legitimates the Soviet political system for an etatist point of view . . . National Bolshevism does not reject communist ideology, though it seeks to minimize it to a minimum needed for legitimacy."[74] Darrel Hammer explained that the fundamental difference between the nationalist nativists and national Bolsheviks was really a matter of institutional loyalty. Whereas the nativists saw the Russian ethnic groups as their source of identity and loyalty, the Bolsheviks saw the powerful Russian-led state as their key concern.[75]

Although these groups differed in their agendas from the late 1960s, both attempted to assume the position of a "loyal opposition" rather than that of outright dissidence. The Brezhnev regime, under the patronage of the Communist Party's chief ideologue Mikhail Suslov, was tolerant, seeing Russian nationalism as a pillar of legitimacy for the regime. Thus, although critical of the Bolshevik regime, the Russian nationalist right increasingly viewed Soviet power as Russia's ultimate defense against the odious West. As the nationalist-Christian publication *Veche* stated, "If you throw off the Bolshevik regime, the Zionists and only the Zionists will come to power."[76] In a similar vein, the nationalist literary critic Vadim Kozhinov described Lenin as the savior of Russian culture from the vagaries of internationalism.[77]

The Soviet regime exhibited a relatively benign attitude toward the nationalist *samizdat* publication *Veche*; although it was closed down after a prolonged semi-clandestine existence, some of its authors were allowed to regroup. Conversely, when Aleksandr Yakovlev attacked Russian nationalism on the pages of *Literaturnaya gazeta*, he was punished with prolonged banishment to Canada. Throughout the 1970s the tenor of such nationalist publications as *Nash sovremenik, Sever, Molodaya Gvardya, Don*, and *Ogonyok* remained unchanged, despite occasional shakeups, especially in 1984, during Yurii Andropov's brief tenure. Nationalist publications continued to articulate the nationalist position with relative impunity; certainly none of them

---

[74] Agursky, *Third Rome*, xv.
[75] See Shtromas and Kaplan *The Soviet Union and the Challenge of the Future*, vol. II..
[76] Quoted in John B. Dunlop, "The Many Faces of Contemporary Russian Nationalism," *Survey* 24: 3 (Summer 1979), 18–35.
[77] Vadim Kozhinov, "On Lenin's Concept of Russian Culture," *Moskva*, no. 11 (November 1986), 183–98.

was subjected to twenty years of repression, as was the case with the liberal literary journal *Novyi Mir*.

As communist ideology receded and nationalism evolved into a potent political force, the direction of Russian nationalism became an issue of major contention in the West. Since all Russian nationalists, from the nativist Solzhenitsyn to the Stalinist Aleksander Prokhanov, rejected Western-style democracy, Western observers were divided as to whether to welcome or fear the rise of Russian nationalism. Some, such as John Dunlop, saw virtue in Russian nationalism as the sole force able to dislodge communism. The antithetical view, often associated with Aleksandr Yanov and Valery Chalidze, was that the difference between nativists and national Bolsheviks was more apparent than real. They noted the position of Genadi Shimanov, who believed that Russia was facing a Zionist–Anglo-Saxon conspiracy that necessitated a communist–nationalist coalition, and cited Shimanov's declaration, "Communism is a vital step to create a Russian renaissance, since it preserved Russia from the West and mobilized its forces."[78] Sergei Semanov called for a "Red–Brown" coalition to save Russia and its greatness from external conspiracy, along with the notion that the Soviet regime could be salvaged by merely shifting the state ideology from Marxism–Leninism to Orthodoxy. In observing the evolution of Russian nationalism, Yanov noted that by the late 1970s it had shifted from an opponent of the autocratic regime to an apologist for it.[79] In fact, Yanov went on to predict that Russian nationalism would undergo three distinct phases, ultimately leading to the reimposition of totalitarianism in Russia. Russian nationalism, Yanov believed, would repeat the nineteenth-century cycle, when Russian nationalism evolved from the liberal nationalism of the 1830s to fascism by 1910; he saw a similar evolution taking place between 1960 and 2000.[80]

Although the long ideological void of the Brezhnev era allowed both the liberals and the nationalists to crystallize into well-defined groups, clustered around different institutions and appealing to different constituencies, neither group foresaw the radical changes that *glasnost* and *perestroika* would usher in, and neither group was prepared to deal with the emerging circumstances. Both groups, the

---

[78] Alexander Yanov, *The Russian Challenge and the Year 2000* (New York: Basil Blackwell, 1974), 237.
[79] Ibid., 251.
[80] Alexander Yanov, "Russian Nationalism: the Ideology of Counter-Reform," *RFE/RL Reports* (special issue), 19 December 1989.

liberals through democratization and the nationalists through a pan-Slavic unitary state, assumed that the preservation of a single state on the territory of the USSR was both desirable and attainable. Among the dissidents, Petr Boldyrev virtually alone rejected the "technocratic" attitude of the liberals, which ignored the passion of non-Russian nationalisms and the national egotism of the Russian right, arguing that the only way for Russia to become a normal democratic state, at peace with itself, was to undertake a rapid and irreversible decolonialization.[81] Boldyrev's characterization of the USSR as a Russian empire and his prescription calling for its dismantlement were rejected by both the liberals committed to *common human values* and the nationalists committed to a *one and indivisible Russia*.

### The rise of Gorbachev and the ascent of liberalism

The ascent of Mikhail Gorbachev to the pinnacle of Soviet power in March 1985 caught both the nationalist and the liberal camps unprepared for the momentous shifts that took place in the Soviet body politic. Gorbachev's initial behavior in office did not indicate that the new Soviet leader would attempt to reform the system but rather that he would try to revive it through administrative fiats and greater vigor and discipline. Gorbachev's initial policies of *uskoreinie* (acceleration), the creation of a new bureaucracy to supervise quality assurance of products *(Gospriemaka)*, and the decision to solve the USSR's alcoholism problem by simple decree suggested that the inertia in the Kremlin would continue unchallenged.

Only in 1986–87, after encountering the depths of the USSR's economic and social plight and the stubborn resistance of the bureaucracy, did Gorbachev take the unconventional step of enlisting the support of the liberal intelligentsia as a means to mobilize public support and to release the creativity stifled by decades of repression and cynicism. Enlisting the intelligentsia against the entrenched officialdom was clearly unconventional in the Russian as well as Soviet historic context. Both the tsarist and Soviet regimes had profoundly distrusted and feared the intelligentsia. It is worth noting, however, that by the mid-1980s some political analysts, both in the USSR and the West, tended to assume that the Soviet population, mostly urbanized and far better educated than its predecessors,

---

[81] Petr Boldyrev, "Russkie za likvidatsyiu svoei imperii (1978)," in *Ukroki Rossii* (Tenafly, NJ: Hermitage Press, 1993), 115–22.

would react to greater openness along patterns similar to those in the West. Fedor Burlatsky, Khrushchev's and later Gorbachev's speech writer, observed that the regime would actually gain strength from democratization. "The [uncensored] press," Burlatsky asserted, "will be the method for democratic control, not control by administration but control with the help of democratic institutions."[82] The sociologist Tatyana Zaslavsaia and the US historian Moshe Lewin assumed that Soviet society was ripe for a fundamental opening, and Lewin argued that Gorbachev was more a symptom than a cause of the democratization of Soviet political life.[83] In a similar vein, Geoffrey Hosking noted that the "population [of the USSR], which in education, lifestyle, and occupation has become so much like the West, should be ready for an open, democratic style of politics."[84]

Gorbachev's growing reliance on the liberal intelligentsia gravely undermined the stability of the USSR. As John Dunlop noted, until 1985 the "democrats" to whom Gorbachev turned in 1988 as a means to dislodge the conservative bureaucracy were not a political force to reckon with, and even after 1988 they consisted of several differing groups. There were those, like Roy Medvedev, Yuri Afanasiev, and others, who at least initially still hoped to salvage Leninism; there were those who sociologist Vladimir Shlapentokh categorized as opportunists;[85] and later they were joined by genuine dissidents such as Sakharov. The conflict that doomed Gorbachev's coalition with the democratic intelligentsia was their intrinsically contradictory agendas. Whereas Gorbachev hoped to be able to unleash the creative forces of the population by enlisting the democratic intelligentsia and simultaneously reinvigorate Leninism from the stupor of the Brezhnev years, many members of the intelligentsia aimed to democratize fundamentally the Soviet political system, even if such democratization led to the end of the communist monopoly of power. The democratic intelligentsia was enthusiastic about *glasnost's* revelations about such taboo topics as the horrors of Stalinism, the current economic plight of the USSR, and the ecologic disasters resulting from high-handed Bolshevik indifference. The airing of taboo topics such as the 1933

---

[82] Robert V. Daniel, *The End of the Communist Revolution* (New York: Routledge, 1993), 16.

[83] Moshe Lewin, *The Gorbachev Phenomenon* (Berkeley: University of California Press, 1989).

[84] Geoffrey Hosking, *The Awakening of the Soviet Union* (London: Mandarin Press, 1990), 4.

[85] Vladimir Shlapentokh, *Soviet Intellectuals and Political Power: The Post-Stalin Era* (Princeton: Princeton University Press, 1990), passim.

famine, the Molotov–Ribbentrop pact, the Katyń massacre, and so on invigorated an intelligentsia hungry to know its own national history.

Instead of reinvigorating Leninism, Gorbachev's (or more precisely Aleksandr Yakovlev's) *glasnost* led to the rapid delegitimization of the regime in both Russia and the smaller republics. The exposure of the cold-blooded terror visited upon Russian culture since 1918 and the economic and ecological malfeasance severely eroded the legitimacy of the regime in Russia. In the outlying republics, the reopening of such issues as the artificial famine in Ukraine (1933–34) and, in the Baltics, the Molotov–Ribbentrop pact and the mass murders fueled separatist tendencies challenging the internationalist ideology under-pinning the regime.

Gorbachev's policy of greater freedom of expression was carried out by officials who remained oblivious to the issue of the nationalities in the USSR. Despite clear warning signs, nationalist tensions were corroding the core of the Soviet states. Neither the riots in Alma-Ata following the removal of Kazakh party boss Diamukhamed Kunayev nor the emergence of popular fronts in the Baltic states evoked a serious reaction from the Kremlin. Notwithstanding the belated admission by Gorbachev at the February 1988 Communist Party plenum that the nationalities problem "is a most fundamental and vital issue," the policy remained one of *ad hoc* reaction to various crises, with no acknowledgment that the Russians or other national-ities were increasingly discontented with the existing order.[86]

Because of the growing contradiction between Gorbachev and his democratic allies, mounting ethnic pressures outside Russia, and disquiet among the "power ministries" controlling the armed forces and security apparatus, Gorbachev in 1990 shifted to the right, attempting to reverse *glasnost* and its destructive effects. Until the late 1980s, many liberal intellectuals continued to see some virtue in an egalitarian planned economy. Although political events in 1989 caused many to rapidly embrace liberalized capitalism, making co-existence between Gorbachev and the intelligentsia untenable,[87] it was Gorbachev's shift to the right that triggered the final abandon-ment of the socialist idea by much of the Westernized intellectual community. The result was a massive exodus of liberal-democrats to

---

[86] See S. Anders Wimbush, Elizabeth Teague, Bohdan Nahaylo, T. H. Ilves, and Iain Elliot, *Glasnost and Empire: National Aspirations in the USSR* (Munich, Washington, DC, and New York: RFE/RL Studies, 1989).

[87] See Jeremy Lester, *Modern Tsars and Princes: The Struggle for Hegemony in Russia* (London and New York: Verso Books, 1995), 89–90.

the camp of Boris Yeltsin, who saw in the assertion of the Russian Republic's sovereign rights a means to break the monopoly on power held by the center.

Although Yeltsin utilized the plight of Russia as a means to expand his power, there is little evidence that he developed a clear idea of how to reform the USSR and divide the powers within it. Many members of Yeltsin's entourage remained convinced Westernizers. The historian Yuri Afanasiev complained that Russia, by following the "Byzantine–Buddhist" political model, had ruined itself and ought to turn to the West. Afanasiev, who openly declared that the two Russian philosophers he admired most were Petr Chaadaev and Aleksandr Herzen, asserted, "The state in Russia has always subordinated society to itself. That was the case before the Soviet regime and during the Soviet period. It represents a certain stable, many centuries-long constant."[88]

Although most of the liberals endorsed Yeltsin's assertion of the sovereign rights of Russia and the other republics, they saw such concessions as an assault on the Soviet monolithic power, not on the integrity of the state as such.[89] Perhaps the philosopher Yuri Burtin encapsulated best the dilemmas of liberal-democrats: "We cannot separate the Russian republic from the center. We look back at history, and the center is somehow ourselves. Even [RSFSR Supreme Soviet Chairman] Yeltsin seems to see Russia's future as the heart of a remade Soviet Union, not something separate from it."[90] Generally, while the liberals continued to believe that the USSR's integrity would somehow survive, few were willing to contemplate George Kennan's prophetic observation:

> If disunity were ever to seize and paralyze the Party, the chaos and *weakness of Russian society would be revealed beyond description*. Soviet power is only a crust concealing an amorphous mass of human beings . . . If, consequently, anything were done to disrupt the unity and the efficacy of the Party as a political instrument, Soviet Russia might be changed overnight from one of the strongest to one of the weakest and most pitiable national societies.[91] (emphasis added)

The ascent of a new liberal elite hastened the disintegration of the

---

[88] John B. Dunlop, *The Rise of Russia and the Fall of the Soviet Empire* (Princeton: Princeton University Press, 1993), 114.

[89] John B. Dunlop, *The New Russian Nationalism* (New York: Praeger, 1985), 95.

[90] Vera Tolz, "The Democratic Opposition in Crisis," *RFE/RL Report on the USSR*, 3 May 1991, 3.

[91] George F. Kennan, "The Sources of Soviet Conduct," *Foreign Affairs* (July, 1947) 566–82.

USSR in several ways. Faced with a surge of nationalist and democratic mobilization, especially in the Baltics and western Ukraine (areas that had been Sovietized for a relatively shorter period),[92] the once-powerful provincial party bosses, mainly Brezhnevite holdovers, could no longer count on the center for protection and were confronting nationalist demands. As a result, the old communist elite had two options: either confront the growing democratic nationalist pressure without the certainty of firm support from the center or reinvent themselves as champions of nationalism. As the center's will and the ability to restore discipline continued to decline, local Communist Party bosses followed the lead of Lithuania's Algirdas Brazauskas and took up the banner of nationalism.[93] As nationality became the strongest and the most secure basis for political mobilization, the old elite rushed toward newly discovered nationalism, prompting the philosopher Grigori Pomerants to observe that in the USSR "nationalities have become converted into political parties."[94]

Despite the growing nationalist turmoil in the outlying republics, Russian liberals continued to view the nationality question as a secondary issue. Not only did they ignore the weakness of Russian society, they even deemed Soviet society sufficiently cohesive to preserve the USSR. In 1988, when Yuri Afanasiev published a collection of thirty-five articles by leading democrats under the title *There Is No Other Way*, not a single article was devoted to the nationality issue.[95] To the extent that the liberals did address the nationality issue in the USSR, most took a position similar to that of the pre-World War I Austrian socialists Renner and Bauer, supporting the existence of a federal structure as an antidote to a (particularly Russian) nationalist-chauvinist reaction.[96] Sakharov, in his "Constitution of the Union of Soviet Republics of Europe and Asia," envisioned a new, truly federal system where Tataria would enjoy the same rights as Ukraine and

---

[92] For a broad discussion of the role of the Habsburg Lands, acquired by Stalin in 1939–45, in the disintegration of the USSR, see Roman Szporluk, "After Empire: What?" *Daedalus* 123: 3 (Summer 1994), 21–40.

[93] For an excellent description of the metamorphosis of communists to nationalists in Ukraine, see Solomea Pavlychko, *Letters from Kiev* (New York: St. Martin's Press, 1992).

[94] Grigori Pomerants, "Po tu storonu zdravogo smysla," *Isskustvo kino* 10 (1989).

[95] Yuri Afanasiev, ed., *Inogo ne dano* (Moscow: Progress, 1988). Similarly, scant attention is paid to the national question in the collection edited by Gavril Popov, *Obratnogo khoda net* [There Is No Return] (Moscow: Progress, 1990).

[96] This view, expressed by Andrannik Migranyan, is quoted in Shlapentokh's *Soviet Intellectuals.*

Estonia.[97] He confidently stated, "With proper democratic procedures I don't think that anything [i.e., any part of the USSR] will be lost."[98] Yeltsin and his liberal supporters recognized that Russia's status had to be changed, and that Russian assertiveness might well be the only way to dislodge the communist oligarchy. But few were prepared to see that Russian assertiveness was leading to the demise of the Soviet Union. As Aleksandr Tsipko noted on the pages of *Izvestia* in October 1991:

> [The] thousands, indeed millions, of Russian voters who were drawn into the struggle of the RSFSR, who dreamed of having their own president, never, it now becomes clear, considered the immediate consequences of the policies they have supported. They did not understand that the idea of a sovereign RSFSR would invariably lead to the split of the historic nucleus of the state, that it would invariably push both Ukraine and Belorussia, not to speak of Kazakhstan, toward separation from a sovereign RSFSR.[99]

In their protracted struggle with Gorbachev and the center, many Russian liberal-democrats to the very end remained oblivious to the implications of the assertion of Russian sovereignty. The Brest Agreement of December 1991 among Boris Yeltsin, Leonid Kravchuk, and Stanislav Shushkevich that dissolved the USSR and replaced it with the Commonwealth of Independent States (CIS) drew an optimistic response from the liberals. Commenting on the agreement, Len Karpinsky, the editor of the liberal *Moscow News*, stated, "The treaty signed in Brest looks good because it launches, at long last, the process of integration." Galina Staravoitova, at the time Yeltsin's adviser on nationality issues, predicted, "The Brest Agreement gives us the hope for a future confederation."[100] Clearly, while the liberal-democrats embraced Yeltsin's Russia-centered struggle against the center, very few were aware that by following such a course they were invariably furthering the disintegration of the USSR and with it the historic Russian state. If most liberals were oblivious to the possibility that democratization might lead to the disintegration of the USSR, fewer still recognized that a potential Russian nationalist reaction might be triggered by the collapse of the USSR.

Andrannik Migranyan was one of the few to note the dangerous

---

[97] See draft of the constitution in *Russkaia mysl'*, 22 December 1989; also Andrei Sakharov, "Stepin' svobody," *Ogonyok*, no. 31 (1989), 26–27.

[98] As quoted in Ed Hewett and Victor Winston, eds., *Milestones in Glasnost and Perestroika: Politics and People* (Washington, DC: Brookings Institution Press, 1991), 145.

[99] Ibid., 61.     [100] *Moscow News*, 18 December 1991.

potential lurking behind the collapse of the USSR. Migranyan warned that Westernizing liberals were fundamentally misreading the state of mind of the Russian masses. It would be a mistake, he believed, to misinterpret the absence of a Russian nationalist reaction to the disintegration of the USSR. The Russian masses, according to Migranyan, numbed by decades of the communist's use of nationalist symbols, initially confused nationalism with discredited communism. However, once the Russians had to deal with the issue of a huge Russian diaspora in the territories of former USSR, realized that they were living in a national state whose legitimacy was based on defending a Russian national identity, and began to associate the collapse of their empire and the drop in their standard of living with liberal democracy, a nationalist collectivist reaction would sweep the land.[101]

The growth of the liberal movement after 1987 placed the Russian conservative camp in an awkward position. Although in the early 1960s the Soviet regime viewed Russian nationalism as its main threat and the initial right-wing opposition was uncompromisingly anti-Soviet, by the late 1960s Russian nationalism, if not fully satisfied with the status of the Russians within the USSR, was nonetheless substantially co-opted by the Soviet political establishment. Even Aleksandr Prokhanov, one of the most vocal nationalist publicists, who continues to believe that the October Revolution was a brutal imposition of foreign domination on Russia, declared that the "enmity between the Party and the people ended in 1942 . . . The people forgave the Party, came to trust it, to accept it as the only possible power . . . Stalin gathered together the debris of tsarism . . . and created his own empire."[102] Valentin Rasputin, the prominent nativist writer, observed that although initially communism was a foreign imposition on Russia, "Russia digested communism and placed it in the service of statehood."[103]

Given the strong link between many nationalists and the powerful central state, Gorbachev's acceptance of liberals (some perceived as non-Russian) alienated the conservatives. As Prokhanov complained, "Our recent masters from the Soviets and the Party trace their lineage from those who took power by force [in 1917] . . . from those who shot the tsar with his daughters and heir . . . and who drove the whole

---

[101] Andrannik Migranyan, "Russia's Fate," *Nezavisimaia gazeta*, 14 November 1991, 5.
[102] Dunlop, *The Rise of Russia*, 173.
[103] Interview with Valentin Rasputin, *Sovetskaia Rossiia*, 23 January 1992, 4.

peasant Russia out of their homes into the cold."[104] Simultaneously, however, Yeltsin's drive to turn Russian nationalism against the all-powerful central state disoriented the nationalists. The schism between the CPSU and the nationalists sapped the energy of the nationalist camp in its struggle with the liberal onslaught.

In 1989 the growing power of the liberals, along with assertive claims by national minorities, prompted the doyen of the Village School of Russian nationalist writers, Valentin Rasputin, to suggest that Russia should withdraw from the USSR. However consistent with the ideas of other Russian nationalists, from Aleksandr Solzhenitsyn to Vladimir Balakhonov, it seems that Rasputin's remarks were made in a spirit of, as *Moscow News* described it, "polemical exaggeration."[105] Solzhenitsyn's suggestion that the Soviet empire ought to be reduced to its Slavic core was scorned by many Russian nationalists. Furthermore, even though some nationalists did call for the dissolution of the Soviet empire, the governing assumption was that Russia would not be bound by the borders imposed on it by the Bolsheviks, and that Ukraine and Belarus would remain united with Russia.[106]

The years 1987 to 1991 were a period of severe disorientation for Russian nationalists. Before 1985, Brezhnevite Soviet elites entered a "political contract"[107] and developed a symbiotic relationship with the nationalists. Thus, Gorbachev's ability to purge many traditional communists and replace them with liberals, including the nationalist's *bête noire* Aleksandr Yakovlev, in a sense orphaned much of the nationalist bloc. The nationalists were further disoriented by splits among those who favored the perpetuation of the empire and the nativists, monarchists, and Stalinists. With the dispirited nationalist camp lacking a unifying theme, the nationalist publication *Nash Sovremenik* attempted to utilize the threat of "foreign conspiracy" as a source of cohesion. Notwithstanding the efforts by the editors of *Nash Sovremenik*, profound differences among many nationalists toward communism and regarding Russia's future direction prevented the emergence of of a successful conservative front. The inability of the nationalist groups to form a unified bloc was reflected in the plethora

---

[104] Dunlop, *The Rise of Russia*, 173.

[105] Krasnov, *Russia Beyond Communism*, 245.

[106] Eduard Voldin, "A New Russia in a Changing World," *Literaturnaia Rossiia*, 26 January 1990, 3–4.

[107] See Yitzhak Brudny, "The Heralds of Opposition to Perestroika," in Hewett and Winston, eds., *Milestones in Glasnost and Perestroika*.

of nationalist publications that surfaced during 1989–90.[108] Russian nationalists and communists were also discomfited by Yeltsin's ability to mobilize large segments of the Russian working class under a Westernizing nativist banner.

### The collapse of the USSR and the demise of the liberal paradigm

There are many unanswered questions about the aborted coup of 19–21 August 1991. Whether the coup was a pathetically bungled operation by desperate party apparatchiks fearing the new Union Treaty that was due to be signed a few days later or a provocation planned by Gorbachev as a pretext to impose dictatorial rule will not be answered for a long time to come. The fallout of the failed coup in many ways was reminiscent of the Kornilov affair in 1917, when a bungled attempt by the military to save the faltering Kerensky government discredited the very regime it had hoped to save. The August 1991 coup triggered a chain reaction whose effects are still far from complete. The collapse of the coup neutralized the traditional power ministries (armed forces and the security apparatus) and denied the central regime the ability to resort to intimidation as an instrument of policy. Many communist leaders of non-Russian republics, whose position as intermediaries between the center and the restless populace had increasingly been challenged by *glasnost*, at first supported the coup, then did a sharp about-face and became champions of national independence. A cascade of declarations of independence soon followed. Hence, the dissolution of the USSR and the democratization of Russia occurred almost as an accidental by-product of a series of events, rather than through an evaluative political process, and created a political situation with which few were prepared to cope. The defection of the republics robbed the center and Gorbachev of any remnants of legitimacy they might have had, making the collapse of the all-Union government a foregone conclusion leading to the emergence of Russia, within its 1954 frontiers, fully independent, and governed by Yeltsin and his liberal coalition.

The complete disintegration of the USSR and the speed with which it happened were anticipated by very few in the Soviet Union or abroad. For many of the newly independent states the task would be

---

[108] Among the new oppositionist newspapers to surface between 1988 and 1991 were *Delo, Den' (Zavtra), Edinstvo, Golos Rossii, Istoki, Molniia, Pamiat', Vestnik Khristianskoi Demokratii, Za Rossiiu, Zemshchina*, and scores of others.

to create a national identity after centuries of submission; for the Russians there awaited the no less daunting task of finding a post-imperial identity and destiny. A torturous and dangerous process had begun.

## Liberal-democrats in the post-Soviet era

The disintegration of the Soviet Union and the contraction of Russia's European frontiers virtually to its pre-Petrine configuration dealt a severe blow to all groups across the Russian political spec- trum. It was liberal-democrats, however, who found it most difficult to adjust to the new circumstance. Seeing communist dictatorship as the key issue confronting the Soviet Union, they gave scant thought to the possible collapse of the USSR. Not only did the democrats assume that all citizens of the Soviet Union subscribed to common human values, they actually thought that separatism had been fanned by the slow pace of democratization under Gorbachev and that full democracy would dampen the separatist tendencies.[109] As late as May 1991, *Izvestia*'s Aleksandr Bovin perceived the nationality crisis as primarily an issue for former socialist countries other than the Soviet Union and saw more democracy as the only way to resolve nationalist tensions.[110] Thus, while credited with the responsibility for playing a key role in ending communist rule in Russia, the liberal-democrats were also charged with responsibility for the break-up of the Soviet Union. Initially, many liberals reacted to the agreement ending the USSR and the creation of the Commonwealth of Independent States as steps toward genuine confederation or perhaps even a pan-Slav confederation that might extend to incorporate Poland and Bulgaria, thus creating a "Slavic chamber within the common European home."[111] Ukraine's insistence on full independence, the inability of Russia to avoid entanglement in the ensuing instability in Central Asia and the Caucasus, and the issue of the huge Russian diaspora across the former USSR created a profound psychological trauma that rapidly discredited the liberal-democratic movement and marginalized it politically in a manner reminiscent of the February 1917 revolution.

---

[109] See Lilia Shevtsova, "Where the Crisis Stands," *Izvestiia*, 17 September 1990.
[110] Aleksandr Bovin, "The Crisis of Socialism and the Nationalities Question," *Izvestiia*, 11 May 1991, 4.
[111] Alexander Rahr, "'Atlanticists' vs. 'Eurasians' in Russian Foreign Policy," *RFE/RL Research Report* 1: 22 (29 May 1992), 17.

The new reality faced by the democrats, who along with Yeltsin seized power in Russia, caused a very early crisis in that camp, leading to a simultaneous polarization and radicalization. The crisis had become particularly severe because, as Dmitri Furman noted, most of the puported democrats who came to power with Yeltsin were not political amateurs and idealists of the generation of Andrei Sakharov and Ales Adamovich but rather opportunistic "migrants" from *Staraia Ploshad'* (the headquarters of the CPSU) to the White House (head-quarters of the Russian government) – whose interest in retaining power was far greater than their commitment to any specific idea.[112]

As a result, shortly after the collapse of the USSR there was a mass exodus from the liberal-democratic camp, with many of its former members either defecting to the nationalists or joining the reborn communist parties. As Viktor Bondarev noted, "If you listen to their speeches, it is difficult to tell former democrats from the most active 'patriots' of today."[113] Aside from the desire to break the CPSU's monopoly on power, the broad coalition operating under the rubric of Democratic Russia *(DemRossia)*, which won crucial political victories in 1990 and 1991, had no other agenda. Thus, following the August 1991 events, a process of rapid disintegration set in.[114] In fact, Democratic Russia started to splinter even before the attempted coup, with the party's chairman, Nikolai Travkin, insisting that the union must be preserved at all costs.[115]

The collapse of the Soviet Union rapidly led to hostile feelings toward the liberals, many of whom were seen as responsible for causing the collapse and, as it now seemed, the possible destruction of Russia. The editor of the liberal newspaper *Moscow News*, Len Karpinsky, declared that, to most Russians, a Russia without Ukraine was an unreal entity.[116] The relatively liberal newspapers *Izvestiia* and *Komsomolskaia pravda* blamed the liberals for the collapse of the USSR and said they should resign from power.[117] Following the 1991 failed coup, several leading members of Democratic Russia, including Sergei

---

[112] Dmitri Furman, "From Sakharov to Khasbulatov," *Nezavisimaia Gazeta*, 3 September 1991, 3.

[113] Allen Lynch, "Postcommunist Political Dynamics: *Ex Uno Plura*," *RFE/RL Research Report* 3: 1 (7 January 1994), 5.

[114] See Julia Wishnevsky, "The Rise and Fall of Democratic Russia," *RFE/RL Research Report* 1: 22 (29 May 1992).

[115] See Nikolai Travkin and Arkadi Murashev, "Krov'-Kto za nee otvetit?" *Demokraticheskaia Rossiia*, 14 June 1991, 5.

[116] See Vera Tolz and Elizabeth Teague, "Russian Intellectuals Adjust to Loss of Empire," *RFE/RL Research Report* 1: 2 (10 February 1992).

[117] Ibid.

Shakhrai, Sergei Stankevich, Nikolai Travkin, Yevgeni Ambartsumov, and Oleg Rumantsiev, defected to the nationalist-statist camp. The former Olympic gold medalist Yuri Vlasov, who made his political debut by denouncing Stalinist terror from the podium of Gorbachev's Supreme Soviet, also crossed to the nationalist camp, declaring, "A democratic path is damaging to Russia – a country of which very little remains at present. It needs its own path of development. Only statists can define this path – no one else."[118] The shift of many former democrats toward nationalist ideologies was a repudiation of what Valery Vyzhutovich described as "Russian liberals' fanciful dream to blend democracy with national [ethnic] patriotism."[119]

Further damaging the liberal-democratic cause was the break in the alliance between blue-collar groups and the liberal camp. Blue-collar workers, especially miners in the Kuzbass and Vorkuta regions who supported Yeltsin in his struggle with Gorbachev and the center, rapidly grew disillusioned with the liberals and their embrace of neo-conservative economics cum brazen property seizure by the nomen-klatura under the façade of privatization. Boris Kagarlitsky, a member of the Moscow city soviet and an activist in the emerging trade union movement, charged that the Soviet intelligentsia (unlike its Russian predecessors, whose concern was the suffering of common people) had no agenda other than denouncing Stalinism. Therefore, once the regime allowed the intelligentsia to settle its score with Stalin, it effectively co-opted that group, reducing it to an interest group committed to Thatcherite neo liberalism and manifesting little or no concern about its implications for Russia's realities. Much like traditional Russian elites in the past who supported either autocracy or dictatorship of the proletariat, some liberals, such as Andrannik Migranyan and Igor Klyamkin, called for a dictatorship by democrats to force market reforms from above. In fact, Kagarlitsky argued that the contemporary Russian intelligentsia was reduced to mere self-serving intellectuals who were repeating the eighteenth-century experiment with Westernization that would create a Western façade benefiting only the "enlightened" few. For the vast majority of Russians, Kagarlitsky believed, Westernization would be yet another revolution from above, which in the Russian context would become increasingly undemocratic.[120]

---

[118] Yuri Vlasov, *Pravda*, 13 May 1992.
[119] Valery Vyzhutovich, *Moscow News*, 15 July 1992.
[120] Boris Kagarlitsky, *The Disintegrating Monolith* (London and New York: Verso Press, 1992), esp. chs. 2 and 10.

In essence, the unforeseen collapse of the USSR, along with the sharp economic decline and profound psychological disorientation, resulted in the rapid transformation of the liberal-democratic movement from a mass movement to a small and increasingly defensive political grouping. Those who continued to identify with liberal views after the events of 1991 retained a consistent vision about Russia's future direction and its place within the international system. Despite profound disappointments with the pace of Russia's integration into the international system, liberals continued to believe that the source of Russia's travails lay in its insistence on a messianic or at least unique role within the international system rather than on building a democracy based on a market economy.[121] Furthermore, most liberals, while regretting the collapse of the Soviet Union, continued to argue that any attempt to re-establish the old structure would not only ruin Russia financially but would also require the use of coercion, thereby dashing all hopes for a real democracy.[122] Yuri Afanasiev bitterly lamented, "On the verge of the twenty-first century, Russians have yet to accept the notion of a single world belonging to humanity; to recognize themselves as a component of that world."[123] In a similar vein, Vladimir Bibler stated that Russia would not be able to construct a civil society unless it abandoned the notion of a "single national idea."[124] The historian Marina Pavlova-Sil'vaskaia, in an essay taking stock on the first anniversary of the collapse of the USSR, observed that Russia would remain a great power only if, in addition to its size and mineral and military wealth, it armed itself with democracy and linked itself economically with the Group of Seven rather than indulging in "Great Russian delirium" (velikorusskii ugar).[125] In economic terms, liberals continued to advocate a rapid transformation to a market economy and called for intensified efforts to provide assurances to foreign investors in order to induce an adequate inflow of capital into the Russian economy.[126] Domestically, Russian liberals, personified by Yegor Gaidar, were eager to launch a rapid market-

[121] S. Alekseev, "Nash shans," Novyi mir, no. 4 (1993), 137–45.
[122] See Denis V. Dragunskii's comments in "Russkaia ideia i novoe rossiiskoe gosudarstvo: problemy, napravleniia, perspektivy."
[123] Yuri Afanasiev, "'Narodovlastie' protiv demokratii," in God posle avgusta: Gorech i vybor, ed. Iu. Burtin and E. Molchanov (Moscow: Literatura i Politika, 1992), 112.
[124] Vladimir Bibler, "Demokratom byt' trudno," in Burtin and Molchanov, God posle avgusta, 179.
[125] Marina Pavlova-Sil'vaskaia, "U rossii est' shans ostatsia velikoi derzhavoi," in Burtin and Molchanov, God posle avgusta, 151.
[126] Boris Pinsker, "Pervaia popytka pervaia neudacha. Chto dal'she?" in Burtin and Molchanov, God posle avgusta.

oriented transformation analogous to the one administered in Poland during the tenure of Leszek Balcerowicz.

Although the liberal-democrats were stunned by the disintegration of the Soviet Union, development of a post-imperial paradigm and a vision of Russia's role within the international system on the part of staunch liberal-democrats evolved slowly. By and large, most of those who still identified themselves as liberals continued to argue that Russia had no usable history (not even medieval Novgorod).[127] The entire notion of a Russian national idea, on which nationalists based their argument, was rejected by the liberals as a phenomenon that would reduce the Russian people to hostages of a bureaucracy committed to the notion of empire and would ultimately lead to Russia's further isolation within the family of nations.[128] The liberals, therefore, saw no solution for Russia's political suffering other than a rapid adoption of the Western model. Despite growing bitterness directed at what they perceived as petty nationalism on the part of the Baltic states, Georgia, and Ukraine, the liberals generally agreed that Russia should put its imperial mentality behind it and view the demise of the Soviet Union as an opportunity to free itself from economic burdens, which for Russia were not sustainable.[129] They regarded any attempt to reintegrate Russia with other former Soviet states as a means to resume Russia's role as a source of subsidies and thus slow its transformation to a market economy. Russian liberals strenuously opposed any notion of expanding the ruble zone to accommodate Belarus, or any other country for that matter. To the extent the liberals envisioned a role for Russia in the "near abroad," such a notion was based on the belief, as Fedor Shelov-Kovedyaev, one of Yeltsin's early advisers on CIS relations, asserted, that Russia could regain a leading role within the CIS only on the basis of its ability to carry out successful reforms.[130] Georgi Arbatov, a longtime Brezhnev confidant and a relative moderate in foreign policy matters, stressed that while Russia should do all it could to interest former Soviet republics in integration, integration itself could be attained

---

[127] Afanasiev, " 'Narodovlastie' protiv demokratii." in Burtin and Molchanov, *God posle avgusta.*

[128] See Vladimir Gurvich, "Natsional'naia ideia i lichnost'," *Novyi mir,* no. 5 (1993), 205–08.

[129] Nikolai Petrov and Andrei Treivish, "Praise for Isolationism," *New Times,* no. 44 (1992), 6–8.

[130] See John Lough, "Defining Russia's Relations with Neighboring States," *RFE/RL Research Report* 1: 20 (14 May 1992).

only if Russia repeatedly proved to the rest of the CIS that it had no imperial ambitions.[131]

The liberal expectation that Russia could easily deny both its Soviet experience and its imperial identity was based on several assumptions. First, with its immense mineral wealth, trained labor, and technological base, Russia would be able to negotiate the transformation to a market economy with relative ease. Second, by Russia's pursuing a foreign policy supportive of the international system, the international community would be prompted to separate democratic Russia from totalitarian USSR and elicit a substantial economic contribution to incorporate Russia into the world economy as quickly and painlessly as possible. Although distressed by the downfall of the USSR, Russian liberals such as Saint Petersburg mayor, Anatoli Sobchak, believed that before long the CIS states would have "their Strasburg," thus creating supranational institutions that would make the dissolution of the USSR less complete and less painful for the Russians. Furthermore, Russian liberals from Yeltsin on down, firmly believing that Russia had distanced itself from the Soviet Union and anticipating transparent borders among the states of the former USSR – all sharing common human values – assumed that the fate of the Russian diaspora would not degenerate into a source of contention. The impracticality of the liberal paradigm was sardonically described by *Moscow News*:

> You will recall the enthusiasm of our liberal publicists for the all-powerful magic of the market economy that would automatically determine everyone's worth and remunerate everyone according to their merit. Unemployment was expected to break people from their lazy ways; the collapse of the empire was expected to make all nations happy; the democratic electoral procedures ought to have brought the best candidates to power and so on. *Such were the banalities we were stupefying ourselves with.*[132] (emphasis added)

A more fundamental problem of the Russian and, indeed, most liberal European intellectuals was noted by Tony Judt, "[the intellectuals] became critics of the Soviet imposed regime *not in the name of the oppressed nation* but on behalf of the individual citizen and the idea of freedom and rights."[133] Judt observed that this preoccupation of

[131] Aleksandr Goltz, *Krasnaia zvezda*, 20 (November 1992), 3.
[132] Viktor Malukhin, *Moscow News*, no. 32 (5 August 1992).
[133] Tony Judt, "The End of Which European Era?" *Daedalus* 123: 3 (1994), 12 (emphasis added).

liberal intellectuals profoundly weakened their political as well as moral authority:

> Intellectuals and the nation-state have a close symbiotic relationship in modern European history. The fragmentation of this link signals a crisis for both parties. Deprived of intellectual justification for their existence and lacking an empire or empires from which they seek liberation, nation-states can only be grounded in economic and political necessity or local interest.[134]

Waning popular support for the liberals and relentless attacks by communists and nationalists forced Yeltsin to jettison his close identification with the liberals and rely more on centrist actors such as Viktor Chernomyrdin. Exiting Yeltsin's circle of liberals were Gennady Burbulis, Oleg Bogomolov, Galina Staravoitova, Yegor Yakovlev, and finally Yegor Gaidar and Boris Fyodorov. While some departed from the democratic camp because of personality clashes with Yeltsin, others, not wanting to be tainted with the responsibility for the disintegration of the USSR, simply switched to the nationalist camp. In the ironic words of Vice-President Aleksandr Rutskoi: "The members of the party nomenklatura have hurled themselves toward nationalism, like people on their way to catch a plane to the West."[135]

Events following the collapse of the Soviet Union, plus a lack of consensus on economic policy or a clear doctrine for the international role of a post-Soviet Russia, continued to fragment the liberal camp. Liberals were increasingly perceived as an arrogant elite with little regard for the price that fascination with the West and Western advice was exacting from the Russian masses. Oleg Bogomolov, a former liberal-democrat, commenting on Gaidar's liberalization of the ruble, lamented, "If the 'operation' fails, the 'surgeons' will hardly be disqualified. They will safely take cushy jobs, become ambassadors or representatives of international organizations or professors in foreign universities. But the victims ruined by the radical experiment will have to lift the country from ruins."[136]

This perception of liberals as a heartless elite consisting of the children of the former nomenklatura pursuing policies with little contact with the masses had become increasingly popular throughout Russia – an image that was bolstered by the fact that the liberals made scant effort to establish a political base outside Moscow and other

---

[134] Ibid. For a description of the identity crisis befalling Russian intellectuals, see David Remnick, "Exit the Saints," *New Yorker*, 18 July 1994.

[135] *Izvestiia*, 31 January 1992.

[136] *Moscow News*, no. 49, 2 December 1992.

urban centers and rarely bothered to consult regional leaders when momentous decisions were made. Another factor contributing to the growing demise of the democrats was that, by virtue of their support of the right of self-determination for the republics, they were held accountable by the Russian opposition for the disintegration of the USSR and the potential disintegration of the Russian Federation. After all, if Slavic Ukraine can part ways with Russia, why not Tataria, or Chechnia, or even Siberia?

As a result, Nikolai Travkin, whose Russian Democratic Party was one of the first to leave the Democratic Russia coalition precisely because of his belief that the collapse of communism must not be attained at the cost of the disintegration of the USSR, accused the democrats of the Russian polity of bringing about the break-up of the Soviet state. In a sense, the Russian liberals were caught in a bind that made it impossible for them to maintain a consistent and therefore credible position. Fearful of the rise of the right and politically isolated, they were compelled to support Yeltsin in his showdown with the Supreme Soviet despite Yeltsin's patent disregard for the country's laws and constitution, and again in his electoral contest with Gennadi Ziuganov. Dreading the rebirth of personalist autocracy in Russia, however, the liberals initially opposed Yeltsin's effort to transfer power from the legislative to the executive branch of the government. Following the electoral success of the right in December 1993, the liberals reversed themselves once again and embraced Yeltsin as their last line of defense against the right. Although Yeltsin survived the bloody showdown with the Supreme Soviet, the liberals' image as defenders of a society of law was tarnished. In fact, the whole issue of the liberals' relationship with Yeltsin had become a divisive one within the liberal camp. While the liberal parties in the state Duma continued to support Yeltsin's imposed constitution, some members became alarmed that the liberals had made a Faustian bargain by supporting despotism in order to preserve reforms.[137] Many liberals were shocked when, following a call on Yeltsin in March 1993 to resort to extraordinary means against the Supreme Soviet, Yeltsin arbitrarily reimposed censorship and forced the mass expulsion of Central Asians from Moscow.[138]

A second obstacle, helping to erode the position of the liberals, was

---

[137] See Dzhulietto K'eza, "Skoro budet pozdno," *Literaturnaia gazeta*, no. 5 (2 February 1994).
[138] See Julia Wishnevsky, "Liberal Opposition in Russia," *RFE/RL Research Report* 2: 44 (5 November 1993).

the issue of closer relations with Belarus and Ukraine. Notwithstanding the shock of losing Ukraine and Belarus, which continued to
resonate across Russian society, the notion of re-creating closer relations among the Slavic states fundamentally contradicted the liberal
agenda. Since the restoration of links with Russia in both Belarus and
Ukraine is generally supported by those who either champion a
return to a command economy or want to restore Russian subsidies to
industries in Ukraine and Belarus for political and emotional reasons,
the Russian idea based on the unity of Orthodox Slavs runs counter to
the liberals' agenda of establishing a market economy and completely
breaking with the centralized past. The notion of restoring unity
among the Slav states of the CIS, which remained popular among the
Russian masses, increasingly became the preserve of Russia's centrist
and nationalist politicians, with Grigory Yavlinski becoming one of
the few liberal politicians advocating rapid integration of Belarus.

The historic legacy of the liberal-democrats remains ambiguous.
They may well have been the power that toppled the communist
autocracy and implemented essential, albeit painful, reforms, but the
price was very high, and the ultimate outcome remains uncertain. The
dilemma of Russian liberals was captured by Viktor Malukhin of
*Moscow News* with these words:

> The [liberal] advocates of transnational leveling-out have made the
> "Russian idea" and the "Russian path" almost dirty words here.
> Similarly our intelligentsia's "internationalism" manifested itself at
> the dawn of perestroika in reckless support for various popular
> fronts which eventually made narrow-minded men presidents and
> led nationalist governments to ignore basic human rights.
>
> Today we are faced with a truly diabolical dilemma: to follow the
> mediocre and mercenary democrats along the road to primitive
> capitalism, or to rally around narrow-minded, aggressive fanatics
> heading for George Orwell's *1984*.[139]

### Post-Soviet Russian nationalism

Much as the liberals who banded together after the failed
coup of August 1991 represented a spectrum of views and aspirations,
with opposition to Bolshevism the unifying factor, the new political
groups opposing Yeltsin and Gaidar also represented a broad coalition
with differing agendas, strategies, and goals. Despite the absence of
well-established political parties and given the tendency of the

[139] Malukhin, *Moscow News*, 5 August 1992.

various political movements to fragment – often as a reflection of a clash of personalities rather than profound beliefs – a rough sketch of the opposing political forces can be drawn. Basically, the opposition movement in Russia consists of three main components: statists, communist-nationalists, and nativists. Although all three groups decry the current situation in Russia, initially there were marked differences both in terms of each group's perception of Russia's past and in terms of their vision of Russia's role in the future.

The statists, at times described as centrists, are a political grouping made up primarily of "Red directors" in the mold of Arkadii Volsky, Yuri Skokov, and others. In terms of their view of Russia's past, the position of the statists is that both Russia's tsarist and Soviet pasts provide a worthy heritage, and therefore Russia must seek guidance from both pre-1917 and post-1917 experiences. Intellectual role models of the statist group, to the extent that they had them, included the nineteenth-century philosopher-historian Boris Chicherin and the tsarist conservative reformer Prime Minister Petr Stolypin. While accepting the notion that Russia's economy will require reform, this group eschews any type of reform that will lead to a rapid decline in industrial production or growing Russian dependence on Western economies. Given the statist commitment to maintaining high levels of industrial output, the explicit assumption is that the state will continue to play the decisive role in the economy. Rapid social and economic change such as that advocated by the liberals, according to the centrists, is bound to lead to turmoil, endangering the integrity of Russia itself.[140]

Seeing the collapse of the USSR as a tragedy, this group continues to be committed to a multinational state. In fact, Volsky went so far as to assert that indeed there was a genotype *'homo soveticus.'* The Eurasian entity, according to the centrist-statists, represents a single community consisting of different peoples who form in Valery Chelidze's term "symphonic members of 'assimilated stock.'"[141] The statists believe that ultimately large parts of the USSR will converge once again, into a single economic space across the USSR, with political and military convergence to follow.

In terms of their perception of Russia's place within the international system, the statists strongly advocate the so-called Eurasian view, whereby Russia will form the core of a conglomeration of Slavic and Turkic peoples occupying the Eurasian landmass – an alignment

---

[140] Lester, *Modern Tsars and Princes*, 175.    [141] Ibid.

that would enable these peoples to avoid a position of perennial economic, and therefore political, disadvantage *vis-à-vis* the West. The Eurasian idea, often associated with Petr Savitskii, Nikolai Berdiaev, Prince Nikolai Trubetskoi, and other émigré thinkers in the 1920s,[142] has been espoused later by the philosopher Lev Gumilev, who argued that "Eurasia is not merely a huge continent, it contains in its center a *super ethnos* bearing the same name."[143] According to Gumilev, this vast landmass, between the Yellow and the Black seas, was united three times: first by Khanate Tatars, then by Siberian Mongols, and finally by Russia. This union, Gumilev argues, was the leg of a cultural tripod consisting of the Muslim world to the south, Eurasia in the center, and the Atlantic Germano-Latin to the west. If Russia is to preserve its cultural heritage, it must maintain a culturally non-threatening union with the Turkic people or face a cultural annihilation inflicted by the West. Some advocates of the Eurasian idea go further, insisting that this idea is the ultimate manifestation of Russian imperial nationalism ("Russians are Eurasia's Romans"). They have contended that the foundation of the Russian national identity is based on love of vast, open space (*porstornost'*) and communal unity (*obshchennyi sobornost*). Since, according to many statists, Russians cannot exist as Russians outside a Russian state, making a multi-national Russian state across Eurasia is vital to the survival of Russians as a people.[144] Sergei Stankevich, a spokesman for the Centrists and a former state councilor to President Yeltsin, declared that: "Russia's mission in the world is to initiate and support a multilateral dialogue of cultures, civilizations and states. Russia, the conciliator, Russia connecting, Russia combining . . . A charitable state, tolerant and open within the limits drawn by law and goodwill, but formidable beyond those limits. A country imbibing West and East . . . "[145]

Although the Eurasian school originated among Russia's émigrés, it would be a fallacy to assume that its notions were accepted universally even among nationalist emigrants. The émigré theologian Georgi Florovski, who initially supported Eurasianists, later classified Eurasianism as the "Third Maximalism," which, like communism and fascism, would provide moral justification to legitimize empires.

[142] See Petr Savitskii, "Geopoliticheskie zametki o russkoi istorii," reprinted in *Voprosy istorii*, no. 11–12 (1993), 120–57.
[143] Lev N. Gumilev, *Ot rusi k rossii: ocherki etnicheskoi istorii* (Moscow: Ekoproc., 1992), 297 (emphasis added).
[144] See Alexander Iudin, "Apologia natsionalizma," *Den'*, no. 38 (September 1993), 24–30.
[145] Lester, *Modern Tsars and Princes*, 176.

The second political group to emerge in opposition to the liberals was an array of unreformed communist nationalists coming under the guise of Nina Andreyeva's hard-line Stalinist faction, Gennadi Ziuganov's Russian Communist Party, and the Agrarian Party, representing the interests of collective farms. The traditional communists differed from the statists in several ways. The historic period of reference for the communists, unlike the statists, remained the post-1917, or better yet post-1929, Soviet experience. Although like the statists the communists were committed to a multinational state, they rejected the theocratic underpinning of politics, insisting on a secular state. Furthermore, whereas the statists saw the possibility of a partial restoration of the USSR, the communists continued to insist on a full restoration of the Soviet Union, though they were somewhat ambiguous about the Baltic states. Although eager to avoid another Cold War with the West, the communists continued to view Russia as a leader of a world order that is at odds with the existing Western liberal model and expected Russia to resume an anti-status quo posture. Whereas the statists draw their historical inspiration from the Eurasian school of the 1920s, the communist-nationalists regard Nikolai Ustrialov, head of the *Smenovekh* movement of the 1920s, as the intellectual forefather of their political outlook. Unlike the Eurasianists, whose concern was the cultural integrity of Russia, the communists were preoccupied with the military power of Russia and with Russia's status as a great power within the international system. With large numbers of former military and security officials as well as party bureaucrats in its ranks, segments of the communist alliance have taken an extreme nationalist position and have inveighed against anti-Russian Judeo-Masonic conspiracies in ways reminiscent of the pamphlets of the Russian proto-Nazi Fedor Vimberg, in the 1920s.

A third opposition group to emerge from the ruins of the Soviet Union is the nativists. Like the statists and the communists, these Slavophile nationalists are also represented by a broad spectrum of opinions, ranging from Russian fascists, the anti-Semitic *Pamyat*, reactionary clerics, and monarchists to nativist nationalists in the school of Solzhenitsyn. Despite profound differences in attitudes and perceptions, all segments of this group shared several common positions. In terms of their view of Russian history, they all have tended to idealize pre-revolutionary Russia[146] while totally rejecting the post-

---

[146] A typical reflection of this view is Stanislav Govorukhin's documentary film, *Rossiia kotoruiu my poteriali* [Russia Which We Have Lost], 1992.

revolutionary experience. In economic terms, the nationalists have rejected the Western model as devoid of morality and spirituality. But, unlike the statists and communists, who envision the continuation of a multinational entity, most nativists have insisted on a theocratic Russian state consisting of the territories populated by Orthodox East Slavic peoples. Unlike other opposition groups, the nativists alone among the nationalists reject the idea of Eurasianism as yet another entanglement that will distract Russia from its spiritual and economic needs.[147] As a source of political inspiration, the nationalists base their political philosophy on the cultural heritage of rural Russia, as well as on the political institutions that preceded the Petrine reforms.[148]

Between the neo-communists and statists, who are eager to re-establish a Great Russian state pursuing a global foreign policy in defiance of the West, and the nativists, who attribute much of Russia's misfortune to its imperial posture and believe that Russia's first order of business is the healing of the land and the people, the liberals have had to reckon with a formidable opposition. Although the differences between the nativists and imperialists over foreign policy seem substantive, on a broader philosophical plane there is a great deal of commonality between the two groups. As Yeltsin's adviser, Andrannik Migranyan, observed:

> During the years of perestroika, a de facto split over tactical principles occurred among Russia's nationally oriented intellectuals. Some of them consistently held anti-communist positions and were consistent advocates of reviving Russia without communists . . . Others . . . held the position of using the Russian Communist Party, an actually existing structure that existed throughout the country . . . After the failure of the putsch and the de facto elimination of the Russian Communist Party, the question that divided the nationally oriented Russian intellectuals was removed for all practical purposes.[149]

Despite different roots and vantage points, Russia's nationalists and communists have found it remarkably easy to coalesce. Some nativist nationalists, such as Aleksandr Solzhenitsyn and Ksenia Myalo, have felt that the Eurasian idea will again shoulder Russia with an imperial

---

[147] For Solzhenitsyn's rejection of the Eurasian idea as articulated by Kazak president Nursultan Nazarbayev, see interview with Solzhenitsyn, Ostankino Television, 22 July 1994.

[148] For a comparative study of political groupings in Russia, see Stephen D. Shenfield, "Post-Soviet Russia in Search of Identity," in *Russia's Future: Consolidation or Disintegration*, ed. Douglas W. Blum (Boulder, CO, and Oxford: Westview Press, 1994), 5–17.

[149] Migranyan, "Russia's Fate."

burden, whereas "Atlanticism" would place Russia in a position of permanent inferiority. Even those isolation-bound nationalists, however, have continued to insist that Ukraine and Belarus, as well as other areas where Eastern Slavs constitute a majority, should be a part of a unitary state.

In reality, the gap between the former communist Reds and the nationalist Browns (or Whites, as they prefer) has almost vanished. Despite their claims to an internationalist ideology, Soviet communists have in fact adopted Great Russian nationalism as one of their key legitimizing features since the period of high Stalinism.[150] Gennadi Ziuganov, the current leader of the Russian Communist Party, has repeatedly stressed that the communist idea is nothing more than an updated version of the Russian idea. In terms of their respective views of Russia's place in the world and the preservation of the Russian empire, the communists have been more than happy, as Boris Ishboldin predicted in 1946, to substitute the Eurasian idea for the Marxist–Leninist idea as a justification for the empire.[151] Furthermore, under the rubric of collectivism (sobornost'), both nationalists and communists have found it easy to adopt a common opposition to Russia's Westernization. As the Russian nationalist writer Eduard Limonov noted, it has been a long time since the Reds became pink and the Whites moved left.[152] Another nationalist writer, Sergei Kirginyan, declared, the liberal's "attacks on communism deprived Russia of its national idea."[153] A consistent theme in both nationalist and communist publications is that Russia faces a mortal threat from rootless democratic "Februarists,"[154] who are keen to reduce Russia to an appendage of the West.

The emerging fusion of many nationalists and communists has received the support of the Russian Orthodox Church, which realized that the break-up of the Soviet Union would trigger the creation of autocephalous churches in Ukraine, Moldova, Estonia, and possibly Belarus, destroying the centuries-old edifice of Russian Orthodoxy. Furthermore, under pressure from the extreme rightist émigré church and fearing that liberal democracy and its strong pro-Western orientation will further encourage the penetration of the lands of Rus' by the

---

[150] See Gennadi Ziuganov, *veriu v Rossiiu* (Voronezh), 1995.
[151] See Ishboldin, "The Eurasian Movement," 64–73.
[152] Eduard Limonov, "K natsional'noi revoliutsii," *Den'*, no. 23 (June 1993), 13–19.
[153] Sergei Kirginyan, "Counteraction," *Nash sovremennik*, no. 7 (1992).
[154] Referring to the democratic Kerensky revolution that took place in February 1917, to be overthrown by the Bolsheviks in October (November) 1917.

Roman Catholic and Protestant churches, the Russian Orthodox Church has allied itself with the anti-liberal coalition, seeing in it a foundation for self-preservation. Large segments of the Russian Orthodox Church, including the Orthodox Brotherhood, openly approved of the Red–Brown coalition as a means of saving Russia from the Judeo-Masonic conspiracy.[155] Patriarch Alexei II, while distancing himself from the position of Metropolitan Ioann of Saint Petersburg (who, among other things, supported the veracity of the notorious anti-Semitic tsarist forgery *The Protocol of the Elders of Zion*), nevertheless endorsed the Eurasian idea[156] along with Ioann and took an activist position in campaigning to preserve, and later restore, the Soviet Union.[157]

Not all nationalists endorsed the emerging alliance with communists, however. Aleksandr Solzhenitsyn steadfastly denounced communism altogether. Similarly, the émigré Cossack writer Mikhail Nazarov continued to insist that it was the Whites who defeated the anti-national forces of communism and that there could be no alliance with an anti-national force that was a twin of Western materialism.[158]

The premodern notion of a society based on communal bonds (*Gemeinschaft*) remains the underlying assumption of most opposition groups, all to various degrees embracing the philosophy of Ivan Ilin in synthesizing Russian traditionalism with Bolshevism in a search of an "organic democracy." Given their reliance on communal bonds, the central feature of society for these groups is not the individual but the Russian state (*gosudarstvennost'*).[159] The opposition rejects Western parliamentarism and Western economic models as systems alien to Russia, opting instead for a "Third Way" in the form of corporatism. Unable to agree on what Russia is, opposition groups reject the current frontiers of the Russian Federation and view the CIS as a transitional arrangement that will have to be rectified. More ominously, the groups subscribe in varying degrees to the belief that

---

[155] Dimitry V. Pospietovsky, "The Russian Orthodox Church in Post-communist CIS," in *The Politics of Religion in Russia and the New States of Eurasia*, ed. Michael Bourdeaux (Armonk, NY: M. E. Sharpe, 1995).

[156] See Metropolitan Ioann, "Tvoreniem dobra i pravdy," *Sovetskaia Rossiia*, no. 15 (May 1993).

[157] See John Dunlop, "The Russian Orthodox Church as an 'Empire Saving' Institution," in Bourdeaux, *The Politics of Religion in Russia and the New States of Eurasia*.

[158] Mikhail Nazarov, "O Kransnom i belom" *Den'*, no. 31 (August 1993), 8–14.

[159] In a symposium organized by the Gorbachev Foundation under the rubric "Rossiia kotoruiu my obretaem" [Russia which we are discovering], *Novyi mir*, no. 1 (1993), 3–44.

Russia was dismembered by a plot planned by either Anglo-Saxon imperialism or a Judeo-Masonic conspiracy and see the emerging post-Soviet order as patently unjust, in a manner reminiscent of the stab-in-the-back theories prevalent in Weimar Germany.

### Russia adrift and in search of an identity

It would appear that a new paradox has come to dominate the politics and future prospects of contemporary Russia. Some liberals, realizing that a transfer to a market economy will be a very long process and impossible without the emergence of a propertied middle class, are hoping for some sort of "authoritarian spasm" (in the mold of Augusto Pinochet or perhaps Aleksander Lebed) that would abort the rise of a nationalist right and allow the middle class to break through. It is this fear that garnered the support for Yeltsin's position during his confrontation with the Supreme Soviet in 1993 and during the presidential elections of 1996.

Conversely, members of the Red–Brown coalition, sensing that the mood of the population is shifting in their direction, have become strong supporters of the legislative and electoral process. Some opposition leaders, such as Vladimir Zhirinovsky, and to a lesser degree Gennadii Ziuganov, make no secret of the fact that their strategy, like that of the Algerian Islamic Salvation Front, is to use the democratic electoral process as a method to put an end to the democratic experiment.

The "accursed question" – what is Russia and where does it fit within the international system – is far from resolved. As Russia's short-lived fling with Westernization appears to be waning, the country continues to drift, searching for a usable history and a paradigm that will enable it to regain its balance. Several answers are offered as to why Russia is experiencing these profound difficulties in finding its new destiny. Some of the difficulties are by no means unique to Russia. No transition from empire to post-imperial status is easy. Even France, with a far more developed sense of national identity than Russia's and despite highly favorable economic conditions in post-World War II Europe, found the transition from an empire to a state difficult; so difficult, in fact, that the country came to the verge of a civil war. The economic decline, the overt criminalization of society, and unrealistic expectations of Western economic aid have clearly fed Russia's, as well as most post-communist states' disenchantment with the Western economic and social model.

Yet, despite all these problems, Russia's attempt to reinvent itself appears to be more trying than that of most other polities. Alexei Kiva has argued that the fundamental defect in Russian society that explains its praetorian outlook on politics lies in the nature of its intelligentsia. According to Kiva, the Russian intelligentsia never cured itself of early-nineteenth-century romanticism and continues to impose an absolutist view of history and politics. Echoing Berdiaev's complaint that the Russian intelligentsia oscillated "between euphoria and apocalypse," Kiva has maintained that it is irrelevant whether the intelligentsia embraced radical Marxism in the late nineteenth century or extreme right-wing nationalism in the late twentieth century, for the result is the same, since both extreme views tend to perpetuate myths while depriving Russia of an opportunity to develop a normal identity and sense of history. Liberalism and democracy are weak in Russia because neither of the two lends itself to the political absolutes so very dear to the Russian intelligentsia.[160] The tendency of the Russian intellectual to oscillate between exaltation and despair was best conceptualized by the late Russian literary critic and cultural historian Yuri Lotman. In his last work, *Culture and Explosion (Kultura i vzryev)*, Lotman argued that Russian culture, unlike that of the West, "embodies an underlying binary logic of opposition."[161] Thus, groups and individuals conceptualize social life in terms of absolutes which brook no compromise. "The past is regarded not as a foundation of organic growth, but as a source of error that must be completely destroyed. Total destruction must precede creation, and so creation takes place in a void. Means and ends are thus separate, and the longed-for new world can only be constructed on the utter ruins of the old, which is wholly corrupt."[162]

Russian anti-liberal political forces remain fragmented not only among the competing personalities of Gennadi Ziuganov of the Russian Communist Party, Vladimir Zhirinovsky of the Liberal Demo-cratic Party, Aleksandr Barkashov of the Russian National Unity Party, and Ilya Konstantinov of the National Salvation Front, but also among those who participated in the October 1993 clashes – Aleksandr Rutskoi, Albert Makashov, and Ruslan Khasbulatov – and those who have accepted, however reluctantly, the political order imposed

---

[160] See Alexei Kiva, "Intelligentsiia v chase ispytanii" [Intelligentsia in a Trying Hour], *Novyi mir*, no. 8 (1993), 160–78.

[161] See McDaniel, *The Agony of the Russian Idea*, 17.

[162] Ibid.

by Yeltsin. As a result, the significant electoral gains by the opposition did not translate into actual control of Russian state policy. Nevertheless, the shift in the mood of Russia's body politic has polarized and altered the conduct of Russia's statecraft.

The centrists, who were judged to be the strongest bloc in the Supreme Soviet and willing, albeit reluctantly, to come to terms with the post-Soviet reality, all but disappeared as political actors following the December 1993 elections. Former centrists, such as Rutskoi, started to talk in terms of the restoration of the superpower. Sergei Shakhrai, Yeltsin's deputy prime minister, publicly declared that the dissolution of the USSR by Yeltsin, Kravchuk, and Shushkevich was "a betrayal of the interests of the Soviet state."[163] Vladimir Shumeiko, another close aide to Yeltsin and later the chairman of the Federation Council, enthusiastically endorsed Kazakhstan president Nursultan Nazarbayev's call for a Eurasian Union, declaring that the CIS was not a satisfactory form of alliance.[164] Yeltsin's formerly liberal foreign minister, Andrei Kozyrev, shifted his rhetoric from advocating common human values to insisting on international respect for a "Russian sphere of influence" across the former Soviet Union.

### The elections of 1996 and their aftermath

Russia's elections of 1996, for a new Duma and for the president, reflected what Yuri Lotman described as the "binary logic of opposition." Unlike the elections in Central Europe, where the competition between the government in power and its challengers (even if former communists) was couched in terms of who can take the country toward a market economy most efficiently, the presidential elections in Russia turned out to be a referendum on Russia's communist past. President Yeltsin and his main challenger, Gennadi Ziuganov, offered two radically different readings of Russia's history, and hence radically different and mutually exclusive visions of the future. Once again Russia's masses were confronted with two "truths" that brook no compromise. The Russian people, consulted about their future, for the first time gave an ambiguous answer. The elections to the Duma resulted in a humiliating rejection of the liberal pro-Yeltsin parties, as the number of voters opting for left-wing

---

[163] See Victoria Clark, "Russia: Yeltsin's Floundering Opposition," *The Observer*, 10 July 1994.
[164] Reuter, 7 April 1994.

parties surged from almost 11 million to over 24 million;[165] in terms of parliamentary representation, the leftist-nationalist alliance garnered 271 seats, while parties with a pro-Western orientation secured only 152 seats.[166]

In the parliamentary elections the Russian voter seemed to have rejected reforms and opted for a return to the certainties of communism, but in the presidential elections, which Yeltsin presented as a referendum on communism, and despite his abysmal public standing (in 1995 only 3 percent of the electorate completely approved of his performance),[167] Yeltsin managed to defeat Ziuganov. While the Russian political elites continue to engage in their traditional praetorian politics, the Russian masses continue to be confused and their hopes and aspirations remain contradictory.

Russia continues to experience a profound crisis of identity. The Russian populace has not managed to break with the past, to which it cannot go back, but it has not yet developed a paradigm for the present or a vision for the future.

Regardless of whether they classify themselves as "Atlanticists" or "Eurasianists," for most Russians the West remains the "other" and thus the ultimate measure of Russia's own self-worth and sense of success or failure. The fundamental unanswered question is whether or not Russia will continue to build its national identity as a part of the Western family of nations, even if this process would require it to accept the loss of empire and a reduced, though still very significant, role within the international system – a process that will increasingly fuse the notion of the Russian ethnic identity with that of a Russian state. Alternatively, Russia will revert to a self-perception not as a nation-state, but rather as a "civilization" or a "world" – a multiethnic entity whose voice in the West will be carried, as Tsar Alexander I remarked, through Russia's two eternal allies, its army and its navy.

Russia today continues to drift. Unable to accept its current predicament, Russia has yet to redefine itself in a manner that will help it regain an identity that can find a political center of gravity. While recognizing that there may be no return to the anti-status quo of 1991, most Russians are "haunted by the specter of a defeated nation," seeking the culprits responsible for its downfall and a new Mikhail Romanov to end its "Time of Troubles."

---

[165] Jerry F. Hough, Evelyn Davidheiser, and Susan Goodrich Lehmann, *The 1996 Russian Presidential Elections* (Washington, DC: Brookings Institution Press, 1996), 53.
[166] Ibid., 55.        [167] Ibid., 39.

# 7    Russia's foreign policy reconsidered

> Having lived gloriously for a long time [nations] are unable to break
> with their past, whatever they do. They experience its influence at
> the very time they work to destroy it. In the midst of their out-
> standing transformations, they remain in the essential aspects of
> their character and destiny the product of their history. Even the
> most daring and powerful revolution cannot abolish national tradi-
> tions that have existed for a long time.
>
> François Guizot, *Essai sur l'histoire de France* (1824)[1]

> As a result of imperialist and civil wars, Russian temporarily
> disappeared from the horizon as a Great Power. Russia is coming
> back to the international stage. Let us hope that the day is at hand
> when her reappearance will be felt so strongly, that no one will dare
> to contradict her voice.
>
> *Izvestia*, 7 December 1922

> Do not think of Russia as a dead tiger. It is a great state that will
> demonstrate its might. It is necessary to be attentive in the conduct of
> relationships with Russia: It is never simple diplomacy – it is never a
> simple country.
>
> Deng Xiaoping[2]

If both its geopolitical position and the inherent set of values underlying its notion of the "national interest" shape a state's foreign policy,
then currently no other foreign policy is subject to greater pressure
and disorientation than that of post-communist Russia. Within the
short space of three years the Russian people have seen the ideology
that dominated their polity for seven decades de-legitimized. Worse
still, they have lost the vast territories that for centuries they considered their own and have witnessed the disappearance of an imperial
status that has been part and parcel to Russia's national being since at

---

[1] Quoted in Hans Kohn, "Soviet Communism and Nationalism," in *Soviet Nationality
  Problems*, ed. Edward Allworth (New York: Columbia University Press, 1970), 44.
[2] Robert Blackwell and Sergei Karaganov, eds., *Damage Limitation or Crisis? Russia and
  the Outside World* (Washington, DC, and London: Brassey's, 1994), 240.

least the sixteenth century. Given the speed and magnitude of the changes, Russia's delineation of its national interest and, therefore, its foreign policy, is very complex. Unlike other empires in the annals of history, the Russian empire did not collapse from a military defeat in a long, debilitating struggle, as did the Austro-Hungarian or Ottoman empires, nor was the Russian imperial retreat a long-drawn-out process in the manner of the West European colonial empires, who were given an opportunity to recast their identity within the European community or the Western bloc as a whole. The bulk of the Russian empire was dissolved almost as an afterthought by a polity that, because of a power struggle between Gorbachev and Yeltsin, temporarily rejected the ideology that sustained this empire.[3] The collapse was so swift and so unexpected that Russia's foreign minister Andrei Kozyrev, admitted, "We were prepared for a confederation, or a federation – and did not conceal that we were for a renewed union";[4] he later added, "I have not dreamed of the dissolution or the disappearance of the Soviet Union."[5] As Kozyrev and other Yeltsin supporters acknowledged, the purpose of the declaration of Russia's sovereignty was to use Russia's dominant position within the USSR as a means to demolish Gorbachev's power base rather than to establish a separate Russian state.

As a result, unlike most emerging polities whose future in the world was considered and debated by an elite before its birth, the Russian polity had neither the opportunity nor the interest to devise a post-imperial role or to articulate a new identity and myths independent of an imperial legacy. No national identity, possibly excepting pre-World War I Hungary, was so very deeply tied to its empire; therefore, Russia's path toward a new self-concept is bound to be slow, fitful, and controversial.

The issues of Russia's predicament and the appropriate foreign policy paradigm to actualize its goals and ambitions remained inadvertently tied to the different Russian groups' definitions of Russia. By 1992 three major clusters of opinion emerged in the Russian body politic (liberal, conservative, and centrist). Each had its own distinct definition of Russia's national identity, and consequently, each developed a different foreign policy paradigm. Although within each

---

[3] Michael McFaul, "Revolutionary Ideas, State Interests, and Russian Foreign Policy," in *Political Culture and Civil Society in Russia and the New States of Eurasia*, ed. Vladimir Tismaneanu (Armonk, NY: M. E. Sharpe, 1995).

[4] *Trud*, 4 August 1992.

[5] Interview with Andrei Kozyrev, *RFE/RL Research Reports* 3, no. 28 (15 July 1994).

cluster of opinion a continuum of views can be found, each group seems to operate consistently within a certain broad perception of Russian national identity and to advocate an appropriate foreign policy reflecting that identity.

### The liberal Atlanticist school

The liberal Atlanticist school, consisting mainly of the remnants of the broad coalition that toppled Gorbachev and propelled Yeltsin to power, has not deviated from its original approach to Russia's place in the international system. This group, although increasingly discredited, remains a vocal presence in several prominent publications as well as among the various research institutes.

The basic view of the liberal school partisans is that Russia's tragedy lies in its repeated bouts of "messianism cum belief in its inherent uniqueness," which demands that it reject the existing world order. Russia, according to the proponents of this school, will become a normal, prosperous, and democratic country only when it abandons all pretensions to "uniqueness" or "manifest destiny." Such pretensions have required it to defy the international system, have imposed a siege mentality, and have resulted in a process that perverted Russia into an autocratic state with a chronically militarized economy. In addressing the issue of whether Russia is culturally part of the "East" or the "West," the liberals adamantly insist that Russia, its uniqueness notwithstanding, is a pillar of Western culture and civilization. They note that while Russia's music and literature are major components of Western civilization, Russia shares no analogous commonalities with its eastern or southern neighbors. Liberal thinkers have repeatedly stressed that the Tatar domination of Russia did not result in a cultural symbiosis with the East as some Eurasianists would have it, but was instead a foreign occupation that scarred Russia's psyche for centuries. Furthermore, Russia's expansion to the east and south did not reflect Russia's preoccupation with its Asian roots but was instead a vain effort by a polity riddled with inferiority complexes to remain in the ranks of the European powers.[6] Russia's imperial expansion, especially in the late nineteenth century, was guided by the desire to remain among the major "civilizing" nations and to fence off an

---

[6] See Nikolai Kolikov, "Rossiia v kontekste global'nykh peremen," *Svobodnaia mysl'*, no. 2–3 (1993).

economic sphere of influence, rather than by a cultural bias toward Asia.

According to the advocates of the liberal paradigm, Russia's hope for salvation lies in rapid integration with the "North" (the G-7 group). In practice, the most important element of that policy would be an alliance with the United States. Accepting the notion that Russia is a sprawling landmass surrounded by three concentric, hierarchical circles of countries, the liberals consider the states in the most distant ring Russia's top priority. Thus, the West, primarily the United States, comprises the most important circle, with countries adjacent to the former Soviet Union taking second priority and the CIS, although pivotal for Russia both in cultural and economic terms, the least significant in Russia's quest to become a "normal" country.[7] Despite their recognition of Russia's historic links to the CIS, the liberals have generally believed that any reintegration of states within the CIS would lead to a reassertion of power by the *nomenklatura*, as well as the re-establishment of a command economy.[8]

According to the liberals, the importance of the United States to Russia lies in the fact that the United States, in addition to being the sole remaining superpower, remains the world's sole power without historic enmities arising out of territorial disputes in the eastern hemisphere. Thus, the United States, while posing no risk, can complement Russia's quest for stability along its lengthy borders. As a result, according to most liberal thinkers, the US presence in Japan and Germany does not threaten, but rather enhances Russia's position, as a Japan or Germany tightly bound to the United States as their ultimate guarantor is unlikely to assume an anti-status quo posture that might be injurious to Russia's security needs. The centrality of the United States in Russia's foreign policy in the liberal paradigm was further emphasized by Alexei Bogaturov, Mikhail Kozhokin, and Konstatin Poleshakov of the US and Canada Institute, who have argued that the United States can be a vital calming presence in Russia's relations with the former republics of the Soviet Union. While Germany views the states of Eastern Europe as its natural sphere of influence, its interests are bound to clash with those of Russia; only the United States, with its truly global foreign policy, is capable of

---

[7] See Andrei Zagorskii, Anatolii Zlobin, Sergei Solodovnik, and Mark Khrustalev, *Posle raspada SSSR: Rossiia v novom mire* (Moscow: MGIMO, 1992).
[8] Sergei Markov, "Russian Political Parties and Foreign Policy," in Tismaneanu, ed., *Political Culture and Civil Society in Russia*, 137–54.

meeting the security concerns of Eastern Europe without threatening Russia.[9]

Some liberal thinkers such as Sergei Blagovolin took this thesis further, asserting that the only way for Russia to ensure that it is not separated from Europe by a string of hostile states is to support the admission of Poland, Hungary, and others into NATO, since such membership would stabilize them politically and reduce their paranoia and hostility vis-à-vis Russia. Similarly, close cooperation between the West and the CIS states would reassure these states that they are not dealing with Russia from a position of inferiority and would thereby allow for the rapid establishment of normal relations between Russia and its new neighbors. The speed of Russia's normalization of these relations with other CIS states would be directly proportional to Russia's integration into the West.[10] Blagovolin and many other liberals felt that the real threat to Russia's long-term security lay in growing instability in Afghanistan and Central Asia, as well as unpredictable developments in China, a country where political reform has not matched economic reforms, making the potential for the emergence of either an aggressive or unstable China a distinct possibility. Sensing that the main threat to Russian, as well as international, security lies along the north–south axis, Blagovolin went on to suggest that Russia urgently embark on the development of a defense doctrine compatible with those of the Western powers.[11] The liberals believe that in alliance with the West, Russia, as long as it is not impoverished or isolated, can contain Islam-driven instability and develop a normal relationship with China. Given the fact that the key aim of the liberals would have been to ensure that Russia indeed became a part of the North, had they retained political power, they would have been willing to make painful political concessions including the eventual return of the Kuril islands to Japan.[12] In a similar vein, most liberal analysts have tended to view a greater Turkish presence in the Caucasus and Central Asia, Polish influence in Ukraine, and Finnish influence in the Baltic states as factors that

[9] Aleksei Bogaturov, Mikhail Kozhokin, and Konstatin Poleshakov, "Natsional'nyi interes v rossiisskoi politike," Svododnaia mysl', no. 5 (1992), 36–42.
[10] See Sergei Blagovolin, "O vneshnei i voennoi politike Rossii," Svobodnaia mysl', no. 18 (1992).
[11] P. Mustafin, "There Is No Imminent Threat to Russia, but Military Danger Does Exist," Krasnaia zvezda, 6 June 1992.
[12] See Douglas W. Blum, ed., Russia's Future: Consolidation or Disintegration? (Boulder, CO, San Francisco, and Oxford: Westview Press, 1994), 134.

would help stabilize Russia's neighbors and thereby add to its security.

The belief that the United States is Russia's natural ally was similarly extended to the economic sphere. Most liberals assumed that the end of the Cold War would result in a multipolar world in which several economic blocs, consisting of the European Union, the North American Free Trade Agreement, and ASEAN, would fiercely compete for economic hegemony. Russia's liberals recognized that Russia itself was far too weak to attempt to form an economic pole of its own and therefore would have to join another.

Of the three emerging global poles, the United States appeared by far to be the most compatible with Russia's needs. The United States, as the most powerful supporter of stability in the international system, could appreciate Russia's role as a containment wall against Islamic fundamentalism and as a possible ally against any other anti-status-quo power. With its global outlook, the American approach to trade is more open to the rest of the world and far less susceptible to parochial interests than Europe and Japan. Finally, while Russia cannot escape a legacy of warfare and suspicion in its relationship with Germany, Japan, and even China, a relationship with the United States is not burdened by such a violent history. Russian liberals, believing that the ability of the United States to enforce a *Pax Americana* is receding, consider it obvious that the United States will need Russia as a partner in order to sustain a balance within the international system's delicate structure.[13]

Interestingly, while the Western states grew in importance among the liberals, an antithetical attitude toward the "near abroad" evolved. Despite the fact that the near abroad contains lands that many Russians perceive as inseparable parts of Russia, writings by proponents of the liberal school often perceive the near abroad as a burden that prevents Russia from modernizing and achieving its full potential as a great power. In fact, Nikolai Kolikov of the Gorbachev Foundation has asserted that the entirety of the Russian empire served no other purpose than to enable the Russians to overcome a deep inferiority complex *vis-à-vis* the West. Liberals believe that the onus of Russia's historic responsibility in the near abroad can only be eased by the West taking an active role in the reconstruction of these areas. Russia also needs close cooperation with the Western world, particularly the

[13] See Nikolai Kolikov, "Rossiia v kontekste global'nykh peremen," *Svobodnaia mysl'*, no. 2–3 (1993).

United States, to complete the denuclearization of its near abroad. Furthermore, liberals are convinced that only vocal insistence from the West can ensure that the rights of the Russian diaspora in the former Soviet republics are respected.[14] Zagorskii, Zlobin, Solodovnik, and Khrustalev have also asserted that the sole purpose for creating the CIS was the development of a mechanism for the controlled disintegration of the USSR to rid Russia of an historic impediment that has been retarding its social and economic development. Russia, according to Zagorskii and his colleagues, can only enter the group of Northern core states by pursuing reformist economic policies, a process that is incompatible with a CIS-centered policy.[15] Even liberals such as Alexei Arbatov, who have bitterly criticized Kozyrev's pro-American policy, have remained extremely wary of any deep Russian involvement in the near abroad, fearing that any such involvement might rekindle an imperial ideology and smother the nascent Russian democracy.[16] Given their ambivalence toward Russia's deepening involvement in the CIS, some of the proponents of the liberal paradigm have welcomed Turkish and Iranian influence in Central Asia as a means of divesting Russia of its commitments to the periphery.[17] To the degree that a selective integration with some CIS states is possible, most liberals tend to believe that it is attainable only should Russia become a role model of economic and political reform, while simultaneously abandoning all hint of hegemonic intentions. In 1992–93, Kozyrev's initial foreign policy, which appeared to dovetail almost mechanically with that of the United States, did upset some liberals who accepted the centrality of the United States in Russian foreign policy but asserted that Russia needed a distinct foreign policy of its own in order to facilitate its process of nation building. According to this view, the United States must accept the notion that while Russia's global interests are similar to those of the United States, they are not identical, and in some areas are contradictory. Thus, analysts such as Alexei Arbatov, Alexei Pushkov, and others reject the idea that Russia's foreign policy toward its large trading partners should be hostage to America's standards of respect for human rights, or that the United States should dictate Russia's arms export policies,

---

[14] Ibid., no. 2–3 (1993).    [15] See Andrei Zagorskii et al., *Posle raspada SSSR'*.

[16] Alexei Arbatov, "Russian Foreign Priorities after the 1990s," in *Russian Security After the Cold War: Seven Views from Moscow*, ed. Teresa Pelton Johnson and Steven E. Miller (Washington, DC, and London: Brassey's, 1994).

[17] See Alexander Rahr, "'Atlantists' vs. 'Europeanists' in Russian Foreign Policy," *RFE/ RL Research Reports*, 18 May 1992.

and so on. These analysts argue that Russia is far too large and too proud to play the role of junior partner; therefore, Kozyrev's policy of *a priori* deference to the United States was neither healthy nor sustainable. While agreeing with Kozyrev that Russia's national identity was eroded by totalitarianism, many liberals were stunned if not outright offended when Kozyrev asserted that contemporary Russian foreign policy is similar to that of post-World War II Italy, Japan, and Germany, when these countries abandoned their totalitarian past and joined the family of civilized nations.[18] Most Russians have found it difficult to accept comparisons between the USSR and the defeated fascist powers.

Despite growing reservations about Kozyrev within the liberal camp, however, the centrality of an intimate relationship with the United States has remained fundamental on both economic and geopolitical grounds. As Alexei Pushkov noted, it is vital for Russia to join the North, and the key lies "in Washington, not in Beijing or Tripoli."[19] Looking at the Russian dilemma from a national security perspective, Alexei Arbatov noted that the first priority for Russia's foreign policy is to prevent the emergence of regional hegemony in Europe, the Far East, and South Asia, a goal that might not be realized without intimate cooperation with the United States.[20]

While liberal analysts attribute a great deal of importance to close economic relations with the European community and East Asia, they believe that these relations are less important to Russia's security. The perception among Russian liberals remains that without America's global presence, Russia's relationship with a German-led European Union and Japan would soon deteriorate into a state of permanent competition and increasing tension, allowing other players immediately on Russia's rim – such as China, Iran, and the East European states – to exploit that rivalry to their own ends.

The liberal paradigm initially had the support of many within the Russian government as well as the intelligentsia. The supremacy of the liberal conception as the shaping force of Russia's foreign policy turned out to be short lived. Several of the basic assumptions underpinning the liberal paradigm failed to materialize. Western aid, which

---

[18] "Preobrazhennaia Rossiia v novom mire," Conference at the Foreign Ministry, 26–27 February 1992, official statement published in *Mezhdunarodnaia zhizn'* (March–April 1992).

[19] Alexei Pushkov, "Is an Alliance with the West Possible?" *Moscow News*, 26 February 1992.

[20] Gerard Holden, *Russia After the Cold War: History and the Nation in Post-Soviet Security Politics* (Frankfurt and Boulder, CO: Westview Press, 1994), 13.

was supposed to facilitate Russia's process of joining the "North," turned out to be far smaller than the liberals assumed, and when delivered, the aid was often misspent with little visible impact on the lives of the Russian masses. Divesting itself of the burden of empire turned out to be far more difficult and drawn out than Russia had expected. It was not until 1993 that Russia managed to fully assert its exclusive control over its own currency, and, despite the dissolution of the USSR, Russia continued to spend as much as 10 percent of its gross domestic product in subsidies to the CIS, thus slowing Russia's ability to reform its economy. Despite the active participation of the West, particularly the United States, in attempting to moderate the relationships among the former Soviet republics, the negotiations to denuclearize Ukraine proved slow and unpredictable. Russia derived even less satisfaction from the West's ability to ensure that the alleged abuses of the Russian diaspora were addressed. The West's reluctance to take on the issue of the Russian-speaking population of the Baltic states and its willingness to admit Estonia into the Council of Europe provoked Russian sensitivities. Finally, the perception that the United States assumed the role of global leader without regard for Russia's peculiarities and interests irked wide segments of the Russian polity. By the time the Russian Federation had celebrated a year of its independence, the liberal paradigm was fending off assaults from across the political spectrum of Russia while its supportive political constituency was rapidly vanishing. In general, one of the main reasons for the decline of the liberals in terms of both Russia's domestic and external politics was their inability to articulate a clear vision of Russia's future, allowing the other groups to dominate the debate about the Russian Idea and whether it could ever be actualized.[21] The disenchantment with the West rapidly trickled down to the popular level. In 1991, 54 percent of Russians welcomed foreign business, while 34 percent opposed it; by 1995 its support had dropped to 33 percent, while the opposition had ballooned to 59 percent.[22] Similarly, between 1993 and 1996 the percentage of Russians who believed that the United States would take advantage of Russia's weakness climbed from 51 percent to 71 percent.[23] As we shall see, the collapse of the liberal foreign policy paradigm, paralleling Russia's

---

[21] See Lena Jonson, "The Foreign Policy Debate in Russia: In Search of National Interest," *Nationalities Papers* 22: 1 (1994).

[22] Richard B. Dobson, *Is Russia Turning the Corner? Changing Russian Public Opinion 1991–1996* (Washington: USIA, September 1996), 14.

[23] Ibid., 72.

domestic politics, saw a migration of many of its original adherents to the centrist and even the nationalist camps.

### The centrists

It appeared from the outset that Kozyrev's liberal Atlanticist policy corresponded poorly to Russia's psychological needs following the collapse of the USSR. As Gerard Holden noted:

> the USSR perished in the course of this westward reorientation [in the Perestroika era]. The leadership of the Russian successor state then committed the country to further re-orientation in the shape of marketization of the economy and multi-party politics, but the new state was territorially more isolated than any Russian state had been for centuries and, as we have seen, somewhat at a loss for a new legitimizing state ideology.[24]

The fugitive notion of joining the West proved to be an approach that found little emotional resonance within the Russian polity, especially when it became clear that the once mighty Russian state had shrunk to the role of a supplicant. As Sergei Stankevich noted, in order for a foreign policy in Russia to have a broad support it needs a "mission."[25] Much as the break-up of the USSR caused many liberals to move to the right on domestic issues, an analogous shift has occurred within Russia's foreign policy community, leading to the emergence of a "centrist" camp and a "Eurasian" camp. As with the other two groups, the centrist position is not a uniform position but rather a broad continuum of opinion, but several broad generalizations characterizing their outlook can be observed. Much like the liberal Atlanticists, Russian centrists, while recognizing Russia's Asian and Turkic roots, assert that Russia is a part of the West, that Russia has no natural allies in Asia, and that Russia's national security is linked to a cordial relationship with the West.[26] However, whereas most Atlanticists tend to take the liberal view that Russia has no usable history and therefore must fundamentally break with its past, centrists, while decrying Russia's autocratic and totalitarian history, insisted that Russia neither can nor should discard its past or its status as a great power entirely, and that Russia should continue pursuing its own distinct national interest. Critiquing the "missionless" nature

---

[24] Holden, *Russia After the Cold War*, 146.     [25] Ibid., 166.
[26] Alexander Vladislavev and Sergei Karaganov, "The Idea of Russia," *Mezhdunarodnaia zhizn'*, no. 12 (1992).

of Kozyrev's foreign policy, Alexei Bogaturov of the US and Canada Institute noted:

> A historically verified truth has been confirmed once again: At the stage of construction of a nation-state, the national idea, in one form or another, of necessity plays an integrative role. It is necessary to struggle for control over national aspirations and direct them into a moderate/liberal channel. Attempts to ignore the specific nature of national expectations only increase the chances that there will be a revival of a totalitarian ideology . . . Russia's foreign policy philosophy should not, of course, set us at odds with the rest of the world, but it should uphold our right to our own specific characteristics, to our specific way of seeing concrete international problems . . . Only at first glance is Atlanticism leading to the improvement in Russia's relations with the West. In fact this mindless following of our western partners is only compromising the West in the eyes of the Russian people, giving rise to anti-foreigner sentiments and rocking the ship of the state.[27]

Where the Atlanticists and centrists appear to differ most is in their ranking of priorities assigned to Russia's foreign policy. Although accepting the "concentric ring" premise, the importance they attribute to each of these rings differs from that of the liberals. Unlike the liberals' assumption that Russia's ability to integrate into the "North" is essentially contingent on its ability to divest itself of the lingering imperial burden imposed by the CIS, the fundamental assumption of the centrists is that Russia's economic, cultural, and political links to the first circle are such that Russia will have to remain the pillar of both political and economic stability across the space of the former USSR. While most centrists concede the irreversibility of the disintegration of the USSR, and many have remained averse to the use of force in relations within the CIS, most embrace the view that Russia's predominant economic weight within the CIS, as well as the presence of Russophone populations in the "near abroad," are legitimate tools of Russian policy. Whereas the liberal Westernizers tend to view Russia's relationship with the CIS in the context of interstate relations, as we shall see later, the nationalists and communists view the issue of the CIS as an issue of internal Russian politics; it is the centrists who coined the term "near abroad," indicating their ambivalent attitude toward the first concentric circle around Russia.[28] It is worth men-

---

[27] Alexei Bogaturov, "Post Elections Russia and the West," *Nezavisimaia gazeta*, 29 December 1993.

[28] Sergei Markov, "Russian Political Parties and Foreign Policy," in Tismaneau, ed., *Political Culture and Civil Society in Russia*, 137–54.

tioning Sergei Karaganov's observation that this renewed interest in the CIS states stems from two distinct sources within Russian society. On the one hand, there are the people who always look at Russia's foreign policy through a geopolitical prism and therefore attribute great importance to the CIS states as a vital ingredient of Russia's strategic depth. On the other, there is the new liberal bourgeois; initially, they had opposed any involvement in the CIS as a process retarding Russia's economic modernization. However, as this group's interest and source of income shifted from the import and resale of consumer goods mainly with countries outside the CIS to manufacturing goods for sale within the CIS, the CIS regained its importance.[29] Michael McFaul described the centrists' policy toward the CIS as essentially a corporatist foreign policy dominated by the economic interests of various Russian industries, giving impetus to a greater Russian economic role while opposing debilitating economic integration or military involvement.[30]

Much like the Atlanticists, the centrists assert that Russia, culturally as well as politically, is a part of the West; indeed, they are determined to integrate Russia into the "core" of the international system. However, whereas many Atlanticists reduce the CIS to a secondary consideration whose problems will be resolved in the context of Russia's relationship with the West, the centrists believe that unless Russia re-establishes close and intimate relations with the CIS, Russia will become isolated and marginalized within the international system. Although few centrists believe that the re-creation of the Soviet Union is possible or even desirable, nevertheless the governing assumption among centrists is that in light of historic, economic, and geopolitical realities Russia should not forgo a "special relationship" with the former republics of the Soviet Union. The prominent centrist Sergei Karaganov advocates an "enlightened post-imperial integrationist course."[31] Explaining the desirable relationship between Russia and other former states, Vyacheslav Dashichev noted:

> The era of empires, the creation of spheres of influence and the filling of political and military vacuums is part of the past. It has been supplemented by regional integrative organizations of sovereign

[29] Sergei Karaganov, "Russia's Elites," in Blackwell and Karaganov, *Damage Limitation or Crisis? Russia and the Outside World.*
[30] Michael McFaul, "Revolutionary Ideas, State Interests, and Russian Foreign Policy," in Tismaneanu, ed., *Political Culture and Civil Society in Russia.*
[31] *Nezavisimaia gazeta,* 19 August 1992.

states . . . But Russia has vital interests in the former Soviet republics, just as these republics retained vital interests in Russia . . . Russia's national interests consist in promoting the creation in the CIS space of an integrated society that is founded on a socially oriented market economy and democratic values modeled on the European Union. Only this can make the CIS viable.[32]

The prevailing belief among most centrists is that Russia's long-term prospects as a modern democratic state are inseparable from the way it manages its relationship with the former Soviet Union.

The consensus among the centrists is that the immediate challenge posed to Russia's security emanates from the south, where the chaos from Afghanistan threatens to engulf Tajikistan and the rest of Central Asia, and from the Transcaucasus, where the Muslim–Christian struggle could spread up the Volga valley to Russia itself.[33] However, while instability in the south is Russia's immediate priority, in the long run the centrists believe that Russia's ability to become a democratic country integrated into the international system is contingent on its ability to manage its relationship with Ukraine. While an intimate relationship with Ukraine would enable Russia to continue with its political and economic modernization, failure to arrive at a modus vivendi with Kiev could lead to a rebirth of an imperial ideology that would smother democracy in Russia and abort its efforts to become a part of the existing world order, returning Russia to the posture of an anti-status-quo power aligning itself with malcontents in the Third World.[34] In order to avoid the slide toward an imperial mentality, centrists argue that Russia must pursue a "good neighbor policy" and strengthen the CIS to the point where the irrational borders of the post-Soviet states by being fully open and transparent will become politically tolerable, enabling Russia to become a stable democracy. Whereas the Atlanticists believe that democratization and integration into the international system requires Russia to concentrate on bolstering its relationship with the "North" while its relationship with

[32] Vyacheslav Dashichev, "Contrivances of Russia Foreign Policy Thinking," *Nezavisimaia gazeta*, 23 April 1994.

[33] See Alexander Goltz, "Near Abroad or a Community After All?" *Krasnaia zvezda*, 20 November 1994; Suzanne Crow, "Competing Blueprints for Russian Foreign Policy," *RFE/RL Research Reports* 1: 50 (18 December 1992); and Sergei Stankevich, "Preobrazhennaia Rossiia v novom mire," Conference at the Foreign Ministry, 26–27 February 1992, official statement published in *Mezhdunarodnaia zhizn'* (March–April 1992).

[34] See Giorgi Arbatov, "A New Cold War?" *Foreign Policy*, no. 95 (Summer 1994); Vladimir Lukin, "Russia and Its Interests," and Nikolai Travkin, "Russia, Ukraine, and Eastern Europe" in *Rethinking Russia's National Interest*, ed. Stephen Sestanovich (Washington, DC: Center for Strategic and International Studies, 1994).

the CIS will sort itself out as Russia's global position normalizes, the centrists have taken the diametrically opposed view that the achievement of these goals hinges on Russia's ability to contain the chaos along its southern border and to establish a community akin to the European Union in the space of the former Soviet Union.

Another fundamental difference between the Atlanticist views articulated by Kozyrev's foreign ministry and those of the centrists concerns the reading of the status of Russia's national security in the post-Soviet period. The Atlantists assume that Russia's security problems are strictly a result of the USSR's gratuitous confrontation with the West and, therefore, the collapse of the USSR and the end of the Cold War has eliminated any serious security challenges. By contrast, the centrists believe that the collapse of the USSR not only did not resolve, but actually deepened, some of the security problems faced by the Russian state. The centrist position regarding Russia's international position and hence the appropriate foreign policy was systematically articulated by the report of the private yet influential Council for Foreign and Defense Policy chaired by Sergei Karaganov.[35] Under Kozyrev, the foreign ministry tended to view Russia's security dilemmas in a global context, thereby emphasizing its relationship with the United States. The centrists, on the other hand, reason that Russia's security problems are exclusively confined to the Eurasian landmass, an area where US influence is likely to decline. They argue that it is vital for Russia to develop intimate relations with the major powers on the European landmass, namely Germany, India, and China.[36] Most centrists tend to maintain that:

> Moscow is prepared to cooperate with the United States and Europe in stabilizing the situation along our new borders. But Russia cannot blindly follow the West, if only because for the United States and Germany conflicts in the nearby foreign countries are humanitarian and political, while for us they mean bloodshed, economic ruin and the humiliation of our citizens.[37]

Konstatin Pleshakov argued that while the West might well be able to impose stability in the "oceanic littoral" of Eurasia, the control over the heartland of "continental Eurasia" will continue to be subject to tensions among Russia, China, and Islamic nations.[38] Echoing this

---

[35] See *Nezavisimaia gazeta*, 19 August 1992.
[36] For an analysis of the decline of the United States and the rise of Germany in Europe, see Andrei Kortunov, "SNG i zapad," *SSha* 2: 29 (March 1994).
[37] Alexei Bogaturov, "Post Elections Russia and the West."
[38] Konstatin Pleshakov, "Russia's Mission: The 3rd Epoch," *International Affairs* 1 (1993).

centrist sentiment, Alexei Vasiliev of the Africa Institute noted that while a return to tension with the United States would be "self-destructive,"

> Equating Russia's interests with those of the United States is fraught with many dangers . . . A new axis of tension is appearing – a North–South axis, which is to say between the West and primarily the Moslem world. Russia too could be drawn into this confrontation . . . Russia has the longest border with the Moslem world of all European countries, several thousand kilometers in length . . . It is in the interest of both ethnoses [Russian and Moslem] to use all conceivable means to convert inevitable conflicts between them into nonviolent form . . . If conflicts turn into bloody civil strife, this would mean the self-destruction of both Russia and the Turkic Moslem peoples.[39]

The centrists contend that Russia's true partners in addressing chaos in the heart of Asia are not from the West, to whom chaos in the region is a secondary consideration, but are such regional powers as India, Pakistan, Syria, Saudi Arabia, Israel, Egypt, and Iran.

To maintain Russia's influence in the "second circle," consisting of countries next to the former USSR, centrist Sergei Karaganov argued that while it is desirable for Russia to maintain intimate relationships with all CIS states, stability on the European landmass and Russian security are directly linked to Russia's influence in Belarus, Georgia, and Kazakhstan – with Belarus being the link to Central Europe, Georgia to the Caucasus, and Kazakhstan to Central Asia.[40] Given the centrist belief in growing tensions between the United States and Germany, as well as between the United States and Japan, many among its proponents argue that Russia's interests would be best served if efforts were concentrated on maintaining stability on the Eurasian landmass and downplaying links to Washington.[41] The relationship with the United States, albeit important, is viewed primarily in light of Washington's ability to constrain a potentially hostile Japan. Furthermore, whereas the Atlanticists, taking comfort from the improved relationship with Washington, tend to assume that Russia is not facing any imminent threat, the centrists, perhaps because of their preoccupation with the festering problems of the Eurasian landmass, fear that Russia is "geopolitically encircled" by

[39] Alexei Vasiliev, "Assessing Russia's Ties with the Moslem World," *Izvestiia*, 10 March 1992.
[40] See Crow, "Competing Blueprints for Russian Foreign Policy."
[41] See Aleksei Bogaturov, "The Eurasian Support of World Stability," *Mezhdunarodnaia zhizn'* (February 1993).

existing and potential foes. According to the centrists, the greatest immediate threat to Russia is the growing chaos and instability along its southern rim, where religion, modernization, and poverty have created a volatile mix. While the centrists believe that Russia should cooperate with the West in containing the growing threat of destabilization in the heart of Asia, they view this as a limited partnership.[42] However, even in the case of Russia's southern rim, the position of the Atlanticists and the centrists is fundamentally different. Whereas the Atlanticists, eager to divest Russia of the Soviet imperial burden, are willing to see Turkey, Iran, and Saudi Arabia play an expanding role in Central Asia and the Caucasus, the centrists see this area as sufficiently vital to Russia's security to justify direct Russian intervention. Given the vital interest of Russia in stability along its "soft underbelly," the centrists maintain that despite the importance of the United States, Russia cannot allow the US commitment to human rights to dictate Moscow's policy *vis-à-vis* China, Iran, India, and others.[43]

Although most centrists concede that Russia is not facing any imminent threat from the West, they are quick to point out that the West does not really want to see a powerful Russia and that the West's instrument to contain Russia – NATO – was not dismantled but actually "moved" by more than 1,000 kilometers from the Elbe River to Russia's border with Ukraine and Belarus. Given their belief that the West can reimpose containment – this time under much less favorable conditions for Moscow – the centrists are adamant in their opposition to the enlargement of NATO to include Poland and Hungary, along with the Czech and Slovak republics. The centrists' opposition to the expansion of NATO can be explained by their belief that an expansion of NATO would deepen Russia's sense of isolation and betrayal by the West. Furthermore, the prevailing belief among the centrists is that the presence of former Warsaw Pact states in NATO, particularly Poland, will galvanize NATO's sense of purpose as an anti-Russian alliance.[44] Arguing that stability in Europe requires an umbrella organization to supplant NATO, Russian centrists continue to advocate the creation of a collective security body under the

---

[42] See Blackwell and Karaganov, *Damage Limitation or Crisis?*
[43] See Alexei Arbatov, "Russian Foreign Policy for the 1990s," in Johns and Miller, eds., *Russian Security After the Cold War.*
[44] See Vladislav Chernov, "Moscow Should Think Carefully," *Nezavisimaia gazeta*, 23 February 1994; also, Sergei Karaganov, "NATO Expansion Leads to Russia's Isolation," *Moscow News*, 15 September 1993.

aegis of either the Council of Security and Cooperation in Europe or the United Nations, a structure in which Russia will be able to fully participate.[45] Therefore, when the Western allies offered Poland, Hungary, the Czech and Slovak republics, and the successor states to the USSR an affiliation with NATO under the rubric of Partnership for Peace, most centrists, despite profound misgivings, argued that Russia should accept the offer or risk isolating itself further and losing all possibility of affecting the debate within NATO.

Thus, despite their rather skeptical attitude toward the West and their lingering suspicion about the role that some Western powers plan to assign to Russia, it is important to stress that the underlying belief of most centrists remains that Russia's ultimate goal is the establishment of a democratic state with a market economy and that Russia needs to become a major power pursuing its national interest within the context of the existing international order. Despite their severe critique of Kozyrev's early foreign policy, the overwhelming consensus among the centrists remains that it would be a calamity for Russia to resume its role as leader of the anti-status-quo forces within the international system. In a similar vein, although highly critical of the West's discriminatory policies vis-à-vis Russia, the position of centrists remained that Russia's long-term economic prosperity depends directly on its ability to participate in the world economy and that, either within the Russian Federation or the CIS, a return to an autocratic model would be a prescription for disaster.

### The rebirth of Eurasianism

In his review of the evolution of the foreign policy debate in Russia, Andrei Kortunov observed a certain intellectual migration within the Russian body politic. "The liberals became pragmatists [centrist]; and the pragmatists became nationalists." Of the three main schools of Russian politics, perhaps the most complex and disparate is the Eurasian school. This group includes members ranging from monarchists, substantial parts of the Russian Orthodox Church, and Cossacks to extreme nationalists modeling themselves on interwar fascists, to hardline communists in the Stalinist mold. Despite their differences, these factions share a basic consensus about Russia's place within the international system and the interpretation of Russian history.

---

[45] See Arbatov, "Russian Foreign Policy for the 1990s."

One common denominator binding all these groups is their belief that Russia is a distinct civilization whose survival depends on preserving a way of life that is different from, if not contrary to, the civilizations of the West. According to the proponents of this school of thought, the essence of the "Russian idea" is the negation of the West. As Sergei Baburin observed, Russia is a multiethnic civilization on which the West is foisting its "anti-national" democracy, using it as a tool to atomize and dismantle Russian civilization.[46] To join the West would require Russia to deny its spiritual essence. According to most of the Eurasianists, disaster has befallen Russia whenever it has attempted to follow the West's anti-national democratic models.[47] Historically, according to the proponents of this view, Russia never was a Western-style polity bound by a contractual agreement among the various segments of society, but rather an "organic spiritual society" held together by a belief in their "commonality" (*sobornost'*).[48] Going further, Stanislav Goncharov asserted that the Maastricht Treaty of the European Union was an effort by the Atlanticist financial capital to denationalize Europe and in the process turn Russia into its shield against the tide of Islam and a source of cheap minerals. The Russian-led Eurasian bloc, according to Goncharov, was the sole remaining salvation to preserve Russian civilization from the menace of denationalization.[49] The notion of Russia as the last barrier to a "denationalizing Atlanticism" is linked to two traditional Russian notions. First, it once again bestowed upon Russia a messianic task, charging it with "saving" the national heritage of nations and their spirituality. Second, it revived militarism as a repository of Russia's national values, thereby enabling Russia to confront the machinations of the perfidious West. Eurasianists also argue that an additional integral element of the nationalists' *Weltanschauung* is the belief that to retain its spirituality (of which egalitarianism is an important ingredient), Russia will have to strive toward economic as well as cultural autarchy. Therefore, most nationalists, or Eurasianists, not only object to Russia's political integration into the international system but actually argue that economic integration into the international system will reduce Russia to a peripheral mineral exporter that in the process

[46] Interview with Sergei Baburin, *Moscow News*, 12 February 1992.
[47] Elgiz Pozdnyakov went so far as to assert that medieval Novgorod collapsed because of its representative assembly the *Veche*, while the culprit of the collapse of the tsarist empire was the *Duma*. Elgiz Pozdnyakov, "Russia Today and Tomorrow," *Mezhdunarodnaia zhizn'*, no. 2 (1993).
[48] Pozdnyakov, "Russia Today and Tomorrow."
[49] Stanislav Goncharov, "Antievropa protiv evrazii," *Den'*, 13–18 September 1993.

of trying to join the West will become materially and spiritually impoverished.

The Eurasianist outlook on the present is linked to a distinct view of Russia's past. The Westernizers tend to assume that Russia has very little in terms of usable history. Centrists have tended to view Russia's history as a series of attempted, and generally aborted, efforts at modernization. While generally supportive of Peter I, the centrists are ambivalent about the Soviet experience. The historiography of Eurasian nationalists – both monarchists and communists – tends to view the Russian past as a relentless effort to create a just "organic society," an effort that was repeatedly interrupted by the infiltration of a foreign (or foreign-minded) elite committed to frustrating Russia in its historic task.

The collapse of the USSR, therefore, according to most Eurasianists, occurred not because of the inability of the Soviet political system to compete economically nor because of the growing nationalist turmoil, but rather as a result of a conspiracy against the Russian state. Fearful of Russia's military might and increasingly in need of Russia's mineral base, Western powers conspired with the anti-national elite in Russia to dismantle the Great Russian state in exchange for a vague promise to join the ranks of the "civilized nations." But this rush into the arms of the West was not only contrary to the geopolitical interests of Russia, and indeed led to its ultimate collapse, but was contrary to Russia's cultural heritage. In this school of thought, the essence of the "Russian idea" is the blending of Slavic and Turkic peoples bound by the Orthodox faith, which exists in a symbiotic relationship with Islam. Therefore, an affiliation with the West, with its Western Christianity, its Anglo-Saxon materialism, and its hostility to Islam, negates a millennium of Russia's heritage. While few in the nationalist Eurasianist camp have shown interest in a return to a worldwide confrontation with the West, there are varying degrees of nativism and even isolationism within the nationalist camp. The notion of Russia pursuing a foreign policy aimed at making it a pillar (or even a part) of the existing international order was perceived as a disaster on practical grounds and anathema on moral grounds. According to most nationalists and communists, it was a direct outgrowth of Gorbachev's and Shevardnadze's attempt to Westernize Russia; going against its cultural and historic heritage, an opportunistic elite jumped on the bandwagon of separatism following Gorbachev's delegitimization of the Soviet state. The collapse of the USSR, therefore, was a result of a desperate attempt by a corrupt elite to preserve itself and was by no means a reflection of the sentiment of the masses. Therefore, many nationalists and communists argue that the removal of these traitorous elites will invariably lead to a peaceful reconstitution of the USSR.

Therefore, whereas both the Westernizers and the centrists (albeit disagreeing on the terms) see the ultimate goal of Russian policy as the integration of Russia into the world economy and international system, to the nationalist camp the purpose of Russia's foreign policy is to recreate a supranational Russian state. The dichotomy in Russian politics was described by the communist-nationalist *Pravda* as the following: "We have two political parties – the advocates of a strong state and those who oppose them; all others are simply variations on the theme."[50] To apply the same "concentric circles" paradigm, the nationalists believe that the rings decrease in importance as the distance from the Russian heartland increases.

In their view, the first circle consists of the territorial space of the USSR, the second circle the Eurasian landmass, and the third circle the "Atlanticist West." It is in their approach to the first circle that the Eurasianists' division seems to be most acute. While there are communists who continue to believe in the reincarnation of the Soviet Union and nationalists who believe in the rebirth of a Russian unitary state modeled on the tsarist empire, most nationalists and communists assume a more flexible position. Among the nationalists there is a strong body of opinion that accepts Solzhenitsyn's notion of a Russian state built around the core of East Slavdom and Orthodoxy.[51] There are communists who foresee a confederation governed by like-minded (and ultimately centrally controlled) communist parties. However, across the nationalist-communist camp there is a prevailing belief that most, if not all, of the former territory of the Soviet Union is of exclusive Russian interest and actually falls in the domain of Russia's domestic politics.[52] The conservative nationalist camp has responded to the issue of the re-creation of the Russian state in a variety of ways. The Russian Orthodox Church has simply taken the position that the current break-up of "Russia" is a temporary aberra-

---

[50] Viktor Linnik, "Nation's Primordial Cause and the Hour of 'Universal Humanists,'" *Pravda*, 10 March 1993.

[51] Although Solzhenitsyn views the Russian imperial experience as an impoverishment of the Russian people, his notion of a Russian state consisting of the Russian Federation, Ukraine, Belarus, and Russophone Kazakstan accounts for nearly 90 percent of the territory of the former USSR.

[52] Sergei Markov, "Russian Political Parties and Foreign Policy," in Tismaneau, *Political Culture and Civil Society in Russia*, 137–54.

tion that will soon be resolved. The metropolitan Filaret of Minsk, in a letter to the Belarussian scouts, declared that "our fatherland, despite the temporary state of affairs, stretches to the Pacific." Similarly, the Patriarch of Russia, Alexii II, presided over the 1996 Yeltsin–Lukashenko summit aimed at future unification. Vladimir V. Zhirinovsky, among others representing the extreme right of the Russian body politic, proclaimed the need to restore, by force if need be, the pre-1917 frontiers of the Russian state.[53]

While averse to resorting to force, Alexander Solzhenitsyn insisted that, by carrying out a district-based referendum across the former USSR, a state encompassing the Orthodox Slavic core would emerge. On a more pragmatic level, Andranik Migranyan, a former advisor to Boris Yeltsin, while accepting the nominal independence of the post-Soviet states, stated bluntly that the statehood of the post-Soviet states is "transitional" and borders separating the post-Soviet states are "provisional," making it "impossible to mechanically transfer the norms and the rules that existed between the Soviet Union and the countries of the far abroad to relations between Russia and these [former Soviet] republics." According to Migranyan, Russia is challenged by outside players that seek to undermine Russia's presence there: "Both Iran and Turkey are making consistent efforts to establish their own political and economic hegemony in the Caucasus. To a significant extent, behind these regional powers one can detect two groupings battling on a world scale: The West is behind Turkey and the Muslim Fundamentalist movement is behind Iran."[54] Given these circumstances, "Russia will not be able to 'sit out' events occurring outside the borders of the Russia Federation without intervening."[55] In line with the perception that the disintegration of the USSR was an arbitrary act and that both the Islamic world and the West are attempting to gain a foothold in areas vital to Russia's survival, Migranyan suggested that Russia "declare to the world community that the entire geopolitical space of the former USSR is a sphere of its vital interests." Alluding to the American Monroe Doctrine, Migranyan went on to state that "not international structures, not the US or NATO, but Russia should be the factor determining the fate of the

[53] See Natalia Narochnitskaia, "Politika rossii na poroge tret'ego tysiacheletiia," *Mezhdunarodnaia zhizn'*, no. 9 (1996), 26–40.
[54] Andranik Migranyan, "Near Abroad Is Vital to Russia," parts I and II, *Nezavisimaia gazeta*, 12 January and 18 January 1994.
[55] Ibid.

geopolitical space of the former USSR."[56] Yuri Katasonov, describing the priorities of the foreign policy agenda of Russian "patriots," noted that Russia must seek a restoration of a "Great Russian State, where intra-CIS issues will be treated again as 'internal' problems."[57]

Seeing the world primarily through the geopolitical prism of Halford MacKinder, who envisioned Russia as the "strategic pivot" of the Eurasian landmass,[58] the adherents of the Eurasian school generally rank the second circle, consisting of the countries of the Eurasian landmass, as being of secondary priority for Russian diplomacy. In Europe, their first concern is to prevent any possible expansion of the former Warsaw Pact countries into the geopolitical space of the former USSR. Of major concern, therefore, is the possible expansion of Romania into Moldova, the spread of Polish culture – mainly through the Catholic Church – to Ukraine and Belarus, and to a lesser degree, the expansion of Finland's influence in Kerelia and among other Ugro-Finnish people in the Russian Federation. Given the belief that Russia is condemned to an unfriendly and competitive relationship with its immediate European neighbors, many adherents of the Eurasianist school believe that Russia can and indeed must revive its historic alliance with Germany to stabilize its immediate western borders, as well as to create a bloc of continental powers against the ever-pernicious Atlanticism. Alluding to the historic cultural link between Russia and Germany, General Sterligov declared that Russia's future hinges on cordial relations with Germany and the countries' mutual ability to resist an Anglo-Saxon conspiracy to frustrate this partnership. Russia and Germany waged distressing wars against each other during this century "because of tragic concurrence of circumstances or someone's malicious intent."[59]

The Eurasianist camp tends to share an enthusiasm for China, seeing in China a vital partner to contain a resurgent Japan, as well as the model of a country that, instead of attempting to join the West in the mode of Russian liberals, forced the West to deal with it on its own terms.[60] *Pravda* described the difference between China's and Russia's efforts to enter the international system the following way: "While a

---

[56] Andranik Migranyan, "Real and Illusionary Foreign Policy," *Rossiiskaia gazeta*, 9 September 1992.
[57] Yurii V. Katasonov, "National Foreign Policy Priorities," *Russkii vestnik*, no. 9, 26 February–4 March 1992, 4.
[58] Halford MacKinder, "Geographical Pivot of History," *Geographical Journal* 4: 23 (1904), 421–44.
[59] Interfax, 22 September 1992.
[60] Migranyan, "Real and Illusionary Foreign Policy."

promise of $24 billion is merely waved in front of Russia as bait, China in five years has taken and utilized foreign investment totalling $60.9 billion(!) . . . China has achieved this impressive success without giving up a single iota of its sovereignty, its national pride, or its moral values."[61] In addition, the Eurasianists consistently advocate close relationships with India and the Arab world, seeing these vast lands as natural allies against the encroachment of Western Atlanticism.

The issue the Eurasianists have found the most divisive and difficult to resolve is the appropriate response to the rise of Islamic fundamentalism and the pan-Turkic movement. While there is a prevailing feeling that one of the global aims of the West is to use Russia as cannon fodder in its struggle with the Islamic tide and China,[62] a role which nationalists have vigorously rejected,[63] the question dividing the ranks of the nationalists is whether the Muslim south consists primarily of friends or foes of Russia. Russia's early twentieth-century Slavophiles and Eurasianists argued that Russia is an amalgamation of Slavic and Turkic roots, a portentous ancestry giving Russia its cultural distinctiveness and laying the foundation for its unique identity. Their attitude toward Islam was also ambivalent; while clearly bruised by the Mongol yoke, the Russian Orthodox Church felt no more (and possibly less) affinity for Western forms of Christianity than for Islam. While the unifying framework of most latter-day Russian nationalists has been the tendency to view Russia's geostrategic position in accordance with MacKinder's concept of Russia as the pivotal state on the Eurasian landmass, most nationalists and Eurasianists recognize that Russia will have to deal with impoverished, overpopulated Muslim neighbors trying to assert their place within the international system. The response offered by Russia's Eurasianists has been far from uniform. General Sterligov asserted that Russia must "restore the traditional balance of interests between the Islamic world, the Slav countries and Europe."[64] Migranyan, alluding to the decline in Russia's population along with the rapid expansion in the populations of Central Asia, argued that Russia, if it

---

[61] Andrei Krushinskii, "We Can Only Envy Them," *Pravda*, 17 March 1993.
[62] See Goncharov's "Antievropa protiv antievrazii" or Victor Linnik, *Pravda*, 10 March 1993.
[63] Some conservatives asserted that the prospect of Russia's membership in NATO will materialize only if the West sees the utility of such inclusion as a means to contain Islam and China, see Vladislav Chèrnov, "Moscow Should Think Carefully," *Nezavisimaia gazeta*, 23 February 1994.
[64] Interfax, 22 September 1992; Katasonov, "National Foreign Policy Priorities."

is to avoid becoming a minority in any future union or confederation, must prevent Muslim expansion across the Caucasus by supporting Armenia and Georgia, while separating itself from most of Central Asia other than Kazakhstan. He warned of the long-term risk to Russia arising from a far-flung pan-Turkic bloc stretching from Europe to the Himalayas under the hegemony of pro-Western Turkey. To frustrate the emergence of a pan-Turkic union that, if unchecked, would engulf Russia's Muslim population in the Urals–Volga region and pose a direct threat to the viability of the Russian state, Migranyan maintained that, while disengaging itself from direct involvement in Central Asia, Russia must give its support to Iran.[65] If Migranyan's prescription is an attempt to create a *cordon sanitaire* around the Turkic world, relying on Iran and the Christian states of the Caucasus as a means to contain that threat, Zhirinovsky went even further, asserting that the only way for Russia to address the threat posed by pan-Islamism and pan-Turkism was through direct occupation (and annexation) of Turkey, Iran, and Afghanistan, a task that Zhirinovsky had hoped to facilitate through close cooperation with Iraq and India.[66]

If most Eurasianists are divided on how to respond to events in the southern segment of the second ring, the rim of the former USSR, their attitude toward the third circle (mainly the United States) is generally consistent, embracing various conspiratorial theories. Therefore, any attempt to improve the relationship between Russia and the United States draws a hostile reaction. Reflecting a view prevalent among many Russian communists and nationalists, *Pravda* noted that:

> The hegemonic aspirations of the leading imperialist power, the United States, have already undergone sharp intensification . . . The warming relationship between the United States and the USSR's main heir – Russia – are illusory. It did not happen because Russia ceased to be a socialist country . . . it is a consequence of both the sharp decline in the international influence of Russia, which the United States no longer has to confront, and Moscow's unilateral concessions to Washington.[67]

Perhaps the best illustration of the views of the Russian right toward the United States was encapsulated by its attitude toward NATO. Although the liberal Westernizers see NATO and the American global

---

[65] Andranik Migranyan, "Soviet Union Gone to Four Winds," *Megalopolis-Express*, no. 43, 28 October 1992.

[66] "Zhirinovsky Redraws India," Reuter–New Delhi, 7 March 1995.

[67] Boris Kulik, "Tiger Leaves His Cage," *Pravda*, 3 September 1992.

presence as vital elements contributing to Russia's national security, and although the centrists' main concern is the possible exclusion of Russia from NATO rather than objections to the organization as such, Russian nationalists see any NATO effort to expand its contacts with Russia and the former states of the Warsaw Pact as a sinister plan aimed at the further denigration of Russia. Describing NATO and its relationship with Russia, Vladislav Chernov noted:

> By its very nature, because of its intrinsic genetic code, NATO has been, and is now and will continue to be designed exclusively for the military-political containment of the USSR and now Russia . . . Whereas in the past it was a matter of containing Soviet expansion, now the tasks that have been set up are the perpetuation of the breakup of the Soviet Union, weakening Moscow's military-political position and bringing its foreign and military policies under Western control.[68]

Migranyan asserted that Russia's and NATO's interests are so contradictory that "Russia's inclusion in NATO (even if only in prospect) will turn our country into an outpost of this bloc on the borders of the Islamic World and China . . . Russia cannot be on NATO's short leash."[69] Other nationalists argue that joining the Partnership for Peace, let alone NATO, would negate Russia's historic mission: they assert that if Russia joins the partnership for Peace "it will not be able to fulfill the historic mission that, in our dramatic era, Russia alone is destined to fulfill – serving as a bridge between Europe and Asia."[70] Commenting on Russia's membership in Partnership for Peace, Gennadii Zyuganov, head of the Russian Communist Party, observed that its impact on Russia will be similar to Hitler's Barbarossa Plan, which resulted in Nazi Germany's invasion of the USSR.

To some Eurasianists, NATO has become an American instrument for fomenting crises and violence in order to provide a pretext for the United States to bolster its global hegemony:

> The events in Yugoslavia have proven to be a lifesaver for the United States and its allies. NATO's interference in Yugoslavia's affairs under the UN flag was supposed to demonstrate the need for this alliance under new conditions and to justify its existence. The operations in Iraq and Somalia are evidence of such intent . . . If such conflicts do not arise NATO will generate them . . . Any country that

---

[68] Chernov, "Moscow Should Think Carefully."
[69] Andranik Migranyan, "Why Enter If It Is Better Not to Enter?" *Nezavisimaia gazeta*, 14 March 1994.
[70] Yakov Plyais, "The Challenge of Our Times and Partnership for Peace," *Nezavisimaia gazeta*, 20 April 1994.

becomes a member of NATO dooms itself to the role of a political
vassal, of an obedient executor of the US's will and interests.

Seeing in NATO a mortal foe of Russia, the author concluded, "United
Germany, together with NATO, are quietly implementing plans that
they were unable to carry out during World War II."[71] Another *Pravda*
editorial described the Partnership for Peace as an American plot "to
encroach upon the Eurasian geostrategic region, which is vital for
achieving world domination."[72]

### From Atlanticism to centrism

Yeltsin's inital foreign policy was based on a belief that to
break its cycle of authoritarianism, it must abandon any notion of
messianism and integrate itself both politically and economically into
the international system. The dominant school of thought in the
foreign ministry held tightly to the belief, not dissimilar to Francis
Fukuyama's "End of History" notion, that the future of the international system would be shaped primarily by economic determinants.
Believing that the international system was about to experience a new
bipolarity between the developed "North" and impoverished
"South," the Russian foreign ministry attempted to integrate Russia
into the North as an end unto itself, with little or no regard for the
new geopolitical realities confronting Russia.[73] The new Russian
foreign ministry, therefore, continued to proceed with Gorbachev's
foreign policy as devised by Eduard Shevardnadze, redirecting
foreign policy from ideologically-driven confrontation with the West
to a commitment to "common human values," support for international organizations, human rights, ecological protection, arms
control, and so on. [74] Banking on the beliefs that there are no major
disputes or political and economic schisms between Russia and the
West and that the West would be both willing and able to finance
Russia's transformation to a market economy, the foreign policy
shaped by Yeltsin, Genadii Burbulis, Yegor Gaidar, and Kozyrev was
one of almost a unidimensional fixation on the West, particularly the
United States. Kozyrev boldly declared that the G-7 countries were

[71] Boris Poklad, "Post-election Russia and the West at a Crossroads?" *Pravda*, 29
December 1993.
[72] Viktor Vishnyakov, "Russian Recruit in NATO's Waiting Room," *Pravda*, 3 June 1994.
[73] For an exposition of such views see Zagorskii, Zlobin, Solodovnik and Khrustalev,
*Posle raspada SSSR.*
[74] Georgii Kunadze, "Russian Axioms," *Novoe vremia*, no. 10 (1991).

Russia's "natural allies."[75] Finance minister Boris Federov confidently declared that Russia would soon join NATO or its successor organization.[76] Under the aegis of the foreign ministry, Russia quickly accepted America's new arms reduction schemes and continued to support the economic embargo against Iraq, NATO's intervention in Yugoslavia, the curtailment of arms exports, and so on.[77]

Within months of its inauguration, Russia's efforts to join "the ranks of civilized nations," came under heavy criticism, both in terms of conceptual content and execution. Across a broad spectrum of Russian politics the foreign ministry was severely attacked. In their fascination with Russia's new-found friendship with the "civilized world," Russia's diplomats were accused of forgetting that the country was confronting fourteen new neighbors, countries to which Russia remained bound economically, politically, and culturally, as well as in terms of national security. Critics of the foreign ministry argued that, in the absence of the foreign ministry's supervision of the web of intra-CIS ties, these vital relations became almost the exclusive domain of the military, the mafia, and the "Red Directors," contributing to greater tensions and instability along Russia's periphery. Other critics asserted that Russia's fixation on the United States had led to the country's neglect of its Islamic rim, a neglect that could lead to the spread of an anti-Russian Islamic fundamentalism across Central Asia, the Caucasus, and ultimately the Volga valley, threatening the very survival of the Russian state. Finally, many Russians came to believe that Kozyrev's uncritical pro-American policy not only reflected the absence of a clear concept of Russia's national interests but also had led to a series of humiliating concessions to the United States in the vain hope of acceptance into the ranks of the advanced nations. Increasingly, Russians across the political spectrum complained that Washington treated Russia with arrogant patronage rather than as a genuine partner. Russian observers bitterly complained about the United States high-handed effort to end Russia's attempts to export rocket engines to India and submarines to Iran at a time when the United States was aggressively promoting its own arms exports. America's perceived habit of making unilateral decisions in the Balkans also irked many Russian nationalists, while Japan's overt effort to link Western credits to Russian flexibility on the

[75] Andrei Kozyrev, "Russia: A Chance for Survival," *Foreign Affairs* 71: 2 (Spring 1992).
[76] "Russia's Stand Toward NATO," *RFE/RL Daily Report*, no. 186 (30 September 1991).
[77] See Alexei Arbatov, "Russia's Foreign Policy Alternatives," *International Security* 18, no. 2 (Fall 1993).

Northern territories and Kuril islands dispute was characterized by most Russians as a by-product of an uncritical pro-Western policy. Kozyrev's foreign policy was further undermined by the perception that Washington condoned discrimination against Russian-speakers in the Baltic states and hesitated to confront Ukraine about breaking its promise to dispose of nuclear weapons.[78] Even apparently friendly gestures by the West, such as the idea of bringing Russia into NATO or the Strategic Defense Initiative, were perceived as an attempt to bind Russia into a position of inferiority.[79]

By late 1992, Kozyrev's seemingly directionless policy increasingly appeared anachronistic. Russia did not possess either the means or the geopolitical position of the USSR; furthermore, as bipolarity ended following the demise of the USSR, Russia's America-centered foreign policy increasingly appeared to be out of step with the current realities. Kozyrev's defense of his pro-American posture – urging Russia to follow the example of post-World War II West Germany, Italy, and Japan, which used their pro-Americanism to regain international stature[80] – angered many Russians, who felt that Russia did not deserve to be ranked with the defeated fascist powers, and prompted calls for Kozyrev's resignation. As Yevgenii Kozhokin, chairman of the Russian parliament subcommittee on intelligence and international relations, stated, "People of a Western turn of mind – and Kozyrev is one of them – are in danger of losing touch with their native soil. Once they come to power, Westernizers must cease to be Westernizers. *One can be a Westernizer only in opposition*" (Emphasis added).[81] The army daily, *Krasnaia zvezda*, characterized Kozyrev as a failure "for the lack of a comprehensive foreign policy concept, for his tractability vis-à-vis the West, for his intention to give away our missiles to Washington and the Kurils to Tokyo, for his soft glove policy toward Kishinev and the general weakness of the CIS."[82]

By 1992, although Russia was still far from achieving consensus about its foreign policy, it was becoming clear that Russia would have to define its own, as opposed to a Soviet, geopolitical concept and

---

[78] See Blackwell and Karaganov, *Damage Limitation or Crisis?*, 6.
[79] See Alexei Arbatov, "Russia's Foreign Policy Alternatives," *International Security* 18: 2 (Fall 1993).
[80] "Preobrazhennaia Rossiia v novom mire," Conference at the Foreign Ministry, 26–27 February 1992, official statement published in *Mezhdunarodnaia zhizn'* (March–April 1992).
[81] Alexander Vasiliev, "Russian Foreign Policy," *Komsomolskaia pravda*, 3 September 1992, 3.
[82] Alexander Goltz, "Laocon in Smolenskaya Square," *Krasnaia zvezda*, 18 July 1992.

develop a corresponding foreign policy. While there was general agreement that Russia was, and was likely to remain, a great power, across the Russian political spectrum the recognition dawned that Russia was surrounded by three rings in which it had diminished influence and disputable interest. While it was easy to agree on this geographic quandary and the fact that Russia's size and resources had bestowed upon it a role reserved for the larger members of the international community, the appropriate paradigm for achieving its fullest potential remained a controversial issue, bitterly dividing Russian society.

### Russia's foreign policy in perspective: the centrist paradigm

*A new consensus emerging*

The Westernizers' liberal concept of foreign policy could not be anything but a passing phase in the genesis of a lasting Russian foreign policy. The liberal policy, a carryover from the foreign policy of the waning days of the Soviet Union, did not respond to the reality that emerged following the USSR's collapse, nor was it equipped to deal with an entirely new universe of issues that were bound to haunt post-Soviet Russia. The basic assumption that Russia could rapidly join the ranks of civilized nations, politically as well as economically, proved to be false.

Martin Walker, in assessing Russia's initial foreign policy, noted, "One of the world's undisputed great powers temporarily subordinated its foreign and domestic policies to the West's capricious preferences. This state of affairs was never likely to last long, and was of dubious benefit to Russia and the West alike."[83]

The liberals' belief that Russia's relationship with the first circle – the former Soviet republics – would sort itself out in the context of Russo-Western relations also proved to be a folly. The initial failure to recognize that the substantial Russian population outside of Russia would become a *cause célèbre* in the Russian body politic further indicated the absence of compatibility between the new political reality and the foreign policy establishment. Describing the mindset of the Russian foreign policy establishment in the early days of Russia's statehood, Tatiana Shakliena of the US and Canada Institute observed

---

[83] Martin Walker, "Russia and the West: What is to Be Done Now?" *World Policy Journal* 11: 1 (1994), 1.

that Russian foreign policy remained a holdover from the Soviet period fixated on global issues: "As for the Near Abroad, this area for some time was on the periphery of Russian foreign policy, which put emphasis on the relationship with the West in order to integrate into the 'community of civilized nations.' The Russian approach to ethnic conflict management has also been under the influence of this general attitude."[84]

The pro-Western foreign policy was out of touch with the new realities in Russia and consequently failed to develop a significant constituency of support. Even more significantly, the Westernizers' approach appeared to be incompatible with Russia's national interests and at odds with the basic national identity of vast numbers of Russia's citizenry. While many Russians lamented the position of the Russian population in the Soviet Union, Russian national identity, firmly tied to the notion of a "Great Russian state," perceived the collapse of the Soviet Union and especially the departure of brethren Slavs from the Union as a severe blow to vast numbers of Russians. In the mind of many Russians, the culprit behind the collapse of the Soviet Union was Gorbachev's Westernization.

The standing of the Westernizers' foreign policy was further eroded by the centrifugal forces that surfaced in Russia following the collapse of the Soviet Union and Russian independence. The Russian people, to many of whom the collapse of the Soviet Union was a bitter blow, were forced following the creation of post-Soviet Russia to contend with a bewildering cascade of declarations of sovereignty or even outright independence, from Chechnya in the south to Sakha (Yakutia) in the northeast. With Russia's own integrity severely stressed, the liberals' concept of rights of self-determination of nations, the human rights aversion to the use of force in dealing with outright threats of secession, and the insistence on maintaining standards and procedures followed in civilized countries led to the perception that the Westernized foreign policy establishment had not only failed to defend Russia's national interests but was actually contributing to Russia's ultimate disintegration.[85] The perception that in their quest to join the civilized nations the liberals were willing to subject Russia to severe economic dislocation and to surrender

---

[84] Tatiana Shakleina, "Russian Policy Toward Military Conflicts in the Former Soviet Union," in *State Building and Military Power in Russia and the New States of Eurasia*, ed. Bruce Parrott (Armonk, NY: M. E. Sharpe, 1995), 83–108.

[85] See Douglas Blum, "Disintegration and Russian Foreign Policy," in Blum, *Russia's Future*.

"Russian lands" to Japan placed the liberal concept outside the mainstream of Russia's politics.

Russia's transformation to a centrist foreign policy position was the result of an evolutionary process. The watershed event signaling the shift in Moscow's foreign policy was probably Yeltsin's abrupt cancellation of his trip to Japan in 1992, when it became clear that a Russo-Japanese summit would be dominated by a link between Japanese aid and the resolution of the territorial dispute between the two countries.

Rejection of the liberals' foreign policy did not imply a willingness to return to messianism or global confrontation with the West. Russia's Westernizing foreign policy, as Michael McFaul argues, was a "detour" imposed by the expediencies of the Yeltsin–Gorbachev struggle. However, despite the disintegration of the USSR, Russia remained a great power and retained most of its pre-1991 institutions; hence, it was bound to resume a traditional great power diplomacy.[86] In reality, despite vocal criticism by nationalists and hardline communists, subsequent Russian foreign policy generally reflects the centrist conception of Russia's role in the world.

The centrist premises are based on the belief that Russia's paramount goal remains full integration into the international system, but Russia's interests are not, nor can they be, identical to those of the United States. However, ultimately Russia is culturally and psychologically an integral part of the West with a stake in the existing international system; therefore, a new confrontation with the West would be a tragedy for Russia. There is widespread recognition across the Russian political spectrum that it is beyond Russia's capabilities to conduct a global foreign policy[87] and conviction that Russia's security interests are limited to the Eurasian landmass, with its interests in areas beyond the borders of the former Soviet Union limited solely to the economic sphere.

As for Russia's relations with the "near abroad," the centrist attitude is built on the assumption that Russia has vital economic and security interests across the territory of the former USSR. While the overt political reconstitution of the Soviet Union may not be attainable or even necessarily desirable, the CIS must proceed with ever-deeper economic, and eventually political integration, with Russia asserting itself as the uncontested *primus inter pares* within the Commonwealth. However, even within the Commonwealth, Russia seems to be pur-

---

[86] See Arbatov, "Russia's Foreign Policy Alternatives".
[87] See Shakleina, "Russia Policy Toward Military Conflicts," 103.

suing a policy of what Kartunov has referred to as "narrow nationalism," a policy in which Russia utilizes its preponderance to mold an economic and political relationship while avoiding commitments that would place additional stress on its economy, even foregoing an opportunity to recast the empire, as the reluctance to closer ties with Belarus demonstrated.

### Russia and the West

Although the overtly pro-American position of the Russian foreign ministry in the early days of post-Soviet statehood was discredited, the centrality of the West remained a cornerstone of Russian foreign policy. Although the centrist foreign policy prevailing in Moscow is far more willing to stake out an independent Russian position on a wide array of issues – including the Balkan War, North Korea, the removal of sanctions from Iraq, and Arab–Israeli issues – and remains convinced that the success of Russia's transformation is ultimately contingent on Russia itself, it recognizes that the transformation cannot be attained without the cooperation of the West. Simultaneously, early Russian expectations that a quiescent foreign policy by Moscow would result in massive Western economic aid and rapid integration into the G-7 group failed to materialize; in fact, even the much-heralded $24 billion package was not delivered. However, despite Moscow's disappointment and the emergence of areas of disagreement with the West, there is a substantial congruence of interests that makes overall cooperation possible. As Sergei Karaganov explained, "Russia's foreign policy changed without questioning the rapprochement with the West."[88]

Russian centrists did complain that while the United States embraced noxiously repressive regimes such as those in China or Saudi Arabia, Washington protested Russia's relationship with Iran. Also, since the collapse of the USSR, the United States has aggressively expanded its export of arms while applying overt pressure on Russia to curtail its arms deals with India and Iran. The Council of Europe was unwilling to admit Russia because of its treatment of prison inmates and conscripts, but gave immediate membership to Latvia and Estonia despite the Russian perception of mass disenfranchisement of ethnic Russians in those countries; the discrepancy was

---

[88] Sergei Karaganov, "Personal View: Russia Finds an Independent Foreign Policy," *Financial Times*, 21 March 1994.

perceived by most Russians as duplicitous, and it embittered many centrists. However, it is the issue of NATO's continued existence, let alone its expansion to the USSR's former satellites and perhaps former Soviet republics, that is perceived across the Russian polity as the ultimate hypocrisy. Alexei Arbatov, director of the Center for Geopolitical and Military Forecasts, declared that the bipolar security system in Europe must be replaced with "three major pillars: European Community/West European Union (EC/WEU), the United States and Russia."[89] The reversal of US policy regarding the expansion of NATO, from a refusal to address the issue directly to proposals to formulate the guidelines for the expansion of NATO, provoked a firestorm across the Russian political landscape. Given Russia's ultimate need for a stable relationship with Washington, the centrists' foreign policy can be best described as a systematic probing to discover Washington's tolerance for a Russian policy that might be at odds with that of the United States. Actions such as the Russian sale of three Kilo-class diesel submarines to Iran, Moscow's agreement to sell cryogenic rocket engines to India, its efforts to impose a more evenhanded policy by the United Nations in Bosnia, and its support for French efforts to restart the peace process in the Middle East were the result of this probing. Although each of these attempts to pursue an independent foreign policy led to some verbal jostling between Washington and Moscow, ultimately Russia opted to preserve its relationship with Washington rather than to dig in its heels for the sake of great-power status. Despite Yeltsin's statement that commercial deals between the "great nations of India and Russia cannot be interfered with by outside parties," the deal between Moscow and New Delhi was in fact shelved. Similarly, although Moscow did not reverse its decision to sell Iran three outdated diesel submarines, during his visit to Washington in September 1994, President Yeltsin promised that no new arms contracts would be signed with Teheran. Russian eagerness to avoid direct confrontation with Washington extended even to the politically sensitive issues of the Balkans, where despite Russian rhetoric in support of the Serbs, Moscow never blocked any United Nations resolution authorizing NATO's involvement in the Bosnian crisis, nor did it ultimately lift the economic embargo imposed in Yugoslavia even after Belgrade broke with the Bosnian Serbs. Moscow's effort to retain Washington's good graces was even more dramatically illustrated by the fact that despite

[89] Arbatov, "Russian Foreign Policy for the 1990s," 26.

domestic sensitivity on the issue of the Russian-speaking diaspora in the former Soviet Union, Russia, with American prodding, withdrew its forces from the Baltic states without directly linking that presence to the political rights of Russophones in Latvia and Estonia. Similarly, although the Russian defense ministry has contended that conventional forces in Europe reduction agreements were signed by the USSR and therefore do not correspond to the existing reality and must be revised, the Russian government, faced with a consistent American refusal to reopen the matter, has not pressed the issue thus far. And despite Yeltsin's statements that Russia will not tolerate the "expansion of NATO to the borders of the Russian Federation" and the threats that a "Cold Peace" will succeed the "Cold War" in the European arena, Yeltsin has not at any time closed the door to a strong Russian link to the West. Recognizing that Russia might not be able to abort the expansion of NATO, Yeltsin, instead of resorting to Soviet-style threats and confrontation, noted that he is confident that the United States and Russia will be able to reach an agreement on the outstanding issues affecting NATO and, therefore, "Russia should prepare its own fallback maneuver," which according to Yeltsin means the inclusion of Russia in the political arm of NATO.[90]

One of the paradoxes of the end of the Cold War is that Russia, no longer a superpower, remains the sole country with a presence in and interests that stretch across the Eurasian landmass, thereby making it a vital ingredient of stability in these regions.

It is perhaps because Russia remains Washington's sole approximation of a pivotal power in Eurasia, without which there can be no stability, that the position of the United States and of the Russian centrists found a certain symbiotic expression.

Thus, although the relationship between Russia's centrists and Washington is free of the romance and mutual admiration typical of the initial phase of Russian foreign policy when Westernizers dominated, both parties have managed to find sufficient congruence to retain a working, if at times strained, relationship. An unresolved issue that may well ultimately derail the existing modus vivendi between Russia and the United States is the question of Russia's relationship with the European members of the CIS. While UN Ambassador Madeleine Albright stressed that the United States did not give Russia carte blanche to assert itself in the European parts of the CIS, Russian centrists increasingly appear to assume, as Kortunov

[90] TASS, 5 December 1994.

wrote: that "The only really sensitive issue is the Baltic states; here a Russian imperialist policy might confront a tough American response. Otherwise, one could expect that even a gradual reabsorption of Ukraine by Russia in some form would be met with indifference, if not understanding, by the United States."[91] Despite the growing tensions between Moscow and Washington, Russia's centrists continue to believe that the success of Russia's integration into the international system is conditional on a good working relationship with the United States, prompting Yeltsin to call for intensified relations with the Republican-dominated 104th Congress, despite obvious clashes on the road ahead.[92]

The general perception of the centrists is that while the United States will continue to be the sole truly global power, its influence and military presence in Europe is bound to decline as Germany resolves its economic dislocation imposed by the costs of reunification. In economic terms the European Union already has emerged as Russia's largest trading partner, easily surpassing Russia's trade with either its Commonwealth partners or the United States.[93] In light of the Russian perception that the European Union is bound to become a major political actor in the international system, Russia is energetically attempting to deepen its European link, at times exploiting the differences between Washington and the European Union. On the issue of the war in Bosnia and the question of enlarging NATO, Russia found a more receptive ear among Western Europe's major powers than in Washington. Both the European Union's secretary, Jacques Delors, and Britain's prime minister, John Major, expressed reservations about the expansion of NATO. Even Germany's chancellor, Helmut Kohl, who has long advocated the eastward expansion of NATO, urged a go-slow attitude, noting that "It is quite important that it [NATO's expansion] happen in such way that the security of Russia is heeded and built in."[94]

The United States rejected Russia's proposals to expand the Organization for Security and Cooperation in Europe (OSCE) as the main institution guaranteeing security in Europe and ridiculed Saddam Hussein's recognition of Kuwait's sovereignty, brokered by Kozyrev,

---

[91] Andrei Kortunov, "Russia and the United States," in Blackwell and Karaganov, *Damage Limitation or Crisis?*, 306.
[92] *Nezavisimaia gazeta*, 9 November 1994.
[93] John Lloyd, "Russian Trade Turns Westward," *Financial Times*, 24 November 1994.
[94] "Russia Will Eventually Accept Bigger NATO – Kohl," *Reuter European Community Report*, 6 December 1994.

but the French position on both issues was far more in line with that of Russia. France joined Russia in calling for the end to sanctions against Iraq and in insisting that Europe should not be allowed to fragment into blocs, which the French argued is bound to occur if NATO admits the Višegrad group as new members.[95] The growing Russian orientation toward Western Europe was articulated by Kozyrev, who, during his official visit to Paris, declared:

> The historic link between France and Russia, along with the present partnership between our countries, looks like one of the central supports for the construction of new Europe . . . This will open additional opportunities for our work in Europe and serve to strengthen our strategic interaction with the key European partners – France, Britain, and Germany. This will not be a partnership against the United States. It will be a partnership with them, but one in which Europe has its own voice and in which Moscow's voice within the European chorus is heard loudly enough.[96]

Russia's relations with Britain historically reflected the view that improved relations with Britain are a channel to improved Russian relations with Washington. Every Soviet leader from Khrushchev to Gorbachev launched his Western diplomatic offensive with a visit to London. However, because Russia believes that British foreign policy is governed by the dictum of a "special relationship" with Washington, Anglo-Russian relations tended to be cordial but superficial. Anglo-Russian relations acquired new substance following the US decision to stop enforcing the arms embargo against Bosnia in November 1994. British observers perceived America's sudden reversal not only as a move that endangered British troops in the Balkans, but, more important, as an American reversion to unilateralism, if not outright isolationism.

At the Paris meeting of Kozyrev, French Foreign Minister Alain Juppé, and British Foreign Secretary Douglas Hurd, Britain broke ranks with Washington and endorsed expanding the authority of the OSCE[97] and agreed to seek "European solutions" to its security needs. This strange Anglo-American rift led the London-based *Sunday Telegraph* to declare that a "divorce" had taken place. However, while "the United States will move on, always the eligible bachelor, Britain will have to find solace in a tentative alliance with France and

---

[95] See "Russia, France Warn Against New Barriers in Europe," *Reuter European Community Report*, 17 November 1994.
[96] ITAR-TASS (World Service), 15 November 1994.
[97] *Reuter European Community Report*, 17 November 1994.

Russia."[98] These shifts in Europe's political landscape gave sufficient encouragement to Kozyrev to declare that both NATO and the OSCE are relics of the Cold War and that a pillar of Europe's security should be "the historic Russo-French alliance."[99]

Moscow's relationship with Germany is experiencing a slow yet noticeable change. Although Germany remains Russia's largest creditor and trading partner, the role that Germany plays in Russian foreign policy has changed dramatically. Whereas during the past two decades West Germany, and later a unified Germany, acted as Russia's primary advocate in Western councils,[100] Germany, now fully sovereign and fearful of being on the front line should chaos befall the former Soviet bloc, finds itself in a contradictory position. German Defense Minister Volker Rühe, fearing that under current conditions Germany will be forced to deal alone with any dislocation east of the Oder River and raising the specter of "singularity" and constraint by the burden of history, has become a vocal advocate of rapid NATO expansion to Central Europe, despite Moscow's objections. It is interesting to note that German foreign policy analysts, while rejecting Russia's demand to turn NATO from an alliance into a collective security system as a ploy to denude NATO of its cohesion,[101] continue to voice the belief that "an enlargement of NATO to include the Višegrad group states in conjunction with a contractual security partnership between NATO and Russia within the framework of the North Atlantic Cooperation Council will probably turn out to be the best possible solution."[102] German Foreign Minister Klaus Kinkel, aware that to be meaningful a NATO guarantee will need an overt US commitment that the US Congress may be reluctant to endorse, and cognizant that should Russia revert to an anti-status-quo position the democratization of Russia, Central Europe, and possibly Germany itself could be compromised, advocated an expansion of NATO concomitant with an overarching agreement with either Russia or the CIS. Therefore, it is Germany that appears to be most respectful of

---

[98] Ambrose Evans-Pitchard, "Focus on the Crumbling Alliance: It's America First and NATO Nowhere," *Sunday Telegraph*, 20 November 1994.

[99] Alan Philip, "Moscow Looks Back to the Treaty of the Tsars, with a Hint of Déjà Vu," *Sunday Telegraph*, 20 November 1994.

[100] Ilya Prizel, "Russia and Germany, the Case of a Special Relationship," in *Post Communist Europe: Crisis and Readjustment*, ed. Andrew A. Michta and Ilya Prizel (New York: St. Martin's Press, 1993).

[101] See Gerhard Wetting, "Moscow's Perception of NATO," *Aussenpolitik* 11 (1994), 123–33.

[102] Lothar Ruhel, "European Security and NATO's Eastward Expansion," *Aussenpolitik* 11 (1994), 115–22.

Russia's proposals to upgrade the OSCE to an intermediary organ between its members and the United Nations, hence giving the Kremlin greater voice in shaping a Europe-wide agenda.[103] Although the German proposal falls short of the Russian notion of a "co-guarantee" to Central Europe by the CIS and NATO, even Germany's modest efforts to accommodate Moscow have met with criticism. NATO's Deputy Secretary General Sergio Balazino charged that any accord along these lines would compromise NATO's independence, stating emphatically, "There will never be a clause or understanding whereby Russia can interfere or have a say in NATO's life."[104] The proposal of a co-guarantee also drew criticism from Central European states, Britain, and the United States. An accommodation with Russia along this track was criticized for several reasons. The Central Europeans contended that any agreement between NATO and Russia would equal "16 plus 1" and once again reduce the Central European states to an object of a "neo-Holy Alliance" between Russia and Germany, evoking a historic legacy that Warsaw, Prague, and Budapest are eager to put behind them. Ukraine, and to some degree Belarus, were alarmed by the prospect that any agreement between NATO and the CIS would in effect be an agreement between NATO and Russia, significantly eroding these young countries' fragile independence; Ukraine's President Leonid Kuchma decided not to accelerate the process of NATO's expansion in a manner that Russia might find provocative.[105] Finally, the mere fact that today Germany and Russia manage their own relations without NATO supervision, as was the case until 1990, raised qualms in Washington, since an intimate relationship between Bonn and Moscow robs the Atlantic link of some of its fundamental missions. While the Russo-German relationship is no longer between a superpower and an insecure semi-sovereign entity, there remains a significant overlap between Russia's and Germany's interests. Chancellor Kohl, despite strenuous Japanese objections, remained the most consistent advocate of full Russian membership in the G-7, while Russia was the first permanent member of the Security Council of the United Nations to endorse permanent status for Germany as well.

[103] Bruce Clark, "Russia and West Split on Europe's Security," *Financial Times*, 10 October 1994.

[104] Daniel Sneider, "Russia Prepared to Join NATO," *Christian Science Monitor*, 27 May 1994.

[105] R. Jeffrey Smith, "Danger is Seen in Rapid NATO Expansion," *Washington Post*, 23 November 1994.

Unlike Russian nationalists, who view an alliance with Germany as the means of destroying the current international system, the Russian centrists recognize that any attempted repetition of an alliance with Germany in the mode of Rapallo (or, worse still, the Molotov–Ribbentrop pact) is futile as well as dangerous. However, in equal measure, Russian centrists seem to be keen on not repeating Russia's policy of the last century, where Russia became the West's main tool to contain Germany, a process that led to the destruction of tsarist Russia and the bankruptcy of the Soviet Union. A concern articulated by some Russian centrists is that, while for Russia Western Europe is both a model and a cultural home, Western Europeans tend to pay attention to Russia only when it is either threatening or essential to retaining a balance of power on the continent. A Russia that is neither a threat nor a necessity tends to be ignored by its Western neighbors, re-enforcing a belief in Russia that ultimately its two allies, as Nicholas I stated, are "the army and the navy."[106]

The policy pursued by Russia's centrists toward the United States and the European Union is one of accommodation, despite disagreements with the United States over the Balkans, the sanctions against Iraq, and NATO's expansion and friction with the European Union over trade issues, the question of Russian membership in the Council of Europe, and the dispute over the rights of ethnic Russians in Estonia and Latvia.

Moscow's policy toward its former allies in the Warsaw Pact has remained far more passive and reactive, often articulated only in response to these countries' overtures toward either NATO or CIS states along Russia's borders. Karaganov's observation that good relations with the CIS's European neighbors are desirable but not immediately attainable has typified Moscow's policy toward most of its former satellites, but it was particularly accentuated toward Poland. While recognizing, and indeed encouraging, a resumption of damaged trade relationships with former Council of Economic Mutual Assistance countries, Russia's centrist attitude toward Poland and to a lesser degree toward Hungary and the Czech Republic is hampered by several complicating factors. On an emotional level, Russia's centrists consider their country the prime victim of Stalinism and therefore bitterly resent any attempt to assign them the burden of guilt for Stalinist savagery. This opinion surfaced several times during

---

[106] See Igor Maksimchev, "Russia and Western Europe," in Blackwell and Karaganov, *Damage Limitation or Crisis?*, 173.

Russo–Polish relations. Yeltsin's adamant refusal during Lech Wałęsa's visit to Moscow in May 1992 to accept responsibility for the massacres of Polish officers in the Katyń Forest was a case in point of the burden of history casting its long shadow on Moscow's relationship with its erstwhile satellites. In a similar vein, Warsaw's celebrations of the fiftieth anniversary of the Warsaw Uprising in August 1994 rekindled Russian ire at Warsaw when Russians perceived that President Yeltsin was invited to apologize for Soviet inaction during the uprising. The notion that a Russian president would be invited to Warsaw to commemorate a World War II event on equal footing with Germany's President Roman Herzog provoked a sense of indignation at Poland's ingratitude toward its liberators. Thus, while Russia's centrists believe it may well be in Moscow's interest to have a good relationship with its former satellites in general and Poland in particular, these relationships remain constrained not only by a differing reading of their mutual history in Warsaw and Moscow, but by the fundamentally different agendas of Moscow and the former satellites. While the basic assumption of Russia's centrists is that Russia's foreign policy must reflect Russia's great-power status, the Eastern Europeans, and Poles in particular, although welcoming the resumption of trade links with Russia, see any resumption of Russia's role as a great power allied with other great powers as a *prima facie* assault on their sovereignty.[107]

Poland's vocal attempts to join NATO and the Suchocka government's attempt to embolden the governments of Belarus and Ukraine to resist closer integration with Russia evoked an angry reaction across Russia's wide political spectrum as a means of building a *cordon sanitaire* around Russia. Thus, although in the economic sphere the Russo–Polish relationship started to show signs of revival – with both parties agreeing to be partners in building a natural gas pipe from Yamal in the Urals to Germany and entering negotiations to co-produce the Sukhoi-39 aircraft – both Poland's and Russia's elites continued to be too hemmed in by the past and by powerful constituencies at home to fully normalize that relationship. However, in the case of Poland, Russia's foreign policy establishment seems to be cognizant of the fact that an overtly hostile position toward Poland would merely strengthen its resolve to join NATO. The Russian ambassador to Warsaw, Yuri Kashelev, admitted that Russia views

---

[107] Peter Hardi, "Eastern Europe and Russia," in Blackwell and Karaganov, *Damage Limitation or Crisis?*

NATO as an unfriendly organization; nevertheless, if Poland were to join NATO, he could not "imagine [Russia] to be so offended that we would stop trading or talking."[108]

The prevailing chill between Moscow and its former Warsaw Pact satellites was articulated by Kozyrev, who noted that, under the current circumstances, in terms of Russia's priorities, the countries of Eastern Europe ranked behind the West and the CIS.[109] Although Russia's relationship with Poland continues to be dogged by historic memories, with the Russian centrists' belief that there is little that Russia should or can do to alter the relationship, the relationship with the other former satellites is somewhat less controversial. Although both the Czechs and the Hungarians expressed an interest in joining NATO, those expressions were couched in far milder terms; furthermore, while Prague and Budapest insisted on an acknowledgment of a historic wrong inflicted by the USSR on these countries in 1968 and 1956, nevertheless both were placated by far milder statements.[110]

On the whole, Russia has maintained a working relationship with its former satellites. Despite tensions over the role of Russia's 14th Army in the Transdneister, Russia's relationship with Romania has remained cordial. Similarly, despite clear divergence between Russia and Hungary on the issue of the Yugoslav crisis, with Russia being pro-Serb and Hungary viewing Belgrade as a menace, the relationship between Moscow and Budapest remained cordial. Russia's Patriarch Alexei II traveled to Budapest and asked for Hungarian forgiveness for Russia's role in the suppression of the 1956 uprising;[111] Russia and Hungary defused the issue of Soviet debt to Hungary through transfers of Russian weapons to Budapest; and although Hungary expressed its desire to join NATO, its former foreign minister, Geza Jeszensky, stressed that Hungary's main goal is European integration, an integration that stretches from Vancouver to Vladivostok.[112]

The only two countries where Russia has managed to re-establish a significant presence are Bulgaria, a country with a tradition of

[108] Interview with Ambassador Yuri Kashlev, *Gazeta Wyborcza*, no. 255, 2 November 1994.
[109] Stanislav Kondrashov, "Vostochnaia evropa i rossiia," *Izvestiia*, 1 December 1993.
[110] For example, during his visit to Prague in September of 1993 Yeltsin limited his reference to the 1968 invasion to the statement, "We wish to draw a final line under the totalitarian past connected with the inadmissible use of force against Czechoslovakia in 1968," *Moscow News*, 1 September 1993.
[111] Emil Varadi, "Russia's Patriarch Apologizes to Hungary for 1956," *Reuter*, 4 March 1994.
[112] "Kozyrev Meets Jeszensky, Goncz and Boross: Regional Security, Bilateral Ties," Hungarian TV1, 21 February 1994.

Russophilia, and Slovakia, thus far the only country outside the CIS to sign a military protocol with the Russian Federation.

## The southern rim

It is perhaps on its southern rim that Russia's shift from a Western-oriented foreign policy to a centrist policy of narrow nationalism finds its greatest expression. Initially Russia's policy toward the former Soviet republics of the Caucasus and Central Asia was one of indifference bordering on contempt. The fact that the decision to dissolve the Soviet Union and replace it with a Commonwealth of Independent States was made by the three Slavic republics (Belarus, Russia, and Ukraine) was clearly a reflection of the marginal position that the Caucasus and Central Asia occupied in the minds of Russia's policy makers during the immediate post-Soviet period. Kozyrev openly derided any intimate relationship with Central Asia as a reversion to "*Aziatchina*," invoking the despotic imagery associated with the term. Initially Russian liberals viewed the Caucasus and Central Asia as a bastion of personalistic fiefs in the mold of Brezhnevism that would only retard Russia's progress toward democracy, a market economy, and integration into the West. It is noteworthy that during Yeltsin's struggle with Gorbachev, Yeltsin's reformers tended to ally themselves with the Baltic Western-oriented nationalists, while Gorbachev sought solace among the conservative "Sovietized" leadership in the south. Following the collapse of the USSR, as Elizabeth Valkenier observed, aside from the Russian military, other Russian political institutions all but ignored the region.[113] Russia's apparent lack of interest in the region created a vast vacuum that Iran, Turkey, and the United States all scrambled to fill. It was symptomatic of the changed political terrain of Central Asia that visits by US Secretary of State James Baker and Iran's Foreign Minister Ali Akbar Valayti to the region long preceded the visit of a senior Russian delegation.

This policy of indifference to the southern rim was predicated on the belief that Russia would be able to rapidly integrate into and shift its trade pattern toward the West. Another initial underlying assumption of the Westernizers was that Russia could insulate itself from the region's problems and that, in fact, the region would be stabilized

---

[113] Elizabeth Kridl Valkenier, "Russian Policies in Central Asia: Change or Continuity?" *SAIS Review* (Summer/Fall 1994).

mainly as a result of the efforts of Turkey and the Western powers. Consequently, forays into the region by Turkey, Iran, and the United States met no objections from the Russians.[114]

The decline in importance of the southern rim did not last long.[115] The Russian security establishment, which from the start had felt that Islamic fundamentalism might spread to the Russian Federation and threaten the integrity of the Russian state itself, continued to insist that Russia's viability as a state depended directly on its ability to counter Islamic fundamentalism by waging local, low-intensity conflicts, and to contain the chaos emanating from Afghanistan at the borders of the USSR rather than those of the Russian Federation.[116] Chechnya's unilateral declaration of independence from the Russian Federation, and ultimately its repression, illustrated the fragility of Russia's body politic when dealing with its southern rim.

The Russian-speaking diaspora in Central Asia (nearly 12 million strong), increasingly confronting the rise of indigenous nationalism, rapidly galvanized into a lobby demanding an assertive Russian policy defending the ethnic Russians against these threats. Finally, the fall of Yegor Gaidar as Russia's chief architect of a market economy, along with the obvious difficulties of the Russian industrial sector's attempts to be competitive and to gain access to Western markets, created a powerful industrial lobby that increasingly viewed Central Asia as an economic opportunity rather than a burden.

By mid 1993, Russian foreign policy along its southern periphery has taken a decisively centrist turn. Avoiding burdensome economic commitments, even if it necessitated the expulsion of the new states of the region from the ruble zone, and rejecting calls by Kazakhstan's President Nursultan Nazarbaiev to create a Eurasian Confederation, nevertheless Moscow recognized that in order to pursue its "narrow national interests" Russia had vital geostrategic, political, and economic interests that required a long-term activist policy. Guided by the centrist concept of Russia as the pivotal Eurasian power, Russian foreign policy after May 1992, when signing of the Tashkent Accord created a regional defense alliance, shifted from showing indifference

---

[114] Mohiaddin Mesbahi, "Russia, the Regional Powers, and International Relations in Central Asia," in Adeed Dawisha and Karen Dawisha, eds., *The Making of Foreign Policy in Russia and the New States of Eurasia* (Armonk, NY: M. E. Sharpe, 1995).

[115] See Robert Legvold in *The Strategic Triangle: Russia, China, Japan, the United States in East Asia*, ed. Michael Mandelbaum (New York: Council of Foreign Relations Book, 1995).

[116] See Nina Kodrova, "The Status Quo But Not Within 'Our Borders,'" *Moscow News*, 20 October 1993.

toward the region to adopting the view that the region insulates Russia from the sea powers across the southern fringe of the Eurasian landmass and against militant Islam and a potentially threatening China. Robert Barylski, analyzing the historic link between Russia and its southern periphery, noted that Russia's standing as a great Eurasian power is contingent on its ability to dominate the economic resources of Central Asia and to create a "transcivilizational partnership between East Slavic and North Islamic peoples."[117] It was the recognition of this fact that prompted Kozyrev to abandon his ill-disguised contempt for "*Aziatshina*" and to admit that "[Russia] must not choose between East and West. Russia always had interests here [in Central Asia] and these interests must be preserved. We are both here [in Asia] and there [in Europe]. We have no inferiority complex."[118]

To consolidate Russia's security interests, the Kremlin resorted to several strategies. In the Caucasus, Russia, by shifting its support, dexterously utilized the conflict between Armenia and Azerbaijan over Nagorno-Karabakh, forcing both states to enter the CIS and to accept Moscow as the regional hegemonic power and arbitrator. Georgia, which in its heady days of early independence rejected any affiliation with the CIS, was brought back to the CIS as a result of a civil war and the secession in Abkhazia, which was aided by the Russian army. In the cases of Tajikistan and Azerbaijan, Russia did not hesitate to support a coup against an objectionable regime in Tajikistan and plunged directly into the civil war raging among the local clans.

To ensure that its security interests are honored, Russia signed a series of bilateral and multilateral agreements allowing for collective security under Russian auspices, and military basing rights in most former Soviet republics along Russia's southern fringe. Bolstered by professional border guards and units relocated from eastern Germany, Russia managed quickly to reassert itself as a regional leader by placing all these countries in its sphere of influence.

Realizing that its standing as a great power is heavily dependent on its ability to dominate its southern periphery, Russia, after a year-long interval, moved energetically to restrain the influence of outside players. When several Central Asian countries attempted to move toward closer economic cooperation with Turkey, Russia's Deputy Prime Minister Shokhin made it clear that these countries would have

---

[117] Robert V. Barylski, "The Russian Federation and Eurasia's Islamic Crescent," *Europe Asia Studies* 46: 3 (1994).

[118] Liana Minasyan, "Kozyrev's 'Eurasian' Ties," *Nezavisimaia gazeta*, 1 February 1994.

to choose between Moscow and Ankara and forced the Central Asian states to abandon the notion of using Turkey as a counterweight to Russia's presence. Russia reacted angrily when Turkey hosted a summit of heads of state of Turkic countries, accusing the Turkish government of "brainwashing" the Turkic people into "dangerous nationalism."[119] As if to make the point that Russia would be capable of, and possibly willing to, undermine the stability of an overly assertive Turkey, shortly after the pan-Turkic meeting Russia's foreign ministry, ignoring Turkey's protest, authorized a conference of the Kurdish National Congress in Moscow.[120]

Ordinary diplomatic calculations aside, a key issue for Russian activism in Central Asia is the control of access to the Caspian Sea basin's vast reserves of oil and gas. Russia is not only self-sufficient in energy but actually a major energy exporter. However, it is the conviction of many Russian politicians that Russia's economic well-being and its standing as a great power depend on its ability to control access to the energy resources of the region. Russia's interest in the energy resources of the region consists of two elements. The first is an insistence upon Russian participation in the various multi-national efforts to develop the oil fields of Kazakhstan and Azerbaijan. In both cases Russian oil companies have been given shares of stock in the ventures despite the fact that the Russian enterprises did not contribute significant capital toward the development of these fields. A far more important dimension of Russian policy toward the region lies not in Moscow's attempt to obtain a share of the energy reserves of the Caspian basin, but in a forceful policy to retain control over access of these energy resources to world markets.

Russia's interest in controlling Central Asia's access to world markets is propelled by several economic as well as geopolitical considerations. Russia's hard-pressed economy will clearly benefit from pipeline construction across its territory and from transit fees that such pipelines will generate. Nevertheless, it is geopolitical considerations that motivate Russia to insist upon the control of access to the energy riches of the Caspian Basin. As one Western oil executive lamented, "Russia does not seem so interested in making money as keeping all these countries under its thumb."[121] Seeing the region as a key to Russia's ability to play a major role on the Eurasian

[119] ITAR-TASS, 19 October 1994.
[120] *Xinhua*, 26 October 1994.
[121] Steve LeVine and John Lloyd, "Asian Oilmen's Troublesome Pipe Dream," *Financial Times*, 23 November 1994.

landmass, Russian analysts have noted that as long as Russia retains control over access to the energy resources of Central Asia, Russia will remain the largest player among energy-exporting countries, enabling it along with Saudi Arabia to influence the price of energy and giving Moscow significant political clout in its relations with energy-producing and energy-consuming states. Believing that dominance over Central Asia gives any outside power a policy instrument to affect the policies of a host of pivotal countries (China, India, Iran, Turkey, and other countries in the Middle East), Russian political analysts increasingly see a vital national interest in preserving Russia's status as the hegemon in the region. Given the importance that Russia attributes to its ability to control access to the energy sources of the region, Russia continues to insist on hegemony in the region, obstructing alternate routes to the region's energy. The Kremlin aborted the deal to develop the accord between Azerbaijan and a Western consortium, insisting that no agreement can be consummated until Russia is guaranteed that the pipes linking the energy-producing regions traverse its territory. Sergei Karaganov, a presidential advisor, stated bluntly that there is "no chance that the deal [between Azerbaijan and British Petroleum] will stick if the pipeline goes south [via Turkey] . . . Russia is interested that we control the pipeline."[122] In order to eliminate Turkey as a competitor offering an alternate access route to Russia, Moscow, along with Armenia, hinted that the Kurdish insurrection in eastern Turkey might well become a means to contain Turkish ambitions in Central Asia.[123] In response to Ankara's growing reluctance to allow supertankers through the Bosporus straits, Russia entered intense negotiations to build a pipeline between Varna, Bulgaria, on the Black Sea and Alexandropolis, Greece, bypassing the Bosporus straits and eliminating Turkey altogether from the energy-transport circuit. Recently Russia broached with Croatia the possibility of extending Russian oil pipes to the Adriatic Sea.

Russia's efforts to reassert hegemony in Central Asia encountered difficulties not only with Turkey but with Iran as well. The war in Tajikistan assumed a degree of competition between Moscow and Teheran, with each side accusing the other of prolonging the crisis.[124]

[122] Jim Hoagland, "Russia Still Playing 'The Great Game,'" *Washington Post*, 27 September 1994.
[123] Barylski, "The Russian Federation," 404.
[124] Gennadii Charodeyev, "Iranians' Arrogance a Turnoff for Former Soviet Muslims," *Izvestiia*, 8 July 1993.

A far more important bone of contention between Russia and Iran was Azerbaijan's decision to take advantage of Western deepwater drilling technology to explore oil reserves off the shelf of the Caspian Sea. Iran, hoping to see Azeri oil transported across Iran to the Persian Gulf (or alternately across Iran and Turkey to the Mediterranean) endorsed the Azeri venture, with the Iranian national oil company agreeing to join the Western consortium set to exploit the field. Russia, although obtaining a 10 percent share for its petroleum concern Lukoil, blocked the deal, invoking the 1921 and 1940 treaties between the USSR and Iran stipulating that the Caspian Sea could not be subject to any development without the consent of all countries bordering it.[125] The centrist politicians who dominate Russia's foreign policy have no interest in repeating Alexander II's conquest of the region or Stalin's efforts to carry out a forced Russification of the region, nor have they shown interest in returning to the Leninist position of utilizing the "Peoples of the East" as a means to undermine the international system, but a clear hegemonic policy has emerged.

It was in the Caucasus and Central Asia that Moscow seemed least constrained in resorting to force within the former USSR, even if such policy leads to friction with the United States. Some Russian analysts have gone so far as to suggest that it is in Central Asia that an American expansion may well lead to Russia's diminution as a great power and to the resumption of the Cold War.[126] The fear of America's presence in Central Asia has alarmed Russian economic and security circles. President Nursultan Nazarbaiev's visit to Washington in February 1994 and the US decision to raise aid to Kazakhstan from $91 million to $396 million caused the business daily *Kommersant* to insist that Russia must take a more activist policy in defending its interest in that country's oil fields.[127] Given the immense importance that Russia attributes to control of the energy wealth of the region, Russia has not hesitated to assert its claims even when these claims clashed openly with those of Western powers. In the Tengiz field in Kazakhstan, developed by a consortium led by Chevron, Russia received a 10 percent stake coming out of the share of the Azeri government. In the case of Azeri gas fields developed by a consortium

[125] Dmitrii Chelishev, *Inter Press*, 17 November 1994.
[126] See Liana Minasyan and Alexander Igantenko, "America's Policy in Central Asia," *Nezavisimaia gazeta*, 10 March 1994.
[127] Serge Tsekhmistrenko, "US Guarantees Kazakhstan Oil Exports via Russia," *Kommersant*, 17 February 1994.

led by British Gas, Russia's Gazprom insisted on and got a 15 percent stake taken out of the share of the Western investors.[128]

Russia's proprietary attitude in the Caucasus and Central Asia resulted in an assertive policy defying international standards and undertakings. Not only did Russia have a hand in the overthrow of several regimes that it found objectionable, but in the case of Azerbaijan, where there was an attempt to set up a peace force under the sponsorship of the OSCE, Russia responded by supporting the coup against the independent-minded Azeri President Abulfez Elchebey, (who invited the OSCE monitors as well as Turkish investment) replacing him with Haider Alieyev and using Russian forces as peace monitors. It was in reference to Central Asia and the Caucasus that Russian diplomats from Kozyrev down asserted a Russian "Monroe Doctrine." Yevgenii Primakov, director of the Russian intelligence establishment, bluntly observed that Central Asia is squarely within Russia's sphere of influence, a sphere that Russia is prepared to defend.[129]

While Russia's assertive policy in Central Asia and the Caucasus did not elicit a direct American response, a reticence motivated by US fear of Iranian and Muslim fundamentalism replacing the vacuum that would follow a Russian disengagement, the impact of Russia's policy on Turkey was profound and long-lasting. The collapse of the USSR gave Turkey hope for the establishment of a dominant political and economic presence across the vast lands of Central Asia. Turkish interest in the region had several motivations. The end of the Cold War reduced Turkey's importance to the Western powers. The continuing repression of the Kurds increasingly alienated Turkey from the European Union, making the prospects of Turkish membership in that organization remote. Since the collapse of the USSR, Ankara has made tremendous efforts to find a new role within the international system. In the Middle East, Turkey energetically pursued a policy of establishing a customs union with both Israel and the Arab nations. However, it was the former Soviet possessions in Central Asia that appeared to offer the greatest possibility for Turkey to define its new international position. Turkish leaders believed that Turkey, with its linguistic and cultural affinity as well as its status as a model of a secular Muslim state, would enjoy an advantageous position in the region. In economic terms, Turkey, with a large oil export facility in

---

[128] Steve Levine and Robert Corzine, "Russia Set to Get Share of Kazakhstan's Largest Gas Field," *Financial Times*, 8 November 1994.

[129] Serge Shevykin, *Nezavisimaia gazeta*, 30 November 1993.

the Mediterranean at Yumurtalik that was idle because of the embargo imposed on Iraq, would offer these countries ready access to the world market. Finally, US Secretary of State James Baker's effort to avert the spread of the Iranian brand of Islamic fundamentalism led the United States to encourage Ankara to establish a presence in the region, with the assumption that this presence would receive political as well as economic support from the United States. Russia's assertive policy on the pipeline issue, as well as overt pressure to reduce Turkish presence in the region, resulted in growing tension between Ankara and Moscow, as well as between Turkey and the United States, leading some officials of the Turkish government, such as former Foreign Minister Vahit Halefoglu, to complain that the "United States' indifference to Russia's moves to spread its influence in our part of the world suggests a hidden understanding."[130]

Russia's foreign policy toward the former Soviet Central Asian republics is brazenly assertive, motivated in large part by the belief that the United States, for domestic as well as geopolitical reasons, has neither the will nor the ability to act in the region aggressively. However, Russia's policy toward countries on the border of the former Soviet Union remains cautious and restrained. Fearing that it may become the front line in the confrontation between Islam and the West, Moscow's policy in the Middle East and the subcontinent is one of subtlety, restraint, and a clear desire to deepen these relationships without becoming part of either the intraregional conflicts or the regions' conflict with the West.

Given the narrow nationalist policy pursed by the Kremlin, Russia's policy in many ways resembles early-twentieth-century tsarist policy along its southern rim, when Russia sought to ensure maximum economic benefit in the region without allowing tension in the region to develop into either a regional or a global crisis. Thus, despite an obvious displeasure with Turkey resulting from the competition in Central Asia and the Caucasus as well as Turkey's advocacy of rapid expansion of NATO to include Poland, Russia continued to cultivate close economic links with Ankara and advocated an economic community of states bordering the Black Sea. Similarly, though tensions with Iran over exploitation of the Caspian Sea and Tajikistan surfaced, Moscow continued to cultivate working relations with Teheran, expanding economic links by agreeing to sell

---

[130] Sami Kohen, "Turkey, Russia Carve Out Power with Oil Routes," *Christian Science Monitor*, 23 November 1994.

Iran some military weapons, including submarines, and entering negotiations to complete a nuclear reactor whose construction was initiated by the Shah.

Russia's metamorphosis from an ideologically driven superpower with global interests to a regional power pursuing its own narrow interests is illustrated by the evolution of the relationship between Moscow and New Delhi. In the Soviet view, India played several vital roles. The foundation of the relationship was first and foremost ideological. India, with its own version of a centrally planned economy and its position as an unassailable leader of the Non-Aligned Movement, was perceived by Moscow as the USSR's prime non-communist ally in its struggle with the West. In the diplomatic arena, the two countries developed a symbiotic relationship, each defending the other in its moment of international isolation. Thus India used its influence to blunt Third World criticism of the Soviet invasion of Afghanistan, while Russia staunchly defended India's refusal to adhere to the Non-Proliferation Treaty. In geopolitical terms, as the Sino-Soviet dispute deepened, India became the largest recipient of Soviet military equipment as well as the largest Third World trading partner of the USSR. In 1971 the USSR and India signed a Treaty of Friendship and Cooperation that affirmed, among other things, ideological affinity, as well as requiring both sides to consult with each other in case of external aggressive action. The collapse of the USSR destroyed their close relationship, resulting in the collapse of trade between the two countries and the end of their military relationship. The 1971 treaty was allowed to expire at the end of 1991.

In light of the non-ideological nature of Russia's post-Soviet foreign policy, along with its initial pro-Western orientation, India, in the words of Deputy Foreign Minister Greigorii Kunadze, "lost its priority" in Moscow's foreign policy.[131] Soviet–Indian trade, which was based essentially on a barter mechanism, all but collapsed; the flow of Soviet military equipment and spare parts was halted; the Indian government was stunned by Moscow's willingness to sell arms to China and to continue to consolidate its relationship with the West.[132] It was the demise of Russo-Indian relations that was most

[131] Valdimir Berezovskii, "Russia and India – Obstructions Cleared Away," *Rossiiskaia gazeta*, 30 January 1993.
[132] Eugene Bazhanov and Natasha Bazhanov, "Russia and Asia in 1992: A Balancing Act," *Asia Survey* 33 (January 1993).

often cited by *Pravda* and other communist publications as the symbol of Russia's slavish pro-Western orientation.[133]

Relations between Russia and India were revived by President Yeltsin's visit to India in January 1993 and Prime Minister P. Narasimha Rao's visit to Moscow in July 1994. However, these relations reflect Russia's new orientation as a regional power seeking stability in its backyard rather than as a superpower eager to overturn the existing world order. Although in 1993 Russia did sign a new Treaty of Friendship with India, the 1993 version was free of ideological rhetoric, and the clause calling for military consultation during a crisis was dropped, effectively ending the axis to contain China.[134] In fact, during his India visit, Yeltsin stressed that Russo-Indian relations were not aimed at any third party and called for a Russo-India-Chinese bloc as the means to ensure stability in Asia.[135] Even the Russo-Indian military cooperation agreement significantly differed from all previous accords between the USSR and India. Whereas in the Soviet era weapon exports were primarily a political matter with Moscow insisting on remaining the sole supplier of spare parts in order to retain political control, the new Russo-Indian accord called for a transfer of production technology to enable India to produce its own spare parts. Only in the case of the rocket engines issue did Russia, under US pressure, withdraw the offer to supply manufacturing technology and agreed instead to supply India with ready-made engines.[136]

Recent Russo-Indian relations, although close once more, are qualitatively different from those of the Soviet era. Russia and India have a pragmatic relationship in which each country is attempting to ensure its maximum security and economic benefit. Thus, unlike the past, Russia has supported Pakistan's call to turn South Asia into a nuclear-free zone despite India's displeasure.[137] Perhaps the clearest symptom of the different nature of relations is the current Russian and Indian reaction to Islamic fundamentalism. While both Moscow and New Delhi welcomed Ayatollah Khomeini's rise to power in Iran in 1979, seeing his policies – including the seizure of the US embassy in Teheran – as a manifestation of the "change in the correlation of forces

---

[133] Vladilen Baikov, "Yeltsin in India, Works to Repair Relations," *Pravda*, 27 January 1993.
[134] Berezovskii, "Russia and India."      [135] *Los Angeles Times*, 30 January 1993.
[136] *Agence France Presse*, 19 January 1994.
[137] Eugene Bazhanov and Natasha Bazhanov, "Russia in Asia in 1993," *Asian Survey* 34 (January 1994).

against imperialism," in 1994, when India's Prime Minister Rao visited Moscow, the Russo-Indian communique condemned "religious fanaticism" as a destabilizing force in Asia,[138] and both sides took a dim view of the battlefield success of Afghani fundamentalists.

### China and Japan

The shift in Russia's foreign policy from initial, nearly exclusive preoccupation with the Western "third circle" to the countries bordering the CIS is somewhat blurred when it comes to the Far East. In the nineteenth century, Russia's policy toward its Eastern neighbors tended to be marked by increased activism whenever its fortunes in the West declined. Thus, for example, Russia's failure to gain control of the Black Sea straits following the Russo-Turkish War (1878) reoriented Russian attention to Central Asia and the Far East.[139] This pattern of reorientation toward the East was repeated in the late 1980s, when the crumbling and ultimate collapse of Soviet holdings in Eastern Europe and the USSR itself resulted in ever-growing Russian activism in the East.[140] From the very beginning there was consensus that Russia must end its tense stand-off in the Far East and, in fact, must bolster its relationship with Asia and the Far East to compensate for its weakness *vis-à-vis* the West.[141] The main bone of contention between the Westernizers and the centrists was whether the focus of Russia's Eastern policy should be Japan or China. Although both Far Eastern powers were able to attract Russia's attention, the causes of China and Japan were championed by very different groups. Consequently, Japan, whose cause was promoted by the Westernizers, receded as a priority for Russia, while China, popular with both centrists and conservatives, managed to transform itself from a rival to an intimate partner.

The importance of Japan was recognized even by the Soviet leadership in the twilight days of the Soviet Union. In his famous "Vladivostok Speech," Gorbachev broke with the Soviet's standard

---

[138] Irina Grudinina, "Yeltsin and Rao Sign a Declaration Condemning Aggressive Nationalism and Religious Fanaticism," *Segodnia*, 1 July 1994.

[139] See A. V. Ignat'ev, "The Foreign Policy of Russia in the Far East in the Turn of the Nineteenth and Twentieth Centuries," in *Imperial Russian Foreign Policy*, ed. Hugh Ragsdale (New York: Cambridge University Press, 1993).

[140] Hung P. Nguyen, "Russia and China: The Genesis of Eastern Rapallo," *Asian Survey* 33: 3 (March 1993).

[141] For a historic discussion of the role of Asia in Russia's geopolitical view, see Milan Hauner, *What is Asia to Us? Russia's Asian Heartland Yesterday and Today* (London: Routledge, 1992).

degradation of Japan as a mere "American aircraft carrier" to acknowledge that Japan is a "power of front-rank importance."[142] As perestroika gained speed and the Soviet position in Europe deteriorated, Gorbachev, anxious to see greater Japanese economic aid, broke two further taboos by withdrawing traditional Soviet objections to the US–Japanese Security Treaty and acknowledging that indeed there is a territorial issue between Moscow and Tokyo. Such prime Russian Westernizers as Yurii Afansiev and Andrei Sakharov, recognizing the anomaly of the absence of a peace treaty ending World War II and the fact that Siberia and Russia's marine provinces cannot develop without Japanese capital, started to urge their government to transfer the southern Kurils to Japan and set the relationship on a new foundation.[143]

Even before the collapse of the Soviet Union, the issue of a territorial transfer to Japan raised serious objections on a variety of grounds. Nationalists depicted it as an act of treason that would give away "sacred" Russian soil. The military complained that the loss of the islands would compromise the position of the Soviet fleet in the Sea of Okhotsk, while others objected because transfer of these islands would open a Pandora's box of other territorial demands. Others argued that the mineral wealth of these islands was far greater than any Japanese credits, which would have to be repaid anyway. The shock of the disintegration of the Soviet Union and the consequent centrifugal pressures within the Russian Federation heightened many Russians' fears that transfer of these islands would be a national humiliation, as well as another symptom of the endless concessions extracted from Russia in the name of partnership. The liberal *Izvestia* captured the mood of the day by observing, "In Russia it is a question of what the partnership [with the industrial capitalist states] means. Does not this partnership simply mean unilateral concessions to Washington, to Tallinn, and even to Tokyo?"[144]

Japan's insistence on the return of the Northern Territories and Tokyo's direct link between economic aid and territorial concessions drew indignant reactions across the Russian political spectrum. It was Japan's insistence on a resolution of the territorial dispute that became the *cause célèbre* of the Russian right. Valentin Feyodorov, the governor

---

[142] *Pravda*, 29 July 1986.
[143] See Hiroshi Kimura, "Gorbachev's Japan Policy: The Northern Territories Issue," *Asian Survey* 31: 9 (1991).
[144] Stanislav Kondrashov, "Trials and Tribulations of Making Peace with Japan," *Izvestiia*, 14 August 1992.

of Sakhalin, warned that should Russia consider ceding the islands it would provoke both civil disobedience and separatist tension in Russia's coastal provinces. Referring to Georgii Kunadze, one of Moscow's most prominent experts on Japan and the Far East, Feyodorov declared that a man with a German patronymic and Georgian surname had no right to make decisions regarding Russian lands.[145] To intensify pressure on Yeltsin not to make territorial concessions, the parliamentary hearings chaired by the jurist Oleg Rumianatsev concluded with a resolution ruling against transfer of the two major islands claimed by Japan. Japan's persistent demand for a territorial concession, along with ever-widening Russian opposition to any concession, forced Yeltsin to abruptly cancel his long-planned state visit to Tokyo. Commenting on the cancellation of the visit, the semi-official *Rossiskaia gazeta* chided the Japanese, noting that, "When you want a great deal and you want it right away, but at the same time you do not shirk from insulting the feelings of a great and multinational people, you risk getting nothing at all."[146]

Yeltsin's last-minute deferment of his trip to Japan was perceived by many Western observers as a watershed event, the first overt defeat of Kozyrev's pro-Western foreign policy and a reversion to a more traditional Russian foreign policy. The collapse of the talks with Japan and the cancellation of Yeltsin's visit to Japan resulted in backpedalling on Russia's part, with Prime Minister Viktor Chernomyrdin characterizing the Russian view that, regarding the Kuril question, "No such problem exists for us today; we do not intend to discuss it and we are not going to give anything away."[147] Sergei Solodovnik, reflecting a view common in the Russian academic community, noted that Russia will not be able to break into the clique of the great Western powers – the European Union, Japan, and the United States – and that, even if it could, it would still be the weakest link. Given this reality, Solodovnik called on Russia to cultivate its relationship with China and with the "little tigers" of Asia rather than pursuing the unattainable.[148] Although Yeltsin ultimately did make a state visit to Tokyo in October 1993, there was little substantive agreement. Upon leaving Japan, Yeltsin declared that he had suc-

[145] Peggy Falkenheim Meyer, "Moscow's Relations with Tokyo: Domestic Obstacles to Territorial Agreement," *Asian Survey* 33: 10 (1993).
[146] Vladimir Kuznechevsky, *Rossiiskaia gazeta*, 10 September 1992.
[147] *Rossiiskaia gazeta*, 24 August 1993.
[148] Sergei Solodovnik, "Stabilnost' v azii–prioritet rossii," *Mezhdunarodnaia zhizn'*, no. 1 (1992).

ceeded in persuading Japan to separate political issues from economic issues, an assertion promptly rejected by his Japanese hosts.[149]

Of all Russia's major relationships, Moscow's relationship with Japan may well be the one that has changed the least since the Cold War. The Russo-Japanese relationship has become a case study of the inherent limitation of the power of the Westernizers to alter Russia's historic course. The relationship between Russia and Japan has been further complicated by the changes that have taken place in Russia's strategic situation. The Russians fully understand that Washington is the beneficiary of any Russo-Japanese standoff, remembering Theodore Roosevelt's observation that "it is best [that Russia] should be left face to face with Japan, so that each may have a moderating effect on the other."[150] However, despite the absence of a peace treaty between Japan and the USSR ending World War II, a US-dominated Japan did not present a major strategic threat to the USSR, especially given Moscow's reliance on its massive land-based arsenal of intercontinental ballistic missiles. The ratification of the START II agreement between the United States and Russia would force Russia to shift its dependence to submarine-launched missiles, making Russian hegemony in the Sea of Okhotsk all the more essential, and indeed giving a new strategic meaning to the possession of the Southern Kurils.[151] Under these circumstances, Russia's political elites concluded that the cost of pursuing a "Western-oriented policy" was an affront to its national dignity and a strategic loss offering little in return. But Russia's inability to accommodate Japan has not been without serious economic costs. The resultant cool relationship with Tokyo continues to prevent Japanese investment in Russia's Far East. Furthermore, Russia was barred from the Seattle and Jakarta meetings of the Asia Pacific Economic Conference largely because of Japan's clout within that body. Japan proved incapable of blocking Russia's membership in the G-7, nor could it influence the level of aid offered by the industrial West. Furthermore, as Russia's economic reform proceeded, Russia's policy makers recognized that regardless of the orientation of their policy toward Japan, the levels of Western aid would remain far below Russia's expectations and the promised amounts would not always be delivered.

---

[149] Serge Agafonov, "Japanese Think Yeltsin Did Not Understand Them Very Well," *Izvestiia*, 15 October 1993.

[150] Quoted in Stephen J. Blank, *The New Russia in The New Asia* (Carlisle, PA.: US Army War College, 1994), 20.

[151] See Blank, *The New Russia*, 22–24.

Russia's relationship with Japan improved somewhat in 1994 when Tokyo became increasingly concerned about China's expanded power-projection capability and fearful of an American retreat from the eastern Pacific. Despite the Russian sinking of Japanese fishing vessels in the waters off the Southern Kurils, Japan showed greater willingness to aid Russia's battered economy and initiated a joint rescue exercise in the Pacific Ocean.[152] However, the improvement in Russo-Japanese relationships remained slow and continues to depend on domestic nationalist politics in both countries. Russia's anemic economy continues to fail to interest Japan's business community. Russia's public attitude toward Japan does not seem to have changed much since the days of Yakov Malik, a wartime ambassador to Japan, who described Japan as a land where "the flowers do not smell, the birds do not sing, and the women do not kiss."

Russia's relationship with China is perhaps the most blatant triumph of the centrists and their advocacy of a concentration on relations with countries adjoining the CIS. Although there were territorial disputes between Beijing and Moscow, most of them were resolved when Gorbachev opted to rebuild the relationship with China by accepting the middle of the Amur and Ussuri rivers as the demarkation line between the two countries. By the time the USSR disintegrated in 1991, China's "three conditions" to normalize relations – a Soviet pullout from Afghanistan, the end of support for the Vietnamese occupation of Cambodia, and resolution of the territorial dispute – had all been accomplished.

Although the relationship between the USSR and China had largely normalized before the collapse of the Soviet Union, the aftermath of the aborted coup in August 1991 did chill the relationship between the neighbors. The Russian government did not hide its dislike of China's overt support for the hardline coup. Furthermore, some of Yeltsin's liberal associates appeared to be convinced that the communist leadership of China would soon lose power in a manner similar to that of the rest of the former Soviet bloc.[153] However, the chill between the two giants did not last long; every constituency except the Westernizers found virtue in warming up to China. Many Russian nationalists perceived the relationship with China as a means to defy the West and retain Russia's status as a great power rather than an appendage of the West. The nationalist

---

[152] See "A Polite Bow," *The Economist*, 3 December 1994.
[153] Eugene Bazhanov and Natasha Bazhanov, "Russia and Asia in 1992: A Balancing Act," *Asian Survey* 33: 1 (1993), 94.

*Nash sovremennik* euphorically observed that "a rapprochement between the Soviet Union and China always causes fear in the West."[154] Russian right-wing economists, observing the enormous dislocation visited on Russia following Gaidar's reforms, increasingly looked to China as a model of a polity that managed to negotiate a transition to a market economy in a wise manner. Even Yeltsin himself was forced to praise China's "cautious step by step, without repercussions for the population."[155] The Russian armed forces, which always perceived the Far East as a region over which the Russian grip was weak, were delighted to see improved relations with Beijing, remembering Brezhnev's anti-Chinese policy, which made Russia's "nightmare of coalitions" – a situation where the United States, China, and Japan all perceived the USSR as a threat and coalesced against it – come true. The Russian security establishment was further gratified that while Russia had to worry about whether its erstwhile Warsaw Pact allies might join NATO or any other anti-Russian coalition, the Sino-Russian bilateral agreement stated explicitly in Article IV that:

> Both parties will not participate in any form of political or military alliance which is directed against the other party, and will not conclude any form of treaty or agreement with a third country which jeopardizes the national sovereignty and the security interests of the respective parties; no party shall allow a third country to use its territory in a manner which threatens the national sovereignty or the national security interests of the other party.[156]

From Russia's perspective, the 1992 accord was vital because it not only relieved Russia from the "nightmare of coalitions" but also implicitly laid a foundation for a concerted effort to stabilize Central Asia and deal with both pan-Islamic and pan-Turkic challenges.

China's massive purchases of Russian military hardware pleased Russia's military-industrial complex, since these purchases not only provided much-needed revenue, but actually helped Russia retain a portion of its technological base. In addition, the fact that over 1,000 Russian officers found employment in China's armed forces helped to create a powerful constituency favoring China. Furthermore, Russia's large-scale weapon transfers to China helped to deflect Japan's preoccupation from Russia to China. In 1992, Japan appealed

---

[154] Nikolai Fedorenko, "Kitai: otkryvaia budushchee," *Nash sovremennik*, no. 9 (1991), 166.
[155] Bazhanov and Bazhanov, "Russia and Asia in 1992," 94.
[156] Blank, *The New Russia*, 28.

to Russia not to sell additional aircraft to China, and a draft of a Japanese defense white paper identified China, rather than North Korea or Russia, as the main threat to Japan.[157] China's security policies and its import of Russian weapons has created a powerful lobby within the Russian body politic supporting this relationship even if it complicates Russia's relations with either Tokyo or Washington. Relations with China also received a boost from the massive cross-border trade in Russia's Far East. Although there are complaints about the presence of over 1 million illegal Chinese immigrants in Russia's east, and although there are flare-ups resulting from cultural differences, along with complaints that Chinese merchants bring shoddy and contaminated goods, this cross-border trade has nevertheless created a large segment of the Russian population in the Far East whose economic well-being depends upon that trade.

China's economic as well as diplomatic success impressed Russians across the political spectrum. The communist daily *Pravda* stated emphatically:

> We Russians can only envy them. Especially since China has achieved this impressive success without giving up one iota of its sovereignty, its national pride, or its moral values. It is opening its doors to the world economy with its head held high as an equal partner, not as a beggar who can only dream of charity in the form of loans or "humanitarian aid."[158]

In a similar vein, Kozyrev observed that Russia longs to benefit from its relations with China. When asked about China's human rights record, Kozyrev, in 1994, curtly replied, "we do not intend to stir up a big commotion about it."[159]

This desire for an intimate relationship with China is now accepted across the Russian political spectrum, with over 70 percent stating that they support Russia's deepening engagement with China. As Eugene and Natasha Bazhanov observed: "A policy of rapprochement with the PRC emerged as possibly the only issue on which there is consensus in an otherwise fragmented Russian society."[160]

---

[157] Bin Yu, "Sino-Russian Military Relations: Implications for Asia Pacific Security," *Asian Survey* 33: 3 (1993).
[158] Andrei Krushinskii, "We can only envy them," *Pravda*, 14 March 1993.
[159] *Izvestiia*, 1 February 1994.
[160] Bazhanov and Bazhanov, "Russia and Asia in 1992," 94.

### Conclusion: the rise of Primakov and the institutionalization of centrism

Russia has not yet defined its post-imperial identity. The vexing question of who is a Russian, "Russkii," or "Rossianin" has not been answered. Furthermore, the issue of Russian frontiers is far from resolved, with some arguing that Russia must expand to encompass all the Slavic peoples of the former Soviet Union, others calling for a Eurasian superstate, and others seeking a decentralized state within the current confines of the Russian Federation, allowing non-Russian components such as Tuva, Tatarastan, and Chechnya very broad autonomy. However, despite the continuing fluidity in Russia's national identity, a foreign policy consensus appears to have emerged. The appointment of Yevgenii Primakov as Russia's new foreign minister indicated not only the repudiation of the pro-Western policies associated with Kozyrev, but also a symptom of a new consenus of the Russian political elite. Primakov's foreign policy reflects a centrist view so broadly held that during the contentious presidential election of 1996 Primakov alone appeared immune to criticism by either side.

What are Primakov's policies? And how do they reflect the new Russian consensus? The Russian people, both 78 percent of the masses and 92 percent of the elite, recognize that cooperation with the West is vital for Russia.[161] The Russian people recognize that, despite the demise of the Soviet Union, Russia did not divest itself of the imperial burden to maintain order on its periphery, with 64 percent fearing a war in a neighboring country, and thus 51 percent favoring a Russian-imposed peace.[162] Kozyrev's efforts to integrate Russia into the North are perceived by Russians as a failure. Most Russians (71 percent) feel that the West is taking advantage of Russia's weakness, 67 percent view NATO as a threat, and therefore 82 percent favor military parity with the United States.

While most Russians want to cooperate with the West, and indeed recognize that Russia should not engage in (nor is it capable of engaging in) a Cold War with the West; and while few are willing to use force to re-create the USSR, there is a growing sense that Russia's security and prosperity are organically linked to its relationship with the states of the former Soviet Union and security in the periphery of

---

[161] Richard B. Dobson, *Is Russia Turning the Corner?* 70.
[162] Ibid., 65 and 66

the defunct USSR. Describing the areas of vital interest to Russia, Sergei Karaganov noted: "90 percent of its [Russia's] prosperity will depend on Russia's ability to influence the policies of Ukraine, Belarus, Kazakhstan, and other former Soviet republics, and not relations with the United States and Europe, though they will remain extremely important too."[163] However, even within the confines of the CIS, Russian foreign policy, reflecting the pronounced isolationist mood of the Russian public, appears to be following the demands of "narrow nationalism," making the Kremlin's engagements selective and avoiding any deep economic commitments.

Thus, while Russia did not hesitate to use force in Tajikistan to check the spread of Afghani-inspired chaos or to use blackmail in Central Asia to defend its economic interest, the Kremlin resisted the temptation of supporting the Crimea's drive to separate from Ukraine and declined to take up Belarus' offer to integrate with Russia as economically too costly for Russia. In fact, as the CIS entered its third year, Russian posture shifted from one of threats and intimidation to one of co-optation or, as *The Economist* observed, "A doctrine of *Lebensraum* (carving out room to live) is giving way to a Monroe Doctrine (others stay out)."[164]

The policy of selective approach enjoys the support of all three major streams within Russian politics. The remaining Western-oriented liberals fear that a deeper approach in the CIS will economic-ally bankrupt Russia, abort its political democratization, and end all prospects of Russia's joining the ranks of "civilized" nations. The centrists, cognizant of the isolationist mood in Russia as well as the paucity of resources in Russia to pursue an imperial policy, continue to believe that an overly assertive policy within the CIS will under-mine the regime's economic foundation and complicate Russia's relationship with the "second circle," making any prospect of Russia's even partial integration into the international system difficult to attain. Russian nationalists object to a deep involvement in part because of a sense that the populations of the former republics were not grateful for Russia's selflessness within the USSR and in part because of their belief that the new states across the former USSR are little more than artificial creations that do not reflect the political feelings of the Soviet people and consequently are doomed to

---

[163] *Moscow News*, 2 January 1992, 3.
[164] See "Russia and the Near Abroad: A Teddy Bear, After All," *The Economist*, 10 December 1994.

disappear in due course, leading to a reintegration of the Soviet state.[165] In light of Russia's limited resources and a public dogged by the "Afghan syndrome," where a majority of the population is opposed to any intervention by Russia's military anywhere across the CIS, even within the Russian Federation, the current policy pursued by the Kremlin is remarkably noncontroversial. However, the current consensus within the Russian body politic does not reflect a new consensus emerging in Russia, but rather a continued paralysis among diverse political groupings, each with its distinct vision of what constitutes Russia and its mission in the world, and continues to make the search for a consistent Russian foreign policy an elusive proposition. The conduct of Russia's foreign policy continues to be a hostage to Russia's own self-definition.

[165] See Shakleina, "Russia and Military Conflicts."

# 8    Ukraine: the ambivalent identity of a submerged nation, 1654–1945

The term *gente Ruthenus, natione Polonus* served to describe the political and national status and affiliation of the Ruthenian nobility during [the seventeenth century]. In Polish historiography, the emphasis has been on the second part of the definition. It has been interpreted as a class relationship that linked the nobility of Rus' with that of Poland, making both nobilities one political and constitutional body within the Commonwealth. It could be that many Ruthenian noblemen had this understanding of their place and their rights in the Commonwealth. I suggest, however, that the first part of the definition, *gente Ruthenus*, was as prominent in their minds as the second. The Ruthenian nobility as a whole was conscious of Ruthenian national, if not political, identity.     Teresa Chynczewska-Hennel[1]

You have given me a sheepskin coat;
Alas, it does not fit.
The garment of your own wise speech
Is lined with falsehood's wit.     Taras Shevchenko[2]

Little Russia, faithful to the throne and unshakable in the faith cultivates . . . an idea of a past; she in her leisure time mourns over her past independence.     Count Sergei Uvarov[3]

In both Poland and Russia, the carriers of the national idea were well-established political elites, clearly preoccupied with the position of their respective polities *vis-à-vis* neighboring states. Thus, the relationship between the nation and other polities and civilizations became a

---

[1] Teresa Chynczewska-Hennel, "The National Consciousness of Ukrainian Nobles and Cossacks from the End of the Sixteenth to the Mid-Seventeenth Century," *Harvard Ukrainian Studies*, 10: 3/4 (December 1986).

[2] C. H. Andrusyshyn and W. Kinconnel, eds., *The Political Works of Taras Shevchenko: The Kobzar* (Toronto: 1964), 62.

[3] Quoted in Stephen Velynchenko, "Identities, Loyalties and Service in Imperial Russia: Who Administered the Borderlands?" *The Russian Review* 54 (April 1995), 192.

key aspect of their identities. Because Ukraine is an "a-historic" nation, the well-spring of the country's modern national identity consisted of intellectuals pursuing a "restorative agenda" similar to that of the Slovaks, and other long colonized peoples.

The common thread of most "a-historic" nationalisms is a preoccupation with cultural revival and social justice. Independent statehood is viewed as a remote, even unattainable possibility. Because of this, Ukrainian intellectuals, while managing to save the Ukrainian language from complete atrophy and make the politically conscious class aware of the social injustices befalling Ukrainian society, failed to develop a concept of Ukraine as an independent political actor. It is the argument of this chapter that because of the restorative nature of Ukrainian nationalism and the absence of an indigenous political elite, Ukraine, along with Slovakia and Belarus failed to define nationalism in terms of their nations against an "other," and thus failed to retain their independence in the fluid situation that followed World War I.

Ukraine's national identity differs fundamentally from that of either Poland or Russia. Both of these neighbors and former colonial masters were endowed with a conscious political elite, a distinct language, and a clear collective memory of nationhood. These elements, which enabled them to take their right to statehood for granted, were absent in Ukraine. While Poles were debating whether the positivist or the romantic tradition was the appropriate path toward independence and Russians were determining their country's place in world civilization, Ukrainians had yet to develop a distinct political identity. Such an identity did not fully emerge until the very end of the nineteenth century, with independent statehood alternatively viewed as either unnecessary or as an unattainable dream.

Ivan Rudnytsky, in his seminal article "The Role of Ukraine in Modern History," argues that Ukraine is a "non-historical" nation because the eclipse of the Ukrainian state by the Mongol conquest of the thirteenth century, and later, by Polish and Russian domination, prevented Ukrainians from developing a continuous elite and, therefore, a continuous notion of statehood.[4] The independent Ukrainian state of 1917 was heir to neither the seventeenth-century Cossack Hetmanate nor Sich, much less to Kievan-Rus; thus the essence of Ukrainian statehood had to repeatedly reinvent itself. By contrast, although partitioned Poland disappeared as an independent state

---

[4] Ivan Rudnytsky, "The Role of Ukraine in Modern History," *Slavic Review* 22: 2 (1963).

302     National identity and foreign policy

from 1795 to 1918, the *szlachta*, and later the middle class, upheld the Polish national idea, passing it from generation to generation and providing a strong degree of continuity. In Ukraine, however, the Cossacks, who led the 1648 uprising against the Poles, had little in common with Kievan-Rus. The Ukrainian intellectuals who founded Ukrainian identity in the mid nineteenth century had few links to the Cossack host and absolutely none to Kievan-Rus.

Although Rudnytsky is certainly right – the history of Ukrainian nationhood is indeed one of interruption and discontinuity – it may be an oversimplification to argue that imperial powers fully assimilated the Ukrainian elite and therefore disrupted all sense of continuity. As the quotes from Chynczewska-Hennel, Shevchenko, and Uvarov seem to indicate, the Ukrainian elite, despite its Polonization or Russification, did in fact retain a distinct identity and thus retained a link with the "Shadows of [seemingly] Forgotten Ancestors."[5] The Ukrainian elite, whether in the context of the Polish *Rzeczpospolita* or the Russian empire, remained aware that they were different. Ukrainians attained high positions at the Polish and Russian imperial courts and yet retained profoundly ambivalent attitudes toward their imperial identity. It was not the absence of a continuous elite, but rather Ukraine's status as a perennially submerged nation that frustrated the emergence of a truly distinct national elite.

Being a "non-historical" nation, modern Ukraine has had to contend with two fundamental handicaps that "historical" nations have never had to endure: the denationalization of the country's intellectual and cultural elite and a prolonged delay in the establishment of a standardized Ukrainian language. Ukraine – partitioned long before the emergence of a genuine, indigenous national elite – experienced the rapid, albeit reluctant, Polonization (and later Russification) of its elite. As Mark Raeff observed, "One is struck by the fact that at the moment of its subordination to Muscovite Russia, it was Ukraine that enjoyed and exercised a clear cultural predominance: much later in the nineteenth century, at the birth of modern national consciousness, Ukraine had the status of a peasant culture adjudged inferior and harshly repressed."[6] With Ukraine subject to successive domination by multinational empires, both the Polish Commonwealth

---

[5] This is a reference to the literary work of Mykhailo Kotsiubyns'kyi.

[6] Marc Raeff, "Ukraine and Imperial Russia: Intellectual and Political Encounters from the Seventeenth to the Nineteenth Century," in *Ukraine and Russia in Their Historical Encounter*, ed. Peter Potichnyj, et al. (Edmonton: Canadian Institute of Ukrainian Studies Press, 1992), 69.

and the Russian empire managed to co-opt Ukraine's elite, reducing Ukraine's culture to peasant folklore.

After the Cossack and peasant uprising of 1648–49, the Cossacks found themselves too weak to assert full independence and in need of an ally for protection from the Poles. In 1654 the Hetmanate finally concluded an agreement with Muscovy. The Pereiaslav Agreement, as it was called, ultimately undermined Cossack autonomy and hindered the development of a distinct Ukrainian national identity more than did the earlier ties to Poland. Under the agreement, the Cossack nobility (*starshyna*) gained the tsar's protection from the Poles, and later from the peasantry, in exchange for the retention of the Polish *szlachta's* privileges. The Hetmanate, however, remained caught in the middle of the Russo–Polish wars and was partitioned when the Poles and the Russians achieved "eternal peace" with the Treaty of Andrussovo in 1667. On the right (western) bank of the Dnieper, the Hetmanate retained its autonomy until 1714. On the left (eastern) bank, the Russian tsars whittled away at the Hetmanate from the mid-eighteenth century onward. The Hetmanate, as guaranteed by the Pereiaslav Agreement, continued to function as an autonomous body until 1782. The Cossack elite, although enjoying the political rights of the Polish *szlachta* and able to expand their land holdings, were increasingly torn between retaining the tsar's favor and maintaining their position over the increasingly restless peasants.[7] The *starshyna* came to resemble the Russian *dvorianstvo*, which served as an intermediary between the tsar and the masses. The break between the Russian autocrat and the Hetmanate occurred when Hetman Ivan Mazepa, a favorite of Peter the Great, reacted to Russia's failure to defend Ukraine from Polish incursions by joining Sweden against Russia in the Great Northern War. The decisive defeat of Sweden and Mazepa at Poltava in 1709 shattered the uneasy relationship between the Hetmanate and Russia's autocracy, leaving left-bank Ukraine exposed to Peter's ruthless revenge; this exposure resulted in the sacking of the Hetmanate capital Baturyn and the massacre of its 6,000 residents.[8]

Although Peter the Great did not formally liquidate the Hetmanate, the relationship between the tsar and the Cossack elite was irreparably damaged. Despite the election of Ivan Skoropadsky, Peter's hand-picked successor to Mazepa, Peter declared in a June 1723 decree that "from the first Hetman Bogdan Khmelnysky, and even Skoropadsky,

---

[7] See Orest Subtelny, *Ukraine: A History* (Toronto and London: University of Toronto Press, 1990), 159.
[8] Ibid., 164.

all Hetmans were traitors."[9] The relative position of the *starshyna* was further weakened by growing unrest among the peasantry and the centralization of the Russian empire. The Cossack elite faced two unappealing choices: to fully join the Russian service nobility or be swept aside by pressures from above and below. By 1782, when Catherine II formally disbanded the Hetmanate, Ukraine's nobility had struck a Faustian bargain. The Cossack nobility exchanged the subordination of the Hetmanate to Russia for the introduction of Russian serfdom across Ukraine. The era of the Hetmanate as the reservoir of Ukrainian identity thus came to an end.

The Cossacks left a dual legacy in the Ukrainian lands. On one hand, popular Ukrainian folk songs and poetry glorified the Cossack past, creating a national "collective memory" essential for future national revival. On the other hand, most nineteenth-century Ukrainian intellectuals viewed the Cossack *starshynas* as an exploitative, decayed, corrupt elite, largely responsible for the sorry state of the Ukrainian peasantry. Only in the late nineteenth century did Ukraine's leading national historian, Mykhailo Hrushevskyi, break with the historiographic tradition of earlier Ukrainian thinkers and assert that the Cossack was the ultimate embodiment of the Ukrainian spirit of freedom.[10] Thus the Cossack element of Ukrainian national identity was legitimized anew and handed down to the present.

The situation in right-bank Ukraine was more favorable to the development of a distinctive national identity. Much as Teresa Chynczewska-Hennel argued, the Ruthenian nobility, despite its identification with the Polish Commonwealth, emphasized its cultural and political differences with Poland. Zenon Kohut observed that the "Little Russian identity, which emerged in the late eighteenth century, combined Russian imperial culture with an attachment to the Hetmanate and its culture."[11] Paul Magocsi argues that the Russification of Ukraine led not to the desertion or assimilation of native culture, but rather to the acquisition of multiple identities, a phenomenon that has occurred among many subordinated ethnic groups.[12] As with all premodern polities, religion played a formative role.

---

[9] See Michael T. Florinsky, *Russia: A History and an Interpretation*, vol. 1 (New York: Macmillan, 1953), 340.

[10] Mykhailo S. Hrushevskyi, *The Historical Evolution of the Ukrainian Problem* (Cleveland, OH: John T. Zubal, Inc., 1981).

[11] Zenon E. Kohut, "The Development of Little Russian Identity and Ukrainian Nation Building," *Harvard Ukrainian Studies* 10: 3/4 (December 1986), 574.

[12] Paul Robert Magocsi, "The Ukrainian National Revival," *Canadian Review of Studies in Nationalism* 16: 1/2 (1989).

The Ukrainian Orthodox Church was not immune to the pressures of the Polish Catholic Church and the Moscow patriarchate. The Ukrainian Orthodox Church was fragmented initially through the establishment, under Polish auspices, of the Uniate Church after the Union of Brest (1596). For the Ukrainians living in the Polish Commonwealth, religion, whether Orthodox or Uniate, shaped Ukrainian national identity.[13] Later, as the Moscow patriarchate extended its influence to the southwest, the Ukrainian Orthodox Church, particularly in eastern Ukraine, was reduced to a mere administrative unit of Muscovite cultural and political influence and became an instrument of Russification. Following the rapid Russification of the Ukrainian Orthodox Church, Ukrainian historiography throughout the seventeenth century tended to downplay the distinctions between Ukraine and the other East Slavic entities of Belarussia and Russia.[14]

This common religious outlook with Russia further weakened Ukraine's sense of national identity, creating what Harvey Goldblatt described as a dual identity of East Slavs – a supranational community of Orthodox Slavs with a restricted parochial patriotism. With Tsar Alexei Romanov's appropriation of the Orthodox Church as a symbol of the Russian state, the Russian state became "an 'icon' of heaven and the Tsar . . . an icon of God."[15] Peter I's 1720 edict forbidding linguistic differences in ecclesiastic books published in the Hetmanate further bolstered the role of the Orthodox Church as a Russifying state institution. The Ukrainian Orthodox Church, which in the seventeenth century had helped sustain Ukraine's identity during its confrontation with the Poles, had become by the eighteenth century a vehicle of Russification. For example, the church anathematized Ivan Mazepa, and to this day reaffirms it every first Sunday of the Great Lent. The official view of Ivan Mazepa as a manifestation of the Antichrist rather than a defender of traditional Ukrainian rights is captured in an 1850 issue of the Ukrainian journal *Svit*. A nephew asks his uncle, "Who is the worst creature in the world?" The uncle replies, "The

---

[13] See Frank Sysyn, *Between Poland and Ukraine* (Cambridge, MA: Harvard Ukrainian Research Institute, 1988), 26. See also Marian J. Rubchak, "From Periphery to Center: The Development of Ukrainian Identity in Sixteenth Century Lviv," *Canadian Review of Studies in Nationalism* 21: 1/2 (1994).

[14] See Frank Sysyn," Concepts of Nationhood in Ukrainian Writing 1620–1690," *Harvard Ukrainian Studies* 10: 3–4 (December 1986).

[15] Harvey Goldblatt, "Orthodox Slavic Heritage and National Consciousness: Aspects of East Slavic and South Slavic National Revivals," *Harvard Ukrainian Studies* 10: 3/4 (December 1986), 343–45.

devil." The nephew then asks, "And who is next worst to the devil?" The uncle replies, "Mazepa."[16]

By the mid-eighteenth century, the Ukrainian elite on the left bank had accepted its participation in the Russian empire, although resentment over Moscow's violation of the Ukrainian nobility's rights continued to surface in various literary and historical tracts. In a polemical poem entitled "Dialogue between Great and Little Russia," the Ukrainian courtesan Semen Divovych emphatically stated:

> [Great Russia] think not that thou art my ruler . . .
> You are Great and I am Little, we live in a joint land
> Yet we are equal parts of the same body.[17]

The Ukrainian elite's acceptance of union with Russia also manifested itself in the anonymous work *Istoriia Rusov*, which first appeared in an unpublished form in the 1820s. Although critical of Muscovite centralism, it nevertheless reaffirmed the notion that the "Great" and "Little" Russians are "people of the same origin and faith."[18]

The inability of the Ukrainians to assert an identity distinct from that of the Russians continued well into the nineteenth century. The fact that much of the Russian elite, including the future Ukrainophobe Mikhail Pogodin, was infatuated with Ukraine further promoted the notion that while Ukraine might have been culturally distinct, it was an inviolable part of the Russian landscape.[19] Vasyl Sypovtsky observed this Russian fascination with Ukraine:

> Exactly the years 1800–1850, the years of the flowering of romanticism in Russian literature, were characterized by a sharpening interest in the nature, history, and life of the Ukraine (as well as the Caucasus, the Crimea, and Siberia). This "burning" interest in the Ukraine that the Russians have demonstrated, their being "in love" with Ukraine, has dissipated with the gradual reawakening of Ukrainian patriotism and nationalism.[20]

[16] Quoted by Yaroslav Hritsai, "Ivan Franko pro politychnu samostiinist' Ukraïny," in *Ukrainska mysl politychna w XX wieku*, ed. Michael Putaski (Kraków: Uniwersytet Jagiellonski, 1993), 45.

> Khto naihirshyi na sviti?
> Diavol.
> A po diavoli?
> Mazepa.

[17] Ibid., 45. See *Ukrainskii Vopros* (St. Petersburg, 1914), 48.
[18] Ivan L. Rudnytsky, "Fraciszek Duchinski and His Impact on Ukrainian Political Thought," in *Essays in Modern Ukrainian History*, ed. Peter L. Rudnytsky (Edmonton: Canadian Institute of Ukrainian Studies, 1987), 195.
[19] See Paul Bushkovich, "The Ukraine in Russian Culture 1790–1860: The Evidence in Journals," *Jahrbücher fur Geschichte Osteuropas*, vol. XXXIX (1991).
[20] Ibid., 340.

In short, the Russian empire's policies of co-optation and proprietorship succeeded, at least partially, in acculturating Ukraine's political elite.

The demise of the Ukrainian language as a means of cultural expression also stunted the growth of a Ukrainian national identity. By the end of the nineteenth century more than 20 million people spoke Ukrainian. Nevertheless, the absence of a nationally active cultural elite and the enforced partition of the Ukrainian lands led to the atrophy of the Ukrainian language. Over time, a substantial number of foreign words entered the Ukrainian vernacular. As George Thomas observed, Linguistic "purism is the epiphenomenon of nationalism . . . In the Slavic world, where the language question is almost always a factor in nationalism, at times of heightened national consciousness a tendency toward maximal differentiation between languages concerned may be anticipated."[21] The extraordinary difficulty of re-establishing the purity of the Ukrainian language substantially hindered the formation of a Ukrainian national ideal and the growth of national pride.

When modern Ukrainian nationalism finally made its appearance in the mid-nineteenth century, idealists were more concerned with containing Russian centralization and avoiding the total assimilation of Ukrainian culture by Russia and Poland than with anything else.[22] As Paul Wexler noted, "The threat of displacement by Russian or Polish runs as a leitmotiv through Ukrainian linguistic discussion."[23] Aware that the preservation of their language was key to preventing their full assimilation, Ukrainian intellectuals had to overcome the prevailing opinion that Ukrainian was "an arbitrary melange of Russian and Polish."[24] The struggle to raise the Ukrainian language from the status of a peasant dialect to that of a "civilized" tongue was starkly reflected on the pages of *Osnova* (1861–62), the first Ukrainian–Russian journal to be published in Saint Petersburg. *Osnova*'s editors declared, "Ukrainian is gradually coming into use in the company of educated people, in their conversation and writings."[25] Despite Shevchenko's successful efforts to create a literary Ukrainian lan-

---

[21] George Thomas, "Slavic Nationalism and Linguistic Purism," *Canadian Review of Study of Nationalities* 16: 1–2 (1989).

[22] See Igor Torbakov, "Mezhdu moskvoi i malorossiei ustanovilas' dvukhmyslennye otnoshenie: Ukraintsy glazami russkikh v XVII–XVIII vekakh," *Nezavisimaia gazeta*, 26 May 1994.

[23] Paul Wexler, *Purism and Language: A Study in Modern Ukrainian and Belorussian Nationalism (1840–1967)* (Bloomington, IN: Indiana University Press, 1974), 41.

[24] Ibid., 45.    [25] Raeff, "Ukraine and Imperial Russia."

guage, the standardization of the Ukrainian language was not completed until the twentieth century.[26] As late as 1905, newspaper publishers still had to contend with the absence of a universally accepted Ukrainian syntax.[27] Yet, as George Shevelov noted, it was "a linguistic development that gave birth to a political movement."[28]

Although Ukrainian national identity was clearly emerging by the mid-nineteenth century, the sources of the national identities emerging on the two banks of the Dnieper were very different. On the right bank in the west, the catalyst to the budding Ukrainian identity was a classic interaction between a people and an "other," leading to the type of *ressentiment* that is the basis for many national identities in Central and Eastern Europe. The cultural and religious pressure from the 1569 Union of Lublin, which shifted control of Ruthenia (Ukraine) from the loose Polish–Lithuanian Commonwealth to the far more centralized kingdom of Poland, resulted in an early backlash. The clash between the Ruthenians and Poles initially occurred on religious grounds, stemming from Ruthenian resentment of the intrusion of "Polish faith" (Latin Catholicism), and prompting the Orthodox Metropolitan of Kiev, Petro Mohyla, to found an academy whose purpose was "to educate clergy and laymen to defend . . . Orthodoxy, so as to enable them to polemicize with [other denominations] and to propagate native Ruthenian culture and language."[29] The anti–Polish reaction, which was initially triggered on the basis of religion, soon evolved into the recognition of a distinct Ruthenian history based in the glorious past of Kievan-Rus.[30] The sense of reaction to the "other" in right-bank Ukraine was further sharpened by the dense presence of Jews, who dominated the urban crafts and acted as intermediaries between the Ruthenian peasantry and the Latin-Catholic Polish gentry, as administrators or leasees.[31]

[26] See Paul R. Magocsi, "The Language Question as a Factor in National Movement," in *Nation Building and the Politics of Nationalism: Essays on Austrian Galicia*, ed. Andrei Markovitz and Frank E. Sysyn (Cambridge, MA: Harvard University Research Institute, 1982), 237.

[27] John S. Reshetar, Jr., *The Ukrainian Revolution, 1917–1920: A Study in Nationalism* (Princeton: Princeton University Press, 1952), 30.

[28] George Shevelov, "Evolution of the Ukrainian Literary Language," in Ivan L. Rudnytsky, ed., *Rethinking Ukrainian History* (Edmonton: Canadian Institute of Ukrainian Studies, 1981), 227.

[29] Jerzy Borzecki, "The Union of Lublin as a Factor in the Emergence of Ukrainian National Consciousness," *The Polish Review* 41, no. 1 (1966), 46.

[30] Ibid., 48.

[31] See M. J. Rossman, *The Lords' Jews: Magante Jewish Relations in the Polish Lithuanian Commonwealth during the 18th Century* (Cambridge, MA: Harvard University Press, 1991).

While national identity developed along the standard Central European path in right-bank Ukraine, the conditions in left-bank (eastern) Ukraine were very different. Whereas the gentry in right-bank Ukraine tended to be Polish, in the left bank most of the landlords were Russified Ukrainians (often of Cossack descent) who shared their language and religion with the peasant masses. In right-bank Ukraine, the middlemen between the lords and peasants were Jewish; because left-bank Ukraine was outside the Jewish pale of settlement, Jews were absent from the local social landscape. Their absence in left-bank Ukraine had a paradoxical effect. On the one hand, the absence of Jews as competition for lenders, crop marketers, and suppliers of consumer goods and farm implements made the peasants dependent on the gentry's monopolist credit and marketing facilities, leading to markedly lower incomes on the left bank of the Dnieper. The Russian philosopher Boris Chicherin carried out an exhaustive study at the end of the nineteenth century comparing incomes on both sides of the Dnieper and observed the following: "Everyone who has been in touch with local life knows that the Russian Kulak is ten times worse than any Jew . . . I can bear witness that the business activities of the Jews do not ruin the peasantry but, quite to the contrary, contribute substantially to their prosperity."[32] On the other hand, the absence of a visible "other" slowed the formation of a national identity.

In the absence of a clear ethnic identity and an easily recognizable collective memory, the initial problem confronting Ukrainian nationalist intellectuals in left-bank Ukraine was how to preserve a cultural identity recognizable throughout all of the ethnically Ukrainian territories. In light of this historical context, Ukrainian national identity emerged in the nineteenth century almost as a reaction to the nationalism of the "other." In fact, as Orest Pelech argues, the efforts of Nicholas I and his minister of education, Count Sergei Uvarov, to forge a distinct Russian national identity as a new source of legitimization of post-Napoleonic, post-Decembrist Russia contributed to the birth of modern Ukrainian nationalism.[33]

However, the physical remoteness of the Russian "other" and its co-optation of Ukraine's indigenous elites led to the very slow gestation of a Ukrainian identity – an identity focused on social and

---

[32] Quoted in Rudnytsky, *Essays in Modern Ukrainain History,* 290.
[33] Orest Pelech, "The State and the Ukrainian Triumvirate in the Russian Empire 1831–1847," in *Ukraine Past, Ukraine Present,* ed. Borden Krawchenko (New York: St. Martin's Press, 1993), 4–12.

cultural rather than political issues. Thus, when modern Ukrainian nationalism first appeared in the guise of the Brotherhood of Saints Cyril and Methodius (1845–47), the founders, Mykola Kostomarov and Panteleimon Kulish, aimed not to create a separate Ukrainian state but to find the Ukrainian people a place within a non-autocratic, pan-Slavic, Orthodox entity. The first bylaw of the Brotherhood clearly stated, "We hold that the spiritual and the political union of the Slavs is the true destiny to which they should aspire."[34] Rejecting both Russian autocracy and Polish "aristocratic democracy," the founders of the Brotherhood believed that "every nation should have its own government and should subscribe to complete equality of citizens regardless of their birth, religious beliefs, or social status."[35] In a similar vein, a manifesto calling on Ukrainian peasants to rebel evoked the *Haidamaky,* the epic poem describing the bloody Ukrainian uprising against the Polish nobility, and their struggle against the landlords for justice rather than for nationhood.[36]

Despite its considerable abundance and diversity, the basis of much of nineteenth-century Ukrainian historiography is cultural and ethnographic, rather than political. As nineteenth-century Ukrainian historians tirelessly gathered the remnants of the vanishing world of the seventeenth-century Ukrainian Hetmanate, they by and large treated its political aspects with disdain.[37] They mainly concerned themselves with the survival of Ukrainian culture, which in their view could be achieved only through the emancipation of the peasantry and the attainment of social justice. Mykola Kostomarov, notwithstanding his spirited defense of Ukrainian individuality versus Russian collectivism, equated the emergence of a Ukrainian nationalism with the emancipation of the peasant. As for Ukraine's political future, Kostomarov viewed the Hetmanate as a "wilted tree,"[38] deservedly supplanted by a larger pan-Slavic entity. In fact, he saw Ukrainian history not as a struggle against foreign domination, but as a struggle between the peasant masses and an exploitative elite. Ukrainian

---

[34] See George S. N. Luckyj, *Young Ukraine: The Brotherhood of Saints Cyril and Methodius, 1845–1847* (Ottawa and Paris: University of Ottawa Press, 1991), 85.

[35] See Basil Dmytryshyn, *Imperial Russia: A Source Book, 1700–1917* (Orlando: Harcourt Brace Jovanovich, 1990), 261. It should be noted that by "religious equality" the authors mean various Christian denominations.

[36] Ibid., 267.

[37] See Dmytro Doroshenko, "The Survey of Ukrainian Historiography," *The Annals of the Ukrainian Academy of Arts and Sciences in the United States* 5–6: 4 (1957).

[38] Ibid., 72.

nationalism was a quest for social justice in a pan-Slavic context, rather than a quest for political independence. Kostomarov's *Book of the Genesis of the Ukrainian People* was similar in style and substance to Adam Mickiewicz's *The Book of the Polish Nation and of the Polish Pilgrims* (1832). However, for Mickiewicz, Poland's loss of independence represented the equivalent of the crucifixion of Christ – Poland's suffering atoned for all of "pagan" Europe. Kostomarov agreed that the Slavs and Slavs alone truly embraced the spirit of Christ. Poland's Christian values, however, had degenerated as Poland developed into a brutal aristocratic state, enserfing its people and the Ukrainians. Russia too had degenerated into an autocracy; only Ukraine retained the true Slavic-Christian egalitarianism, incompatible with either autocracy or aristocracy. It was Ukraine's mission to reawaken the true Slavic spirit now dormant in both Russia and Poland.[39] Kostomarov put his vision in the following words:

> And Ukraine shall rise from her grave and shall again appeal to all brethren Slavs, and they shall heed her call, and Slavdom shall rise and there shall remain neither Tsar nor tsarevich, neither tsarina nor prince, neither count nor duke, neither Illustrious Highness nor Excellency, neither sir nor nobleman, neither serf nor servant; neither in Muscovy nor in Poland, neither in Ukraine nor in Czechia, neither in Croatia nor in Serbia nor in Bulgaria.[40]

Nonetheless, despite Kostomarov's deep love for Ukraine, he saw little in terms of "usable history" to warrant Ukrainian independence.

Taras Shevchenko, a thinker who came closest to the idea of separate Ukrainian statehood, in his preface to *Haidamaky* wrote "Thank God, it [the fighting] is all over, moreover when you recall we are all children of the one mother, we are all Slavs . . . Let the Slavic land be covered with wheat like gold, be undivided forever from sea to sea."[41] Although very conscious of Ukraine's distinct heritage, Shevchenko considered Ukrainian independence irretrievable:

> Once there was the Hetmanate,
> It passed beyond recall;
> Once it was we who ruled ourselves,

---

[39] This idea is developed by Andrzei Walicki in *Philosophy and Romantic Nationalism: The Case of Poland* (Oxford and New York: Clarendon Press, 1982); N. I. Kostomarov, *Book of the Genesis of the Ukrainian People* (New York: Research Program on the USSR, 1954).

[40] Luckyj, *Young Ukraine*.

[41] Quoted in George S. N. Luckyj, *Between Gogol and Sevcenko* (Munich: Wilhelm Fink Verlag, 1971), 143.

> But we shall rule no more . . .
> Yet we shall never forget
> The Cossack fame of yore![42]

Panteleimon Kulish provided an even starker reading of Ukrainian history. He perceived the Ukrainian Cossack elite as a mob with an irrepressible destructive instinct, but with neither the will nor the fortitude to address the grievance of the Ukrainian peasantry whose rebellion had a class rather than an ethnic component. Since the decayed Ukrainian elite was incapable of building anything of enduring value, Kulish openly dismissed the political insignificance (*nichtozhestvo*) of Little Russia,[43] asserting that it was only natural that the "southern" and "northern" tribes of Rus should merge.[44]

The noted mid-nineteenth-century Ukrainian historian Mykola Drahomanov, one of the founders of the Brotherhood of Saints Cyril and Methodius, continued the tradition of seeing the Ukrainian question as a social rather than a national issue. Arguing that national liberation can be attained only through the establishment of human rights, Drahomanov maintained:

> [The] Ukrainian people will have better prospects if they strive for the social and political freedom within the states in which they live, with the help of other peoples also subjugated by these states . . . It would be best for Ukrainians not to advance national ideas but rather autonomist and federalist ones.[45]

Seeing little importance in national independence, Drahomanov found true virtue in the predicament of the Ukrainian people, insisting that the Ukrainians can "bypass the problem of independent statehood and work toward a non-authoritarian stateless order."[46] Oxana Rybak also demonstrated the social rather than ethnic basis of Ukrainian nationalism. She noted that one of the early foundations of Ukrainian national identity was the birth of Ukrainian feminism and its acceptance by the intellectual elite as a vital ingredient of the national agenda.[47]

More typical of urban nineteenth-century nationalism, Ukrainian nationalism also manifested itself as a class phenomenon in its

[42] Ibid., 135.
[43] Ivan L. Rudnytsky, "The First Ukrainian Political Program: Mykhailo Drahomanov's 'Introduction' to *Hromadu*," in *Essays in Modern Ukrainian History*, 273.
[44] Ibid., 273.    [45] Ibid., 264.    [46] Ibid., 271.
[47] Oxana Rybak, "Ukraïnskyi zhynochyi rukh u konteksti teorii sotsializmu i natsional'noho vidrodzhennia, kinets' XIX – pochatok XX stolittya," *Ukrainska mysl polityczna w XX wieku*, ed. Michal Putaski (Kraków: Uniwersytet Jagiellonski, 1993), 73.

attitudes toward the Jews. Unlike in Russia – where "the Jewish question" was increasingly presented as a religious, and later racial, issue – to the Ukrainian intellectuals it remained very much a social issue. The Ukrainians resented the Jewish presence in the Ukrainian countryside, where their commercial activity was perceived by most Ukrainians as detrimental. This was believed to be the result of tsarist repression and marginalization of the Jews, rather than an inherent "Jewish defect." As a result, unlike Russian, Polish, Romanian, French, German, and Hungarian anti-Semitism, which took on an increasingly racial and "scientific" coloration in the late ninteenth century, Ukrainian intellectuals continued to view the Jews as a legitimate community in the mosaic of the country's population. However, they lamented the economically "dysfunctional" role of the Jew, which in their view was a direct outgrowth of their persecution. Despite his glorification of the *Haidamaky* uprising that resulted in the death of thousands of Jews, Taras Shevchenko joined other Ukrainian luminaries, such as Kulish and Marko Vovchok, in condemning the Russian empire for its persecution of the Jews. In a letter to *Russkii vestnik*, they wrote:

> For centuries now the Christian nations comprising the Russian Empire have stigmatized the globe-wandering Jewish tribe with names such as scoundrels, traitors, deceivers, enemies of God and man. And the indignation of the Russian society and government, which was unable to entice the Jews by humane methods unto the path of truth and good, has not manifested itself in merely words. Like beasts of prey, Jews have been exiled, drowned, burned, and slaughtered. Would it not be unnatural for these victims of the blind rage of fanatics to abandon the customs for which they had been despised and adopt the ways of their oppressors?[48]

Drahomanov, although critical of Jewish commercial activity in the Ukrainian countryside, saw a solution to the "Jewish question" in the total political emancipation of the Jews, the re-establishment of Jewish communal autonomy, and the encouragement of Jewish socialism. Such reforms would also contribute to breaking the monopoly of the elite in power in Ukraine and Saint Petersburg.[49] Drahomanov and his circle worried that failure to reorganize society in Russian Ukraine would result in an anti-tsarist explosion and violence against the Jews

---

[48] Quoted in V. Lvov-Rogachevsky, *A History of Russian Jewish Literature* (Ann Arbor, MI: Ardis Press, 1979), 107.
[49] Rudnytsky, "Mykhailo Drahomanov and the Problem of Jewish Ukrainian Relations," in *Essays in Modern Ukrainian History*.

"much more unjust than the bloody specters of the seventeenth and eighteenth centuries."[50]

By espousing political autonomy and social enfranchisement of the Jews, Ukrainian thinkers on the whole took a more liberal, humanistic approach to resolving social problems than Polish and Russian nationalists, who generally advocated assimilation. At the beginning of this century, when a series of anti-Semitic "show trials" in Hungary, Bohemia, and France all resulted in the initial conviction of the accused, the very different attitude of the Ukrainian intellectuals toward the Jews became evident. In Ukraine, Mandel Beylies, charged by the tsarist regime with "ritual murder," was fully exonerated by a Kiev jury, despite political pressure for a guilty verdict. It is noteworthy that Henry Abramson, in his study of the bloody pogroms that swept across Ukraine in 1919, observed that, despite the ferocity of their violence against Jews, Ukrainian peasant anti-Semitism was unique in Europe, in the sense that it was devoid of coherent ideological underpinnings.[51] Resolving social problems may have taken precedence over gaining national independence, but it was not the exclusive domain of the left-bank historians.

The attitude of the right-bank, Polonized Ukrainian elite toward independence was marginally different. Despite the infatuation with the Ukrainian peasant (*khlopomanstvo*), the right-bank elite "could not conceive of an independent state for the Ukraine, except as a part of Poland."[52] Though critical of the Poles for dismissing the Ukrainian masses in deference to the Polish cause, Volydymyr Antonovych was of the same opinion as his left-bank counterparts: "The Ukrainian people do not possess the aptitude to form an independent state."[53] However, the friction with both Poles and Jews in right-bank Ukraine and particularly in Galicia led to a faster crystallization of a distinctly ethnic agenda. In 1848, while the left-bank intellectuals of the Cyril and Methodius society were still dreaming of an autonomous Ukraine within a pan-Slavic state, in Galicia, despite prevailing illiteracy, the Ukrainian Supreme Council (Holovna Rada) presented the Reichstag

---

[50] Quoted by Moshe Mishkinsky, "The Attitude of the Ukrainian Socialists to Jewish Problems in the 1870s," in *Ukrainian–Jewish Relations in Historical Perspective*, ed. Peter J. Potichnyj and Howard Aster (Edmonton: Canadian Institute of Ukrainian Studies, University of Alberta, 1990), 63.

[51] Henry Abramson, "The Scattering of Amalek: A Model of Understanding the Ukrainian Jewish Conflict," *East European Jewish Affairs* 24: 1 (1994) 39–47.

[52] Doroshenko, "Survey of Ukrainian Historiography," 174.

[53] Quoted in Rudnytsky, "First Ukrainian Political Program," in *Essays in Modern Ukrainian History.*

in Vienna with 200,000 signatures demanding the partition of Galicia between Poles and Ukrainians.[54]

Even Hrushevskyi, whose historiographic approach bridges the chasm dividing Galicia and Russian Ukraine, argued that the solution to the Ukrainian question was not statehood but rather a social restructuring of the Russian and Austro-Hungarian empires and a continued emphasis on social, rather than ethnic, issues as the crux of the Ukrainian question. Reflecting his populist rather than nationalist orientation, he stated, "The interest of the working people is the highest form of common good."[55] In a similar vein, Ivan Franko (1856–1916), Galicia's national poet, continued to advocate socialism as a solution to Ukraine's predicament until the last decade of his life. Thus, at the end of the nineteenth century, despite the surge of political nationalism across most of Europe, Ukrainian historiography continued to avoid the issue of political self-determination for Ukraine. Dmytro Doroshenko, summing up the activities of the Ukrainian intellectuals during the nineteenth century, lamented, "The Ukrainian journal *Osnova* was in its social and political program merely a 'South Russian' variant of Russian democratic liberalism. . .The time of the *Osnova* did not produce any political or national program."[56]

The prevailing idea among Ukraine's political thinkers – that the social and political problems of Ukraine were an extension of all-Russian problems – had a strong impact on Ukraine's literary development. As George Grabowicz noted, throughout the nineteenth century Ukraine's political and literary output was haunted by a "deeply ingrained sense of dependence, of having derived from something else (*vtorynnist'*)."[57] This dependent state of mind conceived of Ukrainian literature as a mere "addendum to the Imperial Russian Literature."[58] Ukrainian authors residing in the Russian empire wrote in Russian as much as (if not more than) in Ukrainian, while in Galicia, Ukrainian authors exhibited a similar tendency with Polish or German. George Grabowicz points out that Ukrainian authors adopted a defensive strategy as a means to retain their distinct persona:

---

[54] Jan Kozik, *The Ukrainian National Movement in Galicia 1815–1849* (Edmonton: Canadian Institute of Ukrainian Studies, University of Alberta, 1986), ch. 16.

[55] Doroshenko, "Survey of Ukrainian Historiography," 270.

[56] Ibid., 250.

[57] George S. Grabowicz, "The Politics of Culture in Today's Ukraine," Eighth Annual Ivan Franko Lecture, 12 April 1993, Carleton University, Ottawa.

[58] Ibid.

[This] was the hegemony of populism. From the mid nineteenth century well into the twentieth, Ukrainian populism of *novodnytsvo* became the matrix and the touchstone of artistic, cultural and political action . . . any divergence from the realist canon and populist premises was seen as un-Ukrainian or even anti-Ukrainian. That this impeded cultural and artistic (and indeed political) development goes without saying."[59]

This canon of populist-socialism with internationalism as the solution to the "Ukrainian question" was remarkably similar to the views of the Jewish Bund, which also saw socialism and internationalism as the answer to the Jewish question. The main difference between the Ukrainian and Jewish socialists was their perception of socialism's foundation. Whereas the Ukrainians viewed the peasantry as the popular foundation of their socialism, the Jews considered the rapidly growing proletariat in the empire's western borderlands to be their base.

By the beginning of the twentieth century, the Ukrainian intelligentsia had successfully established a Ukrainian cultural presence across Ukraine. The political agenda in Russian Ukraine, however, remained firmly socialist and federalist in nature.[60] The belief in socialism as the road to salvation was by no means limited to Russian Ukraine. As noted before, only in the last decade of his life did the Galician–Ukrainian poet Ivan Franko lose his attachment to socialism and begin to consider political nationalism as the means of resolving Ukraine's untenable predicament. As late as 1904, Dmytro Antonovych, writing in the Ukrainian publication *Pratsia*, declared that the Ukrainian question was an issue invented by an insignificant Ukrainian bourgeoisie.[61] Marian Melenevskyi of the Ukrainian Workers' Party rejected the notion of a state based on ethnicity, arguing instead for a loose confederation of communities residing in Ukraine: "Ukraine is everything that exists on its ethnographic territory, irrespective of the language."[62] Nonetheless, in their desire for cultural autonomy, Ukrainian intellectuals were inconspicuously, and most likely unconsciously laying the foundation for a clear political

[59] Ibid.
[60] Olga Andriewsky, "The Politics of National Identity: The Ukrainian Question in Russia, 1904–12," Ph.D. dissertation (Ann Arbor, MI: University of Michigan), 33.
[61] Quoted by Dmytro Doroshenko, *Z istorii ukraïns'koï politychnoï dumky za chasiv svitovoï viiny* (Prague, 1936), 5.
[62] Andriewsky, *Politics of National Identity*, 22.

agenda and, in the process, following what Miroslav Hroch believed to be the natural course toward full national development.[63]

Even though national independence was not officially on the agenda of most Ukrainian intellectuals before World War I, the transformation from cultural to political separatism could be readily discerned. The Ems Decree, which banned the Ukrainian language in the Russian empire from 1876 through 1905, gave rise to an unprecedented level of contact between the Ukrainian communities in the Austrian and the Russian empires. Austrian Galicia, the only Ukrainian territory where the Ukrainian language and culture thrived (a process which was reinforced by clashes with the Polish nobility leading to demands as early as 1848 to separate Ruthenian Galicia from the Poles[64]) became a haven for Ukrainian intellectuals from Dnieper Ukraine. The influx of Ukrainians from the Russian empire to the Austrian empire engendered throughout Ukraine the cultural components of nation building, ranging from Shevchenko's literary accomplishments to the myth of the Cossacks as an all-Ukrainian national mythology. Galicia, with a far freer and more developed political life, provided a model of political mobilization that Ukrainian politicians utilized in the Russian empire following the revolution of 1905.

Another vital component of nation building that came as a result of the expanding contacts between Ukrainians from both empires was the standardization of the Ukrainian language. Debates over the use of the Latin or Cyrillic alphabet and the nature of pure Ukrainian rose to the forefront again as Ukrainians from both sides of the Zbruch River intermingled. Ukrainians generally agreed that the Poltava dialect, with some Galician contributions, should be recognized as the standard literary language. Persistent demands by west Ukrainians to establish a Ukrainian language university in Lemberg (Lviv) also gained momentum.[65]

This contact between Ukrainians from the Russian and Austrian empires transformed the basis of Ukrainian national identity from religion and class to language and ethnicity. Mykhailo Hrushevskyi's historiography served not only to bolster a sense of distinctiveness,

---

[63] Miroslav Hroch, *Social Preconditions of a National Revival in Europe* (Cambridge: Cambridge University Press, 1985).

[64] Jan Kozik, *The Ukrainian National Movement in Galicia 1815–1849* (Edmonton: Canadian Institute of Ukrainian Studies, University of Alberta, 1986), ch. 15.

[65] See Paul R. Magocsi, "The Language Question as a Factor in National Movement," in Markovits and Sysyn, *Nationbuilding and the Politics of Nationalism*.

but also, as John Armstrong wrote, to provide a scientific rationale to a past "before time,"[66] a key ingredient of every national mythology.

As Olga Andriewsky has illustrated, the intelligentsia of Russian Ukraine had not yet conceived of a clear political agenda toward full national development before 1905. Its chief goal was the abolition of the Ems Decree. Because of the Ukrainian intelligentsia's emphasis on socialism and federalism, when the Russian empire, as a result of the disastrous war with Japan, suddenly entered the so-called constitutional period (1905–14), the Ukrainian political elite was ill-prepared to translate its cultural agenda into a clearly defined political vision and mobilize the population. In the 1906 elections to the Duma, not a single Ukrainian was elected to represent "southwest Russia,"[67] and in 1907, "Ukrainians found it difficult to elect even one Duma representative who would admit to being a nationally conscious Ukrainian."[68] For the Ukrainian movement, the constitutional period of the Russian empire amounted to a transitional period, when the nationally conscious elite, no longer satisfied with the mere abolition of the Ems Decree, continued to envision the future of Ukraine in the context of democratic federalism, banking heavily on the support of the liberal Russian factions in the Duma.

The euphoria at the outset of the constitutional regime and the subsequent repeal of the Ems Decree did not last very long. The Russian government continued to view any manifestation of Ukrainian nationalism as part of an elaborate German or Austrian intrigue to dismantle the Russian empire. In 1909 the government launched an anti-Mazepa campaign with Prime Minister Petr Stolypin forbidding the registration of "foreign societies, including Ukrainian and Jewish, regardless of their goals."[69] Similarly, the Russian liberal elite's attitude to Ukrainian national assertiveness remained one of indifference or, as in the case of Petr Struve, leader of the Constitutional Democratic Party (Kadets), one of hostility driven by fear for the unity of the "Russian" people.

The hostility of the Russian liberal elite to Ukrainian national concerns distressed Ukraine's nationalists. Replying to Struve's attack on Ukrainian culture and nationalism, Bogdan Kistiakovsky, the quintessential liberal and a contributor to the collection of essays *Vekhi*, summed up the dilemma of the Ukrainian intellectual in imperial Russia as follows:

[66] John A. Armstrong, *Ukrainian Nationalism* (Englewood, CO: Ukrainian Academic Press, 1990).
[67] Ibid., 231.    [68] Ibid., 242.    [69] Ibid., 361.

> As for myself I was born in one of the biggest and, therefore, russified Ukrainian cities; the family into which I was born was highly educated and therefore, to a considerable degree also russified. I know not only Russian and Polish but also foreign languages, I even write in them; and till now I have not ceased to curse my fate for not being educated in my native [Ukrainian] tongue; I curse it for the fact that as a child I rarely heard the songs and melodies of my own country, that my imagination was not being molded by native fairy tales, that my first acquaintance with literature was not in my native language, in a word that I was alien to the people among whom I lived, alien to my own nation . . . Here [among Russian liberals] the Ukrainian question is suppressed or ignored, sometimes it even provokes annoyance as a hindrance to various matters, notably Russian–Polish understanding.[70]

The growing disillusionment among Ukrainian intellectuals with their Russian counterparts prompted some Ukrainians to conclude that the answer to the Ukrainian question required nothing less than a complete break with Russia. The pamphlet *Samostiina Ukraina* (Independent Ukraine) articulated a new militant tendency emerging in Russian Ukraine. Its author, Mykola Mikhnovskyi, was a member of the radical People's Party, whose 1904 pamphlet declared "Muscovites, Jews, Poles, Hungarians and Romainians are the enemies of our nation." Mikhnovskyi joined in the Struve–Kistiakovsky controversy, writing in the Ukrainian-language journal *Snip*:

> And now Ukrainians have finally [come to the point] where their Russian liberal allies have declared them to be a "real state and national evil." That's how Russian liberalism wants to repay Ukrainians for their former "collaboration." Today the liberal mask has dropped . . .[71]

Although Mikhnovskyi represented a new and assertive view of the Ukrainian question, his views remained marginal in Russian Ukraine. Interestingly, even the People's Party, in the platform they shared with the Radical Democratic Party, called for an Ukrainian Assembly (Sejm) with authority to deal only with Ukraine's internal issues, leaving finance, foreign affairs, and defense as imperial issues." Despite their nationalism, they were content to settle for

---

[70] Bogdan Kistiakovsky, "K voprosu o samostoiatel'noi ukrainskoi kulture: pis'mo v redaktsiiu," *Russkaia mysl'* (May 1911).
[71] Andriewsky, *Politics of National Identity,* 416.

autonomy rather than independence.[72] Most radical nationalists, however – such as Dmytro Dontsov, Volodymyr Doroshenko, and Andrii Zhuk – and other east Ukrainian nationalists continued to opt for a national renaissance in Galicia, where the regime was less repressive and the Ukrainian population far more responsive to outright independence.

Despite its disappointment with Russian liberals, the Ukrainian elite in Russian Ukraine remained committed to a federalist, all-Russian solution rather than full independence. In a book published in 1914 by the journal *Ukrainskaia zhizn'* and edited by Volodymyr Vynnychenko and Semen Petliura (both future leaders of independent Ukraine), some authors insisted that the genesis of the Ukrainian nation dated to the prehistoric break-up of the Slavic tribes into distinct groups. They believed that Russia's centralizing policies led to Ukraine's cultural, economic, and moral decay, leaving Ukraine as the most backward and illiterate region in European Russia.[73] Nevertheless, the authors of the book declared that "the notion of separatism is alien to most Ukrainians."[74] The authors ended their manifesto with a call for the end of the "enserfment of the Ukrainian language" and its use in local schools, courts, churches, and other institutions. Although the authors appeared to favor economic autonomy, the answer to the Ukrainian question seemed to lie in the federalization of the Russian empire, a goal to be achieved through "law-based, evolutionary means."[75]

Despite the oft-declared commitment of Ukrainian intellectuals to the integrity of the Russian empire, the Russian state remained suspicious of Ukrainian loyalties; the massive 1912 study by the imperial censor in Kiev indicates that the tsarist state continued to view Ukrainian nationalism as a potential threat to the integrity of the empire.[76] On the eve of World War I, national consciousness in Russian Ukraine remained in a transitional phase, where cultural and political agendas were becoming increasingly intertwined and mutually reinforcing. By the early twentieth century, Ukrainian literature, which in the middle of the nineteenth century concentrated on

---

[72] Hugh Seton-Watson, *The Decline of Imperial Russia 1855–1914* (New York: Frederic Praeger, 1961), 233–234.

[73] "Ukrainskii vopros" (St. Petersburg: Izdaniie redaktsii zhurnala *Ukrainskaia zhizn'*, 1914), 108.

[74] Ibid., 196.    [75] Ibid., 126.

[76] See Sergei Shchegolev, *Ukrainskoie dvizheniie kak sovremennyi etap Iuzhno-Russkogo separatizma* (Kiev: Kushnerov, 1912).

Ukraine's native roots, had mutated into a "militant and program-matic" tool to serve a clearly political cause.[77] The evolution of the political orientation of the Ukrainian body politic was demonstrated in Kiev in 1914, when the celebrations of Shevchenko's centenary turned into a massive political demonstration against the prevailing political and social order.

The situation in Galicia was remarkably different. Tempered by conflicts with the Roman Catholic Polish gentry and supported by an elite of a semi-hereditary clergy of a distinct church, the Ukrainian population had developed a degree of political activism unknown in the Russian empire. Ever since Maria Theresa awarded the Uniate Church equality with the Roman Catholic Church in 1774, Ukrainians had remained one of the most loyal peoples of the Habsburg monarchy.

The struggle of the Ukrainian intelligentsia in Galicia consisted of two basic phases. The first phase came in the mid-nineteenth century when young intellectuals embarked on transforming vernacular Ukrainian into a literary language – even over the objections of the Uniate hierarchy.[78] The second phase was their struggle against the Polish minority in eastern Galicia, to reorganize the empire along Austro-Slavic lines. Until 1867 Galicia's Ukrainians saw their future within the multinational Habsburg monarchy. The reorganization of the Habsburg empire into the Dual Monarchy of Austria-Hungary made it clear that Vienna would not grant the Slavs equal footing in the empire. The national awakening came to Galicia only in the 1870s. Only in the last decade of the nineteenth century did Galicia's cultural activism acquire a component of political separatism. Operating under the more liberal conditions of the Habsburg empire and supported by better-defined national institutions, the Galicians had by the 1890s at last acquired a national identity with a distinct political character.[79]

By the late nineteenth century, all major Ukrainian political parties in Galicia had adopted independence as a part of their political

[77] See George G. Grabowicz, "Province to Nation: Nineteenth Century Ukrainian Literature as a Paradigm of National Revival," *Canadian Review of the Studies of Nationalism* 16: 1–2 (1989).

[78] See Peter Brock, "Gente Ruthenus, Natione Polonus: The Case of Ivan Vahylerych," in *Folk Culture and Little People: Aspects of National Awakening in East Central Europe* (Boulder, CO: East European Monographs, 1992).

[79] See John Paul Himka, "Young Radicals and Independent Statehood: The Idea of a Ukrainian Nation State, 1890–1895," *Slavic Review* 42: 2 (Summer 1982).

platforms. The 1899 platform of the National Democratic Party of Galicia stated: "The final goal of our striving is the achievement of cultural, economic, and political independence for the entire Ukrainian–Ruthenian nation and its unification in one body politic."[80] The issue of national identity, however, had yet to be fully resolved. In Galicia, as in Russian Ukraine, Ukrainian national aspirations remained closely tied to the issues of social justice and utopian socialism.[81] Moreover, shortly after the National Democratic Party declared itself for independence, the Russophile Ruthenian Council proclaimed the national and cultural unity of Galicia's Ruthenians with Russia.[82] Still, by the early twentieth century, pro-independence pamphlets published in Galicia – such as Iulian Bachynskyi's *Ukraine Irredenta* (1898), Mykola Mikhnovskyi's *Samostiina Ukraïna* (*Independent Ukraine*, 1902), and Ivan Franko's *Poza Mezhamy Mozhlyvoho* (*Beyond the Limits of the Possible*, 1900) – had laid the intellectual foundation for independence (*samostiinist'*).[83]

In Russian Ukraine, calls for independence remained the domain of the lonely voices of Shevchenko,[84] Mikhnovskyi, the young Zionist leader Vladimir Zeev Zhabotinskii,[85] and the Russian anarchist Mikhail Bakunin. They predicted Ukraine's emergence as an independent nation, which, while remaining close to Russia and Poland, would have to avoid the hegemony of either of its neighbors.[86] As far as Ukrainian historiography was concerned, the mainstream continued to be preoccupied with cultural and social issues, with a populist reading of history remaining the dominant force. Mykola Porsh, the chief ideologue of the Social Democratic Party in Russian Ukraine, continued to champion the cause of federalism. Ivan Franko, assessing the situation in Dnieper Ukraine following the 1905 Revolution, lamented:

[80] Ivan L. Rudnytsky, "The Fourth Universal and its Political Antecedents," in *The Ukraine, 1917–1921: A Study in Revolution*, ed. Taras Hunczak (Cambridge, MA: Harvard Ukrainian Research Institute, 1977), 191.

[81] See Rybak, "Ukraïnskyi zhynochyi rukh."

[82] Nicholas J. Andrusiak, "The Ukrainian Movement in Galicia," *The Slavonic Review* 14 (1935–36). It is noteworthy that during the first free elections held in Galicia in 1907, Russophile candidates gained five of the twenty-seven seats assigned to the Ukrainian community.

[83] Even in the case of Franko, there was a slow progression toward embracing the concept of independence. See Hritsai, "Ivan Franko pro politychnu samostiinist' Ukraïny."

[84] For the evolution of Shevchenko's views, see Luckyj, *Between Gogol and Sevcenko*.

[85] See Vladimir Zeev Zhabotinskii," Urok iubleiia Shevchenko," in *Izbrannoe* (Jerusalem: Biblioteka Alia, 1978), 144–52.

[86] *Letters of Mikhail Bakunin to Alexander Herzen and Nikolai Ogarev* (Geneva, 1896).

> Since the way of life in Russia has grown more liberal, the Ukrainian intelligentsia now faces the formidable task of molding the huge mass of ethnic Ukrainian people into a Ukrainian nation, an integral cultural body able to live a cultural and political life on its own.[87]

Reflecting the pre-World War I national agenda, the Ukraine Committee, a lobbying group operating in the West, issued a pamphlet in 1914 that reiterated the Ukrainian goal of turning Russia into a "federal state in which each nationality would enjoy complete autonomy."[88]

Even though Ukrainian peasants took an active part in defending their specific interests during the convulsions of 1905–7, Ronald G. Suny observed, "Almost everywhere the nationalist movements were either strengthened or fatally weakened by the nature of their class base."[89] In the case of Dnieper Ukraine, with the exception of a small intelligentsia, national identity almost exclusively overlapped with the class identity of the peasantry. Inasmuch as the peasant base of Ukrainian nationalism in the late nineteenth and early twentieth centuries checked foreign cultural penetration, as Richard Pipes noted, Ukrainian nationalism remained dependent on "the politically disorganized, ineffective, and unreliable village."[90]

The collapse of the tsarist empire in February of 1917 caught the Ukrainian elite, along with the rest of the world, unprepared. Ukraine's political elite, steeped in the tradition of federalism, lacking independent administrative mechanisms, and confronting a skeptical, non-Ukrainian urban population, initially viewed the Ukrainian revolution as part and parcel of the "all-Russian Revolution." Although the Society of Ukrainian Progressives in Saint Petersburg (Tovarystvo Ukraïnskykh Postupovtsiv) demanded the introduction of the Ukrainian language in Ukraine's courts, schools, and churches along with an end to the detention of Ukrainian intellectuals and Uniate clergy, it did not challenge the integrity of the empire. In its first "Universal" declaration, the Ukrainian National Council (Rada), meeting under the banner "Long Live Autonomous Ukraine in a Federated

---

[87] Ivan Franko, *Zibrannia Tvoriv* 45 (Kiev: Naukova Dumka, 1986), 404.

[88] Yaroslav Fedortchouk, *Memorandum on the Ukrainian Question in its National Aspect* (London: Francis Griffith, 1914), 9.

[89] Ronald Grigor Suny, "Nationalism and Class in the Russian Revolution: A Comparative Discussion," in *Revolution in Russia: Reassessments of 1917*, ed. Edith Rogovin Frankel, Jonathan Frankel, and Baruch Knei-Paz (New York: Cambridge University Press, 1992), 224.

[90] Richard Pipes, *The Formation of the Soviet Union: Communism and Nationalism, 1917–23* (Cambridge, MA: Harvard University Press, 1954), 149.

Russia,"[91] continued to depict its role as a guarantor of Ukrainian democracy and declared itself the true representative of "the peasants, workers, and toilers." Although the First Universal stressed the Ukrainian demands aimed at the provisional Russian government, the Rada declared, "Let Ukraine be free without separating from all of Russia, without breaking with the Russian state."[92] Volodymyr Vynnychenko, the head of the Ukrainian government, stressed that "Ukrainian separatism died with its (tsarism's) *raison d'être*."[93]

This ambivalence toward independence held sway even as the Russian center continued to disintegrate. In its Third Universal, issued in November 1917 following the Bolshevik coup, the Rada, uncoerced by the Russian-dominated center, continued to view the future of Ukraine within a supranational structure: "Without separating ourselves from the Russian Republic and maintaining its unity, we shall stand firmly on our soil in order that our strength may aid all Russia, so that the whole of Russia may become a federation of equal and free people."[94] Even the Fourth Universal, the Rada's declaration of independence, issued in January 1918 during a Bolshevik offensive into Ukraine, maintained the possibility of "federative ties with the People's Republics of the former Russian state."[95]

Strikingly, all four declarations, promulgated as they were by a beleaguered Ukrainian leadership in response to a rapidly deteriorating situation, reflect a preoccupation with class and social issues. The issue of Ukrainian statehood was almost an afterthought. The uncertain political direction of the intellectuals dominating the new government in Kiev was manifested in the fact that they, unlike Finnish, Polish, or West Ukrainian nationalists, failed to use their demobilized compatriots from former imperial armies as a basis of a new national army. The tasks facing the new and inexperienced leadership were indeed daunting; the leaders of independent Ukraine were unable to address or resolve effectively the severe social issues of the day. Ukrainian governments lacked both the internal mechanisms and external conditions to claim legitimacy.[96] The historian John Reshetar aptly observed that the Ukrainian leadership was psycholo-

---

[91] Reshetar, *Ukrainian Revolution*, 52.
[92] Taras Hunczak, *The Ukraine, 1917–1921: A Study in Revolution* (Cambridge, MA: Harvard University, 1977), 382.
[93] Reshetar, *Ukrainian Revolution*, 52.
[94] Ibid., 388.     [95] Ibid., 395.
[96] See Rudolf A. Mark, "Social Questions and National Revolution: The Ukrainian National Republic in 1919–1920," *Harvard Ukrainian Studies* 14: 1/2 (June 1990), 113–31.

gically unprepared to deal with the rapidly evolving situation: "The Ukrainian leaders had the disadvantage of having to move from what was essentially an a-political cultural nationalism, to autonomy and federalism, and finally to independent statehood, within one year."[97] Much of Ukraine's march toward independence in 1917 was driven by a peasantry downtrodden by the agrarian situation. When the independent Ukrainian government failed to address their concerns promptly, peasant support rapidly melted away. The urban Russian and Polish populations by and large remained indifferent, if not overtly hostile, to the notion of Ukrainian nationalism.[98] The Jewish population was initially supportive of the Rada because of its recognition of the Jews' "personal and communal" freedoms; however, the inability of the Rada to stop the pogroms conducted by anarchist peasants and government troops led to rapid disillusionment with Ukrainian statehood.[99] The lack of support in urban centers caused Isaak Mazepa to lament that "even our Kiev gave us no help during the revolution."[100]

With an uncertain Ukrainian leadership in Kiev fighting the Bolsheviks, President Woodrow Wilson's commitment to "one and indivisible Russia," and the resurgence of a Poland eager to resume its *mission civilisatrice* in the *kresy* (borderlands to its east), Ukraine's efforts to end its status as a "submerged nation" failed. The collapse of both the Galician and the Dnieper Ukrainian states, coupled with the very different Ukrainian policies pursued by the Polish Second Republic and Soviet Russia, divided the Ukrainian population more than it had been in 1914. After more than six years of continuous war across their territory, Ukrainians found themselves divided not only between two empires, as was the case before 1914, but between radically different ideologies and very different concepts of statehood. These divisions undermined any concerted drive on the part of the Ukrainians to determine their own destiny as a nation. As brief as Ukraine's experiment with independence was, however, the politicization of the

---

[97] John S. Reshetar, "Ukrainian and Russian Perceptions of the Ukrainian Revolution," in Potichnyj *Ukraine and Russia in Their Historical Encounter*, 145.

[98] For a good illustration of a mocking attitude toward the notion of Ukrainian independence, see Mikhail Bulgakov's *Belaia Gvardia* [The White Guard] (Letchworth, Herts.: Bradda Books, 1969).

[99] See Henry Abramson, "Jewish Representation in Independent Ukrainian Governments of 1917–1920," *Slavic Review* 50: 3 (Fall 1991), 542.

[100] Quoted in Bohdan Krawchenko, "The Social Structure of the Ukraine in 1917," *Harvard Ukrainian Studies* 14: 1–2 (June 1990), 100.

Ukrainian national identity had become a reality that could no longer be ignored.[101]

As noted previously, before World War I there were two distinct concepts of Ukraine among Ukrainian intellectuals. In Galicia, Ukraine was perceived, though not exclusively, as an ethno-political concept that would be achieved only with Ukraine's attaining full independence; the Dnieper Ukrainians viewed Ukraine as a distinct cultural entity whose emancipation would be attained only within the context of reform of the Russian empire as a whole. The dichotomy of visions would deepen after 1921 and split the Ukrainian nationalist movement for the next two generations.

### The policy of *korenizatsiia*

As noted in chapter 6, before the October Revolution, Lenin and other Bolshevik theoreticians paid scant attention to the nationalities question. Large segments of the Bolshevik party deeply resented the accommodation of national minorities. Nevertheless, the Bolsheviks' initial policy appeared to support many of the goals of the Ukrainian intellectuals, including cultural autonomy, federalism, and socialism. Indeed, when the vast majority of Ukrainians found themselves part of the new Soviet state, the Bolshevik leaders, chastened by the experience of the civil war, had developed an understanding of the need to co-opt "native" nationalism if it were to hold on to power.

The Bolsheviks' difficult conquest of Ukraine (as with most of the former tsarist empire) and their failure to rally the Polish proletariat against the Piłsudski-dominated regime convinced most Bolsheviks that nationalism was a political force to be reckoned with. They had initially believed, as Stalin stated in 1904, that "not the national, but the *agrarian* question will decide the fate of progress in Russia; the national question is a *subordinate* question" (emphasis added).[102] Notwithstanding the weakness of the post-war regime and its inability to reform the agrarian structure, the Bolsheviks recognized that they would have to accommodate nationalism. Even Stalin, despite his consistent advocacy of Russian-based centralism, attacked the tsarist policy of reducing Ukraine to an appendage of Saint Petersburg and

---

[101] See John S. Reshetar, "The Ukrainian Revolution in Retrospect," *Canadian Slavonic Papers*, 10 (1968) 129–32; see also Omeljan Pritsak and John Reshetar, "The Ukraine and the Dialectics of Nation Building," *Slavic Review* 22: 2 (June 1963).

[102] Robert S. Sullivant, *Soviet Politics and the Ukraine 1917–1957* (New York and London: Columbia University Press, 1962), 7.

called for the return of Ukrainian cultural objects from the Hermitage to Kiev.[103]

Despite the inability of Ukrainian nationalists to sustain an independent Ukrainian state, they nevertheless managed to awaken a Ukrainian nationalism between 1917 and 1920. Lenin prevailed on the Ukrainian Bolsheviks to enter into an alliance with the *Borotbisty*,[104] the party of Ukraine's indigenous leftists, in spite of the *Borotbisty*'s demands for separate Ukrainian military units and representation in the Comintern.[105]

Along with the New Economic Policy, the weakness of the Bolsheviks in Ukraine and their tactical concessions to Ukrainian nationalism ushered in one of the most illustrative periods in Ukrainian history. To many Ukrainian socialists and communists, the policy of *korenizatsiia*, which promoted Ukrainian language and culture, greater social justice for the peasantry, and the recognition of Ukraine as an equal partner within the Soviet Federation, seemed to fulfill the vision advocated by Kostomarov and other early framers of Ukrainian nationalism. Seeing the realization of many of their goals, former Rada leaders such as Hrushevskyi and Vynnychenko returned to Soviet Ukraine and attempted to play a role in Ukraine's reconstruction. This policy even allowed for a separate Ukrainian delegation at the Riga negotiations with Poland. Similarly, in branding the Russian Orthodox Church as pro-monarchist, Lenin's regime tolerated the reemergence of the Ukrainian Autocephalous Church.[106] In his study of Ukraine under the leadership of the national Bolshevik, Mykola Skrypnyk, James E. Mace noted, "Skrypnyk's Ukraine can in some ways be seen as the fulfilment of the demands of the Ukrainian Central *Rada* put forth in 1917."[107]

The situation in Ukraine, however, remained chronically unstable. Ukrainian nationalism could no longer be appeased with the agenda

---

[103] Joseph Stalin, "O natsional'nikh relikviiakh," *Izvestia*, 13 November 1917.

[104] In 1922 only 24 percent of the members of the Ukrainian Communist Party were Ukrainians, while 72 percent were Russian. See John S. Reshetar, Jr., "National Deviation in the Soviet Union," *The American Slavic and East European Review* 12: 2 (April 1953), 162.

[105] See V. Lenin, "Kintseve slovo na VIII konferentsii RKU(b) v pytanni pro radians'ku vladu na Ukraini 3 hrudnya 1919 r.," *Lenin Sbornik* 32 (1919), 550–51; see also Pipes, *Formation of the Soviet Union*, 146.

[106] John Reshetar, Jr., "Ukrainian Nationalism and the Orthodox Church," *The American Slavic and East European Review* 10 (1951).

[107] James E. Mace, *Communism and the Dilemmas of National Liberation: National Communists in Soviet Ukraine 1918–1933* (Cambridge, MA: Harvard Ukrainian Research Institute, 1983), 230.

of the 1917 Rada, and its proponents demanded ever greater autonomy. To the Bolshevik leaders of the Soviet Union, concessions to nationalism would remain tactical until such time "agrarian relations" could be reconfigured by a more stable Soviet power. In other words, while the Ukrainians considered *korenizatsiia* as the first step toward ever greater Ukrainian autonomy, the Bolsheviks saw it as a mere tactical concession to be reversed once the Soviet Union was ready to achieve a higher plane of social development. Given those conflicting agendas, a clash between Ukrainian particularism and Bolshevik centralism became an ever-increasing probability.

Following the introduction of the New Economic Policy, the Ukrainian intelligentsia and the party elite felt assured that Ukraine had at long last entered a phase of prolonged decentralization and would ultimately attain national independence. This notion of distancing Ukraine from Russia and, as Mace observed, drawing Ukraine into the ranks of the nations of Europe[108] permeated the Ukrainian intelligentsia. One of the first manifestations of the desire to utilize the Ukrainization of the country's political and cultural life to distance Ukraine from Russia was the so-called Khvylovy controversy.

Mykola Khvylovy, one of the most popular writers of the time, criticized Ukrainian authors for aping Russian literature and entrenching Ukraine's "psychological servility" to Russia. "Our orientation must be toward West European art, its style, its examples,"[109] he wrote. Khvylovy believed Ukrainian writers should seek their inspiration from the European renaissance and Greco-Roman art; in other words, Ukraine's cultural direction should separate from Russia's Byzantine orientation.[110] Seeing the relationship with Russia as psychologically and culturally damaging to Ukraine, Khvylovy asserted that Ukraine's current relationship with Russia was temporary and that the ultimate goal must be independence from Russia: "Ukrainian society, once strengthened, will never agree with its actual, if not *de jure* decreed hegemon, the Russian competitor."[111]

What started as an aesthetic and literary issue was rapidly turning into a political issue, with the definition of Ukraine's identity and its relationship with Russia becoming basic issues. Oleksandr Shumsky, a

---

[108] Ibid., 211.
[109] Basil Dmytryshyn, *Moscow and the Ukraine 1918–1953* (New York: Bookman Associates, 1956), 94.
[110] See George S. N. Luckyj, *Literary Politics in Soviet Ukraine 1917–1934* (Durham, NC and London: Duke University Press, 1990).
[111] Dmytryshyn, *Moscow and the Ukraine*, 98.

former member of the *Borotbisty* and Commissar of Education, came to Khvylovy's defense. He argued that Ukrainization had failed and led to stagnation. He likened Soviet Ukraine to a submissive (and perfidious) servant of the Bolshevik center,[112] reviving the tradition of *khaluistvo* through which pre-revolutionary Ukrainian nationalists would simultaneously subscribe to Ukrainian nationalist literature and the Russian chauvinist *Kievlianin* as a means to appear politically correct, come what may.[113] What started initially as a literary and philosophic debate soon mutated to a political and economic challenge. The economist Mykhailo Volobuev claimed that the October Revolution did not really alter the economic status of Ukraine within a Russian-dominated state, further firing the controversy over Ukraine's status within the Soviet state. Calling the Ukrainian budget "fiction,"[114] Volobuev felt Ukraine would be far better served if it had direct economic dealing with the world economy, a demand the Bolshevik regime construed as an assault on the integrity of the Soviet state.

Growing Ukrainian demands for autonomy were not limited to segments of the disgruntled intelligentsia, but were also found within the Communist Party itself. Mykola Skrypnyk, the leader of the Ukrainian Bolsheviks, consistently championed not only the cultural and linguistic Ukrainization of political life but, more important, the expansion of Ukraine's political autonomy from Moscow. Unlike other nationalists, Skrypnyk avoided anti-Russian rhetoric. Nevertheless, he once bluntly stated, "A single unified Russia is not our slogan, we can never adopt such a slogan."[115]

Besides successfully carrying out cultural Ukrainization, Skrypnyk's leadership established a Ukrainian territorial army with Ukrainian as its language of command. While these units did not amount to much more than a part of a general reserve, the sheer existence of specifically Ukrainian units re-enforced the notion of Ukrainian statehood. Under the aegises of *korenizatsiia*, Ukraine kept a diplomatic presence within Soviet embassies and other trappings of political independence. Concerning ideology, Matvii Iavorskii, the party's court historian, developed a theory that Ukraine's social development, along with the socialist revolution, was strictly a Ukrainian phenom-

---

[112] Ibid., 106.
[113] See Andriewsky, *Politics of National Identity.*
[114] See Isaac Mazepa, "Ukraine under Bolshevist Rule," *The Slavonic Review* 12 (1933–34), 335.
[115] Sullivant, *Soviet Politics and the Ukraine*, 68.

enon and not linked to events in Russia.[116] The head of the All-Ukrainian Central Committee, Heorhii Petrovskyi, despite decades of unflinching loyalty to Bolshevism, lamented, "Ukraine is almost as rich as France, while the budget of Ukraine is similar to that of the Moscow (city) council."[117] Skrypnyk's drive for political independence peaked in the late 1920s when Ukraine's leadership made territorial demands on Russia, claiming that areas where ethnic Ukrainians formed a majority should not remain part of the Russian Federation.[118] To Skrypnyk, deepening socialism ran parallel with the devolution of the Soviet state.

In the late 1920s, the Bolshevik regime faced two potentially mortal threats: a large, well-to-do peasantry, and ethnic separatism throughout the Soviet Union. To centralize the Soviet Union, appease the urban proletariat, and build a great power, Stalin launched the first Five-Year Plan. This program of forced industrialization would be financed by "Russia's internal colony," the countryside. Ukraine, with its huge and increasingly prosperous peasantry and its deeply entrenched *korenizatsiia*, represented a threat to Stalin's notion of nation building.

The suicide of Mykola Skrypnyk in the summer of 1933 reflected, both metaphorically and practically, the ultimate irreconcilability of Ukrainian nationalist aspirations and Bolshevik centralism. The Bolsheviks initiated an assault on Ukrainian separatism, which consisted of several steps. It started with an attack on Ukrainian intellectuals in 1929–30, accusing the Ukrainian Academy of Science and its members,[119] along with the Ukrainian Autocephalous Church, of links to an *émigré* separatist group, the Union of Free Ukraine, resulting in Hrushevskyi's exile and unexplained death. Soviet attacks on Ukrainian nationalism soon spilled over to include Ukraine's urban professional class (the Shakhty trials in 1928), and in an artificial famine and the starvation of millions of Ukrainian peasants (1932–34).[120] A popular folk poem prevalent in Ukraine in 1934 captured the predicament of the Ukrainian masses:

> To kolhosp went our mother
> To kolhosp went our dad

[116] Mace, *Communism and the Dilemmas*, ch. 7.
[117] Mazepa, "Ukraine under Bolshevist Rule," 335.
[118] Mace, *Communism and the Dilemmas*, 214.
[119] See Heorhii Kasianov, *Ukraïns'ka intelihentsiia 1920kh-30kh rokiv: sotsiial'nyi portret ta istorychna dolia* (Kiev: Vik Publishers, 1992).
[120] See Robert Conquest, *Harvest of Sorrow* (New York: Oxford University Press, 1986).

> Kids are roaming unattended
> Begging for their daily bread
> Bread and lard are gone for good
> Soviet power stole our food.[121]

The destruction brought down on Soviet Ukraine in the 1930s reduced the vitality of the Ukrainian population to an eerie listlessness. The Ukrainian intellectuals' socialist-federalist notion that the Ukrainian question could be solved in a broad Slavic-socialist context also fell victim in this period.

### The case for integralism

Meanwhile, the Poles regarded the western Ukrainian territories of Galicia and Volyn as integral parts of the Second Republic. Having drifted from the Jagiellonian tradition advocated by Paderewski (and to a lesser degree by Piłsudski) toward a political expression of the "Polish Nation," Poland began to view all minorities as impostor populations. According to much of the Polish elite, the optimal future for these ethnic groups was either Polonization or emigration.[122]

The rejection of the Jagiellonian tradition among large segments of the Polish population, as reflected in the views of Roman Dmowski and the Kraków historical school, clearly influenced Galicia's Ukrainians. The unwillingness of the Polish elite to accept Ukrainian national aspirations as equal to those of the Poles was particularly evident in Galicia. As early as 1848, Prince Czartoryski's agent Francizek Duchinski lamented "[t]hat we [the Poles] have allowed the Ruthenians in Galicia to take by force from us what we should have given at their first request – their language – in our unparalleled carelessness . . . if we do not want the Ruthenians to make a revolution, then let us Poles make it for the Ruthenians in response to their just wishes."[123] The bitter interethnic struggle in Austria-Hungary had given impetus to an ethnic rather than a social identity. The interethnic clash was particularly bitter in eastern Galicia, where the

---

[121]     Matka v soziu, batko v soziu,
          hlodni dite po dorozi,
          nema khliba, nema sala,
          bo radianska vlast zabrala.

[122] See Bogdan Budurowycz, "Poland and the Ukrainian Problem 1921–1939," *Canadian Slavic Papers* (December 1983).

[123] Jan Kozik, *The Ukrainian National Movement in Galicia 1815–1849* (Edmonton: Canadian Institute of Ukrainian Studies, University of Alberta, 1986), 365.

Polish gentry was determined to retain its dominant status through a feudal order over the Ukrainian peasantry.[124] Similarly, in Russian Ukraine, where the Union of Russian People found more than half of its membership, Russian nationalism manifested itself most strongly. Fanned by the ultra-Russian nationalist newspaper *Kievlianin*, the Union presented a clear model of a new, narrow Russian nationalism growing in popularity and appeal.

In the last decades of the nineteenth century and the early twentieth century, theories of nationalism, particularly in Central and Eastern Europe, were profoundly influenced by the revolutionary scientific discoveries of the era. Charles Darwin's theory of the natural selection of species and Herbert Spencer's application of that theory to economics and politics fueled narrow and belligerent nationalist fervor across Europe. The popularization of Gregor Mendel's study of genetics encouraged the belief that the behavioral traits of different ethnic and racial groups are not a product of religion or social environment, but rather of immutable profound characteristics. This belief was a departure from the "rationalist" view that had dominated Western thinking since the eighteenth century. Finally, Louis Pasteur's illustration of how invisible foreign bodies can invade a healthy body and overwhelm it found a political echo, especially in the case of relations with the Jewish minority, which was becoming less ghettoized and more difficult to detect in society.[125] It should be stressed that the mutation of liberalism, under the influence of modern economics and science, into a xenophobic, racist, and authoritarian political mode was a Europe-wide phenomenon.[126]

The first manifestation of such narrow nationalism in Ukraine was, perhaps, Mikhnovskyi's 1902 pamphlet *Samostiina Ukraïna* (*Independent Ukraine*), in which he coined the slogan "Ukraine for the Ukrainians." Challenging the mainstream inclusivist views of Ukrainian national identity, Mikhnovskyi stated, "All the evils which the Ukrainian people have suffered are derived from the fact that until recently they did not view their cause nationally, but only socially . . ."[127]

---

[124] Philip Pajakowski, "Dynamics of Galician Polish Conservativism in the Late Ninteenth Century," *Jahrbücher für Geschichte Osteuropas*, vol. XLIII (1995), 19–29.

[125] *The Protocols of the Elders of Zion* was fabricated by the tsarist secret police precisely to popularize the notion of covert Jewish infiltration with the ultimate goal of domination and destruction of traditional European society.

[126] See Carlton J. H. Hayes, *A Generation of Materialism 1871–1900* (New York, Evanston & London: Harper Torchbooks, 1941).

[127] Quoted in Alexander J. Motyl, *The Turn to the Right: The Ideological Origins and Development of Ukrainian Nationalism 1919–1929* (New York: East Slavic Monographs, 1980), 9.

In a statement reflecting the ideology of Mikhnovskyi's Ukrainian People's Party, the notion of narrow nationalism was expressed even more clearly: "All people are your brothers, but Russians, Poles, Hungarians, Rumanians and Jews – these are the enemies of our nation as long as they rule over us and exploit us. Respect the activists of your homeland, hate its enemies . . ."[128] Although Mikhnovskyi and his followers represented a minority view in Ukrainian intellectual thought, they laid the basis for the integralist ideology of the 1920s.[129] Ukrainian nationalist thought could not help but be influenced by the intellectual forces shaping Europe during the 1920s and 1930s. The drift toward right-wing fascist ideology in western Ukraine was reinforced by Poland's failure to address either the individual or communal grievances of the Ukrainian population, as well as by the fact that Ukraine's expatriate intellectuals congregating in Vienna, Berlin, and Prague were exposed to the fascist ideas that were fashionable in these cities.[130]

The ideology of the Ukrainian right shared several key features with other right-wing movements prevalent in the 1920s. Like its European counterparts, Ukrainian integralism was in essence a revolt against the principles of the Enlightenment and the French Revolution that dominated the European intellectual mainstream at the end of the nineteenth century.[131] Ukrainian integralism also rejected the fashionable early-twentieth-century socialism. As Zeev Sternhell observed, "Fascism represented a synthesis of organic nationalism with the anti-materialist revision of Marxism. It expressed revolutionary aspirations based on a rejection of individualism, whether liberal or Marxist."[132] The drift to the right sweeping across Europe took hold in Ukraine because of the bitter experiences of World War I, the 1917 Revolution, and the destruction of two Ukrainian states. This trend eventually influenced the statist school (*derzhavnytska shkola*) of Ukrainian historiography, which demanded the establishment of an independent

---

[128] Quoted in Yury Boshyk, "Jewish Ukrainian Relations in Imperial Russia," in *Ukrainian–Jewish Relations in Historical Perspective*, ed. Peter Potichnyj and Howard Aster (Edmonton: Canadian Institute of Ukrainian Studies, University of Alberta, 1990), 181.

[129] See Mykola Horelov, "Istorychni sproby modeliuvannia ukrains'koï derzhavnosti v XX stolitti," *Politychna Dumka* 4 (1994), 93.

[130] M. Makin and J. Toman, "Prague: City of Russians, Ukrainians, and Eurasians," *Cross Currents* 9 (1990), 69–71.

[131] Zeev Sternhell with Mario Sznaider and Maria Aseri, *The Birth of Fascist Ideology* (Princeton: Princeton University Press, 1994).

[132] Ibid., 6.

Ukrainian state[133] and rejected the rationalist socialist model advocated by earlier Ukrainian intellectuals. The statist school adopted a potent and narrow nationalist notion of Ukraine. For Galician Ukrainians, as Alexander Motyl has argued, the defeats suffered by the Ukrainians between 1917 and 1921 were clearly linked to the inability of the Ukrainian elite to raise national interests above ideological interests.[134]

From 1920 on, the intellectual leaders of the Ukrainian right created a strong synthesis of nationalism and right-wing ideology.[135] Viacheslav Lypynskyi, the luminary founding father of the statist school, rejected the populist-rationalist view of earlier Ukrainian thinkers. He stressed that only a "mystical ideal" can motivate the masses to heroic exploits. To be effective, the masses must be led by an "aristocracy." In an argument similar to that of Oswald Spenagler in *The Decline of the West*, Lypynskyi saw societies going through three stages: first, ochlocracy or social underdevelopment; second, classocracy or high organic development; and third, democracy or degradation and decline.[136] The tragedy of Ukraine, according to Lypynskyi, was that the intellectuals opted for the third stage, ignoring its destructive potential. Lypynskyi dismissed Ukraine's intellectuals as opportunists who discovered Ukrainian statehood only after Russia discarded them.[137] Nevertheless, believing that there could be no nation without a state, Lypynskyi insisted that the basis of a state must be territorial, not ethnic or religious.[138] Despite his rejection of the totalitarian police state, which he associated with Russian centralism, Lypynskyi, like many right-wing thinkers of his time, saw two threats to Ukraine's long-term viability: nomads from the east and the "rapacious, democratic world capitalism."[139]

Lypynskyi represented a traditional variant of right-wing ideology. Dmytro Dontsov, however, became the ultimate ideologue of Ukrai-

[133] See Borys Krupnytsy, "Trends in Modern Ukrainian Historiography," *The Ukrainian Quarterly* 6, no. 4 (1950).
[134] See Alexander Motyl, *The Turn to the Right*, 2.
[135] Aside from features reflecting Ukraine's distinct situation, the intellectual basis of Ukraine's right was part of the larger mainstream view prevalent at the time across Eastern Europe. See Peter F. Sugar ed., *Native Fascism in the Successor States 1918–1945* (Santa Barbara, CA: ABC-Clio, 1971).
[136] Oswald Spengler and Charles Atkinson, *Decline of the West* (New York: A. A. Knopf, 1939); Wsevolod W. Isaiw, "The Political Sociology of Vjacheslaw Lypyns'kyj," *Harvard Ukrainian Studies* 9: 3/4 (December 1994).
[137] Ibid., 299.
[138] See Eugene Pyziur, "V. Lypynskyj's Idea of Nation," *Harvard Ukrainian Studies* 9: 3/4 (December 1994).
[139] Ibid., 325.

nian integralism and its hyper-nationalism. Dmytro Dontsov articulated an even stronger rejection of socialism. He defined it as the "equality of slaves before the powerful ruler and master."[140] Rejecting the notions of democracy and rationalism and expounding on social Darwinism, Dontsov stated: "[Aggression] is not merely plundering, but also the fulfilment of a social function and public interest . . . There are superior and inferior nations . . . The right of the stronger races to organize peoples and nations to consolidate extant and spread its culture and civilization."[141] Dontsov is associated with the term integral nationalism (*chynnyi natsionalizm*), which gave rise to the myth of a homogeneous Ukrainian peasantry engaged in a fight for survival against Jews, Poles, and, most important, Russians.[142] To Dontsov, Ukraine's pivotal position in the racial and cultural struggle between the East and the West, between Russia and Europe, provided the foundation of Ukrainian national identity.[143]

Although right-wing nationalism belonged to the *Zeitgeist* of all Europe, the Ukrainian plight made integralist ideology even more attractive to the Ukrainian population outside Soviet Ukraine. The tenor of Poland's increasingly nationalist politics became apparent when its president, Gabriel Narutowicz, was assassinated in 1922 for his lack of nationalist fervor. Poland's failure to respect Ukrainian communal rights, as solemnly promised to the League of Nations, and its annexation of Galicia, embittered the Ukrainian population even more. Writing in 1921, Oleksa Burantovych warned:

> It may well be that only through the downfall of Poland will the nations of Eastern Europe attain their freedom. Poland has learned nothing from its history; the 150 year long lesson [of Poland's subjugation by other powers] turned out to be too short.[144]

The Polish government's policies of Polonizing minorities and encouraging Polish settlement in Galicia among the land-hungry Ukrainian peasants further fueled anti–Polish sentiment and led to a prolonged small-scale insurrection in east Galicia. The Ukrainian sense of victimization deepened, as Motyl has observed, when a French jury acquitted Samuel Schwartzbard, the Jewish assassin of

---

[140] Quoted in Boshyk, "Jewish Ukrainian Relations in Imperial Russia," 181.
[141] Dmytro Dontsov, *Natsionalizm* (London: Ukrainska vydavnycha spilka, date unknown), 283.
[142] See Dmytro Dontsov, *Rossiia chy evropa?* (Kiev: 1992).
[143] See Oleksa Burantovych, *Ukraïns'ka ideolohiia revoliutsionoï doby* (Lviv and Vienna: Ukraïns'kyi Prapor, 1922), 9.
[144] Ibid., 7.

Semen Petliura. Petliura was a controversial leader whose career spanned early involvement with socialism to the ouster of the Hetman, Pavlo Skoropadsky, and attempted leadership of an anarchic "army" consisting of peasant bands. Although there is ample indication that Petliura abhorred the pogroms carried out by troops nominally under his command,[145] Petliura's troops, and thus by association Petliura himself, were culpable for mass murder in the minds of many Jews of Ukraine.

Previously disliked by many Ukrainians for his socialist tendencies and his willingness to surrender eastern Galicia to Poland in return for a Polish alliance against the Bolsheviks, Petliura thus became a martyr and a national icon. His assassin's acquittal came to symbolize the contempt that the Western democracies allegedly harbored toward Ukrainians. The Ukrainian population could draw the only obvious conclusion: despised polities that broke with democracy (the Bolsheviks and the Poles) attained their goals, while those that adhered to their populist democratic traditions (the Ukrainians) continued to suffer the indignity of colonialism.

Initially, the Soviet policy of *korenizatsiia* found favor among Ukrainians in Poland and contributed to the rapid growth of the Communist Party of Western Ukraine (KPZU). The Khvylovy controversy and the subsequent repression of Ukrainian culture, however, discredited the communists in western Ukraine, reducing their presence from a mass movement to a fringe group that was eventually expelled from the Comintern. By the 1930s, following the end of *korenizatsiia* and the artificial famine, the KPZU was largely displaced by a right-wing nationalist movement.[146] Poland's drift from a quasi-parliamentary republic to the *Sanacja* regime, run by a group of pseudo-fascist colonels, undermined the standing of the legal Ukrainian National Democratic Organization and further facilitated the rise of the ultranationalist Organization of Ukrainian Nationalists (OUN).[147] By the late 1930s, the Ukrainian population, attracted by the power of Nazi Germany and fascist Italy, moved from the conservative *Falangist* nationalism of the 1920s to ultra-right-wing nationalism.[148] The

---

[145] See Semen Petliura, *Satati* (Kiev: Dnepro, 1993), 183–85.

[146] See Alexander J. Motyl, "The Rural Origins of the Communist and Nationalist Movements in Wolyn Wojewodztwo, 1919–1939," *Slavic Review* 38: 3 (September 1978).

[147] See Oleksander Zaiets, "Nationalizm i natsional'na demokratiia: vitoky konflikty (1920–1930 rr.)," *Suchasnist'*, 2 February 1994.

[148] See Wolodomyr Kosyk, *The Third Reich and the Ukrainian Question 1934–1944* (London: Ukrainian Central Information Centre, 1991).

nationalist publication *Nasha Klich* described the transformation in the following manner: "There is now a sociopolitical system which is developing around the world: in one country, it manifests itself as Fascism; in another, as Hitlerism; and here we call it Nationalism."[149]

The Ukrainian right's hope that a Bolshevik–Nazi war would result in the emergence of an independent Ukraine under Nazi suzerainty failed to materialize, as Berlin refused to entertain such notions.[150] Having already awarded Transcarpathian Ukraine to Hungary, the Germans handed over Ukrainian territory west of the Southern Bug to Romania and incorporated Galicia into its *Generalgouvernement Polen*. What was left of Ukraine was divided between the *Reichskommissariat Ukraine* and military administration under the *Wehrmacht*. Furthermore, during the period of German occupation of Ukraine, OUN activists discovered that their highly nationalist and exclusivist ideology found little resonance in Soviet Ukraine, especially in left-bank Ukraine with its highly mixed Ukrainian and Russian population.[151] The first and only aim of western Ukrainian nationalists had been national independence. When co-operation with the Nazis failed to yield statehood, their independent ideology and activities led the Nazis to turn on them, ultimately forcing the OUN to wage a futile war against both Germany and the USSR. Nevertheless, the activities of the OUN, and later the Ukrainian Insurgent Army, which carried on its struggle against Soviet troops until the early 1950s, divided the Ukrainian people's notion of a national myth. Although western Ukraine's epic struggle against both Nazism and Bolshevism created a new national ethos in Galicia, to most Ukrainians, World War II was the Great Patriotic War of the USSR, in which over 3 million Ukrainians served with distinction in the Soviet armed forces. They considered the victory over fascism their own.

The paradigms of both *korenizatsiia* and integralism were destroyed in the course of World War II. The dwindling number of believers in *korenizatsiia* Soviet propaganda during the war drove home the point that a union with Russia based on an equal partnership was as unattainable under Stalin as it had been under Tsar Alexander II. To the nationalists, the defeat of Germany and the rapid acceptance by the West of Soviet hegemony across Eastern Europe gave proof that an

---

[149] *Nasha Klich*, 3 June 1938.
[150] For the ideology and activities of the different factions of the Organization of Ukrainian Nationalists during World War II, see John A. Armstrong's classic, *Ukrainian Nationalism*.
[151] Ibid., ch. 11.

armed struggle with Moscow was futile and that the integralist struggle against "the Russians" was a misguided one, both tactically and strategically. In a prescient analysis in 1943, D. Shakhai (Iosyp Pozchaniuk) foresaw what would become the ultimate means to attain Ukrainian independence. Instead of striving to destroy the "Moskal" empire, through alliances with either Nazi Germany or the West, Ukrainian nationalists would have to understand that the Bolshevik political structure "is not in the interests of the Russian people, but in the interests of a plutocratic internationalist clique . . . [T]he fate of Bolshevism and its empire depends *in greater measure* upon the Russian people than upon external intervention. We are also struggling for a Russian state – 'freedom for nations, freedom for individuals' must also apply to the Russians."[152] Writing in 1949, O. Hornovy (Osyp Diakiv) emphatically stated that "[t]he separation of Ukraine from Russia is thus directed not against the Russian people, but solely against the Russian–Bolshevik imperialists, whose overthrow is also in the interests of the Russian people . . . We are striving for the closest possible political, economic, and cultural cooperation with the Russian people . . ."[153] While the aforementioned voices may well have represented a minority view among Ukrainian nationalists in the 1940s, they nevertheless represented the erosion of the Dontsovian concept of nation, creating for the first time a common ground with politically conscious Ukrainians disillusioned with *korenizatsiia*, thus laying the basis for a modern Ukraine-wide identity.

The Soviet victory in World War II drove home to the Ukrainians the point that neither *korenizatsiia* nor integral nationalism provided an adequate solution to the Ukrainian question. After 1945, Soviet Ukraine, now consisting of most of the traditionally Ukrainian lands, had to find a new paradigm to express its national agenda – one molded by politicians, not intellectuals.

[152] D. Shakhai, "Our Tactics With Regard to the Russian People" in *Political Thought of the Ukrainian Underground 1943–1951*, ed. Peter J. Potichnyj and Yevhen Shtendera (Edmonton: Canadian Institute of Ukrainian Studies, University of Alberta, 1986), 283–317 (emphasis in the original).
[153] O. Hornovy, "Our Attitude Toward the Russian People," in Potichnyj and Shtendera, *Political Thought of the Ukrainian Underground 1943–1951*, 322.

# 9    Ukraine after World War II: birth pangs of a modern identity

[The] twentieth century having dragged Ukraine astray . . . has thrown it in the last decades back to the same crossroads of historical choice in which it found itself in the first decades of the century.

Oksana Zabuzhko, 1991[1]

I don't think that at present it is even possible to think about independence for Ukraine, because we do not have the economic, cultural or political background for such a step. It's absurd.

Yurii Pokal'chuk, early member of Rukh, 1989[2]

After World War II, Ukraine followed the psychological paradigm described by Arnold van Gennep in his book *Rites of Passage*.[3] In this model, unifying peoples undergo a three-stage transformation. In the first stage of the process, a community senses what Gennep calls *separation*, in which it realizes that it is discontented with its traditional identity, but has not yet envisioned a clear alternative. In this stage, a group identifies itself by comparing itself with an other and noting differences. The first stage is followed by a transitional phase which Gennep refers to as *liminality*. In this phase, the group adopts a new identity, but has not shed its old identity entirely. Thus, the group in question may identify itself as a part of both its traditional identity and its new identity, or as a distinct subset of the traditional group. The final stage of *aggregation* occurs when the group has embraced a new identity, and by fully incorporating values and symbols particular to the group, completely discards its previous identity. The story of post-World War II Ukraine follows Gennep's model closely. However, because of the vast differences which have arisen from the

---

[1] Oksana Zabuzhko, "The Philosophy of the National Ideal: Ukraine and Europe," *Zustrichi* 1 (1991), 94.

[2] Roman Solchanyk, *Ukraine from Chernobyl' to Sovereignty* (Edmonton: Canadian Center of Ukrainian Studies, University of Alberta, 1992), 33.

[3] Arnold van Gennep, *The Rites of Passage* (Chicago: University of Chicago Press, 1961)

disparate historical experiences and collective memories of the regions, coupled with Ukraine's size and relative lack of country-wide symbols, Ukraine's "Rite of Passage" has been an uneven process, such that different sectors of the polity at any one time are in different stages of the "passage." This has resulted in an incoherent and at times contradictory evolution of national identity and with it a murky development of a foreign policy agenda to defend an as yet poorly defined "national interest."

The purpose of this chapter is to explore the stages of Ukraine's "Rite of Passage" from a perennial vassal of the Kremlin to an independent nation, and how this process has effected both the emergence of Ukraine's national identity and its foreign policy. In the following pages, I will attempt to address two trends in post-World War II Ukraine. First, during the entire postwar period one can observe a relentless expansion of the Russian language and ever greater ethnic intermixing across the former USSR. Simultaneously, as Robert J. Kaiser observed, this increasingly mobile demographic redistribution and cultural integration did not ease the national self-consciousness of the non-Russian population or lead to any visibly successful Russification.[4]

Second, despite temporary setbacks, most of the postwar period in Ukraine was characterized by slow but almost continuous "Ukrainization" of the country's communist party, its economy, literary, and academic life, and even the Orthodox Church in Ukraine, consolidating a Ukrainian national identity on an unprecedented scale. Although in 1945 the development of Ukraine's consciousness did not begin at the same point throughout the country, nor, when the Soviet Union collapsed did it reach the same stage of development in all areas, Ukraine had begun to identify itself, not as a Russian *oblast,* but as a Ukrainian nation.

World War II initially deepened the schism between the western and Soviet Ukraines. In the former, thousands fought against the Soviet army, and even with the German *Wehrmacht*, while in the latter, millions fought with the Red Army. Nevertheless, the fallout from the war laid the foundations of the contemporary Ukrainian national identity. First, the postwar Ukrainian entity encompassed almost all of the ethnically Ukrainian territories within its borders for the first time ever. Second, the Yalta settlement, which enshrined the

[4] Robert J. Kaiser, *Geography and Nationalism in Russia and the USSR* (Princeton: Princeton University Press, 1994).

Curzon Line as the border between Poland and Soviet Ukraine, removed Poland as a major factor in Ukrainian politics, leaving only Russia as the focus of Ukrainian debate. Third, the expulsion of the Poles from western Ukraine and the Nazi-inspired slaughter of the Jews forever changed the character of Ukrainian cities. For the first time since the early nineteenth century, the populations of Lviv and Kiev were overwhelmingly Ukrainian, thereby accelerating the rise of a Ukrainian urbanized class that was also politically aware. The urbanization of western Ukraine transformed Galicia from an agrarian to an industrial region and narrowed the socio-economic gap between it and the rest of Soviet Ukraine.[5] Fourth, and perhaps most important, as Yaroslav Bilinsky noted, the inhabitants of Ukraine began to identify themselves as Ukrainians rather than as Little Russians, Russians, or simply "locals."[6] Finally, Stalin's success in obtaining a seat in the United Nations for Ukraine changed it, under international law, from a Soviet province to an at least nominally sovereign entity. The experiences of both parts of Ukraine following the war advanced the notion of a common Ukrainian identity and created a Ukraine-wide agenda.[7] An instrumental setback, which pushed both parts of Ukraine to find a new paradigm of national identity, was the profound disappointment of its expectations following World War II.

For most west Ukrainians, Russia posed the ultimate threat to Ukraine and the international order. Therefore it was necessary for Ukraine to solicit Western support for independence by offering itself as a bastion against a final conflict with Russia. By the end of the war, many had come to view this position as misguided and catastrophic in its impact on the Ukrainian people. Having failed to attain statehood after the Nazi invasion, west Ukrainian nationalist leaders, including Metropolitan Andrii Sheptytskyi, banked on the inevitability of a clash between the Soviet Union and the West. They hoped that this conflict would prompt the West to support the Ukrainian cause.[8] These hopes

[5] See David Marples, *Stalinism in Ukraine in the 1940s* (New York: St. Martin's Press, 1992), 111.

[6] Yaroslav Bilinsky, *The Second Republic: The Ukraine after World War II* (New Brunswick: Rutgers University Press, 1964), 284.

[7] For an elaboration of the impact of post-World War II events on Ukraine see Ivan L. Rudnytsky, "The Soviet Ukraine in Historical Perspective," *Canadian Slavonic Papers* (Summer 1992).

[8] Sheptytskyi supported the formation of the SS division Halychina, not as a means to ally Ukraine with the Third Reich, whose defeat was looming, but rather as a means to induce the West to cooperate with Ukraine in the impending war with Bolshevism, see Orest *Subtelny, Ukraine: A History* (Toronto: University of Toronto Press, 1990), 472.

also failed to materialize. The West not only accepted the Elbe River in Germany as the outer perimeter of the Soviet empire, but the British and US intelligence communities judged Ukrainian national identity too weak to be taken seriously. They even considered Ukrainian national identity a product of German expansionist ambitions.[9] A note prepared by the British Foreign Office on the eve of the Yalta Conference bluntly stated:

> The only possible alternative [to Soviet Ukraine], namely the creation of an independent Ukrainian State, is a goal for which certain extremist Ukrainian nationalist organizations have *agitated*, but these movements owed much of their strength in the pre-1939 period to the fact that they were fostered and financed by the Germans for their own ends. In any case, the creation of an independent Ukrainian state would at this late stage in East European history be quite inconceivable; *the only practical possibility of uniting all Ukrainians in a single political unit lies in the incorporation of the Western Ukraine with the Ukrainian Soviet Republic.* (emphasis added)[10]

A 1948 National Security Council report reflected the low expectations of the United States for an independent Ukraine: "While the Ukrainians were an important and a specific element of the Russian Empire, they have shown no sign of being a 'nation'. . . It should be noted, as stated above, we would not encourage Ukrainian separatism. . . ."[11] In Washington's view the Ukrainians, unlike the peoples of the Baltic states, lacked a will to independence worthy of US support. Soviet propaganda held that all Ukrainian nationalists – whether associated with the Organization of Ukrainian Nationalists (OUN) and SS Halychina, which had collaborated with Nazi Germany, or with the non-collaborating Ukrainian Insurrectionary Army (UPA) – were Fascist organs with no place in the emerging European order. In a memo to Secretary of State James Byrnes, Dewitt C. Poole noted, "the cause of Ukrainian nationalism became

[9] Ukrainian nationalism was viewed as part of foreign intrigue by different groups at different times; the Poles seeing an Austrian plot in 1848, tsarist Russia seeing a Habsburg plot during World War I, and Soviet Russia seeing a German plot in 1939.
[10] "Note Prepared for Yalta by B. E. Pares, the Northern Department, British Foreign Office, 22 February 1945, Dealing with the Ukrainian Minority in Eastern Poland," in *Anglo-American Perspectives on the Ukrainian Question 1938–1951*, ed. Lubomyr Y. Luciuk and Bohdan S. Kordan (Kingston, Ont.: The Limestone Press, 1987), 157–158.
[11] "Note to The National Security Council, Washington, by S. W. Souers, Executive Secretary, August 18, 1948, on US Objectives with Respect to Russia and the Issue of Ukrainian National Liberation," in Luciuk and Kordan, *Anglo-American Perspectives*, 209–211.

enmeshed with the German expansion east."[12] US support for the Ukrainian insurgency, which continued until the mid-1950s, was minimal and ineffective.

In eastern Ukraine, those who had hoped that a Soviet victory over Nazi Germany would open a new chapter in their lives soon faced a similarly bitter disappointment. As the Soviet army drove the last Germans from Ukraine in 1944, the Soviet government took steps to address Ukraine's economic and political interests. Rumors spread that the Soviets would not reinstitute completely collectivized agriculture, which had been anathema to rural Ukrainians. In February 1944 the USSR Supreme Soviet amended the structure of the USSR government, ostensibly transferring power from Moscow to the republics. Ukraine was specifically promised separate republican military units, as well as a separate foreign ministry and separate representation in the United Nations. By a decree signed by Soviet President Mikhail Kalinin, the Soviet army established the Khmelnytsky Order of Valor, and the city of Pereiaslav was renamed Pereiaslav-Khmelnytsky.

In cultural politics, the Ukrainian Academy of Sciences, reopened in Kiev soon after the city's liberation after operating in Ufa during the war, was encouraged to step up its output and emphasize Ukraine's past without the ritual affirmation of inspiration from and love for Russia. The Kremlin's attempt to co-opt Ukrainian nationalism reached its peak in March 1945 when the Soviet cultural establishment lavishly praised pre-revolutionary Ukrainian composer Mykola Lysenko, famous for setting Shevchenko's nationalist poems to music, on the 103rd anniversary of his birth. For a brief period it appeared that the Soviet government would live up to its promises of a genuine federal system, cultural autonomy, and a separate international profile. But whatever illusions the people of Soviet Ukraine might have had were shattered at an official victory banquet when Stalin proposed a toast "to the health of the Russian people because it is the most outstanding nation of all included in the Soviet Union."[13]

Stalin's toast, rather than the overtures he made toward Ukraine before Germany's collapse, revealed his political direction. The last years of Stalin's rule were characterized by paranoia, especially

---

[12] "D. C. Poole, Associate Public Liaison Officer, United States Delegation to the San Francisco Conference, 14 May 1945, Regarding Conversation with Representatives of the Ukrainian Congress Committee on the Ukrainian Situation in Europe," Luciuk and Kordan, *Anglo-American Perspectives*, 157.

[13] Robert S. Sullivant, *Soviet Policies and the Ukraine 1917–1957* (New York: Columbia University Press, 1962), 248.

during Andrei Zhdanov's demands for cultural conformity, as the regime clung to Russian nationalism as its main source of legitimacy and increasingly resorted to the repression of all nationalities that might challenge Russian hegemony. Some smaller nationalities, such as the Chechens and Crimean Tartars, were accused of collaboration with the Nazis and deported *en masse* to Central Asia. In Moldova, where Sovietization proved difficult to implement, Moscow orchestrated an artificial famine that resulted in the death of thousands. With the outbreak of the Cold War and the founding of the State of Israel in 1948, what was left of the Jewish community now incurred Stalin's wrath. Stalin charged the Jews with "cosmopolitanism" and proceeded to liquidate the Jewish intelligentsia. Stalin's campaign against the Jews reached its climax when *Pravda* "uncovered" a plot led by Jewish doctors to murder the top Soviet leadership. Mass arrests followed, while plans for the deportation of the Jews to Birobidzhan were made. Only Stalin's unexpected death in March 1953 aborted these plans.[14]

For Stalin, the Ukrainians represented the ultimate threat to the integrity of his empire. Between 1945 and 1953, Ukraine endured forced recollectivization during the famine of 1946, the forced unification of the Greek Catholic Church with the Russian Orthodox Church, and a renewed attack on any manifestations of "bourgeois nationalism" in art and culture. Nikita Khrushchev, then first secretary of the CPU (Communist Party of Ukraine), linked Ukrainian nationalism with German revanchism. Following close upon Khrushchev's repressive policies, Stalin's brutal henchman Lazar Kaganovich returned to Ukraine and launched a massive purge of the party and state institutions. These experiences served to narrow the psychological gap between east and west Ukrainians, though visible differences remained.

Until Stalin's death in March 1953, the leadership of the CPU, primarily members of the "class of 1938," conducted an open war against Ukrainian national identity and culture. Although the campaign was similar in tone and scope to the one waged against Ukraine in the 1930s, this time Ukrainians were far too exhausted and listless to protest, let alone mount serious opposition.[15] Since Kiev had become the cultural center of Ukrainian language activity after World War II,

---

[14] See Nora Levin, *The Jews in the Soviet Union Since 1917* (New York: New York University, 1988).
[15] Some opposition within cultural circles apparently did occur. See Sullivant, *Soviet Policies*, 263.

there were relatively few native east Ukrainians able to fill these posts. From 1950 on, a steady stream of west Ukrainian intellectuals moved to Kiev, while nationalist intellectuals from the east, such as Viacheslav Chornovil and Levko Lukianenko, natives of the Cherkassy and Chernihiv oblasts respectively, moved to Lviv. In the process a common identity began to coalesce. As early as 1954, the post-Stalinist "thaw" had already set in for Ukrainians. Khrushchev's rise to power heralded several fundamental changes in the Kremlin's attitude toward Ukraine. The leaders in Moscow, themselves recovering from Stalin's despotism, quickly realized that in order to prevent another personal dictatorship, some decentralization was essential.

The drive to decentralize, initially launched by Lavrenti Beria and later adopted by Khrushchev, had a profound impact on Ukraine. Khrushchev had built much of his career in Ukraine in the 1930s and 1940s and viewed it as his power base. At the outset of the post-Stalin power struggle, he made a friendly gesture toward Ukraine by replacing the first secretary of the CPU, Leonid Melnikov, a Russian, with Oleksii Kyrychenko, a Ukrainian. Bohdan Khmelnytsky, previously depicted as an enemy of the peasantry, was rehabilitated and portrayed as a historic and prescient leader who had foreseen the need to "reunite" Ukraine with Russia. During the celebration of the tercentennial of the Pereiaslav Agreement, Khrushchev not only rewarded Ukraine with the Crimea, he also promoted it to the status of what Bilinsky called "the second republic," second only to Russia in terms of its importance for world socialism, and within the hierarchy of republics of the USSR. Soviet historiography was moderated, and in 1957 the Kremlin launched *Ukraïns'kyi Istorychnyi Zhurnal* (*The Ukrainian Historical Journal*). While Soviet historiography held on to its basic tenets of "one core nation" and "Pereiaslav reunification" and continued to reject Hrushevskyi's theory of an independent Ukrainian history, Ukraine was depicted as a partner and sovereign state following the October Revolution, rather than as an appendage of Russia.[16] Thus, the Soviets restrained Ukrainian historians from making nationalist claims while encouraging their Russian counterparts. Nonetheless, Ukrainian historiography had been re-established.[17]

By the mid-1950s, the CPU leadership had realized that, barring a

[16] See Stephen M. Horak, "Ukrainian Historiography 1953–1963," *Slavic Review* 24: 2 (June 1965).
[17] See Jaroslaw Pelenski, "Soviet Ukrainian Historiography after World War II," *Jahrbucher fur Geschichte Osteuropas* (1964).

return to Stalinist methods, it would have to come to terms with the Ukrainian population. Therefore, in addition to allowing greater expression of Ukrainian culture and initiating a new drive for greater use of the Ukrainian language, after the Twentieth Congress of the CPSU in 1956, the communist leadership made a concerted effort to draft native west Ukrainians (*mistni kadry*) into the communist apparatus. The dilemma facing the Ukrainian political elite was how to accommodate Ukrainian national aspirations and retain legitimacy in Ukraine while at the same time preventing nationalism from lurching down the slippery slope of separatism as in the 1920s. This dilemma would persist essentially unchanged for the next thirty-seven years.

If the communist elite had to find a way of accommodating both nationalism and internationalism, Ukrainian dissidents and nationalists had to synthesize the virtues of *korenizatsiia* and integralism. The Kremlin's history of brutality and broken promises had discredited *korenizatsiia* as a route to national salvation. International apathy toward the Ukrainian cause and association of the OUN with the German war effort, together with the ultimate defeat of the UPA by the Soviets, showed that integralism and the concomitant armed struggle had also failed to provide a solution to the Ukrainian question. Ukraine's experience from 1930 to 1953 proved that both the west Ukrainian political paradigm *and* the Soviet Ukrainian paradigm were illusory. A united Ukraine would have to mold a new identity and find a new paradigm.

As Ivan L. Rudnytsky has said, Ukraine's political elite was very much aware that, while Soviet Ukraine embodied "a compromise between Ukrainian Nationalism and Russian Centralism . . . neither of the parties [had] accepted the existing compromise as a final settlement."[18] With the end of Stalinist totalitarianism, the task of Ukraine's communists was to reconcile the contradictory demands of Ukrainian nationalism and Russian centralism. Kenneth C. Farmer, in his study of nationalism in post-Stalinist Ukraine, noted that since 1956 Ukraine had been caught between two competing myths, the myth of proletarian internationalism and the myth of national patrimony.[19] This dichotomy between nationalism and internationalism spilled over into the Ukrainian dissident movement that emerged in

[18] Ivan L. Rudnytsky, "Soviet Ukraine in Historical Perspective," *Essays in Modern Ukrainian History* (Edmonton: University of Alberta, 1987), 236, 239.
[19] Kenneth C. Farmer, *Ukrainian Nationalism in the Post-Stalin Era: Myth, Symbols and Ideology in Soviet Nationalities Policy* (The Hague, Boston, London: Martinus Nijhoff Publishers, 1980).

the late 1950s. Whereas west Ukrainian dissidents extolled the importance of Ukraine's ethnocultural identity, the dissidents in Russophone Ukraine tended to concern themselves with issues of social justice and human rights broadly defined.[20]

Although the Ukrainian body politic appeared passive after four brutal decades, the Soviet leaders understood that they were succeeding in co-opting only the urban population, which associated Soviet power with improvements in the standard of living. Two vital segments of Ukraine's population remained recalcitrant: the peasants and the highly educated urban intellectuals. The rural population considered collectivized agriculture, with its exploitative policies of the state and the monopoly on tractors and plows via the machine tractor stations (MTS), modern-day serfdom.[21] To address the concerns of the rural population in Ukraine and the other Soviet republics, Khrushchev abolished the MTS system and permitted the collective farms to own their implements. Improvements in the economic conditions in the rural areas during the Khrushchev era, which continued and even increased under Brezhnev, pacified the turmoil in the Ukrainian countryside in the post-World War II period.

Given the elite's fear of cultural nationalism mutating into political nationalism, the co-optation of the urban intelligentsia proved to be far more complex. In the cities, anti-Soviet sentiment coalesced around the most educated segments of the population, which increasingly perceived a direct relationship between professional success and denationalization. The Harvard Interview Project echoed this conclusion: "The higher the occupational group, the higher was the portion of those who claimed that nationality was a significant factor in career advancement."[22] Reacting to the contradictory demands placed on the intellectual layer, where professional advancement could be attained only through acculturation, the Ukrainian political elite attempted to co-opt the young intelligentsia with greater tolerance and occasional support of Ukrainian culture and language and to retain political control to the point of often appearing more doctrinaire and inflexible than the Russian center, making Ukraine's cities some of the most volatile in the USSR, a volatility which was reflected by recurring crack-downs and campaigns to restore ideological reliability.

[20] Ludmilla Alexeyeva, *Soviet Dissent: Contemporary Movements for National, Religious, and Human Rights* (Middletown, CT: Wesleyan University Press, 1985), 28.
[21] Bilinsky, *The Second Republic*, 290.
[22] Ibid., 289.

In the late 1950s and early 1960s, Kiev experienced a limited cultural renaissance, but political repression of any challenge to the existing order continued unabated. On the one hand, the authorities rehabilitated Volodymyr Sosiura's patriotic poem "Love Ukraine"; the liberal journals *Dnipro* and *Vitchyzna* printed new, nationally inspired, avantgarde works of Ivan Dziuba and Maksym Rylskyi; and Oles Honchar published his obliquely anti-Soviet novel *Sobor* (Cathedral). In 1958 the CPU reversed its Zhdanovite criticism of Ukrainian music and operas, such as *Velyka Druzhba, Bohdan Khmelnytskyi,* and *Vid Shyrokoho Serdtsa*, and allowed their performance within Ukraine.[23] On the other hand, Ukraine's KGB continued its political repression, and members of the United Party for the Liberation of Ukraine were arrested and sentenced. In 1961 the historic heart of Ukrainian Orthodoxy, the Kiev Pecherska Lavra monastery, was declared unsafe and cleared of its remaining monks. The archbishop of Chernihiv, after a show trial, was sentenced to a long prison term.[24] The attacks on the Church in Ukraine coincided with Khrushchev's anti-religion crusade, as well as pursuit of his policy of *slianie* (blending) of the Soviet people. Borrowing a page from tsarist policy at the beginning of the twentieth century, the party elite adopted anti-Semitism as a tool of state propaganda in order to deflect the anti-Russian mood of Ukrainian nationalists. This official anti-Semitism peaked when the Ukrainian Academy of Sciences published Trokhym K. Kichko's pamphlet *Judaism without Embellishments.*[25]

In the wake of Khrushchev's thaw, national identities throughout the USSR, particularly in Ukraine, began to reappear, greatly alarming the Kremlin. Khrushchev responded with the doctrine of *sliianie,* the blending of the nationalities of the USSR into the Soviet people. *Sliianie* was accompanied by a change in language policy that made instruction in the "native" language of the republics subject to parental discretion. These policies resulted in a mass exodus of children living in the cities from Ukrainian language schools to Russian language schools. Nationalist intellectuals perceived both policies as an assault on Ukraine's culture and heritage. The policies also resulted in greater tension between the CPSU and the CPU, and

---

[23] Hryhoryi Kas'nov, *Nezgodni: ukrainska intelihentsiia v rysi opory 1960–1980kx rokiv* (Kiev: Lebid Press, 1995), 15.
[24] B. R. Bociurkiw, "The Orthodox Church and the Soviet Regime in Ukraine, 1953–1971," *Canadian Slavonic Papers* (Summer 1972).
[25] Trokhym K. Kichko, *Eiudaizn bez prykras* (Paris: Cercle d'études Franco-Ukrainnes,1964)

between the CPU and the Ukrainian intelligentsia. The position of Ukraine's political elite was underscored by Khrushchev's decentralization of the economy into *Sovnarkhozy*, which led to the transfer of most industrial activity to local jurisdiction and created both a cultural and an economic agenda for Ukrainian intellectuals.[26] The Ukrainian political elite reacted to the growing contradictions between the Kremlin and Ukraine's nationalist intelligentsia by attempting to accommodate both constituencies, intensifying repression of political dissent on the one hand and asserting cultural separateness on the other.

The attempt to reconcile the agendas of the CPU and the national intelligentsia reached its zenith during the tenure of Petro Shelest (1963–72) as leader of the Ukrainian Party. Shelest, who personified the deep contradictions among the Ukrainian elite in the post-Khrushchev era, saw that communist legitimacy, as well as his own, depended on the support of the Ukrainian population. To muster that support, he had to improve living standards and broaden cultural autonomy. At the same time, he understood that the survival of the Soviet political system, in which he truly believed, required complete conformity.

Shelest defended Ukraine's economic interests, becoming a most persistent lobbyist for agricultural subsidies from Moscow and investment in Ukrainian mining, and new terms of trade for agricultural goods. He also challenged the Kremlin's enthusiasm for large, wasteful development projects in Siberia. In the cultural sphere, Shelest elevated Ukrainian culture and the Ukrainian language to a level unheard of since the period of *korenizatsiia*. For the first time since the days of Khvylovy in the 1920s, Russia's economic and cultural hegemony came under fire as Shelest charged, "nationalist and great power chauvinism have always been the two faces of bourgeois policy and ideology on the nationality question."[27] In many ways, Shelest's political conception did indeed resemble the perceptions of the 1920s Ukrainian leadership. His beliefs required a visceral devotion to Ukraine's cultural legacy *and* a heartfelt commitment to Marxism–Leninism.

Shelest's dual loyalties were only partially successful. Although they produced a revival of Ukrainian arts and letters during the

---

[26] Orest Subtelny, *Ukraine: A History* (Toronto, Buffalo, and London: University of Toronto Press, 1990), 505.

[27] Borys Lewytzkyj, *Politics and Society in Soviet Ukraine 1953–1980* (Edmonton: Canadian Institute of Ukrainian Studies, University of Alberta, 1984), 97.

waning days of the Khrushchev era, the security apparatus and large segments of Ukraine's bureaucracy never subscribed to Shelest's policies. Thus, while Shelest continued to support the Ukrainian cultural revival, and probably directly supported Ivan Dziuba's treatise *Internationalism or Russification* (1965) where Dziuba using Leninist argumentation charged that the Kremlin, in the name of internationalism, was uprooting Ukraine's culture in favor of Russian cultural hegemony,[28] he could not prevent the arrest of nationalists and dissidents. Dziuba's track presented the Kremlin with an unusual dilemma, on one hand, it could be easily justified as yet another "Euro-communist" manifestation, on the other, given the fact that Dziuba's work was published by Ukrainian émigrés in Canada, it was a clear challenge to the Soviet state. In 1965 more political arrests took place in Ukraine than in the previous eight years combined. By 1966, as the Brezhnev–Suslov team moved increasingly away from communist ideology toward Russian nationalism and material co-optation for legitimacy, Shelest's mixture of native nationalism with internationalist ideology fell out of favor with the Kremlin.

The divergence of agendas became increasingly clear as the Brezhnev leadership took its first steps toward détente with the West, downplaying the unrelenting conflict with the capitalist West, though without renouncing socialism or the ideological struggle. Brezhnev led the Soviet Union in a new direction in Soviet domestic and foreign policy, stressing Russian nationalism at home and détente with the West externally. The first indication of divergence between Shelest and Brezhnev became visible during the Czechoslovak crisis in 1968. Initially the Kremlin had taken a tolerant position toward Alexander Dubcek's liberalization, while Shelest, along with Poland's Władysław Gomulka and East Germany's Walter Ulbricht, depicted Dubcek as a product of Zionism and West German revanchism and demanded his removal.[29] The ideological schism between Shelest and the Kremlin deepened during the 24th Congress of the CPU (1971). Shelest, after lavishly praising Ukraine's unique cultural achievements, attacked deviations from socialism and exhorted his audience to "intensify the ideological struggle"[30] with the West. Two weeks later, Brezhnev, addressing the 24th Congress of the CPSU, called on the "great

[28]  Ibid., 114.
[29]  See Jiri Valenta, *Soviet Intervention in Czechoslovakia, 1968: Anatomy of a Decision* (Baltimore and London: Johns Hopkins University Press, 1981).
[30]  Ibid., 125.

Russian people, [who] have played their role in the creation and consolidation of this mighty Union of peoples,"[31] to endorse détente.[32]

The showdown between the two notions of the Soviet state – Brezhnev's Russian orientation with less emphasis on internationalism and Shelest's native nationalism with an internationalist ideology – came just before President Richard Nixon's official visit to the USSR in May 1972. The visit, which included a stop in Kiev, prompted Shelest to tell Brezhnev that Nixon would not be welcome in Ukraine, and he added, "I shall not shake the hand that has been bloodied in Vietnam."[33] In April 1973, on the eve of Brezhnev's departure for his first visit to Bonn, Shelest was removed from office and replaced with the servile Volodymyr Shcherbytskyi. Petro Shelest's fall from grace illustrated that as far as the Kremlin was concerned, devotion to Marxism–Leninism was not a substitute for loyalty to the "leading role of Russia" within the USSR. Ukrainian nationalism could be tolerated by the Kremlin only so long as it did not become politicized; Shelest's political use of Ukrainian nationalism was clearly unacceptable to the Kremlin. The new Ukrainian party leader was a product of the Ukrainian elite, which preferred strong links with the Soviet center for its survival. In 1974 during the celebration of the fiftieth anniversary of the founding of the USSR, the Kremlin unleashed a concerted attack on non-Russian nationalism. With Shelest's removal, Ukraine's second effort to accommodate national aspirations with an internationalist ideology ended in failure. Despite Shelest's ambiguous legacy and ultimate failure, the combined impact of Khrushchev's thaw and Shelest's national communism left an indelible mark on the Ukrainian consciousness and national identity.

Brezhnev's neo-Stalinism did not have the same catastrophic impact on Ukraine as high Stalinism had. Nevertheless, Shcherbytskyi dutifully carried out an accelerated program of Russification. Brezhnev's 1977 constitution curtailed much of the autonomy that Ukraine had enjoyed, despite the willingness of the regime to resort to arrest, exile, and intimidation.[34] Ukraine was subjected to the most severe

[31] Ibid., 126.
[32] Anatoly Dobrynin, *In Confidence: Moscow's Ambassador to America's Six Cold War Presidents 1962–1986* (New York: Times Books [Random House], 1995), 218.
[33] Raymond L. Garthoff, *Detente and Confrontation: American–Soviet Relations from Nixon to Brezhnev* (Washington, DC: The Brookings Institution, 1985), 100.
[34] David Kowalewski and Cheryl Johnson, "The Ukrainian Dissent: A Statistical Profile," *The Ukrainian Quarterly* 40: 1 (Spring 1984), 51.

form of repression in the USSR. By the end of 1976, thirteen of every twenty male political prisoners under "special" regime were Ukrainians. Of all female political prisoners in the USSR, one-quarter were Ukrainians.[35] There were, though, many differences between Stalin and Brezhnev. First, Brezhnev's method of rule relied primarily on co-optation of an atomized polity rather than on coercion. With economic policies based on massive transfers to agriculture and excessive generosity toward the military-industrial complex, living standards in Ukraine continued to improve, thereby pacifying large segments of the population. Furthermore, unlike Stalin, who in 1924 launched the doctrine of "socialism in one country," implying the withdrawal of the USSR from the international system, Brezhnev pursued a policy of détente as a means of reviving a sagging economy. As a result, he was far more constrained in his ability to root out dissidents.

At first, Ukraine's dissidents were not visibly different from other intellectuals who came of age in the 1960s, though Ukrainian *shistydesiatnyky* quickly distinguished themselves from dissidents in Moscow. As noted in previous chapters, Russian dissidents generally belonged to two groups: "Westernizers," whose chief goal was the democratization of the USSR, and nationalists, who deplored the Soviet cultural denuding of Russia. With the decline of ideology in Brezhnev's USSR and the growing emphasis on Russian nationalism, the Soviet regime managed to arrive at a *modus vivendi* with the Russian nationalists by accommodating their cultural agenda. Thus the Soviet authorities managed to split the Western-oriented democrats and the nationalists agitating in Russia.

The Ukrainian *shistydesiatnyky*, like their peers throughout the USSR, reacted to Khrushchev's thaw by preoccupying themselves with the universal human condition.[36] But when Ukrainian intellectuals started to uncover Ukraine's long-suppressed past, the Soviet security apparatus cracked down on them. While the Kremlin under Brezhnev tolerated, and even encouraged, the publication of Russian nationalist Village Prose, it banned Honchar's novel *Sobor* and suppressed any movement to restore Ukraine's historic churches or revive any other vestiges of a collective national memory. As Russian dissidents split into opposing camps during the 1970s, Ukrainian democratic and nationalist movements began to converge.

Despite the growing symbiosis of national assertion and democracy,

---

[35] Alexeyeva, *Soviet Dissent: Contemporary Movements for National, Religious, and Human Rights*, 46.

[36] George Luckyj, "Turmoil in the Ukraine," *Problems of Communism* 7 (1968).

Ukrainian dissidents still failed to develop a unified front. Drawing on its historic roots, dissent in Ukraine broke into two distinct orientations. The first, personified by Dziuba, challenged Moscow's nationality and economic policies as a violation of "Leninist standards." The other, represented by Valentyn Moroz, drew on the violent integralist fascist ideology of Dmytro Dontsov. The two orientations, national communists and neo-integral nationalists, tended to split along regional lines, with easterners, such as Dziuba and Leonid Pliushch, trying to combine nationalism with neo-Marxism, and westerners, such as Moroz and Ivan Hel, holding an integralist position. As Rudnytsky observed, however, both orientations represented a throwback to the two authoritarian traditions that had dominated Ukraine for most of the twentieth century and were out of step with most of the far more moderate Ukrainian population.

Meanwhile, events in Poland began to have an effect on Ukraine. Ever since Gomulka had successfully defended the prerogatives of national communism in Poland, Ukrainian dissidents had viewed Poland as a model, middle-sized Slavic state that managed to retain a modicum of independence and defend its culture. Solidarity's challenge to the Soviet regime and Pope John Paul II's defense of the Ukrainian Greek Catholic Church[37] inspired Ukrainians and prompted the poet Vasyl Stus to exclaim in a *samvydav* publication, "Long live the volunteer in the cause of Freedom! The Poles' defiance of Soviet despotism fills us with joy, and their national uprisings amaze us."[38]

By the 1970s, the Ukrainian dissident movement had combined the two intellectual legacies. The national communists increasingly moved toward cultural and political autonomy, if not outright independence, while the neo-integral nationalists rejected fascism. Both agreed that self-determination had to be attained through legal and peaceful means. The shift away from integral nationalism toward pluralism was accompanied by a shift of the center of dissident activity from Lviv to Kiev.[39] Rudnytsky described this new Ukrainian dissent under Brezhnev as "national patriotic." It was a movement that was alarmed by the eclipse of the Ukrainian language and Ukrainian culture and distressed by the excessive servility of the CPU

---

[37] See Ivan Hvat, *The Catacomb Ukrainian Catholic Church and Pope John Paul II* (Cambridge, MA: Harvard University Ukrainian Studies Fund, 1984).

[38] Quoted in Elizabeth Teague, *Solidarity and the Soviet Worker: The Impact of Polish Events on Soviet Internal Politics* (New York and London: Croom Helm, 1988), 177.

[39] Farmer, *Ukrainian Nationalism*, 178–79.

to Moscow. It was open and inclusive, following the path set by the poet Vasyl Symonenko, closely linking nationalism with democracy, the rule of law, and pluralism. Most Ukrainian dissidents characterized themselves as Marxists and federalists and found inspiration in the socialist bloc countries, not in the USSR.[40]

The shift from universal themes to an increasing preoccupation with nationhood was also reflected in the arts. The painter Opanas Zalyvakhas, defying the prevailing trends, called for "art on a national basis." As the political repression of the early 1970s radicalized Ukrainian dissent, a similar shift began to take place in the underground *Ukrainian Herald*, traditionally a champion of human rights. In 1974, the journal raised the issue of colonial domination of Ukraine. As Kenneth Farmer noted, although Ukrainian dissent was a creature of romantic intellectuals, intellectualism and rationalism, rather than romantic nationalism, remained the cornerstones of their value system.[41] Danylo Shumuk, a dissident and a political prisoner in both Poland and the USSR, summed up the views of many in the Ukrainian dissent movement:

> Only democracy can save mankind from the dangers of the rightist as well as leftist brands of tyranny. Only the unrestricted right, guaranteed by law, for all citizens to express, advertise, and defend their ideas will enable the people to control and direct the policy of the government . . . Where opposition does not exist, there can be no control over government policy . . . I have reached these conclusions after many years of thinking, stock-taking, and analysis, and they led me to adopt a critical attitude to both communists and Donstovan nationalists.[42]

While rejecting the forced Russification of Ukraine, the dissident movement in Ukraine eschewed anti-Russian sentiments, viewing the Russian people themselves as victims of the Soviet empire.[43] The 1980 programmatic declaration of the Ukrainian Patriotic Movement stated that "freedom for Ukraine will bring freedom for the Russian and other nations enslaved by the existing regime."[44]

The make-up of the Ukrainian Helsinki Group, whose leadership included Russians, Jews, Estonians, and Lithuanians, reflected the movement's commitment to a non-exclusive notion of nationalism.

[40] Luckyj, "Turmoil in the Ukraine," 20.
[41] Farmer, *Ukrainian Nationalism*, ch. 3.
[42] Rudnytysky, "Political Thought," in *Essays in Modern Ukrainian History*, 482.
[43] Jaroslaw Bilocerkowycz, *Soviet Ukrainian Dissent. A Study in Political Alienation* (Boulder, CO: Westview, 1988), 64–65.
[44] Rudnytysky, "Political Thought," 483.

Nevertheless, the group refused to be distracted by issues that did not relate directly to the implementation of the Final Helsinki Act, creating a degree of alienation between the dissidents in Moscow and Kiev.[45] The focus of the Helsinki Group on the cultural rights of Ukrainians diminished its international profile. It also forced the dissident workers in the Donbas to turn to dissidents in Moscow as a means of articulating their grievances.[46]

The narrow preoccupation of the Helsinki Group, however, did not mean that minority issues did not concern the Ukrainian intelligentsia. Inspired by Western notions of democracy, Ukrainian intellectuals, despite a state-sponsored anti-Semitic campaign and the popularity of anti-Semitic stereotypes among broad sectors of the population, consistently defended Jewish religious and cultural rights and saw the Jews as a vital ingredient of the country's mosaic.[47] In a similar spirit, some Ukrainian dissidents, led by General Petro Hryhorenko, took up the issue of the deportation of the Crimean Tartars.[48]

By the mid-1980s, Ukraine once again had a well-defined dissident movement, whose broad agenda ranged from merely increasing Ukraine's autonomy to achieving full independence in the framework of democratic pluralism. Led by humanist intellectuals and reacting to the human tragedy of this century, Ukraine's dissidents reached a consensus that democracy and independence would be attainable as the USSR democratized.

Although both the means and ends of democracy and independence were well defined, the dissident movement in Ukraine remained weak and vulnerable. First, the number of dissidents remained minute. Bohdan Krawchenko, in his 1972 study of Ukrainian society, identified only 942 active dissidents in Ukraine.[49] Second, in addition to its small numbers and chronic weakness, the dissident movement was unable to formulate a clear political position that appealed to the working class.[50] While the intellectual dissidents were stumbling in their efforts to reach the masses, Ukraine's

---

[45] Alexeyeva, *Soviet Dissent: Contemporary Movements for National, Religious, and Human Rights*, 52.
[46] Ibid.
[47] Note Dziuba's speech at Babi-Yar, Pvalychko's poem "Farewell."
[48] See Petr Grigorenko, *The Grigorenko Papers* (Boulder, CO: Westview Press, 1973).
[49] Bohdan Krawchenko, *Social Change and National Consciousness in Twentieth Century Ukraine* (Edmonton: Canadian Institute of Ukrainian Studies, University of Alberta, 1987), 250.
[50] See Bohdan Nahaylo, "Ukrainian Dissent and Opposition after Shelest," in *Ukraine after Shelest*, ed. Bohdan Krawchenko (Edmonton: Canadian Institute of Ukrainian Studies, University of Alberta, 1983), 37.

churches, and the Greek Catholic Church in particular, were building up grassroots organizations as defenders of Ukrainian national identity. The Greek Catholic Church, which since the late eighteenth century had represented west Ukrainian identity, had been disbanded in 1946 following the Council of Lviv and forcibly united with the Russian Orthodox Church. Nevertheless, the church remained ubiquitous in western Ukrainian life. In 1961, out of approximately 11,000 legal Orthodox parishes throughout the USSR, 8,500 were located in western Ukraine.[51] Most of these were perceived by the Kremlin as fronts for the underground Church, also known as the Catacomb Church. Fearing that the Greek Catholic Church had retained its grip on the west Ukrainian population, the Russian Orthodox Church attempted to bolster its legitimacy in Ukraine by making the Church more Ukrainian.

In 1966, for the first time since the eighteenth century, a Ukrainian was appointed Metropolitan of Kiev. Two years later, the first Ukrainian language prayer book was published. After 1969, all Ukrainian bishops were ordained in Kiev. The effort to Ukrainize and co-opt the church paralleled the efforts to Ukrainize the communist party and co-opt the young intellectuals. To stress the growing autonomy of the Ukrainian Church, the Kiev Patriarchate allowed the establishment of a nominally independent Department of External Affairs in 1969.[52] Still, the new Ukrainian clergy of the 1960s were loyal to the Soviet state. During a visit to the United States, Metropolitan Filaret of Kiev declared that "all" Ukrainians wished to belong to the Russian Orthodox Church.[53] The mere fact that the Orthodox Church, in competition with the ghost of the Greek Catholic Church, had to legitimize itself as a Ukrainian institution reinforced the sense of national identity among many Ukrainians who had not yet been affected by the nationalism of intellectuals in Kiev and Lviv. As a result, the Russian Orthodox Church in Ukraine, which since the days of Peter I had been a tool of Russification, found itself imitating the Greek Catholic Church four centuries earlier.

The Poles had established the Greek Catholic Church as a means of assimilating Ukrainian peasants to Catholicism. The Greek Catholic Church, however, transformed itself into a national institution. By 1970, the Russian Orthodox Church in Ukraine had reversed the role

---

[51] Bociurkiw, "The Orthodox Church and the Soviet Regime," 193.
[52] Ibid., 209.
[53] Quoted in Frank E. Sysyn, *The Ukrainian Orthodox Question in the USSR* (Cambridge, MA: Harvard Ukrainian Studies Fund, 1987), 19.

it had played since its incorporation into the Moscow Patriarchate in 1686. Now, reluctantly, the Orthodox Church became a carrier of Ukrainian national identity. It should be noted that the Ukrainization of Ukraine's Orthodox Church, much like the Ukrainization of the Communist Party in Ukraine, initially meant to legitimate the country's subservience to the Kremlin. However, the mere appearance of a distinct Ukrainian Church created for the first time an institution with its own interests which in time would vary with the patriarchate in Moscow. The growing nationalization of the Russian Orthodox Church in Ukraine had a limited impact on curtailing the presence of the Greek Catholic Church in western Ukraine. Many Greek Catholic Church clergymen ostensibly joined the Russian Orthodox Church, but remained what Vasyl Markus described as a "church within a church,"[54] profoundly attached to their traditional church. A smaller, more determined group joined the well-developed, illegal Catacomb Church, which enjoyed a degree of tolerance from the local authority.[55]

Ukraine's political landscape reflected all the paradoxes of the Brezhnev era. On the one hand, Ukraine retained the Shcherbytskyi leadership, one of the most hard-line, homogeneous political elites in the USSR, with its legitimacy in Moscow rather than among Ukrainians. At the same time, without the assistance of the Western media, Ukraine developed a resilient democratic opposition consisting of intellectuals from the broad grassroots network of the Greek Catholic Church in western Ukraine and nationalist intellectuals in Kiev, and even with some limited popular appeal in eastern Ukraine.

The majority of Ukrainians, however, remained atomized and apathetic. They had endured seventy years of harsh dictatorship – even in the context of Bolshevism. As the dissident poet Ivan Drach noted, "If they clip your nails in Moscow, they cut off your fingers in Ukraine."[56] The repressive Shcherbytskyi government, combined with the passivity of the population, slowed the arrival of glasnost in Ukraine. Decades of strong-arm rule and unquestioning loyalty to Moscow had formed an elite dependent on the survival of the Soviet Union.

---

[54] Vasyl Markus, *Religion and Nationalism in Soviet Ukraine After 1945* (Cambridge, MA: Harvard Ukrainian Studies Fund, 1985), 70.

[55] Ibid., 71.

[56] Quoted in Bohdan Krawchenko, "Glasnost and Perestroika in the USSR," in *Echoes of Glasnost in Soviet Ukraine*, ed. Romana M. Bahry (York University, Ont.: Captus University Press, 1989), 11.

Ukraine's drive to liberalization was further stymied by a mental state resulting from centuries of Polish and Russian colonial rule. As Oksana Garbowicz, drawing an analogy to Frantz Fanon's study of the Algerian case,[57] aptly observed:

> As Jung observed there is a clear relationship between the level of repression and a society's hypocrisy . . . Projection of the ruling society's collective shadow is highly damaging to the subordinate group. Since the dominant group is always perceived by the colonized people as superior, the colonized progressively identify with these projections and internalize them – that is, they come to believe these features as their own . . . the colonized people are forced not only to carry, but also to act, the shadow side of the dominant culture. In addition, the colonial subjects, because of their political and economic subordination in general, cannot project their own negative qualities (their collective shadow) unto the oppressor, but are forced to turn it against themselves.[58]

Given the broadly held belief in many Ukrainian circles that their own culture was inferior, and given the fatalism common among long-colonized people, the nationalist intellectuals found little popular support for their efforts, ensuring that Ukraine (other than its western periphery) would remain one of the most conservative and pliant polities in the USSR.

Shcherbytskyi's political machine included several powerful interlocking political clans. This political machine was supported by an impressive economic foundation. Ukraine not only enjoyed the status of a key producer of agricultural goods but also was home to a large part of the Soviet Union's metallurgy industry and large parts of the USSR's military-industrial complex. Both of these economic sectors were favored by the Brezhnev regime and received massive subsidies. The CPU *nomenklatura* exploited its privileged position and appropriated vast sectors of the Ukrainian economy as *de facto* private fiefs.

While a synthesis between nationalist and liberal national communists had been forming, the disaster at the nuclear power plant in Chernobyl in April 1986 accelerated the process, temporarily uniting both the national communists and the nationalists. The Kremlin's callous handling of the catastrophe accentuated Ukraine's quasi-colonial status. The disaster at Chernobyl was soon followed by the revelation of mass graves of victims of Stalinism in Kuropaty, Belarus,

---

[57] Franz Fanon, *Black Skins, White Masks* (New York: Grove Press, 1967).
[58] Oksana Garbowicz, "The Legacy of Colonialism and Communism," in *Perspectives on Contemporary Ukraine* 2: 2 (March–April 1995).

and Vynnitsa, Ukraine. These two seemingly unrelated events increasingly reinforced and accelerated the sense of bankruptcy in the notion of an ideologically based multinational state, energizing Ukraine's quasi-dormant nationalism.[59] The catastrophe came to symbolize the sorry state of Ukraine's environment and the neglect of Soviet rule, as Roman Solchanyk noted, and the nuclear power station also became a metaphor for Soviet misrule in general. People began talking about "a linguistic Chernobyl," "a cultural Chernobyl," and other such terms.[60] The Chernobyl disaster propelled the small, seemingly insignificant movement into a mass movement. Although the Ukrainian political elite continued to rule as "Little Russians," the rise of mass politics forced the Ukrainian *nomenklatura* to recognize that it might have to adopt the national cause if it wished to hold on to power, especially as the power of the Moscow center was receding.

As Ukrainians, in the wake of glasnost, began to catch up to their counterparts across the Soviet Union, the Ukrainian political elite tried at first to ignore them. Unlike the Baltic communist parties, which attempted to harness the energy of the intellectuals through popular fronts, and the Moscow elite, which competed in the recruitment of liberal intellectuals for Mikhail Gorbachev's central government or Boris Yeltsin's Russian government, Leonid Kravchuk, then the secretary for ideology of the CPU, insisted that a popular front was both unconstitutional and unnecessary in Ukraine. In his view, the CPU fulfilled all political modernizing functions.

The stubborn inertia of the CPU led to the defection of the intellectuals from the communist party to more liberal groupings, particularly the Ukrainian Popular Movement (*Rukh*).[61] Ukraine's hard-line regime continued to meet any challenge to its authority with harassment and intimidation and forced Ukrainian dissidents to seek protection through the authorities in Moscow. Only the direct intervention of Mikhail Gorbachev and the support of the CPSU forced the CPU to publish the draft program of *Rukh* in *Literaturna Ukraïna*, the organ of the Union of Ukrainian Writers.[62] In its draft program, *Rukh* presented itself as "a movement which recognizes the leading role of

[59] Raymond Pearson, "The Making of 89: Nationalism and the Dissolution of Communist Eastern Europe," *Nations and Nationalism* 1: 1 (1995), 69–79.
[60] Roman Solchanyk, *Ukraine: From Chernobyl' to Sovereignty* (Edmonton: Canadian Institute of Ukrainian Studies Press, University of Alberta, 1992), xii.
[61] See Taras Kuzio, "Restructuring from Below: Informal Groups in Ukraine under Gorbachev, 1985–89," in *Ukrainian Past, Ukrainian Present*, ed. Bohdan Krawchenko (Edmonton: University of Alberta, 1993).
[62] Ibid., 84.

the Communist Party [and] whose aim it is to assist the Communist Party in creating and working out a democratic mechanism."[63] Whereas the Baltic communist parties moved increasingly toward accommodation of the democratic forces challenging their power, the CPU continued to resort to brutal force. As late as October 1989, one month after the "retirement" of Shcherbytskyi, the city of Lviv experienced its own "bloody Sunday" when OMON troops broke up a procession commemorating the anniversary of the city's founding.[64] The sclerotic communist leadership faced a decline in its meager popularity. Disasters, such as Chernobyl and economic chaos in the Donbas, inflicted heavy damage on Ukraine and the CPU.

Nonetheless, the *nomenklatura* elite held on to power. As long as the challenge to their power remained fragmented, the ruling elite could play off the conflicting agendas of the splintered opposition movements.[65] Four key groups dominated the Ukrainian opposition: disillusioned Marxists, such as Dziuba; nationalists under Moroz's successors; democrats, clustered around the Helsinki Group; and industrial workers of the Russian-speaking east.

The agenda of the intellectuals in west Ukraine and Kiev called for democracy and the reversal of decades of forced Russification. They saw perestroika and, more important, glasnost as the means of furthering their goals. In contrast, the agenda of the coal miners and metal workers in the Donbas aimed to prevent any economic modernization that would reduce subsidies or shift coal production from Ukraine's nearly exhausted mines to the richer deposits of Siberia.[66]

The miners' protest passed through two distinct phases. The first phase began in July 1989 and was clearly economic. The miners held their demands to calls for better wages, safety equipment, pensions, soap, and other such limited goals. By 1990, however, the miners' protest had turned political, demanding an end to the autocratic rule of Moscow's all-union ministries and the adoption of local self-management.[67] Once the miners had turned on the center, *Rukh*'s

---

[63] Draft Program of the People's Movement of Ukraine for Restructuring (Rukh), February 1989.

[64] See E. Mikhailovskaia, *Ukraina: Politicheskiye partii i organizatsii* (Moscow: Panorama, 1992), 56.

[65] See Julian Birch, "The Nature and Sources of Dissidence in Ukraine," in *Ukraine in the Seventies*, ed. Peter J. Potichnyj (Oakville, Ont.: Mosaic Press, 1974).

[66] See David R. Marples, *Ukraine under Perestroika: Ecology, Economics and the Worker's Revolt* (New York: St. Martin's Press, 1991).

[67] Lewis H. Siegelbaum and Daniel Walkowitz, *Workers of the Donbas Speak: Survival and Identity in the New Ukraine 1989–1992* (Albany, NY: State University of New York, 1995).

leadership was able to build a coalition consisting of nationalists, moderates, and miners. The nationalists sought independence in order to preserve Ukrainian culture and the Ukrainian language. The moderates believed greater autonomy would put an end to exploitation by Moscow and lead to a better life. The miners, as stated, wanted better working and living conditions. The success of *Rukh* in building this coalition, bridging diverse interests and identities, was an unprecedented achievement that would not be repeated.

The convergence of various dissident movements culminated with logistical support from the communist authorities and formed a human chain stretching from Lviv to Kiev in 1990. This demonstration, which according to some accounts exceeded a million people, illustrated the phenomenal growth of the Ukrainian national movement, the new alliance between Ukraine's restless dissidents and the traditionally passive population, as well as its limits. Although this enormous chain was impressive, it remained very much a right-bank Ukraine affair. The Russified cities of the east did not take part; the human chain did not extend to either Kharkiv or Odessa, Ukraine's second- and third-largest cities, respectively.

Despite the opposition's growing unity, the CPU still believed that the CPSU would at some point reverse Gorbachev's liberal policies. Developments at the center were an aberration soon to be corrected. Accordingly, the Ukrainian political elite continued to resist the democratization of Ukrainian political life. In November 1989, the Ukrainian Supreme Soviet, increasingly dominated by national communists, adopted legislation making Ukrainian the official state language. When Yeltsin asserted Russia's sovereignty on June 12, 1990, Ukraine's leadership took another full month before emulating Russia on July 16. Yet even as perestroika and glasnost continued to erode Soviet power, the Ukrainian population remained remarkably atomized, making mass mobilization in Ukraine slow and uneven.[68]

Perhaps nothing indicated more clearly the difference between the Ukrainian party and the Baltic and Soviet communist parties than the failed coup of August 1991. Whereas Yeltsin and Leningrad Mayor Anatolii Sobchak organized mass opposition to the coup and the Baltic republics seceded from the Soviet Union, Ukraine's communist leadership under Kravchuk actually supported the coup, seeing in it

---

[68] Ukraine's state of political atomization may be most succinctly reflected in the Ukrainian folk expression: "Moia khata s kraiu nicheho ne znaiu" [My Home is on the Outskirts, I Do Not Know a Thing].

the end of Gorbachev's policies. The collapse of the coup induced the communist elite to embrace full political independence for Ukraine, but only as a means of self-preservation. Despite the odious past of the CPU, the process of adaptation by the old *nomenklatura* proved remarkably easy.

Even after the coup, the ability of the *nomenklatura* to manipulate the electorate in Ukraine remained undiluted. In March 1991, Ukraine's communist elite had rallied 70 percent of the electorate to support a "reformed Soviet Union." Eight months later, Ukrainians endorsed independence by an overwhelming majority of around 90 percent. Such a turnaround did not represent a revolution as much as the atomized nature of the Ukrainian polity and the elite's ability to agitate in the Soviet tradition, hindering democratic political mobilization and genuine political debate. As Alexander Motyl noted, the outcome of the 1991 referendum on independence was the product of a month of Soviet-style agitation and propaganda rather than genuine political dialogue about the country's future.[69] The elite of the defunct CPU marketed Ukrainian independence as a way to stop the broadly perceived economic exploitation by Russia. Even on this critical issue, however, it tolerated no genuine debate.

Until 1991 the Ukrainian *nomenklatura* had viewed its relationship with Moscow as a source of power and legitimacy. Following the failed coup and the rapid democratization in Russia, it became clear that further association with Moscow threatened the CPU's hold on power. The shift in the Ukrainian elite's attitude, from supporting a reformed union to supporting full independence, reflected their re-evaluation of self-interest. The rapid shift at the top bewildered the Ukrainian population. The Ukrainian sociologist Viktor Stepanenko described the population's attitude to the referendum on independence as follows: "Everyone is hoping for something better. They know what they do not want, a fraction of them know what they want, but no one knows how to achieve it."[70] Analyzing the reaction of the Ukrainian masses to democratization, the philosopher Oleh Bilyi noted:

> [Democracy] was understood by the mass consciousness as an ordinary resolution of a plenary session of the CPSU Central Committee. The only difference was that this "resolution" was based on

[69] Alexander J. Motyl, *Dilemmas of Independence: Ukraine after Independence* (New York: Council of Foreign Relations Books, 1993), 49.

[70] Viktor Stepanenko, "Ukrainian Independence: First Results and Lessons," *The Ukrainian Review* 40 (Summer 1993), 40.

real faith in a bright future . . . The main specificity of the induced
myth of democracy was the old schemata of catechism. In other
words, the affirmation of democracy was implemented in the mass
consciousness with the aid of traditional Stalinist ideological
methods, by way of endless scanning of the above-mentioned
identities in the question and answer forms and on the pages of
periodicals and on TV screens.[71]

As is often the case with post-colonial countries, the old native elite,
emboldened by the departure of the powerful mother country, proceeded to assert its authority and use the rhetoric of nationalism for
legitimization. Similarly, it no longer had to account to either the
external elite or its own citizenry. In the heavily atomized Ukrainian
society, with the overwhelming majority of the population fundamentally apolitical, Ukraine's communist elite succeeded in reinventing
itself. Paradoxically, the collapse of the USSR actually bolstered the
political and economic standing of the Ukrainian communist elite.
According to some estimates, as much as 85 percent of Ukraine's fixed
capital belonged to all-union ministries. With independence, the
Ukrainian *nomenklatura* gained control over this social property and
thus the country's wealth. This not only resulted in the stillbirth of
economic pluralism, an essential component of modern democracy, it
also led to the "re-monopolization" of the Ukrainian economy and an
even further tightening of the *nomenklatura*'s grip on the country.[72] In
reality, despite the nationalist rhetoric of the *nomenklatura*, especially
during the Kravchuk period, the Ukrainian communist elite was
etatist rather than truly nationalist. The main concern of the elite was
to preserve their political and economic hegemony over the territory
of Ukraine, with nationalism being a secondary issue.

Ukraine's historic commitment to social justice and the fear among
Ukrainian intellectuals that excessive pluralism would weaken
Ukraine's fragile statehood enabled Kravchuk to build a coalition in
which the democratic elements, including the leadership of *Rukh*, were
willing to overlook the CPU's oppressive past in order to strengthen
the Ukrainian state. By remaining committed to the defense of social
justice, Kravchuk appealed to industrial eastern Ukraine, where
workers feared economic liberalization would erode their privileged
economic position. Kravchuk's discovery of nationalism allowed him

[71] Oleh Bilyi, "Nihilism and Political Phantoms of the Post Communist Period," *Political Thought* 4 (1994), 114–15.
[72] See Serhii Rozhkov, "Ukraina: remonoploizatsia zamist' reform," *Politychna Dumka* 1: 5 (1995).

to co-opt large segments of the intellectuals and west Ukrainians who insisted on a sovereign and independent Ukraine. The industrial and agricultural oligarchy believed that Kravchuk, a member of the old guard, would not adversely affect their interests. Thus, Ukraine's communist elite harnessed the opposition and built a new power base, preserving their leading role in Ukrainian politics. As a result, the elite's economic and social policies continue to hamper Ukraine in its post-communist transition. Despite occasional rhetoric calling for fiscal austerity, successive governments have continued to subsidize both industry and agriculture. Between 1992 and 1995, this led to hyperinflation and a rapid depreciation of the currency.

The inflationary monetary policy pursued by the Ukrainian government retarded the formation of a civil society in several ways. Since economic success in Ukraine hinged on access to government subsidies, export licenses, arbitrary tax, and custom regulation, economic activity in Ukraine remained on the whole the preserve of the old party elite.[73] The hyperinflationary policies, while ultimately destructive to the national economy because they eroded savings and discouraged investment, served to bolster the political power of Ukraine's political elite. Virtually all economic actors, predominantly members of the *nomenklatura*, remained beholden to the state's credit and license policies.

The structure of the economy in Soviet Ukraine also played into the hands of the communist elite in Ukraine. The breakup of the USSR enabled the Russian elite involved in the energy and non-ferrous metals sectors to indulge in the wholesale export of readily saleable items, such as energy, non-ferrous metals, diamonds, and lumber, opening Russia to foreign presence and creating independent economic players with considerable economic and political power. The Ukrainian economy, however, is built on agriculture and an antiquated manufacturing industry geared to military production. There were few readily marketable manufactured goods. As a result, the collapse of the USSR led to relative economic isolation and the consolidation of a monopolistic structuring of the Ukrainian economy. This in turn created further economic distortions, discouraged foreign

---

[73] The abuse of licensure as a means to contain and extort from any emerging entreprenurial class manifested itself in November 1995 when the government passed a decree of a license fee of 4 million Krb. ($22) for all those engaged in commerce. The Lviv oblast amended the ordinance by issuing such licenses only to graduates of commercial institutes, triggering a black market in false diplomas.

investment, and further consolidated the elite.[74] Whereas many officials in Russia saw the collapse of Soviet trading patterns as a means of freeing themselves from disadvantageous relationships with the former Soviet republics and CMEA members, the Ukrainian elite realized that the only way for it to survive was to reinforce rather than dismantle Soviet-era economic distortions.

More important, however, has been the failure of privatization in Ukraine. Privatization is important to the transition because it tends to promote economic efficiency and can create independent economic players and pluralize society. Vaclav Klaus, prime minister of the Czech Republic, once remarked that privatization in the Czech Republic intentionally aimed at breaking the power of the communist-era oligarchy. In contrast, Ukraine's Prime Minister Yevhen Marchuk told the Supreme Rada in October 1995 that "privatization cannot be an end in itself."[75] Given the glacial pace of privatization in Ukraine, by Klaus' criteria, the power of the Ukrainian elite is far from broken.

While Ukraine's economic woes have captured the media's attention, a far more serious crisis continues to permeate Ukrainian politics: the crisis of national identity. Most Ukrainians, throughout the country and from all walks of life, support Ukraine's independence. The purpose and modality of Ukrainian statehood, however, are far from resolved. For most Ukrainian intellectuals, Ukraine, unlike Russia, is an inseparable part of Central European civilization. Whereas Muscovy's formative experience was the Tatar yoke, Ukraine's was the European traditions conveyed by Poland. Through the Polish–Lithuanian Commonwealth, Ukraine experienced the major European intellectual events, such as the Renaissance, the Reformation, and the Counter-Reformation, and had its own Baroque tradition. Most Ukrainian intellectuals believe that Ukraine's three centuries in the Russian empire and the Soviet Union unnaturally detached Ukraine from its natural cultural orbit. The primary purpose of Ukraine's independence was to return Ukraine to its natural state. As Dziuba emphatically stated, "Ukrainian history is a part of European history and not that of the Russian periphery."[76]

Along with distance from Russia's cultural, political, and economic

---

[74] For a comparative study of the liberalization of the Ukrainian economy, see *Nations in Transit: Civil Society, Democracy and Markets in East Central Europe and the Newly Independent States* (New York: Freedom House, 1995).

[75] Mattew Kaminski, "Ukraine Mixes its Economic Signals," *Financial Times*, 12 October 1995.

[76] Ivan Dziuba,"Ukraiina i svit," in *Quo Vadis Ukraine?* (Odessa: Maiak Publishing House, 1992), 11.

sphere of influence, Ukrainian statehood required strenuous efforts to rebuild links with Poland, Lithuania, Hungary, Slovakia, and the Czech Republic. As the historian Yaroslav Dashkevich has stated, many Ukrainian intellectuals felt that any association with Russia, including the Commonwealth of Independent States (CIS), was an act of treason since it forced Ukraine to cooperate with its "biggest enemy."[77] As a result, the ideology of a nationalism oriented toward Central Europe was accepted by Ukraine's political elite as a means of self-preservation and legitimization in a post-Soviet environment. The elite's co-optation of this dissident ideology had several unforeseen consequences.

First, the notion of "scientific Marxism–Leninism" was replaced by "scientific nationalism."[78] The first government of Ukraine discovered that the Central European Ukrainian idea, as articulated by intellectual dissidents and adopted by President Kravchuk, did not sit well with wide sectors of the population. The Ukrainian government's efforts to revive or create national myths and symbols proved a painful process that at times deepened debates over the essence of the Ukrainian ideal rather than resolving them. As Zenon Kohut noted, while some symbols and myths (such as the Zaporizhzhian Cossack Hetmanate, Ivan Mazepa, or Stalin's famine as an anti-Ukrainian genocide) were readily accepted, others (such as the activities of OUN–UPA in World War II) remained anathema to vast numbers of Ukrainians.[79] Even Hrushevskyi's school of historiography remained controversial among the millions of Ukrainians who had grown up believing Moscow to be the heir to Kievan-Rus and the bond between the "fraternal Russian and Belarussian peoples" to be eternal. It was not long before another Ukrainian concept arose, referred to here as a "national Slavic concept."

The national Slavic concept, which began in the Russophone areas of eastern and southern Ukraine, differed from the Central European concept in several ways. While supportive of Ukrainian independence to end what was perceived as Russia's economic exploitation and hegemony, the national Slavs continued to argue that independence

---

[77] See Yaroslav Dashkevich (round table discussion) in "Derzhavnij ustrij ta formi pravlinnia v ukrainii," in *Quo Vadis Ukraine?* 159–66.

[78] See Evgenii Bystritskii. "Pochemu natsionalizm ne mozhet byt' naukoi," *Politychna Dumka* 2 (1994), 33–40.

[79] See Zenon Kohut, "History as a Battleground: Russian Ukrainian Relationship in Historical Consciousness in Contemporary Ukraine," in *The Legacy of History in Russia and the New States of Eurasia*, ed. S. Frederick Starr (Armonk, NY: M. E. Sharpe, 1994).

was a means of attaining equal partnership with Russia, rather than escaping the Tatar East. In general, the national Slavs firmly believed in Ukraine's distinct culture and value system, and most accepted Hrushevskyi's thesis of Ukraine's distinct historic origins. Proponents of this view, however, argue that regardless of Moscow's claim to the inheritance of Kievan-Rus, Ukraine and Russia are bound by Byzantine Orthodox Christianity, common ancestry, three centuries of common statehood, and shared experiences, such as World War II. This has produced a cultural and human commonality that cannot simply be abandoned for either Central Europe or the West.[80]

The current political schism in Ukraine is unique because the divisions in Ukraine are not over the economic direction of the country but the meaning of Ukrainian statehood and identity. In Ukraine, perhaps more than in any other successor state to the USSR, there is a consensus on economics. Both the left and the right seem committed to gradualism, opposing both Poland's shock therapy and Russia's "wild east" capitalism. In fact, the economic debate that does exist is often couched in terms of defining national identity and devising a polity reflecting that identity. The schism over the national idea was clearly reflected in the summer of 1994, when Ukrainians elected Leonid Kuchma over incumbent President Leonid Kravchuk. During the campaign, Kuchma stressed the symbiotic relationship with Russia, while Kravchuk emphasized his efforts to build a distinct Ukrainian state.

The parties of the moderate right, consisting of *Rukh*, the Democratic Party of Ukraine and the Ukrainian Republican Party, all share a basic vision. While committed to the democratic process and to minority rights, they envision Ukraine as a unitary state with a central government dedicated to the gradual but systematic Ukrainization of the educational system, civil service, and armed forces. All three of these parties see Ukraine as a Central European state integrated into the European framework culturally, economically, and politically, and perceived by the international community as a fortress against the non-European East or, more specifically, Russia. The left-wing bloc in the *Rada*, consisting of the Communist Party of Ukraine, the Communist Party of Crimea, the Socialist Party of Ukraine, and the Peasant's Party of Ukraine, has its own vision of Ukrainian statehood. Whereas the moderate right insists on a unitary state, the left demands a

[80] See Orest Subtelny, "Russocentrism, Regionalism, and the Political Culture of Ukraine," in *Political Culture and Civil Society in Russia and the New States of Eurasia*, ed. Vladimir Tismaneanu (Armonk, NY: M. E. Sharpe, 1995).

bilingual and bicultural, federated Ukraine, with the transfer of most of the power to the local level, and each region pursuing its own economic and linguistic policies. In short, the moderate right emphasizes Ukraine's European heritage and the left stresses the features that Ukraine shares with Belarus and Russia.

Since Ukraine's independence, the political center has declined in numbers while a visible polarization of the political spectrum has taken place. The largest centrist faction in the *Supreme Rada* is the Interregional Bloc for Reforms. It advocates "controlled reforms" and a strategic alliance with Russia. Only the tiny parties – the New Wave Party, the Party of Democratic Rebirth of Ukraine, and the Christian Democratic Party of Ukraine, which collectively hold less than 2 percent of the seats in the *Rada* – articulate a centrist position on questions of economic transition and Ukraine's place in the world. Paradoxically, Ukraine's anti-democratic fringe parties on the extreme left and right, much like the country's body politic, also support economic gradualism and a mixed economy where the state plays a key role. As with the rest of the Ukrainian body politic, the extreme right in Ukraine is preoccupied with the question of national identity.

The extreme right in Ukraine consists of two major camps. The "nativist-nationalist camp" consists of splinter parties such as the State Independence of Ukraine, the Social National Party of Ukraine, and the Organization of Ukrainian Nationalists in Ukraine. The ideology of the nationalist bloc calls for a hierarchical, authoritarian state and is committed to opposing decadent Western "liberalism," which it considers "non-Ukrainian" and a tool of "Jewish-Moskal hegemony."[81] Ukraine, according to the nativist-nationalists, must work for the disintegration of Russia. The key goal of this grouping, however, is the creation of an ethnically homogeneous state, free of the impurities that have allegedly denied Ukraine its historic destiny.

A far more important group within the undemocratic right is the Ukrainian Nationalist Assembly (UNA), which takes an "imperial" view of Ukrainian identity. Like the nativists, UNA favors a hierarchical, corporatist polity that rejects Western liberalism as a foreign ideology designed to enslave Ukraine to the interests of world capital. There are, however, several key distinctions between UNA and the nativists. Whereas the nativists view Ukrainian identity as a blood relationship derived from common ancestry, the UNA considers it possible to acquire a Ukrainian identity. The leader of the UNA

---

[81] Roman Koval', *Pidstavy natsiokratii* (no publisher, 1994), 16.

faction in the *Rada*, Dmytro Korchynsky, noted, "By joining the UNA, any person becomes a Ukrainian." Whereas the nativists confine their political space to ethnographic Ukraine and see their main foe as ethnic minorities living in that space, the UNA ideology calls for a Eurasian bloc, stretching from the Adriatic Sea to the Pacific Ocean, centered in Kiev.[82] Ukraine's special mission, according to UNA, is to reconstitute Eurasian civilization across the former Soviet bloc. The main rival that the UNA must confront is not the minorities residing in Ukraine, but Russian hegemony, which usurped the historic position of Kievan-Rus Ukraine. UNA's ability to transcend the narrow national definition of Ukraine appeals to the great power nostalgia prevalent across the former Soviet Union and articulates an economic position opposing what it sees as the imposition of foreign solutions on Ukraine. UNA has therefore found resonance throughout Ukraine, making it one of the few political parties with a national presence.

The anti-democratic extreme left in Ukraine is represented by the Party of Slavic Unity. This fringe group's ideology is based on the belief that the twenty-first century will witness a struggle among civilizations: West European civilization, American–Israeli civilization, East Asian civilization, and Orthodox-Slavic civilization. Only through a pan-Slavic polity can Slavic civilization survive. Ukraine must stress its shared Slavic identity with other Slavic peoples rather than obsess about its own particularism.

The anti-democratic splinters have found scant support among Ukraine's masses, and their parliamentary representation remains minuscule. Still, the potential of the anti-democratic positions may be greater than their numbers suggest. Given the successful co-optation of the intellectuals by the old elite and the sense of political anomie in Ukraine, members of the radical fringe could present themselves as the sole source of opposition with an authentic, coherent, consistent political platform. Despite its electoral insignificance, the anti-democratic right has managed to radicalize the tenor of the political and economic debate in Ukraine, with the ruling elite trying to co-opt many of its ideas. The radicalization of the debate over Ukraine's identity has manifested itself not only in the political center's demise but, more ominously, in the radicalization of the democratic left and right.

On the left, the Socialist Party's calls for "socially just privatization"

---

[82] Oleksander Kovalenko, "Geopolytuchny orentatsyiina na mokrom piske," *Natsionalist* 18: 1 (1994), 14.

and integration with the CIS have been overshadowed by the Communist Party's hostility to Ukrainian nationalism and calls for an end to economic reforms and a confederation with Russia. On the right, both *Rukh* and the republican parties have drifted away from an inclusive, "post-integral nationalism" and toward defensive and exclusive nationalism.[83] The polarization taking place over the identity of Ukraine and its place in the international system has led to flare-ups over issues that in most other countries might go completely unnoticed.

For example, President Kuchma's decision to travel to Moscow to celebrate the fiftieth anniversary of the victory over Nazi Germany provoked accusations in western Ukraine that he was celebrating a "genocidal victory" and a "crime against humanity." The decision by various Ukrainian oblasts to terminate Russian television broadcasts, mainly due to the non-payment by Russia for use of air time, has provoked bitter recriminations between the Russophones and the authorities.[84] The former accuse the authorities of "fascist nationalism," and the latter accuse the Russophones of "Bolshevism" or a reversion to "the Little Russian complex," reviving the chasm between Ukraine's left and right in a manner reminiscent of the divide within the Ukrainian dissident movement during the late 1950s and early 1960s, when the actors in the western and eastern parts of the country were concerned with starkly different issues. Few political actors have been able to bridge the gap. While in the Russian-speaking east there has been a growing chorus of complaints about "forced Ukrainization" and even violence when the dubbing of the popular soap opera *Santa Barbara* was switched from Russian to Ukrainian, the nationalist intelligentsia feels that independent Ukraine has failed to nourish the country's distinct culture. The former dissident poet Ivan Drach, during the opening of the Congress of the Ukrainian Intelligentsia, lamented:

> We, representatives of Ukraine's intelligentsia, attest to the following: with the exception of the 1930s, when the Bolsheviks rooted out practically all the leaders of our culture, sciences, and technology, and destroyed a third of the Ukrainian nation, *Ukraine has not gone through such a de-Ukrainization as we have today [1995].*[85]

---

[83] The change in the mind set of Rukh was reflected in the Conference of Ukrainian Intellectuals discussed below.

[84] Matthew Kaminski, "Ukraine's Old Guard Kills Off TV News," *Financial Times*, 15 February 1996.

[85] Marta Kolomayets, "Intelligentsia Notes Continuing Threat to Ukrainian Culture," *The Ukrainian Weekly* 62: 47 (November, 1995), 19 (emphasis added).

The emergence and consolidation of regional political parties is a worrisome symptom of the growing polarization of Ukraine. With the existence of a relative consensus about the country's economic agenda, the debate about Ukraine's long predicament and the essence of Ukrainian statehood shifted to foreign policy and the crucial relationship with Russia.

Ukraine's "Rite of Passage" is by no means complete; the dynamics of Ukrainian nationalism continue not to be synchronized, leading to different "national" agendas advocated by various regions. While, after five years of independence the Ukrainian state is accepted as a legitimate entity across most of the country, there is little agreement as to the purpose of that statehood. The regional differences that played a crucial role in shaping the fortunes of Ukraine during the 1917–20 tumult and during World War II, continue to beset the Ukrainian polity. Key issues such as whether Ukraine is to become a culturally unitary state or bilingual, whether Ukraine is part of the "European" or "Eurasian" civilization, which Ukrainians served their country's needs during the Second World War, and many others remain a salient presence in Ukraine's political life. Until a time when such basic issues of national identity will be settled, Ukraine's political posture, both at home and abroad, will remain halting and uncertain.

# 10 Foreign policy as a means of nation building

The collapse of the Soviet Union and Ukraine's subsequent attainment of independence may well prove to be the most propitious developments in Eastern European history since the collapse of the Ottoman, German, and Habsburg empires after World War I. Unlike the disintegration of the older empires, which occurred after four years of war, the recent proliferation of East European states was the result of the sudden Soviet implosion. Almost overnight, Ukraine was transformed from a compliant fiefdom of the Communist Party of the Soviet Union and its Ukrainian satrapies into one of Europe's largest states, located between a disgruntled Russia and an enlarging NATO. And unlike the post-Versailles states, which basked in the glow of international attention, Ukraine's independence went almost unnoticed by the international community. Although such countries as Hungary, Poland, and Canada quickly recognized Ukraine's independence, the United States and Germany first tried to breathe life into the faltering Soviet Union and then focused on Russia. Both the suddenness and remoteness of Ukraine's independence complicated its sense of nationhood.

This rapid metamorphosis deprived Ukraine of several vital building blocks of nation building. Because of its peaceful, almost uneventful transformation, Ukraine lacked a unifying national mythology and heroes. Although some nationalists called for a new, distinct Ukrainian political and cultural awareness, especially in foreign affairs and language policy, most Ukrainians found this agenda unappealing. Furthermore, Ukrainians could neither look to a common national experience for a "usable past" nor follow Israel's example and use their own experience of genocide (The Great Famine) as a nation-defining experience because, in George Grabowicz's words, "the perpetrators of its [Ukraine's] former suppression, and at the very least the co-conspirators of this policy [of suppression], are still part of the establishment."[1] This lack of national cohesion was soon revealed when the original grand coalition of Russian-speaking blue-collar workers, *nomenklatura* of the Soviet-era Communist Party of Ukraine (CPU), and democrats, who had secured 90 percent of the votes for Leonid Kravchuk and independence in 1991, disintegrated.[2]

Ukraine, apart from Galicia, unlike the emerging polities of Slovenia, Slovakia, or Croatia, had never embraced a solely ethnic identity that could tie its political and national agendas together. Not only does Ukraine have an ethnic Russian minority population of 20 percent, but the divide between Ukrainian- and Russian-speaking Ukrainians has hindered what Dominique Arel calls the "nationalization" of the state.[3] Despite President Kravchuk's attempts at nationalization, regional divisions largely negated his plans, as the 1994 presidential elections demonstrated. The majority of support for the "nationalist" Kravchuk came from west of the Dnieper while the populist Russophone east gave its mandate to Leonid Kuchma, who had concentrated on the disastrous condition of the economy to the exclusion of all other issues, including nationalism.[4] Kravchuk's defeat demonstrated that large segments of Ukraine's population are not sufficiently nationalistic to allow nationalism alone to provide politicians with sufficient legitimacy to remain at the political helm. Kravchuk, unlike Franjo Tudjman in Croatia or Slovakia's Vladimir Meciar was unable to use nationalism as a substitute for economic performance. Furthermore, in the case of Ukraine, the use of nationalism, with Russia as the "other," not only did not galvanize the population but actually deepened the regional divisions across Ukraine. Given the historic, cultural, and psychological fissures across Ukraine, the use of nationalist rhetoric divided rather than consolidated the polity. For these reasons, Ukraine became a state without a clear sense of national identity and legitimacy and remains plagued by these deficiencies to this day.

Some Ukrainian observers have argued that had Ukraine's elite, namely the *nomenklatura* and nationalist intellectuals, pursued wiser

[1] George S. Grabowicz, "The Politics of Culture in Today's Ukraine," Ivan Franko Lecture at Carlton University, Ottawa, 12 April 1993.
[2] Marta Kolomayets, "Intelligensia Noted Threat to Ukraine's Culture," *The Ukrainian Weekly* 43: 47 (19 November 1995).
[3] Dominique Arel, "Ukraine: The Temptation of the Nationalizing State," in *Political Culture and Civil Society in Russia and the New States of Eurasia*, ed. Vladimir Tismaneanu, New York and London: M. E. Sharpe, 1995).
[4] For the role of nationalism in Kravchuk's political strategy, see Taras Kuzio, *Ukraine: the Unfinished Revolution*, Institute for European Defense and Strategic Studies (UK): (London: Alliance Publishing, 1992).

economic policies, they could have legitimized an independent Ukraine just as the *Wirtschaftswunder* helped legitimize West German democracy in the 1950s. This argument fails to note, however, that such an economic revival would have required radical reform and the evisceration of the former CPU *nomenklatura*, which, in the words of Oleh Havryslyshyn, had become a "rentier-capitalist" elite, whose profits depended on the economic system remaining highly dirigist and regulated by the state."[5] As a result of the elite's hold on both industrial and farm production, Ukraine's economic development bears far greater resemblance to the stagnation, corruption, and exploitation of natural resources that Frantz Fanon described in sub-Saharan post-colonial countries in Africa, than to the other states of Eastern Europe, let alone the Asian tigers.[6]

Furthermore, Ukrainians were led to believe that independence would bring with it economic prosperity. Economic reforms proved to be too few and were often carried out in response to reforms in the Russian Federation, such as the liberalization of prices and the elimination of the ruble zone. As a result, Ukrainians found themselves both psychologically disoriented and financially devastated. In contrast to Poland, where by 1990 the economy had effectively collapsed leading most citizens to accept Finance Minister Leszek Balcerowicz's radical reforms as a vital step to "returning to Europe," neither Ukrainian nationalists nor leftists seriously contemplated liberal economic reforms.

Accordingly, Ukraine's political elite conformed to a familiar post-colonial pattern: it sought political legitimacy through the manipulation of foreign policy. Such action has traditionally served as an instrument in nation building among post-colonial, "non-historical" entities that view themselves, in Mark von Hagen's words, as "innocent victims of other nations in a litany of heroic but ultimately tragic (previous) struggles for national independence."[7] Ukraine proved no exception to this pattern as Kravchuk ignored the need for economic reform in favor of an assertive, nationalistic foreign policy. Kravchuk's experience suggests that nationalism plays a less significant role in Ukraine than elsewhere in Eastern Europe, and Kravchuk's embrace of an assertive foreign policy at the expense of

---

[5] Oleh Havryslyshyn, "Ukraine's Economic Crisis and Western Financial Assistance," *Political Thought*, no. 3 (Kiev, 1994), 164.

[6] I owe the analogy to Fanon to George S. Garbowicz's article, "Ukrainian Studies: Framing the Contexts," *Slavic Review* 54: 3 (Fall 1995).

[7] Mark von Hagen, "Does Ukraine Have a History?" *Slavic Review* 54, no. 3 (1995), 665.

necessary economic reforms eventually led to his downfall. While Poland and the Czech Republic attempted to establish identities as modern European nations through bold economic reforms, Kravchuk focused only on foreign policy to increase Ukraine's visibility abroad and to gain domestic support at home. Most important, his foreign policy called for an equitable distribution of formerly Soviet assets, international (especially Russian) recognition of Ukraine under international law, and the establishment of a Ukrainian army. Initially, this assertiveness found broad support across the Ukrainian political spectrum. Ukraine's centuries-old history as an "invisible nation," and its division betwen Poland and Soviet Russia shortly after the end of World War I,[8] provided the psychological basis for this support.

### Development of Kravchuk's foreign policy

Support for Kravchuk (an astounding 90 percent of the electorate in 1991) resulted from his success in uniting such disparate groups as the old *nomenklatura* and nationalist dissident intellectuals during the heady early days of independence. However, the ideals espoused by the pro-independence camp enjoyed such success because they were general. Independence meant different things to different people. The *nomenklatura* interpreted independence as freedom *from* instability, namely the tumultuous events resulting from the rapidly decaying authority of Soviet power in Moscow, while foreign policy stood at the periphery of their concerns. In contrast, nationalist intellectuals saw independence as the chance to establish an assertive foreign policy, lest Russia once again attempt to subjugate Ukraine. Nationalist interest in economics proved as superficial as the *nomenklatura*'s interest in foreign policy. Most of the nationalists came from the fields of history, law, or the fine arts. Not surprisingly, the divergent interests of the two groups allowed the nationalists to fashion Ukrainian foreign policy in their own image, while the *nomenklatura* focused on consolidating its economic privileges, thus ushering in hyperinflation and economic instability.

Although the nationalists were by no means monolithic, virtually all agreed on foreign policy matters. They espoused Mykhailo Hrushevskyi's theory of a unique Ukrainian identity grounded in an anti-Russian, pro-Western orientation, rejecting the Russian interpretation

---

[8] Poland's forced annexation of Galicia was confirmed by the Council of Allied Ambassadors in March 1923.

of the 1654 Pereiaslav Agreement as an act of "reunification" with Russia, and viewed Ukraine's reintegration into Central Europe and the West as essential. Furthermore, they called for a policy of standing up to Russia, not only to carve out an independent international profile for Ukraine, but also to establish an image as a European outpost defending the civilized world against Asian Russia. Specifically, the nationalists viewed integration into Central Europe as the most effective means of guaranteeing stability and long-term integration into the West as a whole. Not only would integration help to anchor Ukraine's identity firmly in the West, it would also provide security against Russian advances. Taking the nationalists' cue, Kravchuk proceeded to focus on Western integration and assert Ukraine's independence from Russia. In May 1992, at the beginning of his presidency, he declared that Poland would soon take over Russia's role as Ukraine's main economic partner.[9] Almost all nationalists assumed that Russia would soon rediscover its traditional hostility toward the West and once more expand beyond its borders. Ukraine would become a modern-day *antemurale christatis* to contain its eastern neighbor. As Kravchuk's defense minister, Konstantyn Morozov, stated:

> It is probably by now axiomatic that an independent, powerful, democratic Ukraine makes Russia as an empire impossible, and conversely, as soon as Russia swallows up Ukraine, she will become an imperial super-state, with her foreseeable inclination towards a renewed Cold War. I do not think that this would please the peoples of the developed countries . . . By appeasing growing Russian ambitions, the US government encourages conflict between the western and eastern regions of Ukraine.[10]

Relying on the above noted constructs the Kravchuk team formulated a list of the central assumptions of the Ukrainian foreign policy paradigm:
1 Russia alone poses an immediate threat to the existence of the Ukrainian state.
2 Before long, Russian imperialism will resurface to threaten the international system.
3 Russia's acceptance of Ukraine is merely provisional, and before long Russia will try to impose its will on the Ukrainian people.
4 Ukraine's natural allies in containing Russia are not the West

---

[9] *Życie Warszawy*, 20 May 1992.
[10] Konstantyn Morozov, "Ukrainian Independence in the International Context," *Perspectives on Contemporary Ukraine* 2: 2 (January–February 1995).

Europeans and Americans, given their shaky historical record of support, but the Central European states once under Soviet hegemony. Therefore, Ukraine should revive Piłsudski's vision of a Baltic–Black Sea Bloc including the Višegrad group (Hungary, the Czech Republic, Slovakia, and Poland), Turkey, and, possibly, Germany.[11]

5 Within the Commonwealth of Independent States (CIS), Ukraine should steadfastly block any efforts by Russia to turn the organization into a supranational, neo-imperialist Russian puppet, but instead support other independent-minded CIS states to resist potential Russian aggression.

6 Ukraine should raise its international profile by fostering special relations with countries containing large populations with Ukrainian roots (e.g. Canada, the United States, Israel, Australia, and Brazil).

Ukraine's most influential nationalist group, *Rukh*, also shared many of the same concerns. Referring to a medieval enemy of Kievan Rus, Ivan Drach even described Boris Yeltsin as someone who "suffers from an Andrei Bogolyubskyi complex."[12] In addition to backing Kravchuk's measures in general, *Rukh*'s leaders proposed several more security initiatives, including the following:

1 More intensive security and economic cooperation with the Baltic–Black Sea Bloc.

2 Ukraine's withdrawal from the CIS.

3 A carefully neutral, bilateral foundation of relations with Russia based on Ukrainian national interests.

4 In general, a greater focus on guarded neutrality and national interests in order to avoid enervating alliances.[13]

5 An economically egalitarian approach to European integration, aimed at preventing great economic disparities between nations.

Initially, this Western focus of Kravchuk's foreign policy did not inspire the same level of support in Russian-speaking eastern and southern Ukraine as it did among nationalist intellectuals. Nevertheless, Russia's economic implosion in 1992, combined with rampant

---

[11] Ihor Koval, "Ukraina i vostochnaia evropa v poiskakh regional'noi bezopasnosti," in *Ukraian i rossia: Osnovnye napravlenia vneshnepolitichskoi diatel'nost*, ed. S. E. Appatov and B. A. Schmelov (Odessa: Logos Press, 1994).

[12] Andrei Bogolyubskyi, the prince of Suzdal-Rostov (in modern-day Russia), sacked Kiev in 1169. See Ivan Drach, "Will Russia Repent?" *The Ukrainian Quarterly* 40: 3 (Autumn 1993) 3.

[13] The All-Ukrainian Congress of the Popular Movement, "Rukh," *A Concept of State Building in Ukraine* (Kyiv, December 4–6, 1992) 12.

poverty and the rapid growth of organized crime, gave Kravchuk's Western paradigm legitimacy as a viable alternative and won general support both at home and abroad. Among the other countries that emerged from the Soviet Union, the Baltic states enthusiastically embraced Ukraine's foreign policy, as did the newly independent nations of the Transcaucasus, especially as their own links with Russia deteriorated. All in all, Kravchuk's foreign policy enjoyed considerable success in establishing Ukraine as a player on the international scene during the first months of independence.

### Kravchuk's Russia policy

Above all else, Kravchuk stressed the importance of distancing Ukraine from Russia on both practical and symbolic levels. One of his first acts as president was to unilaterally move Ukraine out of Moscow's time zone, a move that created tremendous confusion with the jointly operated railroad and airway systems. On a more pragmatic level, he led the drive to resist the Kremlin's efforts to turn the CIS into a supranational body. In arms control negotiations, he defied Russia's claim that Russia was the sole successor state to the USSR, insisting instead that Ukraine held the right to represent its positions independently rather than through Moscow's "collective voice" for the four new nuclear powers.

Perhaps the most contentious issues were those involving former Soviet property located in the newly independent states and Soviet foreign debt. Ukraine alone among the post-Soviet states insisted on assuming both debts and property in proportion to each republic's population (which, in the case of Ukraine, was 18 percent of the former Soviet Union), while the other Soviet republics agreed to let Russia retain Soviet property in exchange for assuming responsibility for Soviet debt. Kiev feared that, unless it adhered strictly to international law, the international community would relegate Russo-Ukrainian relations to an "internal Russian affair," as with Chechnya. Ukraine's deputy prime minister, Ihor Yukhnovsky, openly stated that Ukraine's legalistic rationale for taking on its share of Soviet debt was an effort to conform to international law.[14]

Ukraine's defense policy also defined Ukrainian national identity "against" Russia. Painfully aware of the territorial losses of the seventeenth century and, more recently, during Ukraine's brief period

[14] *Moscow News*, 20 January 1993.

of independence in 1917–20, Kravchuk called for an extravagant security budget, including an army of 400,000 men, an ocean-going fleet, and Ukrainian ownership of nuclear weapons inherited from the USSR. Although this agenda angered the West, it went further in raising Ukraine's profile abroad and enjoyed popular support.

Initially, Kravchuk's foreign policy scored several major victories at home and abroad. Ukraine, previously the perennially invisible nation, had finally managed to assert itself on the international stage, securing diplomatic ties with more than 100 countries. Ukraine's insistence on autonomous participation in arms control reduction talks, including the Lisbon Conference, where the newly independent states agreed to relinquish their part of the Soviet nuclear arsenal in accordance with the START (strategic arms reduction talks) Agreement, further solidified Ukraine's credentials as an independent state. Its smooth assumption of vast amounts of Red Army material guaranteed that it would be one of the few post-Soviet states without any Russian military presence. Within the CIS, Ukraine successfully thwarted the Kremlin's efforts to promote a unified economic and defense policy; this policy included supporting Georgia's territorial integrity, backing Azerbaijan's position in the Nagorno-Karanbakh conflict, and supplying weapons to both countries as well as volunteers to Georgia.[15] For Kravchuk, however, reorientation toward Central Europe was just as important as standing up to Russia.

### Ukraine and Central Europe

While the relationship with Russia deteriorated into acrimonious exchanges over the Black Sea Fleet, Soviet debts and properties, and disputed borders, Ukraine's relations with Central Europe made a much more propitious start. Poland not only promptly recognized Ukraine (the first non-CIS country to do so), but also signed the Treaty of Good Neighborliness (May 1992), which renounced all territorial claims, thereby resolving the central conflict that had impeded the normalization of relations between the two peoples since the seventeenth century. Hungary also agreed to a similar treaty that, among other things, guaranteed minority rights in both countries. Outside Eastern Europe proper, Ukraine reached an accord with Turkey calling for a Black Sea "cooperative zone." In short, Kravchuk's

---

[15] See Ukrainian Centre for Independent Political Research, *UNA-USPD: Faces of Ukrainian Nationalism*, no. 5 (Kyiv, June 1995).

careful cultivation of Central European ties seemed to reap substantive awards.

Despite these victories, however, Kravchuk gravely miscalculated both the agendas of his Western partners and the ability of his CIS allies to resist Moscow's encroachments. Although the Višegrad states welcomed Ukraine as an independent Eastern European state and signed agreements on environmental, trade, and cultural issues, their own economic and security priorities differed fundamentally from Ukraine's agenda. First and foremost, the Višegrad group sought membership in the European Union at the earliest possible moment.[16] This aim fueled their reform efforts and justified the economic pain behind the economic reforms, which started in 1990. In economic terms, seeing their future prosperity linked to a rapid shift of their production to more high value-added items, marketable in the wealthier economies, these nations cut their economic links with the impoverished East and concentrated on the lucrative markets in the West. The only substantial trade between Central Europe and the CIS that survived was for Russian energy imports and participation in energy infrastructure projects, ventures that included Belarus and Poland but not Ukraine.

By contrast, the Ukrainian *nomenklatura*'s consolidation of its control over the Ukrainian economy soon guaranteed that stagnation and decline, rather than reform, would characterize the Ukrainian economy. As a result, Ukraine's economy remained one of the least reformed in the former Soviet bloc, even in traditionally strong areas like agriculture. Although Kravchuk reoriented Ukraine's political profile from Russia to the West, he unwittingly increased Ukraine's economic dependence on Russia. By aborting a single economic space, Kravchuk alienated Moscow and hastened the imposition of higher prices for Russian energy imports, thereby saddling Ukraine with excessive debt. The debt to Russia grew very rapidly not only because of the gross inefficiency of its industrial users, but also because a vast amount of Russian energy was still available at prices below world levels and was simply resold by a corrupt elite pocketing the profits. Consequently, a basis for substantive economic cooperation between unreformed Ukraine and radically reforming Central European markets remained illusory.

Security issues also divided Ukraine and Central Europe. While

---

[16] In fact, the Višegrad group was formed under pressure from the European Union (EU) to induce the postcommunist states to formulate a joint approach to the EU.

both camps viewed a potentially resurgent Russia as their primary threat, their specific proposals for containing Russia had almost nothing in common. The Soviet collapse and the emergence of an independent Belarus and Ukraine separated Central Europe from a direct Russian threat.[17] This new geopolitical reality raised Višegrad hopes for membership in NATO. In contrast, Ukraine's proposal of a Baltic–Black Sea Bloc won virtually no support in Central Europe, except for some right-wing fringe Polish politicians and President Lech Wałęsa, who saw a regional military alignment as an inter-mediary step toward full membership on NATO. Most Central European politicians feared that such an alliance would reduce their chances for NATO membership and a good working relationship with Russia and, at the same time, again relegate Central Europe to its historical position as a gray zone.

As noted before, while in Central Europe the notion of a "Third Bloc" was the agenda of a fringe, Kravchuk's foreign policy establish-ment saw these proposals as a final push out of Russia's orbit. With a potential total population of 100 million and potential access to the world's third largest nuclear arsenal, the bloc (in Kravchuk's eyes) could effectively ensure the region's security and thwart Russian expansionism, thereby winning Western support. His arguments, however, failed to win support from the Višegrad countries. Further-more, Kravchuk undermined his own credibility regarding security issues with his intransigence toward the Lisbon Protocols' demand that Ukraine turn over its nuclear weapons to Russia for destruction.

By 1993, Kravchuk's foreign policy was becoming increasingly controversial and ineffective. Ukraine's relationship with Central Europe failed to move beyond vague affirmations of support, while vital cooperation on security and economic concerns proved impos-sible. The divergence of agendas became even starker in 1993 as the Višegrad nations officially began their drive for NATO membership. To shore up US support, the Central Europeans began to downplay their sympathy for Ukraine in light of its reluctance to abide by the Lisbon Protocols. Despite NATO's insistence that no outside power could veto its expansion, the Višegrad countries also began to culti-vate closer ties with Russia in the hope of deflating its opposition to NATO expansion. Although rhetorically the governments of the Czech Republic, Hungary, and Poland insisted that their drive to join

---

[17] Russia, of course, did retain a foothold in Central Europe by holding on to the enclave of the Kalinigrad district.

NATO was a sovereign decision, these countries remained aware that a rift with Moscow would only complicate their drive toward NATO membership.

To counter the deterioration in relations, Ukraine tried to strengthen its own ties with Central Europe by hosting official visits from Poland's president, foreign minister, premier, and defense minister in the spring of 1993. In April, Kravchuk proposed a "Central European Initiative," consisting of the Višegrad group, the Baltic states, Ukraine, and Belarus – but not Russia. Although Polish President Lech Wałęsa responded positively to the proposal during his May visit, the plan went nowhere. The plan was fatally crippled the following month when Yeltsin informed Poland that Russia might tolerate NATO expansion, thus implying that closer ties to Ukraine could possibly ruin Polish hopes for NATO membership. Poland dropped further talk of a Central European initiative, leaving Kravchuk isolated and embarrassed when he met Yeltsin at Massandra, in September of 1993, to discuss Russian demands to resolve the Black Sea Fleet issue.

### Ukraine and the West

Ukraine's relationship with the West, particularly the United States, revolved primarily around nuclear disarmament. Accordingly, as Washington continued to insist on Ukrainian adherence to the Lisbon Protocols and Kravchuk resisted, their relationship soured. Until visits by Ambassador to the CIS Strobe Talbott in May 1993 and Secretary of State Warren Christopher in October, the American–Ukrainian relationship consisted primarily of haggling over the nuclear issue. Only after these two visits did Washington switch from a policy of single-minded insistence on disarmament to a focus on trilateral negotiations. Ultimately, this move led to the Trilateral Accord in January 1994, which established a mechanism to oversee the dismantling of the Ukrainian arsenal. Nevertheless, Kravchuk never fully overcame his international reputation for deceit and unreliability. Despite the attention lavished on the reforming economies of Central Europe by the US government and business community, Kravchuk refused to confront Ukraine's disastrous economic decline and bring his nation into the international economic community.

Ukraine's relations with Western Europe also failed to blossom. Attempts to revive Ukraine's historic, and sometimes dubious, relationship with Germany quickly deteriorated.[18] Kravchuk attempted to cultivate Germany by visiting that country even before the demise of the Soviet Union and by promising to resettle parts of the German population scattered across the former Soviet Union. Relations between Germany and Ukraine, however, started poorly, when Kravchuk failed to fulfill his promise to resettle ethnic Germans in Ukraine who had been deported to Central Asia and Siberia from the Kherson region after World War II. The German Green Party insisted that Ukraine move swiftly to decommission its dangerous power stations. Furthermore, as long as thousands of Russian troops remained on East German soil, Chancellor Helmut Kohl preferred to maintain the best of relations with Russia to expedite withdrawal. Thus, Bonn, also frustrated over Ukraine's non-compliance with the Lisbon Protocols, kept a distance from Russo-Ukrainian disputes. Unlike the countries of Central Europe, Russia, and the Baltic states where, following the Cold War, a German economic and political presence became ubiquitous, the levels of German exchange with Ukraine remained low.

France, hoping to establish a counterbalance to a unified Germany, also played up to Russia and thus took a dim view of Ukraine's efforts to keep Russia out of Europe. Finally, lingering frustration over Kiev's inability to adequately handle the effects of Chernobyl negatively affected relations with Western Europe. Ukraine continued to insist on energy independence, which meant relying on notoriously unsafe nuclear reactors. This only brought a great amount of Western criticism of Ukraine's policy as short-sighted, irresponsible, and dangerous. Kravchuk's intransigence and misplaced assertiveness created a perception of Ukraine as a spoiler state bent on obstructing the emergence of a new security system stretching from Vancouver to Vladivostok.

### Demise of Kravchuk's foreign policy

Kiev's souring relations with Moscow triggered the economic and political crises that doomed both Kravchuk and his foreign policy. Immediately following the December 1991 Belovezhsk Agreement among Russia, Ukraine, and Belarus, which officially dissolved the USSR and created the CIS, Moscow and Kiev engaged in a bitter exchange over the future status of CIS states. The two governments

---

[18] See Hans-Joachim Torke and John-Paul Himka, eds., *German–Ukrainian Relations in Historical Perspective* (Edmonton & Toronto: Canadian Institute of Ukrainian Studies, 1994)

fundamentally differed over whether the CIS should follow independent or collective – and Russia-dominated – economic and defense policies. Kiev called for a civilized divorce codified in autonomous, bilateral agreements between states, while Russia insisted on a "joint economic and security space." Ukraine promptly established its own defense ministry, while Russia recognized former Soviet Marshall Dmitry Shaposhnikov as the official CIS defense minister.

Russia also continued to exert considerable economic control by insisting that the ruble remain the sole or dominant currency throughout the CIS. In 1990–91, Kravchuk had already introduced the *karbovonets* as a temporary Ukrainian currency in hopes of stopping Russian commuters from draining Ukraine's relatively well-stocked stores. At the same time, however, Kravchuk was unwilling to discipline the grossly inefficient economy and continued to keep heavily subsidized industries and agriculture afloat by permitting the Central Bank of Ukraine to issue massive ruble-denominated credits. Thus, members of the *nomenklatura* managed to maintain their grip on the economy and, not surprisingly, hyperinflation seized Ukraine.

In the meantime, Russia's foreign policy, led by the "Atlanticist" Andrei Kozyorev, focused on the United States, Western Europe, and China and, for the most part, downplayed relations with the so-called near abroad. This strategy affected Ukraine in two ways. On one hand, Kravchuk continued to derive economic benefits from the old Soviet–Ukraine relationship, such as ruble credits and low energy prices, and thus avoided difficult economic decisions. On the other hand, Russia's willingness to prop up other CIS economies without a coherent policy confirmed Ukraine's suspicions that Russia had become too disoriented to play a further role in Ukraine's internal development. Finally, the extreme poverty in Russia between 1991 and 1992 convinced Ukrainians, even in the Russophone east, that Kravchuk's foreign policy best served Ukrainian interests by ending centuries of political and economic exploitation.

Although the Russian government was slow to realize that the Belovezhsk Agreement would not in fact create a Russian-dominated CIS including Ukraine, it quickly realized that a radical break from traditional Soviet economic policies was essential. On 1 January 1992, Deputy Prime Minister Yegor Gaidar freed most prices in the Russian Federation, thus inducing a prolonged period of Russian hyperinflation. With most prices in Russia suddenly exceeding those in Ukraine, Russians began flocking to their Ukrainian neighbor, causing a hemorrhage of goods and an explosion in prices on the black market. Kiev responded by increasing public expenditures, paid for by cheap ruble-denominated credits. In November 1992, the Russian Central Bank in turn *de facto* expelled Ukraine from the ruble zone. As a desperate last resort, Kravchuk ordered increased printing of *karbovontsi*. Together, these disastrous policies caused Ukraine's inflation rate to skyrocket from 91 percent in 1991 to 1,210 percent in 1992, finally peaking at 4,735 percent in 1994. In the meantime, Ukraine slid into the production decline characteristic of all post-centrally planned economies, with its gross domestic product dropping 12 percent in 1991 and another 23 percent in 1994.[19]

Once Russia recognized that it could no longer control the CIS as a supranational body, Russia changed its diplomatic behavior. It gave up the idea of a CIS-based defense ministry and established its own in May 1992. At the same time, two assertive, anti-Russian ex-Soviet states which initially avoided membership in the CIS – Georgia and Azerbaijan – were brought to heel by Moscow's effective manipulation of proxy armies in the regions of Abkhazia and Armenia. At the same time, Ukraine's support for such independent-minded states backfired as Russia's tactics forced both entities back into its orbit. The bloody coup against Georgian dictator Zviad Gamsakhurdia, followed by the Russian-backed Abkhazi defeat of the Georgian army in the autumn of 1993, forced a humbled President Eduard Shevardnadze to toe the Russian line and accept membershp in the CIS and a Russian military presence on Georgian soil. Azerbaijan's new president, Haider Aliev, a former member of the Soviet Politburo, showed similar obedience after the Russian-backed coup against elected President Abulfaz Elchibei in August of 1993. With the loss of these allies, Ukraine found itself increasingly isolated within the CIS.

At the end of 1993, Kravchuk's strategy had stalled on all sides. The Ukrainian economy had sunk to such depths that it had become the sick man of the CIS, even by its own anemic standards. Diplomatically, Ukraine was locked in a stalemate with Russia, isolated from the United States, and ostracized by both Western and Central Europe. Central Europe remained focused on strengthening ties with the West, while keeping Russia at bay and ignoring Ukraine. Though Kiev failed to carry out its promises of nuclear disarmament, it lacked real operational control over most of its strategic weapons, creating

---

[19] European Bank for Reconstruction and Development, *Transition Report 1995: Economic Transition in Eastern Europe and the Former Soviet Union*, 1995.

tensions with the West, but not giving Ukraine any significant deterrent benefit *vis-à-vis* Russia. Paradoxically, it was President Kravchuk who signed the Trilateral Agreement with Russia and the United States in January of 1994 that resulted in the transfer of all nuclear weapons from Ukraine to Russia. Nevertheless, Kravchuk's personal credibility as a reliable partner for the West never recovered.

Even domestically, Kravchuk's Western-oriented policy had lost support in all regions except western Ukraine.[20] Kravchuk's confrontational style in dealing with Russia did not accurately gauge Ukrainian sentiment. Despite a profound sense of grievance against Russia, most Ukrainians continued to perceive themselves as a nation sharing a history and culture with their neighbor. In a 1995 survey, only 5 percent of Ukrainians considered themselves European, and 39 percent viewed Russia as Ukraine's most important ally.[21] While 53 percent felt that Russia would attempt to reincorporate Ukraine, only 16 percent, mostly west Ukrainians, feared such a move.[22] For 55 percent, "confederation with Russia, Kazakhstan, Belarus, and other former Soviet Republics rather than remaining a sovereign and independent state" better served the interests of Ukraine.[23] In other words, Kravchuk's Western-oriented foreign policy did not correlate with the self-image of the Ukrainian population.[24]

These strains were further complicated by the strength of the *nomenklatura*, who argued that the strained relationship with Russia visibly damaged Ukraine's chances for economic stability. Although most had initially welcomed the Soviet break-up and transfer of assets to Ukraine, Ukraine's drastic decline had begun to hurt them as well. Indeed, their largest source of real income had become Russia's exports (or credits) of subsidized oil to Ukraine, which were subsequently sold on world markets at high international prices. Parliament responded to the situation by forcing new elections on the president.

[20] In 1991, during the contest against Viacheslav Chornovil, Kravchuk garnered less than 25 percent of western Ukraine's vote (see Henry Huttenbach, *Analysis of Current Events*, Association for the Study of Nationalities, no. 12 (1991)). During the 1994 elections, Kravchuk got over 90 percent of western Ukrainian votes in his contest with Leonid Kuchma.
[21] *Central and Eastern European Eurobarometer*, no. 3 (February 1993) 28 and 62.
[22] "Ukrainians Seek Security Links in Diverse Ways: Closer Ties Sought with Russia, NATO," *Opinion Analysis, USIA: Office of Research and Media Reaction* 15 (March 1995).
[23] "Ukrainian Public Wants Security Arrangements with NATO and CIS," *Opinion Analysis, USIA: Office of Research and Media Reaction* 15 (March 1995).
[24] According to a sociological study carried out by the Ukrainian Academy of Science, 69 percent of ethnic Ukrainians would marry an ethnic Russian, while only 25 percent would marry a Ukrainian from the diaspora and 15 percent a Pole.

At the same time, Kravchuk finally caved in to US pressure and concluded the Trilateral Agreement with President Bill Clinton and Yeltsin, which provided the mechanism for removing nuclear weapons from Ukrainian territory in exchange for nuclear reactor fuel and security guarantees.

Two competing groups emerged in late 1993. On one side stood Kravchuk and his supporters, the former party elite and the pro-Western nationalists, trying to hold on to their power. On the other side stood the industrial barons of the East, led by former missile-maker, Leonid Kuchma, who was now forging an alliance with the largely Russophone workers and calling for restoration of close ties with Russia. Although both groups stemmed from the former *nomenklatura*, these groups represented different segments of the former Soviet elite. Whereas Kravchuk's supporters often were drawn from the communist party bureaucracy, Kuchma's powerbase was the economic elite - the industrial and agricultural bosses of the old communist system. While the party bureaucracy could only claim legitimacy by recasting themselves as nationalists, Kuchma's supporters could run on the basis of their managerial competence.

As a result, the 1994 presidential elections became an extension of the centuries-old debate between the nationalist, pro-Western concept of western Ukraine and the right-bank and the pro-Russian stance of the left-bank industrial elite. Kravchuk asserted that "the people of Ukraine built a sovereign democratic European state,"[25] while Kuchma claimed, "We need an economic union. Ukraine needs it more, and Belarus even more. Russia needs it less; however, we all need it."[26] Accordingly, the final election totals showed a clean split along this historic axis. Kravchuk won the provinces (oblasts) along the southern borders of Vinnytsia and Cherkassy and west of the Dnieper River, which corresponded roughly to the territories annexed by Poland under the 1667 Treaty of Andrusovo with Russia. In addition, within the territories of the Polish frontier of 1939, Kravchuk received more than 83 percent of the votes. In Luhansk, Donetsk, and Crimea, parts of which arguably had never been core territories of Ukraine before Stalin and Khrushchev, Kuchma collected 79 percent or more of the votes.[27]

---

[25] Quoted in Zenovia A. Sochor, "Political Culture and Foreign Policy: Elections in Ukraine 1994," in *Political Culture and Civil Society*, 216.

[26] Radio Moscow, 13 January 1993.

[27] See David R. Marples, "Ukraine After the Presidential Elections," *RFE/RL Research Reports* 3: 31 (August 1994), 7–13.

Kuchma's election initially polarized the Ukrainian population. Panicky nationalists feared that Kuchma would surrender Ukraine's independence. Not only in western Ukraine, but also among nationalists throughout the country, the result of the presidential elections seemed to be a harbinger of rapid reintegration with Russia. Before the election, *Rukh* leader Viacheslav Chornovil said, "It is impossible to vote for Kuchma. It is impossible because Russia is betting on him."[28] The Russian ultranationalist publication *Zavtra*, which often brandishes its own version of Eurasianism, agreed with its Ukrainian antagonists on this issue, celebrating the fall of "the traitor Kravchuk." In truth, though, the election was a referendum on Kravchuk's foreign policy, not on sovereignty itself. Kuchma represented a different, and ultimately more popular, reading of Ukrainian history. He hailed not only from Ukraine's most populous region, but also an area where Ukrainian nationalisn is largely free of the integralist notions associated with Galica and the small east Ukrainian intellectual elite. Although Kharkiv and the east did provide many of the early Ukrainian nationalists in the mid-nineteenth century, their idea of nationalism rarely viewed the Russophones as the traditional "other." However despite apocalyptic fears that the new administration would return Ukraine to Moscow's orbit, especially once he staffed much of the central administration with people from his native Dnepropetrovsk, [29] Kuchma's team developed a nuanced policy that sought to end Kiev's isolation and redress its relationships with both Russia and the West, which managed to improve the country's international standing without compromising its sovereignty.

### The Eurasian foreign policy of Leonid Kuchma

The 1994 presidential elections in Ukraine represented a watershed on several levels. The peaceful transfer of power from one democratically elected president to another set a precedent unknown in the millennium of Byzantine–East Slavic history. Just as significantly, the defeat of Kravchuk not only represented the rejection of his economic policies and world outlook, it heralded the arrival of left-bank Ukraine as a unified and assertive political player. Traditionally,

[28] Sochor, "Political Culture and Foreign Policy," 217.
[29] According to the Ukrainian Center for Independent Political Research, by 1995 Kuchma had transferred about 150 functionaries from his native Dnepropetrovsk to Kiev.

Ukrainian activism had centered on Kiev and western Ukraine, while left-bank Ukrainians remained politically dormant. As a result, nationalist intellectuals based in Kiev and Lviv set the political agenda of all of Ukraine during the tumultuous period of 1989–91. Although left-bank Ukraine had served as the home of the Cossack Hetmanate and led Ukraine's national revival in the 1840s, its strain of nationalism fundamentally differed from that of the right bank and became a potent force after Ukraine won its independence in 1991. While west Ukrainian identity developed in reaction to various "others," such as Poles, Jews, or Russians, east Ukrainian identity rested on vague notions of a mythical Cossack democracy and resistance to remote autocratic rule. Furthermore, whereas right-bank Ukrainians – and more extremely, Galicians – viewed Ukraine's forced extradition from its historic Central European orbit as the root of its misfortunes, left-bank Ukrainians perceived Central European cultural influence as an intrusion while at the same time rejecting Russian centralism. To left-bank Ukrainians, the causes of Ukraine's misfortune lay not in the displacement of their nation but rather in their own failure to put their house in order. Examples of this, they argued, ranged from the invitation to the Varangians to govern Kievan-Rus in the ninth century to Khmylnytskyi's Pereiaslav Agreement in the seventeenth century, and to Hetman Pavlo Skoropadsky's attempt in 1918 to link Ukraine's independence to Wilhelmine Germany and the Soviet Union. As a result, left-bank Ukrainians came to view Ukraine as a distinct linguistic entity within the Slavic Orthodox world, while right-bank Ukrainians saw themselves as a distinct part of Central Europe.

In light of these divisions, Kravchuk's foreign policy was not only politically shortsighted, attracting unwanted attention from Russian nationalists, but it also alienated the large Russophone population in the east and south, who considered a close relationship with Russia an integral part of their identity. President Kravchuk's foreign minister, Anatoli Zlenko, asserted, "Ukraine is opening itself to the world and Europe and promoting ties that have been denied over the last decades . . . NATO [is] the basis of security in Europe."[30] Yuri Pavlenko, a senior researcher at the Ukrainian Academy of Sciences, writing in *Politychna Dumka* (*Political Thought*), noted that all emerging alliances are "civilizational" (i.e., West European, Pan Islamic, etc.),

---

[30] Anatoly Zlenko, "The Foreign Policy of Ukraine: Principles of Shaping and Problems of Implementing," *International Affairs (Moscow)* 1 (1994) 16–17.

making it imperative for Ukraine to be part of the "oriental-Christian Eurasian domain."[31] He argued that Kravchuk's strategy of using the CIS structure as a step toward attaining a "divorce" from Russia had backfired, allowing Russia to consolidate its control over the Commonwealth, given the absence of a strong countervailing presence such as Ukraine.

Intellectual criticism of the Western orientation of Kravchuk's foreign policy was growing. Professor Serhiy Sherghin of the Ukrainian Institute of International Relations argued that Ukraine ought to emphasize Ukraine's historic ties to the Eurasian bloc, despite the strong "anti-Oriental" groups that traditionally provoked fear of the Asian threat and wanted to look to the West for allies.[32] Furthermore, he maintained that as a result of this mindset, Ukraine was adopting a Eurocentric linear view of history that distorted both Ukraine's Oriental niche and its relationship with the West.[33] Eurasianism, as propagated by Sherghin and other intellectuals, differed from Russian Slavophilia, which is fundamentally hostile to the West, and from the position of Ukraine's extreme right, which called for the re-establishment of a Pan-Slavic state with Kiev rather than Moscow at its center. Eurasianists reject the notion that Ukrainian independence must be synonymous with Russophobia or must discard centuries of cultural and political history shared with Russia. Kuchma articulated this notion of Ukraine's identity during his inaugural speech:

> Historically, Ukraine is part of the Euro-Asian cultural and economic space. Ukraine's vitality and important national interests are now concentrated on this territory of the former Soviet Union . . . We are also linked with . . . the former republics of the Soviet Union by traditional scientific, cultural, informational, and family ties.[34]

In a similar vein, during his triumphant visit to Washington in November 1994, President Kuchma proclaimed, "Russia is our great neighbor . . . We are connected by a thousand-year history."[35]

Not surprisingly, the specific goals of Kuchma's foreign policy also reflect this fundamental philosophical shift away from Kravchuk and the Central European school. Whereas Kravchuk viewed military

---

[31] Yuri Pavlenko, "Ukraine and Modern Civilizations," *Politychna Dumka Kyiv* 3 (1994) 189.

[32] Serhiy Sherghin, "A Eurasian Way for Ukraine?" *Political Thought* 2 (1994) 139.

[33] Ibid., 140.

[34] Quoted in Stephen R. Burant, "Foreign Policy and National Identity: A Comparison of Ukraine and Belarus," *Europe-Asia Studies* 47: 7 (November 1995) 1138.

[35] Quoted in ibid., 1138.

weakness and potential Russian aggression as the main threats to Ukraine's sovereignty, Kuchma argued that priority should be given to fostering a healthy political and economic life to ensure the long-term viability of the Ukrainian state. As a result, while both schools of thought understood the importance of Russian recognition of Ukraine's legitimacy and the primacy of the Russian threat, they offered different prescriptions to address these needs. The Kravchuk camp argued for a "return to Europe" and the creation of a bloc to contain Russia. The Eurasian school, on the other hand, believed that closer ties with the West would provoke a Russian attempt to reassert control over Ukraine, pointing to previous examples such as the clash between Latin Catholicism and Orthodoxy in the seventeenth century, Bolshevik resistance to Piłsudski's expansion in 1920, and the popular World War II belief that a conflict between Stalin's USSR and the West would arise and lead to Ukraine's true liberation. Therefore, concluded the Eurasians, Ukraine should attempt to integrate Russia into the international order and remove its psychological need to control its "western borderlands." In other words, multipolar cooperation should take precedence over Western alliance.

By late 1994, Kuchma's Eurasia-oriented team had developed the following policy prescriptions:

1 The greatest threat to Ukraine's statehood is rooted in its anemic economy, which delegitimizes Ukrainian statehood among its citizens and creates the conditions for a popular reintegrationist agenda.

2 Nuclear weapons on Ukraine's soil not only fail to enhance the country's security, but actually hurt its chances for economic recovery by alienating Washington. The disposal of nuclear arms can win badly needed financial compensation as well as US involvement in Ukraine's security.

3 The West has an interest in Ukraine's economic success, since economic decline can quickly trigger waves of economic refugees flooding Europe. The economic collapse of Ukraine will most likely tempt Russian intervention and end all hope of a lasting democratic transformation in both Ukraine and Russia. For this reason, Ukraine needs aid from the West to ensure economic growth.

4 Ukraine should remain in the CIS, not only because many of its citizens wish to retain an institutional link with the former Soviet republics but, more importantly, because Ukraine can stall Moscow's drive to turn the CIS into a supranational entity. In the absence of a Russo-Ukrainian friendship treaty institutionalizing

Ukraine's current borders, the CIS remains the sole instrument legitimizing Ukraine's borders with Russia.

5 It is vital for Ukraine to improve both economic and military relations with Russia that remain subject to international law. This way Russia cannot call into question Ukraine's sovereignty.

6 Conversely, Ukraine's relations with Central Europe, especially Poland, should focus on a variety of bilateral issues but hold limited strategic value.

### Ukraine and the West

The three main obstacles blocking improved relations between Kiev and Washington were the American frustration over Ukrainian nuclear disarmament, Ukraine's sluggish pace of economic reform, and Washington's focus on Russia at the expense of the other post-Soviet states. Ukrainian–American relations began to change after June 1993, following the Massandra meeting in which Yelstin forced the alienated Kravchuk to submit to his *diktat* and agree to turn over the Black Sea Fleet. Washington's initial assumptions about Russian behavior within the CIS were being re-evaluated as Russia overtly increased support of Abkhazian separatists in Georgia and military involvement in Moldova's breakaway Trandniestra region. The United States feared that Russia's tendency to capitalize aggressively on CIS instability across the former Soviet Union might remain an integral part of its foreign policy.[36] Moreover, growing tensions in Moscow between Yeltsin and the Russian Supreme Soviet, led by its speaker Ruslan Khasbulatov, suddenly raised new doubts over the viability of Russia's political and economic reform. As US–Russian relations foundered, US–Ukrainian relations improved.

By autumn 1993, while still insisting that Ukraine comply with the Lisbon Protocols and the Non-Proliferation Treaty, the United States linked, albeit indirectly, Ukraine's nuclear disarmament with broader security and economic needs. On 14 January 1994, Ukraine, Russia, and the United States signed the Trilateral Agreement, which required Ukraine to dismantle its entire nuclear arsenal by June 1996. From the Ukrainian perspective, the Trilateral Agreement was significant on several scores. First, Ukraine finally received economic relief. Second, by becoming a direct partner of Ukraine in nuclear disarmament,

---

[36] See Ilya Prizel, "The United States and a Resurgent Russia: A New Cold War or a Balance of Power Recast?" in *Does Russian Democracy Have a Future?* ed. Stephen J. Blank and Earl H. Tilford, Jr. (Carlisle Barracks, PA: US Army War College, 1994).

instead of leaving the issue up to Russo-Ukrainian relations or negotiating with the CIS over Ukraine's head, the United States established its presence in the region. Third, Ukraine won security assurances from Russia, the United States, the United Kingdom, and, later, both France and China (the recognized nuclear powers and the permanent members of the UN Security Council).[37] A breakthrough in US–Ukrainian relations occurred under Kravchuk, with the signing of the Trilateral Accord and his visit to Washington in March 1994, when he secured $350 million to expedite disarmament and another $350 million in economic assistance. Ultimately, however, Kuchma proved far more effective at projecting trust and reliability and at securing more substantive diplomatic agreements.

The election of Kuchma, following Ukraine's cooperation on nuclear disarmament and its greater commitment to macroeconomic stabilization, led to rapid improvement in US–Ukrainian relations. The US government invited Kuchma for a state visit in November 1994, thus bestowing upon Ukraine greater status as a potential strategic partner and promises of US foreign assistance in an amount exceeded only by US funds to Israel and Egypt. As US relations with Moscow became even more strained over Russian sales of weapons and nuclear reactors to Iran, increasingly close Sino-Russian relations, and Russian attempts to assert control over the Caspian basin, US–Ukrainian relations continued to improve rapidly. By 1995, US–Ukrainian relations had become a vital component in US European policy. Ukraine preceded Russia as a member of both the Council of Europe and NATO's Partnership for Peace (PFP). While Russia proved an awkward member of the NATO force sent to implement the Dayton Agreements, Ukraine's contingent in the Balkans actually assisted the Clinton administration in arming Bosnia as part of the US exit strategy of building a well-armed Bosnian state. Unlike the Kravchuk era, when official US visits to Ukraine were rare and dominated by bitter controversy, Ukraine hosted not only President Clinton, high cabinet officials, and military delegations, but military exercises of US, Slovak, Hungarian, and Ukrainian troops in the summer of 1995 under PFP.

The nascent Kiev–Washington relationship continues to encounter serious difficulties. For its part, other than linking some economic aid to disarmament, the United States did not broaden its scope beyond

---

[37] See Sherman Garnett, "The Sources and the Conduct of Ukraine's Nuclear Policy," in *The Nuclear Challenge in Russia and the New States of Eurasia*, ed. George Quester (Armonk, NY: M. E. Sharpe, 1995).

the nuclear issue, and most recently has focused on Ukraine's alleged export of military technology to China, Iran, and, possibly, Libya.[38] The absence of a unifying agenda between the two countries, combined with Washington's growing frustration over Kiev's economic reforms, may result in a relapse into poor relations between the two states. The United States will continue to attach significance to its relations with Ukraine, as Kiev represents the primary barrier to a Russian drive to reestablish a superstate within the CIS. In the absence of overt Russian aggression, however, both states need a broader agenda to nurture that relationship.

Ukraine's relations with Western Europe followed a similar path to that of the relationship with the United States. In the aftermath of the disintegration of the USSR, most West European states paid scant attention to Ukraine and the other non-Russian CIS states. Germany's main objective was to ensure the withdrawal of the remaining former Red Army units on East German soil. France, having belatedly recognized the inevitability of German reunification, sought Russian cooperation to revive a modified Franco-Russian *entente cordiale*. Italy attempted to capitalize on FIAT's historic presence in Russia and to expand upon its economic presence in Russia. Furthermore, the surprisingly rapid and quiet collapse of the USSR left a perception among West Europeans that the independent states of the CIS were bound to return to Russia.[39]

The Ukrainian issue that concerned Europeans more than the United States during Kravchuk's presidency was the Chernobyl nuclear power plant and the safety of nuclear reactors located in Ukraine. Much as the United States fixated on nuclear weapons, the European Union focused on Chernobyl. The Europeans accused Ukraine of bad faith and foot-dragging in closing down dangerous reactors. In turn, Ukraine claimed the European Union had failed to provide adequate funding for the clean-up of the Chernobyl plant and the construction of a new sarcophagus to house the ruins of the destroyed reactor. While Kravchuk managed to improve Ukraine's relationship with Poland and Central Europe, Ukrainian relations with the European Union continued to languish. Only in the last days of the Kravchuk era and under Kuchma's leadership did Ukraine

---

[38] Bill Gertz, "Ukraine and Libya Forge a 'Strategic' Alliance," *Washington Times*, 10 June 1996.

[39] Angela Stent, "Germany and the Post-Soviet States," in *The International Dimension of Post-Communist Transitions in Russia and the New States of Eurasia*, ed. Karen Dawisha (Armonk, NY: M. E. Sharpe, 1997), 197–216.

achieve a *rapprochement* with Western Europe, particularly with the United Kingdom and Germany.

Like the United States, the West Europeans rediscovered Ukraine as they reassessed Russia's long-term intentions. Their concern increased when Russian's Duma made territorial claims on Ukraine in Crimea in July 1993. Russia's heavy-handed role in overthrowing the pro-Turkish regime in Azerbaijan and limiting British Petroleum's activities in the Caspian basin startled Britain. Russia's not-too-subtle struggle with Turkey alarmed Bonn and London. Both Western countries viewed Turkey as the foundation of stability on Europe's east Mediterranean flank and a pillar against fundamentalist Islam. By 1996, in light of Yeltsin's agreement with Belarusan President Aleksyandr Lukashenka to form a union of sovereign republics and the Russian State Duma's passage of a non-binding resolution annulling the Belovezhsk Agreement, Western Europe was actively seeking closer ties with Ukraine. Furthermore, the British government recognized that the Ukrainian fear of becoming a buffer zone between Russia and the NATO countries, rather than Russian intransigence, could complicate NATO's expansion if the security concerns of Ukraine and the Baltic states remained unresolved. Accordingly, the British government began going to great lengths to assure Ukraine of its support, and British Foreign Secretary Malcom Rifkind became one of the most consistent advocates of increased aid to Ukraine and stronger ties between Western Europe and Ukraine. In relations with Germany, Kuchma once again proved far more adept at diplomacy than his predecessor, visiting Bonn in the summer of 1995 and signing agreements to promote a Ukrainian–German economic partnership.

In May 1996, Rifkind and his German counterpart, Klaus Kinkel, made a joint visit to Kiev, their only joint visit of that year apart from their trip to Turkey.[40] The European Union's commissioner for external relations, Hans van den Broek, bolstered this drive to support Ukraine by declaring that an independent Ukraine served as a crucial element of European security.[41] By the spring of 1996, Kuchma was speaking of European Union membership as a "strategic aim," while hastening to add that such an aim remained contingent upon economic reform rather than simply offering itself as an emergency brake to Russian expansionism.[42]

---

[40] Reuters, "Britain, Germany to Show Support for Ukraine," 2 April 1996.
[41] *Agence France Presse*, 21 May 1996.    [42] Radio Ukraine, 23 March 1996.

### Ukraine and Russia

Russia remains the greatest dilemma for Ukraine. Ukraine's elites are haunted by the Pereiaslav complex and unable to develop a clear notion of the national interest *vis-à-vis* Russia.[43] Similarly, Ukraine's population is deeply divided over the issue, with large segments embracing the nationalist view of Russia as Ukraine's worst enemy, while millions of others perceive Russia as a fraternal nation, deserving of a special relationship with Ukraine.[44] This special relationship does not entail annexation, but rather closer cultural and economic ties. In 1995, a public opinion poll revealed this ambivalence by reporting that 67 percent of ethnic Ukrainians had a favorable view of the Pereiaslav Agreement (15 percent unfavorable), while support for their country's independence was 61 percent in favor and 31 percent against.[45]

As the newly elected Ukrainian president, Kuchma's greatest challenge was to reconcile Kravchuk's policy of a distinct, sovereign Ukraine subject to international law with a policy of strengthening ties to Russia as demanded by the left in the Rada. Given Kuchma's electoral mandate and the evolving perception that Russia should remain a close partner of Ukraine in light of the disastrous state of the Ukrainian economy,[46] Kuchma initiated several symbolic moves that reflected this closer orientation to Russia.

In contrast with the Kravchuk era, when Russian speakers were often depicted as traitorous Janissaries, Kuchma informally decentralized language policy to permit the linguistic coexistence of Russian and Ukrainian. Instead of stressing Ivan Mazepa's uprising, Peter I's suppression, and the Famine of 1933 as Ukraine's formative experiences, Kuchma lauded Ukraine's contribution to the "Great Patriotic War" and observed the tercentennial of the Black Sea Fleet by authorizing his press service to state, "The [Black Sea] fleet was built and perfected by our common Ukrainian and Russian predecessors

---

[43] Taras Kuzio, *Ukrainian Security Policy* (Westport and London: Praeger Books, 1995), 4 and 13.

[44] Ibid., 14.

[45] See N. M. Guboglo, "The Disintegration and Synthesis of Identity in Post Soviet Space and Time (The Case of Ukraine)," in "Peoples, Nations, Identities: The Russian–Ukrainian Encounter," ed. Mark von Hagen, *The Harriman Review* (Spring 1996) 14600.

[46] Zenovia A. Sochor, "No Middle Ground? On the Difficulties of Creating a Consensus in Ukraine," *Harriman Review* (Spring 1996), 58.

who stood at the cradle of the glorious traditions and protected our common motherland."[47]

Kuchma's policy displayed several fundamental departures from Kravchuk's foreign policy on a practical level as well. While Kravchuk strove to minimize Ukraine's relations with Moscow and undermine Russia's involvement in the CIS by supporting Azerbaijan's war against Armenia and Georgia's war against Abkhazian separatists, Kuchma adopted a far more pragmatic course. Kuchma believed that the centrifugal forces that had torn apart the USSR had peaked and that Russia's activities in the near abroad simply represented a return to a natural equilibrium. Efforts to prevent the emergence of this equilibrium could prove counterproductive, if not outright dangerous. While Kravchuk sought to reduce links between the two countries and return to Europe, Kuchma saw no contradiction between restoring vital economic relations with Russia and simultaneously strengthening those with the West. For Kuchma, the main threat to Ukraine's independence was not a resurgent Russia but rather the economic collapse of Ukraine or the country's becoming a buffer between NATO and a Eurasian bloc. Accordingly, Kuchma's policy achieved greater military and security cooperation with Russia while maintaining Ukraine's visibility within the international diplomatic arena.

Kuchma reversed Kravchuk's policy and actively encouraged the resumption of broken economic ties. In a wide array of industries, from nuclear power to the vast military-industrial complex inherited from the USSR, Kuchma encouraged the emergence of joint Russo-Ukrainian enterprises.[48] Economic disputes that emerged – such as debates over transit fees for Russian oil and gas or competition for construction of a pipeline linking the Black Sea with Western Europe – have thus far been treated as normal business issues rather than warfare by other means. Fiercely guarding its sovereignty, Ukraine has refused to join Russia and the other CIS states in the formation of a customs union. Ukraine did, however, sign a bilateral free trade agreement with Russia, which enabled Ukraine to derive most customs union benefits while keeping its sovereignty intact.

Kuchma quickly jettisoned the Baltic–Black Sea axis proposal to allay Russian fears and cooperated with Russia in a variety of military activities. Although Kiev claims neutrality and even refused to join

---

[47] TASS, 6 May 1996.
[48] Yaroslav Bilinsky, "Ukraine, Russia, and the West: An Insecure Security Triangle," *Problems of Post-Communism* (January–February 1997), 27–33.

the Tashkent Treaty, which creates a loose military alliance and a single military space within the CIS, Kiev did agree to participate in a CIS joint air-defense system, began joint training of officers with Russia, and sold Moscow 32 SS19 intercontinental ballistic missiles in November 1995. The latter package also included 160 bombers, more than 300 cruise missile delivery systems,[49] and industrial facilities for producing heavy bombers.[50] In return, Russia agreed to provide Ukraine with a facility to test its new *Sich* rocket. The exchange ensured that Russia's nuclear arsenal would remain modern and effective until 2015 and signaled Ukraine's acceptance of Russia as a nuclear power rather than a state that must be contained by military opposition.

Kiev's new policy of accommodation has had political ramifications as well. Its rejection of the original policy of using the CIS as a means to a civilized divorce and its abandonment of support for anti-Russian forces in the CIS led to a Treaty of Friendship with Armenia. It supported the election of the pro-Russian Haidar Aliev regime in Azerbaijan. Rather than tolerating heroes' funerals for Ukrainian nationalists killed fighting Russia in either Abkhazia or Chechnya, as Kravchuk had done, Kuchma's foreign minister, Henadii Udovenko, branded such Ukrainian nationalists "criminals."[51]

Kuchma's efforts notwithstanding, however, the relationship continues to be dogged by Moscow's unwillingness to accept Ukraine as a fully sovereign state. Two issues continue to plague the relationship: the future of the Black Sea Fleet's bases and the international status of the CIS. Despite Kuchma's willingness to compromise, the issues of the bases and Russian political acceptance of Ukraine's sovereignty have thus far prevented the two Slavic giants from signing a Treaty of Friendship.

Crimean bases remain the most contentious issue. However, because Kuchma realizes that Ukraine does not have the means to expel the Russian fleet, the two sides have recently compromised and Ukraine has agreed to allow a continuing Russian presence at the ports. But, while Kiev insists that Russia must sign a 10– to 25–year lease,[52] Russia refuses to commit itself to any specific length of time. Even more problematic is the conflict over the Sevastopol base, which Russia claims as its own. Ukraine says it will lease necessary facilities

[49] Interfax News Agency, 27 November 1995.     [50] TASS, 29 March 1996.
[51] Victor Timoshenko, "Kiev's Balanced Stand," *Nezavisimaia gazeta*, 18 May 1996, 3.
[52] Sergei Balykov, "Ukraine Reports Russo-Ukrainian Treaty on Friendship Ready," ITAR-TASS, 21 March 1996.

in Sevastopol to accommodate the Russian fleet, but only on its own terms, and considers the Russian demands an affront to its sovereignty.

Russian politicians across the spectrum view the CIS as a first step toward a new Russian-dominated supranational entity. While Kuchma recognizes this drift as understandable, he has continued to insist on a "special relationship" for Ukraine that will not impinge on its sovereignty. Moscow has consistently perceived this move as aggressive and disruptive. Nevertheless, although Russo-Ukrainian relations continue to be marred by acrimonious exchanges between Russian "patriot-communists" and Ukrainian "nationalists" over the bases and other issues, Kuchma has largely succeeded in establishing a special relationship with Russia and the CIS while simultaneously preserving Ukraine's sovereignty. By strengthening its military ties with the CIS, Ukraine may have begun a reluctant shift toward military integration with the supranational body.[53]

Most important, the shift from Kravchuk's Western orientation to Kuchma's Eurasian paradigm recognized that Ukraine's security depended on a healthier relationship with Russia. While Eurasian foreign policy sought and achieved nuclear disarmament, ending Ukraine's isolation and improving its relationships with both the West and Russia, Ukraine's neutrality remains sustainable only in the absence of a bipolar international system. Ukraine's neutrality is being called into question as NATO moves to include Poland, Hungary, and the Czech Republic, increasingly raising tensions between Russia and the West.

### NATO expansion and Ukraine's transformation into a buffer zone

While both Kravchuk and Kuchma welcomed the US presence in Europe under NATO as an essential component of European stability, Ukraine's political elites continue to fear that rapid expansion will rekindle the Cold War and turn Ukraine into a buffer between two massive blocs. In such an event, Ukraine would find itself in a particularly precarious situation, for it lacks most of the traditional requirements for neutrality. Ukraine does not have an independent and viable economy, a reliable and well-organized military, or even

---

[53] See British American Security Information Council, "NATO Enlargement and Ukraine," *Basic Papers*, no. 16 (11 April 1996).

fully demarcated, recognized, and defensible borders with Russia.[54] Ukraine must both ensure a Western, mainly US, presence in Central Europe and prevent a return to bipolarity and heightened tensions with Russia. Ukraine's position regarding NATO's expansion is therefore subtle and nuanced.

Unlike Russia, Ukraine does not consider NATO a potential source of aggression nor does it accept Russia's position that an external power can exercise veto power over the decisions of other sovereign states. Similarly, Ukraine did not adopt Belarus's position that NATO expansion directly threatened to turn Ukraine and Belarus into buffer states.[55] On the other hand, Kiev declined to follow the Baltic states in their support for NATO expansion to include all the post-Soviet CIS states except Russia. In short, Ukraine's NATO policy hedges both sides. Kiev does not fear the expansion of NATO but rather a new division of Europe. Despite its mild reaction to the enthusiasm for NATO membership displayed by the Višegrad countries, Kuchma remains well aware that NATO expansion would alarm both Russophiles and Russians in Ukraine, ultimately tearing into the fabric of Ukrainian society, and would infuriate Russian nationalists in Moscow. As a result of this cautious policy, Kiev dispatched troops to Bosnia to enforce the Dayton Accord, but followed the Russian example of not placing its troops under direct NATO command.

Ukrainian Foreign Minister Henadii Udovenko articulated this dilemma by urging "NATO to reconsider thoroughly its role in modern Europe and develop in an evolutionary process from a collective defense organization into a collective security organization, thus becoming a possible nucleus for a future all-European security system that would encompass other mutually complementary institutions." Reflecting Kiev's anxiety over its ability to sustain a policy of neutrality, he remarked that Ukraine "still adheres to the policy of non-participation in military alliances and has not put the issue of NATO membership on the agenda for the time being."[56] Although it has studiously avoided a Russian-style direct confrontation with the Višegrad states over NATO expansion, its policies are fundamentally at odds with those of Poland. Poland has rejected Ukraine's call for a

[54] Boris Glebov, "Ukraine Raises Border Issue," *Current Digest of Post-Soviet Press*, no. 41 (20 October 1995), 2.
[55] Stephen R. Burant, "Foreign Policy and National Identity: A Comparison of Ukraine and Belarus," *Europe-Asia Studies* 47: 7 (November 1995).
[56] Henadii Udovenko, "European Security and NATO Enlargement: Ukraine's Perspective," *NATO Review* 43: 16 (19??) 15–18.

Europe-wide collective security system, which Kiev sees as necessary to avoid bipolarity, calling it a Russian-inspired, latter-day "holy alliance" intended to serve as the Kremlin's tool in setting Central Europe's security agenda.[57] While not objecting to the expansion of NATO as such, Ukraine indicated its support for a binding treaty between NATO and the former states of the USSR, again backing the Russian, rather than Western position.

Differences over the US-led Partnership for Peace (PFP) have also emerged. Ukraine has joined the PFP, enthusiastically participating in joint exercises and cooperation between the general staffs of both countries, and has cultivated its own special relationship with the United States, without damaging its special relationship with the CIS. Not surprisingly, it has come to view the PFP as a vital institution for mitigating the possible return of a bipolar international system. For Poland, however, the PFP serves only as a hastily conceived intermediate step, obstructing Warsaw's full membership in NATO.

### Conclusion: the Ukrainian paradox

On the surface it would appear that Ukraine, under the stewardship of President Kuchma became more, rather than less vulnerable to the whims of its troubled neighbors. Economically, Ukraine remains linked to Russia with nearly half of its imports and 42 percent of its exports traded with Russia.[58] In addition, after a brief effort to create an armed establishment capable of fending off a potential Russian threat under the tenure of General Morozov, President Kuchma and his first defense minister Valerii Shmarov proceeded to rapidly, and chaotically, downsize the army, virtually eliminating it as a credible fighting force.[59] Instead, Kuchma and Shmarov proceeded to revitalize the Ukrainian military-industrial complex, a process which led to an ever deeper collaboration with Russia. Five years into its independence, Ukraine has yet to develop a clear defense doctrine or restructure the armed forces. The Ukrainian army today retains its Soviet-era offensive structure and its military districts continue to be configured against an offensive from the West.

---

[57] See Arthur Rachwald, "Poland Looks West," in *Post-1989 Poland: Challenges of Independence*, ed. Andrew Michta and Ilya Prizel (St. Martin's Press, 1995).

[58] Paul D'anieri, "Dilemmas of Independence: Autonomy, Prosperity and Sovereignty in Ukraine's Russia Policy," *Problems of Post-Communism* (January–February 1997), 17.

[59] See Taras Kuzio, "Crisis and Reform in Ukraine," *Jane's Intelligence Review* 8: 10 (October 1996) and 8: 11 (November 1996).

It still has not created a military contingent that could meet a possible challenge from the north or the east.[60]

Kuchma has assumed an ambiguous position with regard to NATO. While not objecting to its expansion, Kiev has insisted on a slow expansion and a "legal" charter between NATO and the former states of the Soviet Union.[61] Ukraine several times raised the hope of developing a special relationship with NATO, and agreed to participate in NATO's "Sea-Breeze '97" exercise in the Black Sea, planned for August 1997. In April 1997, however, the Ukrainian navy commenced on a series of joint exercises with the Russian controlled Black Sea Fleet,[62] de facto acknowledging the legitimacy of its presence in Crimea.

While to the outsider Kuchma's policy may appear to be detrimental to Ukraine's national interests, the reality is that this policy of bolstering Ukraine's international presence while remaining sensitive to Russia is a reflection of a national consensus prevalent across the country's body-politic. While, in late 1996, 21 percent of Ukrainian respondents felt that Russia was the main threat to Ukraine's security, 40 percent also felt that Russia should be Ukraine's main source of security. Only 15 percent saw Western Europe and merely 6 percent saw the United States as a possible source of security for Ukraine.[63]

The agendas of Russia and Ukraine remain different. Large parts of the Russian elite continue to believe in a return to "Slavic-fraternity," making it impossible for Moscow to agree to a normal state-to-state relationship with Ukraine which would institutionalize this separation. Ukraine, meanwhile insists on clear-cut and open diplomatic relations without any "special relationship." In reality neither of the parties is sufficiently strong and stable to enforce its agenda. Russia lacks the political will, elite cohesion and both the economic and military means to force a "Slavic fraternal relationship" on Ukraine. Ukraine, in turn, given its continued economic dependence on Russia and the continued psychological link of many Ukrainians to Russia cannot fully abandon what is de facto a special relationship with its northern neighbor. Given the economic and psychological state of the

---

[60] See Yaroslav Bilinsky, "Ukraine, Russia, and the West: An Insecure Security Triangle," Problems of Post-Communism (January–February 1997), 27–33.
[61] Raisia Stetsyura, "Ukraine Insists on a Document with NATO," ITAR-TASS, 15 April 1997.
[62] "Black Sea Begins Exercise; Ukrainian Navy Participate for the First Time," Interfax 16 April, 1997.
[63] "Russians and Ukrainians Differ in Their Views of NATO and the US," USIA Office of Research and Media Reaction Opinion Analysis, 24 January 1994, M-12–97.

Ukrainian polity, Kiev is bound to continue the current policy of retaining a *de facto* special relationship with Moscow while insisting on a total *de jure* separate international presence.

Over the past two years, Kuchma's team has managed to achieve a broad consensus at home, and attain a level of recognition abroad unprecedented in Ukraine's history. Despite the unrelenting economic crisis, regional divisions, and territorial disputes with Romania and other neighbors, Ukraine remains an island of calm and stability, free of ethnic strife and tensions with its neighbors. Increasingly, countries around the world are coming to recognize Ukraine as an essential, integral part of Europe's emerging security architecture.

However, both its internal and external security are fragile. As long as Ukraine remains "the borderland" between civilizations, its long-term security will depend on external recognition and support of those civilizations, a process that Ukraine can influence marginally at best. A return to bipolarity in Europe may well be catastrophic to Ukraine's security and statehood. Thus, the only two consistent themes of Ukraine's foreign policy under President Kuchma remain the utilization of Ukraine's diplomatic influence to prevent the return of bipolarity to Europe, and to remove Ukraine from its precarious position as the rallying cry of a frustrated Russian nationalism. In both endeavors, his policies appear to be effectively steering Ukraine into the twentieth century.

# Conclusion: national identity and politics in the age of the "mass man"

It is the task of education to give each human being a national form, and so direct his opinions and tastes that he should be a patriot by inclination, by passion, by necessity. On first opening his eyes a child must see his country, and until he dies, must see nothing else.

Jean-Jacques Rousseau[1]

Patriotism is stronger than class hatred and usually stronger than any kind of internationalism.

George Orwell[2]

When mass opinion dominates the government there is a morbid derangement of the true functions of power. The derangement brings about the enfeeblement verging on the paralysis of the capacity to govern.

Walter Lippmann[3]

## "Mass-man's" nationalism in the post-modern age

The prevalent belief of the last few decades, that nationalism and national idenitity are the products of an intellectual elite's ideas having been coopted by a cynical political elite, had led scholars to believe that nationalism would wither away with the rise of democracy and education. This "withering away" never materialized. Today, national identity remains the key marker of political identification. The popular notion of the 1970s popularized by Jurgen Habermas that Germans limit themselves to *Verfassungs Patriotismus* devoid of a historically understood national consensus was swept away by the short-lived waves of popular nationalism when Germany reunited on the basis of a historic national identity.[4]

---

[1] Quoted in Michael Howard, *The Lessons of History* (New Haven and London: Yale University Press, 1991), 145.

[2] See Brian Jenkins and Spares A. Sofos, *Nation and Identity in Contemporary Europe* (London: Routledge, 1996), 90.

[3] Walter Lippmann, *The Public Philosophy* (New Brunswick: Transaction Books, 1989).

[4] See Wolfgang J. Mommsen, "Nationality, Patriotism, and Nationalism," in Roger

In fact, the growing internationalization of modern politics has resulted in the progressive alienation of the population from many political institutions leading to an even greater reliance on "national" identity. What has changed this century is the rise of the "mass man" and the transfer of the custodianship of national identity from an intellectual elite, with its traditional leanings toward "romanticism" or "messianism," to a popular level, and with it a new, generally narrower, and more parochial definition of nationalism. Jose Ortega y Gasset in his *Revolt of the Masses* written in the 1920s noted that the popularization of politics led to the demise of elite politics and, with it, an end to politics driven by lofty ideas.[5] The trend throughout the Western world is toward ever greater parochialism and a narrower interpretation of nationalism, and consequently of the national agenda. Indicative of this non-ideological mindset is the emergence of the Liga Norte in Italy, the demise of Czechoslovakia (mainly on economic grounds), and the fact that while 40 percent of Germans admitted that they are indifferent to their national flag, the vast majority identified with the country's economic miracle.[6] In the United States public tolerance of political scandal seems to be directly linked to its perception of its own well-being. James Grant argues that the reason that the Whitewater affair failed to capture the public's attention was because it occurred at a time when the Dow Jones Industrial Index was racing toward the 7,000 level,[7] inducing presidential candidate Bob Dole to lament, "Where is the outrage?" Conversely, the public's interest in Watergate ran deep since it coincided with the greatest economic downturn since the great depression.

Paradoxically, while national identity today is driven far less by lofty universalist ideas and is, in fact, far more parochial, narrow, and pragmatic than in previous times, the strength and the appeal of nationalism today is greater than during any period following World War II. Yet if, as Hans Kohn argues, early-nineteenth-century nationalism was triggered by the decline of religion and an aversion to the emerging "cold etatism," late-twentieth-century nationalism seems to be driven by the disorienting effects of a global economy and a

Michener, ed., *Nationality, Patriotism and Nationalism in Liberal Democratic Societies* (St. Paul, MN: Paragon House, 1993), 2.
[5] See Jose Ortega y Gasset, *The Revolt of the Masses* (New York: W. W. Norton, 1957).
[6] Gred Knischewski, "Post War National Identity in Germany," in Jenkins and Sofos, *National Identity*, 131.
[7] James Grant, *The Trouble with Prosperity: The Loss of Fear, the Rise of Speculation and the Risk to American Savings* (New York: Times Books, 1996)

popular sense of impotence in the face of a relentless economic and hence social turmoil.

The contemporary political trends in the world, along with the rapid development of a truly global economy, have resulted in a significant decline in the authority of political institutions, which are increasingly perceived as "non-national," and with it a return to some sort of national "primordial community" as the key political point of reference. The electoral triumph of right-wing nationalists in Austria and France, the secessionist pressure in Quebec, the *de facto* economic partition of Belgium, and the severe tensions straining the integrity of Britain, France, and Spain are all symptomatic of the resurgence of nationalism, and the relative decline of the "non-national" democratic state.

Another indicator of the emergence of neo-nationalism is the decline across the democratic West in the levels of electoral participation; and in the successes of the "national" parties at the expense of the "mainstream parties." The electoral gains in France by Jean Marie Le Pen's National Front are symptomatic of the "revolt of the masses" against the rapid exposure of French society to the vagaries of a global economy. This can also be interpreted as a rejection of elite hegemony over the country's messianic foreign policy, which has led to France's endless commitment to its former colonies and resulted in massive population inflows from the former empire. Similarly, in the United States, the persistent electoral presence in the political arena of politicians such as Ross Perot and Pat Buchanan is testimony to the enduring resilience of parochial nationalism.

In advanced democracies, institutions moderate the rise of narrow neo-nationalism. In the countries of Eastern and Central Europe, where the roots of the political institutions are far shallower, national identities, which remain in Max Weber's parlance the primary intellectual "switchmen," set the direction and content of politics in the region. For this reason, nationalism will remain a more profound influence in Eastern Europe than in the more established political entities of Western Europe or North America.

### The decline and fall of Messianic nationalism

The national identities in Eastern and Central Europe fall into two distinct categories. A messianic nationalism is prevalent among the "historic" nations (Poland, Hungary, and Russia), and a restorative nationalism is common to " non-historic" nations, such as

Ukraine, Slovakia, the Czech Republic, and Finland. Restorative nationalism is usually triggered by a perceived sense of imminent acculturation of a smaller people by a larger "universal" culture. Hence, restorative nationalism generally has a far less ambitious agenda.

The so-called "historic" nations of the region (Poland, Hungary, and in its unique form Russia) are those which have retained an indigenous elite as a bearer of the national idea – an elite whose collective memory is linked to an entity that transcends the narrow ethnic definition of the nation. Whether it was the Polish Romantics' fixation on the Commonwealth with its civilizing mission or the Russian elite's (be it Orthodox or Marxist) preoccupation with a task beyond Russia's confines, the national agenda of the "historic nations" has had a strong element of messianism and has defined the missions of its respective countries in universal terms. In almost all cases, this messianic vision has resulted in foreign policies characterized by aggressive, imperialistic stances with regard to neighboring nations. Historically, devolution from a 'civilization' to a nation does seem to facilitate easier adaptation to the international system. This is demonstrated by the comparative experiences of China, which perceived itself as a civilization and Japan, which perceived itself as a nation.[8] In comparative terms, Japan's adaptation to the modern international system proved to much easier than that of China, where the bloody Cultural Revolution in the late 1960s was yet another convulsion by a polity that viewed itself as a civilization with a universal mission.

In the case of Ukraine, the Czech lands, Slovakia, the Baltic states, and other "non-historic" nations, the aristocracy was alien linguistically and, in some cases, religiously. The carriers of the national idea were largely the emerging literate intelligentsia, which saw a moral obligation to save and preserve a vanishing culture. Although eventually the nationalism of "non-historic" peoples, whether Ukrainians, Czechs or Finns, did cross over from the strictly cultural sphere to the political domain, the thrust of "non-historic" nationalism remained restorative, leading from the start to a parochial paradigm devoid of messianism and grandeur.[9] The restorative nature of the national

---

[8] John Breully, *Nationalism and the State* (Chicago: University of Chicago Press, 1993), 243.

[9] See Zdenek Suda, "Slovakia in Czech National Consciousness," in *The End of Czechoslovakia*, ed. Jiri Musil (Budapest, London, New York: Central European University Press, 1995).

identities of these nations was demonstrated by their policies in support of the status quo.

While Poland and Russia are not unique in having an elite serving as the repository for the national idea, the differences between these two countries and Western Europe (or even Germany) are broad and fundamental. In Western Europe (e.g., England or France) there was a rural gentry that transmitted the notion of national identity, national institutions, and civil society to the rural population. In Poland and Russia, though, this link between the rural peasant population and the aristocratic elites was all but non-existent. The Polish gentry (*szlachta*) conceiving itself as being of a different racial make-up from the peasantry, often relied on the Jews as intermediaries between them and "their" peasants, regardless of whether they were ethnically Poles, Ukrainians, Lithuanians, or White Russians. In Russia, service-nobility (*dvorianstvo*), exploiting estates granted by the crown and to which they did not have permanent title, were generally absent altogether. The Polish intelligentsia, which crystallized in the late nineteenth century was often of aristocratic origins and those who were not of noble origins rapidly acquired the mannerisms and the messianic world-view of the traditional elite. In Russia, although most of the intelligentsia did not stem from the aristocracy and often remained antagonistic to it, they, whether right or left wing, invariably developed a messianic mission viewing Russia as a means to a larger goal. In general, messianic notions of society are a direct outgrowth of elite politics which rarely find instinctive resonance on the popular level.

In Western Europe, the rise of the middle class and its successful seizure of power ultimately democratized these countries and freed them from the various messianic mythologies prevalent in that part of the world. As early as 1919 Joseph A. Schumpeter, in analyzing the origins and sources of imperialism, noted:

> The orientation toward war is mainly fostered by domestic interests of the ruling classes who stand to gain from a war policy, whether economically or socially . . . [Imperialism] is an atavism in the social structure, in individual, in psychological habits of emotional reaction. Since the vital needs that have created it have passed away for good, it will gradually disappear, even though every warlike involvement, no matter how non-imperialist in character, tends to revive it.[10]

---

[10] Joseph Schumpeter, *Social Classes: Imperialism* (Cleveland and New York: Meridian Books, 1968), 65.

Schumpeter observed that with the popularization of politics from an elite to the bourgeoisie, the messianic vocation of a society was eroding and ultimately would disappear. Therefore, the imperialist urge of the elite would be "condemned to political impotence."[11] The evolution from an aggressive imperialist drive to a parochial orientation, according to Schumpeter, is linked to the democratization of economic life. The rise of bourgeois capitalism delegitimated the imperialist urge, giving rise in Great Britain to the "Little Englanders" and a growing public apathy toward imperial adventures. Schumpeter's argument was based on his observations in Britain, a country where there has been a slow but continuous shift of the locus of power from an elite to a more popular level over the last two centuries. He concluded that with political and economic democratization, the British body politic shifted from an aggressively imperialistic foreign policy to one guided by the interests of the middle class which, while global in orientation, are without the elite's imperialism. Schumpeter attributed British imperialism in part at least to the psychological needs of the elite.[12] Writing nearly forty years later, Seymour Martin Lipset in his authoritative *Political Man the Social Bases of Politics* affirmed that one of the effects of economic modernization and consequent democratization is the de-ideologization of politics in the developed West.[13]

Samuel Huntington, linking economic modernization to political development in terms of a widening of the electoral base, argues that this leads to parochialization.[14] In a somewhat similar vein Richard Pipes asserts that the urge for territorial expansion is generally associated with overpopulated agricultural countries, whereas industrial countries are generally concerned with access to markets. Therefore, urbanized industrial countries such as Poland, Ukraine and Russia, enjoying relatively free access to markets, are not as likely to be prone to territorial expansionism.[15]

---

[11] Bernard Semmel, *The Liberal Ideal and the Demons of Empire: Theories of Imperialism from Adam Smith to Lenin* (Baltimore and London: Johns Hopkins University Press, 1993), 169.

[12] For a critical discussion of Schumpeter's theories, see Wolfgang Mommsen, *Theories of Imperialism* (Chicago: University of Chicago Press, 1980).

[13] See Seymour Martin Lipset, *Political Man: The Social Bases of Politics* (Baltimore: Johns Hopkins University Press, 1981), chs. 13, 15.

[14] See Samuel P. Huntington, "The West and the World," *Foreign Affairs*, 75: 6 (November–December 1996).

[15] Richard Pipes, "Weight of the Past: Russian Foreign Policy in Historical Perspective," *Harvard International Review* 19: 1 (Winter 1996/7).

A historic overview of Western societies tends to support this thesis. While during the Boer War (1898–1901) even London's beggars supported the government in its dealings with their "rebellious subjects,"[16] by 1956 Britain's imperial escapades in Egypt were rejected by broad sectors of the British public. Interestingly, the most popular British prime minster this century, who left office in a "blaze of glory," was the "nativist" Stanley Baldwin, whereas the "messianic" Winston Churchill was rejected at the end of World War II in favor of the "nativist" Clement Attlee. Similarly, democratization in the United States altered the course of America's international posture. After women got the vote, more than doubling electoral participation, the elections of 1920 resulted in a rejection of Wilsonian universalism in favor of Warren Harding's "normalcy."

It should be noted that the parochialization of politics, resulting from mass politics, does not imply isolationism or withdrawal. A case can be made that the Republican administration, while relying on their parochial paradigm to remain in power in the United States during the interwar period, pursued a foreign policy no less, and perhaps more, activist than their democratic predecessors. The difference, however, was that whereas Wilson presented his policies in messianic terms, such as "waging war to end all wars" or "making the world safe for democracy," the Republican administrations presented their policy as the "business of America is business" or "dollar diplomacy," themes revolving around "parochial" US interests.

The parochializing impact of modern nationalism is well illustrated by the 1991–95 civil war raging in the former Yugoslavia. Throughout history, wars in the Balkans have been perceived almost by definition as a means to actualize the universalist nationalizing ideology of a host of European polities. For Russia, they have been seen as an opportunity to revive its pan-Slavic mission; for the Italian nationalist right, they have presented a chance to reclaim Italy's "historic" patrimony; and for the Austrian and German empires, they have been used to extend German influence over Catholic Croats and Germanized Slovenes. A war in the Balkans, in the context of nineteenth or early-twentieth-century European nationalism, would have triggered a host of universal-messianic European nations to join the fray as a means of self-actualization, as occurred during the two world wars. Because of the emergence of late-twentieth-century parochial nationalism, however, the war in the Balkans has had a less dramatic impact.

[16] Semmel, *The Liberal Idea.*

With the possible exception of the stance taken by the theocratic, authoritarian Iran, the recent war in the Balkans not only failed to trigger a conflict among competing "civilizational" nationals, but actually led the European governments to resist entanglement in the quagmire.

In the West, mass politics has arisen from an expanding franchise and the progressive democratization of these societies. In Russia and Poland, "national identities" were the product of an educated class, who, regardless of their social origins, led lives separate from the atomized peasantry. The physical, psychological, and often linguistic and religious[17] separation between the elite and the peasantry was so broad that their relationship was akin to that of a colonial master and a colony. For the peasantry of Eastern Europe, the educated elite was "them," an alien, incomprehensible body. As a result of this genesis, the national idea was not based on national institutions or even a common culture, but was grounded in some variant of the universalist-messianic idea embedded in the collective memory (or collective agenda) of the elite. Whether anchored in the Polish elite's romantic notion of being an "apostle among adulterers," and linked to the collective memory of the Polish–Lithuanian Commonwealth or in the Russian elite's collective agenda of Pan-Slavic brotherhood, both socialism and internationalism were in concert with the universalist idea that the indigenous state was primarily a means to a universal goal. This strong universalist-messianic feature of the elite nationalism of these Slavic peoples contributed to the atomization of the general population and its alienation from the political leadership. In both cases the overwhelmingly rural population rightly perceived itself as being used as a means to achieve some larger agenda. Therefore, the messianic national ideas of the Polish and Russian elites were alien, antagonistic and largely incomprehensible to the greater population and therefore essentially irrelevant.

It was only in the early twentieth century, with its increase in urbanization, literacy, and mass politics, that the Eastern European elite felt compelled to extend the notion of "the nation" to the popular level. In Poland, the rise of literacy and greater national consciousness produced both by urbanization and the impact of emigrants returning

---

[17] Although the Polish gentry did share a language and religion with the peasantry, the gap nevertheless was as broad as in Russia and Ukraine. The Polish elite perceived itself as a different racial caste and commonly referred to the peasantry as cattle (*bydło*). In the Russian empire, the gentry's attitude toward the peasantry, viewing them as chattel, is immortalized in Nikolai Gogol's novel, *The Dead Souls*.

from Western Europe and north America to the countryside, re-enforced and popularized the notion of Polishness. Since messianic ideas held little appeal for the masses, a shift was required. To varying degrees, messianic elites in both Poland and Russia combined the national idea with the concept of *ressentiment*. Across Eastern and Central Europe, elites embraced the politics of *ressentiment* as a means of legitimizing their position and spreading the national idea to the masses. Both the Russian empire in the late nineteenth century and Poland in the interwar years saw their respective elites resort to state-sponsored xenophobia and exclusivity (e.g. anti-Semitism in both countries, anti-Catholicism in Russia and anti-Germanism in Poland). In both cases, a narrow political elite failed to develop either demo-cratic or corporatist-style links to the general populace, relying on a mix of *ressentiment* and *the mission civilisatrice* of the titular nationality as the foundation of the political order. In the early twentieth century (in Poland's case until World War II), the universities, elite institutions at that time, were the hotbeds of messianism and intolerant nation-alism. Although pre-1917 Russian universities did not serve as a bastion of Russian nationalism, they did remain the key exponents of a messianic mission of one sort or another. Thus, both Poland and Russia emerged as polities governed by a messianic elite, relying on state-sponsored xenophobia and intercommunal tension to legitimize themselves and their pursuit of an aggressive foreign policy. This was the case in pre-World War I and Soviet Russia and in Poland until World War II.

The post-World War II communist experiences of Poland, Russia, and Ukraine fundamentally altered the basis for nationalism in all three countries. The old messianic elite notions – whether the pre-World War II Polish elite's fascination with the Commonwealth and perception of Poland as a great civilizing power or the old Russian Bolshevik ideas of "world revolution" – gave way to a more opportu-nistic ideology. The new communist elites in Poland, Russia, and Ukraine, while not abandoning universalist verbiage, relied on eco-nomic performance, coercion, and carefully titrated internal politics of *ressentiment* as the means to remain in power with a modicum of legitimacy. The messianic façade of a cynical elite, on one hand, and the rapid improvements in the educational level of the populace, on the other, led to a dramatic delegitimization of the communist elite and its universalist ideology.

The dramatic improvement in educational levels in the three countries transformed them from quasi-literate, rural societies into literate, highly urban societies. This striking increase in educational levels hastened the demise of the messianic idea, promulgated by the state, and simultaneously undermined the ability of the state to rely on the politics of *ressentiment*. Not only could the better educated populations of Eastern Europe easily discern the double-talk of the state, but the universities quickly became the source of an educated group who may have been nationalist but were not messianic. The politics of *ressentiment* retained its appeal primarily among blue-collar workers and on the fringes of the intelligentsia.

Sociologists and political scientists, from Schumpeter to Zbigniew Brzezinski, have argued that imperialism and democracy cannot coexist. This premise can also be expanded to the study of nationalism and national identity, that is, that popular national identity and messianism cannot coexist. Michael Howard in his essay, "Ideology and International Relations," aptly noted the incompatibility of popular national identity and internationalism (messianism):

> We must never forget that the primary and instinctive loyalties of human beings are to small local communities they know best and of which they and their families formed part. Parochialism came before nationalism. The creation of national self-consciousness was, for the mass of mankind, a widening of horizons not a narrowing of them. Progress toward a higher ideology, a system of cultural values transcending national boundaries, is possible for a highly educated minority, but in making such progress that minority is in danger of distancing itself from the mass of fellow-countryman, if not losing touch with them altogether.[18]

National identity remains the main, if not the sole, glue of all societies. However, whereas the identity of the established democracies is grounded in their developed political institutions, East European societies and Russia, with their feeble institutions and weak civil societies, must rely on nationalism as their key pillar of cohesion, and it is essential for their societies to function. In the absence of strong political institutions or great economic gravitation to various internal foci, it is a sense of nationalism that links Vladivostok to Saint Petersburg in Russia, Galicia to Donbas in Ukraine, or even the industrial western part of Poland (*Polska A*) to the backward, agrarian northeast (*Polska B*).

The "democratization" of national identity in the "historic nations"

---

[18] Michael Howard, "Ideology and International Relations," in *The Lessons of History*, 148.

was marked by the passage of the custodianship of the national identity from the elite to the popular level. This phenomenon reshaped the agenda of these nations' identities, leading to the decline of messianism and allowing the rise of parochial nationalism, which has facilitated Polish and Russian accommodation to their current post-imperial realities. Popular nationalism, the nativist nationalism that has always prevailed in Ukraine, did not entirely prevail in Russia and Poland until after World War II. Popular nationalism, while it may well be defensive and xenophobic, is not messianic and has little or no interest in "civilizing" other cultures. It was this displacement of the elite's messianic-universal nationalism with popular nativist nationalism that facilitated the relatively easy Polish adaptation from a paradigm based on the Commonwealth to policies based on ethnographic "Piast Poland." The rise of Russian popular nationalism, epitomized by the nativist Village Prose literary school, facilitated Russia's separation from a universalist idea and, consequently, led to the collapse of the Soviet empire in a virtually bloodless manner.

Perhaps one of the greatest paradoxes of communist rule in Eastern and Central Europe is that it democratized, and thus parochialized, nationalism across the region. With the exception of fringe groups, modern Polish nationalists do not consider the essence of Polish nationalism to be "rescuing" the Ukrainians in the name of a "superior" civilization, nor does the Polish body politic seem to miss the days of "pacification" campaigns against its Ukrainian minority. Although anti-Semitism is still endemic across wide sectors of Polish society, as in other developed societies there is an inverse relationship between education and anti-Semitic bias. In contemporary Russia (unlike imperial Russia of the nineteenth century), fighting in the Caucasus is not perceived as a romantic adventure, a "civilizing mission," nor as part of the Russian nation's faith (sud'ba). Rather, it recalls the ghost of an unloved empire that the Russians would rather put to rest. Although most Russians continue to regret the collapse of the USSR, attempts by the communists to denounce the 1991 agreement to dissolve the USSR backfired. Even in the case of Belarus, despite its cultural and linguistic affinity with Russia, Belarussian overtures toward integration drew only muted popular support.

Although the "politics of ressentiment" continue to be a feature of all three polities, this aspect of nationalism is primarily confined to the least educated layers of the urban population. This is true despite severe economic dislocation and the fact that all three countries have recently witnessed massive movements of populations across their borders and the revival of a host of minority cultures whose existence was suppressed by decades of communism. Remarkably, this new multiculturalism has not thus far evoked the much-feared xenophobic reaction.

The rise of nativist national identity in Poland and Russia is allowing these countries to conduct a pragmatic foreign policy which is far less at odds with their neighbors and the international system than at almost any other time in history. This neo-nationalism, while it can be mobilized in "defense" of the "nation," does not lend itself to a struggle in the name of messianism. President Roosevelt, although cognizant of the threat to the United States posed by German Nazism and Japanese militarism, was only able to bring America into World War II following the attack on Pearl Harbor, when he could mobilize America's "defensive nationalism." Unlike the elitist Woodrow Wilson who took America into World War I for lofty messianic reasons, the populist Roosevelt had to rely on the more utilitarian fear of direct invasion to garner and sustain public support for entering into a war on the European continent. As the continuing oscillation between universalism and nativism demonstrates, even in a developed institutional polity such as the United States two visions of nationalism can coexist simultaneously, with neither ever fully subsuming the other.

Similarly, following World War II, the United States did not assume a global role in the name of a "manifest destiny," the concept so dear to various elites in the United States in the nineteenth century, nor were they imperialists in the mold of Theodore Roosevelt and Henry Cabot Lodge. Rather, the US emerged as a "reluctant empire" responding to a perceived threat to its own survival. As Ronald Steel insightfully noted:

> Anti-communism as an ideology was a response not only to stalemate abroad, but also to the insecurities of life at home, where traditional values have been uprooted. To those whose sense of security had been destroyed by the extreme mobility of American life, who felt threatened by the demands of racial minorities for equality, and who were humiliated by the impersonality of an increasingly bureaucratized society, ideological communism served as a focal point of discontent. It could not allay these anxieties, but it could explain them in a form that was acceptable to those who saw as many enemies within the gates as they saw outside. The McCarthyism and the witch-hunts of the 1950s, which so debased American intellectual life and spread a blanket of conformity over

the government, were a reaction to this insecurity, acts of self-exorcism by a people tormented by demons.[19]

In general, societies that rely on nativist nationalism, while they may not be inherently as aggressive as messianically-oriented societies, can still be volatile. Unlike stable political institutions, nationalism (even nativist nationalism) exists as a reflection of the "other," resulting in an inherent tension in external relations. Thus, for example, the evolution of Poland's national identity and with it, Poland's international posture, is linked to how the Poles perceive the process of their "return" to Europe. A successful integration into Western Europe's political, economic, and cultural institutions will hasten the development of civil institutions in Poland, lessening their reliance on "defensive" nationalism, leading to a more accommodating interaction with the international system. Ukraine's national identity, although devoid of messianism, will continue to be shaped by its interaction with Russia and integration into the international system. A non-threatening relationship with Russia will reduce its propensity to embrace defensive nationalism and leave it confined to the political fringe. Conversely a threatening relationship with Moscow or the emergence of powerful centrifugal forces may well lead to an aggressive nationalism.

The transition of Russian identity from a messianic to a nativist form is far behind that of Poland. Whereas Polish nativism can be traced to the positivist movement of the nineteenth century, a true nativist movement did not emerge in Russia until the late 1950s, when the rise of "village prose" gave meaning to a new perception of the Russian reality. And, while Poland's messianic idea was physically annihilated in a series of military defeats, the Soviet imperium imploded faster than large elements of the Russian polity could adjust to the loss of its empire. Given that the Russian messianic identity did not experience its "Waterloo" and that even a post-imperial Russia has retained the trappings of a great power, large sectors of the Russian body politic have yet to embrace a clear, post-imperial identity. The question of whether the "near abroad" will ultimately become a foreign or a domestic issue in Russian politics will be very much an outcome of the evolution of Russia's national identity.[20] Prolonged economic decline, a sense of humiliation from the outside

[19] Ronald Steel, *Pax Americana: The Cold War – How it Grew and What it Means* (New York: The Viking Press, 1967), 24.
[20] See Reno Lukic and Allen Lynch, *Europe from the Balkans to the Urals: The Disintegration of Yugoslavia and the Soviet Union* (Oxford: Oxford University Press, 1996), ch. 17.

or the plight of the Russian diaspora may trigger a defensive nationa-listic reaction, leading to an assertive foreign policy, even though such a policy would only deepen Russia's crisis.

The analogy between the current Russian state and Weimar Germany can easily be extended to the realm of national identity, where, in reaction to perceived humiliation, defensive "nativist" nationalism was evoked. It is particularly worrisome that German nationalists in the 1920s and the Russian nationalist philosopher Lev Gumelev both evoke the fear of the extinction of their particular ethnic identity as justification for aggressive and xenophobic nationalism. The attacks of the Russian right on the soulless modern Westernization of Russia are reminiscent of the Weimar Republic's debate of "Amer-icanism versus *Kulturkritik.*" Along with the politicization of the status of the Russian diaspora, this all may serve to provoke an assertive, salvationist nationalism which, although devoid of messianism, may trigger violence in Russia's long and ill-defined periphery.

### Scenarios for post-modern nationalism in Poland, Russia, and Ukraine

The emergence of a sovereign Poland, Ukraine, and Russia was not the result of an elite nationalism driven by a universal idea. In all three cases it was the triumph of Ortega y Gasset's "mass man," rather than some sort of latter day romanticism. Poland's long struggle for independence was a struggle for national freedom and perhaps the possibility to join the affluent West, rather than an effort to recast a civilizational sphere between the Baltic and the Black Seas. Russia's declaration of sovereignty which set the stage for the demise of the Soviet Union was couched by Yeltsin as a means to save Russia from oblivion and decay rather than as an effort to re-invent Russia as a standard-bearer of a grandiose, universal ideal. Ukraine's December 1991 referendum on independence was also presented to the Ukrai-nian people as a choice between prosperity in an independent Ukraine or poverty within the context of the USSR. Ukraine's independence referendum was devoid of the idealistic notions of Ukraine serving as a social model, common to earlier Ukrainian nationalists of the past.

Today's nationalism, despite the critical role that it continues to play in shaping the three countries in question, in all three countries is a nationalism largely devoid of messianic ambitions or belief in a universal mission. Instead, nationalism is a consequence of the rise of the "mass man" and his adjustment to the collapse of the ideological age. Thus, given the influence that national identity has historically had on external relations, what future foreign policies are the three polities are likely to pursue in the future?

## Poland

Perhaps nowhere in the region was the notion of a "return to Europe" a stronger and more prominent feature of the political myth than in Poland. The sacrifices made during the long communist ordeal were justified in part by the promise of a "brilliant future" within the context of a return to an idealized West. To most Poles, a "return" to Europe had both a strong psychological as well as economic component and its success will be measured on two planes. On the one hand, many Poles are very eager to be included in Western institutions ranging from the Council of Europe, OECD, NATO, or the European Union (while simultaneously shunning any possible affiliation with Eastern Europe). On the other, the legitimacy of this process invariably depends on the country's ability to negotiate an economic return to Europe in which the gap between Poland and its Western neighbors declines and ultimately disappears.

Skeptical voices notwithstanding, postcommunist Poland has dramatically improved its economic performance, becoming one of the fastest growing economies in Europe and perhaps in the world. Nevertheless, even at these rapid rates of growth, it would take the Poles more than a generation to attain the income levels of the poorer members of the European Union and far longer to match Austria, Germany, or Scandinavia (countries by which most Poles measure success or failure). Should the Polish body politic lose its patience with this slow "return" to Europe, what political and hence diplomatic turns in Poland could one anticipate? Even today, though, Poland's return to Europe is fraught with ambiguity. The infatuation with Western culture which earlier was endemic across Polish society has started to recede. Western values are no longer accepted by Poles as eagerly and as uncritically as they once were. Even the drive to join NATO, which is supported by approximately 80 percent of the population, is controversial; 52 percent of Poles believe that despite NATO membership, the West will continue to deal with Russia over Poland's head, and only 23 percent believe that the West would defend Poland in case of a Russian attack. Clearly, Poland's "return" to Europe is tenuous and precarious.

However, given the homogeneity of the Polish population and their strong national identity, Poland is unlikely to face separatist region-alism akin to that of Spain or Italy. Conversely given that the custodianship of Poland's national identity is held by the "mass man," Poland is not likely to revert to a messianic polity attempting to reclaim a civilizational sphere. But, should Poland's return to the West turn out to be longer or harder than most Poles anticipated, Poland's current flirtation with Western style politics can easily deteriorate to a Polish version of Populist-Peronism.[21] The intellectual basis of Polish Peronism most likely will be based on the argument that Poland's economic and cultural dealings with the perfidious West led to the country's economic and moral impoverishment, and reduced Poland to a peripheral position not commensurate with Poland's contribution to Western culture and its defense. A relapse into populist parochial nationalism would combine a *ressentiment* of the "internationalist" status of the modern economic order with the rhetoric of national aggrandizement cum populist redistributive policies. Adam Michnik in his description of modern Polish populism characterized it as a still unnamed ideology with the following features: "There is a bit of fascism in it and a bit of communism; a bit of egalitarianism and a bit of clericalism; a radical critique of the Enlightenment and the harsh language of moral absolutism."[22] It is worth noting that populism is not merely a rejection of modernity but rather a defensive reaction of the threatened "mass man." Vladimir Tismaneanu has noted:

> Populism is a larger discourse that integrates nationalism in a structure of expectations and demands for protection from the drastic changes imposed by political and economic modernization. This "national-populism" . . . is a response to deep seated and excruciating fears of failure. It is not inherently anti-modern, but it expresses the yearning among many strata for not being ostracized, excluded or abandoned during the on going seismic transformation.[23]

In domestic terms a turn to Peronist-style nationalism would lead to the abandonment of the liberal economic policy, and a movement toward a greater state role in the economy, along with growing xenophobia and anti-capitalist (i.e., liberal Western) attitudes. In terms of foreign policy, while not resuming its "civilizing" mission of the

---

[21] See Vladimir Tismaneanu, "The Leninist Debris or Waiting for Peron," *East European Politics and Societies* 10: 3 (Fall 1996).

[22] Adam Michnik, "Gray is Beautiful: Thoughts on Democracy in Central Europe," *Dissent*, Spring 1997, 17.

[23] Vladimir Tismaneanu, *Fantasies of Salvation* (Princeton: Princeton University Press, forthcoming).

past, a Peronist Poland will likely become a more insistent advocate of the Polish minorities in neighboring countries, while simultaneously seeking a position of geo-political as well as economic leadership in an independent bloc of countries lying between the Baltic and Black Seas. A rise of Polish populism would most likely quickly resonate in the two countries where Polish influence is most profound, triggering the rise of populism in Ukraine and Lithuania and severely testing the delicate political balance of these young countries. The potential emergence of Polish Peronism would not only destabilize the painful economic recovery of postcommunist Europe, but might very well contribute to the re-emergence of a "grey zone" between Russia and Germany with all its historic pitfalls.

Despite Poland's dramatic economic recovery in the last five years, exclusive anti-modernist populism did re-emerge on the Polish political landscape. The political agenda of the opposition's Solidarity Electoral Alliance (AWS) led by Marian Krzaklewski, and even more overtly Jan Olszewski's Movement for the Reconstruction of Poland (ROP), manifested distinct clericist-integralist features, earning Mr. Olszewski the designation as the Polish Le Pen. The 1997 debate over the new Polish constitution accentuated the rift between the modernizing agenda of the current government (consisting of former communists) and the populist opposition calling for a constitution based on "Catholic Values," "natural laws," and "organic society," reviving a populist clericist tradition in Polish politics.[24]

### Ukraine

While the Ukrainian vote for independence in 1991 was not explicitly aimed at a "return" to the West, only a minority of the country's population saw national independence as a good within itself. The "mass man" of Ukrainian politics of the 1990s who opted for independence did so in the belief that national independence will end economic servitude to Moscow and hence lead to improved economic conditions in Ukraine. Should national independence fail to provide for a visible improvement in the lot of the country's suffering, what direction will Ukraine's national identity be likely to pursue? Given the historically nativist nature of Ukrainian nationalism, even if its attempts to Westernize were to fail, Ukraine is not likely to turn

---

[24] See Marek Bakkowicz, "Akcje Naszej Akcji," *Tygodnik Malopolski-AWS*, 21 December 1996.

toward irredentism. Furthermore, in light of the deep regional divergence in Ukraine, it is unlikely to develop a Ukrainian version of Peronism, since that model presupposes a strong and clear national identity as a basis to rally against both "internationalism" and the "world order."

Should Ukraine's efforts to become an effective Western polity fail, the "mass man" of Ukrainian politics is most likely to follow the example of its Italian, Canadian, British, or Spanish counterparts – a situation in which specific regions try to arrange independent relationships with outside players, while minimizing the power of the central national government.

The growth of regionalism has stressed the national unity of even such established polities as those mentioned above. The situation in Ukraine, however, is different for both internal and external reasons. Internally, the differences across Ukraine are differences not only of language, religion, or economic interest, but more importantly are derived from historic experience and collective memory. The absence of a common collective memory makes Ukrainian identity more malleable than that of Poland, giving the regions a freedom to define or redefine the legitimacy of the national government on a scale unknown in most other countries.[25] Furthermore, while it is normal in the age of global economic integration for some regions to develop more intimate relationships with neighboring countries than with the rest of the nation, Ukraine's situation is different in light of the historic attitudes of its neighbors. The fact that British Columbia trades more with the US than with the rest of Canada may put the provincial government occasionally at odds with the national government in Ottawa. Nevertheless, this situation does not mean that the U.S. will attempt to detach the Canadian west from the rest of the confederation.

In the case of Ukraine, it is far from clear that economic interdependence between eastern Ukraine and the Russian federation will remain a rational economic process and not lead to an attempt by some in Russia to bifurcate the Ukrainian state. The growth of regionalism is a Europe-wide phenomenon which has led to devolution of power in these polities and, therefore, to greater democratization and vitality within these polities. Regionalism in Ukraine, though, may well lead to an even greater control of the regions by

[25] See Andrew Wilson, *Ukrainian Nationalism in the 1990s: a Minority Faith* (Cambridge: Cambridge University Press, 1997). See also Paul S. Pirie, "National Identity and Politics in Southern and Eastern Ukraine," *Europe-Asia Studies* 48: 7 (November 1996), 1079–104.

political clans (a European version of war lordism) resulting in less democracy, more political atomization of the population, and even a possible break-up of the state and severe civic disorder. There are several issues which might destabilize Ukraine and sunder its tenuous cohesion. The crucible of Crimea, which heretofore was well managed by all sides was, however, never resolved, and may trigger a major inter-Ukrainian crisis, given the deep division throughout Ukrainian society over whether a compromise with Russia is either possible or desirable. In international terms, the potential atrophy of Ukraine might very well create a vacuum that could rekindle imperial ambitions among segments of the Russian elite, which could easily destabilize the delicate balance in Europe.

### Russia

In Russia, a nativist understanding of nationalism has replaced the messianic version of the past. However, given that Russia has yet to determine its own boundaries, even a nativist interpretation of its identity may lead to strife. Even though the majority of Russians welcomed the demise of the Soviet empire and are focused exclusively on narrow Russian interests, most have yet to reconcile themselves to the loss of Sebastopol or northern Kazakhstan, creating the potential for mobilizing the popular identity in "defense" of "sacred Russian soil." Furthermore, the plight of the Russian diaspora in Central Asia and the Baltic states or the sense of a threat from an external actor may well allow the regime to galvanize "nativist" nationalism in perceived self defense.

The situation in Russia is far more complex than in either Poland or Ukraine. While the Russian "mass man" is no more inclined to endorse a messianic paradigm for his country than his counterpart in either Central or Western Europe, it was the Russians in fact who brought about the demise of the Soviet Union and its messianic idea.[26] The pacific attitude of the Russian masses was well documented by the massive public opinion poll conducted by Yuri Levada. In his book *The Simple Soviet Man*,[27] Levada observed that nearly 45 percent

---

[26] See Roman Szporluk, "The Fall of the Tsarist Empire and the USSR: The Russian Question and Imperial Overextension" in *The End of Empire? The Transformation of the USSR in Comparative Perspective*, ed. Karen Dawisha and Bruce Parrott (Armonk, NY: M. E. Sharpe, 1997).

[27] Yuri Levada, *Sovetskii Prostoi Chelovek: Opyt Sotsal'nogo Portreta na Rubezhe 90kh* (Moscow: Inter-Center, 1993).

of the Russian population felt that Russia had no adversaries. However, the Russia situation is complicated by several facts which leave open a host of possible outcomes of the Russian transformation.

Much like Poland, a sense of economic malaise and rejection by the West may well lead to a populist backlash leading to a Russian version of Peronism, a rejection of the liberal model, and a return to redistributive dirigism. While by the late 1980s most Russians were indeed very dissatisfied with their political and economic situation, it is not clear that the Western concept of freedom and democracy has been internalized by most Russians. An enduring feature of the way many Russians understand "democracy" is as an expression of economic egalitarianism and the necessary absence of glaring economic disparities, making the transformation of Russia into a modern economic and political entity a complex and unpredictable process.[28] This deeply ingrained notion of equating democracy with economic egalitarianism also makes the country prone to Peronist style populism.

Given Russia's weak national identity and enormous regional differences, it is not to be excluded that Russia will devolve under its centrifugal forces leading to the rise of regional sub-states, with some pursuing a liberal economic model, and others reverting to authoritarianism of one sort or another. In fact, given the very different policies pursued by local governments ranging from liberalism in Nizhni-Novgorod to the quasi-authoritarian policies of mayor Yuri Lushkov in Moscow, to the Marxist–Leninist model implemented by the authorities in the Ulianovsk region, a case can be made that Russia has already started the process of economic disintegration and accelerating regionalization.

A far more threatening scenario which may well reemerge in Russia is a return to aggressive imperialism. While it is most unlikely that the Russian "mass man" will succumb to a new (or the revival of an old) messianic idea, there are some danger signs. On the popular level, the demise of the Soviet Union has yet to be internalized by the broad Russian masses. The current Russian state remains unreal for most Russians, as the leftist Russian intellectual Boris Karalitsy noted: "The Russian Federation so far is not a state in the sense of the full definition of the notion of the state, but just a piece of Russian territory run by Yeltsin's administration. Once the regime changes, the defini-

---

[28] See Hugh Ragsdale, "The Constraints of Russian Culture," *National Interest*, no. 33 (Fall 1993), 68–72.

tion of this notion will change as well."[29] The collapse of the USSR
was so swift and unexpected that a certain air of unreality continues
to prevail in Russia, and while only a tiny minority would advocate
the use of force to recreate the USSR, nostalgia for the past is palatable
(76 percent of Russians feel Ukraine should unite with Russia).[30]

On the popular level, the population, while bewildered by the
current "unnatural" Russian state, has neither the will nor the drive to
recreate a "Greater Russia" or to indulge in messianism or irredentism
of any sort. On the elite level, however, two troubling trends can be
observed. Among nationalist intellectuals, the current Russian state is
perceived, much as post-Trianon Hungary was viewed by Hungarian
nationalists in the 1920s, as an absurd aberration that emerged due to
a Western conspiracy. At one point, the illegitimacy of the current
Russian state reached such a degree that rejection of the 1991 Agreement to dissolve the USSR had become the shibboleth of Russian
politics. Virtually all Russian politicians, ranging from the liberal
Yavlinskii who called for the reincorporation of Belarus to the populist
mayor of Moscow, Lushkov, who laid claim to Sevastopol have
attempted to build their political base on the notion of recasting a
greater Russian state and reversing the current "unnatural" state of
affairs. The overwhelming rejection by the Russian Duma in April,
1997 of Yeltsin's efforts to return German art seized by the Soviet
troops during World War II, and the popularity of that decision, is
symptomatic of how difficult it is for many Russians to resign
themselves to the current reality.

Although there is no will on the popular level to change the current
situation, given the profound cognitive dissonance prevalent in
Russian mass politics and the increasingly revisionist state of mind
among some of Russia's intellectual and political elites, there is a real
danger that a successful "translation" of the intellectual elite agenda
may well move the Russian body politic in a direction in which the
rhetoric of "defensive" and "restorative" nationalism could become
aggressive. This might lead to the mutation of the current feeling of
political anomie into a self-conscious ideology. Despite the fact that
only 9 percent of the Russian population appears willing to make
sacrifices in their lives or fortunes to recreate the USSR,[31] the lack of

[29] Quoted in Sergei Giorgiev, "Rhetoric and Reality: Post-Soviet Policy in the Near
Abroad," *Harvard International Review* 19: 1 (Winter 1996/97), 20.
[30] Opinion Analysis, United States Information Agency, M12–1997.
[31] Angela Stent and Lilia Shevtsova, "Russia's No Turning Back," *Foreign Policy*, no. 103
(Summer 1996).

legitimacy of the current Russian state among ordinary Russians is palpable in Russia's popular culture, especially in popular music. The popularity of groups ranging from the popular "Heavy Metal" band, *Metal Corrosion*, widely popular among the young with its hit lyric "kill the darkies (*sunerev*)," to the neo-Soviet band *Lyube* whose top selling CD in 1996, *Kombat*, blended traditional militarism and chauvinism, to the very popular ballad *Lieutenant Galitsyn (Poruchik Galitisyn)*, in which the rape of Russia is a theme, indicates that despite the passivity of the Russian "mass man," elite rejection of the current Russian state has seeped into the popular consciousness. It is worth noting that Antonio Gramsci in the *Modern Prince*[32] argued that universal suffrage and the rise of the "mass man" did not result in the drowning out of elite agendas but rather provided the polity with a means with which to judge the ability of the elites to promulgate their programs. Clearly, large segments of the Russian elite have not given up their imperialist ambitions. Whether these elites manage to galvanize the defensive instincts of nativist Russian nationalism toward aggression remains an open question.

Fritz Stern in his classic *The Politics of Cultural Despair: A Study in the Rise of Germanic Ideology*[33] demonstrated that the success of Hitler and the National Socialists lay not in their capacity to inflame the public's passions against the humiliation of the Treaty of Versailles or the illegitimate Weimar Republic, but rather in their ability to translate the agenda of anti-modernist nationalist intellectuals, who cultivated their aggressive agenda for decades before Hitler's ascent of power. Similarly, despite the elite anti-Semitism prevalent in German intellectual circles since the 1880s, this initially did not translate into a pogrom. In fact, Hitler's early efforts to organize a boycott of Jewish businesses drew little or no popular support.[34] David Schonebaum, in *Hitler's Social Revolution*,[35] pervasively showed that the success of Nazism was largely due to their reconciliation of the new industrial state with the *volkish* tradition of the German bourgeoisie and hence, their ability to utilize a modern state to achieve an anti-modernist agenda. While history rarely repeats itself, several uncomfortable analogies can be

[32] See Antonio Gramsci, *The Modern Prince and Other Writings* (New York: International Publishers, 1968).
[33] Fritz Stern, *The Politics of Cultural Despair: A Study in the Rise of Germanic Ideology* (Garden City, NY: Anchor Books Doubleday & Co, 1965).
[34] See Saul Friedlander, *Nazi Germany and the Jews: Years of Persecution 1933–1939* (New York: HarperCollins Publishers, 1997), 18–25.
[35] David Schonebaum, *Hitler's Social Revolution: Class and Status in Nazi Germany 1933–1939* (New York and London: W. W. Norton and Co., 1996).

drawn. Large segments of the Russian intellectual elite view the current Russian state as quasi-legitimate at best. Russia's small bourgeoisie, concentrated almost exclusively in the urban areas, feels trapped between government by kleptocracy on one side and, on the other, a tumultuous and dangerous disenfranchised blue-collar lumpen proletariat and an "intellectual proletariat" consisting of the tens of thousands of disenfranchised scientists, engineers, and military officers. They are both eagerly seeking a leader who will restore order without drawing Russia into yet another "social experiment" or bout of "internationalism." Because large segments of the population vacillate between passive indifference to the Russian state and outright hostility, the country may well be ripe for a "restorative ideology" based on the restoration of Russia's dignity as a great power, desiring hegemony across much of the former Soviet space. With its historically conservative foreign policy, Russia even under a nationalist guise is unlikely to become the "mad dog" of international politics in the mode of Nazi Germany.[36] However, the conservative nature of Russian politics does not preclude an assertive turn.

There are several unknowns which will continue to trouble Russia in the future. Russia, which was always a "one-legged" power (relaying solely on its military might) saw its army all but disintegrate. Russia was left a great power solely by virtue of its nuclear potential, a situation with no historic precedent. The Russian polity has yet to internalize its defeat in Chechnia, and the debate over what caused the worst humiliation of the Russian army since the Russo-Japanese war has yet to work itself through Russian society.

It is far from clear how the clash between the "nationalizing nationalism" of the new states of Russia's periphery and some republics within the Russian Federation itself, and the "Russian homeland nationalism"[37] of the Russian-speaking population in many of the former Soviet states will resolve itself. What is clear, however, is that both the successor states' "nationalizing" nationalism, and the diaspora's "homeland" nationalism are based on the concept of "nationality" rather than citizenship, and hence have the potential to lead to conflict. The mass migration of Russians from Central Asia and particularly from northern Kazakhstan, accentuates the lack of synergy between the Russian "nation" and the Russian state. This mass migration is viewed by most Russians as a humiliation and the

[36] I owe this term to David Schonebaum.
[37] See Roger Brubaker, *Nationalism Reframed: Nationalism and the National Question in the New Europe"* (Cambridge: Cambridge University Press, 1996), ch. 4.

abandonment of historic land, adding to the delegitimization of the current configuration. Given the "inward" nature of the "nationalizing" nationalism prevalent in most post-Soviet states, and the growing "expansionary" nationalism of the Russian elite, there is certain to be tension between Russia and its periphery, which may further kindle Russia's "defensive nationalism." The ethnic diaspora of formerly imperial people has historically galvanized irredentist nationalism in its respective mother countries fomenting conflict between the former empire and its new neighbors. The cases of the *Volkdeutsch* Germans across Eastern Europe, the Magyars outside Hungary after the Trianon truncation of Hungary in 1920,[38] the Turks in Cyprus, and the Russian Cossacks in northern Kazakhstan all demonstrate the ability of the diaspora to mobilize "nativist" aggression. Although the definition of Russian identity remains fugitive, often being an admixture of ethnic, linguistic, cultural, and sociological criteria, the issue of the Russian diaspora has become imbedded in the Russian political discourse, deepening the crisis of identity that has befallen Russia.[39]

As I have suggested, national identities are neither permanent nor immutable. In time polities do adapt to new circumstances, develop new mythologies, and recast themselves. These new identities can result in different concepts of national interest and therefore new foreign policies. This process is inevitably slow and painful and generally requires a generational change. Poland and Ukraine, by virtue of having regained their political independence, can use that independence as a basis for a legitimizing mythology, and with it a new identity. Post-imperial societies are bound to go through a much longer period of political anomie, accompanied by a profound elite and popular disorientation. This is particularly true of Russia where their imperial and national identities are so throughly intertwined. As Geoffrey Hoskins aptly noted, while "Britain had an empire, Russia was an empire."[40] Russia's painful path to devise a post-imperial national identity, and to devise a political system reflecting Russia's cultural needs, is bound to be a slow and torturous process, which will continue to reverberate across the Eurasian landmass.

---

[38] See Bela Kiraly and Laszlo Veszpermy, eds., *Trianon and Eastern Europe: Antecedents and Repercussions*, War and Society in East Central Europe, vol. XXXII (Boulder, CO: Social Science Monographs, 1995).

[39] See Neil Melvin, *Russians Beyond Russia: The Politics of National Identity* (London: The Royal Institute of International Affairs, Pinter Cassel Imprint, 1995), ch. 2.

[40] Quoted by Szporluk in "The Fall of the Tsarist Empire and the USSR."

# Index

Hlond, Cardinal, 80
Howard, Michael, 413
Hroch, Miroslav, 14, 18, 317
Hrushevsky, M., 188, 189, 304, 315,
  317–18, 327, 330, 366, 367, 375
human rights, 22, 101, 115, 200–1,
  268, 296, 354–5
Hungary, 26, 27, 65, 138, 145, 147, 243,
  254, 255, 277, 279, 314, 337, 372,
  381, 393, 407, 424
Huntington, Samuel, 18, 409

Ilin, Ivan, 234
imperialism, 174, 408–9, 413, 423
India, 5, 19, 32, 35, 194, 252, 253, 254,
  261, 262, 270, 271, 284, 288–90
industrialization, 13, 48, 51–2, 54, 75,
  76, 83
institutions, 23, 31
intellectuals, 3, 13, 14, 163, 404, 405,
  407–8
  see also intellectuals, Russian;
    intellectuals, Ukrainian
intellectuals, Polish, 92, 93, 94, 104,
  125, 142, 149, 408
  in Khrushchev period, 86, 88–91
  and minority groups, 99–100
  and peasantry, 49–50
  post-war, 79–82, 84, 86
  see also political elites, Polish
intellectuals, Russian, 154, 157, 163,
  166, 168, 172, 175–7, 179, 181,
  192–3, 195, 197–204, 211, 408,
  424, 426
  émigrés, 186–8, 207–8, 230
  failure of, 236
  liberal-democrat, 225–6, 232, 235
  and Ukraine, 318–20
  and Westernization, 18, 160–5,
    166–8, 195, 214, 219, 222, 233ff.,
    238
  see also political elites, Russian
intellectuals, Ukrainian, 14, 23, 301,
  302, 304, 309, 328, 347, 349, 359,
  366, 369, 370
  and democratic opposition, 357, 360

failure of, 373–4
and fascism, 333–7
and independence (1919), 314–26
and Jews, 355
and nationalist foreign policy, 375,
  389
and Russian Revolution, 323–6
and Stalinism, 330–1, 344–5
  see also political elites, Ukrainian
intelligentsia see intellectuals
international relations theory, 14–20
internationalism, 41, 180, 183, 316,
  346, 350, 413
Ioann, Metropolitan of St. Petersburg,
  234
Iran, 5, 33, 35–6, 245, 246, 253, 254,
  259, 262, 270, 271, 280, 281,
  284–5, 287–8, 289, 394
Iraq, 262, 265, 273, 274, 287
Ireland, 6, 17
Islam, 5, 33, 40, 252–3, 256, 257, 259,
  261–2, 265, 282, 289–90, 395
Israel, 20, 253, 286
Italy, 6, 16, 405, 410
Ivan IV, Tsar, 157

Jagiellonian tradition, 50, 56–7, 62, 86,
  96, 97–8, 128, 331
Jansina-Kania, Aleksandra, 59
Japan, 18, 190, 242, 244, 246, 253, 260,
  265, 266, 269, 290–6, 407
Jaruzelski government, 115
Jaworsky, Rudolf, 25
Jefferson, Thomas, 23
Jerschina, Jan, 76–7, 79
Jews, 8, 16, 24, 34, 40, 45, 47, 50, 52–3,
  63–5, 67, 68, 78, 107, 164, 174,
  194, 308, 309, 313–14, 316, 325,
  332, 336, 341, 344, 348, 355
  see also anti-Semitism
John Paul II, Pope, 97, 100–1, 107,
  138, 141, 353
Joselewicz, Colonel Berek, 45
Judt, Tony, 225–6

Kaganovich, Lazar, 344

Ukrainian national identity (*cont.*)
and foreign policy, 375–8, 388–92
and independence (1918), 324–6
national communists and, 353, 358
"non-historical," 301–2
and Orthodox Church, 305, 310
and the "other," 308–10
and the people, 412–13
and rationalism, 354
revival of, 358–9
and social justice, 310–12
stages of, 339–41ff.
Stalin and, 330–1, 343–5
weakness of, 302–3, 305–7, 358, 372–3
and Westernization, 160–6
and World War II, 337–8, 340–1
*see also* Ukraine; Ukrainian foreign policy; Ukrainian state
Ukrainian Nationalist Assembly (UNA), 368–9
Ukrainian School of Polish literature, 45
Ukrainian state, 2, 301–2, 316, 366, 367, 373, 391
Ukrainians, ethnic, 26, 45, 46, 47, 50, 54, 61, 63, 66, 67, 68, 73, 78, 98, 99, 100, 107, 108, 125, 144, 373, 396, 402
Uniate Church, 139, 166, 174, 305, 321, 323
Union of Lublin (1569), 308
United Kingdom *see* Great Britain
United Nations, 255, 276, 341, 343, 393
United States, 1, 16, 17, 19–20, 29, 34, 35, 87, 145, 147, 201, 295, 297, 405, 410
and Central Asia, 280, 281, 285, 286–7
parochial nationalism in, 406, 415–16
and Poland, 110–11, 115, 122, 135
rationalist foreign policy of, 21–3
and Russian foreign policy, 242–7, 252, 253, 254, 262–4, 264–6, 270–8

and Ukraine, 343–4, 351, 382, 385, 386, 392–4
universalism, 5–7, 19–20, 21–3, 30–1, 39, 55, 155, 163, 180, 186, 194, 411
Ustrialov, Nikolai, 231
Uvarov, Count Sergei, 302, 309

Vatican, 77, 80, 83, 88, 141–2
*see also* Roman Catholicism
Vernadsky, George, 157, 160
Village Prose school, 194, 203, 206, 207, 218, 352, 414
Vilnius, 149, 150
Visegrad group, 120, 135, 147, 274, 275, 380, 381, 382, 400
Vlasov, Yuri, 222
Volga valley, 265
Volhynia, 63, 78, 140, 158
Volsky, Arkadii, 229
Volyn, 331
Vovchok, M., 313
Vynnitsa, 359
Vynnychenko, Volodymyr, 320, 324, 327

Wałęsa, Lech, 6. 102, 103, 107, 108, 127–8, 130, 135, 136, 138, 140, 142, 144–5, 278, 381, 382
Walicki, Andrzej, 39, 41, 51
Walker, Martin, 267
Wandycz, Piotr, 72
Weber, Max, 15, 33
Weimar Group, 135
Weimar Republic, 29, 417, 425
Weintraub, Wiktor, 44
West, the, 18–19, 26, 28–9, 93, 95, 406
and détente, 91–2, 115, 195, 350
and Poland, 41–2, 46, 57, 71, 73–4, 81, 86–7, 96–7, 98, 117, 131–2, 134–5, 146–8
and Russia, 160–6, 175–6, 197–201, 205, 210, 222, 234, 238, 240–8ff., 256, 264–9, 270–80
and Ukraine, 341–2, 350–1, 383–3, 391, 392–5

# Cambridge Russian, Soviet and Post-Soviet Studies